1991

Issues
in
Insurance

Volume II

Issues in Insurance

Volume II

EVERETT D. RANDALL, CPCU, CLU

Director of Underwriting Education
American Institute for
Property and Liability Underwriters

Editor

Fourth Edition • 1987

AMERICAN INSTITUTE FOR
PROPERTY AND LIABILITY UNDERWRITERS
720 Providence Road, Malvern, Pennsylvania 19335-0770

© 1987
AMERICAN INSTITUTE FOR
PROPERTY AND LIABILITY UNDERWRITERS, INC.
All rights reserved. This book or any part thereof
may not be reproduced without the written
permission of the publisher.

Fourth Edition • December 1987

Library of Congress Catalog Number 87-71983
International Standard Book Number 0-89463-050-4

Printed in the United States of America

Contributing Authors

Barbara D. Stewart, B.S. Mrs. Stewart is the President of Stewart Economics, Inc., a consulting firm that specializes in the insurance business. Her work involves strategic and business planning, analyses of insurance operations, studies of insurance markets and their competitive problems and opportunities, and evaluations of insurance organizations. Mrs. Stewart earned a B.S. degree in economics and business administration from Beaver College in Glenside, Pennsylvania, and then studied economics at the graduate level at New York University. Her professional career has included economic research, investment management, and performance measurement for the investment banking firm of Wood, Struthers and Winthrop and investment systems consulting for Bradford Computer Systems. From 1974 to 1981 she was Corporate Economist for The Chubb Group of Insurance Companies. She has published several papers on the profit cycle and other economic subjects relating to insurance. She was named Insurance Woman of 1987 by the Association of Professional Insurance Women.

David C. Sterling, B.S., CPCU, CLU, ChFC, CIC, AIM, ARM, AU, ALCM, APA, AAI, ARP, AIC. Mr. Sterling is a Secretary at The Hartford Insurance Group where he is involved with the General Liability line of business with responsibility for pollution liability insurance, commercial umbrella insurance, new product development, market segmentation activities, and industry affairs. He also has responsibility within The Hartford for implementation of the Insurance Services Office, Inc. (ISO) Commercial Lines Simplification program. Mr. Sterling is a graduate of Bryant College with a B.S. in Business Administration. He has lectured on the subject of environmental impairment liability insurance and has been active in industry affairs regarding this subject.

Michael P. Duncan, B.S., JD, CPCU   Mr. Duncan is Assistant Vice President and Assistant General Counsel of Allstate Insurance Company in charge of the Personal Property and Casualty Insurance Law Division of the Law and Regulation Department. He served as Director of Insurance of the State of Illinois in 1976 and 1977. He has published papers on insurance guaranty funds and was Chairman of the National Committee on Insurance Guaranty Funds in 1982. From 1983 to 1986 he was Chairman of the Industry Advisory Committee to the NAIC Guaranty Fund Task Force.

M. Moshe Porat, Ph.D., CPCU   Dr. Porat is Associate Professor of Risk Management and Insurance at Temple University. He received his undergraduate degree in economics and statistics from Tel Aviv University. His M.B.A. is from the Recanati Graduate School of Management at Tel Aviv University. He completed his doctoral work at Temple University. Prior to his academic work, Dr. Porat served as deputy general manager of a large international insurance brokerage firm and as an economic and financial consultant. Dr. Porat authored four monographs on captives and their use in risk management. He has published numerous articles on captives and other financial and risk management topics. He has served as a consultant to public and private organizations including the United Nations, the Government of Bermuda, the Pennsylvania Bar Association, the Pennsylvania Manufacturers Association, and the CIGNA Corporation.

Table of Contents

V. Risk Management ~ *Identification and Measurement of Exposures; Alternatives*

VI. Pollution Liability Insurance ~ *Coverage; The Marketplace; Marketing Pollution Liability Insurance; Coverage Issues; Underwriting the Pollution Exposure*

VII. Future ~ *EIL Insurance and the Pollution Exclusion; The Pollution Exposure*

VIII. Summary and Personal Observations

I. Introduction

II. Dealing with Insolvent Insurers

III. Concept and Origin of Insurance Guaranty Funds ~ *Federal Proposals and NAIC Reaction*

IV. NAIC Model Act ~ *State-by-State Variations*

V. How Post-Assessment Guaranty Funds Work

VI. How Funds Have Performed ~ *Prevention and Detection of Insolvencies*

VII. Challenges of a Multi-State System ~ *Residence of a Corporation; Triggering Guaranty Fund Obligations*

VIII. NAIC Activity Since 1969 ~ *Early Activity; Deductibles; Scope of Coverage; Claims-Made Policies; Funding; Attempts to Quantify the Funding Issue; Policy Committee Report*

IX. Prospects for the Future ~ *Issues in a Multi-State Liquidation System; Guaranty Fund Issues; Liquidator and Guaranty Fund Relations; The Future*

MONOGRAPH 7

Regulating Workers Compensation Groups*

I. INTRODUCTION

Traditionally, employers have met their obligations under state workers compensation laws by obtaining workers compensation insurance from private insurance companies or state funds or by satisfying state requirements for becoming qualified self-insurers. State workers compensation agencies, which typically have the responsibility for regulating self-insurers, have established requirements for becoming a qualified self-insurer that recognize both the nature of the workers compensation risk and the social orientation of the program. One effect of these requirements has been that only large employers have been able to qualify as self-insurers.

There has been a growing trend over the past several years for states to enact legislation permitting smaller employers to pool their risks in entities known variously as workers compensation group self-insurance pools, funds, or associations. Approximately half of the states permit these entities to one degree or another. For purposes of

*This monograph is a Study Committee report to the NAIC, reprinted with the permission of the National Association of Insurance Commissioners (NAIC). The Introduction to the monograph explains some of the background of the issue and when the Study Committee report was adopted by the NAIC. Following the Study Committee report is a copy of the "Private Employer Group Workers Compensation Self-Insurance Model Act," which was adopted (in its current form) at the June 1984 meeting of the NAIC.

1

brevity, this report will refer to them as "workers compensation groups" or simply "groups."

Individual state approaches to workers compensation groups vary considerably. In some states groups are regulated in a similar fashion to self-insurers. In some other states the regulation applicable to groups approaches the kind of regulation applicable to insurance companies. Finally, there are states that at least for a time placed regulatory responsibility for groups with state agencies not usually involved with workers compensation matters.

While the principal motive for the formation of workers compensation groups seems to be to reduce costs, the primary concern of public policy makers should be the solvency of groups and their ability to pay workers compensation benefits as required by law. The present diversity of regulatory approaches indicates a lack of consensus on the nature and extent of regulation appropriate for workers compensation groups and on the state agency to provide it. Until more is known about this, it is possible that workers compensation groups are being inadequately regulated in some states, while in others the degree of regulation they receive may be more than is necessary. Adverse effects can occur in either case.

At its June 1982 meeting the National Association of Insurance Commissioners (NAIC) accepted the recommendation of the Workers Compensation Task Force that a study be performed of the regulation of workers compensation groups. A Study Committee was appointed in August 1982 to conduct a balanced study of workers compensation groups to develop a better understanding of their characteristics and the type of regulation appropriate for them. The Study Committee was not asked to produce model legislation but to analyze carefully the regulatory issues associated with workers compensation groups. For this reason, the Study Committee members, who are listed in Exhibit 7-1, were chosen for their ability to contribute to the study and to achieve a reasonable balance of competing interests.

For those readers who are not familiar with workers compensation groups, the Study Committee presents in Section II a review of their structural, operational, and financial characteristics. This section concludes with a comparison of how workers compensation groups are similar to or different from self-insurers and various types of insurance companies.

Section III provides an overview of the regulation of workers compensation groups and identifies the states that permit such groups and the state agencies that have regulatory jurisdiction over them. This section also includes a listing of citations to state laws and regulations on workers compensation groups.

In Sections IV through VII the Study Committee discusses in some

Exhibit 7-1
NAIC Study Committee on the Regulation of Workers Compensation Group Self-Insurance Associations

James W. Newman, Jr.
Committee Chairman
Senior Vice President
American Insurance Association
85 John Street
New York, New York 10038

Keith T. Bateman
Assistant Vice President
Alliance of American Insurers
20 North Wacker Drive
Chicago, Illinois 60606

Newton P. Black, CPCU, CFE
Supervisor, Self-Insurance Division
Tennessee Department of Insurance
114 State Office Building
Nashville, Tennessee 37219

Daniel Blum
Insurance House of Lafayette
1116 Coolidge Boulevard
P.O. Box 52848
Lafayette, Louisiana 70505
(Representing the National
    Association of Professional
    Insurance Agents)

J. Howard Bunn, Jr.
Vice President
National Association of
Independent Insurers
2600 River Road
Des Plaines, Illinois 60018

Timothy R. Campbell
Assistant Vice President
Aetna Life & Casualty
151 Farmington Avenue
Hartford, Connecticut 06156

Richard I. Fein
Senior Vice President
National Council on
Compensation Insurance
One Penn Plaza
New York, New York 10019

John H. Lewis
Attorney-At-Law
Box 330550
Coconut Grove, Florida 33133

K. Gordon Flory
Secretary-Treasurer
Louisiana AFL-CIO
P.O. Box 3477
Baton Rouge, Louisiana 70821

Brenda M. Fluker
Senior Attorney
Liberty Mutual Insurance Company
175 Berkeley Street
Boston, Massachusetts 02117

Larry D. Gaunt, Ph.D., CPCU
Professor of Insurance
College of Business Administration
Georgia State University
University Plaza
Atlanta, Georgia 30303

Bradley K. Harmes
Deputy Director
Virginia Municipal League
P.O. Box 753
Richmond, Virginia 23206
(Representing Public Risk &
    Insurance Management
    Association)

Richard Heydinger
Director, Risk Management
Hallmark Cards, Inc.
P.O. Box 437
Kansas City, Missouri 64141
(Representing Risk and Insurance
    Management Society)

Donald L. Jones
Coordinator, Risk Management Pool
Service Program
National League of Cities
1301 Pennsylvania Avenue, N.W.
Washington, D.C. 20004

Robert J. Sullivan
Vice President
Crum & Forster Insurance Companies
305 Madison Avenue
Morristown, New Jersey 07960

Robert L. Larsen
President
Insurance Administration Center
1480 Renaissance Drive
Park Ridge, Illinois 60068
(Representing the National
    Association of Wholesalers-
    Distributors)

Continued on next page

Herman B. Lightsey, Jr.
Auditor, Self-Insurance
South Carolina
Industrial Commission
1800 St. Julian Place
Columbia, South Carolina 29204

Daniel J. Miller
President
Florida AFL-CIO
135 S. Monroe
Tallahassee, Florida 32302

J. Maurice Miller, Jr.
Attorney-At-Law
Mays, Valentine, Davenport & Moore
P.O. Box 1122
Richmond, Virginia 23208

S. Allen Norris
Workers' Compensation Self-
Insurance Consultant
2850 Delk Road, Apt. 7-H
Marietta, Georgia 30067

Richard R. Rousselot
Director, Workers' Compensation
P.O. Box 58
Jefferson City, Missouri 65102

Robert J. Sullivan
Vice President
Crum & Forster Insurance Companies
305 Madison Avenue
Morristown, New Jersey 07960

Joseph W. Tasker, Jr.
Chief Examiner
Georgia Insurance Department
236 State Capitol
Atlanta, Georgia 30334

Richard D. Teubner, CPCU
Rich & Cartmill, Inc.
3365 E. Skelly Drive
Tulsa, Oklahoma 74125
(Representing the Independent
Insurance Agents Association)

Gilbert Waters
President
Waters Insurance Management Corp.
2540 South Trail
Sarasota, Florida 33579

Study Committee Staff

Mark R. Fradkin, CPCU
Senior Research Associate
American Insurance Association
85 John Street
New York, New York 10038

James D. Zarnowski, Esq.
Senior Research Associate
American Insurance Association
85 John Street
New York, New York 10038

detail four important aspects of workers compensation groups: (1) their organization and administration, (2) the obligations of groups and their members, (3) the ways in which rates are established and profits and losses are distributed, and (4) the methods used to guard against insolvency. Each section identifies a number of public policy issues, discusses why the issues are important, presents various points of view on the issues, and describes how current laws and regulations treat the issues.

Section VIII focuses on the regulatory process with emphasis on the knowledge, skills, and abilities needed by regulators of workers compensation groups. This should be of particular interest to legislators who are faced with establishing an appropriate regulatory approach for workers compensation groups and assigning regulatory responsibilities to state agencies in keeping with their levels of interest and capabilities. Other general aspects of the regulatory process are also discussed in Section VIII.

The report concludes with an Overview in Section IX, which contains a listing of the principal workers compensation group regulatory issues addressed by the Study Committee.

Some of the descriptive material in Sections II through VIII is included primarily to inform and to indicate to which state laws and regulations public policymakers can refer for information about specific regulatory approaches. Much of this material is presented by the Study Committee without comment. There are, however, a large number of issues discussed in the report that the Study Committee considers to be particularly important. In almost all of these instances, the Study Committee presents its recommendations, which are in italics in the text.

These recommendations, together with the information and analysis in the report, should assist legislators, insurance regulators, workers compensation administrators, and others in constructing suitable approaches to regulating workers compensation groups.

II. WHAT ARE WORKERS COMPENSATION GROUPS?

In simple terms, a workers compensation group is a cooperative pooling arrangement through which a number of employers jointly meet their workers compensation obligations. Typically, the form and nature of the cooperative arrangement and important operational features of workers compensation groups are governed by state law and regulation.

The principal attraction of workers compensation groups is the perception that employers can obtain workers compensation coverage at lower cost than if they purchased the coverage individually from insurance companies. Related to this is the retention of investment income for the benefit of employer members. Employer trade associations have shown interest in workers compensation groups because it permits them to provide additional services to their members. Some employers joined workers compensation groups because they believed that the group offered a level of service superior to that offered by insurance companies. In some cases employers have joined groups to obtain workers compensation coverage not readily available from insurance companies.

The purpose of this section is to present an overview of the structural, operational, and financial characteristics of workers compensation groups. Where appropriate, differences between public and private employer groups are noted. The section concludes with an analysis of how workers compensation groups are similar to and different from insurance companies and self-insurers. The background information in this chapter should be valuable for those readers who are not familiar with workers compensation groups.

Structure

Employers in a variety of industries have established workers compensation groups. Industries in which groups appear most often include local governments and public school districts, builders and general contractors, health care facilities, automobile dealers, lumber manufacturing and wood products, roofing and sheet contractors, and retail merchants. Most of the industries are characterized by a large number of employers of small to moderate size.

In most states workers compensation groups have been formed by already existing groups of employers, such as industry trade associations or associations of governmental entities. Although some workers compensation groups have multi-industry membership, the membership of most groups is drawn from a single industry.

Workers' compensation groups are usually unincorporated associations or trusts. Another type of organization, used by governmental and educational agencies in California and Texas, derives its existence from joint powers provisions, which permit two or more public agencies to exercise jointly any power an agency can exercise individually. The rules or bylaws under which groups operate are established by the sponsoring organization in conformity with relevant state laws or regulations governing workers compensation groups. The employer members of a group are bound together by their execution of an indemnity agreement and by the group's bylaws. These documents establish many of the key operational elements of the group including the naming of the first governing board, the naming of an administrator, the establishment of guarantees of the group's financial status, and in some cases, the designation of the claim service company.

Most indemnity agreements include a provision binding group members jointly and severally to pay the unsatisfied obligations of the group that may arise from workers compensation claims and awards. The use of joint and several liability is typical in workers compensation groups formed by private employers. Groups organized by local governmental units and school districts sometimes do not incorporate joint and several liability. Whether or not joint and several liability is present, members are obligated to pay their premiums to the group as determined by the trustees.

Joint and several liability provides the ultimate financial security for a workers compensation group. While premium payments and various financial security arrangements are expected to be sufficient to meet the obligations of the group and its members, if they are not, a member may be required to pay a share of any deficit or the entire deficit. If a group has a projected shortfall in funds needed to meet its obligations, additional funds may not actually be needed until several years have passed because of the long-tail nature of workers compensation claims. The group could use investment income, reduce dividends, suspend advance premium discounts, or impose assessments on its members to raise the additional revenues as they are needed.

The governing board of a workers compensation group has responsibility for the group's operations and financial condition. Specifically, the board's responsibilities include admitting new group members, selecting the administrator and service companies, obtaining excess insurance, and establishing dividend distribution policies.

In most cases, members of the governing board are selected by and from the members of the sponsoring organization and the group. In some cases, such as school board groups, each employer member of the group is represented by a person designated by the individual school board.

Operations

Day-to-day management of a workers compensation group usually is provided by a professional administrator. Group administrators may be individuals, independent specialized organizations, or subsidiaries or affiliates of insurance companies or brokers. A few groups use their own employees to perform some administrative and other functions.

The services that groups most often obtain from service companies are (1) claims handling and rehabilitation, (2) purchase of excess insurance and bonds, (3) loss control and safety engineering, (4) actuarial, (5) data processing and (6) compliance with state filing requirements. With respect to claims handling and loss control, service companies perform the same functions that insurance companies perform. The service companies receive, investigate, reserve, pay, and in some cases, controvert claims. They keep appropriate records and make filing with state workers compensation agencies. Contracts for claims handling generally stipulate that the service company will continue to handle all claims that occur in the contract period. In cases where service companies are changed, this could result in a group having different claims handled by different companies at the same time.

Workers compensation groups have developed safety and loss control programs, which can be important factors in their ability to keep overall costs low. Repeated lack of cooperation with loss control efforts is one reason used by groups to terminate members.

Groups collect and maintain essentially the same experience data as insurance companies, although there are important differences. Groups are usually not required to file data with rating organizations, but they need the data, nevertheless, to calculate experience modifications, dividends, assessments, and final premiums based on audited payrolls.

The pricing decisions of the governing board of a workers compensation group are circumscribed by the need to maintain adequate loss reserves, the excess insurance company, and the laws and regulations of the state in which the group operates. In most cases, newly formed groups use rating organization classification plans and rates. Groups that have been operating sufficiently long to collect credible data may sometimes establish rates based on their own experience. The premiums for individual group members are affected by their own experience through the experience rating plan in effect in the state and by the advance premium discounts that most groups are permitted to give.

All workers compensation groups establish what are variously termed claims funds or loss funds to comply with state regulatory requirements. The function of these funds is to retain a sufficient amount of premium for payment of claims and claim-related expenses of the group. As initially established, loss funds may be considered analogous to the permissible loss ratio of an insurance company. In most cases, the amount in the loss fund is determined by the group's retention percentage under its aggregate excess insurance coverage.

Another fund established by groups, generally called the trustees' fund, contains monies under the control of the trustees that are not part of the loss fund. In practice the trustees' fund corresponds to the expense provision in insurance company rates. Payments from this fund typically are made for such purposes as loss control services, excess insurance premiums, legal services, accounting services, and outside premium auditors.

The primary way in which group members realize lower workers compensation costs is through dividends paid following the conclusion of a policy year. There are a variety of state regulatory approaches as well as different methods by which groups determine eligibility for dividends and the amounts to be refunded. State regulation generally determines the minimum waiting period after the close of each policy year after which a group may declare dividends and specifies how much surplus in excess of incurred losses and loss expenses the group must retain in the loss fund. Groups are typically required to wait from six months to a year or longer after expiration of the policy year before paying dividends. All states regulating group dividends require approval before dividends can be paid so regulators can determine whether loss reserves adequately provide for loss development and losses that have occurred but have not yet been reported to the group.

Groups usually pay dividends from funds generated from savings due to better than average loss experience and relate them to each employer's premium volume and loss history on a sliding scale. Expense savings and investment income on the group's funds are typically segregated from loss experience savings and are usually refunded on a pro-rata basis not related to either the size or loss history of each employer.

Because groups usually do not refund initially all projected surplus from a fund year, funds may accumulate during the early years of a group's operation. As the claims from each fund year develop, the group can better estimate ultimate loss payments. Typically, this results in gradually increasing dividends for a number of years. A continuing group member's annual dividend may be the sum of pro-rata expense and investment surplus, plus an experience dividend based on the losses of both the group and the member. In most groups, an employer is eligible for only those dividends arising from the fund years of its membership. Although it is the policy of most groups to pay a dividend only to employers who are members at the time the dividend is declared, some groups differentiate in their dividend policies between employers who terminate their membership voluntarily and those who are terminated involuntarily. Some groups do not continue to pay dividends to members who terminate their membership voluntarily. In these cases, the receipt of future dividends is a strong incentive for employers to remain in the group and to cooperate with loss control programs.

The establishment of underwriting standards is a responsibility of the governing board, as is the acceptance, declination, or termination of employers. Primary underwriting factors include loss history, cooperation with loss control efforts, and an employer's credit history and liquidity. A number of public sector groups do not refuse to accept or terminate employers for underwriting reasons.

Finance

The financial characteristics of workers compensation groups are dictated to a considerable degree by state statutory and regulatory requirements. These range from general proof of ability to administer and pay workers compensation claims to very specific methods of assuring financial strength.

In most cases, workers compensation groups meet their initial and ongoing working capital requirements by collecting an advance premium from members, which normally amounts to 25 percent of estimated standard premium. In addition, groups are frequently required to make a security deposit with the state in the form of cash, securities, an irrevocable letter of credit or a surety bond to provide additional financial protection.

Well-run workers compensation groups maintain their solvency through a combination of prudent actions such as underwriting carefully, handling claims properly, promoting safety and loss control among their members, establishing loss reserves conservatively and protecting their members with adequate excess insurance. Excess insurance, which pays after individual claims reach a certain size or after claims in the aggregate reach a specified limit, is particularly significant for groups because they are usually much smaller in size than most insurance companies.

Although state requirements vary, most groups have specific excess coverage, i.e., insurance that covers in excess of the amount retained by the group for a specific accident. Recently, excess insurance policies with unlimited specific excess coverage for all statutory benefits have become available in several states.

In addition states usually require aggregate excess insurance and specify minimum amounts of coverage in terms of flat dollar amounts, percentage of annual premium, or percentage of anticipated losses. The purpose of aggregate excess insurance is to limit the sum of individual retained losses of a group to a stated amount. When this occurs, the excess insurance company pays all additional losses up to its limit of liability. The retention level for aggregate excess insurance is usually a percentage of earned premium. Groups usually obtain specific and aggregate excess insurance from the same insurance company.

Although final responsibility for investments of workers compensation groups rests with the governing board, implementation of investment policy is handled differently by various groups. Some groups give investment authority to their treasurers, while in other groups it is the professional administrator who makes investment decisions, usually with approval and authority from the governing board or an investment committee.

Because of regulatory restrictions, most groups place their funds in conservative investments such as obligations of the state of domicile, United States Government securities, and bank certificates of deposit. Other investments may include bankers' acceptances, bonds, and repurchase agreements. Groups are typically prohibited from investing in common stocks, mortgages, or real estate.

Workers compensation groups maintain and submit to a regulatory authority a variety of records and reports reflecting the financial condition of the group and its members. Although requirements vary among the states, groups typically submit periodic and annual financial reports, certified audits of fund accounts, and reports on premium payments and claims. In some cases they report on the net worth of their members.

In some states, workers compensation groups pay premium taxes. More commonly, groups pay the same types of assessments that insurance companies and self-insurers pay for the support of the workers compensation agency. In states where groups are regulated by the insurance department, they may also pay some types of fees or assessments to cover the costs incurred by the insurance department.

Although workers compensation groups do not participate in insurance company insolvency funds, in a few states they participate in guaranty funds with self-insurers. In most cases, groups contribute to Second Injury Funds, but there is less uniformity regarding participation by groups in other special funds. Groups have not been required to participate in the residual market mechanisms operated by insurance companies.

Comparison of Workers Compensation Risk Bearing Alternatives

The preceding sections described workers compensation groups and how they operate. This section compares workers compensation groups with self-insurers and several types of insurance companies. These comparisons will provide useful background information and understanding for the in-depth discussion in the remaining sections of this report on the public policy issues involved with the regulation of workers compensation groups.

Exhibit 7-2 presents concise summary descriptions of the intrinsic characteristics of several workers compensation risk bearing alternatives. To facilitate comparisons that are pertinent for this report, some alternatives, such as captive insurance companies and state funds, are excluded. Also, the summary descriptions of self-insurers and insurance companies are couched in workers compensation terms, even though both are often involved with other types of risks. Finally, the summary description of workers compensation groups more accurately describes groups of private employers, which are the most numerous, than groups of public employers because of the reference to joint and several liability.

Exhibit 7-2
Intrinsic Characteristics of Risk Bearing Alternatives

Workers Compensation Group	A not-for-profit unincorporated association or trust that assumes the workers compensation risks of its members. Members are jointly and severally liable without limit to meet the workers compensation obligations of the group and all of its members.
Self-Insurer	A large corporation or governmental subdivision that retains its own workers compensation risk and, as differentiated from "non-insurance," typically has a plan or budget for paying claims.
Reciprocal Exchange	A not-for-profit unincorporated association through which each subscriber transfers its workers compensation risk and assumes the workers compensation risks of all other subscribers. Subscribers do not retain any of their own risk of loss but, in the case of assessable reciprocals, are liable for assessment up to some multiple of premium. In the case of non-assessable reciprocals, subscribers are not liable for assessment.
Mutual Insurer	A not-for-profit non-stock corporation that assumes the workers compensation risks of its policyholders. Policyholders do not retain any risk of loss but, in the case of assessable mutual insurers, are liable for assessment up to some multiple of premium. In the case of non-assessable mutual insurers, policyholders are not liable for assessment.
Stock Insurer	A for-profit stock corporation that assumes the workers compensation risks of its policyholders who do not retain any risk of loss and who are not liable for assessment.

The references in Exhibit 7-2 to assumption of risk by workers compensation groups and insurance companies needs some explanation. In this context risk refers to chance of loss and does not refer to legal liability. An employer can transfer its workers compensation risk even though it does not transfer its workers compensation liability. In fact, many state laws state that an employer purchasing coverage from an insurance company or joining a workers compensation group is not relieved of the liabilities imposed by workers compensation law with respect to its employees.

There is an important difference between self-insurers and workers compensation groups. While a self-insurer retains and is responsible for its own workers compensation risk, a workers compensation group is a separate entity formed by many employers to assume their workers compensation risks. Even though a group member's joint and several liability is analogous in certain respects to the retention of risk by self-insurers, the analogy is not strong. As a matter of practice, groups try to arrange their financial affairs, i.e., collecting premiums, establishing loss reserves, and purchasing surety bonds and excess insurance, so that joint and several liability is never utilized and they never have to make an assessment. Several states have approved specific excess insurance policies that pay statutory benefits, which a number of groups have purchased voluntarily, that reduces this likelihood further.

As the entries in Exhibit 7-2 show, workers compensation groups, reciprocal exchanges, mutual insurance companies, and stock insurance companies share a number of important characteristics, although there are some differences. Groups, reciprocal exchanges, and mutual insurance companies are all not-for-profit organizations controlled by their respective members, subscribers, and policyholders. With stock insurance companies, non-assessable mutual insurance companies, and non-assessable reciprocal exchanges, an employer's workers compensation risk is transferred unconditionally in exchange for a premium. A public group without joint and several liability and a private group with a comprehensive excess insurance program have risk characteristics substantially the same as those of a non-assessable mutual insurance company.

With assessable mutual insurance companies and reciprocal exchanges there is an initial transfer of risk; however, in both cases individual employers remain contingently liable for assessment if financial resources are insufficient to pay losses. The liability for assessment of employers who insure with mutual insurance companies or reciprocal exchanges is limited to a stated multiple of their premium. Members of workers compensation groups have in practical effect an unlimited liability for assessment. The earlier statement about groups minimizing the possibility of assessment applies equally to assessable mutual insurers and reciprocals. It is fair to say that none of these entities ever expects to make assessments.

With this background the remainder of the report discusses public policy issues related to appropriate regulatory requirements for workers compensation groups as risk assuming organizations and the state agencies that provide this regulation.

III. REGULATORY OVERVIEW

State workers compensation laws, enacted early in this century to replace the tort system with a structured benefit system for compensating injured workers, led to a higher degree of state government involvement in workers compensation insurance than is the case for other lines of insurance. State insurance departments and workers compensation agencies have long had important responsibilities regarding workers compensation insurance and the workers compensation system.

Insurance departments have responsibility for administering the insurance laws of the state. With respect to workers compensation insurance, the insurance department's activities are directed primarily toward (1) regulating the financial condition of insurance companies to guard against insolvency and (2) exercising review and approval authority over rates charged by insurance companies to ensure that rates are not excessive, inadequate, or unfairly discriminatory.

Workers compensation agencies have responsibility for administering the workers compensation laws of the state. This involves primarily (1) ensuring the fair, prompt, and efficient delivery of workers compensation benefits to injured workers and (2) resolving disputes between employers and workers as they arise.

Early in the history of workers compensation, some, usually very large, employers sought permission to meet their workers compensation liabilities with self-insurance programs. Because workers compensation agencies were responsible for ensuring that employers complied with the requirements of the workers compensation law, these agencies were given the authority to approve or disapprove self-insurance programs. Over time, workers compensation agencies developed reasonably uniform approaches to regulating self-insurance programs, including requirements on minimum size, financial reports, and security deposits. In carrying out their responsibilities regarding self-insurers, workers compensation agencies evaluate and monitor the financial well-being of those employers who have applied for and been granted the privilege of self-insuring their workers compensation obligations. This activity is similar in purpose to the regulation of insurance company financial condition performed by insurance departments.

Employers too small to implement acceptable self-insurance programs have argued that they should be able to join with other employers to meet their workers compensation obligations as a group. Because these workers compensation groups seemed to have characteristics similar to both insurance companies and self-insurers, it was not always clear how they should be regulated and by whom. The states that permit workers compensation groups have arrived at a variety of answers regarding the nature, extent, and location of regulatory authority for workers compensation groups. Exhibit 7-3 lists the states that permit workers compensation groups, indicates whether public or private groups are permitted, and identifies the agency responsible for their regulation.

When the term "regulation" or "regulatory authority" is used in this report, it refers to oversight, review, and approval activities of a group's formation, structure, pricing and financial affairs unless the context indicates another meaning. These terms are not used in this report to refer to the important claim-related activities of workers compensation agencies, which are applicable to groups just as they are to self-insurers and insurance companies.

Most of the thirty states allowing workers compensation groups permit both public and private employers to join groups, but not the same group. There are seven states, however, that permit either all public employers or some types of public employers to form groups, but do not permit private employers to do so. Colorado permits public employer groups as well as groups made up of physicians and health care institutions.

An important decision that must be made when legislation is enacted permitting workers compensation groups is the state agency that will have regulatory authority over the groups. The evidence indicates a diversity of opinion on this. Fifteen states have assigned regulatory authority to the workers compensation agency, while in eleven states the insurance department has this responsibility. Colorado has split the responsibility with the insurance department responsible for public groups and the workers compensation agency responsible for physician and health care institution groups. Connecticut has dual regulation with both the workers compensation agency and the insurance department having responsibility. Texas and Tennessee permit public groups without any regulatory oversight.

Almost all of the states enacting workers compensation group laws prior to 1979 placed regulatory authority for groups with the workers compensation agency. Of the recent laws, those enacted in 1979 or after, most place regulatory authority with the insurance department.

States permitting workers compensation groups usually have explicit statutory authorization for the existence of groups as one permissible method by which employers can meet their workers compensation obligations. For example, the Virginia Compensation Code states that:

Every employer subject to this Act shall secure his liability thereunder by one of the following methods:

Exhibit 7-3
States Permitting Workers Compensation Groups

State	Type of Employers Allowed to Form Groups	Regulatory Agency
Alabama	Public and Private	W/C Agency
Arkansas	Public and Private	W/C Agency
California	Public only	W/C Agency
Colorado	Physician or Health Care Institutions	W/C Agency
	Public	Insurance Dept.
Connecticut	Public and Private	Insurance Dept. and W/C Agency
Florida	Public and Private	W/C Agency
Georgia	Public and Private	Insurance Dept.
Illinois	Public and Private	Insurance Dept.
Iowa	Public and Private	Insurance Dept.
Kansas	Private	Insurance Dept.
Kentucky	Public and Private	W/C Agency
Louisiana	Public and Private	Insurance Dept.
Maine	Public and Private	Insurance Dept.
Maryland	Public Only	W/C Agency
Michigan	Public and Private	W/C Agency
Minnesota	Public and Private	Insurance Dept.
Missouri	Public and Private	W/C Agency
New Hampshire	Public and Private	W/C Agency
New Jersey	School Boards	Insurance Dept.
New Mexico	Public only	Insurance Dept.
New York	Private and Counties	W/C Agency
North Carolina	Public and Private	W/C Agency
Oklahoma	Public and Private	W/C Agency
Oregon	Public and Private	W/C Agency
Rhode Island	Public and Private	Insurance Dept.
South Carolina	Public and Private	W/C Agency
Tennessee	Public only	None
Texas	Public only	None
Virginia	Public and Private	Insurance Dept.
Washington	School Districts	W/C Agency

(In Pennsylvania, some school districts have formed a workers compensation group even though this is not explicitly authorized by statute. Potential members of the group must apply to the W/C Agency for permission to self-insure on an individual basis.)

1. Insuring and keeping his liability in an insurer authorized to transact the business of workers compensation insurance in this State,
2. Receiving a certificate...from the Industrial Commission authorizing such employer to be an individual self-insurer, or
3. Being a member in good standing of a group self-insurance association licensed by the (insurance department).

In addition to authorizing workers compensation groups and identifying the agency responsible for their regulation, statutory language is needed to implement a regulatory scheme. The most common approach is delegating authority to a regulatory agency in a statute containing a grant of rule making authority and guidelines or parameters regarding the areas to be regulated. The agency then promulgates a regulation providing the needed regulatory detail. Several states have followed this approach, e.g., Arkansas, Illinois, Louisiana, and Virginia. Some other states have a more generally-worded grant of authority that gives the workers compensation agency or insurance department more flexibility in developing its regulatory approach. Alabama, Kentucky and Oklahoma are in this category. This approach, however, may be challenged as an improper delegation of authority by the Legislature. For example, the Oklahoma Attorney General rendered an opinion in November 1982 that the Oklahoma statute did not comply with a recent state Supreme Court decision requiring the Legislature to "establish its policies and set out definite standards for the exercise of an agency's rulemaking power." California and Texas represent another variation in that they have used the joint power authority approach to permit public employers to form groups.

Exhibit 7-4 sets forth specific citations to statutes and regulations for the thirty states permitting workers compensation groups. This listing should be helpful to anyone interested in examining individual state approaches to regulating workers compensation groups. The statutes and regulations cited in Exhibit 7-4 provide the basis for the many individual state references contained in the following chapters. The Study Committee made a considerable effort to ensure the accuracy of the information in Exhibit 7-4 and the later state references; however, the report may not reflect all new laws or regulations or amendments thereto.

Because of the focus on individual state references, the report does not refer in the following sections to the model regulation adopted in 1980 by the International Association of Industrial Accident Boards and Commissions (IAIABC). Nevertheless, the Study Committee acknowl-

Exhibit 7-4
Citations and Effective Years of Statutes and Regulations

State	Type of Group	Statutes		Regulations	
		Citations	Years	Citations	Years
Alabama	Public	Act 265, Laws 1981	1981	R-100 through R-111, Rules for Group S-1'ers under Ala. W.C. Law	1981
	Private	Ala. Code S. 25-5-9	1965		
Arkansas	Public	Ark. Stat. Ann. S.81-1336 (a) (3)	1979	Rule 5, Part III Arkansas W.C. Rules of the Commission	
	Private	Same	1979	Same	
California	Public	Cal. Gov't. Code. S.6500	1975		
		Cal. Lab. Code. S.3700	1978		
Colorado	Public	Colo. Rev. Stat. S.8-44-110	1981		
	Physicians or Health Care Institutions	Colo. Rev. Stat. S.11-70-101	1977		
Connecticut	Public	Munic: Conn. Gen. Stat. S.7-479a	1979	Conn. Agencies Regs. S.31-284-5 (Informal W.C. Board Guidelines - not part of Administrative Code)	
	Private	Labor: Conn. Gen. Stat. S.31-328, S.31-284	1949	Same	
Florida	Public	Fla. Stat. Ann. Title 30 S.440.57	1937	Chapter 38F-5, Rules of the Dept. of Labor and Employment Security, Division of W.C.	
	Private	Same	1937	Same	
Georgia	Public	Ga. Code Ann. S.114.6a	1981	Ga. Admin. Comp Ch. 120-2-34	1982
	Private	Same	1981	Same	
Illinois	Public	Ill. Rev. Stat., Ch. 48, pars. 138.4a and 172.39a	1980	Dept. of Insurance Rule 29.01	
		Ill. Rev. Stat. Ch. 73, pars. 799, 1013, 1065.3, 1065.501, 1065.11a	1980		
	Private	Same	1980		
Iowa	Public	Iowa Code S.87.4 - Public Groups first allowed in 1981	1913		
	Private	Same - Private Groups first allowed in 1930's	1913		

State	Type	Statute	Year	Rule/Regulation
Kansas	Private	K.S.A. 44-505; 44-532; 74-711, 712, 713, 714, 716, and 719 K.S.A. 1982 Supp. 44-566a and 44-573	1983	803 K.A.R. 25.025
Kentucky	Public	Ky. Rev. Stat. S. 342.350	1977	
	Private	Same	1977	
Louisiana	Public	Municipalities and Parishes: La. Rev. Stat. Ann. 33.1343	1979	Proposed Ins. Dept. Rule No. 4 (Interlocal Risk Mgt. Agencies)
	Private	Labor and Workmen's Comp: La. Rev. Stat. Ann. 23:1191-93	1979	Proposed Ins. Dept. Rule No. 8 (Group Self-Ins.)
Maine	Public	39 M.R.S.A. S.23.4-23.5	1973	Dept. of Bus. Reg., Bur. of Ins., Ch. 250
	Private	39 M.R.S.A. S.23.4-23.5, 23(2-A), (4)	1979	
		24-A M.R.S.A. S.601-16	1980	
		39 M.R.S.A. S.23-23-A	1982	
Maryland	Public	Chapter 666, Laws 1981	1982	Proposed C.O.M.A.R. 14.09.02
		Chapter 410, Laws 1982	1982	
		Chapter 704, Laws 1982	1982	
Michigan	Public	Mich. Comp. Laws S.418.611	1974	Michigan Workers' Disability Compensation Administrative Rules 408.43
	Private	Same	1974	
	Nonpublic Nonprivate Health Care Facility			
Minnesota	Public	Minn. Stat. S. 471.98, 471.981, 471.982	1980	4 M.C.A.R. S.1.9285-99
	Private	Minn. Stat. S.176.181	1979	
Missouri	Public	Mo. Rev. Stat. S.287.280	1982	8 Mo. Admin. Code 50-3010 Rules Governing Self-Insurers
	Private	Same	1982	
New Hampshire	Public	N.H. R.S.A. S.281:9, II	1947	N.H. Dept. of Labor Admin. Reg. No. III-C-101
		Groups first allowed by reg.	1975	1975
	Private	Same	1975	Same
New Jersey	School Boards	N.J.S. 18A	1983	
New Mexico	Public	a. State (Mandatory) N.M. Stat. Ann. S.15-7-6	1977	
		b. Munic. (permissive) N.M. Stat. Ann. S.32-62-2	1979	
		N.M. Stat. Ann. S. 11-1-1 to 11-1-7	1978	

State	Type of Group	Statutes Citations	Statutes Years	Regulations Citations	Regulations Years
New York	Private	N.Y. Work. Comp. Law Art. 4 S.50.3-a (McKinney 1966)	1966	N.Y.W.C. Board Rules and Reg. Sec. 315,316 (1982)	
	Counties	N.Y. Work. Comp. Law Art. 5 S.60-75 (McKinney 1955)	1955		
North Carolina	Public	N.C. Gen. Stat. S.97-7	1929	Rules of the Industrial Commission, Rule V	1977
	Private	N.C. Gen Stat S.97-93	1929	Same	
Oklahoma	Public	51 O.S. S.167 85 O.S. S.2b, 185 Same	1978 1981 1982		
	Private	85 O.S. S.149.1, 1.2(E)	1981	Rule 39 of the Rules of the Oklahoma WC Court	1981
Oregon	Public	Ore. Rev. Stat. S.656.430	1981	O.A.R. 51-405-998	1981
	Private	Ore. Rev. Stat. S. 656.430, 656.506, 656.614	1981		1982
Rhode Island	Hospitals	R.I. Gen. Laws S.28-36-1.1 (repealed)	1980		
	Public	R.I. Gen. Laws S.28-47	1982		
	Private	Same	1982		
South Carolina	Public	S.C. Code Ann. S.42-5-20	1972	S.C. Industrial Commission Memo. 7/1/79 Revised1/1/82	
	Private	Same (but groups existed earlier)		None	
Tennessee	Public	T.C.A. S.29-20-401, S.12-9-101 (Interlocal Coop.)	1979 1967		
Texas	Public	Tex. Stat. Ann. Art. 8309h S.4	1974		
Virginia	Public	Va. Code S.65.1-104.2	1979	Department of Insurance, Regulation 16	1980
	Private	Same	1979		
Washington	Sch. Districts and/or other Ed'l. Svce. Districts	Chapter 191, Laws of 1982	1982	Proposed W.A.C. 296-15-026	1982-83

The letter "S" is used as an abbreviation for "Section"

edges the important contribution this model represents and the use made of it by many states.

IV. ORGANIZATION AND ADMINISTRATION

A workers compensation group is more than a collection of employers. It is a separate entity with important workers compensation responsibilities. Because of the state's interest in seeing that benefits are paid to injured workers and others as required by law, the state needs to be sure that workers compensation groups are properly organized and administered. While this does not guarantee success, a workers compensation group that is properly organized and administered is more likely to function effectively over the long run than one that is not.

Membership Requirements

The minimum number of members a workers compensation group must have is an important question regarding the structure of groups. The use of the term "group" implies more than one member, but it does not provide any guidance as to the number of members a group should have to enhance its chance of success. The most frequent approach is to state, as the Alabama, Kentucky and Virginia laws do, that "two or more employers" may be licensed or approved as a group. A few states, such as Missouri and New Hampshire, do not state a number requirement, which implies that as few as two employers could form a group. Some of the more recent workers compensation group laws have established a higher minimum for the number of members in a group. Kansas and Louisiana require five or more employers, while Georgia and Oregon require ten or more.

In addition to the total number of members, regulators have an interest in the relative size of members to assure an adequate spread of risk. If one large employer represents substantially all of a group's net worth or premium volume, the group may have real difficulty if that employer has bad loss experience, has severe financial difficulties, or withdraws from the group.

An important issue regarding the organization of workers compensation groups is how similar the activities, and therefore the risk characteristics, of group members should be. The early workers compensation groups had essentially homogeneous membership because they were developed by existing trade associations or associations formed to meet employers workers compensation needs. Some of these single-industry groups traditionally have included employers operating on the periphery of their industries in a support or service capacity. In recent years some groups have departed consciously from the homogeneous membership approach by accepting members from a variety of industries.

The argument for requiring homogeneity of membership has several elements. Employers in the same industry have in-depth knowledge of the workers compensation risk characteristics of their business. They should be able to judge with greater confidence the risks of joining a "same industry" workers compensation group than they would if they were considering joining a group with diverse membership. The group itself would be better able to evaluate potential members' likely loss experience, commitment to safety, and credit worthiness. These points are significant for a workers compensation group because of the joint and several liability assumed by each member. Also, a homogeneous group should be able to develop and implement specialized claim handling rehabilitation, safety, and engineering services for the group's members.

The principal argument in favor of membership heterogeneity is the benefit associated with the insurance concept of spread of risk. Adverse business conditions or a hazardous exposure in one industry would have less effect on a heterogeneous group than on one whose members were all in the affected industry. A second argument is that in some states there may not be enough employers in the same industry to form a group of sufficient size. In this case, a strict homogeneity requirement may foreclose the possibility of groups being formed. In other states, a homogeneity requirement may not stand in the way of groups of at least the minimum size being formed, but it could prevent groups from reaching a size where significant operating economies occur. A third argument is that there are groups that have operated successfully with heterogeneous memberships.

With only a few exceptions, states require some relationship between members of workers compensation groups. A few states, including Michigan, say simply that members must be in the same industry. New Hampshire goes further and defines that required relationship as being employers "having similar trades, businesses, occupations, professions, or functions." A third group of states, represented by Florida, Rhode Island, and Virginia, use the phrase "common interest" in describing the relationship required of members or potential members. This is usually defined to mean membership in a trade association or engaging in the same or similar types of business. Georgia requires that members of private groups must be bona fide members of a trade or professional association and must have "similar governing industry classification." The new Kansas law contains the following requirements: (1) a group must consist of five or more employers who are members of the "same bona fide trade or profession-al association," (2) the association must have been in existence at least five years, and (3) members must be engaged in the "same or similar type of business."

Recently, two states have relaxed their homogeneity requirements. Illinois, which had language in its workers compensation group law requiring members of groups to have "similar risk characteristics," has expanded this language to permit groups whose members belong to "a bona fide professional, commercial, industrial or trade association." Some groups permitted by this new language will probably be more heterogeneous than groups formed under the "similar risk characteris-tics" language. In Minnesota, the "same industry" requirement was eliminated. Now, "two or more employers, whether or not they are in the same industry," are permitted to form a workers compensation group. This change creates the possibility that public and private employers will join the same group. This possibility is explored in the section on public groups.

The members of the Study Committee have different opinions on the homogeneity/heterogeneity issue. Some believe that heterogeneous groups are de facto insurance companies. These members believe that at some point groups and insurance companies are so similar that for a number of public policy reasons, including competitive fairness, they should be regulated in the same manner. Other members believe that heterogeneity does not make a group an insurance company, but the increased spread of risk in heterogeneous groups provides greater protection against severe losses in a single industry resulting from either inherent hazards or economic reverses. Further, they maintain that heterogeneous groups are simply an alternative method of providing workers compensation coverage to employers who do not choose to obtain this coverage from insurance companies, may be unable to qualify as self-insurers, or do not choose to self-insure.

The Study Committee believes that the homogene-ity/heterogeneity issue should be reviewed carefully by those con-cerned with the regulation of workers compensation groups in each state.

There are two aspects of the many references in state laws and regulations to trade associations that need further elaboration. First, a number of states with homogeneity requirements permit a workers compensation group to be formed by members of a trade association without further definition of what they mean by "trade association." Do these states intend for trade associations with heterogeneous member-ships to be able to form groups? Some trade associations are substantially homogeneous but have some members with different risk characteristics. Do these states intend for a trade association's membership policies to take precedence over a "same industry" or "similar risk characteristic" requirement? If these are not the intended results, states will need to set forth more precisely their intentions regarding trade association membership.

There are many who believe that if a trade association sponsors a workers compensation group, the group would have more continuity and a better chance of success than if a number of previously unrelated employers were brought together solely to form a group. Georgia, as indicated earlier, does not permit groups to be formed except by a trade or professional association. An important question is whether the trade association must have a reason for existence other than to serve as a means of complying with the workers compensation group membership requirements. Only a few states have addressed this question explicitly. Georgia defines "trade association," in part, as an..."association which is engaged in substantial activity for the benefit of its members, other than the sponsorship of a 'group'...." Kansas recognizes membership in a trade association only if the trade association has been in existence for five years, while Missouri requires eight years. There is precedent for this approach in the insurance laws of many states that prohibit so-called "fictitious" groups, which are groups of individuals or businesses brought together solely for the purpose of obtaining insurance at favorable rates.

The Study Committee believes that if a state wants to have a trade association requirement, the requirement should be stated in terms of membership in a bona fide trade association.

Most states have recognized the practical value of having the workers compensation risks of all parts of a business handled by the same entity. Michigan, Oklahoma, and Virginia, for example, all permit different businesses owned or controlled (which usually means a majority interest) by a member of a group to join the group.

In many states the ability of public employers to join workers compensation groups is set forth explicitly in the law; however, this is not always the case. In Virginia, for example, any employers having a common interest may join a group. This generalized approach permits public entities to join a group, but does not answer with precision the question of whether municipalities, counties, and school boards can all join the same group. Several states, such as Missouri and South Carolina, permit public employers of the same type of governmental unit to join a group. Some other states define specific types of public employer groups, and do not let governmental units of one type join a group with governmental units of another type. For example, Georgia lists four categories of public groups: municipalities, counties, school boards, and hospitals.

A regulator whose law contains a homogeneity requirement has the task of making judgments in specific cases that are technically difficult and sometimes politically sensitive because there is no clear line of demarcation between homogeneity and heterogeneity. The more detailed the homogeneity criteria developed by the regulator the less room there is for flexibility in handling special cases.

Group and Member Approval Procedures

Each state permitting workers compensation groups has developed a framework of structural, operational, and financial requirements that groups must meet before they are given regulatory approval. In some cases, the requirements extend to individual members as well as to the group as a whole. It is the regulator's duty to determine, after a careful review, that a potential group complies with the state's requirements and will be able with reasonable certainty to meet its obligations under the law. The process of reviewing a group's application and associated documents to make the required determinations and judgments is the first and one of the most important aspects of the regulation of workers compensation groups.

Because of varying requirements and regulatory philosophies, the form of the application and the number and nature of the other documents required to be filed with the regulator before an application is acted upon vary considerably from state to state. Nevertheless, this documentation falls generally into the following categories:

Category	*Examples*
Group organizational documents	indemnity agreement, bylaws, designation of board and administrator, service agreements
Group financial information	security deposit or bond, confirmation of excess insurance, pro forma financial statements, proof of premium deposits
Information about each member	application, current financial statement, list of annual premiums, proof of premium deposits

The review and approval process contains within it few public policy issues not discussed elsewhere in this report. There are, however, two aspects of this process that deserve specific attention. These are (1) specification of the indemnity agreement and (2) reg-

141.199

ulatory involvement in the admission of individual members to the group.

The indemnity agreement is the principal organization document of a workers compensation group. It performs the same function for groups that the subscriber's agreement performs for reciprocal exchanges. While states typically require joint and several liability of members to be set forth in the indemnity agreement, many do not go much further in specifying the content or form of the agreement.

A number of states specify that a group's indemnity agreement must conform to an indemnity agreement approved by the regulator. It is not clear whether this means there is a standard form of the agreement to be used by all groups or that groups have some flexibility in developing their agreements as long as they meet the regulator's approval. Kentucky goes a little further in stating that the indemnity agreement must be in the form prescribed by the workers compensation agency. The form, however, is not specified in Kentucky's regulation.

Alabama and Florida require that a group's indemnity agreement conform to the form of the indemnity agreement set forth in their regulations and contain all of its provisions. They do permit other provisions to be added that are not inconsistent with the required agreement.

Oklahoma and Virginia take a different approach. They specify in their regulations that certain provisions are to be included in an "indemnity agreement and power of attorney," but they allow additional provisions. An agreement must set forth the rights, privileges, and obligations of each member and of the group and the powers of the administrator. The agreement, which is subject to the approval of the regulator, must contain provisions on (1) joint and several liability, (2) the appointment of an administrator to accept service of process and to act for and bind the group and its members, and (3) the group's right to substitute administrators and revoke the power of attorney.

The specification by the regulator of the form of the indemnity agreement has the advantage of assuring that all workers compensation groups are similar in their essential features. This is important because of the uncertain impact of alternative wording, particularly in the event of adverse experience. *The Study Committee believes that each state should prescribe certain minimum uniform substantive provisions for all indemnity agreements, but should permit workers compensation groups to add, subject to regulatory approval, other provisions they need because of their particular circumstances.*

The second approval issue concerns the degree of regulatory involvement in the admission of individual employers to a workers compensation group, whether initially or after a group has formed and begun operation. The fundamental issue is whether regulatory focus on the group as a whole is sufficient. Some people argue that if the regulator assures that a group is of reasonable size, is organized and structured properly, has adequate financial security arrangements, and follows sound administrative and operational practices, it is not necessary for the regulator to exercise prior approval over the admission of individual employers to the group. Advocates of this position point out that the information available to regulators and the knowledge, skills and abilities of regulatory staffs do not permit them to make judgments about individual employers with a high degree of certainty and that the time the regulator spends in analyzing individual employers would better be spent monitoring and evaluating the financial condition and performance of the group.

There is an array of arguments presented by those in favor of the regulator having the authority to review and approve individual employers before they can join a group. One argument is that this approval process helps the regulator, if it is the workers compensation agency, to know how each employer is complying with the workers compensation law. Another argument is that the regulator needs to have information about individual employers to enforce the state's laws and regulations concerning homogeneity, net worth requirements, etc. The principal argument, however, is that a group's ultimate ability to meet its obligations is the joint and several liability assumed by each member. Therefore, the regulator should be authorized to assess the capability of each employer and to prevent an employer from joining a group if it does not appear to have sufficient resources to assume and carry out its responsibilities.

The differences of opinion described above are reflected in current regulatory practice. Maine, Michigan, Oklahoma and Virginia specify that an employer's membership in a workers compensation group must be approved by the regulator. For example, the Virginia law states that the regulator shall not grant authorization for an employer to become a member of a group unless it receives satisfactory proof of the employer's solvency and of the employer's financial ability to meet its obligations as a member. In addition, the Virginia law gives the regulator the authority to "review and alter any decision approving an employer as a member of a group...." In Georgia and Arkansas, the regulator has the right to disapprove or reject any application for membership. The approach used by Florida appears to be a compromise between the differing positions on individual employer approval. In Florida, the regulator has prior approval authority over members of a group when it is formed, but does not have prior approval authority over employers who join a group after it is formed. The Florida regulator, however, does have the authority to terminate an employer's membership in a group whether the employer was an initial member or joined subsequently. Most other states do not address specifically the regulator's responsibility for approving or disapproving individual members. It is not clear in these states whether regulators have any role other than ensuring that minimum standards are met and, perhaps, being notified of new members.

The Study Committee notes that a workers compensation group has a compelling interest in admitting and retaining only solvent employers who are able to meet their joint and several obligations and other membership responsibilities. It does not appear to be necessary for a regulator to perform this function for groups. Therefore, *the Study Committee believes that the principal focus of regulatory efforts should be the performance and financial condition of workers compensation groups rather than approving or disapproving individual employers for membership in groups.* If a state has a homogeneity or individual employer net worth requirement, the regulator may need to get information on new or prospective group members to enforce these requirements. A regulator, however, may be able to monitor compliance with membership requirements through a well-conceived program of on-site examinations and periodic reports.

Governing Board

Because a workers compensation group is a cooperative arrangement among employers who voluntarily join together to meet their workers compensation obligations, the group's governing board has a special role in assuring that the group is organized and administered in conformity with state requirements and meets its obligations to injured workers. For this reason most workers compensation group laws and regulations devote considerable attention to the governing board. The principal issues regarding the governing board concern the membership and structure of the board and its duties and responsibilities.

While many states use terms such as "board of trustees" or "members' supervisory board," the more general term "governing board" will be used in this report so as to not indicate any preference among terms actually used.

The members of a group's governing board are usually chosen by the group's membership. States such as Arkansas, Florida, Michigan and Missouri refer to the governing board as a group of members elected or appointed by the workers' compensation group. Oklahoma and Virginia say that the governing board is the representative body selected by the members. In Georgia, the governing board is chosen by the mutual agreement of the group members in accordance with state regulations and with the bylaws of the group.

An important membership issue is whether the governing board must be made up entirely of group members or whether a group can select non-group members to serve on its board. Because most states do not prohibit non-group members from serving on the board, it appears they recognize the value of having non-group members who have special expertise on the board. Arkansas, Florida, Maine, and Michigan specify that group members must be a majority of the board. Oklahoma and Virginia, however, require at least three-fourths of the governing board to be group members. Alabama states that the entire board must be members of the group or directly involved with the group in a supervisory or administrative capacity. If an Alabama group wants to appoint someone not meeting these requirements, it can seek approval from the regulator.

Equally important is whether there are types of individuals who are not permitted to be a member of the governing board. States may decide that the nature of the duties and responsibilities they assign to the governing board makes it inappropriate for some people to serve on the board. Arkansas, Florida, Maine, Michigan, and Missouri specify that an owner, officer, or employee of the service company may not serve on the governing board. Oklahoma and Virginia extend this bar to any parent or affiliated company of the service company under contract with the group. Kentucky prohibits employees or agents of a service company from serving on the board.

Most states seem to be satisfied with establishing general requirements regarding the membership of governing boards, as described above. Georgia, however, places itself directly into the process followed by workers compensation groups to establish their governing boards. The appointment of any board member is subject to the approval of the Insurance Commissioner. Each prospective board member must submit a detailed application to the Insurance Commissioner and a copy of any proposed contract entitling the person to any indirect compensation from the group for services performed or sales or purchases made to or for the group. The application must also be submitted to the group itself.

After describing how the governing board is to be established, most states set forth a substantial list of duties and responsibilities for the board. In many states, these duties and responsibilities are assigned directly to the board. In some states the duties and responsibilities are not specifically assigned to the governing board, falling instead upon the group itself. In a few other states, a mixed approach is used in that some duties and responsibilities are assigned to the board and others are assigned to the group. In the latter two instances, states probably intend for the governing board to handle all of the duties and responsibilities on the group's behalf.

There is considerable diversity among the states in the way they approach the specific duties and responsibilities of the governing board, even though some of the diversity is more form than substance. For illustrative purposes, the discussion below will focus on the approach used by Arkansas, Florida, and Maine. Several other states, however, including Alabama, Louisiana, Michigan, Minnesota, Missouri, Oklahoma, and Virginia, have many of the listed duties and responsibilities and in some cases a few additional ones.

To ensure the financial stability of the group's operation, the governing board is directed to "take all necessary precautions to safeguard the assets of the group." These precautions cover a wide range of operational and financial control topics such as (1) the designation of a service company and/or an administrator, (2) an annual audit, (3) limitations on borrowing from or for the group, (4) controlling and investing group funds, and (5) requiring that the group's funds be used only for workers' compensation purposes. Some of the precautions listed by other states include making active efforts to collect delinquent premium payments, monitoring the financial conditions of each member to assure that each member is able to fulfill its obligations, not extending credit to individual members for payment of premium, and assuring that payroll audits are conducted as required. All of these precautions are standard financial controls and safeguards that mark any well-run organization of a similar nature.

The governing board is directed to develop a set of bylaws or a trust agreement that the group members shall agree to. The bylaws or trust agreement shall contain, but not be limited to, the qualifications for membership, the method of selecting members of the governing board and their terms of office, and the method of amending the bylaws or trust agreement. If regulators are concerned about any negative consequences of self-perpetuating boards, they may want to require that a group's bylaws contain provisions guarding against this possibility.

In addition to the bylaws or trust agreement, the governing board is directed to adopt written policies on a variety of topics. These policies, which are to be binding on the administrator and any service company, are required to assure that the governing board is actually exercising its policymaking responsibility and giving direction to the administrator and service company. The written policies are to cover such topics as investment of assets, frequency and extent of loss control and safety engineering services to members, size of the revolving claims fund, rules on payment and collection of premiums, membership termination procedures, delineation of authority granted to the administrator and service company, and procedures for resolving disputes between members and the group and for dealing with members with excessive losses. Some other states require the written policies to set forth the basis for determining surplus distributions, assessments to make up deficits, and premium contributions.

In addition to establishing written policies, the governing board is also directed to review at least annually the performance of the service company, loss control and safety engineering services, investment policies, delinquent debts, cancellation procedures, admission of new members, and the administrator's performance. Some other states include claims handling and reporting, excess insurance coverage, and payroll audits. The governing board is required to review these matters so that it knows how the group is operating and whether state laws and regulations and its written policies are being adhered to.

To assist the regulator in understanding how the group is to operate, a copy of the current bylaws or trust agreement and the written policies must be on file in the regulator's office. Any change in the bylaws or trust agreement or in the written policies must be filed with the regulator at least 30 days prior to the effective date.

The governing board of a workers compensation group is a key element in the group's successful operation. *The Study Committee believes that for the governing board to function effectively, group members should constitute more than a simple majority of the governing board, no administrator or person associated with either the administrator or any service company should serve on a governing board, and the governing board's principal duties and responsibilities should be set forth in the law or regulations.*

Administrator

While the governing board of a workers compensation group has the primary policy making and oversight responsibility, the administrator (or fiscal agent) manages and directs the group's day-to-day activities. Almost all workers compensation groups, even the very large groups, rely upon the services of an administrator. The administrator's role in a workers compensation group raises a number of issues regarding (1) who can be an administrator, (2) the administrator's duties and responsibilities, (3) security requirements and (4) regulatory approval. States vary considerably in their treatment of these issues.

While it is clear that many state laws and regulations envision that a separate entity will function as a group's administrator, no state explicitly requires this or prohibits an employee of the group from serving as the administrator. Many states, including Alabama, Arkansas and Florida, simply require the governing board to appoint an administrator without further definition of who that can and cannot be. Oklahoma and Virginia permit an administrator to be an individual, partnership, or corporation. Georgia is the only state that refers directly to the possibility that an administrator can be an employee of the group.

Of considerably more importance is the relationship between the administrator and the service company that handles the group's claims. Of the states that address the administrator, most, including Florida, Maine and Virginia, provide that the administrator shall not be an owner, officer, or employee of the service company. Louisiana extends this prohibition to any affiliate of the service company. These states, among others, include within the list of specifically required precautions that the governing board must take to safeguard the assets of the group the designation of an administrator to administer the group's financial affairs. It appears that they do not want a single entity, such as a service company that also functions as the administrator, to have virtually complete control of the day-to-day affairs of the group. These states seem to envision the administrator performing an important oversight function with respect to the service company on behalf of the members of the group.

Not all states erect a barrier between the administrator and the service company. Arkansas and Kentucky, for example, allow the service company and the administrator to be the same. Alabama is silent on this point. Also, the other states whose laws and regulations include no mention of the administrator would seem by their inaction to have no concern about the administrator functioning as the service company, or vice versa.

While many states do not go beyond the statement that the administrator is to administer the financial affairs of the group, Michigan and Missouri do. They specify that the governing board may delegate authority for specific functions to the administrator. These functions include, but are not limited to, such matters as contracting with a service company, determining the premium charged to and refunds payable to members, investing surplus funds, and approving applications for membership. The functions delegated must be set forth in the governing board's minutes. Georgia goes further and states that there must be a contract between the group and a non-employee administrator that sets forth the powers of the administrator and the general services to be performed. The agreement may include any restrictions on the exercise of the administrator's powers.

States, such as Alabama, Arkansas, Florida, Maine, and Virginia, that refer only to the administrator handling the fiscal affairs of the group, probably do not intend this as a limitation on the functions that the administrator can perform. Nevertheless, there is an ambiguity in these states not present in Georgia, Michigan, and Missouri.

Because the principal responsibility of the administrator is to look after the group's fiscal affairs, there is a natural concern about mishandling or misappropriation of the group's funds by the administrator. States such as Alabama, Arkansas, and Florida have addressed this concern by requiring the administrator to furnish a fidelity bond with the governing board as obligee in an amount sufficient to protect the group against the misappropriation or misuse of any funds or securities. Typically, the governing board is permitted to set the amount of the bond. Evidence of the bond must be filed with the regulator prior to approval being granted to establish the group. Oklahoma and Virginia, however, require that the regulator rather than the governing board determine the amount of the bond. Georgia and Illinois go much further. They have detailed requirements regarding both the nature and amount of bond coverage. Georgia requires both a $100,000 bond and a $100,000 errors and omission or other appropriate liability insurance policy. The amount of the bond required by Illinois begins at $20,000 for groups having assets under $500,000 and increases according to a formula based on the amount of the group's assets.

Most of the states that address the administrator give it only limited treatment in their laws and regulations. They seem to be satisfied with requiring each group to have an administrator, requiring the administrator to provide a security bond, and addressing the relationship between the administrator and the service company. These states do not seem to have any interest in approving administrators or intruding into the relationship between the group and the administrator. Georgia and Illinois, however, treat the administrator in considerably more detail. The Georgia and Illinois requirements regarding bonds and insurance were discussed above. Georgia also requires that the agreement between the group and a non-employee administrator be submitted to and approved by the regulator. Both states require a detailed application containing extensive biographical and financial information, as well as information about the compensation to be paid to the administrator. Georgia also gives the regulator the power to determine whether the compensation is reasonable and equitable under the circumstances. Any form of direct or indirect compensation to an administrator or to a corporation or firm in which an administrator is in any way financially interested (other than as provided by law or regulation) is considered by Georgia to be a violation of the administrator's fiduciary responsibility.

A competent administrator is a necessary ingredient for a successful workers compensation group. *The Study Committee believes that the role of the administrator should be addressed specifically in law or regulation, that the administrator and the service company should not have financial interests in each other, and that the*

administrator should be required to furnish a fidelity bond in an
appropriate amount to protect the group against misappropriation
or misuse of funds.

Services

A workers compensation group must provide on behalf of its
members a range of services very similar to those provided by
insurance companies and self-insurers. As discussed in the preceding
section, certain services are usually provided to a group by the
administrator. Other services, those associated with ensuring compliance with the state's workers compensation law, such as handling
claims, loss control, and safety engineering, are typically provided by
service companies. Because the performance of these claim-oriented
services is so important to a group, its members, and employees of its
members, most states have included a number of provisions in their
laws and regulations regarding these services and service companies.
This section will address a number of service-related issues falling into
two broad categories, i.e., the regulator's review and approval authority and requirements needed to ensure that service companies meet
their obligations.

While states vary considerably in the number of services they
require, most identify a number of services and indicate that the
services can be provided by qualified employees of the group or by
contracting with a service company meeting state requirements.
Kentucky, which has the longest list, identifies the following seven
required services: (a) claims adjustment, (b) safety engineering,
(c) purchase of excess insurance, (d) accumulation of statistics and the
preparation of premium, loss and tax reports, (e) preparation of other
required self-insurance reports, (f) development of members' assessments and fees, and (g) administration of a revolving fund. Arkansas,
Florida, and Maine specify claims adjusting, underwriting, safety
engineering, and loss control services. Louisiana, Michigan, Oklahoma,
South Carolina, and Virginia require the first three of these services,
but do not include loss control. Lousiana and Michigan, however, add
the service of providing required reports. Alabama merely refers to
those services necessary to fulfill the employer's workers compensation
obligations.

Several states, including Alabama, Arkansas, Florida, Missouri,
Oklahoma, South Carolina, and Virginia, require regulatory approval of
service companies so that regulators can evaluate the record and
capabilities of a service company before even considering a specific
contractual arrangement it may have with a workers compensation
group. In addition, these states have established grounds, which are

related principally to quality of service and compliance with the workers compensation law, for revoking approval previously given to a service company. Most of the other states not having a prior approval requirement have established similar grounds for disapproving a service company or terminating its service contract with a group. Illinois and Minnesota have particularly well-defined processes for handling this situation.

It is not clear from the sketchy evidence available whether prior approval authority for service companies is justified. Some of the problems occurring in the past would not necessarily have been prevented by subjecting service companies to prior approval. Differences among states regarding prior approval of service companies may be a function of varying regulatory philosophies and of specific local concerns. *The Study Committee believes that whether or not regulators have prior approval authority over service companies, they need to have both the obligation and the authority to monitor the performance of service companies and to take appropriate action against those service companies not performing satisfactorily.*

States typically have established a variety of requirements for service contracts. While some are substantive, such as the requirement that a service company handle claims to their conclusion (which will be discussed in more detail below), most are procedural in nature. Probably the most important of these is the requirement that copies of any contracts with service companies be filed with the regulator in conjunction with a workers compensation group's application. This helps the regulator make necessary judgments about how well the group will be able to meet its service obligations.

The Study Committee believes that regulatory review of a group's service arrangements is needed to ensure that adequate provision is made for performance of essential services; however, it is probably not necessary for regulators to have explicit prior approval authority for every service contract, renewal thereof, or change thereto. Specific minimum standards for service contracts and the regulatory authority to take remedial action, if necessary, should be sufficient.

There are numerous details that states must resolve regarding service contract terms, filing requirements, experience requirements, and other matters relating to the relationship between groups and service companies. Maine, for example, has treated these subjects extensively. The Study Committee, however, focused its attention on two aspects of service contracts and service companies that it considers to be particularly important.

The first issue is whether a service company should be required to have an office within the state and to maintain records at that location sufficient to verify the accuracy and completeness of all submitted reports. There are two views on this. The concern of regulators, as evidenced by the number of states having this type of requirement, is to have records and service company staff readily available so that examinations can be conducted efficiently and questions answered readily. Proximity certainly facilitates the regulatory process. In addition, regulators generally believe that a service company located in state will be able to provide a higher level of service than one located out of state, if all other factors are equal. The in-state requirement, however, may create inefficiencies because some of the larger, multistate service companies may now have or soon develop centralized data processing facilities. These service companies may be able to provide a higher level of service to groups in several states from a centralized office than they could if they had to divide their staff and technical resources into several single-state offices. *The Study Committee believes that the regulators should have the discretion to evaluate alternative service arrangements and not be bound by a strict in-state requirement.*

The second issue concerns how claims services will be handled if either the group or service company ceases operation or one service company is replaced by another. The fact that many workers compensation claims require servicing for a number of years after the year of occurrence makes this a particularly important issue. Regulators want to know that all claims will be handled to their conclusion either by the service company contracting with the group at the time injuries occurred or by another acceptable means.

Several states have addressed the guarantee of services issue by specific provisions in their laws and regulations, by requiring appropriate provisions in service contracts, or both. Florida, Kentucky, Maine, and Michigan each require that any service contract for the adjustment and settlement of claims must include a requirement that the service company will adjust to final conclusion any and all claims that result from an occurrence during the period for which the contract is in effect. Louisiana, Oklahoma, and Virginia have similar requirements except that they add language referring to the possibility that a service company may be relieved of its responsibility or have its responsibilities transferred with the approval of the regulator.

One approach to assuring that funds will be available to pay for the servicing of claims to their conclusion is to require a service company to post a surety bond to secure the performance of its obligations under its service contract with a workers compensation group. Louisiana seems to be the only state requiring a surety bond for this purpose. It requires a service company to post with the regulator a $50,000 surety bond issued by corporate surety authorized to do business within the state.

While a surety bond would provide protection in case a service company was not able to fulfill its obligations directly, it may not be sufficient in the more serious situation where the group itself ceases operation. Here the concern is whether the service company has sufficient economic incentive to fulfill its obligations without requiring the regulator to take legal action against it. It is far better for a willing service company to have financial resources it needs to service claims to their conclusion than for the regulator to threaten the service company with removal of its privilege to operate in the state.

The manner in which a service company is compensated is a factor in whether it has the resources or the incentive to continue servicing claims after a group ceases operation. Most service companies are compensated on a percentage of premium basis, some on a per claim basis, and some on a per closed claim basis. Under the first two of these compensation methods, the service company receives its compensation during the fund year and, if it does not reserve some money for this purpose, it may not have the resources in subsequent years it would need to service continuing claims. The third compensation method solves this problem, but it may result in overemphasis on quick closure of claims. One approach, which no state is using at this time, is to require either the group or the service company to establish a reserve for unearned service fees. While this may be a means of assuring that some financial resources would be available to cover the costs of closing outstanding claims, there are substantial difficulties that limit the use of this approach.

The Study Committee believes that because of the importance of guaranteeing claims service, state laws and regulations should address this subject specifically. This should not be left for negotiation under adverse circumstances. Service contracts for claims services should require service companies to handle to their conclusion all claims and other obligations incurred during the contract period unless the regulator approves a substitute arrangement. The Study Committee also believes that states should give serious consideration to requiring service companies to post an appropriate surety bond to secure their faithful performance.

Member and Group Termination

Because of the cooperative nature of a workers compensation group and the joint and several liability of its members, the termination of a member, whether voluntary or involuntary, can have an impact on the group, the member, and the member's employees. The termination of a group has even more significant consequences. For these reasons, many workers compensation group laws and regulations address several procedural and substantive aspects of terminations to ensure that no employee is deprived of benefits and that each employer shares equitably in the cost of providing these benefits. Not all aspects, however, are discussed in detail in this section of the report. For example, joint and several liability implications and eligibility for dividends will be discussed fully in later chapters.

States such as Georgia, Kentucky, Louisiana, Maine, Michigan, Minnesota, Missouri, Oregon, and South Carolina provide that members of a workers compensation group may elect to withdraw from a group or be subject to cancellation by the group pursuant to the group's bylaws. There is considerable diversity, however, in the notice requirements regarding how much advance notice there is, to whom the notice is given, and whether regulatory approval is required. States range from ten to ninety days in the amount of time that must pass after notice is given before a member's withdrawal becomes effective. States typically require the workers compensation agency to be notified of any termination to enable the agency to monitor individual employer compliance with the workers compensation law, even when the insurance department has regulatory authority over workers' compensation groups.

A few states have imposed a variety of restrictions on and penalties for withdrawal from a group. Illinois, Louisiana, and Minnesota require a one-year minimum term of membership. In addition to their one-year membership requirement, Louisiana and Minnesota impose a 25 percent premium assessment for voluntary withdrawal during the second year of membership and a 15 percent premium assessment for withdrawal during the third year, although under some circumstances the assessment may be waived. In Kentucky, the right to dividends is forfeited for at least two years as a penalty for voluntary withdrawal from a group. Michigan and Missouri state that withdrawing members of groups are ineligible to receive any dividends until the statutes of limitation expire on all open or potential claims for the fiscal years involved.

The restrictions on and penalties for voluntary withdrawal from a group described above deserve further comment. These penalties and restrictions may be viewed by advocates of workers compensation groups as tactics to retain employers in groups once they join. Competitors of groups may see them as a means of discouraging employers from joining groups. Whichever is the case, *it is not clear that a legitimate public policy purpose is served by these penalties and restrictions and the Study Committee does not recommend their adoption.*

While most states limit their requirements to timely notice of withdrawals, Georgia and Oregon go further. Withdrawals in these two states must be approved by the regulator. In Oregon, a group must submit a statement showing the effect of a withdrawal on the net worth of the group and evidence that the employer leaving the group has made alternative arrangements for coverage. In Georgia, an employer wanting to withdraw from a group must submit a special application to the group and the regulator to demonstrate that after withdrawal it will comply with the workers compensation law. The group must notify the regulator of the employer's current standing and state any reasons why the application for withdrawal should not be approved.

With respect to the cancellation of an employer's membership by a group, only a few states go beyond a reference to the group's bylaws. Georgia states that a member may be involuntarily terminated for failure to pay any premiums due the group or for failure to discharge its obligations to the group. Kentucky permits a group to suspend or expel any member due to adverse claims experience or lack of cooperation with safety and loss prevention policies. Also, a member may be expelled for willful failure to report its payroll properly to the group. Other states probably have approved or accepted similar wording in the group's bylaws, but did not see a need for addressing this subject in their laws or regulations.

If regulators have a concern that groups may not apply their underwriting criteria fairly, i.e., that different standards are applied to different employers, then they may want to address this directly in their laws and regulations. Inequitable treatment of individual members can be defined in law as an unfair business practice. To enforce this, regulators could establish an administrative process giving each terminated employer an opportunity to appeal, or regulators could simply wait until an employer alleging unfair treatement contacted them without requiring notice of every termination. Local conditions will probably determine which of these procedures is most appropriate for each state.

A few states give special attention to a workers compensation group member who has undergone a change in legal status or ownership. In Florida and Maine, an employer's participation in a group terminates if there is a change in majority ownership. Typically, if the employer wants to remain in the group, it must reapply for membership. A similar procedure is used in Oregon for a "change in legal entity" which includes, but is not limited to, a partner joining or leaving a partnership, a change from a sole proprietorship, partnership or corporation to another form, or when a non-corporate employer sells ownership to another party.

The Study Committee recognizes that the workers compensation agency needs to be informed if an employer's membership in a workers compensation group is terminated. This is no different from the typical requirement that insurance companies must notify the workers compensation agency if an employer's insurance is terminated. If the insurance department has regulatory authority over a group, it may also need to be notified of a member's termination. The necessity for this, of course, depends on the state's particular requirements and regulatory philosophy. Nevertheless, consistent with its recommendations in Section VI.C regarding the approval and disapproval of individual employers for membership in groups, *the Study Committee recommends that regulators neither be given nor take on the function of passing judgment on the voluntary or involuntary termination of an employer's membership in a group.*

Of more importance than the withdrawal or termination of an individual member is the dissolution of a workers compensation group. Whether the group terminates voluntarily or involuntarily, great care must be taken to assure that the obligations incurred by the group and the individual members during the group's existence are handled properly.

While the voluntary dissolution of a group has rarely occurred, it has happened. Nevertheless, only a few states have addressed this possibility in their laws and regulations. Kentucky requires the group's governing board to give thirty days' notice to the regulator and each member and to pay no dividends without the specific written approval of the regulator for at least three years following the close of each fund year during which it operated. The group must prove to the regulator that satisfactory arrangements have been made for the continued payment and servicing of all outstanding claims. Similarly, Georgia requires the regulator's prior written approval of the group's dissolution and the regulator's determination that all claims and other legal obligations of the group have been paid or adequately provided for. Florida requires that a dissolved group leave its reserves intact. Maine, New York, Oregon, and Rhode Island specify that upon a group's termination the securities or surety bond on deposit shall remain in the regulator's custody for a period from two to five years depending on the state. These states also set forth requirements for a policy of insurance that the regulator will accept when the securities or surety bond are released.

In the event a workers compensation group does not comply with the many requirements imposed upon it by law or regulation, the regulator may need to take enforcement action. In extreme cases, this may involve action to terminate a group's operation.

Unlike its previous recommendation on individual member terminations, *the Study Committee recommends that the subject of the termination of a group be given full treatment in a state's law and regulation so that as many of the procedural and technical questions as possible can be resolved in advance of a group being faced with voluntary or involuntary dissolution.*

V. OBLIGATIONS OF A GROUP AND ITS MEMBERS

When employers join a workers compensation group, with the exception of some public groups, they assume joint and several liability for the workers compensation obligations of the group as a whole and of each member. The principal obligation of groups is to assure that workers compensation claims are paid timely and in full. To assist groups in meeting this obligation, other participants are brought into the claims payment process. Typically, the other participants include a surety company and an excess insurance company. The claim payment interrelationship between the group, its members, joint and several liability, and the other participants is an important focus of this section. In addition, this section discusses a number of public policy issues regarding the obligations of groups and their members for residual markets, special workers compensation funds, and state taxes, fees, and assessments.

Joint and Several Liability

One of the key features of workers compensation groups is the assumption of joint and several liability by each member for the workers compensation liabilities of the group and all of its members. It is the joint and several liability that each member assumes without limit by signing the indemnity agreement that provides the foundation for the group's financial security. While the premium payments, security bonds, and excess insurance programs are expected to be sufficient to meet the group's obligations to injured workers, if they are not, the individual members of the group have to provide whatever additional funds are needed. If some members of the group are not able to pay their share, because of bankruptcy or any other reason, then the remaining members of the group have to provide the funds that these members should have provided.

One situation, which some states have addressed directly and others have not, is the continuing liability of former members of the group for obligations incurred by the group during the former member's tenure. Conceptually, a former member should continue to be liable jointly and severally for all obligations incurred during its period of membership. Allowing the joint and several liability to terminate upon withdrawal from membership may not be fair to continuing members and may jeopardize the benefits owed to injured workers of the withdrawing members. In practice, groups may have difficulty collecting assessments from former members because some of the former members may no longer be in business or may force the group to sue them for payment, particularly if the former members have been out of the group for several years and the assessments are to pay workers compensation benefits to employees of other members of the group.

With this background on the meaning of joint and several liability in workers compensation groups, two public policy issues can be considered. The first issue is the manner in which the joint and several liability requirement is expressed in state law. While states have used a variety of approaches, most seem to be similar in purpose, and it is reasonable to assume that they intend to achieve the same result.

Most states use one of two basic approaches to joint and several liability. States such as Alabama, Arkansas, Florida, Kentucky, Maine, Missouri, South Carolina, and Virginia require language in the indemnity agreement binding each member of the group to comply with the provisions of the workers compensation law. This approach focuses the joint and several liability requirement on the responsibility of the group and its members to pay workers compensation benefits.

States using the other basic approach refer less directly to compliance with the workers compensation law. Instead, they focus on the assumption by the group of the workers compensation obligations of the members. Georgia, for example, requires the members of a group to be jointly and severally liable for all obligations of the group during the entire period of their membership. In addition, Georgia explicitly states that a member terminating either voluntarily or involuntarily remains liable for all of the group's obligations incurred during the period of membership. New York and Rhode Island have a particularly complete requirement. The laws of these states provide the following:

1. The group shall assume the liability of all the members and pay all compensation for which the members are liable under the workers compensation law.
2. A group member is not relieved of its workers compensation liabilities except through payment by the group or the member of required benefits.
3. The insolvency or bankruptcy of a member does not relieve the group from the payment of compensation required during the member's period of membership.

If state laws and regulations and groups' indemnity agreeements and bylaws do not address adequately the respective obligations of present and former members and the time periods the obligations cover, it is possible that litigation may arise at a time when groups need to accumulate funds promptly. Also, the various ways that states have stated their joint and several liability provisions and the numerous fact situations that can occur create uncertainty regarding how regulators and courts will decide specific joint and several liability issues. Existing case law may have limited applicability because traditional situations involving joint and several liability usually involve a fixed number of parties assuming specific obligations.

The Study Committee believes that because joint and several liability provides the foundation for the financial security of workers compensation groups, state laws and regulations should set forth explicitly the extent and term of this obligation.

The second public policy issue involving joint and several liability is whether this requirement is imposed on workers compensation groups formed by public employers such as school boards, cities, and counties. Constitutional or statutory restrictions may prohibit one public entity from assuming the obligations of another. This has caused a few states, such as Florida and Michigan, to modify or eliminate the joint and several liability requirement for public groups. Tennessee, which has public groups only, states explicitly that agreements among group members may provide for the pooling of losses so that any or all of the funds contributed by a participating governmental entity may be used to pay claims for any of the members. In addition, Tennessee addresses the constitutional question by stating that all contributions of financial and administrative resources required by the group's agreement are made for a public and governmental purpose and that all such contributions benefit the contributing governmental entity. Colorado seems to have taken a different approach for hospital and health care groups in that members are not liable except for the payment of their full agreed contribution to the group in accord with the indemnity agreement. Several states are silent on whether public groups are required to have the same joint and several liability that private groups have. It is not clear in these states whether public group members have joint and several liability, although regulators by their own action may permit public groups to form without it.

One point of view on this issue is that if the prohibition of one governmental entity assuming the obligations is statutory, then the legislature can amend this restriction. If the legislature is not willing to do this, then it probably should not let governmental entities form workers compensation groups. Members of workers compensation groups are sharing the risks of others; the benefits that each member receives is the quid pro quo for the obligations it assumes. Viewed from this perspective, the presence of joint and several liability adds financial security to the group and does not pose public policy problems. The absence of joint and several liability for public groups makes them virtually identical to mutual insurance companies and raises the question of why they should not be regulated in the same fashion that mutual insurance companies are regulated.

The opposing point of view is that governmental entities are usually permitted to self-insure their workers compensation risks even without regard to whether they meet the size standards applied to a private self-insurer. The principal reason for this is the power to raise sufficient revenues through their taxing powers to meet their workers compensation obligations. By joining together in workers compensation groups, they are able to achieve a variety of operating efficiencies and economies. It is unnecessary to have joint and several liability in public groups because if the group runs into difficulties, each public member would be able to meet its own obligations and would not need to rely on the resources of other members.

The Study Committee believes that joint and several liability is as important to the financial security of workers compensation groups of public employers as it is for groups of private employers. States should not permit public groups to form without joint and several liability unless they have established with certainty that public employers are prohibited from assuming the legal obligations of other entities. If public groups are formed without joint and several liability, the Study Committee recommends that regulators identify other means of enhancing the capability of public groups to meet their workers compensation obligations.

Claim Payments

There are many participants in the claims payment process of a workers compensation group — the group itself, individual group members, the surety company, the excess insurance company, the service company, and the regulator. The objective of all of these participants should be that each and every workers compensation award is paid timely and in full. Few states spell out in any detail the interrelationships among the claim payment participants. The generally good experience of workers' compensation groups and the newness of most groups means that few regulators, groups, and other participants have had to address the difficult technical and procedural questions that arise if a group has adverse experience.

Before proceeding into a discussion of several claim payment issues, it is probably useful to discuss generally how typical claims payment situations are intended to be handled. Also, important aspects of the claims payment process are discussed in several other sections of the report, including the sections on services, joint and several liability, assessements, required security, reserves, and protection against insolvencies. A thorough understanding of the claim payment process requires knowledge of all of these areas.

Most claims are paid from the group's loss fund. The excess insurance company becomes involved if an individual claim exceeds the group's specific excess retention or if the group's retained losses in a fund year have accumulated to more than the group's aggregate excess retention. In either case the excess insurance company must make payments to the group in accord with the excess insurance policy. If a group has a shortage of funds on hand, there are several actions a group can take in an attempt to cover the shortfall. With sufficient time, the group can avoid having to draw upon its surety bond. If for any reason, however, the group fails to pay required benefits, the surety company may be called upon to provide funds to the group up to the limit of the surety bond. Usually, payments by the surety company are paid to or controlled by the regulator. These payments may be needed for losses below the aggregate excess retention or above the aggregate excess insurance policy limit. If the surety bond is exhausted, the group members may be faced with responding to their joint and several liabilities. If a group is unable to do this, a guaranty fund mechanism may be called upon, if one exists covering workers' compensation groups, to meet the group's obligations. If the excess insurance company is not able to deliver on its contractual promises, the insurance guaranty fund can be called upon if the excess insurance company is a licensed company.

Surety bonds are usually worded to pay upon a workers compensation group's failure or refusal to pay required benefits. Insolvency of the group normally is not required. The principal purpose of the surety bond is to continue the timely payment of benefits while other more permanent steps are taken to overcome the group's financial difficulties. Depending upon the language in the surety bond, the surety company may be able to wait until after group members have been assessed before it has to begin paying benefits. If so, this could considerably delay benefit payments to injured workers. Florida has addressed this problem by requiring a surety bond endorsement making the surety company immediately liable upon any failure of a group to pay required benefits and giving the surety recourse to seek reimbursement against the group and its members.

While there is normally no interaction between the surety company and the excess insurance company, there may be circumstances where conflicts arise. One approach to avoiding potential problems of this sort is the financial security endorsement to excess insurance policies, which has been approved in several states. The effect of this endorsement, which is discussed in more detail in the section on required security, is to include within the excess insurance policy the coverage otherwise provided by the surety bond.

An issue related to excess insurance is that many excess insurance policies are written on a reimbursement only, or indemnity, basis, i.e., the workers compensation group must first make a benefit payment before it can seek reimbursement from the excess insurance company. Under normal circumstances this does not pose particular problems for workers compensation groups. The principal concern of excess insurance companies is that they do not want to become involved in making direct payments to claimants because they are not staffed to provide this service.

Problems regarding excess insurance payments when the insured is not able to or does not make required payments have arisen in Florida. Based on this experience, the regulator added a requirement to the Florida regulation that excess insurance policies must contain a provision permitting the regulator to order "the monies due under the terms of an excess contract or policy be paid directly to the injured employee or such other party as the (regulator) may appoint." This action is to be ordered only if the regulator determines that it is necessary to ensure continued benefits to an injured employee. While a provision of this sort may be troublesome to excess insurance companies and could affect their willingness to offer excess insurance policies in a particular state, a regulator probably would direct payments from excess insurance companies to be made to the regulator himself or to a trustee so that the excess insurance companies would not have to deal with numerous individual claimants.

Some aggregate excess insurance policies contain a minimum loss fund provision. For example, while the policy may be written to cover a group's losses in excess of 70 percent of the group's premium, the policy may state a minimum retention below which coverage is not provided. This may cause particular problems for a new group whose premium volume has not yet reached its intended level or for any group with excessive uncollected premiums. As a result there may be a gap between the loss fund and the point at which the aggregate excess insurance policy takes effect. This gap may have to be covered by assessments of group members or by payments from the surety company.

The Study Committee believes that the regulator should evaluate carefully and in their totality the terms and coverages provided by a group's premium collection program, surety bond, and excess insurance policies to assure that no unnecessary gaps in funding exist and that funds for benefit payments will always be available on a timely basis.

The termination of a group should not create financial problems if the group has sufficient loss reserves and adequate surety bond and excess insurance coverage. If a group is terminating because of adverse experience, however, the loss reserves may not be adequate, and the regulator will have to give careful consideration to assuring that funds are available to pay required benefits. In addition, problems regarding the servicing of claims can arise. This problem is discussed in the section on services.

In most cases termination of an individual member of a workers compensation group should not create any claims problems. First, the terminating member has paid premiums for the period of its membership. Second, depending on individual state requirements, the terminating member remains jointly and severally liable for claims occurring during its membership period.

Residual Market Mechanisms

There are some types of employers that have difficulty obtaining workers compensation insurance. Typically, these employers are in particularly hazardous businesses, have worse than average accident experience for their class, or are of such small size that the premiums do not cover the cost of handling their business. Because these employers are required by law to have workers compensation coverage, the insurance industry has developed residual market mechanisms to meet this need. In some states these mechanisms are required by law, but in most states the insurance industry has implemented them on a voluntary basis.

Workers compensation residual market mechanisms typically are voluntary "pools" composed of insurance companies writing workers compensation insurance in the state. An employer who has been turned down for insurance can obtain coverage from the pool and is assigned to one of a limited number of insurance companies, referred to as servicing carriers, which provide to the employer all the usual workers compensation insurance services including policy issuance, loss prevention, and claims handling. The servicing carrier is reinsured by the pool with insurance companies writing workers compensation insurance in the state participating in proportion to their market share. Through this process, insurance companies share equitably the experience of the residual market. In addition, the residual market experience is included with the experience of other insured employers and reflected in the overall rates charged by insurance companies, except in a few states where separate rate levels are established for the workers compensation residual market.

The growth of workers compensation groups has raised a question about the fairness of the present situation in which groups do not participate in residual market mechanisms. If a workers compensation group refuses to permit an employer to join or if it terminates the membership of an employer for cause, such as poor experience, the employer will usually end up in the insurance industry's residual market mechanism. In addition, while a few groups have been formed by types of employers who frequently were insured in residual market mechanisms, most groups have been formed by types of employers that insurance companies would insure directly. As employers with good loss records join workers compensation groups, the insurance industry is left with an increasing proportion of employers with poor loss records. This serves to increase further the difference between rates charged by the insurance industry, which reflect the extra costs associated with residual market mechanisms, and rates appropriate for employers with good loss records. From the insurance industry's perspective, then, the residual market issue, rather than being a question of fairness between insurance companies and workers compensation groups, is a question of fairness between employers who purchase insurance from an insurance company and employers who join groups.

One response of workers compensation groups to the insurance industry's concern is that groups are more like self-insurers than insurance companies and, therefore, should not be expected to share residual market costs with insurance companies any more than self-insurers are expected to share these costs. Another argument is that most groups are willing to accept employers with poor loss records and keep them in the group by working with them to improve their record. Also, groups claim that in many cases they have taken employers out of the residual market and, as a general rule, do not force employers to withdraw from the group. In addition, there are fairness and procedural issues from the groups' perspective. Because almost all groups are established to serve employers in a single industry, groups believe it is unfair and inappropriate to require them to absorb losses of employers in other industries through a residual market mechanism.

While the workers compensation residual market issue is real rather than theoretical, no state to date has attempted to implement a residual market mechanism combining insurance companies and workers compensation groups. This is due, at least in part, to some difficult procedural and administrative problems. A discussion of these problems and their possible solutions is beyond the scope of this report.

One of the concerns of the insurance industry about insuring former members of workers compensation groups is the possibility that an increased number of claims will emerge in the years following the employer's return to an insured status. To address this concern, a number of states have approved an endorsement program that requires an employer returning to insured status in the residual market to make an additional security deposit that is used if excess losses emerge during the initial three-year period.

The Study Committee does not believe as a general rule that groups should be required to participate in residual market mechanisms; however, this may be appropriate in some states depending on the nature of the voluntary market in general and the residual market in particular. If a state decides to have groups participate in the residual market mechanism, there are methods, such as credit programs, to minimize any adverse effects.

Special Workers Compensation Funds

The nature of the workers compensation system, coupled with the potential long-term payout of benefits, has led state legislatures to establish a number of special funds to meet specifically identified needs. The number and type of special funds vary considerably from state to state, as summarized in the table below.[1]

Type of Fund	Number of Funds
Second Injury	54
Uninsured Employers	21
Benefit Adjustment	18
Rehabilitation	17
All Other	36
TOTAL	146

Four types of special funds constitute about three-fourths of all funds. The most common type of special fund is the second injury fund. It is designed to provide assurance to prospective employers that their liabilities will be limited in the event of further injury to employees with prior physical impairments and, thereby, to encourage employment of the handicapped. Uninsured employers funds exist to provide certain and immediate workers compensation benefits to workers injured while in the employement of employers who fail to insure or legally self-insure their workers compensation risks. Benefit adjustment funds are used to provide payment for periodic adjustment in benefits to reflect increasing living costs. Rehabilitation funds pay additional compensation to incapacitated workers engaged in an approved rehabilitation program. A variety of other special funds exist in only a few states.

While the goals of special funds may vary, they all provide a mechanism for transferring risk and potential liability from an employer to all employers within a state through a pooling mechanism. Special funds are generally financed by fees or assessments based on workers compensation insurance premiums or related to workers compensation benefits. Regardless of the basis for the fee or assessment, the objective is to have each employer pay its fair share because all employers and their respective employees benefit from the special funds. This is the reason why states traditionally have levied fees and assessments for special funds on both insurance companies and self-insurers. Through this process all employers directly or indirectly have provided financing for the special funds.

Because states obtain the majority of the financial support for special funds from insurance companies, some may suggest that workers compensation groups should be exempt from special fund fees and assessments. It is important for public policy makers to focus on this because, depending on the nature and structure of pertinent state laws, inaction by legislators and regulators may result in groups not being required to provide support for special funds.

The argument for requiring workers compensation groups to participate in the financing of special funds is strong. Special funds are employer/employee oriented rather than being oriented toward the particular mechanisms employers choose to meet their workers compensation obligations. States have collected monies for special funds from insurance companies primarily for reasons of convenience rather than for reasons of philosophy. *For these reasons the Study Committee recommends that workers compensation groups and their members participate in special funds in the same manner that self-insurers and insurance companies and their insureds participate.*

State Taxes, Fees, and Assessments

In addition to the fees and assessments associated with the special workers compensation funds discussed in the previous section, states impose a variety of taxes, fees, and assessments on insurance companies, self-insurers, and workers compensation groups. While some states direct these revenues into their general fund to support the broad range of state programs and activities, other states place some of these revenues, particularly fees and assessments, into dedicated funds for the support of the workers compensation agency or the insurance department.

There are several criteria that a "good" revenue source should meet.[2] Two that are pertinent for this discussion are that everyone should pay his or her fair share (the fairness criterion) and that a revenue source should interfere minimally with economic decisions (the neutrality criterion). These two criteria are involved in the public policy decision regarding the taxes, fees, and assessments imposed on workers compensation groups. In addition to marketplace implications of these decisions, the level of revenues available to the state can be affected.

Typically, states impose a tax on insurance premiums which in most states is in lieu of sales taxes, income taxes, and other taxes and fees imposed by state and local governments. The premium tax, which in 1981 produced $3.3 billion dollars nationwide for all lines of insurance, is paid into state general funds by insurance companies and is included by them in the premiums charged to their customers. The tax rate averages around 2 percent of premiums, although there are states considerably above and below the average.

Many states collect a tax on workers compensation insurance premiums from insurance companies as they do for other lines of insurance. Self-insurers do not pay this tax because they are not insurance companies. This is one incentive for a larger employer to self-insure its workers compensation risk instead of insuring it with an insurance company. If workers compensation groups are viewed in a particular state as being like self-insurers rather than as being like insurance companies, the state may decide to exempt groups from the premium tax. One effect of this decision would be to provide added incentive for smaller employers to form or join a group instead of purchasing coverage from an insurance company. Any shift in the market away from insurance companies toward workers compensation groups would result in a reduction in workers compensation premiums and a loss of general revenue funds to the state. Imposing the premium tax on groups would be in keeping with the neutrality criterion, and would leave the state's general revenue fund unaffected by an employer's decision to join a group.

A few states appear not to view workers compensation as a source of general revenue and do not levy the premium tax on either workers compensation insurance premiums or on self-insurers. Instead, both insurance companies and self-insurers usually pay a separate assessment based on premiums or losses to support the activities of the workers compensation agency. This approach recognizes that the workers compensation agency exists to facilitate the workers compensation system and that the cost of administering the agency is a cost that should be borne by all employers, whether insured or self-insured. As a result, workers compensation groups usually are assessed in the same manner that others are assessed. Thus, employers' decisions on the particular mechanism for meeting their workers compensation obligations do not affect the level of funds received by the workers compensation agency.

The growing number of states that have placed regulatory responsibility for workers compensation groups with their state insurance departments face similar revenue and equity questions regarding insurance department fees and assessments. In order to treat insurance companies and groups fairly and to obtain from groups the funds to cover the cost of their regulation, states usually impose the same or similar fees and assessments on groups that are imposed on insurance companies.

Georgia, Virginia, and Kansas illustrate three approaches to treating groups and insurance companies equitably regarding insurance department fees and assessments. The Georgia Insurance Department, which is funded from the state general fund, collects a $300 annual license renewal fee from each licensed insurance company. This annual fee is also collected from workers compensation groups. The primary revenue source for the Virginia Bureau of Insurance, which is funded from a dedicated fund, is an assessment on insurance company premiums. In 1982, the assessment rate was .07 percent. This assessment is also applied to the premiums for workers compensation groups. The new Kansas law establishes a mechanism for identifying regulatory costs associated with groups and collecting fees from groups to cover these costs.

Although not taking a position on the premium tax issue, *the Study Committee believes that workers compensation groups should pay to the workers compensation agency, the insurance department, or both, whichever is appropriate, fees and assessments consistent with those paid by insurance companies and self-insurers.* This is in accord with both the fairness criterion and the neutrality criterion.

A final issue relating to state taxes, fees, and assessments is whether workers compensation groups of public employers are treated differently from groups made up of private employers. In most cases public and private employers pay directly or indirectly the same taxes, fees, and assessments. They pay them indirectly if they insure their workers compensation risks or directly if they are self-insured. Georgia and Rhode Island have created an exception to this general rule by exempting groups of public employers from the workers compensation premium tax paid by insurance companies and private workers compensation groups.

The Study Committee recognizes that the question of whether state taxes are imposed on local governmental entities transcends workers compensation. A state that exempts local governments from the state sales tax and gasoline tax may also choose to exempt a workers compensation group made up of local governmental entities from the premium tax, if it is imposed on workers compensation premiums. *The Study Committee believes that a distinction can be made between the premium tax and a fee or assessment paid to the workers compensation agency or the insurance department and that all groups, whether public or private, should pay the same fees and assessments to cover the cost of their regulation.*

VI. PRICING

Regulation is a common thread running through all elements of workers compensation insurance pricing. In addition to the approved or required rate levels, items such as rating plans, discounts, payment schedules, and retrospective rating factors are required by state law or regulation or are subject to regulatory approval. While various types of workers compensation competitive rating laws, which give insurance companies more flexibility in establishing rates and rating plans, exist in a few states, by far the prevalent regulatory approach involves prior approval of rates and considerable rate uniformity.

The basis of all insurance rate regulation is the requirement that rates should not be excessive, inadequate, or unfairly discriminatory. The public policy objectives underlying these rate standards would seem to apply equally to rates charged by workers compensation groups. Because of solvency implications, a key issue is how much regulatory emphasis to put on rate adequacy. At one extreme are regulatory approaches that could adversely affect the competitiveness of groups. At the other extreme are approaches that could impair the ability of groups to meet their long-term obligations to injured workers.

Given the tradition of heavy state regulatory involvement for workers compensation insurance pricing, there are several aspects of pricing by workers compensation groups that should be addressed. These include (1) development of premium, (2) the timing and amount of premium payments, (3) dividend practices, (4) assessments to make up for a premium shortfall, and (5) data reporting.

Development of Premium

There are three basic issues relating to how the premium for workers compensation groups may be developed. The first issue concerns how rates for new groups should be determined. The second addresses the subject of modifications, discounts, and deviations. The third issue involves the possibility of group-made or group-modified rates.

In most of the states whose laws and regulations address the subject of rates, new workers compensation groups are required to charge members the manual rates published by the National Council on Compensation Insurance or the state rating organization. These are average rates for all insured employers in each class. While some states do not address pricing, Connecticut appears to be unique in granting each group the power to determine its own rates.

The alternative to manual rates would be rates established by the new groups. While this might be attractive to some groups for competitive reasons, there are serious technical difficulties involved in establishing rates based on the prior experience of the original members. In addition, even if the members of a new group had a high degree of homogeneity, the group probably would not have sufficient size to develop credible rates for its members.

The second issue in the development of workers compensation group premiums is the degree to which groups may modify, discount, or deviate from the manual rates they charge their members. Insurance companies use employers' prior loss histories to determine whether employers should pay more or less than manual rates. They apply premium discounts on a sliding scale based on the modified premium of each employer to reflect the lower average expenses per premium dollar of insuring larger employers. The experience rating and premium discount plans used by insurance companies are filed by the National Council or a local rating organization in each state and are approved by the insurance regulator. In most states, insurance companies are permitted to file deviations, which are flat percentage reductions on the basis of favorable overall experience.

All of the states that require use of National Council or other rating organization rates also require workers compensation groups to use the experience rating plan filed in the state. Maine, however, permits groups to use another experience modification plan if its appropriateness can be demonstrated.

Florida, Michigan, and Missouri permit the governing board of a workers compensation group to apply a penalty in excess of the normal premium to any member with unfavorable loss experience so long as the member and the regulator are notified in advance. In Florida, the penalty rate is subject to the prior review and approval of the regulator. While this procedure is similar to the consent-to-rate procedure available to insurance companies under most insurance rating laws, insurance companies are not usually permitted to apply penalty rates for workers compensation insurance.

Premium discount plans are permitted in all states whose laws or regulations address the subject. "Premium discount," however, may be a misnomer for the types of discounts given by groups in most states.

The discounts are typically flat percentage deviations rather than discounts based on premium size.

Although Virginia specifies that groups give no discount greater than the maximum allowed by the non-stock premium discount plan, most states permit a flat deviation for all group members with the limitation that the percentage be approved by the excess insurer. In practice, this means that the excess insurance company is willing to accept a deviated premium as the basis for the group's retention for aggregate excess coverage. Some states with this provision specify a maximum "premium discount" of 15 percent. Missouri applies the 15 percent limitation only during the first year of a group's existence. Maine permits use of a premium discount plan different from the rating organization plan if it is found to be actuarially sound by the regulator. Florida does not allow an advance premium discount if in any given fund year a group will have an unfunded contingent liability.

The Study Committee believes that states should require workers compensation groups to use bureau-developed rates, rating systems, and experience rating plans, particularly in a group's early years, as well as defined premium discount or deviation plans. This approach is preferred because it places regulatory emphasis on long-term solvency even if the resulting premiums eventually turn out to be greater than some groups need to cover their losses and expenses.

Those states that have or are considering competitive rating laws for workers compensation insurance may not have bureau-developed rates that groups can use. Regulators in these states will need to find another method to assure the adequacy of group rates.

The third issue is when and to what extent workers compensation groups should be permitted to establish rates based on their own experience. If a group has credible loss experience, the continued use of bureau-developed rates may not be necessary. If a group is permitted to reduce its rates based on a limited amount of apparently favorable experience, the group could have financial difficulties in later years as losses become fully developed. Three states specify procedures for a workers compensation group to deviate from manual rates in years subsequent to the group's establishment. Michigan permits a group to apply for deviations after three years; Georgia requires only one year of operation. Maine permits a group to apply for downward deviations after three years, but permits a group to apply for upward deviations after only one year. Deviations in rates must be based on experience and must show evidence of prospective rate adequacy. Agreement by excess insurance companies is required.

The Study Committee believes there may be circumstances in which groups should be permitted to deviate from bureau-developed rates and classes or to develop their own rates and classes, although the Study Committee urges regulators to assure that deviations are actuarially appropriate.

Premium Payment Requirements

States have established premium requirements, including required deposits, payment schedules and premium audits, to ensure that groups have sufficient funds to meet their current obligations.

In many states, workers compensation groups are required to have evidence of collecting at least 25 percent of the annual discounted, modified premium prior to inception of each group's fund year. Minnesota, however, requires a deposit premium of only 20 percent. Most states merely require that these funds be deposited before inception of coverage. Kentucky requires deposit at least 30 days prior to inception, and Minnesota requires payment at least 10 days in advance.

Requirements for payment of the balance of the annual premium vary widely among the states. Kentucky, which has the most stringent schedule, requires that groups collect at least one-third of the remaining premium balance each 30 days after inception. Other states permit collection over periods of six months, nine months, and the full policy year on the basis of either monthly or quarterly payments. Louisiana specifies only that a schedule be established for payment and collection of premiums.

Final fund year premiums are based on audited employer payrolls. Additional premiums (or premium refunds) are payable immediately after billing, subject to normal collection terms.

The Study Committee believes that while periodic payment plans are appropriate for workers compensation groups, regulators should be certain that the initial premium deposit and the subsequent payments are received by the group at a rate faster than premiums are earned.

Dividends

The key dividend issues for workers compensation groups are (1) the length of time a group must wait after the end of a fund year to commence dividend payments and (2) the amount of surplus that may be returned at any time. Early payment of large dividends may leave a group without sufficient funds if losses develop adversely. Unnecessarily long delays in paying dividends, however, could reduce the attractiveness of group membership. Another issue is which members are eligible to receive dividends. This involves consideration of both equity and competitiveness. These and other dividend related issues are discussed below.

Most states require a waiting period between the end of the group's fund year and the distribution of any dividends based on that year. The purpose of the waiting period is to assure that loss reserves are sufficient to pay both reported claims and losses incurred but not reported to the group. Alabama, Arkansas, Florida, Maine, Michigan, and Missouri require a waiting period of one year. In Louisiana and Minnesota the period is 18 months. Kentucky requires a two year wait. Oklahoma and Virginia do not specify any waiting period.

States generally take either of two approaches in regulating how much of surplus may be refunded. Most states permit groups to refund any monies in excess of the amount necessary to fulfill all legal obligations for the fund year. Louisiana and Minnesota use a formula that provides for refunds of 50 percent of any surplus in excess of 125 percent of the amount necessary to meet all workers compensation obligations. In these states, a separate calculation must be made annually for each fund year and incremental dividends may be paid each year as losses are paid. When all claims arising out of a fund year have been paid, groups may declare all of the remaining surplus for that year as dividends.

Over the last two decades, doctrines of compensability have expanded. Insurance companies are being required to pay benefits for types of losses not contemplated in the past such as cumulative trauma, long latency diseases, and heart attacks unrelated to workplace injuries. As these doctrines have developed, insurance companies have been called upon to pay claims on policies written years earlier and for which even the most conservative incurred but not reported (IBNR) reserves have proved insufficient. It is not clear that present regulatory control over the timing and amount of dividends for groups adequately takes into account either the problem of long latency claims, such as asbestosis, or the possibility of new types of claims emerging.

The states do not regulate the manner in which groups calculate dividends for individual members, although some states require groups to inform the regulator of how dividends are to be distributed. In practice, groups use methods including flat percentages, sliding scales based on individual members' loss ratios and size of premium, and retrospective rating. Some groups pay sliding scale dividends on claim fund surplus and flat dividends on expense savings and investment income. In general, states permit groups to use different procedures for distributing surplus from the trustees' fund than from the loss fund.

Because dividends typically are not paid until well after the end of the fund year, and because even then surplus for a given fund year may be paid out as dividends over several years, there is an important issue regarding which members are eligible for dividends. If members resign from the group before all surplus funds are distributed for a given fund year, are they eligible for dividends they helped to create? Does the same approach apply to employers whose memberships are canceled or not renewed by the group? What about new members? Are they eligible to receive dividends in a current year which in large part may have come from earlier fund years?

Michigan is the only state specifying that groups may pay dividends to members who have withdrawn from the group. Dividends are not payable, however, until after the statute of limitations has expired on all open or potential cases for the fund year involved. Florida law is silent on this matter and many groups in Florida limit payment of a dividend to current members and members involuntarily canceled. The new Kansas statute specifies that payment of previously earned dividends shall not be contingent on continued membership in a group. Also, Kansas requires that dividends can be paid only to members who remained members for an entire year. The laws and regulations of other states do not address this subject, which permits each group to decide whether it will pay dividends to withdrawn or canceled members for those fund years in which they participated. Insurance companies, on the other hand, are prohibited in some states from making receipt of dividends conditional on renewal of coverage.

Because dividend practices have such potential to impact the financial well-being of workers compensation groups many states, including Arkansas, Florida, Georgia, Maine, Michigan, Oklahoma, and Virginia, require prior regulatory approval for payment of dividends. Alabama, Louisiana and Minnesota require groups to give notice prior to declaration of dividends. Georgia requires that a dividend application must contain a statement by a qualified actuary that the dividend would not impair the group's financial condition. Maine has a similar requirement.

The Study Committee believes that solvency considerations make it necessary for regulators to have prior approval authority over the timing and amounts of dividends for workers compensation groups. Regulators should give serious consideration to ways in which adequacy of reserves can be evaluated and assured. Each group should be required to have an explicit dividend plan made known in advance to each member.

Assessments

While the payment of dividends is the mechanism by which better than expected loss experience and administrative savings are shared among group members, an assessment levied on members is the way that a group obtains additional funds when collected premiums and investment income are insufficient to cover losses and expenses. The ability of groups to make assessments may result from a group's indemnity agreement, its bylaws, or state law. The important issues regarding assessments are when an assessment should be made, who decides if an assessment is to be made, which group members are assessed, and how much individual members can be assessed. The assessment of members becomes an issue upon a finding that the group has insufficient resources to satisfy its obligations, whether in the aggregate or on a fund year basis. A number of subsidiary questions are involved. For example, must the assessment be made immediately upon determination that the group cannot meet its current or future obligations, or may the group continue paying its current obligations for a period of time, if it is able to do so, without being required to make an assessment? Also, are options available other than assessment of members?

Most states that address assessments specify that immediate action must be taken if a deficit exists. The states of Florida, Louisiana, Maine, Michigan, Minnesota, and Missouri specify deficits in any fund year as a cause for action. Connecticut, Illinois, New York, Oklahoma, Rhode Island and Virginia are silent on this point. The states that refer to deficits in any fund year provide that an alternative to assessment is the transfer of surplus from other fund years or from the trustees' funds to eliminate the deficit. This action requires subsequent notification to the regulator. The "any fund year" states also provide that other alternatives acceptable to the regulator may be used in place of assessment, but do not explain what they may be.

The six states that address deficits without reference to particular fund years refer to assessments to cover any deficits. Oklahoma and Virginia, however, permit alternatives to assessment without explaining what they are. Rhode Island requires assessment of the members of an insolvent group after payment of the penal sum of the surety bond.

A determination that a deficit exists and that remedial action is required could come from either the group itself or the regulator. One problem with leaving the decision with the group is that necessary action could be postponed because of the governing board's possible reluctance to impose additional financial burdens on members, even though the governing body probably has earlier knowledge of the deficit than the regulator does.

Most of the states listed earlier take the position that if deficits exist or have not been paid up immediately, the regulator shall order assessment of the group's members. Georgia has a particularly complete provision on this point. Connecticut and Oklahoma require that assessment be made, but do not specify that it will be ordered.

The importance of early action to remedy a deficit should be understood. If a projected shortfall is identified early, it may be possible that relatively small assessments can be collected over several years to fund the deficit without imposing undue financial difficulties on any of the group's members.

The question of which members should be assessed is important because it concerns the liabilities of former group members as well as current members. If employers that left the group are not liable for assessment, either for specific fund years during which they were members or for overall deficits arising from their terms of membership, then a disproportionate share of the workers compensation costs could fall on those employers in the membership at the time of assessment. On the other hand, requirements that former members be assessed may be impractical and inefficient, as former members may refuse to pay voluntarily or may no longer be in business. The costs of legal action against former members may more than offset the additional funds collected. Only Georgia specifies that any member voluntarily or involuntarily terminated shall remain liable for future assessments, although this may be implicit in the requirements of other states.

The Study Committee believes that workers compensation group laws and regulations should set forth clearly (1) the circumstances under which the need for assessments arises, e.g., when a deficit exists, (2) the regulator's powers to act, (3) alternatives to assessments, and (4) which members are liable for assessment.

Workers Compensation Data Reporting

The central issue concerning data reporting is to determine the requirements appropriate for workers compensation groups. Should the requirements be similar to those for insurance companies, or does the nature of groups call for different arrangements? This section is limited to reporting of data for rate making, pricing, and rate verification purposes, and does not include reporting of data about a group's financial condition, which is discussed in the section on financial reports, audits, and examinations.

Insurance companies writing workers compensation insurance are required to supply data to either the National Council on Compensation Insurance or a state rating organization, whichever is licensed in the state. These data usually fall into three categories: financial data for establishing overall state rate levels, Unit Statistical Plan data for establishing classification relativities and experience modification factors, and research and special call data for specific rating projects or studies.

Workers compensation groups in most states are not required to report data to rating organizations, although typically they are required to use rating organization rates, classifications, and experience modification plans in determining their premiums. Kansas is the first state to require groups to report premium and loss data to a rating organization. Groups are required, however, to maintain and report to regulators much of the same data that insurance companies report to rating organizations. For example, almost every state regulating groups requires reporting of members' payrolls by classification. Further, reporting of summary loss data is required in such states as Arkansas, Florida, Louisiana, Maine, Michigan, Minnesota, Missouri, New York, Oklahoma, and Virginia.

The issue of verification poses some serious questions for regulators. Verification of proper classifications, payrolls and rates is performed by rating organizations for insurance companies. The purpose of verification is to prevent competitive abuses, such as misclassifications and intentional understatement of initial payrolls, that artificially lower premiums. The verification function performed by rating organizations includes assistance in selecting proper classifications, with rating organization employees conducting physical inspections of work premises when necessary. While rating organizations limit their premium auditing activities to test audits on a sampling basis, they do compare payrolls on policies with previous audits to determine if patterns of underestimation emerge. To facilitate these functions, insurance companies are required to file a copy of each policy written with the appropriate rating organization for each state in which there is workers compensation exposure.

The rating organizations have personnel experienced in verification; insurance departments and workers compensation agencies do not. If groups are required to use bureau-developed rates, classifications, and experience rating plans and if regulators are to carry out their responsibilities to assure solvency, regulators may have to seek verification assistance from rating bureaus. *The Study Committee believes that verification of classifications, payrolls, and rates for workers compensation groups is an important regulatory tool. Each state should decide how this function should be performed.*

Reporting of rate making data is the most complex and potentially controversial data reporting issue. There are several aspects of this issue that need careful consideration by regulators and others concerned with data collection and utilization. Should states in which workers compensation groups have a large share of the total market or of certain classifications include or exclude group experience? Is it physically possible for groups to report data accurately and completely to rating organizations? If groups are able to report data, what would be the effects of including group data in the workers compensation data bases? In view of the answers to the previous questions, is it appropriate for group data to be included in those data bases? The Study Committee was not in a position to evaluate these questions and does not have a recommendation regarding them.

An additional facet of data reporting concerns availability of data for experience rating. When a previously insured employer joins a workers compensation group or when an employer withdraws from a group and purchases workers compensation coverage from an insurance company, it would be helpful to have the employer's experience readily available for rating purposes. One of the long-standing principles of the workers compensation system is that an employer's workers compensation cost should reflect its past experience and safety record. The calculation of experience modification factors by rating organizations was developed in part to keep employers from being able to "run away" from their experience by changing insurance companies. Also, the availability of experience modification factors has promoted competition among insurance companies.

The growth of workers compensation groups raises the question of how groups should interact with rating organizations regarding experience modification factors. Because groups are usually required to use the same filed experience rating plan as insurance companies, they need the experience data of new members and the ability to use the data, or they need the experience modification factors themselves. Some rating organizations have been reluctant to share these data with groups or with individual employers who are not members of the rating organization. Insurance companies attempting to get employers to leave groups and purchase insurance from them could develop premium quotes more accurately with access to experience data group members.

The Study Committee believes that it would be advantageous for both insurance companies and workers compensation groups to have equal access to employers' experience data for the purpose of calcuating experience modification factors.

VII. FINANCIAL CONDITION

The continued financial well-being of a workers compensation group, so that it can meet its current and future obligations, is of vital concern to the regulator, injured workers, and group members who are usually jointly and severally liable for any deficiencies in the group's funds. Because of the importance of this aspect of the regulation of workers compensation groups, substantial portions of group laws and regulations, as well as considerable regulatory time and effort, typically is devoted to the financial condition of groups. The purpose of this section is to address a number of issues related to the financial resources of groups, required financial security arrangements, various types of reserves, investments, financial reports, audits and examinations, and insolvency guaranty mechanism.

Financial Resources

Insurance departments and workers compensation agencies have relied traditionally upon various types of financial requirements in licensing insurance companies or approving self-insurers. Typically, these requirements include capital and surplus requirements and in some cases reinsurance arrangements for insurance companies and net worth, current ratio, and working capital requirements for self-insurers. The purpose of these requirements is to ensure that insurance companies and self-insurers are large enough and have sufficient financial strength to meet their obligations to policyholders, injured employees, and others. Regulators have similar concerns regarding workers compensation groups. The resources available to the group from its members and the security provided by surety bonds and excess insurance, which will be discussed in detail in the succeeding section, must be sufficient to ensure the group's ability to meet the workers compensation obligations of its members.

There are two regulatory issues associated with financial resource requirements for workers compensation groups. They are (1) the types of resources that should be considered financial resources for groups and (2) the method of determining minimum requirements for groups.

Some states, including Maryland, New Hampshire, and New York, have not established any quantitative financial standards by law or regulation. Instead, they require a potential group to submit proof of its financial ability to pay compensation. This approach gives the regulator considerable flexibility in evaluating potential groups, but it does not provide any guidance to applicants. Alabama, Arkansas, Missouri, and South Carolina have a similar requirement stated in terms of working capital in an amount establishing the combined financial strength and liquidity of the members. Each of these five states, however, combines this qualitative requirement with at least one quantitative standard.

Most of the states permitting workers compensation groups have established one or more quantitative requirements for the financial resources available to a group. The most common requirements are combined net worth of the members and some measure of gross annual premium. Some states have one of these, while several other states have both. Alabama, Arkansas, Kansas, Oklahoma, Oregon, and Virginia have established a combined net worth requirement of $1,000,000, while Florida, Kentucky, and Louisiana have set their net worth requirement at $500,000. The net worth requirements in all of these states seem to be fixed, i.e., they do not vary from one group to another or as the size of a group changes over time. In contrast, Minnesota has a variable net worth requirement equal to the greater of ten times the group's retention or one-third of the current annual premium.

Annual premium volume is a commonly used measure of a group's financial resources. There is even more diversity regarding the annual premium requirement than for the net worth requirement, as illustrated by the table below:

Annual Premium Requirement	States
$100,000	Alabama, Florida, Kentucky, Maine
200,000	Louisiana
250,000	Kansas, Michigan, Oklahoma, Virginia
300,000	Georgia, South Carolina
350,000	Missouri

Several states have established other financial requirements that are used instead of or in conjunction with net worth or annual premium requirements. For example, Michigan, Missouri, and South Carolina have a combined net asset requirement. Alabama, Arkansas, and Florida require a combined ratio of current assets to current liabilities of one to one. Colorado and Illinois have an annual payroll requirement for the group. Georgia requires that 1,000 employees be covered by a group. Illinois has a set of requirements that takes into account the number of employees, gross annual payroll, and years in business of each prospective group member. South Carolina requires each member to have at least $25,000 net worth.

Annual premium appears to be a valid measure of the adequacy of workers compensation groups' financial resources. Below a minimum premium size a workers compensation group probably would not be an economically viable entity because it may not be able to obtain excess insurance or cover its overhead expenses. The combined net worth of members, however, while useful to regulators, has a limitation that regulators should consider.

Regulators seem to view combined net worth of group members as a group's financial resource of last resort, i.e., a measure of the group's ability to give meaning to the members' joint and several liability for the group's legal obligations. The extent to which this approach measures available financial resources is determined by the degree that the net worth of individual members is already committed to their individual businesses. The primary purpose of each member's net worth is to provide a financial base for its business operations, not to support its joint and several liability for workers compensation obligations of other members. Assets that are collateral for business loans may not be available to provide security for workers compensation groups. These are factors that regulators should keep in mind when evaluating the net worth of a group's members.

A practical question for regulators is whether they will be able to continue to monitor the combined net worth of group members after the group has been given approval to operate. This could involve a large amount of regulators' staff time. On the other hand, regulators may want to consider a group's combined net worth in their initial determination of the adequacy of a group's financial resources, even if they do not plan to monitor it closely after the group begins operation.

Financial resource requirements perform a variety of functions. If the requirements themselves are meaningful and if they are maintained at appropriate levels, they serve primarily as a regulatory threshold. This permits the regulator to dismiss applications quickly from employers not large enough in the aggregate to form a workers compensation group with a reasonable chance of success. Also, they offer guidance to employers on the minimum financial resources needed to form a successful group. If financial resource requirements are not kept up to date, however, they will soon lose their ability to serve any useful function.

The Study Committee believes that a combined net worth requirement of $1,000,000 and an annual premium requirement of $250,000 are appropriate minimum requirements for most groups, although these requirements may need to be modified depending on the type of risks involved, state benefit levels, size of minimum loss fund, and the aggregate excess insurance retention. The Study Committee believes, however, that financial resource requirements should not be used by regulators except in conjunction with requirements for financial security arrangements such as surety bonds and excess insurance, which will be discussed in detail in the next section.

Required Security

In addition to financial resources arising directly from workers compensation groups and their members, which is one type of payment guarantee, groups typically purchase other guarantees of payment from excess insurance companies and surety companies. The purpose of these purchased security arrangements is to protect the group, its members, and the members' employees by decreasing the likelihood that the group's financial resources will not be adequate to meet its obligations. These arrangements are so important to the long-term success of workers compensation groups that states permitting groups have established a number of requirements for them. This section discusses these security arrangements and a number of important issues relating to them.

The typical security requirements established by states regulating workers compensation groups include excess insurance and security deposits. Security deposits may take the form of cash or negotiable securities deposited with the state, surety bonds payable to the regulator, and, in some states, irrevocable letters of credit. Most often, groups choose to satisfy security deposit requirements with surety bonds, principally because the premiums for bonds require the smallest commitment of group resources. Since surety bonds are used by the majority of groups, they will be the focus of further discussion of security requirements in this section.

Excess insurance, which is the traditional method used by workers compensation groups to protect themselves against catastrophic losses and high loss frequency, is described in Section II C. A comment is needed to explain why this report refers only to excess insurance instead of referring to both excess insurance and reinsurance. Some people use the terms "reinsurance" and "excess insurance" interchangeably, although they are not synonymous. In Florida the group law refers to reinsurance rather than excess insurance. Even though most groups purchase excess insurance, the Florida regulator has had to accept reinsurance contracts, although these contracts are required to contain the same provisions that excess insurance policies are required to contain. Large, sophisticated groups may arrange reinsurance with one or more reinsurance companies rather than relying on the more traditional excess insurance approach. As a practical matter, these reinsurance arrangements usually involve a fronting insurance company issuing an excess insurance policy to satisfy the state regulatory requirements, passing most or all of the liability on to the reinsurance companies. The Study Committee's references to excess insurance in this report should be interpreted to include those instances where reinsurance arrangements lie behind the excess insurance policy.

Most states require some form of excess insurance. Usually, both specific and aggregate excess insurance are required. Alabama, however, requires specific excess insurance, but does not refer to aggregate excess insurance. Colorado, Iowa, Minnesota, New Hampshire, New York, Oregon, and Rhode Island require excess insurance, but do not refer directly to either specific or aggregate excess insurance and do not establish minimum policy limits. New York's excess insurance requirement is based on the financial condition of the group. New Hampshire's requirement varies depending on the size of the group, type of occupation, and number of employees. The Oregon excess insurance requirement takes into account the members' claim experience, the group's financial stability, and its surety bond.

In states that specify excess insurance limits, $1,000,000 is the lowest amount required. Alabama, Florida, Georgia, and Kentucky require this minimum for specific excess insurance, and, with the exception of Alabama, require it for aggregate excess insurance as well. Among states requiring higher excess insurance limits, Louisiana requires $2,000,000 for each specific and aggregate, Maine requires $2,000,000 specific and an acceptable amount for aggregate, Michigan requires $3,000,000 for each, and Virginia requires $1,000,000 for specific and $5,000,000 for aggregate.

The requirements for surety bonds, which are commonly provided by groups in lieu of cash or security deposits, vary considerably from state to state. Colorado simply states that the bond must be of sufficient size to meet the regulator's approval. In Illinois, Michigan, and New York, the size of the bond depends on the group's assets and financial condition. The lowest specified bond limit is $50,000 in Alabama, Florida, Maine, and South Carolina, although the size of the bond may be increased if warranted by the type of employment, size of the group, or its financial condition.

Several states establish the surety bond requirement as a percentage of the group's annual premium. In Georgia, the requirements are 35 percent for private groups and 15 percent for public groups. Kentucky requires a bond equal to 75 percent of the group's premium but limited to a $250,000 maximum. Minnesota has a 70 percent requirement with a $500,000 maximum. New Hampshire sets the bond requirement for a group at its percentage of risk retention.

In establishing requirements for surety bonds and excess insurance, regulators should consider (1) the purposes of these security devices and (2) the factors that contribute to the need for different requirements from group to group. The purpose of excess insurance is to limit a group's exposure to either large individual losses or large losses in the aggregate. The primary purpose of surety bonds is to provide a temporary source of funds if a group fails to pay required benefits. Further discussion of the claims payment provisions of surety bonds and excess insurance policies is presented in the section on claim payments.

Factors that affect excess insurance needs include the size of groups and the types of employment covered. In general, groups having lower annual premium are less able to withstand the effect of high severity losses, need a lower retention, and require a lower specific excess attachment point than groups with higher annual premium. Groups whose members have greater exposure to high severity losses have higher specific and aggregate excess insurance needs than groups whose members have exposure concentrated in high frequency, low severity types of employments.

Surety bond requirements are principally related to a group's need for working capital to pay current expenses and benefits. While there may be a relationship between retentions for specific and aggregate excess losses and the surety bond limit for a small group, applying a fixed relationship for all groups would result in multi-million dollar surety bond requirements for larger groups. Another factor affecting surety bond limits is the nature of the surety coverage. In some states, if surety bonds are purchased for several years, the limits accumulate or "stack." In other states, the coverage is continuous and the limits do not accumulate. Unless regulators take these differences into account, regulators inadvertently may establish surety bond requirements that are either too high or too low.

It is important for regulators to ensure that excess insurance and surety bond requirements are sufficient. In this regard, *the Study Committee believes that minimum limits for excess insurance and surety bonds should be established, that they need to be adjusted periodically, and that the regulator should have the flexibility to establish higher requirements for some groups based on differences in size, types of employment, and other relevant factors.* In addition to aspects of excess insurance policies discussed in this section and in the section on claim payments, there are other aspects that some states have addressed and others may want to consider such as commutation, cancellation, and renewal provisions.

An issue that pertains to both excess insurance policies and surety bonds is the reliability of the companies providing the guarantees. Based on experience to date, the greatest risk of insolvency for a workers compensation group may be failure of the excess insurance company. Licensed excess insurance companies not only are subject to closer regulatory supervision than unlicensed companies but also provide workers compensation groups with the additional protection afforded by state insolvency guaranty funds. Unlicensed insurance companies, even if they are approved surplus lines companies, do not belong to such funds. Surety bonds typically are excluded from coverage by insurance guaranty funds.

The issue facing regulators, then, is the nature of requirements placed on companies offering either excess insurance policies or surety bonds for workers compensation groups. One approach is to accept at face value any excess insurance policy or surety bond. A somewhat more rigorous approach is to accept excess policies and surety bonds only from licensed companies or approved surplus lines companies. The most restrictive approach is to accept excess policies and surety bonds only from licensed companies. Guaranty fund protection for licensed excess insurance companies would be an important factor in this regard. A variation of the latter two approaches is to differentiate stronger from weaker insurance companies by establishing quality standards based on independent financial ratings in addition to requiring either a licensed or an approved company.

The Study Committee believes that regulators should evaluate the financial strength of companies offering excess insurance policies or surety bonds for workers compensation groups; however, there was not agreement on the best method to do this.

A relatively recent development is the financial security endorsement. This is an endorsement to the excess insurance policy that provides a guarantee of benefit payments similar to a surety bond. It is only offered by a limited number of insurance companies and has been approved in only a few states, including Florida, Illinois, Iowa, Kentucky, Michigan, North Carolina, South Carolina, and Virginia. It deserves the attention of regulators because of its apparent benefits and potential problems. The financial security endorsement has the advantage of having both security devices underwritten by one insurance company presumably familiar with workers compensation groups. It eliminates questions or disputes about precedence of coverage between excess insurance policies and surety bonds, and offers certain economies. Regulators should be aware, however, that workers compensation groups purchasing both excess and surety protection from one source may be more vulnerable than if they purchased these security devices from two sources.

A workers compensation group's financial resources, security arrangements, and joint and several liability are important regulatory issues primarily because they are expected to provide the same type of financial safety for groups that surplus, i.e., the excess of assets over liabilities, provides for insurance companies. In fact, this may constitute the principal regulatory difference between groups and insurance companies. For this reason public policy makers should consider carefully the degree of financial security that groups have without surplus.

Requirements regarding insurance company surplus are of two types. First, there are minimum surplus requirements in all states. This is the amount of surplus that insurance companies must have when they are formed and are required to maintain to retain their insurance license. If an insurance company's surplus drops below the minimum required, the company is said to be "impaired." When this occurs, regulators usually take steps to rehabilitate or liquidate the company. The second type of surplus requirement involves the relationship between an insurance company's premiums and its surplus. Insurance regulators have guidelines regarding this relationship that are designed to keep an insurance company from selling more insurance, i.e., assuming more exposure to loss, than its surplus can support. Viewed from this perspective, surplus is a financial cushion to absorb adverse underwriting or investment experience.

One argument in favor of some type of surplus requirement for groups is that while assessments and joint and several liability may provide financial security for groups, the dollars they represent are not readily available to the group. The surety bond meets part of the need, but it may not be sufficient if the group has serious problems. Even though group members can be expected to respond favorably to modest assessments, it is not certain how group members would respond if large assessments were involved. Law suits might be necessary. As groups grow, even with sufficient loss reserves and adequate surety bond and excess insurance coverage, without a surplus to provide a cushion, they become more and more susceptible to problems resulting from adverse loss and investment experience. Finally, financial security requirements are not unique to workers compensation groups. Many states require insurance companies to make security deposits of cash or securities. Reinsurance is used as often and is as important to the welfare of insurance companies as excess insurance is for workers compensation groups.

The counter to the arguments in favor of a surplus requirement for groups is that the various financial safety devices required of workers compensation groups have proven that they work. When groups have experienced shortfalls, group members have provided the necessary funds. Excess insurance reduces the need for groups for surplus. Groups argue that the security provided by joint and several liability exceeds that provided by surplus because of the unlimited nature of joint and several liability. A mandatory surplus requirement is not needed in addition to joint and several liability and other financial requirements. If a surplus requirement is imposed on workers compensation groups, the joint and several liability should be eliminated.

Reserves

With respect to reserves, workers compensation groups are very similar to insurance companies and quite different from self-insurers.

The practice of maintaining specific reserve funds is necessary for any risk sharing mechanism, although it is essentially foreign to a self-insurer's cash flow approach.

The principal categories of reserves maintained by workers compensation groups are unearned premium reserves, conditional reserves, and loss reserves. Some groups also maintain bad debt reserves.

One approach to regulating reserves for workers compensation groups is by reference to the reserving requirements established for insurance companies. Oklahoma and Virginia take this approach by requiring groups to maintain unearned premium and loss and claim reserves in the same manner as stock and mutual insurance companies. Georgia has the same requirement, but makes it applicable to all groups after their first year of operation. Maine and Illinois set forth loss reserve requirements for groups without reference to insurance company reserves.

In property and casualty insurance accounting, premiums are generally recognized as revenue evenly over the contract period. More specifically, written premiums are placed in the unearned premium reserve, which is a liability account, and are transferred from the unearned premium reserve to premium income accounts on a prorated basis throughout the policy year so that premium is earned at a rate that matches a theoretically uniform exposure to loss over the course of the policy year. Also, unearned premium may have to be returned to policyholders if coverage is canceled before the end of a policy period. The size of the unearned premium reserve relative to annual premium volume depends mainly upon the scheduling of premium payments. If most policyholders pay full advance annual premiums, the reserve will be larger than if premiums are paid in installments.

Without an unearned premium reserve, financial statements for insurance companies or workers compensation groups would not present an accurate picture of their financial condition. There would not be a proper matching of revenued and related losses and expenses. For those workers compensation groups that operate with a common expiration date for all members, this effect would be even more pronounced.

The Study Committee believes that regulators should require workers compensation groups to establish unearned premium reserves to reflect the fact that unearned premiums are liabilities.

Loss reserves are a necessity for workers compensation groups just as they are for insurance companies. The value of loss reserves is that they relate ultimate claim payments, which are made over a period of years, to the year of occurrence so that premiums and losses can be matched and compared effectively for a given year. Also, loss reserves are important because they reflect the true liabilities of a group. Without accurate loss reserves, a group would not be able to evaluate the adequacy of its premium and investment income to judge the appropriateness of dividends or the need for assessments.

As noted previously, some states hold workers compensation groups to some or all insurance company loss reserve requirements. In addition, Maine requires groups to file an explanation of reserving methodology along with the required filing of claim data. Illinois requires groups to maintain sufficient reserves, and can require independent actuarial opinions as to the sufficiency of reserves. Florida requires that groups' loss reserves be reviewed annually by a qualified actuary. The state of Washington permits a group to choose between the State Fund's methodology and its own, providing the group has a history of adequate reserving.

A larger number of states address reserves by requiring that groups maintain a fund, called claim funds or loss funds, for the purpose of paying claims. These funds, which are also discussed in Sections II and Section V, are intended to contain sufficient money to pay claims up to a group's retention limit under its aggregate excess policy. Florida adds that, in the absence of aggregate excess coverage, the loss fund shall be a percentage of the premium allocated to pay losses, as determined by the regulator.

Because most workers compensation groups limit their maximum losses through excess insurance, particularly through aggregate excess coverage, the question may arise whether loss reserving by groups should involve anything more complex than providing funding for the aggregate excess retention. An answer to this question is that as long as a group has not paid out fully its aggregate retention, it must be able to determine some reasonable estimate of the ultimate paid losses if it desires to pay dividends before all claims are closed.

Florida and Maine require an additional form of reserve, known as conditional reserves. These are amounts equal to the required security deposit held by the groups instead of deposited with the state. The purpose of the conditional reserves is to provide a safety factor for adverse development of losses, IBNR and premium shortfalls.

The Study Committee believes that regulators should hold workers compensation groups to standards of loss reserve adequacy that measure the true liabilities of groups and permit regulators to assess accurately their financial condition.

Another type of reserve that regulators may want to consider for groups is a reserve for bad debts. Because the aggregate excess retention limit is initially estimated as a percentage of projected earned premiums, rather than collected premiums, a shortfall in collections will cause a shortfall in deposits to the loss fund. Even if delinquent members' coverage is canceled for nonpayment, which reduces the total coverage in force and the aggregate excess retention, there still may be a deficiency in the loss fund. This is because the delinquent members may have been covered for some period for which no premiums were ever collected. A reserve for bad debts, in an amount based on the historical experience of the group or of other groups, can provide the funds to make up this type of deficiency in the loss fund and avoid the necessity to transfer money from other fund years or to take other action. In Florida and Maine, the conditional reserve serves this as well as other purposes.

In practice, the reserve for bad debts may also be available to protect the group against other contingencies. These might include occurrences such as the failure of an excess insurance company or exhaustion of either specific or aggregate excess coverage. This is not meant to suggest that a bad debt reserve could adequately overcome the effect of a major financial setback but the presence of the reserve could provide some working capital while additional funds were raised by assessment or some other means.

Although no state requires a reserve for bad debts, some groups have established them on a voluntary basis. *The Study Committee believes that regulators should require workers compensation groups to establish reserves for bad debts and should specify the methods by which they are determined.*

Investments

An extremely important financial activity of workers compensation groups is the investment of their assets. While a group's funds could be placed in a checking account to assure that they are available when needed, the members' expectations about dividends as well as competitive pressures in the marketplace compel the group to invest any assets not needed immediately to earn an investment return. This adds an element of investment risk to the workers compensation risk assumed by the group and requires a careful balancing of investment liquidity, yield, and safety. Because this is a complex task and because groups operate without a surplus account (which would otherwise be available to absorb fluctuations in investment values), public policy makers have given considerable attention to investment practices of workers compensation groups, as they have for insurance companies.

Individual states have taken a variety of approaches to regulating investment practices of workers compensation groups. Some states have geared their investment regulations to those for insurance companies while others have taken different approaches. In general, investment regulations for groups have focused on allowed uses of group funds and on general and specific provisions concerning allowed investments.

At least ten states provide that (1) the governing board or the administrator shall not use any premiums for any purpose unrelated to workers compensation; (2) the governing board or the administrator shall not borrow any money from the fund or in the name of the fund without first advising the regulator of the nature and purpose of the loan and obtaining approval; and (3) the governing board may, at its discretion, invest any surplus funds not needed for current obligations, in accord with stated investment restrictions. Arkansas, Florida, and Maine state that the governing board should not make even authorized types of investments with the intent to trade, dispose or sell securities in any manner other than redeeming them at maturity. In addition, these states direct the governing board to purchase securities in such denominations and with dates of maturity to insure that these securities are redeeemable at the same time and in the same amounts as the group's current and long-term liabilities.

Several states make it clear that the governing board is responsible for assuring that the group's funds are invested wisely. For example, Maine states that the governing board is responsible for the safety of any investment of surplus monies or claim reserves, is to be held accountable for any misuse or bad faith misapplication of funds as in a fiduciary relationship, and is to adopt written investment policies in addition to the bylaws. In addition, Maine directs the governing board to review the group's investment policies annually. Minnesota also requires an annual review of investment policy. Kentucky specifies that the safety of any investments that exceed federally-insured amounts is the responsibility of the governing board. Georgia has a particularly complete provision prohibiting any pecuniary interest of workers compensation group officials in any of the group's investments or other financial transactions.

States have taken a number of approaches to the types of investments that workers compensation groups are permitted to make. One commonly used approach is to set forth a number of permitted investment categories. Typically, these include federally insured accounts or certificates, direct obligations of the U.S. Government, bonds secured by the full faith and credit of U.S. political subdivisions (usually restricted to the three highest bond ratings), money market funds that are invested only in U.S. Government or government agency obligations with a maturity of one year or less, repurchase agreements, and high grade commercial paper. These investment categories are notable for their high degree of safety and liquidity. Omitted from the above list of permitted investments are common stocks and direct investments in real estate or mortgages, which these states appear to have decided are not suitable for workers compensation groups.

Some states, however, do give latitude to groups to invest in other categories of securities under certain conditions. For example, Maine states that groups may make other investments acceptable to the regulator that are readily convertible to a payment mode without prospect of significant penalty upon conversion to meet current debts of the group.

Illinois permits groups to invest in direct, unconditional obligations of solvent business corporations and in the obligations of any political subdivision of any state, although for each of these types of investments certain conditions must be met. In addition, Illinois seems to be the only state that places quantitative limits on the proportion of a group's funds that can be invested in certain categories of investments.

Michigan and Missouri specify that deposits in savings and loan associations and commercial banks must be limited to institutions in the state and are not to exceed the federally insured amount in any one account, with certain exceptions.

While several states relate investment restrictions for workers compensation groups to investment restrictions on insurance companies, language accomplishing this is usually used in addition to specific enumeration of other types of allowed investments. Louisiana and Minnesota, for example, state that in addition to specifically allowable investment categories, assets of the group may be invested as provided by state law for a casualty insurance company, except that investment in common stock, real estate, or indebtedness of any member company is prohibited. Georgia also relates its investment restrictions for groups to investments permitted for property/casualty insurance companies. Connecticut relates investment restrictions for groups to the same classes of securities and in the same manner in which funds of domestic life insurance companies are by law required or permitted to be invested. Hospital and health care trusts in Colorado are permitted to invest according to declarations in the trust agreement.

The Study Committee believes that workers compensation groups need and should be permitted to have a reasonable range of investment options. Nevertheless, the Study Committee believes that because of the special purpose nature of workers compensation groups and the particular features of the workers compensation risk, the investment function should always operate to support the group's insurance function. There are types of investments that are either unduly speculative or otherwise inappropriate for groups. For this reason, the Study Committee concurs with those states that prohibit groups from investing in common stocks or directly in real estate or mortgage loans. A group should be permitted, however, to invest an appropriate amount in real estate for its own use.

Financial Reports, Audits, and Examinations

Regulators depend on a variety of financial reports to give them an accurate, reasonably comprehensive overview of the financial condition of a workers compensation group. By analyzing a group's financial reports and comparing them to financial reports for previous periods, regulators are able to detect any unfavorable trends and take appropriate action. Certifications by group officials, audits and certifications by independent auditors, and on-site examinations by regulatory staff are all used in varying degrees as ways to assure that a group's financial reports accurately portray its financial condition. Although the public policy issues regarding financial reports, audits, and examinations are not as significant as some other issues discussed in this report, there is room for improvement and much that states can learn from each other in this important area of regulatory practice.

Most states require that each workers compensation group file an annual statement of financial condition. Typically, this includes a balance sheet, income statement, and various supplemental schedules. In some states, the annual financial statement must be in a form acceptable to the regulator, which would seem to imply that all groups would not necessarily have to use the same report format. In other states, the annual financial statement must be in a format prescribed by the regulator. In some of these states, regulators have prescribed the NAIC Convention Statement Blank, which is the format used by property and casualty insurance companies.

For a variety of reasons regulators may want or need to receive financial reports more frequently than once a year. Newly formed groups or groups showing indications of adverse trends may require relatively close regulatory attention. Some regulators may believe that the special nature of the risks assumed by workers compensation groups means that annual financial reports are too infrequent. For these and possibly other reasons, regulators may want to receive financial reports quarterly or semi-annually. Some states give the regulator specific authority to require some or all groups to submit financial reports more often than annually; some do not. Georgia requires groups to file quarterly financial reports, while Illinois permits the regulator to require quarterly financial reports. Other states, such as Arkansas, Florida, Louisiana, Maine, Minnesota, and Virginia give the regulator discretionary authority to require interim financial reports.

At least seven states require a quarterly status report reflecting such matters as the status of a group's claim fund, the premium income and losses of each open fund year, and a listing of any and all delinquent accounts. In addition, several states require groups to file at various intervals loss reports, frequently called Summary Loss Data Reports, containing loss information by classification and by group member. Louisiana, Maine, and Minnesota, require specific identification of claims reserved in excess of $50,000.

While the reports discussed so far are routine financial and operating reports, some states have established special reporting requirements. For example, Kentucky requires a group to furnish each group member a report setting forth information on premiums, losses, expenses, assessments and dividends. New Hampshire, New York and South Carolina have requirements for reports dealing with paid workers compensation benefits, outstanding death and disability claims, and accidents, respectively.

It is important that regulators are able to get the information they need to monitor the financial condition of workers compensation groups and to get this information in a format and at intervals that regulators deem appropriate. *The Study Committee believes, therefore, that regulators should have the specific authority to prescribe the format of financial and other reports and to require interim reporting in addition to routine annual reports. Also, the study committee believes that while groups do not operate on an interstate basis, the IAIABC and the NAIC should work together to develop uniform formats for as many reports as possible. The initial focus should be on annual and quarterly financial statements and on loss reports.*

It is not sufficient for regulators to receive financial reports at appropriate intervals; regulators must have reasonable assurance that the reports are accurate. The principal means states use to achieve this result is to require certified audit reports by an independent certified public accountant (CPA). The accuracy of other reports, such as quarterly status reports, is often attested to by the administrator, chairman of the governing board, or both.

In addition to requirements regarding the certification or attestation of financial and other reports, many regulators find it useful to have regulatory staff conduct on-site examination of a workers compensation group's records and files. Not only does this help the regulator verify the accuracy of previously submitted financial and other reports, but it also gives the regulator an opportunity to observe the day to day operations of a workers compensation group at close hand. Frequently, on-site examinations permit regulators to learn things about workers compensation groups that are not revealed by submitted reports. While the value of this activity has proven itself in the regulation of insurance companies, on-site examinations are not being utilized as frequently for workers compensation groups.

The next few paragraphs, which describe how several states approach audit and examination requirements, will illustrate both the diversity among states and the commonality of their objectives.

A number of states, including Alabama, Arkansas, Oklahoma, Maine, Michigan, Missouri, and Virginia, require a group's governing board to have the group's accounts and records audited annually and at any other time the regulator requires. Typically, these audits are to be performed by independent CPA's according to generally accepted accounting principles. In Arkansas, Michigan, Missouri, and Virginia, the regulator reserves the right to prescribe the type of audits to be made and a uniform accounting system so that the regulator may determine the solvency of groups.

In Virginia, the regulator may accept an unaudited annual financial report, prepared by an independent CPA, in lieu of an audited report. In this case the regulator may require an additional security deposit or surety bond. Also, the regulator may make or direct to be made an examination into the affairs of any group, member, or service company licensed in the state if the examination is necessary for the protection of the public interest. The manner in which these examinations are to be conducted and the release of any examination report are to be handled in the same way that examinations of insurance companies are handled.

Florida requires representatives of the workers compensation agency to audit the records of each group at least once a year. This audit is in addition to any audit associated with the preparation of required financial reports. In Maine, the regulator may require each group's records to be audited annually by accountants acceptable to the regulator, and may require, as often as the regulator deems advisable, other examinations of the affairs, transactions, accounts, records, and assets of each group and of any person as to any matter relevant to the financial affairs of the group. In both Florida and Maine, a written audit report is to be prepared and submitted to the regulator to become part of the annual compliance review.

In Louisiana and Minnesota, in addition to annual audits of accounts and records by a CPA, the regulator may require a special audit at other times if the financial stability of the group or the adequacy of its monetary reserves is in question. In Kansas, the regulator may make, or direct to be made, an examination of the affairs and financial condition of any pool whenever the regulator deems it necessary, except that each pool is to be examined at least once every five years.

Georgia, which has perhaps the most comprehensive treatment of regulatory examination requirements, specifies that the regulator may examine all affairs that relate to the business of operating a workers compensation group at any time, but must do so at least once every three years. Also, the regulator is specifically granted the authority to require and conduct periodic examinations to verify the solvency of groups in the same manner and under the same conditions as insurance companies are examined. Georgia has record retention requirements to ensure that permanent records are available whenever the examination is conducted. The regulator is to have free access to all accounting and financial records, and the administrator, officers, trustees, employees, and representatives of a group are to aid the regulator as far as it is in their power in making the examination. If at any time the regulator finds the accounts of a group to be inadequate or incorrectly kept or posted, the regulator may employ experts to rewrite, post, or balance such records at the expense of the group being examined if the group has failed to correct such accounting records within 60 days after the regulator has given it notice to do so.

It is essential that regulators of workers compensation groups have confidence in the accuracy and completeness of the financial and other reports submitted by workers compensation groups. *The Study Committee believes that statements made under oath by administrators and officers of groups as to the accuracy of filed reports, certified audits by independent CPAs, and on-site examinations by regulatory staff are all necessary regulatory requirements. Provisions relating to these requirements should be clearly stated in state laws and regulations.*

Protection Against Insolvencies

While insolvencies of either insurance companies or workers compensation groups are rare events, the consequences of their occurrence can be severe. Currently all fifty states and the District of Columbia have statutes requiring property and casualty insurance companies to participate in a state guaranty mechanism covering most lines of property and casualty insurance, including workers compensation insurance. Although workers compensation groups typically have joint and several liability provisions, the ability to assess members for additional funds if needed, and substantial security deposits and excess insurance coverage, public policy makers may still be concerned that a group and its members may not be able at some point to provide workers compensation benefits required by law.

While guaranty funds for property and casualty insurance companies are very similar across the country because they are based on a model law developed by the National Association of Insurance Commissioners, the few states that have developed guaranty mechanisms for workers compensation groups have taken different approaches. There is not a model law available suggesting answers to the many questions that must be resolved in developing a guaranty mechanism for groups. These questions include the following:

1. Is a guaranty fund actually formed, is the regulator given the authority to impose assessments on solvent groups as funds are needed, or are both provided?
2. Are both public and private groups required to participate in the guaranty fund?
3. Are groups and self-insured employers included in the same guaranty fund?
4. Is the guaranty fund funded by advance assessments or by assessment after payments are made from the fund?
5. What is the most appropriate basis for assessments on solvent groups?
6. At what point is the guaranty fund called upon to begin paying benefits?
7. Does the guaranty fund have the right to recover monies paid on behalf of an insolvent group and its members?

There are seven states that have established a guaranty mechanism of one type or another to pay workers compensation benefits to injured employees of insolvent groups. Because of this small number and because of the variations among the mechanisms, each is described below.

Illinois Whenever the regulator determines that a workers compensation group may default on its obligations to pay benefits and that the penal sum of the surety bond or other securities provided by the group are about to be exhausted, the regulator can impose upon and collect from all workers compensation groups an assessment to assure prompt payment of workers compensation benefits.

Maine The Self-Insurance Guaranty Association includes all self-insured employers and workers compensation groups. Very large self-insured employers, e.g., private employers with a net worth in excess of $25 million and counties, cities, and towns with a state assessed valuation equal to or in excess of $300 million, are not required to be members of the Association. The Association assesses workers compensation groups in an amount equal to 1 percent of the total annual standard premium which the members of each group would have paid during the calendar year prior to the year of assessment.

Michigan Each year workers compensation groups are assessed by the Workers Compensation Security Fund an amount equal to one-fourth of 1 percent of the total compensation benefits paid during the preceding year exclusive of payments made for investigations, fees, vocational rehabilitation and burial expenses. If additional funds are needed to maintain solvency of the Security Fund, workers compensation groups may be assessed an additional 3 percent of total compensation benefits paid in the previous year.

Minnesota Workers compensation payments to an injured employee of an insolvent workers compensation group are to be paid from the Special Compensation Revolving Fund, which is the same workers compensation fund used to insure state employees. Minnesota law does not provide for an assessment against all workers compensation groups to provide the monies needed to pay claimants of an insolvent group. The law does provide, however, that the state must make an effort to recover monies paid on behalf of the insolvent group directly from the insolvent group unless the regulator determines that no monies are available. Any monies recovered from insolvent groups are deposited into the state general revenue fund.

New York Whenever the regulator determines that workers compensation benefits may be unpaid because of the default of an insolvent private self-insured employer (which includes workers compensation groups) and that the surety bond or the securities held on the employer's (group's) behalf are about to be exhausted, the regulator can levy an assessment against all private self-insured employers to assure prompt payment of benefits. The payments are made first from state administrative funds, which are then replaced by funds derived from the assessment.

Oregon The workers compensation agency levies assessments against workers compensation groups in amounts necessary to maintain an adequate reserve in the Self-Insured Employer Group Adjustment Fund. The Fund pays benefits to injured employees of an insolvent group only after its security deposit and excess insurance coverage have been exhausted. Additional assessments can be levied at any time against groups if it is determined that the adjustment fund reserves are inadequate to meet injured employee benefit payments of insolvent groups.

Rhode Island The regulator can impose an assessment against members of all workers compensation groups to assure prompt payment of compensation and benefits of any insolvent group.

The members of the Study Committee have different opinions as to how fully injured employees should be protected from the possibility of nonpayment of benefits. Those arguing that additional security in the form of a guaranty fund or an assessment mechanism is not needed for groups point to the various financial security requirements imposed on groups and to the favorable experience of groups. They view the joint and several liability provision as a "guaranty mechanism." Those arguing for additional security point out that uncertainties exist with all of the financial security requirements imposed on groups, including joint and several liability. They believe that substantial, additional protection can be provided for the employees of group members through a post-insolvency assessment mechanism with very little burden being placed on groups until funds are needed to pay benefits on behalf of an insolvent group.

The Study Committee believes that each state should evaluate carefully the financial security requirements it imposes on workers compensation groups and, in keeping with its regulatory philosophy regarding workers compensation benefit guarantees, should make its own decision on whether a guaranty mechanism is needed for groups. Also, the Study Committee believes that if a state decides to establish a guaranty mechanism for groups, the guaranty mechanism should not (1) take the place of any financial security requirements, (2) relieve the members of an insolvent group of their joint and several liabilities, or (3) be prefunded except for minimum administrative expenses.

VIII. THE REGULATORY PROCESS

The preceding four sections discussed a large number of regulatory issues regarding specific aspects of workers compensation groups. The purpose of this section, which concludes the Study Committee's discussion of substantive issues, is to address a number of public policy issues that are focused on the structure and process of regulation itself.

The principal issue here is the assignment of regulatory responsibility for workers compensation groups. With rare exception, regulatory responsibility has been assigned to either the workers compensation agency or to the insurance department. While groups can be regulated effectively by either agency, decisions on the locus of regulation, just as decisions on the nature and extent of regulation, should be made with full understanding of the public policy objectives involved and how those objectives can best be achieved. Other general issues discussed more briefly include implementation and enforcement of regulatory requirements, regulation of public groups, and regulation of groups in existence prior to the effective date of the workers compensation group law.

Assignment of Regulatory Responsibility

Throughout this report the terms "regulation," "regulatory authority," and "regulatory responsibility" refer principally to oversight, review, and approval activities related to a workers compensation group's formation, structure, pricing and financial affairs. This is appropriate because of the report's focus on these matters. Before discussing the assignment of regulatory responsibility, however, it is necessary to take a broader look at workers compensation regulatory activities.

State insurance laws impose many regulatory requirements on an insurance company offering workers compensation insurance. In particular, an insurance company has to satisfy licensing requirements in order to obtain and retain a license to do business, cannot use rates or rating plans unless they are approved by the insurance department, must submit periodic financial reports to the insurance department, and is required to open its books and records periodically for examination by insurance department staff.

An insurance company offering workers compensation insurance is also "regulated" in a number of important ways by the workers compensation agency as part of its administration of the workers compensation laws. The workers compensation policy issued by the insurance company may be subject to the approval of, or specified by, the workers compensation agency. The insurance company has to inform the agency of an employer's identity each time a workers compensation policy is issued, canceled, or nonrenewed to assist the agency in assuring compliance with benefit security requirements. The insurance company has to file a variety of reports with the workers compensation agency so that the agency can monitor and evaluate the timeliness and accuracy of the insurance company's benefit payments. The workers compensation agency may be involved in screening injured employees for referral to rehabilitation agencies. Where there is a dispute about workers compensation coverage or benefits, the workers compensation agency often provides a mechanism for hearing both sides of the dispute and has responsibility for reaching a decision on which side prevails. In reality, an insurance company writing workers compensation insurance probably has more extensive contact with the workers compensation agency than it does with the insurance department.

The previous discussion illustrates the point that, viewed broadly, an insurance company writing workers compensation insurance is "regulated" by both the insurance department and the workers compensation agency. Public policy makers have decided that certain types of activities can be carried out more effectively and efficiently by the insurance department and some by the workers compensation agency. In the discussion to follow, the Study Committee assumes (1) that workers compensation agencies will continue to perform the functions necessary to administer the workers compensation laws and to oversee self-insurers and (2) that insurance departments will continue to perform the functions necessary to administer the insurance laws. There is little reason to believe, and it is not the purpose of this report to suggest, that anything would be gained by shifting or altering these functions.

In deciding how regulatory responsibility (as that term is used in this report) for workers compensation groups is to be assigned, public policy makers should have a clear understanding of the regulatory functions to be performed and the knowledge, skills and abilities needed to perform these functions. Having achieved this understanding, public policy makers will be able to evaluate the existing capabilities of the workers compensation agency and the insurance department to regulate workers compensation groups.

In addition, public policy makers will need to consider carefully how regulatory responsibility for workers compensation groups would fit in or mesh with existing regulatory responsibilities assigned to the workers compensation agency and the insurance department. This is important because if the regulation of groups is thought to be more closely related to the principal focus of one of these two agencies than to the other, the more closely related agency would probably be a more effective regulator.

Both the evaluation of existing capabilities and the closeness of current regulatory responsibility are important in determining whether either the workers compensation agency or the insurance department have within them the staff resources to provide effective regulation of workers compensation groups. If neither agency has sufficient staff with needed knowledge, skills, and abilities, it may be that one agency would be able to provide effective regulation with fewer additional staff resources than would the other agency. While this should not necessarily be the determining factor, it may be of some importance in the present economic environment.

The Study Committee believes that the agency assigned regulatory responsibility for workers compensation groups should have staff possessing an understanding of the workers compensation system and the following specific knowledge, skills, and abilities needed for effective regulation:

1. Knowledge of
    (a) workers compensation classification and rating systems;

    (b) accounting methods appropriate for risk-sharing organization;

    (c) the interrelated claims payment obligations of groups, their members, surety companies, and excess insurance companies;

    (d) actuarial principles regarding loss reserves and loss reserve evaluation techniques;

    (e) investment alternatives, their valuation, and their suitability for groups;

    (f) bankruptcy laws and treatment of insolvencies; and

    (g) rate regulatory techniques, if groups are permitted to establish rates based on their own experience.

2. Skills and abilities to

    (a) evaluate organizational documents to ensure that membership agreements, contracts for services, operating policies, etc. are complete, well-conceived, and meet legal requirements;

    (b) assess homogeneity of members, if applicable;

    (c) evaluate experience and capabilities of administrators and service companies;

    (d) monitor and evaluate a group's overall claim handling performance, e.g., timeliness and accuracy of payments, adequacy of reporting, rehabilitation program and litigiousness;

    (e) assure adequacy of loss control programs;

    (f) examine a group's books and records to determine its financial condition, including particularly the sufficiency of its loss reserves;

    (g) analyze a group's financial statements and understand trends in premiums, losses, and expenses to evaluate appropriateness of dividends, need for assessments, and continued viability of the group; and

    (h) examine a group's operations to assess its marketing program, management and fiscal controls, payroll audits, and investment program.

A careful comparison between the knowledge, skills, and abilities identified above and the capabilities of a workers compensation agency and insurance department may show that the workers compensation agency is more capable in some areas and the insurance department is more capable in others. For example, the workers compensation agency, because it has an immense amount of data about individual claims, is in an excellent position to monitor and evaluate the overall claim-handling performance of groups. The insurance department, on the other hand, has considerable expertise regarding financial reports, investments, and other related financial matters. Public policy makers, then, must weigh carefully the merits of assigning all regulatory functions for groups to one agency or the other or of assigning some functions to one agency and some to the other to take advantage of the agencies' different capabilities.

Although the Study Committee does not offer a specific recommendation regarding assignment of regulatory responsibility because of varying conditions from state to state, *the Study Committee urges public policy makers to give careful consideration to this issue on its merits. The Study Committee also urges public policy makers to assure that the regulator has the authority and the staff resources needed to regulate workers compensation groups efficiently and effectively, whether the regulator is the insurance department or the workers compensation agency or whether regulatory responsibility is divided between the two agencies.*

Implementation and Enforcement

Once decisions are made regarding the nature and extent of workers compensation group regulation and the assignment of regulatory responsibility, public policy makers must ensure that the regulator has sufficient staff resources and enforcement tools to regulate groups effectively. If either the staff resources or the enforcement tools are missing, even the most soundly conceived group law and regulation will fail. In addition to discussing resources and enforcement tools, this section includes a brief discussion of a few other regulatory implementation and enforcement issues.

It is difficult for public policy makers to know in advance the number of staff that will be needed to implement an effective regulatory program for workers compensation groups. As indicated in the previous section, the availability of knowledgeable staff in either the workers compensation agency or the insurance department may be a factor in how regulatory responsibility is assigned. A careful analysis of regulatory requirements and a survey of the experience of other states can help public policy makers make a reasonably well-informed decision regarding the level of staff resources needed initially. The problem with one state basing its staffing decisions on the number of staff used in another state is the difficulty of evaluating the effectiveness of the regulatory program in the other state. For example, in some states regulatory responsibility for groups may be assigned to one staff person who also has other responsibilities. This person may not have time to do more than keep up with some of the paper work. He or she may not have time for careful analysis of applications, financial reports, and other reports; for monitoring the performance of the service companies; or for making on-site examinations. Also, the person may not have the full range of knowledge, skills, and abilities needed to regulate effectively. States that look at the staffing patterns of other states must evaluate these points carefully.

The Study Committee urges public policy makers to provide adequate resources for regulating workers compensation groups. The millions of dollars in benefits that groups will be obligated to pay certainly justifies more than a token amount of resources devoted to their regulation. There is probably no instance where regulatory responsibility for workers compensation groups can simply be absorbed by existing staff within either the workers compensation agency or the insurance department.

In addition to sufficient staff to implement the regulatory program for workers compensation groups, the regulator needs a number of enforcement tools. Most states give regulators the authority to terminate a group or revoke approval previously given to a service company if either are not operating in accord with regulatory requirements. Termination and revocation, however, are extremely serious steps that are probably best reserved for extraordinary situations. Other enforcement tools that regulators need are the ability to suspend operations, to issue injunctions and cease and desist orders, to order corrective actions, and to impose a range of fines. These enforcement tools, combined with an active enforcement program, should permit the regulator to ensure reasonable compliance with regulatory requirements and, more importantly, to minimize the possibility that groups will not operate in a sound, safe manner. Therefore, *the Study Committee believes that the workers compensation group law should provide the regulator with a variety of enforcement tools.*

One set of provisions that states may want to consider including in some form in their workers compensation group law or regulations are those dealing with certain unfair trade practices. For example, false advertising, misrepresentations, defamation, filing of false reports, including false entries in books and records, and engaging in a variety of improper and unethical claims practices are all unfair trade practices. To ensure that participants in the workers compensation marketplace do not engage in unfair business practices, provisions may be needed in workers compensation group laws or regulations prohibiting such practices. This would permit regulators to respond to the concerns that have arisen in some states regarding the business practices of some individuals and firms that promote the formation of workers compensation groups and solicit employers for membership.

Public Groups

There are special legal and political aspects of the formation of workers compensation groups by public employers, such as cities, counties and school boards. As a result public policy makers must face two fundamental issues: (1) are public groups to be regulated at all? and (2) if they are to be regulated, how extensive is this regulation to be? Because states have made different decisions regarding the first issue, it deserves particular attention.

Many states have enacted joint power provisions that permit public employers to join together and perform as a group any function they are authorized by law to perform individually. Because a public employer is typically permitted to self-insure its workers compensation risks, the joint power provision permits public employers to pool their workers compensation risks with other public employers. Advocates of permitting public groups to operate without regulation point out that the joint power provision does not state specifically that a workers compensation group formed under it is to be regulated by the workers compensation agency or the insurance department. This line of reasoning is buttressed by the argument that the revenue raising ability of public employers makes regulation of public groups unnecessary.

There are arguments in opposition to exempting public groups from regulation. First, the joint power provision in laws governing various public employers was put there to permit a wide range of joint activities, not just those relating to workers compensation risks. In fact, joint power provisions were enacted before most states had ever thought that public employers would want to form workers compensation groups. Therefore, the absence of any reference to regulation of public groups does not represent a conscious public policy decision on this point and has no relevance to whether a public group is to be regulated or not. The significance of the joint power provision is that without it public employers would probably not be able to form workers compensation groups at all.

The other argument, based on the ability of public employers to raise revenues through their taxing power, misses the point that a key purpose of regulation is to guard against financial and operational difficulties in risk-sharing mechanisms. While it is significant that public employers have the ability to meet their workers compensation obligations by raising taxes, the controversy and delay in benefit payments that would probably occur when any group—public or private—exhausts its financial resources and reaches the limits of its security arrangements is not in the public interest. The issue is not whether each public employer joining a group would be able to pay all benefits required for their own employees. The issue is how best to minimize the risk of a public group not meeting its workers compensation obligations in a timely manner so that the individual public employers do not have to consider levying taxes to meet their workers compensation obligations.

Most states with workers compensation group laws have required public groups to be formed under them. While many of these laws are relatively new, they do not appear to have caused problems for public groups. For example, the first group formed under the Virginia law was a public group. Texas and Tennessee, on the other hand, have passed special laws permitting public groups to form without any regulation. California, which does not have a workers compensation group law, does not seem to have addressed explicitly the regulation of public groups, although there are a large number of public groups operating there. By implication, one must conclude that California intends for public groups to operate without regulation.

The Study Committee urges public policy makers to weigh carefully the pro's and con's of regulation for public groups and to make a conscious public policy decision on this issue.

For those states that have decided to regulate public groups and for those that will do so in the future, there remains the question of how groups are to be regulated. Public employers have some characteristics similar to private employers, but they are different in important ways. Most states have recognized these differences and have relaxed certain requirements imposed on private groups while retaining others. For example, workers compensation agencies apply the same quality of service standards to public groups that they apply to private groups. Regulatory requirements regarding such matters as adequacy of rates, dividends, loss reserves and financial reports are equally applicable to public groups. There are some requirements that have relevance for private groups but may not for public groups. Joint and several liability, which was discussed at length earlier, is an example. Another is aggregate or individual net worth requirements, which do not have meaning for public employers.

States have responded to the need for variances in regulatory requirements for public groups in different ways. Some states have included specific language in their group laws. Others have relied upon regulators to exercise common sense in not imposing meaningless requirements on public groups.

The Study Committee believes that public groups can be accommodated with little difficulty under any reasonable regulatory framework for workers compensation groups as long as regulators evaluate requirements carefully and do not apply inappropriate requirements to public groups.

An issue that has arisen recently in Minnesota and Florida is whether public and private employers should be permitted to join the same workers compensation group. In Florida, the regulator decided that public employers could not join with private employers in a workers compensation group. The regulator's declaratory statement, dated July 20, 1981, said that by joining a group including private businesses, governmental entities would be acting contrary to a provision of the Florida constitution by lending the state's "credit" to a group of private corporations in that the state through those entities would be potentially liable to be assessed a share of the liabilities of the private corporate members under the law and regulation controlling groups. Recently, the Florida group regulation was amended to prevent public employers that are legally unable to enter into a joint and several liability agreement with private employers from participating in a workers compensation group with private employers.

While the homogeneity requirements in most group laws seem to prohibit public and private employers joining the same group (although the Florida regulator did not not consider this in reaching the decision described above), the Minnesota law was changed in 1981 to permit "two or more employers, whether or not they are in the same industry" to form a group. The City Attorney for the City of Duluth, which currently self-insures its workers compensation liability, asked for and received an opinion from Minnesota's Attorney General on the following question: "Does a city have authority to pool its workers compensation liability with that of private employers in the formation of a group self-insurer?" On November 9, 1982, the Attorney General answered in the negative.

The Minnesota Attorney General's opinion was based principally on the view that the Legislature would have to pass specific enabling legislation to permit public and private employers to join the same workers compensation group. The Attorney General, however, included the following observation:

> It should be noted that as a governmental entity, a city in such a pool would not merely be deciding to cover its own liability, or to pool its liability with other governmental units both of which options are specifically authorized. Rather, it would be subjecting itself to potential liability for claims against private employers, who, unlike the city, may terminate business and thus be unavailable for future assessments in the event of larger than anticipated claims.

Michigan and Alabama allow public and private employers to join the same workers compensation group in limited circumstances—usually involving hospitals. The private members sign a joint and several liability agreement, but the public members do not. In effect, public members must guarantee their own workers compensation liabilities.

States seem to be concerned about public employers being liable for assessments to benefit private employers. Certainly imposition of joint and several liability on a public employer would pose serious risks for individual taxpayers. On the other hand, the absence of joint and several liability for all members of a joint public and private group, in combination with the group actively seeking employers of many different types, makes it for all practical purposes a mutual insurance company without any surplus, and raises fundamental questions regarding the public policy objectives associated with the regulation of both groups and insurance companies.

The Study Committee believes that public and private employers should not be permitted to join the same workers compensation group because this would pose significant regulatory problems, present serious solvency concerns, and stretch the concept of a workers compensation group beyond acceptable limits.

Already Existing Groups

In a few states, workers compensation groups—some public, some private—came into existence before specific laws and regulations were enacted applicable to groups. During this period when groups were not as well known as they have become in the past few years, the workers compensation agency and the insurance department may have been aware of the group's existence but may have been unsure of their regulatory authority. Some states have chosen to "grandfather" these pre-existing groups by making the group laws and regulations applicable only to newly formed groups.

The Study Committee does not believe there are any valid public policy reasons for having some groups subject to regulation and some groups not subject to regulation based on when they were formed. If groups in existence at the time a group law and regulation becomes effective cannot meet the regulatory requirements imposed by the law and regulation, these groups should be given a reasonable period to come into compliance. The requirements imposed by the various state laws and regulations on groups are not so burdensome that any properly organized and operating group could not comply with them.

IX. OVERVIEW

Until a few years ago, an employer met its workers compensation obligations in most states by purchasing insurance from a licensed insurance company or, if it were large enough, by qualifying as a self-insurer. Over half of the states now provide a third method. In these states employers not large enough to self-insure are permitted to join with other employers in cooperative pooling arrangements to meet their workers compensation obligations jointly. The form and nature of these arrangements, commonly known as workers compensation group self-insurance pools, funds, or associations, are governed by state laws and regulations.

Workers compensation groups, which share some characteristics with both self-insurers and insurance companies, are regulated by the workers compensation agency in some states and by the insurance department in others. Almost all of the states enacting workers compensation group laws prior to 1979 placed regulatory responsibility for groups with the workers compensation agency. Of those states enacting group laws in 1979 and after, most placed regulatory authority with the insurance department.

Most of the states permitting workers compensation groups have recognized that the regulation of groups is both necessary and appropriate. Although state laws and regulations pertaining to groups vary considerably in some of their details, typically they address (1) the organization and administration of groups, (2) the obligations of groups and their members, (3) the ways in which prices are established and profits and losses are distributed, and (4) financial resources of groups and methods to guard against insolvency. As is the case with the regulation of self-insurers by workers compensation agencies and of insurance companies by insurance departments, the principal objective of group laws and regulations is to assure that groups have and maintain adequate financial resources to meet their obligations to injured workers and others.

At the direction of the National Association of Insurance Commissioners, the Study Committee conducted a comprehensive review of state approaches to regulating workers compensation groups. The Study Committee's report identifies and analyzes the fundamental public policy and regulatory issues a state must face in developing a group law and regulation. The more important of these issues are listed below under section headings where they are discussed in the report:

IV. Organization and Administration
1. Minimum number of members.
2. Similarity of members' risk characteristics.
3. Specification of the indemnity agreement.
4. Membership, duties, and responsibilities of the governing board.

    5. Qualification and role of the administrator.
    6. Regulatory approval of service companies and service contracts.
    7. Guarantee of claims services.
    8. Regulatory involvement in member and group terminations.
  V. Obligations of a Group and Its Members
    1. Joint and several liability.
    2. Surety bond and excess insurance claim payment provisions.
    3. Involvement of groups in residual market mechanisms and special workers compensation funds.
    4. Appropriateness of premium taxes and regulatory fees and assessments.
  VI. Pricing
    1. Use of approved manual rates and rating systems.
    2. Rate deviations.
    3. Periodic premium payment plans.
    4. Prior approval of timing and amount of dividends.
    5. Assessment procedures
    6. Verification of rates and calculation of experience modification factors.
  VII. Financial Condition
    1. Financial resource requirements.
    2. Excess insurance and security deposit requirements.
    3. Types of and standards for reserves.
    4. Permitted investments.
    5. Financial reports.
    6. Audits and examinations
    7. Need for benefit payment guarantee mechanism.
  VIII. The Regulatory Process
    1. Agency responsible for regulating groups.
    2. Knowledge, skills and abilities needed for effective regulation.
    3. Adequacy of regulatory resources and enforcement tools.
    4. Regulatory treatment of public groups.
    5. Regulatory treatment of already existing groups.

While not its principal charge, the Study Committee was able to reach general agreement on many of the public policy and regulatory issues and to develop recommendations. These recommendations should increase the usefulness of the report to legislators, regulators, and others.

In identifying and analyzing the issues and formulating its

recommendations, the Study Committee did not evaluate workers compensation group regulation in the abstract. By necessity, the Study Committee had to consider existing regulatory structures and the competitive marketplace in which insurance companies, self-insurers, and groups all operate. If legislators and regulators approach decisions regarding the regulation of workers compensation groups in this manner, they will (1) avoid inappropriate incentives or disincentives for employers forming, joining, or leaving groups, (2) achieve more efficient and effective regulation of groups, and (3) come closer to assuring that groups are able to meet their obligations to injured workers and others.

* * *

PRIVATE EMPLOYER GROUP WORKERS COMPENSATION SELF-INSURANCE MODEL ACT*

Table of Contents

---

*The following is a reprint of the model act adopted by the NAIC for private employer workers compensation self-insurance groups. This model act is reprinted with the permission of the NAIC from the *Official NAIC Model Laws, Regulations and Guidelines*, pp. 425-1 to 425-11. The NAIC at its June 1984 meeting also adopted a similar model act to apply to public employer groups. Three primary differences between the private and the public employer model acts (which otherwise are substantially similar) are:

1. Sections 4.B.1. & 2. regarding securities and which are mandatory in the private employer group model act are made optional and are slightly revised in the public employer group model act. A drafting note states that the issue regarding whether a security deposit is necessary must be decided on a state by state basis.
2. The joint and several liability provision of Sections 4.B.5. and 8.C. in the private employer group model act is not included in the public employer group model act.
3. Section 12 regarding taxes and optional Section 20 regarding the guaranty mechanism in the private employer group model act are not included in the public employer group model act.

Two apparent typographical errors do appear in the model act reprinted here. (Since the act is being reprinted as is and any changes would have to be formally adopted by the NAIC at a later meeting, these errors are mentioned in this footnote.) Section 4.A.5. should refer to Section 19, not Section 18. Also, Section 5.A. should refer to Section 23, not Section 21.

Section 1. Scope

The provisions of this Act shall apply to workers compensation self-insurance groups. This Act shall not apply to public employees or governmental entities. Groups which are issued a certificate of approval by the commissioner shall not be deemed to be insurers or insurance companies and shall not be subject to the provisions of the insurance laws and regulations except as otherwise provided herein.

Section 2. Definitions

A. "Administrator" means an individual, partnership or corporation engaged by a workers compensation self-insurance group's board of trustees to carry out the policies established by the group's board of trustees and to provide day to day management of the group.
B. "Commissioner" means the Commissioner of Insurance.
   Drafting Note: See Discussion on the regulation of groups
   by either the insurance department or workers compensa-

tion agency on pp. 72-75 in the NAIC Study Committee report.

C. "Insolvent" or "Insolvency" means the inability of a workers compensation self-insurance group to pay its outstanding lawful obligations as they mature in the regular course of business, as may be shown either by an excess of its required reserves and other liabilities over its assets or by its not having sufficient assets to reinsure all of its outstanding liabilities after paying all accrued claims owed by it.

D. "Net premium" means premium derived from standard premium adjusted by any advance premium discounts.

E. "Service company" means a person or entity which provides services not provided by the administrator, including but not limited to, (a) claims adjustment, (b) safety engineering, (c) compilation of statistics and the preparation of premium, loss and tax reports, (d) preparation of other required self-insurance reports, (e) development of members' assessments and fees, and (f) administration of a claim fund.

F. "Standard premium" means the premium derived from the manual rates adjusted by experience modification factors but before advance premium discounts.

G. "Workers compensation," when used as a modifier of "benefits," "liabilities," or "obligations," means both workers compensation and employer's liability.

> Drafting Note: In those states where workers compensation does not include employer's liability, "employer's liability" should be eliminated from the definition.

H. "Workers compensation self-insurance group" or "group" means a not-for-profit unincorporated association consisting of five or more employers who are engaged in the same or similar type of business, who are members of the same bona fide trade or professional association which has been in existence for not less than five years, and who enter into agreements to pool their liabilities for workers compensation benefits and employer's liability in this state.

> Drafting Note: States may wish to use other terminology to describe groups, e.g., associations, funds, or pools.

> Before a state chooses to delete the language "who are engaged in the same or similar type of business and" it is recommended that the drafter carefully review the discussion of the issues involved, see pp. 22-25 of the NAIC Study Committee report.

Section 3. Authority to Act as a Workers Compensation Self-Insurance Group

No person, association or other entity shall act as a workers compensation self-insurance group unless it has been issued a certificate of approval by the commissioner.

Section 4. Qualifications for Initial Approval and Continued Authority to Act As A Workers Compensation Self-Insurance Group

A. A proposed workers compensation self-insurance group shall file with the commissioner its application for a certificate of approval accompanied by a non-refundable filing fee in the amount of $_____. The application shall include the group's name, location of its principal office, date of organization, name and address of each member, and such other information as the commissioner may reasonably require, together with the following:
   1. Proof of compliance with the provisions of Subsection B of this Section.
   2. A copy of the articles of association, if any.
   3. A copy of agreements with the administrator and with any service company.
   4. A copy of the bylaws of the proposed group.
   5. A copy of the agreement between the group and each member securing the payment of workers compensation benefits, which shall include provision for payment of assessments as provided for in Section 18.
   6. Designation of the initial board of trustees and administrator.
   7. The address in this state where the books and records of the group will be maintained at all times.
   8. A pro forma financial statement on a form acceptable to the commissioner showing the financial ability of the group to pay the workers compensation obligations of its members.
   9. Proof of payment to the group by each member of not less than 25% of that member's first year estimated annual net premium on a date prescribed by the commissioner. Such payment shall be considered to be part of the first year premium payment of each member, if the proposed group is granted a certificate of approval.

B. To obtain and to maintain its certificate of approval a workers compensation self-insurance group shall comply with the following requirements as well as any other requirements established by law or regulation:

1. A combined net worth of all members of a group of private employers of at least $1,000,000. Any such securities shall be deposited with the (state treasurer) and assigned to and made negotiable by the (chairman of the workers compensation agency) pursuant to a trust document acceptable to the commissioner. Interest accruing on a negotiable security so deposited shall be collected and transmitted to the depositor provided the depositor is not in default.

2. Security in a form and amount prescribed by the commissioner which shall be provided by either a surety bond, security deposit or financial security endorsement or any combination thereof. If a surety bond is used to meet the security requirement, it shall be issued by a corporate surety company authorized to transact business in this state. If a security deposit is used to meet the security requirement, securities shall be limited to bonds or other evidences of indebtedness issued, assumed, or guaranteed by the United States of America, or by an agency or instrumentality thereof; certificates of deposit in a federally insured bank; shares or savings deposits in a federally insured savings and loan association or credit union; or any bond or security issued by a State of the United States of America and backed by the full faith and credit of the State. A financial security endorsement, issued as part of an acceptable excess insurance contract, may be used to meet all or part of the security requirement. The bond, security deposit, or financial security endorsement shall be (a) for the benefit of the state solely to pay claims and associated expenses and (b) payable upon the failure of the group to pay workers' compensation benefits it is legally obligated to pay.

   The commissioner may establish, and adjust from time to time, requirements for the amount of security based on differences among groups in their size, types of employment, years in existence, and other relevant factors.

3. Specific and aggregate excess insurance in a form, in an amount, and by an insurance company acceptable to the commissioner. The commissioner may establish minimum requirements for the amount of specific and aggregate excess insurance based on differences among groups in

their size, types of employments, years in existence and other relevant factors and may permit a group to meet this requirement by placing in a designated depository securities of the type referred to in Paragraph 2 of this Subsection.

4. An estimated annual standard premium of at least $250,000 during a group's first year of operation. Thereafter, the annual standard premium shall be at least $500,000.

5. An indemnity agreement jointly and severally binding the group and each member thereof to meet the workers compensation obligations of each member. The indemnity agreement shall be in a form prescribed by the commissioner and shall include minimum uniform substantive provisions prescribed by the commissioner. Subject to the commissioner's approval, a group may add other provisions needed because of its particular circumstances.

6. A fidelity bond for the administrator in a form and amount prescribed by the commissioner.

7. A fidelity bond for the service company in a form and amount prescribed by the commissioner. The commissioner may also require the service company providing claim services to furnish a performance bond in a form and amount prescribed by the commissioner.

C. A group shall notify the commissioner of any change in the information required to be filed under Subsection A of this Section or in the manner of its compliance with Subsection B of this Section no later than 30 days after such change.

D. The commissioner shall evaluate the information provided by the application required to be filed under Subsection A of this Section to assure that no gaps in funding exist and that funds necessary to pay workers compensation benefits will be available on a timely basis.

E. The commissioner shall act upon a completed application for a certificate of approval within 60 days. If, because of the number of applications, the commissioner is unable to act upon an application within this period, the commissioner shall have an additional 60 days to so act.

F. The commissioner shall issue to the group a certificate of approval upon finding that the proposed group has met all requirements or the commissioner shall issue an order refusing such certificate setting forth reasons for such refusal upon finding that the proposed group does not meet all requirements.

G. Each workers compensation self-insurance group shall be deemed to have appointed the commissioner as its attorney to receive service of legal process issued against it in this state. The appointment shall be irrevocable, shall bind any successor in interest, and shall remain in effect as long as there is in this state any obligation or liability of the group for workers compensation benefits.

Section 5. Certificate of Approval; Termination

A. The certificate of approval issued by the commissioner to a workers compensation self-insurance group authorizes the group to provide workers compensation benefits. The certificate of approval remains in effect until terminated at the request of the group or revoked by the commissioner, pursuant to provisons of § 21 of this Act.

B. The commissioner shall not grant the request of any group to terminate its certificate of approval unless the group has insured or reinsured all incurred workers compensation obligations with an authorized insurer under an agreement filed with and approved in writing by the commissioner. Such obligations shall include both known claims and expenses associated therewith and claims incurred but not reported and expenses associated therewith.

Subject to the approval of the commissioner, a group may merge with another group engaged in the same or similar type of business only if the resulting group assumes in full all obligations of the merging groups. The commissioner may hold a hearing on the merger and shall do so if any party to the merger, including a member of either group, so requests.

> Drafting Note: Before a state chooses to delete the language "engaged in the same or similar type of business" it is recommended that the drafter carefully review the discussion of the issues involved, see pp. 22-25 of the NAIC Study Committee report.

Section 6. Examinations

The commissioner may examine the affairs, transactions, accounts, records, assets and liabilities of each group as often as the commissioner deems advisable.

> Drafting Note: It is recommended that this examination requirement be consistent with the existing requirement for examining insurance companies, e.g., not less often than once every three (five) years.

Section 7. Board of Trustees: Membership, Powers, Duties, and Prohibitions

Each group shall be operated by a board of trustees which shall consist of not less than five persons whom the members of a group elect for stated terms of office. At least two-thirds of the trustees shall be employees, officers, or directors of members of the group. The group's administrator, service company, or any owner, officer, employee of, or any other person affiliated with, such administrator or service company shall not serve on the board of trustees of the group. All trustees shall be residents of this state or officers of corporations authorized to do business in this state. The board of trustees of each group shall ensure that all claims are paid promptly and take all necessary precautions to safeguard the assets of the group, including all the following:

A. The board of trustees shall:

1. Maintain responsibility for all monies collected or disbursed from the group and segregate all monies into a claims fund account and an administrative fund account. At least 70% of the net premium shall be placed into a designated depository for the sole purpose of paying claims, allocated claims expenses, reinsurance or excess insurance, and special fund contributions, including second injury and other loss related funds. This shall be called the claims fund account. The remaining net premium shall be placed into a designated depository for the payment of taxes, general regulatory fees and assessments, and administrative costs. This shall be called the administrative fund account. The commissioner may approve an administrative fund account of more than 30% and a claims fund account of less than 70% only if the group shows to the commissioner's satisfaction that (a) more than 30% is needed for an effective safety and loss control program or (b) the group's aggregate excess insurance attaches at less than 70%.

   Drafting Note: Special fund contributions include second injury and other loss related funds. Administrative costs include guaranty fund assessments.

2. Maintain minutes of its meetings and make such minutes available to the commissioner.

3. Designate an administrator to carry out the policies established by the board of trustees and to provide day to day management of the group, and delineate in the written minutes of its meetings the areas of authority it delegates to the administrator.

4. Retain an independent certified public accountant to prepare the statement of financial condition required by Subsection A of Section 11.

B. The board of trustees shall not:

1. Extend credit to individual members for payment of a premium, except pursuant to payment plans approved by the commissioner.

2. Borrow any monies from the group or in the name of the group except in the ordinary course of business, without first advising the commissioner of the nature and purpose of the loan and obtaining prior approval from the commissioner.

Section 8. Group Membership; Termination; Liability

A. An employer joining a workers compensation self-insurance group after the group has been issued a certificate of approval shall (1) submit an application for membership to the board of trustees or its administrator and (2) enter into the indemnity agreement required by Subsection B.5. of Section 4. Membership takes effect no earlier than each member's date of approval. The application for membership and its approval shall be maintained as permanent records of the board of trustees.

B. Individual members of a group shall be subject to cancellation by the group pursuant to the bylaws of the group. In addition, individual members may elect to terminate their participation in the group. The group shall notify the commissioner and the workers compensation agency of the termination or cancellation of a member within 10 days and shall maintain coverage of each canceled or terminated member for 30 days after such notice, at the terminating member's expense, unless the group is notified sooner by the workers compensation agency that the canceled or terminated member has procured workers compensation insurance, has become an approved self-insurer, or has become a member of another group.

C. The group shall pay all workers compensation benefits for which each member incurs liability during its period of membership. A member who elects to terminate its membership or is canceled by a group remains jointly and severally liable for workers compensation obligations of the group and its members which were incurred during the canceled or terminated member's period of membership.

D. A group member is not relieved of its workers compensation liabilities incurred during its period of membership except through payment by the group or the member of required workers compensation benefits.

E. The insolvency or bankruptcy of a member does not relieve the group or any other member of liability for the payment of any workers compensation benefits incurred during the insolvent or bankrupt member's period of membership.

Drafting Note: This language should not be interpreted as negating any other statute or case law limiting defenses.

Section 9. Service Companies

A. No service company or its employees, officers or directors shall be an employee, officer or director of, or have either a direct or indirect financial interest in, an administrator. No administrator or its employees, officers or directors shall be an employee, officer or director of, or have either a direct or indirect financial interest in, a service company.

B. The service contract shall state that, unless the commissioner permits otherwise, the service company shall handle to their conclusion all claims and other obligations incurred during the contract period.

Section 10. Licensing of Agent

Except for a salaried employee of a group, its administrator or its service company, any person soliciting membership in a workers compensation self-insurance group must be licensed as provided (in Section_____of the insurance code).

Section 11. Financial Statements and Other Reports

A. Each group shall submit to the commissioner a statement of financial condition audited by an independent certified public accountant on or before the last day of the sixth month following the end of the group's fiscal year. The financial statement shall be on a form prescribed by the commissioner and shall include, but not be limited to, actuarially appropriate reserves for (1) known claims and expenses associated therewith, (2) claims incurred but not reported and expenses associated therewith, (3) unearned premiums and (4) bad debts, which reserves shall be shown as liabilities. An actuarial opinion regarding reserves for (1) known claims and expenses associated therewith and (2) claims incurred but not reported and expense associated therewith shall be included in the audited financial statement. The actuarial opinion shall be given by a member of the American Academy of Actuaries or other qualified loss reserve specialist as defined in the annual statement adopted by the National Association of Insurance Commissioners.

B. The commissioner may prescribe a uniform financial reporting system for all groups to ensure the accurate and complete reporting of groups' financial information.

C. The commissioner may prescribe the format and frequency of other reports which may include, but shall not be limited to, payroll audit reports, summary loss reports, and quarterly financial statements.

Section 12. Taxes

Drafting Note: A state that imposes a premium tax or other tax on workers compensation insurers will have to decide whether such tax should be imposed on groups. However, a state that dedicates a premium tax or other tax on workers compensation insurance principally for workers compensation purposes, e.g., administration or a special fund, should impose such tax on groups. See pp. 45-47 of the NAIC Study Committee report.

Section 13. Fees and Assessments

Drafting Note: Fees and assessments for second injury funds or other special funds or for administrative funds associated with the insurance department or the workers compensation agency should be imposed on groups in the same manner that they are imposed on insurance companies or self-insurers. See pp. 45-47 of the NAIC Study Committee report.

Section 14. Misrepresentation Prohibited

No person shall make any untrue statement of a material fact or omit to state a material fact necessary in order to make the statement made, in light of the circumstances under which it is made, not misleading, in connection with the solicitation of membership of a group.

Section 15. Investments

Funds not needed for current obligations may be invested by the board of trustees in accordance with (Section_____of the insurance code regarding investments of property and casualty insurers).

Section 16. Rates and Reporting of Rates

A. Every workers compensation self-insurance group shall adhere to the uniform classification system, uniform experience rating plan, and manual rules filed with the commissioner by an advisory organization designated by the commissioner.

B. Premium contributions to the group shall be determined by applying the manual rates and rules to the appropriate classification of each member which shall be adjusted by each member's experience credit or debit. Subject to approval by the commissioner, premium contributions may also be reduced by an advance premium discount reflecting the group's expense levels and loss experience.

C. Notwithstanding Subsection B. of this Section, a group may apply to the commissioner for permission to make its own rates. Such rates shall be based on at least five years of the group's experience.

> Drafting Note: States that have adopted the Alternative Model Workers Compensation Competitive Rating Act should use the following provision in place of Subsections B. and C. above:

> Every group shall use the pure premium rates filed with the commissioner by the designated advisory organization plus an additional amount representing the member's portion of estimated expenses. A group may contract with an advisory organization approved by the commissioner for assistance in developing appropriate rates.

D. Each group shall be audited at least annually by an auditor prescribed by the commissioner to verify proper classifications, experience rating, payroll and rates. A report of the audit shall be filed with the commissioner in a form prescribed by the commissioner. A group or any member thereof may request a hearing on any objections to the classifications. If the commissioner determines that as a result of an improper classification a member's premium contribution is insufficient, he shall order the group to assess that member an amount equal to the deficiency. If the commissioner determines that as a result of an improper classification a member's premium is excessive, he shall order the group to refund to the member the excess collected. The audit shall be at the expense of the group.

Section 17. Refunds

A. Any monies for a fund year in excess of the amount necessary to fund all obligations for that fund year may be declared to be refundable by the board of trustees not less than 12 months after the end of the fund year.

> Drafting Note: In those states where dividends may be paid earlier than 12 months, the time limit should be changed to conform to state practice.

B. Each member shall be given a written description of the refund plan at the time of application for membership. A refund for any fund year shall be paid only to those employers who remain participants in the group for the entire fund year. Payment of a refund based on a previous fund year shall not be contingent on continued membership in the group after that fund year.

Section 18. Premium Payment; Reserves

A. Each group shall establish to the satisfaction of the commissioner a premium payment plan which shall include (1) an initial payment by each member of at least 25% of that member's annual premium before the start of the group's fund year and (2) payment of the balance of each member's annual premium within the first months of that fund year in monthly or quarterly installments.

B. Each group shall establish and maintain actuarially appropriate loss reserves which shall include reserves for (1) known claims and expenses associated therewith and (2) claims incurred but not reported and expenses associated therewith.

C. Each group shall establish and maintain bad debt reserves based on the historical experience of the group or other groups.

Section 19. Deficits and Insolvencies

A. If the assets of a group are at any time insufficient to enable the group to discharge its legal liabilities and other obligations and to maintain the reserves required of it under this Act, it shall forthwith make up the deficiency or levy an assessment upon its members for the amount needed to make up the deficiency.

B. In the event of a deficiency in any fund year, such deficiency shall be made up immediately, either from (a) surplus from a fund year other than the current fund year, (b) administrative funds, (c) assessment of the membership, if ordered by the group or, (d) such alternate method as the commissioner may approve or direct. The commissioner shall be notified prior to any transfer of surplus funds from one fund year to another.

C. If the group fails to assess its members or to otherwise make up such deficit within 30 days, the commissioner shall order it to do so.

D. If the group fails to make the requirement assessment of its members within 30 days after the commissioner orders it to do so, or if the deficiency is not fully made up within 60 days after the date on which such assessment is made, or within such longer period of time as may be specified by the commissioner, the group shall be deemed to be insolvent.

E. The commissioner shall proceed against an insolvent group in the same manner as the commissioner would proceed against an insolvent domestic insurer in this state as prescribed in (Sections of the insurance code regarding liquidation, conservation, etc.). The commissioner shall have the same powers and limitations in such proceedings as are provided under those laws, except as otherwise provided in this Act.

F. In the event of the liquidation of a group, the commissioner shall levy an assessment upon its members for such an amount as the commissioner determines to be necessary to discharge all liabilities of the group, including the reasonable cost of liquidation.

Section 20. Guaranty Mechanism (OPTIONAL)

In the event of a liquidation pursuant to Section 19, after exhausting the security required pursuant to Section 4.B.2., the commissioner shall levy an assessment against all groups to assure prompt payment of such benefits. The assessment on each group shall be based on the proportion that the premium of each group bears to the total premium of all groups. The commissioner may exempt a group from assessment upon finding that the payment of the assessment would render the group insolvent. Such assessment shall not relieve any member of an insolvent group of its joint and several liability. After any such assessment is made, the commissioner shall take action to enforce the joint and several liability provisions of the insolvent group's indemnity agreement, and shall recoup (1) all costs incurred by the commissioner in enforcing such joint and several liability provisions, (2) amounts that the commissioner assessed any other groups pursuant to this Section, and (3) any obligations included within Subsection F. of Section 19.

> Drafting Note: Each state should evaluate carefully the financial security requirements it imposes on workers compensation groups and, in keeping with its regulatory philoso-

phy regarding workers compensation benefit guarantees, should make its own decision on whether a guaranty mechanism is needed for groups. If a state decides to establish a guaranty mechanism for groups, the guaranty mechanism should not (1) take the place of any financial security requirements, (2) relieve the members of an insolvent group of their joint and several liabilities, or (3) be refunded except for minimum administrative expenses.

Section 21. Monetary Penalties

After notice and opportunity for a hearing, the commissioner may impose a monetary penalty on any person or group found to be in violation of any provision of this Act or of any rules or regulations promulgated thereunder. Such monetary penalty shall not exceed $1,000 for each act or violation and shall not exceed $10,000 in the aggregate. The amount of any such monetary penalty shall be paid to the commissioner for the use of the state.

> Drafting Note: The disposition of monetary penalties will have to be set forth by each state according to its own practices.

Section 22. Cease and Desist Orders

A. After notice and opportunity for a hearing, the commissioner may issue an order requiring a person or group to cease and desist from engaging in an act or practice found to be in violation of any provision of this Act or of any rules or regulations promulgated thereunder.

B. Upon a finding, after notice and opportunity for a hearing, that any person or group has violated any cease and desist order, the commissioner may do either or both of the following: (a) impose a monetary penalty of not more than $10,000 for each and every act or violation of such order not to exceed an aggregate monetary penalty of $100,000 or (b) revoke the group's certificate of approval or any insurance license held by the person.

Section 23. Revocation of Certificate of Approval

After notice and opportunity for a hearing, the commissioner may revoke a group's certificate of approval if it (1) is found to be insolvent, (2) fails to pay any premium tax, regulatory fee or assessment, or special fund contribution imposed upon it, or (3) fails to comply with any of the provisions of this Act, with any rules promulgated thereunder, or with any lawful order of the commissioner within the time prescribed. In addition, the commissioner may revoke a group's certificate of approval if, after notice and opportunity for hearing, the commissioner finds that (a) any certificate of approval that was issued to the group was obtained by fraud; (b) there was a material misrepresentation in the application for the certificate of approval; or (c) the group or its administrator has misappropriated, converted, illegally withheld, or refused to pay over upon proper demand any monies that belong to a member, an employee of a member, or a person otherwise entitled thereto and that have been entrusted to the group or its administrator in its fiduciary capacities.

Section 24. Notice and Hearings

> Drafting Note: This section should conform to the state's administrative procedures act and insurance code for notices and hearings resulting in orders of suspension, revocation, cease and desist and monetary penalties.

Section 25. Rules and Regulations

The commissioner shall have power to make rules and regulations in order to implement this Act.

Section 26. Severability Clause

If any provision of this Act, or the application thereof to any person or circumstance, is subsequently held to be invalid, such invalidity shall not affect other provisions or applications of this Act.

Legislative History (all references are to the Proceedings of the NAIC).
1984 Proc. I 704 (adopted)
1984 Proc. II (amended)

Monograph Notes

1. Based on information contained in a paper titled "Special Funds in Workers' Compensation" by Lloyd W. Larson and John F. Burton, Jr., presented at the National Council on Compensation Insurance's Second Annual Seminar on Economic Issues in Workers' Compensation on 19 November 1982.
2. Richard A. Musgrave and Peggy B. Musgrave, *Public Finance in Theory and Practice* (New York: McGraw-Hill Publishing Co., 1980), p. 235.

MONOGRAPH 8

Profit Cycles in Property-Liability Insurance

by Barbara D. Stewart

PREFACE

Profit cycles in property-liability insurance have been noted by the industry and its observers for years, but to the author's knowledge the cycles have never been analyzed as an economic phenomenon. This monograph may be the first attempt to develop an economic theory for the industry's profit cycles. Because the following analysis of property-liability profit cyclicality is original, it has not had the benefit of debate and discussion, not to mention prior authority (it is no accident that footnotes disappear halfway through the monograph). Hence, this work will no doubt treat some issues too much or too little and may omit some points that others believe are relevant to the cyclical process. The author hopes that this first attempt to develop an economic theory for profit cyclicality in property-liability insurance will prompt further thought and writing on the subject. The following is not meant to be the final word, but rather a starting point for understanding the property-liability insurance profit cycle.

I. INTRODUCTION

Profit cycles in property-liability insurance are not new. For years insurers have recognized that the business has its good times and its bad times. Perhaps insurers accepted profit cyclicality in the past because they expected that, over the long pull, the money made in the good times would more than make up for the money lost in the bad times. But recent events have made insurers less certain that this will continue to be the case.

In 1975 the property-liability industry experienced its worst loss in the fifty years for which profits had been recorded. Three years later, profits soared to record highs, only to be beaten down later by price cutting, especially in commercial lines. Industry losses mounted, and by 1984 profitability had sunk even lower than 1975's frightening levels. Insolvency, which rarely occurred during much of the twentieth century, threatened a number of insurers and reinsurers. Both large and small organizations went out of business or were forced to merge with stronger organizations in order to avoid bankruptcy.

The roller coaster of profitability has raised questions about the industry's financial ability to bear the risks, especially the growing liability risks, of modern society. Twice in a decade the insurance industry has reacted to losses by severely curtailing availability of coverage. Buyers have responded with anger and have formed their own insurance companies, some of which compete directly with insurers from whom they previously bought coverage. Legislators in many states have responded to the most recent crisis of availability by demanding new controls on the industry, especially prior approval of rates.

Severe swings in profitability and availability have caused people inside and outside the industry to ask whether property-liability cyclicality can be controlled. Answering that question first requires understanding profit cycles. This monograph is an analysis of the industry's profit cycles. It reviews historical evidence of profit cycles, their causes in the context of economic theory, the phases of a typical cycle, major influences on cycles, whether cycles can and should be controlled, and, finally, the destiny of the individual firm operating in a cyclical business.

This monograph confines its analysis of past cycles to the period following World War II, although profit cycles were evident before that time. In fact, they have occurred over the entire period for which statistics on insurer profitability have been collected. Even so, the end of World War II makes a convenient starting point for the purposes of this monograph. In the prior period, dislocations of the war, and before it the severity of the 1930s depression, complicated the situation of the insurance industry, as they complicated it for every other business at that time. Another reason to start the analysis with the years just following the war is that they marked the beginning of changes in regulation and in industry behavior toward greater competition.

The legal and economic environment for property-liability insurance was substantially changed in 1944 by the U.S. Supreme Court's decision that insurance transactions that cross state lines are interstate commerce.[1] The effect of the ruling was that the federal antitrust laws applied to the insurance business. The pricing practices in insurance—based on the collection of data from many companies, the promulgation of uniform rates, and agreements by many companies to adhere to those rates—clearly violated the antitrust laws as to pricing. Congress enacted an exemption for insurance from much antitrust law, conditioned on an unspecified degree of regulation by the states. As a result, the property-liability insurance business has functioned for the past forty-two years under an uncertain and probably diminishing insulation from the antitrust laws, complicated by changing attitudes of the states toward competition and important changes in the structure and competitive behavior of the industry itself.[2]

For these reasons, property-liability insurance has not been an easy subject for economic analysis. It has been a moving target and, therefore, it counsels caution in looking at any development or behavior except in its temporal context. Although the business generally has become very competitive, and hence more amenable to economic analysis of competitive behavior that underlies this monograph, this was neither always true nor is it true now for every insurance market. One must recognize exceptions and anomalies as well as changes that are part of the historical evolution of insurance institutions.

II. WHAT IS THE PROFIT CYCLE?

According to one dictionary definition, a cycle is

> a series of changes usually but not necessarily leading back to the starting point.[3]

A closely related and perhaps more relevant definition for this monograph states that a cycle is

> a recurring sequence of events which occur in such order that the last event of one sequence immediately precedes the recurrence of the first event in a new series.[4]

The Concept of a Profit Cycle

A profit cycle is a series of changes in some measure of profitability that follow a pattern similar to the pattern in previous and subsequent series of changes in profitability. The measure of profitability may be profits as a percentage of sales or of equity, dollars of profit, growth of profits, or some other measure. The pattern of changes is increases followed by decreases; that is, the profit measure increases for a while and then decreases for a while and then increases and then decreases and so on. The high points of the series are referred to as "peaks," and the low points are referred to as "troughs." A full cycle is the interval from peak to peak or from trough to trough. It does not matter whether one starts with peaks or troughs as long as the ending reference is the same as the starting reference. Exhibit 8-1 shows some theoretical profit cycles and their reference points.

A profit cycle in property-liability insurance traditionally is considered as the period from trough to trough—specifically, the lowest year of profitability to a subsequent lowest year of profitability, with the better years of profitability in the middle. Insurance people often talk of a "cycle" in terms of the worst years of a cycle, probably because they are not concerned about the cycle when times are good. But characterizing the worst profit years as a "cycle" is incorrect. The full cycle includes both the bad years (current and previous) and the good years in between.

The traditional profit measure used to identify cycles is underwriting profitability; hence, the property-liability insurance profit cycle is usually called the "underwriting cycle." Strictly speaking, the profit measure should be total operating profitability, that is, the combination of underwriting income and investment income.

Profit cycles in property-liability insurance can refer to changes in profitability for the whole industry, for a segment of the industry such as stock agency companies or direct writers, for all lines of business, for a combination of lines into a major group such as personal or commercial insurance or for individual lines of business. Cycles can even refer to changes in profitability in one line of business in a single company. This monograph deals with the industry's profit cycles for all lines and for individual lines.

Historical Perspective of Profit Cycles

The profit cycle in property-liability insurance is usually documented with the industry's underwriting results in the form of the well-known and widely used *combined ratio*. This ratio is the sum of two other ratios,[5] the *loss ratio* and the *expense ratio*, which are defined as

Exhibit 8-1
Profit Cycles and Their Reference Points

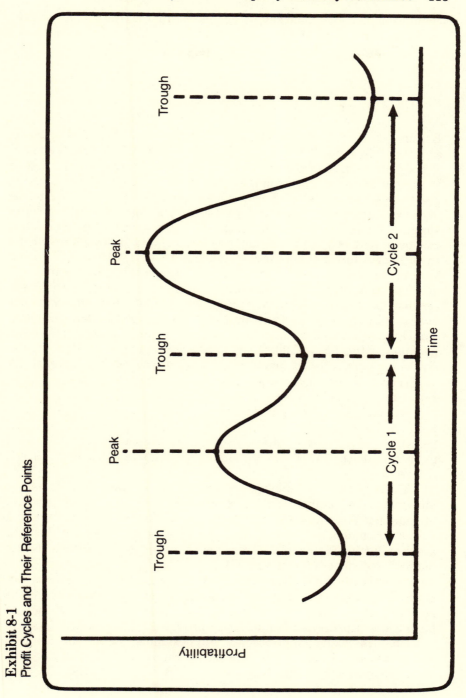

$$\text{Loss Ratio} = \frac{\text{Incurred Losses} + \text{Incurred Loss Adjustment Expenses}}{\text{Earned Premiums}}$$

$$\text{Expense Ratio} = \frac{\text{Incurred Underwriting Expenses}}{\text{Written Premiums}}$$

Because it is a ratio of outgo to income, the combined ratio is arithmetically equivalent to one minus a profit margin, or, more simply, it is an inverse measure of profitability—the lower the ratio, the higher the profit margin. For example, a combined ratio of 92 (industry practice is to express the ratio in percentage terms) suggests an underwriting profit margin of +8 percent; a combined ratio of 108 suggests an underwriting profit margin of −8 percent. (A profit margin can be stated in positive or negative terms, and profitability can be thought of in terms of both profits and losses.)

As mentioned earlier, the profit cycle should be measured by total, not just underwriting, profitability. Underwriting data is used here because industry investment income by line of insurance was not available until recently. However, the industry's profit cycle reference points, its peaks and troughs, are usually the same whether measured by underwriting profitability or by total operating profitability; only the levels of profitability change. (This point is discussed more extensively in Section II under "Integration of Investment Income" and is supported by data in Exhibits 8-11 and 8-12.)

Exhibits 8-2 through 8-8 show the industry's underwriting profitability for all lines and for individual lines of insurance as measured by combined ratios.[7] The ratios are calculated from data published in the A. M. Best Company's annual publication, *Best's Aggregates & Averages, Property-Casualty.*[8]

Underwriting profitability for the individual lines of insurance is illustrated with combined ratios before policyholder dividends. It would be more accurate to subtract policyholder dividends from written and earned premiums before calculating the combined ratios, but the data are not available for all of the years under study—Best's began publishing dividends by line in 1971.

In order to be consistent over time, policyholder dividends are omitted in all years. However, this does not appear to affect the reference points or timing of the cycles. At least it has not done so during the fifteen years from 1971 through 1985 for which data are available to make comparisons. For example, cycles in workers compensation insurance have the same reference points before and after policyholder dividends even though dividends in that line have

Exhibit 8-2
Combined Ratio for All Lines of Property-Liability Insurance† 1945-1985

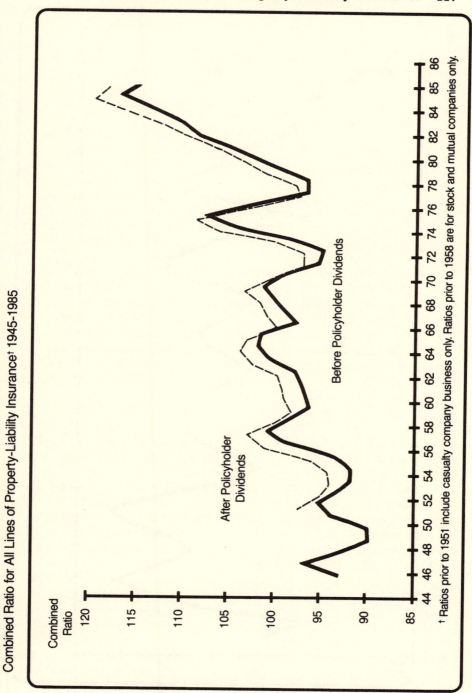

† Ratios prior to 1951 include casualty company business only. Ratios prior to 1958 are for stock and mutual companies only.

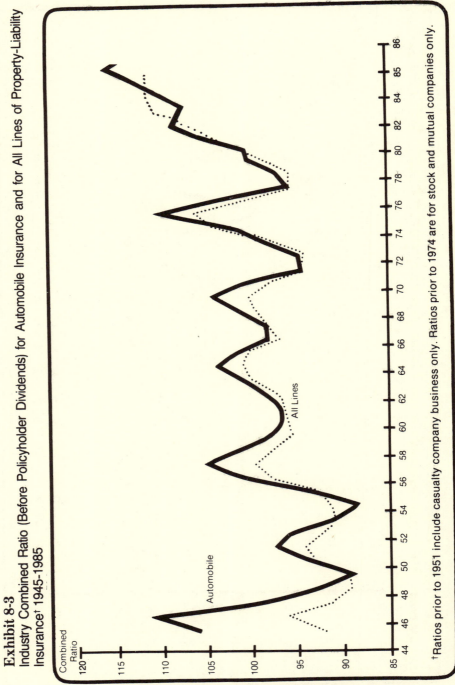

Exhibit 8-3
Industry Combined Ratio (Before Policyholder Dividends) for Automobile Insurance and for All Lines of Property-Liability Insurance† 1945-1985

†Ratios prior to 1951 include casualty company business only. Ratios prior to 1974 are for stock and mutual companies only.

Exhibit 8-4
Industry Combined Ratio (Before Policyholder Dividends) for Workers Compensation Insurance† 1945-1985

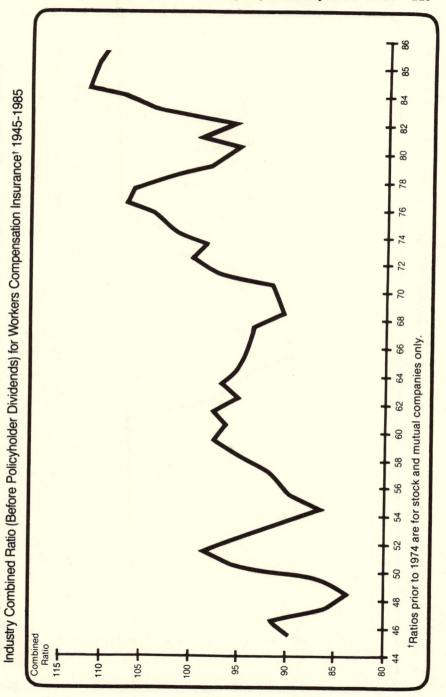

†Ratios prior to 1974 are for stock and mutual companies only.

Exhibit 8-5
Industry Combined Ratio (Before Policyholder Dividends) for Homeowners Insurance† 1955-1985

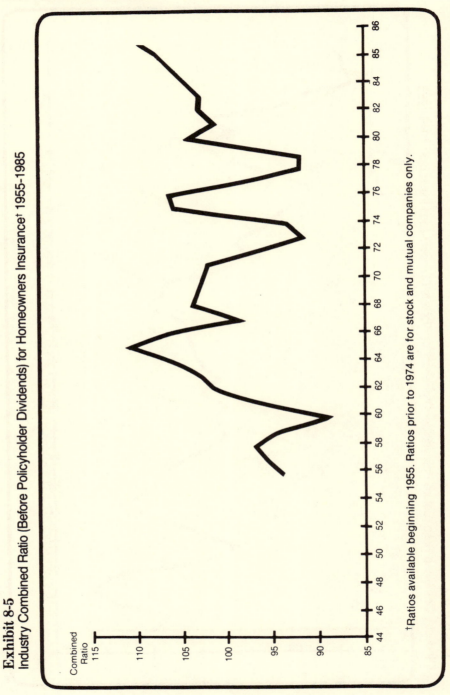

†Ratios available beginning 1955. Ratios prior to 1974 are for stock and mutual companies only.

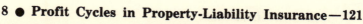

Exhibit 8-6
Industry Combined Ratio (Before Policyholder Dividends) for Commercial Multiple Peril Insurance† 1956-1985

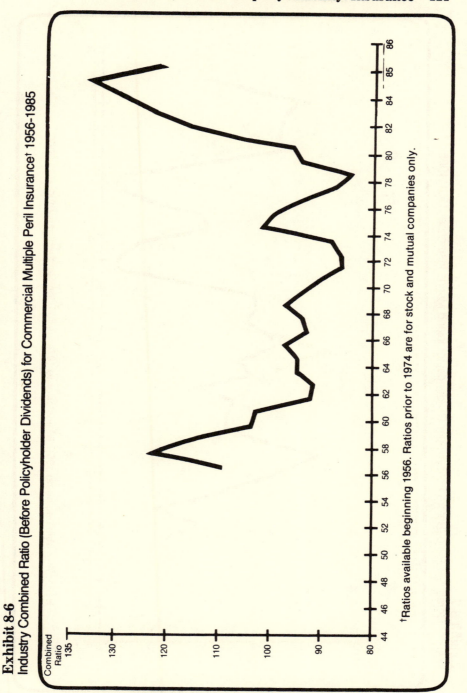

†Ratios available beginning 1956. Ratios prior to 1974 are for stock and mutual companies only.

Exhibit 8-7
Industry Combined Ratio (Before Policyholder Dividends) for Inland Marine Insurance† 1951-1985

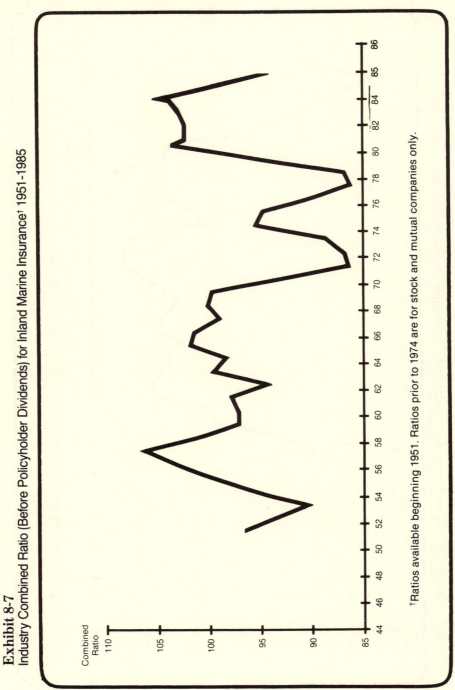

†Ratios available beginning 1951. Ratios prior to 1974 are for stock and mutual companies only.

Exhibit 8-8
Industry Combined Ratio (Before Policyholder Dividends) for Miscellaneous Liability Insurance† 1945-1985

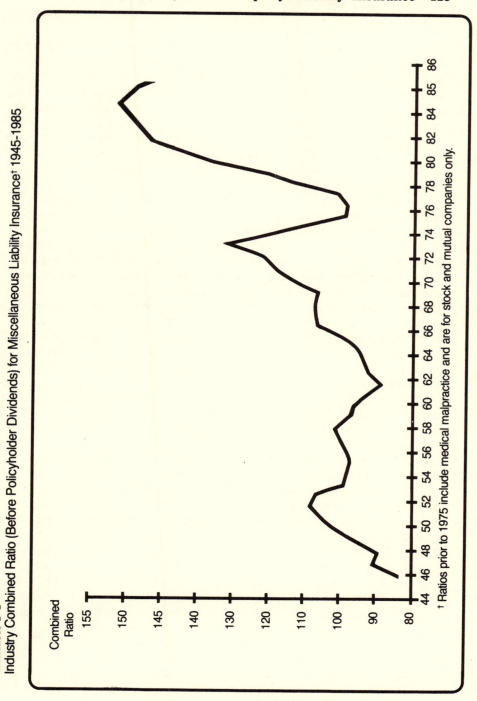

† Ratios prior to 1975 include medical malpractice and are for stock and mutual companies only.

been large and variable, having accounted variously for between 5 percent and 11 percent of earned premiums in those years.

One inconsistency in the combined ratios over the long period covered by the exhibits is the exclusion of reciprocal and Lloyd's results in the earlier years. However, this inconsistency is minor and can be ignored. Stock and mutual companies accounted for 97 percent of the industry's premium volume in 1945, when the data begin, and for 95 percent in 1973, the year before reciprocals and Lloyd's are included.

Exhibit 8-2 shows the industry's underwriting profitability for all lines of property-liability insurance as measured by combined ratios from 1945 through 1985. A definite, recurring pattern can be observed. The combined ratios rise for several years, then fall for several years, rise again, fall again, and so on. These movements in the industry's underwriting profitability are not random. The cycle is visually apparent and can be verified by statistical tests.

Profit cycles reflect economic behavior in a changing economic, legal, and social environment, so they are not as perfectly symmetric or regular as cycles produced by mathematics or studied in the physical sciences. The concept of a cycle does require enough regularity that, at least in retrospect, observers can agree that a recurring sequence of events has indeed occurred; but those events need not be identical in duration, oscillation, or any other feature. That profitability is cyclical does not necessarily mean either that it will return to a given, past level. Cycles can and do occur around rising and falling long-term trends in profitability.

In the forty-one year period under observation there are six peaks and six troughs in the all-lines combined ratios. Thus, as counted in the conventional way from trough to trough in profitability, there are six full profit cycles—1946-1952, 1952-57, 1957-64, 1964-1969, 1969-1975, and 1975-1984. With the combined ratio's inverse measure of profits, the same pattern is counted peak to peak.

Throughout this period, the industry's all-lines profit cycles have been heavily influenced by profit cycles in automobile insurance. Exhibit 8-3 presents the industry's combined ratios for automobile insurance and superimposes on them the all-lines combined ratios from Exhibit 8-2. The automobile combined ratios closely track the all-lines combined ratios. The similarity is not surprising. During this period, automobile insurance premiums each year accounted for roughly 40 percent of total premiums, so underwriting profitability in automobile insurance naturally had a pronounced effect on total underwriting profitability.

Profit cycles can be observed in other lines of insurance. Their timing in other lines is not the same as in the automobile profit cycles; nor are their amplitude and frequency the same. Yet, the cycles are identifiable by inspecting the graphs. For example, the workers compensation combined ratio in Exhibit 8-4 shows that this line of insurance had four profit cycles (1946-1952; 1952-1961, 1961-1976, and 1976-1984) throughout the forty-one years during which the automobile line and the all-lines total had six cycles. Homeowners insurance, which is shown in Exhibit 8-5, has had only two full profit cycles (1964-1975 and 1975-1985).[9] Exhibits 8-6 and 8-7 show that the three profit cycles in inland marine insurance and in commercial multiple peril insurance (1957-1965, 1965-1974, and 1974-1984) coincided with one another and roughly with the third, fifth, and sixth automobile and all-lines profit cycles.[10] Exhibit 8-8 shows that miscellaneous liability insurance had a very long profit cycle from 1951 through 1974 and then a cycle coincident with the other lines from 1974 through 1984.

Exhibits 8-3 through 8-8 also show that the severity of the profit cycles differed from one line to another for the period under study. For example, in the twenty years following its establishment in the market, from 1960 through 1980, commercial multiple peril insurance had a combined ratio over 100 in only one year, 1975. By contrast, in the 1961-1970 decade, homeowners insurance had a combined ratio below 100 in only one year, 1967.

The graphs reveal that despite a definite recurring up and down movement of the combined ratios over the forty-one-year period, no two cycles were ever exactly alike. From one line of insurance to another, the movements occurred at different times and in different degrees; some occurred around a trend and others did not; and the various cycles within individual insurance lines differed from one another.

But despite the differences, the basic recurring pattern of rising and falling profitability still remains in Exhibits 8-2 through 8-8. The observed profit cycles thus suggest a recurring process, which causes profitability to rise for a while, then fall for a while, rise, fall, and so on. Because cycles are a recurring process, they are likely to have common, fundamental causes. These are grounded in the economics of the property-liability insurance business, which are covered in the following section.

III. CAUSES OF PROFIT CYCLES

Profit cycles occur in many industries. The reasons why and the way in which cycles occur in any industry depend largely on two economic characteristics: (1) the structure of the industry and (2) the nature of the supply of and the demand for the industry's products or services.

Structure, supply, and demand are not precise terms or easily understood concepts. They are economic abstractions. Abstractions can never do justice to the rich detail of a complex and changing world, but they are necessary to explain in a systematic and uncluttered way how markets operate. Abstractions are useful in explaining why and how profit cycles occur. Once the cyclical process is understood as a simple abstraction, it is more easily understood in its more complex, real-world dimensions.

Competitive Industry Structure

An industry's structure refers to the degree of competition in that industry. Competition is not the same as rivalry for buyers' loyalty, which goes on in almost any industry, regardless of its structure. In economics, competition is defined by how many companies there are in an industry, by those companies' respective market shares, by whether the industry's products are differentiated, and by whether barriers exist to entry into or exit from the industry.[11]

Economists define an industry as perfectly competitive when the industry has many buyers and sellers of its goods or services, when the sales or purchases of each individual unit are small relative to the total, when the firms produce a homogeneous product, when entry into and exit from the market are easy, and when, as a result of the foregoing, no one buyer or seller can influence the product's price or the actions of others. Perfect competition does not exist in real life. Nevertheless, by examining how closely industries meet the perfectly competitive conditions, economists make relative judgments as to whether one industry is more or less competitive than another and the extent to which competition is working.

The property-liability insurance industry in general has a very competitive structure according to the economic definition. Most insurance markets have many sellers and many buyers, and in most insurance markets no one seller or buyer has a large share of the market.[12] Buyers normally perceive little, if any, difference in sellers' products. Launching or terminating an insurance enterprise usually is less difficult than launching or terminating enterprises of many other types.[13] In classic economic terms the property-liability insurance industry has a very competitive structure because it has low concentration, little product differentiation, and relatively easy entry and exit.[14]

The competitive market structure of the property-liability insurance industry can be appreciated by comparing it with the less competitive structures of the automobile and computer industries. Each of these industries is highly concentrated: the largest seller in each industry has 40 percent of the market.[15] Sellers achieve product differentiation, which is often substantial, through technology, service, performance, and advertising. Large amounts of capital required to manufacture cars or computers create formidable barriers to entry. They also create barriers to exit since capital invested in plant and equipment is not readily adaptable for other uses.

In a perfectly competitive industry no one seller or buyer can dictate prices. Prices are set in the market by supply and demand. Most property-liability insurance markets closely resemble the perfectly competitive model; thus, in most property-liability insurance markets no one insurer has the power to control insurance prices. Rather, insurance prices are the products of decisions made by many sellers and many buyers. Within the context of supply and demand insurance prices are determined by how much the many sellers (insurers) want to sell at what prices (supply) and how much the many buyers (insureds) want to buy at what prices (demand).[16]

Understanding how supply and demand cause insurance prices to change is the key to understanding profitability and cycles of profitability. Prices are equal to cost plus a margin of profit (or loss), so setting a price is, by definition, setting a profit margin. No matter how costs change (and insured losses and expenses can change significantly over time), it is the movement of prices relative to costs, not the movement of costs alone, that determines profit margins.

Demand for Insurance

The demand for property-liability insurance tends to grow steadily over time.[17] Its steady growth is remarkable compared to the volatile demand for many other things that individuals and businesses buy. For example, the demand for automobile insurance edges ahead each year as the stock of cars and the driver population expand. The demand for new automobiles, by contrast, is very erratic. It expands or contracts sharply with changes in buyers' incomes, automobile design, and, in recent years, the availability of gasoline. The demand for most commercial lines of insurance is also relatively steady. For example, when a business firm's sales decline, the firm may purchase a bit less insurance (e.g., inland marine coverage on the lesser amount of goods it ships), but it does not drop its insurance altogether. On the other hand, the same firm may decide to forgo altogether building a new plant or buying a new piece of equipment.

Insurance demand is normally quite steady for two reasons. First, buyers see most property-liability insurance as a necessity, something they would be reluctant to do without and for which there is no readily available or comparably priced substitute. Buyers may object to price increases, but normally they will continue to buy the coverage.[18] In textbook economic terms, insurance demand would be described as having low elasticity with respect to both income and price. Second, buyers cannot store up insurance as they can store up other products they buy, such as automobiles and refrigerators, which can be used for a long time. Insurance contracts have a fixed life, and to keep their insurance protection buyers must purchase renewal coverage immediately upon expiration of the existing coverage.

Insurance demand tends to grow with what there is to insure and with expansion of legal liabilities. Buyers normally increase their insurance limits along with increases in their property values and liability exposures. What there is to insure is largely determined by the growth of the economy and inflation.[19] Liability exposures change with social attitudes and legal doctrine. Economic, social, and legal change do not proceed at a steady, predictable pace, so growth in the demand for insurance is not perfectly stable. But absent a serious dislocation in the economic, social, or legal environment, growth in the demand for insurance should not and generally does not vary dramatically from year to year.

Supply of Insurance

While the demand for insurance increases fairly steadily over time, the supply of insurance is quite variable. This point is critically important to understanding the behavior of property-liability insurance prices. Insurance supply[20] can change drastically and rapidly for two reasons.

First, the supply of insurance, the amount of insurance that insurers are willing to sell at various prices, is a financial rather than a physical matter. How much manufacturing and mining industries, for example, can vary their supply over a short time period is severely limited by the physical nature of their productive assets, that is, their capacity to produce. Expanding physical capital (productive capacity) in manufacturing or mining requires time and effort in building new plants or digging new mines. Contracting capacity is equally difficult because plants and mines are not readily adaptable for other uses.

Financial capital, unlike physical capital, is very flexible. The reason is its mobility. Money and credit can be easily shifted from market to market, country to country, or product to product. The mobility of financial capital in insurance was evident in recent years by various movements of capital into insurance markets: the expansion of Lloyd's,[21] the growth in the number of reinsurers, particularly foreign reinsurers,[22] the creation of captives,[23] the entry of life insurers into property-liability insurance markets, not to mention the reinvestment of established insurers' profits back into the market in the form of physical expansion and increased employment.

The second reason why insurance supply can change quickly is that insurance supply is as psychological as it is financial. Effective supply is really how much insurers want to write. Although insurers and regulators believe there are prudent limits to how much insurers should write relative to their surplus, those limits are elastic, stretching with the needs of the time. For example, if the industry as a whole in 1982 had written at 2.31 times policyholders surplus (the ratio for 1978) instead of at 1.72 times policyholders surplus (the actual 1982 ratio) it would have written $35 billion, or 34 percent, more premiums.[24] Although the lower ratio in 1982 was mainly the result of lower prices, this example illustrates that a slight change in the ratio can make a huge difference in written premiums.

Because insurance supply is both financial and psychological, changes in the supply of insurance can occur as quickly as money can be transferred and can be as volatile as a state of mind. What moves money and minds are expectations of profits. Expectations of acceptable profits encourage existing insurers to sell more insurance and encourage the formation of new insuring companies. Expectations of unacceptably low profits or even losses discourage insurers from selling and may even cause them to leave the business as well as discourage others from entering the business.

Expectations are formed in various ways. Expectations may be formed on the basis of most recent experience—the future level of profitability is expected to be the same as the current or latest known level of profitability. Or, expectations, may reflect the trend of recent experience—if profitability is moving up (or down), it is expected to continue to move up (or down). Expectations may also recognize the profit cycle in property-liability insurance—a decline (or rise) in profitability is expected to reverse itself. How expectations are formed at one time may be different from how they are formed another time, especially if the prior reasoning is found incorrect or if circumstances change. Regardless of how expectations are formed, though, expectations of profits rather than profits themselves are what influence the supply of insurance.

The Economic Model

Because changes in insurance supply tend to be large and sudden, and because changes in insurance demand tend to be small and gradual, changes in insurance supply tend to cause insurance prices to move up or down depending on the direction of the change in supply.

In terms of insurers' actions, changes in insurance supply move insurance prices in the following way. When insurance operations are expected to produce desirable profit margins, insurers attempt to increase their sales and new insurance firms are formed. The supply of insurance expands relative to the demand for insurance if how much insurers want to sell increases more than how much buyers need or want to buy. Elementary economics dictates that when supply exceeds demand, prices must fall. Prices fall because the only way a single company can grow faster or sell more than the growth in demand is to increase its market share. Since every company sells virtually the same product, the only way one company can take sales away from others is to cut prices. Other companies, however, do not want to lose their business; they want to sell, too, so they also cut prices. As a result, everyone's prices fall.

Insurance prices are more than just rates. They are a combination of rates, rating classifications, deductibles, policyholder dividends, payment terms, and other credits and debits. Insurance prices can be changed by anything that changes the present value of the premium received for insuring a fixed exposure. Because insurance prices reflect a number of variables, insurance price cutting takes a number of forms. Insurers can reduce prices in ways other than by marking down the old price. For example, they may loosen underwriting standards, add coverages, increase dividends, increase credits, devise new payment terms, create new risk classifications, add services, or otherwise favor buyers. (An increase in price, of course, would occur by reversing one or more of these price-cutting techniques.)

In inflationary times price cutting can be even more subtle. Prices in real terms can be cut by not raising nominal prices to match inflationary increases in costs. Thus, price "cutting" may simply mean not raising premiums when insured losses and expenses are expected to increase. Since setting a price is essentially the same as estimating costs and adding a margin for profit, price cutting is any deliberate change in the premium or any deliberate increase in what is offered the buyer that reduces profit margins.

Price cutting can continue to squeeze profit margins until, either because of actual operating losses or the prospect of operating losses, insurers no longer want to write business at existing prices. Some insurers may even go out of business. If insurers that remain expect further declines in profitability, they may cut back or discontinue writing the coverage. As insurers curtail their writings and as some drop out of the market, the supply of insurance contracts. Buyers, however, still want to buy. Supply is less than demand, so prices must rise. Prices go up because there are not enough sellers willing to sell at the old price. Prices rise until profitability once again encourages sellers to increase market share or until profitability brings additional sellers into the market. The whole process then starts over.

The economic model for the profit cycle is thus as follows: profit expectations change supply, supply changes prices, prices change profits, profits change expectations, and so on. The cycle is dominated by supply. Variations in supply in relation to relatively steady demand change prices and profit margins. The economic model provides a formal definition of profit cycles in property-liability insurance: profit cycles are the recurring rise and fall of profitability that result from contractions and expansions of the supply of insurance in competitive markets.

The model just outlined describes the cyclical process, but it does not explain what keeps it going. Why does the contraction or expansion of supply not stop at the point where every insurer achieves some minimum acceptable margin of profit and stabilize at that level? Or, in terms of conventional supply and demand curves, why does the quantity supplied, and thus the price, not automatically gravitate towards equilibrium and stabilize there? At that level—equilibrium—no incentive exists for new insurers to enter the business or for existing ones to expand. Insurers are better off employing capital in more rewarding enterprises.

The cyclical process does not end for two reasons: lack of information and lack of coordination. Individual insurers do not and cannot know the precise amount of insurance to supply to reach equilibrium. They have different operating costs and, therefore, different break-even points or minimum acceptable margins of profit. Their perceptions and expectations of future profits or losses develop in different ways. Some insurers may be willing to sustain losses for a long time in order to be prepared to capture market share when other firms leave the market. In self-interest, insurers do not coordinate their actions. Collusion, furthermore, is illegal. Even when prior approval and rating bureaus had more influence on prices, insurers varied supply according to their own situations.

Cycles that result from supply's response to profit expectations are described in textbook economic theory by what is called a "cobweb."[25] The name cobweb is applied because tracing price changes from point to point over time on supply and demand curves produces a diagram that resembles a cobweb. The cobweb is often the economic model for prices and profits in agriculture. In agriculture, as in property-liability insurance, demand is steady and supply is variable, with the result that prices tend to move with changes in supply.

Profit cycles in most other industries, particularly manufacturing, typically are dominated by demand. That is, demand is variable and supply is relatively steady, at least over the short or intermediate term. Changes in prices and profit margins tend to be caused more by changes in demand than by changes in supply. Because demand in most industries tends to rise and fall with changes in the general level of economic activity, profit cycles in these industries tend to coincide with general business cycles.

The insurance industry is different. Since supply, and not demand, is more important in influencing insurance prices and profits, insurance profit cycles need not, and usually do not, coincide with general business cycles and therefore do not coincide with other industries' profit cycles. Exhibit 8-9 shows that for much of the period under review, the timing of profit cycles (expressed as return on sales) for property-liability insurance companies was not the same as the timing for profit cycles for all U.S. corporations. Nor was property-liability insurance profitability contracyclical. It did not consistently move in opposition to profitability for all U.S. corporations. Insurance profit cycles were and still are the result of the industry's own competitive dynamics.

Integration of Investment Income

Investment income is an integral part of the cyclical process just described. As mentioned in Section II of this monograph, profit cycles in property-liability insurance are cycles in total operating profits, the sum of underwriting profit or loss, and investment income. It is the lack of data that confined observation of historical cycles in individual lines of insurance to underwriting results. Following is a discussion of investment income's role in the cyclical process and its effect on the statistical evidence of cycles.

Changes in investment income depend primarily on cash flow and changes in investment yields, in other words, on how much cash is available to invest and on how much financial markets pay for funds invested. Of the two, cash flow is the more important determinant of investment income. If yields rise and insurers have no new money to invest, the only way insurers can take advantage of the higher yields is to sell existing assets and buy new ones. But when market yields rise, the value of insurers' assets fall. Prices of fixed income securities (bonds, notes, bills, preferred stock) automatically fall when interest rates rise. Common stock prices may or may not fall when interest rates rise. Whether they do or not depends on how much other factors, such as earnings and dividend prospects, affect stock prices. Usually, though, rising interest rates depress common stock prices. Insurers are reluctant to sell their lower yielding, and now lower valued, investments for higher yielding ones. The realized capital loss on the sale not only would reduce policyholders surplus, but would also reduce reported net income. When yields fall and asset values rise, insurers may be reluctant to take the reverse action and accept lower current yields in exchange for capital gains. Not only would they give up

Exhibit 8-9
Return on Sales (Before Taxes) for Property-Liability Insurance Stock Companies and for all U.S. Corporations —
1945-1985

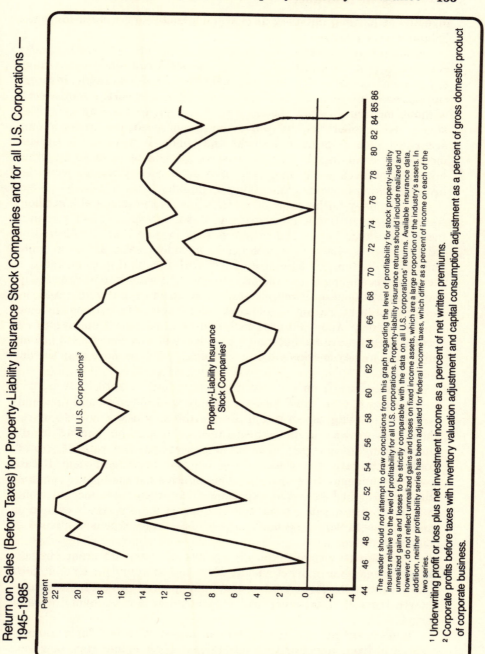

The reader should *not* attempt to draw conclusions from this graph regarding the level of profitability for stock property-liability insurers relative to the level of profitability for all U.S. corporations. Property-liability insurance returns should include realized and unrealized gains and losses to be strictly comparable with the data on all U.S. corporations' returns. Available insurance data, however, do not reflect unrealized gains and losses on fixed income assets, which are a large proportion of the industry's assets. In addition, neither profitability series has been adjusted for federal income taxes, which differ as a percent of income on each of the two series.

[1] Underwriting profit or loss plus net investment income as a percent of net written premiums.
[2] Corporate profits before taxes with inventory valuation adjustment and capital consumption adjustment as a percent of gross domestic product of corporate business.

investment income, but they also would possibly incur an income tax liability on the capital gain.

Changes in investment yields, therefore, do not automatically change investment income. Of course, insurers can always rearrange their mix of assets to change investment income. For example, insurers can increase investment earnings on their existing portfolio of assets, without incurring capital losses, by selling lower yielding securities such as common stocks and reinvesting the proceeds in higher yielding securities such as preferred stocks and bonds. Increasing investment income by changing asset mix, however, tends to be a self-limiting opportunity because trading up to ever higher yielding securities involves taking more risk and giving up liquidity.

New money for investment, or cash flow, is the essential ingredient for making investment income grow. Cash flow consists of premium income less paid losses and expenses plus income that is collected on existing assets. Cash flow technically includes realized capital gains since by definition the sale of an asset with a capital gain means that more cash is coming out of the investment than went into it. Practically, though, additional cash represented by realized capital gains need not be considered in tracing the sources of change in investment income. The influence of the additional cash from realized gains on investment income is only marginal because it can produce more investment income only if the money is reinvested in a security yielding more than the one that was sold.

If cash flow from underwriting operations is zero, that is, paid premiums just equal paid losses and expenses, interest and dividends earned on existing assets would provide the only new money to invest. Then, the growth in investment income would be similar to the compounding of interest in a savings account. The rate of growth would be the rate of interest, or the average investment yield. If cash flow from underwriting operations is negative because paid premiums fall behind paid losses and expenses, then investment income would grow even less because a portion of interest and dividends earned on existing assets would be used to pay losses and expenses instead of being reinvested.

Investment income typically grows at very different, usually higher, rates than market yields. Evidence is found in Exhibit 8-10, which compares stock and mutual companies' investment income growth from 1951 through 1985 against interest rates over the same period.

Investment income growth varies largely with the fluctuations in cash flow from underwriting operations. How much cash flow that underwriting operations produce depends largely on the industry's prices or how much property-liability insurance prices cause premiums

Exhibit 8-10
Investment Income Growth and Interest Rates — 1951-1985

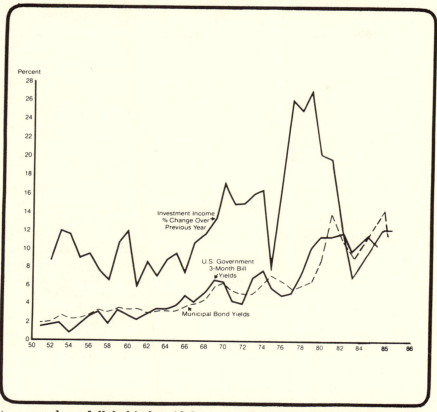

to exceed or fall behind paid losses and expenses. Property-liability insurance prices, in turn, move with the cycle. As insurance prices go up or down over a cycle, they provide more or less cash flow to invest, and, therefore, produce more or less investment income.

Another source of changes in cash flow from underwriting operations is delaying payment of losses. Over the period under study, a growing share of liability business in the industry's sales has increased the average amount of time insurers can hold premiums before paying losses. In the past decade a growing share within liability insurance of coverages that have long payment periods, such as medical malpractice and products liability, has lengthened even more the amount of time insurers can hold premiums. This shift to longer paying liability business, though, has been rather steady. The larger and more variable source of change in cash flow from underwriting operations is changes in insurance prices.

This discussion of insurance prices, cash flow, and investment income makes one important point: insurance prices are the prime mover behind changes in investment income. Prices also determine underwriting results. The expression, "underwriting cycles," then, is still entirely appropriate for referring to cycles in total operating profitability. The prices driving underwriting results also drive total results.

Exhibit 8-11 illustrates how closely the cycles in total operating profitability track the cycles in underwriting profitability alone. It shows stock companies' total operating income (underwriting profit or loss plus investment income) expressed as a percentage of written premiums, together with stock companies' combined ratios for the same period. (Underwriting and investment income expressed as a percentage of written premiums is a "return on sales.")

Each of the two series in Exhibit 8-11 is drawn on its own scale. The combined ratios are presented on an inverted scale, that is, on a scale that declines, so they are an upside down, mirror image of their presentation in earlier exhibits. On an inverted scale the combined ratio series can be interpreted in the usual and straightforward manner that the other profitability series would be interpreted—when the series rises, profitability improves, and when it falls, profitability deteriorates.

Exhibit 8-11 demonstrates that even with investment income included, profit cycles were still clearly discernible, and their peaks and troughs occurred at the same time as the peaks and troughs of the inverted combined ratios. As investment income has grown over the years, underwriting profitability, as measured by the inverted combined ratios, has tended on average to decline over the cycles.

Exhibit 8-12 demonstrates the same cyclical resemblance with total operating profits (underwriting profit or loss plus investment income), this time expressed as a percentage of policyholders surplus. (These figures are similar to the financial analyst's "return on equity.") As in the previous figure, the timing of the cycles is the same.

In summary, the process underlying property-liability profit cycles is the following: profit expectations change supply; new supply changes prices; prices change profits (the combination of underwriting results, cash flow, and investment income); profit expectations change again; and the cyclical process starts over.

In the past when investment earnings were much smaller relative to premiums and to underwriting earnings, insurers' profit expectations usually were based only on underwriting results. Because investment earnings have become more important relative to premiums, profit expectations now include both, and prices reflect both. The cycle goes on, only at different levels of underwriting profitability. More investment earnings have merely raised acceptable underwriting break-even

Underwriting Profit or Loss† Plus Investment Income as a Percentage of Written Premiums and the Combined Ratio†
(Inverted) for Property-Liability Insurance Stock Companies — 1945-1985

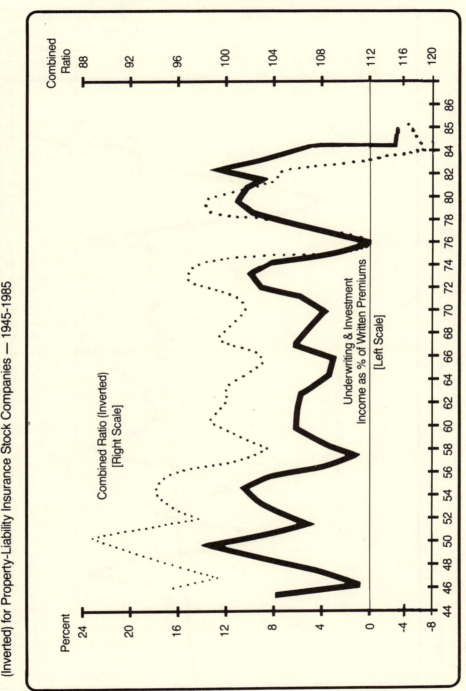

† Before policyholder dividends.

Exhibit 8-12

Underwriting Profit or Loss† Plus Investment Income as a Percentage of Policyholders Surplus and the Combined Ratio†
(Inverted) for Property-Liability Insurance Stock Companies — 1945-1985

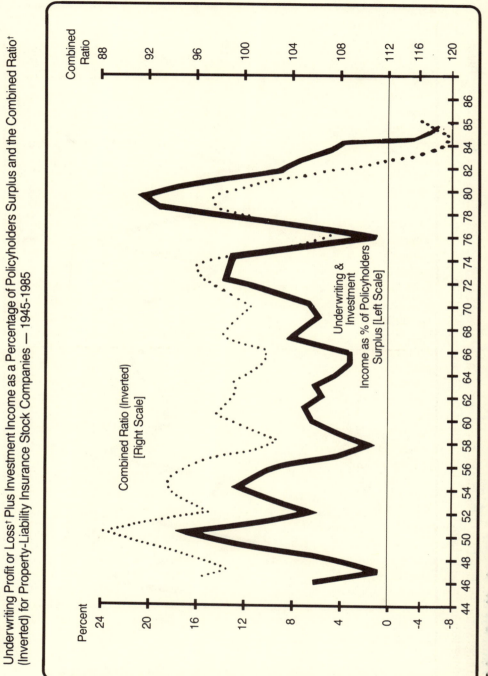

points, with insurers setting particular prices by viewing overall, rather than just underwriting, profit prospects.

IV. A TYPICAL PROFIT CYCLE

The economic characteristics of the property-liability insurance industry are the causes of profit cycles. How competition, the interaction of supply and demand, and price changes produce profit cycles in the real world of insurance may be better understood by a description of what goes on in a typical cycle.

No two profit cycles have ever been exactly alike. Each has had its own idiosyncrasies. Every cycle, though, produces similar attitudes and behavior and consequences in the marketplace. These similarities permit constructing a description of what might be called a typical profit cycle. Again, the necessity of abstracting from reality means that a "typical cycle" will never conform exactly to any one particular cycle of the past.

Just as the general business cycle is divided into three phases— recession, recovery, and expansion— a typical insurance profit cycle can be divided into three phases. They can be called the *reunderwriting* phase, the *competition* phase, and the *crunch* phase.

The three phases are useful for describing and understanding how insurers' competitive behavior drives the direction of profitability and, thus, how behavior creates cycles. These descriptive phases may or may not exactly coincide with statistical peaks and troughs. Profit statistics reflect behavior, but usually with a lag. For example, as noted in the following paragraphs that describe the phases, profitability may peak after the crunch phase has begun and bottom after the competition phase has begun.

Although each phase of the cycle is distinguished by particular market behavior, the transition from one phase to another may not be obvious. Each cycle phase grows out of conditions that developed in the previous one. Individual insurers' profitability may change at different paces, and individual insurers may react differently to market conditions and at different times. Hence, aggregate behavior is always a mixture of reactions and adjustments, and each phase of a cycle contains a progression of change within it. The discussion that follows begins with the reunderwriting phase because common industry practice is to see that phase as the beginning of a new cycle. Perhaps it is only natural to depict a move towards better times as a beginning.

The Reunderwriting Phase

The reunderwriting phase usually begins just after the industry's profitability hits its worst point, or in terms of Exhibits 8-2 through 8-8, near the peak of the combined ratio. Insurers are no longer willing to sell at the prices they had been receiving. They refuse business at old price levels and accept new business or renewals only at higher levels. In states and lines where rates are regulated, companies and rating bureaus scramble after rate increases. Insurers generally become cautious and careful. They comb through existing accounts to correct careless underwriting of the past. They scrutinize new business. They price meticulously according to "the book."

The catchwords of this phase are likely to be "sound underwriting" and "carefully managed growth." Control and caution prevail because even though profitability may improve modestly, insurers are still experiencing low profit margins. Corrective action tends to be greater than improving profit fundamentals would require because during this stage of the cycle, anxious insurers tend to overcompensate on price increases and rate requests. Corrective action tends also to go on longer than improving profit fundamentals would require because insurance accounting systems lag reality. Events change faster than the changes can be reflected in insurers' traditional ratios, thanks to financial accruals, deferrals, average costs, and average prices.

During the reunderwriting phase, companies are concerned with building surplus, which at the time seems inadequate to meet the demand for insurance. The concern for surplus adequacy usually lingers from the previous crunch phase. For example, the spectacular economic boom that followed the end of World War II and the severe inflation that came with the termination of wartime price controls sharply increased insurance needs and demands. Insurers worried, however, that in meeting rapidly growing insurance demands they might strain their capital (as represented by policyholders surplus) beyond reasonable limits. Insurers thus were unwilling to write as much insurance as buyers were willing to buy from them. Insurers felt unable to meet demands in the middle 1960s because a long string of severe hurricanes earlier reduced the availability of reinsurance and therefore diminished their ability to take on large or concentrated risks. In the middle 1970s and middle 1980s, insurers believed their surplus was inadequate for meeting rapidly growing needs for liability coverages.

In the reunderwriting phase of the cycle, insurers pull back or hold down their supply by cautious and restricted writing. Some insurers may leave the market altogether by closing down voluntarily or by having been taken into liquidation. At the same time, the demand for insurance, that is, the desire and ability of persons to buy, continues to grow. Supply is less than demand, so prices rise. Prices rise in a number of ways: explicit rate increases, more stringent underwriting standards, lower policyholder dividends, and whatever else affects the total premium. As prices go up, so do insurer profit margins, and as the reported numbers on insurer profitability improve, the cycle then moves into the next phase, competition.

The Competition Phase

The competition phase of the profit cycle begins when profits are once again generally visible and moving higher. The industry's attention shifts from putting the business back on a sound footing to finding opportunities to grow and increase market share. At this point premium growth is strong because insurers are still benefiting from the previous phase's tougher underwriting standards and from rate and price increases, which most likely overshot the amount necessary to make up for increased costs. Investment income grows more rapidly too as more premiums and widening profit margins provide more cash flow for investment. In this flush of profits, companies open new branches, appoint new producers, and put new life into hiring and training programs. Newcomers enter the business to share in an activity that is expected to be profitable.

The catchwords of the competition phase are "new markets" and "profitable growth." As optimism spreads and as increasingly satisfying financial results feed ambitions for writing more insurance and bring others into the business, the total of all insurers' ambitions to sell and to grow eventually exceeds growth in the demand for insurance. Supply is greater than demand, so prices begin to fall. They fall because individual insurers can grow faster than market demand only by expanding their market shares.

Competition for market share, taking sales away from others, can involve various practices: creating lower-rated risk classifications; applying more relaxed underwriting criteria; paying more generous dividends; permitting additional premium discounts; delaying payment of premiums; charging separate and lesser fees for claims, survey, and other services related to the insurance transactions; or simply cutting the rate. While rate cutting is the easiest form of price cutting to observe, all the other techniques mentioned also effectively reduce prices. The point has already been made that in inflationary times, the failure to increase prices commensurately with rising insurance costs is actually a cut in relative prices.

One insurer's price cuts spur its competitors to cut prices, too. In fact, competitors may be motivated to cut their prices even more in an effort to protect existing relationships and to capture their own larger shares of profitable markets. In the process everyone's prices fall. Soon, dwindling premium growth narrows profit margins. Insurers are unhappy about the new trends, but they cannot stop them. Not to meet a competitor's price would mean to lose business. Since customers tend to view the insurance products of every insurer as essentially the same, customers tend to buy from insurers whose prices are lowest. Insurers who do not match competitors' price cuts, therefore, acquire less new business and lose existing business on renewal. Insurers can tolerate giving up business only for a short time, mainly because they want to cover overhead expenses and keep operations intact. Their natural response is to lower their own prices to remain competitive.

Unable to control the competition, insurers turn to what they think they can control, their own expenses. They may freeze hiring, trim budgets, and postpone funding new projects. However, because a large proportion of insurers' expenses are variable, that is, they vary with the volume of business written, they are not easily reduced. Underwriting, processing, adjusting claims, and other functions must be performed no matter what the level of prices. Expenses such as taxes and commissions are figured as a percentage of premiums, and commissions, when markets are competitive, tend to increase as a percentage of premiums as insurers bid for business from producers. A significant reduction in the expense portion of the premium requires a long-term effort in changing methods of doing business. Hence, in the short term, cutting expenses cannot make up for the decline in prices.

More and more companies ultimately find their underwriting results deteriorating and their investment income growing at a decreasing rate. Investment income may even stop growing and decline because cash premiums are not sufficient to cover expense and loss payments. An insurer may even have to sell assets to pay losses and expenses. As financial problems become increasingly intense, widespread, and frightening, the cycle moves into the next phase, the crunch.

The Crunch Phase

The crunch phase is the critical turning point in the profit cycle. It begins when insurers' profit margins have sunk so low—some are likely to be negative—that their continuing existence is threatened. Although some insurers may leave the business or be forced out by insolvency, a general fear of failure usually brings on the crunch phase. That fear may arise because competition in the preceding phase of the cycle was so ferocious or prolonged or both that losing market share appears a far better course than continuing to suffer losses. The crunch is typically set off, however, by a frightening event or set of events which, by occurring when margins are already competitively beaten down, produces enough financial devastation to cause a general withdrawal from the market. Such jarring events could include severe catastrophes, runaway inflation, collapsing securities markets, social upheavals, or major insolvencies.

For example, the industry was frightened in 1946 by sharply higher loss payments that resulted from the postwar economic boom and inflation. It was frightened in 1951 by ballooning automobile and workers compensation insurance claims, which came with the Korean conflict's inflation and industrial upheaval. In 1965 the scare was produced by the property damage and loss of reinsurance capacity following Hurricane Betsy. In 1974 a sudden erosion of surplus in a stock market collapse and a doubling of inflation were the principal causes of the crunch. Insurers became frightened in 1985 when they realized that a large amount of the reinsurance they had relied upon to write difficult liability coverages would never be recovered and that sound reinsurance might not be obtainable at any price.

As a result of this fear, companies pull back. Expectations change from prospects of profits, however distant, to prospects of losses that are too immediate. Insurers' profitability may continue to fall as insurers learn that reserves need strengthening. They may cancel producer agreements, reduce commissions, withdraw from territories and lines, offer only limited capacity for large or unusual risks, and try to increase their reinsurance. It is not surprising, then, that the catchwords for this phase are "tight markets" and "strained capacity." Some insurers even quit the business voluntarily or are forced out. Sometimes the industry looks for outside help, usually from government. For example, a frightened industry (or at least segments of it) clamored in the 1960s for government-underwritten riot reinsurance for inner city residents; in the 1970s and 1980s the industry asked government to limit the rights of plaintiffs in liability suits.

Other effects of the crunch include government-mandated insurance plans and other involuntary markets. If withdrawals are so widespread that markets cease to function, customers create new insuring organizations of their own, such as mutuals, reciprocals, and captives, or they assume more risk. Adjustments and new arrangements are gradually made. Rating bureaus and insurers vigorously pursue rate increases in state after state. Insurers tighten controls on producers and underwriters, and the reunderwriting phase begins again.

As mentioned, the crunch phase of the profit cycle marks a turning point. It sets in motion the conditions that again make profitability rise. There is no counterpart for the crunch phase at the upper turning point of the cycle; that is, the point at which profitability ceases rising and starts falling. That turn tends to be gradual and smooth and often is not even noticed until it is well underway. The lower turning point, however, tends to be abrupt and causes severe market discontinuities (big changes in availability and prices).

The crunch phase deserves special attention also because the frightening event that starts it typically saves most insurers from gradually competing themselves out of business. In most industries competition forces out excess supply (productive capacity) as participants abandon the business, merge with others, or go bankrupt. Wringing out excess capacity is usually a long, drawn out process because as one supplier pulls out, another with unused capacity can step in to meet demand.

In property-liability insurance, the wringing out in the crunch phase is quick, but it condemns the industry to antagonistic relations with buyers and regulators. A frightening event that halts the competition causes general fear, so there is no reservoir of insurers willing to step in to meet the demand that others are not satisfying. As a result, availability abruptly contracts. Much of the insurer withdrawal, however, is not permanent. Capacity is only sidelined—put aside for use when market conditions are better. The cycle thus perpetuates itself.

Without a frightening event, competition in property-liability insurance could conceivably wring out excess capacity much as it does in other industries. But it is more likely that a permanent wringing out of capacity would occur over a long period of cycles. As each peak and each trough occurs at a lower level of profitability so that the long-term trend of profitability is a declining one, new capital would be discouraged from entering the business even during the better phases of the cycle, and more existing participants would leave or be forced out in the worst phases.

Coincidence of Cycle Phases by Line

While every profit cycle has three phases—reunderwriting, competition, and crunch—not every line of insurance experiences the same phase at the same time. For example, in the late 1960s the automobile insurance business was in a crunch phase, while the general liability insurance business was in a competition phase. Exhibits 8-2 through 8-8 confirm the fact that profit cycles in individual insurance lines prior to the late 1960s did not have the same timing. While some lines of business were in one phase, other lines were usually in one of the other two phases.

The reason for the lack of coincidence probably lies in the

industry's history of monoline companies. Insurance company operations and management remained organized around single lines of insurance even as multiple-line rating laws spread during the 1950s and the 1960s and as monoline companies were placed in corporate families under a common management. Only gradually did insurer corporate thinking shift from the line-by-line approach to a multiple-line, integrated-operations approach. As long as insurers tended to evaluate markets, profits, and prospects by line, profit cycles remained distinctive by line. The net result was that because the good profit phases of cycles in some lines sometimes coincided with and offset the bad profit phases of cycles in other lines, many of the industry's profit cycles, on an all-lines basis, were less severe than they would have been had individual lines' cycle phases coincided.

More recently, insurers have come to evaluate their results from the viewpoint of total operations. In an effort to achieve the best profit margin for the company as a whole, managements are more willing than formerly to coordinate profit goals by line, to allocate marketing resources from one line to another, and to adopt underwriting and pricing practices that do not necessarily maximize profit margins in a single line. For example, many insurers practice *account underwriting*, in which they are willing to write all of an insured's coverages for an acceptable total profit margin rather than demand an acceptable profit margin on each individual coverage. Account underwriting helps competition spread more readily from one line to the next as the insured's account and all its lines of insurance become the object of competition.

Most insurance markets have thus evolved from single product markets to customer markets, and the focus of the competition has shifted along with them. Consolidation in measuring performance, writing business, and judging prospects along customer lines are tending to make the phases of the profit cycles in some individual insurance lines coincide with the phases of the cycles in others. This consolidation has two implications. First, because cycles in single product lines are not likely to offset one another as much as they formerly did, profit cycles for major customer markets, such as individuals (all personal lines) or businesses (most commercial lines), are likely to be more severe. Second, future study of competitive forces and profit cycles in the property-liability business is likely to be concerned more with groups of lines defined by customer need than with single product lines.

V. ROLE OF THE ENVIRONMENT AND REGULATION IN PROFIT CYCLES

Profit cycles in property-liability insurance are a recurring process that is the result of changing profit expectations, which, in turn, produce changes in the supply of insurance. More specifically, a change in profit expectations produces a change in the supply of insurance; the change in supply against fairly steady demand produces a new price and a new profit margin; the new profit margin leads to a change in profit expectations; and the process starts over again.

Property-liability insurance profit cycles, however, are not a closed system. They occur in an external environment affected by natural, economic, social, and legal change. Human responses to a changing external environment can make each cycle depart from the theoretical model and will thus make each cycle differ from one another. Some of the prominent external influences affecting property-liability insurance profit cycles, particularly in recent years, are economic and social inflation and natural disasters. Regulation of insurance by government also has a major influence on profit cycles. The role of the external environment and regulation in influencing profit cycles deserves attention. Principally, they influence the timing and the severity of cycles. This is important, but it should not be confused with the forces that cause profit cycles in the first place. The fundamental forces that cause profit cycles are the competitive dynamics of the property-liability insurance industry. Even if the environment and regulation never changed, profit cycles would still occur as long as the industry remained subject to the same competitive forces.

The Environment

The term "environment" can be used as a catchword for a miscellany of external factors that change the frequency and severity of losses. The environment can be cruel or kind. Hurricanes may be more or less severe; inflation may be mild or rampant; deflation could conceivably occur; social attitudes or legal change may encourage or discourage litigation.

Although the environment influences underwriting results and therefore total profits and profit expectations, it does not cause profit cycles. Profit cycles would still occur even if the external environment were constant or if insurers could perfectly predict how a changing environment would affect their underwriting results. Why profit cycles occur is described in Section III, "Causes of Profit Cycles." As explained there, the property-liability insurance industry has a competitive structure—many participants, homogeneous products, and relatively easy entry and exit. Demand, largely because insurance is a necessity and needs to be continually replenished, is fairly stable. Supply, because it is financial and psychological, is quite flexible. As profit expectations change, supply changes too, thanks to easy entry and exit and to supply's flexible nature. Supply thus can fall behind or move ahead of demand, and prices rise or fall accordingly. The cyclical process continues because the many participants in the business lack both the information and the means to coordinate their actions in order to bring supply and demand perfectly into balance or to maintain an equilibrium.

The role of the environment in the cyclical process might best be described with some examples. Suppose that something in the environment undergoes a significant change, such as a sudden increase in inflation. With it, insurers' costs suddenly go up, and their profit margins immediately fall. If margins collapse as they did in 1974, the competition phase of the cycle might end right then and there. But if margins are merely squeezed as they were in 1979, the competition phase of the cycle might continue, very likely in earnest as it did for the next several years. A natural catastrophe could have been used as the environmental change in the illustration, and insurer reactions to the catastrophe would have been just the same as their reactions to the higher inflation.

The environment can interfere at any point in a profit cycle. The industry's reaction to it will depend on profit expectations at that point. Consider another example. In 1974, liability claims did not explode overnight. The number of claims and monetary settlements grew fairly steadily, although at an increasing rate, over a period of years. While the industry's concern for juridical hazard also grew in the early 1970s, this concern did not check profit optimism or prevent insurers from cutting prices in order to write this business. The revulsion and crunch came later, after the industry realized the extent of its underpricing of many liability insurance products.

The main point of these examples is that prices follow supply through each phase of each cycle. Prices do not follow costs. Insurers' profit expectations determine supply. If the external environment changes those expectations in a way that insurers change their supply, then prices will also change. Insurers' profit expectations may not necessarily be correct. Insurers must estimate their costs in advance. If their estimates are higher or lower than ultimate costs, insurers will supply too little or too much insurance, and the resulting prices will produce profit margins that are higher or lower than insurers expected in the first place.

Insurers' assessment of the environment is reflected in their loss reserves. It would seem natural for that assessment to be optimistic in the competition phase of the cycle and pessimistic in the crunch and reunderwriting phases, so that reserving practices are likely to change over the cycle as follows.

Early in the competition phase when profitability is still high, an adverse environment is not likely to change insurers' feelings of well being and therefore may not make them question the adequacy of their reserves. Later, however, when profits are being squeezed, an adverse environment is more likely to make insurers uneasy about their reserves, but some insurers may choose to ignore the adverse environment because they want to avoid reporting even worse profit margins than are already developing from paid losses and normal reserving practices. Worse margins may hurt insurers' stock prices or their reputations in the marketplace, and worse margins may discourage underwriters from continuing to offer competitive prices.

On the other hand, in the crunch and reunderwriting phases of the profit cycle, because gloom and uncertainty pervade most insurance organizations, the natural tendency may be to overestimate the potential harm of external developments, so reserves are likely to be seen as dangerously inadequate. Since most other insurers are in the same position, they may assume that more bad profit news will not hurt their stock prices or their market reputations. It would be natural to strengthen reserves in the crunch and reunderwriting phases of the cycle, also, because insurers typically want their front line underwriters to be cautious on pricing and are more willing to let business go to competitors.

In summary, because of changing psychology over the cycle, insurers are more likely to add to reserves in the parts of the cycle when profits are at their lowest point and moving up, and less likely to add to reserves in the part of the cycle when profits reach their highest point and are moving down. Inconsistencies in reserving practices, therefore, are likely to exaggerate the shape of profit cycles, making profitability look better than it actually is in the competitive phase of the cycle and worse than it actually is in the crunch and reunderwriting phases.

Reserving practices are thus one more illustration that expectations do not necessarily reflect the external environment and that as a result, prices do not necessarily follow costs.

The environment typically plays its most important role in forcing the end of the competition phase of cycles. At this point, profit margins are likely to be already badly squeezed by competitive price cutting. A severe external shock such as a burst of inflation, a stock market collapse, or a severe hurricane becomes the final straw. The sudden and unexpected loss of capital threatens even the survival of many companies. In fear, individual companies pull back from the market, and the crunch sets in.

Regulation

Regulation of the insurance business has many aspects, but for the purposes of understanding the property-liability insurance profit cycle, the most important aspect is the regulation of insurance rates. Rate regulation directly affects the prices and profit expectations of insurers.

Insurance rate regulation affects the shape of cycles, but it does not cause them. Rate regulation, even where it is most strict, does not rule out competition. Texas has some of the most elaborate rate and form regulation; it also has some of the fiercest competition. Workers compensation insurance is one of the most widely regulated lines; yet it still goes through very distinct underwriting cycles. Competition and cycles coexist with rate regulation because price competition, as already noted, can occur in numerous ways, even without any rate changes taking place—insurers can change prices by changing underwriting standards, policyholder dividends, payment terms, and risk classifications, to name a few well-known devices. Even in automobile insurance where the price is closely tied to the rate, price competition can occur without an insurer's necessarily changing its rate. As its losses and expenses increase, an insurer can indirectly lower its price simply by not raising its rates. Profit margins contract without the explicit price having been changed at all.

Although it does not prevent competition, rate regulation generally tends to reduce price competition and thus the severity of cycles. Automobile insurance provides the best example of this tendency.

The competitive phase of the automobile profit cycle is usually shortened by action that can be taken by a rating bureau. As profit margins decline, typically because rates are not keeping pace with increases in losses, the rating bureau responds by requesting rate increases. The requests on behalf of all member companies create a joint action to raise rates, something no insurer could accomplish by acting alone. As a result, the crunch phase of the cycle may be bypassed, and the cycle may move immediately into the reunderwriting phase. Rating bureaus' actions and regulators' approval speed up the reunderwriting phase because the rate increase serves as a signal to all participants that many organizations are raising prices. Even companies that are not members of the rating bureau can take advantage of the signal. No difficult competitive decision needs to be faced as to whether to raise prices or not because nonmember companies know most of their competitors are raising prices. It is not surprising, therefore, that profit cycles in automobile insurance have been more frequent and more regular than cycles in other lines of insurance.

If regulators in prior approval states do not permit rates to increase enough to offset insured losses and expenses, however, the crunch phase will not be bypassed. Insurers have no desire to write at unprofitable rates. Since they usually are not permitted to cancel insureds, the supply insufficiency tends to hit new applicants. Rate suppression trades higher rates for an availability problem.[26] The crunch will last as long as the rates remain too low for insurers to earn an acceptable profit.

Summary

One of the more fundamental points for understanding profit cycles in property-liability insurance is that although the external environment and rate regulation affect the timing and shape of the profit cycles, it neither creates nor prevents them from occurring. The external environment and rate regulation usually make profit cycles look different from one another. They can alter the length of each phase, the magnitude of the swings up and down, and the average level of profitability from one cycle to the next. The process that creates the cycles, however, remains the same. To restate this process: profitability changes expectations; expectations change supply; supply changes price; and price changes profitability again. Understanding exactly why and how profit cycles occur leads naturally to the question of controlling them.

VI. CAN PROFIT CYCLES BE CONTROLLED?

Profit cycles in property-liability insurance result from competitive forces within the industry. Most insurance markets have many sellers, each of whom sells a relatively undifferentiated product and none of whom has a large enough share of the market to influence the price significantly. Insurers, therefore, tend to be price takers, not price makers. Price is set in the market by the total of all insurers' supply of insurance and all buyers' demand for insurance. Since in competitive markets individual insurers cannot control the price, they can neither prevent profit cycles from occurring nor can they influence their timing or intensity.

If profit cycles are not controllable by any individual insurer, could they be controlled at the industry level by insurers acting together or by government? The answer to that question is that cycles could be controlled only if the property-liability industry became or were made noncompetitive. That could happen in several ways. One way would be for insurers to come together and agree to fix prices and restrict writings, but such anticompetitive behavior is illegal. Another way the industry might become noncompetitive would be for it to undergo fundamental structural change. Competition depends on an absense of concentration, freedom of entry and exit, and lack of product differentiation. Increased concentration, barriers to entry and exit, or substantial product differentiation would tend to restrict competition so that a few insurers might gain sufficient market power to control prices and thereby alter profit cycles. Price regulation is a third way the property-liability industry might be made noncompetitive.

Concentration

One way the industry could become more concentrated is if one or more insurers with sufficient financial resources to withstand an extended period of little or no profitability decided to use that strength to put a number of smaller and weaker insurers out of business. Implementing such a plan might mean that the financially stronger insurers would have to forgo profit and perhaps absorb substantial losses for several years. Whether they could or would want to do so is another matter. Any insurer, irrespective of form of legal organization, is likely to face heavy pressure to abandon a market strategy that is designed to produce heavy losses over a period of years. Regulators, whose overriding concern is solvency, would not be very sympathetic to a strategy that put insurers at risk. Losses could also make the strategy backfire if they damage an insurer's rating and its reputation in the marketplace to the extent that its market share declines rather than grows. The historical evidence, at least for the period under review in this monograph, is that no insurer has been able or willing to tolerate substantial losses for an extended time in order to force competitors out of the market.

Another way of increasing concentration is for one seller (or even several sellers) to increase its efficiency relative to other sellers' efficiency, that is, it can produce and deliver the product at a lower cost than anyone else. The lowest cost producer has an advantage over competitors in two ways. First, the lowest cost producer has the option of charging the lowest price. By undercutting the competition, it can get as many customers as it pleases from other sellers. Second, the lowest cost producer has the option of charging the market price. By charging the market price, the lowest cost producer gets the largest profit margins. Greater profits allow the lowest cost producer to invest more than other sellers in improving and promoting its products and services in order to establish itself more firmly in the market. The most efficient seller, therefore, is able to increase its market share and possibly, in time, the degree of seller concentration in the market.

In property-liability insurance the lowest cost producer can offer the insurance buyer the best price or can collect the largest margins in any phase of the profit cycle, and, therefore, the lowest cost producer is likely to increase its market share over the long pull. In the period under review, various direct writers, because of their lower cost structures and lower prices to buyers, have significantly increased their share of automobile, homeowners, and other insurance markets. These insurers, however, still compete among themselves as well as with other insurers. No one of them is yet in a strong enough position to price its products without giving attention to prices of competitors. Whether relative efficiency will give any insurer such pricing freedom and make the industry less competitive is problematic. This discussion offers little prospect that profit cycles will be avoided merely through increased concentration without other restrictions on competition.

Freedom of Entry and Exit

Restricting freedom of entry and exit from insurance markets is a possible way to reduce competition and thereby to mute or avoid profit cycles. Barriers to entry could be created by government, perhaps at the instigation of insurers already active in the property-liability insurance market. The more likely barriers would be an increase in minimum capital requirements and prohibitions against certain types of organizations selling certain types of insurance.

Legislation might be enacted to raise the minimum capital required to launch or continue a given type of insurance enterprise. Persons without easy access to capital might be barred from entering the business, or companies unable to generate capital internally might be unable to increase their writings. As a result, over time the supply of insurance might be smaller than if the legislation had not been enacted.

Passage of such legislation, however, is unlikely. Existing insurers who would have the most to gain by barring others from the business may not find it in their own best interest to seek such legislation. Aside from the long and difficult process of getting every state to legislate higher entry requirements for domiciled and foreign-admitted insurers is the simple fact that to be effective at all, the entry requirements would have to be raised so high that they might become prohibitive for insurers already in the market. Doubling, even tripling, existing capital requirements would be no serious obstacle to insurance subsidiaries of large industrial conglomerates, to large captive companies, to alien insurers that might seek entry into a given state, or even to new companies, which if they could promise convincingly high returns to investors, could raise capital in financial markets. Capital requirements, then, are not likely to become effective barriers to entry.

More effective in restricting freedom of entry than raising capital requirements would be legislation that banned outright the formation of insuring entities or prohibited certain types of economic organizations from insuring or selling insurance. A well-known current example is in the efforts of insurance organizations and associations to prevent banks and other financial institutions from organizing or acquiring and operating insurance companies or agencies (see monographs 4 and 5 on this subject). Totally apart from the question of whether banks should own and operate insurance companies or agencies, the issue does illustrate a concerted effort to reduce freedom of entry into the insurance business. Several years ago serious attention was given by some states to the question of possible limitations on the freedom of conglomerates to own and operate insurance companies, which was another example of an effort to restrict freedom of entry to insurance markets.

Such barriers to entry, though, tend to work only in the short term. If profits are attractive, in time businesses other than those specifically prohibited from entering will find their way into insurance markets. In order for explicit barriers against outsiders to work, they must continually be reinforced with new legislation to bar newer and newer groups. The opposition of interest groups to such barriers and their lack of economic value would make continually raising legislative barriers an impossible political task.

Product Differentiation

Product differentiation is another way to restrict competition and thus alter profit cycles. If buyers perceived every insurer's products as significantly and importantly different from one another and, therefore, not at all substitutable for one another, price competition would no longer exist. Competition would occur instead on the basis of the perceived qualities of the products. Every insurer, in effect, would have its own monopoly.

Scattered instances of product differentiation exist in the property-liability insurance industry. Some insurers have developed an expertise for insuring difficult or exotic exposures or for serving special classes of insureds. Such expertise, if it requires substantial time and effort to achieve, serves as a barrier to others' providing the same product. Most of the differentiation efforts in insurance are not successful for long, as they tend not to be based on achieving special expertise but instead are based on factors that are readily apparent and easily duplicated by competitors.

By and large, though, insurance is perceived by buyers as much the same, or as a commodity. Products of one seller (insurer) are regarded as the same or as easily substituted by the products of other sellers (insurers). Nothing in the nature of the business suggests that such perceptions will change.

Price Regulation

Regulators could mitigate profit cycles only if they suppress competition in the property-liability industry. Suppressing competition, in turn, would require control over almost every aspect of the business. Rate regulation alone cannot control the profit cycle. As discussed in the section, "Regulation," price competition can occur where prior approval of rates is required. The primary reason is that a rate is not a price, and a price can be changed in ways other than changing the rate, such as by changing underwriting standards, policyholder dividends, payment terms, and risk classifications. From a practical standpoint, government would be faced with an enormous administrative burden if it did try to regulate those variations as well as the multitude of forms and rates. The alternative would be to prohibit such variations; to prescribe standard policies, prices, commissions, deductibles, and so forth; to outlaw surplus lines; to ignore risk management; and to reverse many other developments that have brought to insurance the flexibility and sophistication that it has today.

The requirements for suppressing competition in order to control cycles, however, have not discouraged regulators from trying to control them with rate regulation alone. Several states have recently adopted rating laws that are specifically intended to moderate cyclical swings in insurance prices and availability. The laws are a modified form of prior approval called "flex rating" or "band rating." Flex or band rating permits insurers to change rates within prescribed limits without government approval but requires it for changes outside of those limits. While the intention to moderate the cycle is well meant, it cannot work for all of the reasons stated above.[27]

Prospects for Controlling Profit Cycles

This discussion leads to the general conclusion that while at the industry level profit cycles theoretically could be controlled, such control has little chance of being exercised. The insurance industry is not likely to embrace the necessary methods for changing its competitive structure in the interest of controlling the cycle. Concentration, because it implies the extinction of a large number of existing firms, no doubt would be unpalatable to most industry participants. Barriers to entry into the insurance business are difficult to achieve because they are politically unpopular and because they do not stand up for long. Product differentiation, even assuming buyers would become convinced that the products of insurers are genuinely different, can quickly disappear through imitations.

The industry cannot legally resort to any of the simpler and more direct ways of controlling the cycle by suppressing competition. Insurers cannot agree, for example, to fix prices, to restrict writings in a geographical area or for a product, or to carve up market share. All those agreements would be illegal. State insurance laws and regulations as well as state and federal antitrust laws, prohibit such anticompetitive conduct. Nor can the industry look to regulation for controlling the cycle for it too would mean suppressing competition. Public policy is to encourage competition, not restrict it. Competition is viewed as the superior way of organizing most economic activity. The principle is widely accepted that free markets can do a better job of allocating resources than can powerful business or government officials. Prices that do not reflect supply and demand usually bring inefficiency, waste, scarcity or surplus, and little innovation. Whether profit cycles can be controlled is not the appropriate question. The appropriate question is whether profit cycles *should* be controlled, even assuming they could be controlled.

In general, society benefits from the free flow of goods and services, the impetus to innovate, and the lower prices that result from competition. These benefits do not arise without costs to society, which are significant. They include the following: firms may go out of business causing hardship for persons who lose their jobs and inconvenience for customers who must find new suppliers; some people in society may not agree with how society as a whole, that is, the market, values individuals' skills and attributes; some individuals, through no fault of their own, may not be able to make a living. Society, however, rather than rejecting competition because of its costs, can and generally does look for ways to deal with those costs.[28]

Competition in insurance has benefits and costs as well. Insurance is generally flexible, adaptable, and available. When new needs arise, they are met, either by the existing participants or by new ones. The price of insurance is held down by competitive forces that always develop when profit margins expand to attractive levels. Insurance, however, is not necessarily available to everyone and may be unavailable or exceedingly costly to those who need it most. Market dislocations from time to time make some risks practically uninsurable. Insurers may go bankrupt. These costs are not trivial, but they can be and are being dealt with. For example, the insuring public at large subsidizes specified classes of insureds who represent substandard underwriting exposures. New insuring mechanisms are created as needed. Guaranty funds are established to protect policyholders from insurer insolvencies.

From society's standpoint, then, competition in the property-liability insurance industry should not be lessened just because profit cycles make doing business uncomfortable or difficult for insurers and insureds from time to time.

In summary, no strong force within or outside the industry is likely to limit competition in property-liability insurance markets. Profit cycles, therefore, should continue.

VII. THE DESTINY OF THE INDIVIDUAL FIRM

Profit cycles are an inevitable result of the competitive dynamics of the property-liability insurance business. Since little chance exists that competition will be eliminated, profit cycles will not be eliminated. Individual insurance firms, therefore, will have to continue to manage in a cyclical business.

Profit cycles are one of the most serious challenges facing a property-liability insurance company's management. During the competition phase of a profit cycle, squeezed profits may seriously weaken an organization's ability to withstand external adversity such as inflation or catastrophes. Although choices facing management over the cycle may not have life or death consequences, some decisions could cause the firm irreparable harm. For example, refusal to meet price cuts may mean a permanent loss of business. Squeezed profits may preclude investment in people and technology when those investments would best provide a long-term advantage over competitors. Fear to write in the crunch phase of a cycle may forever impair a company's relations with its producers and with the community.

The individual firm that hopes to be a successful competitor over the long term must try to minimize the harmful impact profit cycles might have on its operations. It also must try to take advantage of competitive opportunities profit cycles might bring. In other words, it must try to outperform its competitors in every phase of the cycle.

In any competitive business two basic strategies are available for establishing a competitive advantage. The first is to attempt to avoid competing on the basis of price by creating a differentiated product or service. The second is to try to win the price competition by having the lowest costs. In insurance each works as follows.

If the individual firm does not want to compete on the basis of price, it needs to remove itself from the competition. In effect, it must try to create its own monopolies through differentiation. If an insurer can convince its buyers that its products or services are different from and better than other insurers' products or services, that insurer can command a different price. Differentiation in insurance can be accomplished in various ways. It might involve offering different coverages, providing exceptional service, uniquely tailoring a product and its delivery to specific customer market segments, or identifying and serving neglected or misunderstood customer markets.

Because successful differentiation invites imitation, insurers that pursue a differentiation strategy must keep searching for ways to protect themselves from potential competitors. This might involve developing proprietary information and systems, building specialized knowledge and experience, or accumulating resources. In general, a successful differentiation strategy requires continually improving existing products and services and developing new markets, which in turn means searching out and responding to society's insurance needs.

The need to find new markets and refine old ones in order to differentiate one's products and services is how an industry renews itself. In fact, individual insurers' efforts to meet insureds' existing needs in better ways and to meet emerging needs are what historically have made property-liability insurance a growth industry.

The other strategy an individual firm can choose for establishing a competitive advantage is to sell an undifferentiated product and to compete on price. In order to compete successfully on price and to gain market share and increase profits over time, the firm must have a cost advantage. The lowest cost producer of an undifferentiated product can beat its competitors in every phase of a cycle because it always can offer what the buyer wants, namely, the lowest price. Developing a low-cost structure in insurance might involve geographic location in a low-cost labor market or use of a relatively more efficient distribution system. However, as with product differentiation, competitors also tend to imitate firms that have lowered costs. So, as with product differentiation, the company with the lowest costs must keep finding new ways to lower its costs in order to stay ahead of its competitors and continue to offer the lowest prices to its buyers.

The property-liability companies that historically have grown faster and profited more than average have been the ones that have been able to differentiate their products and services from everyone else's and to develop low cost structures. Typically, they have used a combination of the two—by line, customer, or other market segment. Differentiation and low costs tend to reinforce one another. Higher-than-average profit margins earned with one strategy permit investing in and developing the other.

The prescriptions of product differentiation and lowest costs are in theory simple and straightforward, but in practice both are very difficult. Creating, holding onto, and profiting by a different product or a low cost structure require imagination, tenacity, daring, and confidence—the imagination to depart radically from the industry's views on the nature of the product and how it should be delivered; the tenacity to take a long-term view and to keep inventing; the daring to risk time, effort, and money in untried methods and ventures; and the confidence to meet challenges alone instead of seeking comfort in numbers.

The successful firms in cyclical, competitive insurance markets do not look for external causes of the industry's profit cycles or try to devise impossible industry solutions. The successful firms always look to themselves, continually searching and finding better and less costly ways to serve society's insurance needs.

Monograph Notes

1. United States v. South-Eastern Underwriters Association et al., 322 U.S. 533 (1944).
2. An account of the spread of competition in the property-liability industry can be found in the National Association of Insurance Commissioners Central Office Staff's *Monitoring Competition: A Means of Regulating the Property and Liability Insurance Business* (Milwaukee, WI: National Association of Insurance Commissioners, 1974), Vol. 1, Part One: "Evolution Towards a More Competitive Rating Environment in the Property and Liability Insurance Business."
3. *Webster's Third New International Dictionary* (Springfield, MA: G. & C. Merriam Company, 1968), p. 563.
4. *Wester's Third New International Dictionary.*
5. The source of industry data for this monograph is A.M. Best Company, Oldwick, NJ. This company has compiled the most consistent and comprehensive set of aggregate industry data for the longest period of time. Prior to 1982, A.M. Best did not publish aggregate investment income data for individual lines of insurance.
6. The rules of mathematics prohibit adding ratios with different denominators, so the combined ratio is an approximate measure of underwriting profitability. However, the denominators of the loss ratio and expense ratio are similar enough that the combined ratio provides a reasonably consistent estimate of underwriting profitability for the period under review.
7. Tables containing the data used in Exhibits 8-2 through 8-8 appear in the appendix to this monograph.
8. Industry ratios for 1974 and subsequent years were taken directly from the sections labeled "Cumulative By Line Underwriting Experience—Industry" in the 1979, 1983 and 1986 editions of *Best's Aggregates & Averages*. Ratios prior to 1974 were calculated by the author as follows. Each annual edition of *Best's Aggregates & Averages* contains ten years of underwriting data for stock companies and for mutual companies in the sections labeled "Cumulative By Line Underwriting Experience—Stock" and "Cumulative By Line Underwriting Experience—Mutual." (Prior to 1951, data were available for casualty companies only.) Since ten years of data are presented, only a few editions are needed to calculate aggregate combined ratios for stock and mutual companies for 1945 through 1973. Dollar totals for stock and mutual companies' written premiums, earned premiums, losses (derived by multiplying earned premiums by the loss ratio), and expenses (derived by multiplying written premiums by the expense ratio) must be calculated before deriving the aggregate loss ratios, expense ratios, and combined ratios.
9. Because homeowners insurance had been introduced only a few years earlier, the 1957 peak may have more to do with anomalies in the numbers

during a period of unusually fast growth than with a profit cycle. Nevertheless, a ferocious rate war erupted over the new policy's propriety and rating. The sudden drop in the combined ratio in 1966 was not a cyclical trough, but more likely reflected reserve takedowns following the realization of how heavily Hurricane Betsy losses were reinsured. The rise in the combined ratio in 1980 was, in retrospect, not a peak, but reflected unusually bad weather losses that year.

10. The secondary peak in the commercial multiple peril combined ratio in 1968 does not appear to be a cyclical peak, but rather a temporary interruption, most likely due to urban riot losses, in a cyclical decline of the combined ratio from 1965 through 1971.

11. See Robert L. Heilbroner and Lester C. Thurow, *The Economic Problem*, Third CPCU Ed. (Englewood Cliffs, NJ: Prentice-Hall, Inc. 1984), Chapters 25 and 27.

12. Notable exceptions exist. In a few specialized insurance markets, for example, in boiler and machinery insurance and in some geographical areas certain companies may have monopolistic or near-monopolistic market positions.

13. For example, entry is facilitated by low capital requirements, generally available and undifferentiated technical knowledge, and a distribution network that is already in place (independent agents and brokers). Exit is facilitated by reinsurance. But as is true for any business, participants can face significant practical problems in entering, such as developing credibility in the marketplace, or leaving, such as regulatory requirements for writing certain lines of business.

14. How well the property-liability insurance industry meets conditions for competitiveness is more extensively discussed in the Arthur D. Little, Inc. 1967 report to the American Insurance Association, *Prices and Profits in the Property and Liability Insurance Industry*, pp. 44-55.

15. Judging levels of concentration first requires defining the relevant market, which frequently is a difficult and much debated matter, particularly for antitrust reasons. If the relevant market for General Motors were more narrowly defined as domestic automobiles, its share would be 55 percent, and if the relevant market for IBM were defined as mainframe computer systems, its share would be 70 percent.

16. Not all insurance prices move with supply and demand. The most notable exceptions are automobile insurance prices, which in some states are subject to regulatory approval. If regulatory authorities do not permit prices to rise (or fall) with the forces of supply and demand, that is, they set ceilings over prices (or floors under prices), shortages (or surpluses) will appear. For a full explanation of why this must happen, see Heilbroner and Thurow, *The Economic Problem*, chapter 22.

17. The demand for insurance and the supply of insurance cannot be measured. Premiums are neither demand nor supply. Premiums represent the quantity of insurance bought (or sold) and the price at which it was bought (or sold). That particular quantity may still leave some demand unmet or some supply left over.

18. As always, notable exceptions exist. Large commercial insurance buyers in

increasing numbers are turning to retention or "self-insurance" and cash management plans to replace traditional insurance coverages.

19. The effect of inflation on insurance premiums is discussed in the monograph, "Inflation and Property-Liability Insurance," found in Volume I of the third edition of this text.

20. Popular insurance jargon often refers to insurance *supply* as insurance *capacity*. Practically speaking, the words are interchangeable, although in a strictly technical sense, they have slightly different meanings. *Supply* is used in this monograph because it is the correct term in classic economic theory.

21. Lloyd's membership increased from 6,257 members in 1972 to 19,100 members in 1981. See *The Insurance Director & Year Book (Post Magazine Almanack) 1982/83* (Middlesex, England: Buckley Press Limited, 1983), p. 232.

22. A.M. Best counted 62 U.S.-owned and U.S. branches and foreign-owned stock reinsurance companies in 1974 and 147 such stock reinsurance companies in 1981. See *Best's Aggregates & Averages, Property-Liability*, 36th Ed. (Oldwick, N.J.: A.M. Best Company, 1975), pp. 110, 112, 114 and *Best's Aggregates & Averages, Property-Casualty*, 43rd ed. (Oldwick, N.J.: A.M. Best Company, 1982), pp. 86, 88.

23. Since many captives are inactive, perhaps a more relevant proxy than the number of captives for capital entering insurance markets is the volume of business written by captives, which has been estimated to have increased from less than $1 billion in 1970 to $4.7 billion in 1980. See *The Changing Property and Casualty Commercial Lines Markets* (Hartford, CT: Conning & Company, 1980), p. 20, and the monograph, "The Use of Captives in Risk Management," in this text.

24. *Best's Aggregates & Averages, Property-Casualty*, 40th ed. (Oldwick, NJ: A.M. Best Company, 1979), p. 3 and *Best's Aggregates & Averages, Property-Casualty*, 44th ed. (Oldwick, NJ: A. M. Best Company, 1983), p. 3.

25. See Heilbroner and Thurow, *The Economic Problem*, pp. 362-363, for a description and diagram of a "cobweb."

26. Why price ceilings create shortages is explained in Heilbroner and Thurow, Chapter 22.

27. The reasons why flex rating or band rating cannot work are outlined in Richard E. Stewart, *Remembering a Stable Future (Why Flex Rating Cannot Work)* (New York: Insurance Services Office, Inc., and the Insurance Information Institute, 14 January 1987).

28. An enormous amount of literature exists on the case for competition, its benefits and costs, and how it does work and could work better in the real world. A concise, yet comprehensive, survey of the benefits and costs of competition can be found in Frederic M. Scherer's *Industrial Market Structure and Economic Performance*, 2nd ed. (Chicago: Rand McNally College Publishing Company, 1980), Chapter 2: "The Welfare Economics of Competition and Monopoly."

Selected Readings

Heilbroner, Robert L. and Thurow, Lester C. *The Economic Problem*, Third CPCU Ed. Englewood Cliffs, NJ: Prentice-Hall, Inc., 1984.

Arthur D. Little, Inc., *Prices and Profits in the Property and Liability Insurance Industry*, Report to the American Insurance Association, November, 1967.

National Association of Insurance Commissioners (Central Office Staff), *Monitoring Competition: A Means of Regulating the Property and Liability Insurance Business, Volume I*, National Association of Insurance Commissioners, 1974.

Scherer, Frederic M. *Industrial Market Structure and Economic Performance*, 2nd ed., Chicago: Rand McNally College Publishing Company, 1980.

Appendix

This Appendix contains the data used in the graphs in Exhibits 8-2 through 8-12. The data are provided for the benefit of any reader who might be interested in more detail than provided by the graphs.

Data for Exhibit 8-2
Industry Combined Ratio for All Lines of Property-Liability Insurance[†]
1945-1985*

Years	Combined Ratio Before Policyholder Dividends	Combined Ratio After Policyholder Dividends	Years	Combined Ratio Before Policyholder Dividends	Combined Ratio After Policyholder Dividends
1945	92.3	NA	1963	99.9	102.0
1946	95.9	NA	1964	101.2	103.2
1947	91.7	NA	1965	100.7	102.6
1948	89.2	NA	1966	97.1	99.0
1949	89.5	NA	1967	98.2	100.2
1950	93.3	NA	1968	99.5	101.5
1951	94.4	96.7	1969	100.6	102.5
1952	92.3	94.4	1970	98.4	100.1
1953	91.1	93.4	1971	94.7	96.4
1954	91.4	93.7	1972	94.3	96.2
1955	93.1	95.4	1973	97.3	99.2
1956	98.2	100.6	1974	103.7	105.4
1957	100.0	102.2	1975	106.6	107.9
1958	97.3	99.6	1976	101.3	102.4
1959	95.5	97.7	1977	96.0	97.2
1960	96.0	98.2	1978	95.9	97.5
1961	96.5	98.6	1979	99.1	100.6
1962	97.2	99.1	1980	101.4	103.1
			1981	104.1	106.0
			1982	107.7	109.6
			1983	109.9	112.2
			1984	116.1	118.0
			1985	114.6	116.3

NA = Not Available

[†] Ratios prior to 1951 include casualty company business only. Ratios prior to 1958 are for stock and mutual companies only.

* Source: *Best's Aggregates & Averages*, A.M. Best Company.

Data for Exhibit 8-3
Industry Combined Ratio (Before Policyholder Dividends) for Automobile Insurance and for All Lines of Property-Liability Insurance[†] 1945-1985*

	Automobile		All Lines
Year	Combined Ratio	Year	Combined Ratio
1945	106.0	1945	92.3
1946	110.8	1946	95.9
1947	99.2	1947	91.7
1948	93.1	1948	89.2
1949	89.2	1949	89.5
1950	93.8	1950	93.3
1951	97.7	1951	94.4
1952	96.0	1952	92.3
1953	91.0	1953	91.1
1954	88.7	1954	91.4
1955	93.4	1955	93.1
1956	101.6	1956	98.2
1957	105.3	1957	100.0
1958	101.4	1958	97.6
1959	98.1	1959	95.8
1960	96.8	1960	96.2
1961	97.2	1961	96.7
1962	98.8	1962	97.3
1963	101.4	1963	100.1
1964	104.3	1964	101.2
1965	102.2	1965	100.9
1966	98.6	1966	97.2
1967	99.0	1967	98.4
1968	102.2	1968	99.7
1969	104.8	1969	100.6
1970	101.7	1970	98.6
1971	95.0	1971	94.9
1972	95.3	1972	94.5
1973	99.2	1973	97.5
1974	102.0	1974	103.7
1975	110.4	1975	106.6
1976	104.0	1976	101.3
1977	96.0	1977	96.0
1978	97.1	1978	95.9
1979	100.6	1979	99.1
1980	100.9	1980	101.4
1981	105.8	1981	104.1
1982	108.5	1982	107.7
1983	107.6	1983	109.9
1984	116.1	1984	111.4
1985	114.6	1985	111.4

[†] Ratios prior to 1951 include casualty company business only. Ratios prior to 1974 are for stock and mutual companies only.

* Source: *Best's Aggregates & Averages*, A.M. Best Company.

Data for Exhibit 8-4

Industry Combined Ratio (Before Policyholder Dividends) for Workers Compensation Insurance† 1945-1985*

Year	Combined Ratio	Year	Combined Ratio
1945	89.0	1965	93.1
1946	90.5	1966	92.6
1947	85.3	1967	92.3
1948	83.7	1968	89.7
1949	86.1	1969	90.3
1950	94.2	1970	90.7
1951	96.9	1971	96.0
1952	93.5	1972	98.1
1953	89.9	1973	96.9
1954	86.2	1974	99.9
1955	89.0	1975	101.1
1956	90.2	1976	104.2
1957	91.4	1977	103.3
1958	94.2	1978	99.4
1959	96.0	1979	96.4
1960	95.0	1980	93.4
1961	96.0	1981	97.1
1962	93.9	1982	94.0
1963	95.4	1983	101.9
1964	93.9	1984	112.0
		1985	109.5

† Ratios prior to 1974 are for stock and mutual companies only.
*Source: *Best's Aggregates & Averages*, A.M. Best Company.

Data for Exhibit 8-5
Industry Combined Ratio (Before Policyholder Dividends) for Homeowners
Insurance† for Stock and Mutual Companies 1955-1985*

Year	Combined Ratio	Year	Combined Ratio
1955	93.9	1971	97.5
1956	95.9	1972	92.0
1957	96.8	1973	93.6
1958	94.4	1974	105.7
1959	88.9	1975	106.2
1960	96.8	1976	97.2
1961	101.6	1977	91.7
1962	103.2	1978	92.0
1963	106.7	1979	98.6
1964	111.0	1980	104.9
1965	106.6	1981	101.4
1966	99.0	1982	103.5
1967	104.0	1983	103.2
1968	103.6	1984	106.0
1969	102.9	1985	112.0
1970	102.5		

† Ratios available beginning 1955. Ratios prior to 1974 are for stock and mutual companies only.

* Source: *Best's Aggregates & Averages*, A.M. Best Company.

Data for Exhibit 8-6
Industry Combined Ratio (Before Policyholder Dividends) for Commercial Mutiple Peril Insurance† 1965-1985*

Year	Combined Ratio	Year	Combined Ratio
1956	109.2	1971	85.8
1957	122.3	1972	86.1
1958	114.6	1973	88.2
1959	103.2	1974	100.9
1960	102.3	1975	98.4
1961	91.6	1976	93.3
1962	91.2	1977	86.7
1963	94.2	1978	84.1
1964	94.4	1979	92.5
1965	96.7	1980	98.0
1966	92.3	1981	106.0
1967	93.2	1982	115.6
1968	96.4	1983	122.6
1969	93.3	1984	134.5
1970	89.8	1985	121.1

† Ratios available beginning 1956. Ratios prior to 1974 are for stock and mutual companies only.

*Source: *Best's Aggregates & Averages*, A.M. Best Company.

Data for Exhibit 8-7
Industry Combined Ratio (Before Policyholder Dividends) for Inland Marine Insurance[†] 1955-1985[*]

Year	Combined Ratio	Year	Combined Ratio
1951	96.5	1968	99.8
1952	93.4	1969	99.5
1953	90.3	1970	92.8
1954	95.5	1971	86.1
1955	99.2	1972	86.6
1956	103.4	1973	88.4
1957	105.9	1974	95.1
1958	100.3	1975	94.6
1959	97.1	1976	89.6
1960	97.1	1977	86.0
1961	97.5	1978	86.5
1962	94.3	1979	94.9
1963	99.3	1980	102.1
1964	98.0	1981	102.1
1965	101.5	1982	102.1
1966	101.1	1983	102.7
1967	98.8	1984	106.0
		1985	95.8

[†] Ratios available beginning 1951. Ratios prior to 1974 are for stock and mutual companies only.

[*] Source: *Best's Aggregates & Averages*, A.M. Best Company.

Data for Exhibit 8-8

Industry Combined Ratio (Before Policyholder Dividends) for Miscellaneous Liability Insurance[†] 1945-1985*

Year	Combined Ratio	Year	Combined Ratio
1945	81.1	1965	93.0
1946	87.1	1966	96.5
1947	86.3	1967	102.7
1948	91.5	1968	103.5
1949	96.9	1969	103.9
1950	99.7	1970	103.2
1951	102.4	1971	109.1
1952	100.9	1972	113.9
1953	94.7	1973	116.1
1954	94.4	1974	125.0
1955	93.5	1975	115.6
1956	94.3	1976	106.5
1957	96.6	1977	99.6
1958	97.1	1978	96.9
1959	94.1	1979	97.6
1960	93.0	1980	106.6
1961	90.4	1981	115.3
1962	87.4	1982	128.6
1963	90.8	1983	137.5
1964	91.5	1984	151.1
		1985	145.3

[†] Ratios prior to 1975 include medical malpractice. Rates prior to 1974 are for stock and mutual companies only.

*Source: *Best's Aggregates & Averages*, A.M. Best Company.

Data for Exhibit 8-9
Return on Sales (Before Taxes)*

Year	Property-Liability Insurance Stock Companies[1]	All U.S. Corporations[2]
1945	7.5	NA
1946	0.1	16.5
1947	3.2	18.3
1948	8.8	21.0
1949	13.4	19.8
1950	8.6	21.8
1951	5.0	21.7
1952	7.5	19.5
1953	9.4	18.3
1954	10.5	18.0
1955	8.5	20.6
1956	3.7	18.7
1957	1.2	17.7
1958	4.4	16.1
1959	6.1	18.3
1960	6.3	16.9
1961	6.0	16.7
1962	5.8	17.8
1963	4.2	18.3
1964	3.4	18.8
1965	3.1	19.7
1966	6.6	19.2
1967	6.1	17.6
1968	5.0	17.2
1969	4.2	15.3
1970	5.7	12.6
1971	9.9	13.6
1972	10.8	14.1
1973	9.0	14.2
1974	3.5	11.8
1975	0.7	12.6
1976	5.2	13.8
1977	10.7	14.6
1978	12.3	14.5
1979	11.5	13.3
1980	10.3	10.8
1981	9.5	10.2
1982	7.5	7.9
1983	4.4	10.4
1984	-2.4	11.6
1985	-2.9	11.6

NA = Not Available

The reader should not attempt to draw conclusions from these data regarding the level of profitability for stock property-liability insurers relative to the level of profitability for all U.S. corporations. Property-liability insurance returns should include realized and unrealized gains and losses to be strictly comparable with the data on all U.S. corporations' returns. Available insurance data, however, do not reflect unrealized gains and losses on fixed income assets, which are a large proportion of the industry's assets. In addition, neither profitability series has been adjusted for federal income taxes, which differ as a percent of income on each of the two series.

[1] Underwriting profit or loss plus net investment income as a percent of net written premiums.

[2] Corporate profits before taxes with inventory valuation adjustment and capital consumption adjustment as a percent of gross domestic and product of corporate business.

*Source: *Best's Aggregates & Averages*, A.M. Best Company; *National Income and Product Accounts of the United States*, Bureau of Economic Analysis, U.S. Department of Commerce.

Data for Exhibit 8-10
Investment Income Growth and Interest Rates 1951-1985*

	Percentage Change Over Previous Year of Investment Income[†]	Average Percentage Yield on Domestic Municipal Bonds	Average Percentage Yield on U.S. Government 3-Month Bills
1951		2.0	1.5
1952	8.8	2.2	1.7
1953	12.0	2.7	1.9
1954	11.7	2.4	0.9
1955	9.1	2.5	1.7
1956	9.5	2.8	2.6
1957	7.8	3.3	3.2
1958	6.6	3.2	1.8
1959	10.6	3.6	3.4
1960	12.0	3.5	2.9
1961	5.8	3.5	2.4
1962	8.7	3.1	2.8
1963	7.1	3.2	3.2
1964	8.9	3.2	3.5
1965	9.6	3.3	3.9
1966	7.3	3.8	4.9
1967	10.8	4.0	4.3
1968	13.8	4.5	5.3
1969	13.1	5.8	6.7
1970	17.2	6.3	6.4
1971	16.9	5.5	4.3
1972	15.3	5.2	4.1
1973	16.2	5.2	7.0
1974	16.5	6.3	7.8
1975	8.4	7.1	5.8
1976	17.6	6.6	5.0
1977	26.6	5.7	5.3
1978	25.3	6.0	7.2
1979	27.3	6.5	10.1
1980	19.2	8.6	11.4
1981	19.8	11.3	14.0
1982	12.5	11.7	10.6
1983	7.2	9.5	8.6
1984	10.6	10.1	9.5
1985	10.5	9.1	7.5

† Stock and mutual companies' data from 1951 through 1967. Consolidated industry data from 1968 through 1985.

* Source: *Best's Aggregates & Averages*, A.M. Best Company; *Survey of Current Business*, Bureau of Economic Analysis, U.S. Department of Commerce; *Selected Interest Rates and Bond Prices*, Statistical Release G. 13, Supplement to Banking & Monetary Statistics, Section 12, Board of Governors of the Federal Reserve System.

Data for Exhibit 8-11

Underwriting Profit or Loss† Plus Investment Income as a Percentage of Written Premiums and the Combined Ratio† for Property-Liability Insurance Stock Companies 1945-1985*

Year	Underwriting + Investment Income as Percent of Written Premiums	Combined Ratio
1945	7.5	95.8
1946	0.1	98.8
1947	3.2	96.3
1948	8.8	91.2
1949	13.4	87.6
1950	8.6	93.0
1951	5.0	97.1
1952	7.5	94.4
1953	9.4	93.1
1954	10.5	93.6
1955	8.5	94.9
1956	3.7	100.5
1957	1.2	102.9
1958	4.4	100.0
1959	6.1	97.8
1960	6.3	98.4
1961	6.0	99.4
1962	5.8	99.0
1963	4.2	101.0
1964	3.4	101.9
1965	3.1	101.9
1966	6.6	98.0
1967	6.1	98.9
1968	5.0	100.0
1969	4.2	100.6
1970	5.7	99.3
1971	9.9	95.8
1972	10.8	95.4
1973	9.0	98.2
1974	3.5	105.0
1975	0.7	107.5
1976	5.2	102.0
1977	10.7	97.0
1978	12.3	96.6
1979	11.5	99.6
1980	10.3	102.4
1981	9.5	104.9
1982	7.5	108.7
1983	4.4	111.8
1984	-2.4	119.0
1985	-2.9	116.5

† Before policyholder dividends.

* Source: *Best's Aggregates & Averages*, A.M. Best Company.

Data for Exhibit 8-12

Underwriting Profit or Loss[†] Plus Investment Income as a Percentage of Policyholders Surplus and the Combined Ratio[†] for Property-Liability Insurance Stock Companies 1945-1985*

Year	Underwriting + Investment Income as Percent of Policyholders' Surplus	Combined Ratio
1945	5.7	95.8
1946	0.1	98.8
1947	4.2	96.3
1948	12.6	91.2
1949	17.2	87.6
1950	10.5	93.0
1951	6.3	97.1
1952	9.7	94.4
1953	12.7	93.1
1954	11.2	93.6
1955	8.4	94.9
1956	3.8	100.5
1957	1.4	102.9
1958	4.6	100.0
1959	6.5	97.8
1960	6.9	98.4
1961	5.5	99.4
1962	6.1	99.0
1963	4.0	101.0
1964	3.2	101.9
1965	3.1	101.9
1966	8.3	98.0
1967	7.3	98.9
1968	6.0	100.0
1969	6.6	100.6
1970	9.2	99.3
1971	14.2	95.8
1972	13.9	95.4
1973	13.5	98.2
1974	7.6	105.0
1975	1.4	107.5
1976	9.7	102.0
1977	20.1	97.0
1978	21.7	96.6
1979	18.5	99.6
1980	14.5	102.4
1981	13.9	104.9
1982	10.1	108.7
1983	5.8	111.8
1984	-3.7	119.0
1985	-4.5	116.5

[†] Before policyholder dividends.

*Source: *Best's Aggregates & Averages*, A.M. Best Company

MONOGRAPH **9**

Environmental Impairment Liability: An Insurance Perspective*

by David C. Sterling, CPCU, CLU, ChFC, CIC

I. INTRODUCTION

Elixirs of Death

For the first time in the history of the world, every human being is now subjected to contact with dangerous chemicals, from the moment of conception until death. In the less than two decades of their use, the synthetic pesticides have been so thoroughly distributed throughout the animate world that they occur virtually everywhere. They have been recovered from most of the major river systems and even from streams of groundwater flowing unseen through the earth. Residues of these chemicals linger in soil to which they may have been applied a dozen years before. They have entered and lodged in the bodies of fish, birds, reptiles, and domestic and wild animals so universally that scientists carrying on animal experiments find it almost impossible to locate subjects free from such contamination. They have been found in fish in remote mountain lakes, in earthworms burrowing in soil, in the eggs of birds—and in man himself. For these chemicals are now stored in the bodies of the vast majority of human beings, regardless of age. They occur in the mother's milk, and probably in the tissues of the unborn child.[1]

---

*The author wishes to thank William C. Aldrich, Vice President, Government Relations, The Hartford Insurance Group, for his work on the Superfund section of this monograph.

The pollution of the environment is an extremely unfortunate by-product of the industrial age and its technology. While the effects of many existing and potential pollutants on the ecology of the earth have yet to be understood, the general public has become increasingly aware of the damages caused by and potential dangers of pollutants.

Media "events" surrounding the situation at Love Canal, Three Mile Island, Bhopal, and Times Beach have given widewpread exposure to the impact of toxic and hazardous substances. Interested citizen and environmental groups have increased the public's awareness and have spurred on the promulgation of federal and state-level legislation designed to safeguard the environment. Along with legislation, there is an increasing amount of litigation involving pollution incidents. Many experts believe that the amount of litigation will continue to increase dramatically as more and more such incidents come to light.

One of the central issues with regard to pollution litigation focuses on the following question: Who will bear the financial burden for cleaning up the environment as well as the damages for the injuries and property damage that emanate from pollution incidents? If the pollution problem is as large as suspected, will there be sufficient financial resources to respond? The latency period for some diseases may span thirty or forty years prior to manifestation. The possibility exists, therefore, that the polluters cannot be identified, may be out of business, or simply may be unable to respond financially.

Examples of the tremendous costs involved are numerous. *Village of Wilsonville, IL* v. *SCA Services, Inc.* involved a state Environmental Protection Agency (EPA)-approved landfill that had to be moved at a cost of $20 million after being declared a nuisance.[2] The Dutch government is seeking over $16 million from a large chemical company for the costs of cleaning up a closed hazardous waste dump.[3] A Swiss chemical company settled for $7 million in a case involving the dioxin contamination of Sevesco, Italy.[4] But these are mostly payments for cleanup costs. "Superfund" (an act described later in this monograph) spent more than $33 million just to buy property in Times Beach, Missouri before even beginning major cleanup operations.[5]

The cost of defending pollution claims is enormous. Class action suits are certain to escalate, and evidentiary procedures are likely to be eased by the courts. Precedent set by cases involving asbestos, Agent Orange ($180 million out-of-court settlement[6]), and DES, for example, likely will influence the outcome of litigation involving pollution cases.

Although the insurance industry has been involved with insuring the pollution exposure for several decades, it was not until the passage in 1976 of the Resource Conservation and Recovery Act (RCRA) financial responsibility requirements that a concerted effort was made to insure environmental impairment liability (EIL) exposures.

What, then, should be the insurance industry's role in the future in regard to EIL coverage? At this time, there are some proposals and legislation in Congress as well as in some of the states that would make it difficult, if not impossible, for the insurance industry to continue to respond. The private insurance sector requires a reasonable opportunity to make a profit, and undue legislative constraints will create obstacles in the path of further development and growth of this limited market and, in fact, may lead to its demise.

This monograph will look at the EIL problem primarily from an insurance perspective. First, the monograph will examine the dimensions of the pollution exposure. Next, the common law and statutory responsibilities and liabilities will be examined. The monograph will then look at the risk management alternatives with regard to the EIL problem followed by a discussion of the insurance developed for this exposure and the market for that insurance. Finally, the author will look at the future of this problem, summarize it, and make some personal observations.

II. DIMENSIONS OF THE POLLUTION EXPOSURE

The contamination of our world is not alone a matter of mass spraying. Indeed, for most of us this is of less importance than the innumerable small-scale exposures to which we are subjected day by day, year after year. Like the constant dripping of water that in turn wears away the hardest stone, the birth-to-death contact with dangerous chemicals may in the end prove disastrous. Each of these recurrent exposures, no matter how slight, contributes to the progressive buildup of chemicals in our bodies and so to cumulative poisoning. Probably no person is immune to contact with this spreading contamination unless he lives in the most isolated situation imaginable.[7]

Although environmental pollution has been ongoing for generations, the consequences of some of these activities and the potential number of sites involved are just now becoming known. The estimates vary from 2,000 to 5,000 as to the number of hazardous waste sites that could be included on the EPA National Priorities List of sites requiring cleanup action.[8] According to the EPA National Priorities List, the state with the largest number of sites is New Jersey, followed by New York, Michigan, and Pennsylvania. There are various estimates of the total number of hazardous waste dump sites located in the United States, but there seems to be some consensus that the number is between 25,000 and 50,000. Another estimate indicates that there may be as many as 1,200 abandoned chemical dump sites located across the country.[9]

The EPA estimated in 1984 that 150 million metric tons of hazardous waste must be disposed of annually by United States industry. Another 300 million metric tons are being stored, treated, or incinerated at the point of production.[10]

Few communities are truly insulated from the toxic waste exposure. Many municipalities operate sanitary landfills and sewage treatment plants, own underground fuel tanks, and grant permits to firms to dispose of hazardous wastes in sewer systems the municipalities' sanitary landfills. Until recent years, and even now in some cases, municipalities have not adequately monitored who is disposing what in their landfills. Underground fuel tanks also pose a problem for municipalities. It is hard to estimate when a tank might begin to leak since local soil conditions and the type of tank play a role in the time that will elapse before a tank begins to leak. The EPA has estimated that there are 796,000 motor fuel tanks (not limited to those owned by municipalities), and as many as 35 percent of them may be leaking, some as much as six gallons of fuel a day.[11]

It might be helpful to look at some definitions and explanations of some of the terminology used with landfills and dumping, which are so often used in conjunction with the exposures faced by municipalities. One source states (italics are those of this author):

> *Open dumping* involves the deposition of wastes on the land with little or no regard for environmental and/or public health protection. *Sanitary landfills* are utilized for municipal solid wastes. At these facilities, solid wastes are spread in thin layers and compacted. Cover material is then applied. A *secure chemical landfill* (see Exhibit 9-1) is an excavation which is utilized to store and contain hazardous waste and leachate. *Leachate* is contaminated liquid which is found in landfills. It is formed where water enters the landfills via precipitation and mixes with the waste. A landfill must:
>
> 1) Protect ground water and surface water.
> 2) Contain waste and leachate.
> 3) Provide for the collection, removal, and treatment of leachate.
> 4) Control gas emissions.
>
> Liners
>
> The bottom, sides, and any areas of a landfill which are likely to come in contact with leachate should be covered with a liner which is designed and built to achieve containment of fluids during the life of the landfill. This prevents escape of hazardous constituents to surrounding soils and ultimately to the groundwater. Liners generally fall into one of two categories—clay or synthetic. A landfill should have at least one liner, and the material used must be resistant to the chemicals it will encounter in the wastes and in the leachate. The liner must be strong enough to withstand the forces it will encounter

during installation and operation. This requires a base which supports the liner to prevent failure.[12]

In view of these and other municipal operations, there are a number of municipalities with toxic waste problems today. The City of Philadelphia filed a $30 million lawsuit against a chemical company and others for cleanup and related costs arising out of a municipal dump. In this case, two city employees were bribed to allow a transporter to dump toxic materials into a city dump.[13] Although Hooker Chemicals and Plastic Corporation (which was acquired by Occidental Petroleum Corporation in 1968) has been the name most often associated with the Love Canal incident and with having to pay for the damages associated therewith (and has been held responsible in court for most of those damages), the town and local school board in the area were also held jointly liable for a settlement likely to reach into the tens of millions (suits in that settlement sought over $2 billion).[14] Suits against Hooker have sought over $10 billion in damages.[15]

Finally, the insurers for Jackson Township, New Jersey refused to defend or provide coverage for the township when it was faced with a $51.5 million lawsuit arising from the contamination of wells due to persons illegally dumping toxic wastes in the township landfill. These insurers were only providing the general liability coverage and denied coverage on the grounds the pollution was not sudden and accidental. This township, like many municipalities, had no separate pollution policy in addition to tis general liability coverage.[16] A later decision by a New Jersey Court on the coverage and defense issue for one of the insurers, however, found in favor of the township (*Jackson Township Municipal Utilities Authority* v. *Hartford Accident and Indemnity Company*). The court stated that "sudden" does not have to be an instantaneous happening and that if pollution damage could be viewed as unintended, it could constitute an accident.[17]

Just as most communities are not immune from the toxic waste exposure, it is difficult to determine which firm will have a pollution exposure. A high percentage of manufacturing and processing firms use hazardous chemicals in various processes and create hazardous waste as a by-product. One estimate indicates that 80 percent of the companies (that is, manufacturers, processors, and so on) that generate hazardous waste dispose of it on their own property. For an example of how pollution might result from a manufacturing process, see Exhibit 9-2.

Farming operations, through the use of pesticides, herbicides, and fertilizers, also pose a threat to people and their environment. In Connecticut's Tobacco Valley, ethylene dibromide (EDB) has shown up in a number of wells. In a mid-1970s Michigan case, tons of animal feed became contaminated with polybrominated biphenyl (PBB), an extreme-

Exhibit 9-1
Secure Chemical Landfill*

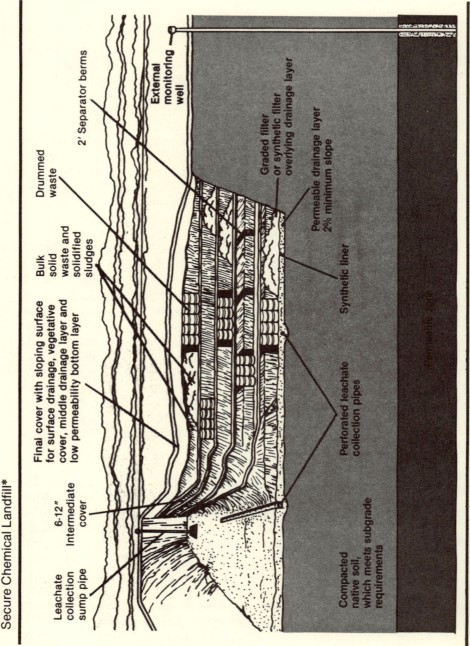

* Reprinted from *Technologies and Management Strategies for Hazardous Waste Control*, Office of Technology Assessment, Congress of the

Exhibit 9-2
Track Chemicals Flow — Some Potential Pollution Exposures*

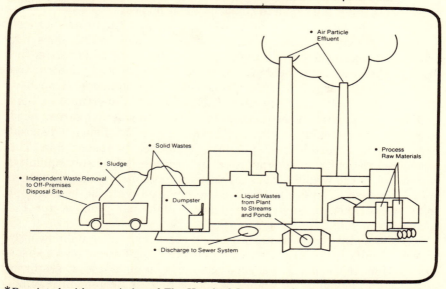

*Reprinted with permission of The Hartford Insurance Group from *Don't Find Out About Pollution Liability By Accident,* pp. 9 and 10.

ly toxic fire retardant. Property damage losses arising from this contamination and the subsequent destruction of many animals may reach $1 billion.[18] *Silent Spring* describes the farm exposure in the following manner:

> If the farmer scrupulously follows the instructions on the labels, his use of agricultural chemicals will produce no residues larger than are permitted by the Food and Drug Administration. Leaving aside for the moment the question whether these legal residues are as "safe" as they are represented to be, there remains the well-known fact that farmers very frequently exceed the prescribed dosages, use the chemical too close to the time of harvest, use several insecticides where one would do, and in other ways display the common human failure to read the fine print.
>
> Even the chemical industry recognizes the frequent misuse of insecticides and the need for education of farmers. One of its leading trade journals recently declared that "many users do not seem to understand that they may exceed insecticide tolerances if they use higher dosages than recommended. And haphazard use of insecticides on many crops may be based on farmers' whims."[19]

Chemical manufacturing as well as many other industrial and manufacturing operations present significant pollution exposures. In the past and even in some instances today, such firms have disposed of their toxic wastes on their own premises using lagoons, settling ponds, or by discharging the waste to adjacent water bodies.

One of the most significant exposures for a firm can be its choice of a hazardous waste disposal facility. If the chosen facility does not properly manage and handle the disposal of the hazardous waste, the firm could end up being held strictly, jointly, and severally liable if the site becomes a target of a Comprehensive Environmental Response, Compensation and Liability Act (CERCLA or Superfund) action. Companies that entrust the disposal of their toxic waste to others need to be especially sensitive to the quality and capability of such a disposal firm and make certain that the firm is financially responsible. The amendments to the Superfund made in 1986 (described subsequently) responded to the inability of many firms to obtain adequate insurance coverage. Organized crime has become involved with the handling of toxic waste and this may pose yet an additional problem for the unsuspecting manufacturing company.[20]

Additionally, firms acquiring other companies may unknowingly pick up significant pollution exposures (Occidental Petroleum's acquisition of Hooker Chemical is a good example). In instances where firms have been in business for a long period of time, management may not be aware of past disposal practices—employees who would know may have retired or passed away—until they are confronted with a problem or a claim.

Not only is the pollution exposure pervasive, but the cleanup costs involved are tremendous. Additional examples not yet mentioned are those occurring at sea and would include the 1967 Torrey Canyon supertanker grounding ($7.8 million paid by the ship's owner), the 1969 drilling spill off the coast of California (damage of over $1 billion), and a 1970 Gulf of Mexico spill (resulting in claims for over $100 million in damages suffered by oyster and shrimp fishermen.)[21] Even Congress is recognizing the scope of the problem. Superfund was originally set up as a $1.6 billion fund. The amendments passed in 1986 increased this to $9 billion.

In all of these situations, because of the complexity of the claims and the issue of cause and effect over what can be very lengthy periods,[22] defense costs are expected to be very high also. One study reported that for asbestos claims the average total cost was $95,000, of which approximately $35,000 (or about 37 percent) was for total defense litigation expenses.[23]

The question remains: Who will fund these losses? Certainly the insurance industry should not be expected to do so; in any event, because of the magnitude of the problem, it probably could not. Society and industry eventually will have to come to grips with the issue.

III. COMMON-LAW RESPONSIBILITY[24]

Environmental impairment liability tort actions, an area of the law coming before the courts on an increasing basis, are largely grounded in the principles of common law. Persons or firms involved with the handling, storage, or disposal of hazardous substances or wastes should realize that apart from any statutorily imposed liability, fines, and costs of compliance with regulations, there exists a well established body of common law that supports cases for recovering costs of personal injury and damage to property.[25]

One person has summarized his thoughts regarding this and the possible criminal liability involved by saying:

Costs associated with the compelled compliance with the generally comprehensive federal environmental regulation statutes and associated state regulatory schemata can be very substantial, but the ultimately critical considerations for those who are being regulated and for any person or entity manufacturing or processing or disposing or transporting hazardous wastes or toxic substances will be the extent of potential exposure for civil and criminal liability for their actions or failures to act. Once the variety of fascinating issues and litigating questions of administrative authority and procedure arising under "RCRA" and "Superfund"...etc., have been largely completed, and once, in particular, the U.S. EPA and the corresponding state agencies have delineated standardized permit and regulatory procedures, compliance costs will become substantially predictable and the administrative process will generally become orderly.

In stark contrast to this general predictability and procedure is the current and future specter of potentially unlimited and largely unpredictable exposure to civil and criminal liability.

Such civil liability, primarily sounding in tort...and the relief may well include compensatory and punitive damages, civil penalties and often-times extraordinary affirmative or prohibitive injunctive relief. The significant hazards of potential criminal liability, corporate and individual, are present at various levels of jurisdictions, federal, state and local....

[T]he amounts of corporate asset base subject to jeopardy and the expense arising from such potential liability exposure will ultimately be of greater concern to management and clients than the very costly and complex matters of compliance [not to mention] criminal charges and convictions.

Multi-million dollar verdicts for substantial personal injuries and punitive damage awards in the tens of millions are no longer exceptional.... Even at the present time, many lawsuits have been filed by private-party plaintiffs alleging damages for amounts ranging from a million dollars for pollution of two residential water wells allegedly resulting from leachate leakage of unspecified chemicals from a dump site (See, e.g., *Ballard* v. *South Carolina Recycling and Disposal, Inc., et al.,* Court of Common Pleas, Lexington County, South Carolina, 12/8/80) to the roughly $20,776,000.00 of complaint-specified damages claimed in the "Love Canal" litigation *(United States, et al., v. Hooker Chemicals and Plastic Corp., et al.,* Civ No. 79-990 and associated cases, USDC W.D.N.Y. 10/18/80)....[26]

The common-law approaches on which lawsuits can be based include nuisance, trespass, negligence, and strict liability. Nuisance and trespass are actions relating to activities that interfere with the possession of land. *Nuisance* involves interference with another's use and enjoyment of land. *Trespass* is an interference with an owner's exclusive right of possession of land.

Nuisance

Actions involving nuisance have generally been brought in air pollution cases where the plaintiff's enjoyment of his or her land is hindered by noxious fumes. However, nuisance can be the basis in other situations where pollutants interfere with individuals' rights to enjoy and use their property: "Interferences including vibration, raising of the water table, pollution of streams, loud noises, and the effects of toxic dust or gas are common invasions of this interest."[27]

Trespass

Trespass as an action is not often allowed by the courts in pollution liability cases because there may be no visible intrusion on the land. However, at least one court granted a plaintiff damage for injury to his land caused by fluoride compounds. This court stated that the plaintiff's interest in the exclusive possession of his land could be violated even "by a ray of light, an atomic particle, or by a particulate of fluoride."[28]

Closely related to nuisance in terms of interfering with the enjoyment of land is the situation involving the interference with another's water rights, which is an aspect of the law in its own right. If riparian owners cannot use the water for purposes to which they are accustomed, they are entitled to relief. Just as one has the right to have the water flow to his or her land in its usual quantity (that is, without diversion), one has the right to expect the water to be naturally pure.[29]

Negligence

An individual may also allege that someone has caused environmental damage or harm to others through his or her own negligence. Traditional negligence principles require all people to conduct themselves in a manner so as not to cause a forseeable risk of harm to others. Such principles require that the "offending party's" conduct must be linked to the harm alleged by the individual claimant. This party may be held liable in situations where he or she fails to warn others of known or potential dangers or fails to take proper precautions to prevent harm. Liability may also involve failure to choose a responsible disposal facility for hazardous wastes. One court has granted both compensatory and punitive damages to a plaintiff whose dairy business was disrupted when cattle drank water contaminated by pollutants that the defendant permitted to flow into a creek on the plaintiff's property. The defendant knew that a harmful condition existed but failed to take corrective action.[30] When statutes provide for standards of care or conduct, deviation from those standards may be considered conclusive evidence of negligence.

Strict Liability as an Alternate Theory

Finally, courts have also allowed pollution and hazardous substance suits on strict liability grounds, which imposes liability without regard to negligence. Liability may be found even in cases where the activity is one that is accepted and beneficial to society, and liability may be held regardless of any precautions taken.

Strict liability can logically be applied to any activity that is likely to cause harm simply because of its nature (for example, storing toxic wastes). An early English case, *Rylands* v. *Fletcher*, established the precedent of imposing strict liability for anything brought onto one's land that is not naturally there and that is likely to cause great harm. The advantage to plaintiffs in strict liability cases is that the plaintiff can recover without proving negligence on the part of the defendant.

Even in the states whose courts have not accepted the *Rylands* v. *Fletcher* strict liability doctrine, a similar outcome based on other grounds, such as nuisance, has been reached. Some courts have held that even though the defendant was not negligent, he or she had *unreasonably* interfered with another's use of land and was therefore liable.[31] Other grounds also used essentially to find strict liability include harm caused by *ultrahazardous activities* (blasting is usually given as the best example).[32] Following this line of reasoning, strict liability has gradually been used in cases involving less "ultrahazardous" activities. A revised version of this rule applied it to *abnormally dangerous activities*.[33] As might be expected, courts have been turning more and more toward strict liability in pollution cases.[34]

Defenses

In cases based on common-law liability involving activities that result in pollution, defendants have found little protection in traditional statutes of limitation. Such statutes generally require plaintiffs to begin a lawsuit within a prescribed period of time following an occurrence. However, many states in pollution and other cases allow plaintiffs to bring a suit within a certain period of time after the plaintiff first becomes *aware* of an injury or violation of property rights, not after the pollution or injury takes place. This greatly increases the opportunity of a person to bring a suit within the time allowed by statute. Because of this change, a lawsuit may be brought by an injured person based on an activity that occurred many years in the past, thus making it difficult to properly defend the lawsuit. Hooker Chemical, which is still in the midst of defending and paying claims, first began dumping at Love Canal in 1947.[35] The 1986 Superfund amendments preempted state laws on this subject and made the "clock" start running on the date the plaintiff knew or reasonably should have known of the causal connection between his or her harm and the exposure to the hazardous substance.

Apportionment of Damages

Another area of importance involves how courts will apportion damages among a variety of defendants. Courts are not only applying traditional damage theories, but also are developing new theories to make recovery by plaintiffs easier in situations where they may not be able to prove which specific defendant is responsible for the harmful conduct. If several companies discharge pollutants or engage in other parallel activities, all may be found jointly and severally liable. Partly because of this, what otherwise might have been a small property damage suit against one firm can become an enormous lawsuit if a class action suit is filed, as in the cases of Love Canal and Three Mile Island. These class action suits tend to be highly publicized and very emotional if there is evidence of possible bodily injury. Understandably, both of these factors can work to the disadvantage of the defendant when a jury of peers from the same area is involved. Cases can also involve highly technical scientific issues that are difficult to defend and resolve, resulting in lengthy trials and high legal costs.[36]

Expansion of Liability

Professor Sheila Birnbaum comments that she sees an attitude approaching hysteria regarding pollution and that people perceive a huge problem, which the press keeps magnifying. People think they are affected when they are not. But, she states, it makes little difference if they are affected or not, since they are now filing lawsuits based upon being "at risk." Although most courts have refused to find in favor of persons just because they live near a dump and have an increased chance of becoming ill later, she sees a runaway problem if courts start finding otherwise. Mental distress is a closely related problem. She noted that when the government agreed to buy out Times Beach property owners, those just outside the area to be purchased also wanted relief. If new dioxin contamination sites are discovered, she asks whether, "all the home-owners in Missouri ultimately will demand compensation for depreciated property values and mental distress."[37]

It is important to realize that common-law principles are being applied by the courts to activities that cause pollution in a manner that provides injured parties a wide range of opportunities to obtain compensation for their injuries or damage to their property. These principles, in conjunction with legislation, are at the same time reducing the ability of defendants to successfully defend such suits.

IV. STATUTORY REQUIREMENTS

Since the late 1950s, there has been a proliferation of federal legislation regulating various aspects of the handling, storage, transportation, and disposal of toxic substances and hazardous wastes. Among the more noteworthy of these environmental laws are the Clean Air Act (CAA), the Comprehensive Environmental Response, Compensation and Liability Act of 1980 (CERCLA—also known as "Superfund"), the Clean Water Act (CWA), the National Environmental Policy Act (NEPA), and the Resource Conservation and Recovery Act (RCRA). Of these, RCRA and CERCLA (Superfund) have major impact on firms whose activities involve hazardous and toxic substances or wastes.

Resource Conservation and Recovery Act (RCRA)

RCRA, enacted in 1976, is one of the most far reaching and complex of the various laws regulating the environment. The expressed purpose of RCRA is to "promote the protection of health and the environment and to conserve valuable material and energy resources." In accomplishing this objective, RCRA sets forth regulations that provide for "cradle-to-grave" regulation of toxic and hazardous substances or waste materials. It requires the EPA to identify and define the characteristics of toxic and hazardous substances or wastes subject to the regulation, as well as establish standards, and permits programs involving the generation, treatment, storage, and disposal of such substances or wastes.

In addition, RCRA has established an elaborate manifest (record keeping) system whereby hazardous waste is tracked from the time it leaves a plant until it is disposed of. Should it be necessary at a later date, the "paper" trail will document all parties who were involved with the handling of the hazardous waste.

One of the most important aspects of RCRA legislation, however, has been its establishment of financial responsibility requirements for hazardous waste management facilities, known as treatment, storage and disposal facilities (TSDFs). Because a significant number of generators (manufacturers/processing firms) that produce hazardous waste disposed of it in the past on their own property, they fall within the TSDF requirements. Also, a generator that retains more than 1,000 kilograms of hazardous waste for more than ninety days also becomes subject to the TSDF financial responsibility requirements. Insurance is one method of satisfying the RCRA financial responsibility requirements, summarized as follows:

Requirements for Existing Facilities (Interim Permitted Status—Existing as of 19 November 1980)

1. *Sudden Accidental Occurrences*
   The owner or operator of a TSDF must demonstrate financial responsibility for bodily injury and property damage to third parties of at least $1 million per occurrence with an annual aggregate limit of liability of at least $2 million. This coverage must be exclusive of legal defense costs and must be in effect by 15 July 1982.

2. *Nonsudden Accidental Occurrences*
   An owner or operator of a surface impoundment, landfill, or land treatment facility that is used to manage hazardous wastes must demonstrate financial responsibility for bodily injury and property damage to third parties of at least $3 million per occurrence with an annual aggregate limit of liability of at least $6 million. This coverage must also be exclusive of legal defense costs. There is a phase-in requirement for existing facilities for nonsudden accidental occurrence coverage as follows:
   (a) by 15 January 1983 for facilities with annual sales in excess of $10 million,
   (b) by 15 January 1984 for facilities with annual sales between $5 million and $10 million, and
   (c) by 15 January 1985 for all other such facilities not included in (a) or (b).

Requirements for New Facilities (Not in Existence as of 19 November 1980 An owner or operator of a new hazardous waste management facility must submit evidence of insurance to the appropriate regional EPA administrator at least sixty days before the date on which hazardous waste is first due to be received for treatment, storage, or disposal. The insurance must include coverage for both sudden accidental occurrence (at least $1 million per occurrence with an annual aggregate limit of liability of at least $2 million) and nonsudden accidental occurrence (at least $3 million per occurrence with an annual aggregate limit of liability of at least $6 million) and must be effective before the initial receipt of hazardous waste.

Additionally, owners and operators of hazardous waste management sites must demonstrate annual financial responsibility with respect to closure and post-closure care of the sites by one of the following means: a trust fund, a surety bond, a letter of credit, a test demonstrating financial strength, or an insurance policy.

Superfund (CERCLA)

Superfund (as CERCLA generally is known), which was passed in 1980, is designed to accomplish the following:

1. allow the federal government to provide emergency response and cleanup funds with respect to a release or a substantial threatened release of hazardous substances into the environment,
2. authorize the federal government to recover cleanup costs from responsible parties, and
3. provide funds for the cleanup of inactive disposal sites.

Superfund is largely financed by petroleum and certain chemical taxes plus direct federal appropriations to be used in response to an actual or threatened release of a substance that poses a substantial danger to the public health or welfare. This fund initially totaled $1.6 billion. Superfund is not intended to respond to damages for personal injury or loss of use of property. Third parties must sue in tort or under other laws for these damages.

Superfund imposes strict liability on the responsible parties involved with hazardous substances for all government response costs and all for damages for injury to, destruction of, or loss of natural resources. It should be noted that while RCRA deals with hazardous wastes, Superfund's scope is considerably larger in that it involves hazardous substances in addition to wastes. The potential liability can be as high as $50 million, and the liability cannot be transferred.

The way in which the provisions of Superfund are interpreted is very important to firms that come under the law. Although there is little disagreement that the liability under the act is both strict and retroactive, there is disagreement as to whether the provisions are (1) joint and several or (2) several. The disagreement arises because the act simply states (although not in these exact terms), "entities shall be liable for. . . . " In defining what is meant by "liable," the definition section of the act refers to the Clean Water Act for its interpretation of liable and liability. However, the Clean Water Act is not definitive either. Thus, the interpretation rests on case law in which findings from case to case have been mixed to date. Some courts have held in favor of a joint and several interpretation and others have held in favor of several. Many of the courts in the latter case have not actually used the term several, but by their action of apportioning liability according to negligence or fault, they have interpreted the law severally by implication. In trying to enforce the law, the EPA has generally interpreted the provisions of the law as being joint and several.

The strict liability provisions of the act pose serious implications for insurance companies. It should be noted that RCRA and CERCLA per se do not change or impose liability with respect to damages sought by third parties for personal injury or damage to property—the traditional tort remedies must be relied upon. CERCLA only applies to government response costs and damage to natural resurces.

Sean Mooney, in an Insurance Information Institute paper entitled *Toxic Wastes: The Insurance Issues,* identifies the insurance industry's concerns if the liability provisions of Superfund were to be joint and several as well as strict and retroactive:

> . . . joint and several liability . . . is a particular problem for insurers because this provision makes it difficult to quantify potential losses. The insurer of a small machine shop might find itself paying for waste site damages mainly caused by other businesses dumping in the same waste site due to joint liability provisions. The creation of a strict liability system means that incentives to avoid harm, which normally flow from reasonable behavior, are discarded. Traditionally, tort law has excused defendants who can prove the reasonableness of their actions. This has been acceptable because it seems to be just and because it encourages better behavior. Under strict liability, the party which acts reasonably will find itself in no better position that the party that does not. Retroactive liability means that an insurer may end up paying claims for losses which were not contemplated at the time of issuance of the insurance policy.[38]

Sean Mooney provided the following legal definitions in his paper:

> *Strict Liability:* imposes liability on a defendant, regardless of whether the defendant was negligent. For example, a person who stores dangerous explosives on his property would be liable for

damages if an accident occurs, even though all necessary precautions to prevent an accident had been taken.

Joint and Several Liability: the plaintiff may sue one or more of the parties to a liability separately or all of them together, at the plaintiff's option. One party can be forced to pay all damages, even though its actions contributed only a small fraction to the cause of injury or damage.[39]

The financial responsibility requirements of Superfund may be met by the purchase of an insurance policy. The insurer would then file a financial responsibility statement making the insurer a "grantor" under the act. The law then allows for direct action against such guarantor. In addition to such direct action, the guarantor loses its normal defenses, and if a guarantor is found to be acting in "bad faith," it will also lose its limits of liability stated in the policy. This opens the insurer to unlimited liability for claims authorized under Superfund.[40]

As enacted, Superfund did not address victim compensation. However, it did stipulate that a study of the issue should be made. Subsequently, a study group (referred to as the 301(e) Study Group) comprising twelve lawyers was appointed to study the issue. Their plan for addressing toxic waste victim compensation was proposed in late 1982. A two-tier system of compensation was advanced. Tier I benefits would be administered under a federal no-fault system similar to workers compensation. The benefits would be paid without consideration for liability. The benefits of the full judicial system would be available to injured parties under Tier II of the plan. However, even though the plan calls for courts to litigate such cases, these cases would be tried utilizing modified federal rules that would make it easier for plaintiffs to prevail. As Sean Mooney's paper concludes:

The problem with the 301(e) Study Group proposal is that it advocates a radical departure from the present common law system. If the group's proposals were to be implemented, they would enable a plaintiff to collect damages based on the presumption that the injuries or disease were caused by exposure to certain hazardous substances even if this causal relationship could not be proved, and even though there had been no negligence on the defendant's part. Moreover, specific industries would be taxed to pay for the funds administered under Tier I of the program regardless of whether individual companies within those industries had exercised proper care in disposing of their toxic wastes. Such proposals virtually eliminate any incentive for companies to expand resources to dispose of their wastes in a careful or responsible manner, a situation which runs counter to the fundamental principles of insurance as well as tort law.

In fact, there is some question as to whether the industries involved would be able to afford the insurance premiums needed to cover the risks to insurers, or whether insurance could even be written in such circumstances.

Moreover, the cost to society to fund such an all inclusive compensation program would be staggering. Thousands of claims could be filed each year for all types of diseases allegedly caused by exposure to toxic wastes. A conservative estimate of Tier I claims payment alone exceeds $26 billion.

The victim compensation proposals by the 301(e) Group are under study by Congress at the present time. The Superfund Act provides no statutory timetable for such legislation.[41]

Superfund Amendments and Reauthorization Act (SARA)

In 1986 Congress passed the Superfund Amendments and Reauthorization Act (SARA), which reauthorized Superfund with an appropriation of $8.5 billion (plus an additional $500,000 in motor fuel taxes) covering the period from 1 January 1987 through 31 December 1991. In addition to providing more than a five-fold increase in the Superfund taxes, SARA includes a number of new provisions that are likely to produce dramatic increases in the Superfund liabilities that will be imposed on responsible parties and their insurers. It is also possible that the provisions will have far-reaching legal implications.

For example, under the new act, the EPA must meet a number of deadlines in its cleanup activity at sites on the National Priorities List (NPL). The cleanup standards are also much more stringent than those applicable under prior law. The combined effect of these requirements is expected to be a significant increase in both the number of sites being cleaned up and in the average cost of cleanup per site.

The new act also establishes several new types of costs that the EPA may recover as "response costs" from responsible parties. Potentially the most significant of these is included in a section of the act titled Health Related Authorities. Under this section, the government is required to perform health assessments at several hundred sites that are considered national priorities not later than 10 December 1988. If the assessments indicate a significant risk to human health, the EPA is directed to take necessary steps "to eliminate or substantially mitigate" the risk. These steps could include provision of alternate water supplies and relocation of affected individuals. The cost of such steps ultimately falls on responsible parties.

Another significant new response cost relates to the activities of response action contractors, that is, those who are hired to clean up the sites. Because of the difficulties these contractors have had in obtaining insurance, EPA is authorized to "hold them harmless" from liability. These costs of indemnification are response costs under the act.

The issue of compensation to individuals that was the subject of the 301(e) Study Group continued to receive a great deal of attention during the congressional deliberations on reauthorization. Proposals to incorporate a federal cause of action for personal injury and property damage in the Reauthorization Act were defeated. As a compromise, however, SARA does include a provision preempting state statutes of limitation applicable to personal injury and property damage actions due to exposure to hazardous substances. As described, the federal standard requires that the commencement date for determining the period within which actions must be brought be the date the plaintiff knew or reasonably should have known (date of discovery) of the causal connection between harm and exposure to the hazardous substance. This provision overrides statutes in some states that measure the limitation period from the date of exposure or injury, which can be much earlier in time. This provision is likely to revive a substantial number of cases in these states.

It is also possible that EPA cleanup deadlines and the provision in the Health Related Authorities section will cause an increase in lawsuits. The mere study of health at actual sites is bound to make the public more aware of personal injury and property damage. If there are actual findings of adverse effects, the number of suits will increase even more.

Another section of SARA that is likely to have the same effect is titled Community Right-to-Know. This contains elaborate provisions requiring facilities to notify local authorities of the existence of hazardous substances and releases, who will, in turn, notify the public.

The problems involving insurability under CERCLA led Congress, in enacting SARA, to authorize the establishment of risk retention groups for pollution liability. The regulatory criteria embodied in the more generally applicable Rick Retention Act Amendments of 1986 are made specifically applicable to the risk retention groups authorized under SARA.

New financial responsibility requirements will be established with respect to leaking underground storage tanks. They will cover exposure to liability from both bodily injury and property damage. The required amounts of financial responsibility are to be determined through EPA rule making, but the act does specify a minimum coverage of $1 million per occurrence for tanks containing petroleum. The EPA is authorized to suspend the requirements if financial responsibility mechanisms prove to be unavailable. The General Accounting Office (GAO) is directed to conduct a study of the availability of pollution insurance for owners and operators of petroleum storage and distribution facilities. The study is to be completed within fifteen months after date of enactment of SARA.

SARA also directs the GAO to conduct a study of the insurability of Superfund exposures. The study is to be completed in the fall of 1987. As of this writing, GAO is in the middle of the project and is interviewing insurers and others to determine the reasons for the difficulties in insuring these exposures.

Other Legislation

In addition to the preceding acts, the Clean Air Act and Clean Water Act, among others, establish standards, fines, and penalties that apply within certain jurisdictions. The possibility of criminal liability may exist. For example, the Clean Air Act presents the possibility of criminal liability for "any responsible corporate officer" of a firm that violates the statute or an administrative order issued by the federal government relative to the act (42 U.S.C. Section 7413(c) of the Clean Air Act). The Clean Water Act was amended in 1987 to provide $18 million in funds for the construction of sewage treatment facilities and $2 million for the cleaning up of waterways in the United States.

The Motor Carrier Act of 1980 (as amended in 1985) deals with the transportation of hazardous substances. The law breaks down these substances into two groups. The first refers to "defined" hazardous substances and requires truckers hauling such substances to carry $5 million of liability insurance. The second group includes "nondefined" hazardous substances and requires that truckers carrying such substances carry $1 million of liability insurance.

Individual states can, of course, enact their own environmental legislation, which may be more stringent than that of the federal government (such legislation cannot require less than the federal requirements). Minnesota enacted its Environmental Response and Liability Act of 1983, which established a $5 million Superfund for cleaning up waste sites and property damage. The strict provisions in this act, which were cause for concern for the insurance industry, may result in some reduction in pollution liability insurance capacity for Minnesota pollution risks. Massachusetts has recently increased its own financial responsibility requirements, which include coverage for intangible property damage and a possible pyramiding or stacking of limits of liability when companies certify financial responsibility under the Massachusetts Act.

It is apparent that as time goes on, more states will enact their own special laws, perhaps making it increasingly difficult for the insurance industry to continue to provide a market for pollution liability insurance. The end result of some of the federal proposals may have a similar effect.

V. RISK MANAGEMENT

"Risk management refers to the functions of identification, measurement, and control of pure risks whether insurable or uninsurable."[42]

Identification and Measurement of Exposures

The first step in the risk management process is to identify a firm's pollution exposures (see Exhibit 9-3). One useful approach is to track the flow of chemicals that a firm uses through the various storage, processing, and disposal stages (see Exhibit 9-2). It is important to keep in mind that in order to treat an exposure, it must first be identified. No two firms are likely to have identical pollution exposures.

In order to conduct an effective and systematic assessment of a firm's pollution exposures, someone in the firm should be familiar with the environmental regulations that apply to that firm. At the same time, someone with an engineering or environmental background who understands the manufacturing operation should be involved with the assessment effort. If the resources are not available internally, it may be necessary to secure assistance from a firm or insurance company that specializes in providing risk assessment/site evaluation services or environmental audit services. If a firm fails to understand, implement, or comply with environmental regulations, it may subject itself to fines and criminal actions as well as set the stage for pollution liability losses.

The objectives of [an] assessment are to identify potential risks, to evaluate such risks, and to take steps to control, reduce, or eliminate identified risks.

Factors to be considered in [an] assessment include:

- Potentially hazardous characteristics of raw materials, products, by-products, and wastes
- Storage, transportation, and disposal of toxic and hazardous substances and waste materials
- Current practices in engineering design, facility operation, management, employee training, maintenance of pollution controls
- Pathways of exposure, and local geology, hydrology and meteorology
- Population along potential pathways of exposure, including high risk groups such as the elderly and infants
- Complaints and claims made
- The potential for interruption of, or damage to, property [nearby], such as other businesses and industry, transportation facilities, farms, recreational facilities, and water supplies

Exhibit 9-3
Risk Management Decision-Making Flow Chart*

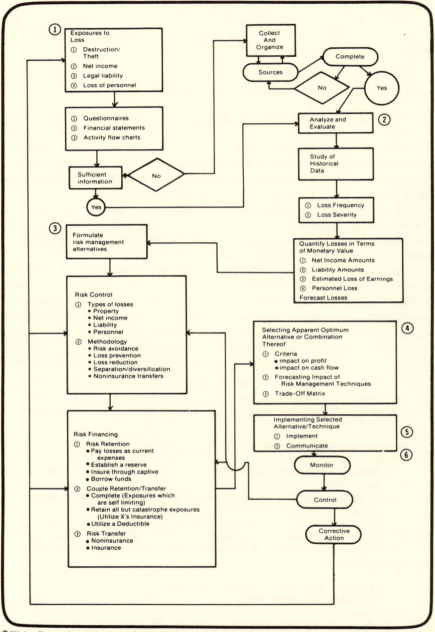

*This flow chart is based partially upon the format of a flow chart developed by Bindranath Maharajh, Balmain Village, Trinidad.

- The probability of sudden or non-sudden release of hazardous or toxic substances[43]

When a firm performs a pollution assessment, it should recognize that pollution exposure may exist in one or more of the following areas:

- Destruction of tangible property
- Loss of net income through decreased revenues or increased expenses resulting from an accidental event
- Legal liability to others (including employees)
- Loss of services of key personnel

For example, pollution may contaminate the firm's own drinking water or water that is needed in a pure state for certain manufacturing processes. Of course, pollution may physically corrode or otherwise impair the use of tangible property. With respect to the potential for loss of net income, a firm found to be operating with a high level of contaminants in the air could be forced to close down by the state of local EPA or health department. Significant expenses could be incurred in the cleanup of contaminated property.

Occupational disease is a significant problem in the workplace; employers with a pollution problem could end up with a substantial workers compensation insurance price tag and lose some of their most productive workforce at the same time. Firms should also consider the possibility of losing the services of key personnel due to disease, disability, or death resulting from pollutants, contaminants, or irritants.

One article pointed out that risk assessments are on the upswing:

The consultants disagree about the reasons for the upswing, but among those cited are tougher enforcement of federal laws by the Environmental Protection Agency and growing worries among corporate managers about the threat of pollution lawsuits.... Normally, consultants base their assessments on information from the company's own records and the records of its outside waste disposal firm, as well as on plant inspections and interviews in which the consultants review plant conditions, waste disposal practices, geological conditions, and other factors.

Most risk assessments don't include such technical procedures as soil sampling or groundwater monitoring, though in some cases consultants might suggest that these be done.

Several consultants also differentiate between a risk assessment and an "environmental audit," a more comprehensive review that could include checks of a company's compliance with federal, state and local pollution laws and the setting up of ongoing, environmental review procedures within the company.[44]

Alternatives

The following risk management alternatives exist for the pollution exposure:

- *Risk Control*
    1. *Risk avoidance*—the manufacturing process could be modified to eliminate the use of certain toxic substances.
    2. *Loss prevention*—develop a "closed" processing system where the toxic by-products are continually recycled.
    3. *Loss reduction*—substitute less toxic chemicals.
    4. *Separation/diversification*—separate highly active (volatile) toxic substances from other substances. Arrange for special handling and disposal.
    5. *Noninsurance transfers*—arrange for someone else to conduct the process.
- *Risk Financing*
    1. *Retention*—retain a part of the exposure. An example would be for a firm to utilize a deductible approach. The risk could retain all but catastrophe losses. Due to the catastrophic potential of pollution liability and the astronomical legal defense costs that could be involved, the pollution exposure should *not* be retained in its entirety.
    2. *Couple retention with transfer*—retain part of the risk through a deductible approach and transfer the remainder of the exposure to an insurance company. Of course, in some instances a noninsurance transfer might be appropriate (for example, a hold-harmless agreement could be used instead of insurance to transfer a part or all of the exposure to a third party).
    3. *Risk transfer*—transfer the entire pollution exposure to an insurance company. Again, as in (2) above, the appropriateness of a noninsurance transfer could be considered, such as hold-harmless agreements.

As mentioned, it is imperative that any hazardous waste disposal firm the company decides to use be evaluated very closely. An effort should be made to require the disposal firm to agree to effect a hold-harmless agreement in favor of the generator or manufacturer. This agreement should be backed up with appropriate pollution liability contractual insurance, and the generator should obtain a certificate of insurance identifying the hold-harmless agreement and the contractual coverage. The disposal firm's pollution liability policy should be scrutinized carefully to make certain that it provides adequate coverage as well as high enough limits of liability. Whether the policy is written on an occurrence or a claims-made basis is also important. The generator should also request to be named as an additional insured on the disposal firm's pollution policy. Likewise, manifests and shipping records should be carefully maintained. Careful documentation may provide the critical ingredient in successfully defending a pollution liability lawsuit at a later date.

It is essential that firms review their loss control programs, potential liabilities, and the environmental laws that govern their operation relative to pollution. One writer warns of the potential legal and financial liabilities if firms do not do so. Although senior management and corporate counsel think that their current operations and precautions are adequate, discussions and surveys tend to indicate otherwise. This writer argues that the lack of knowledge of senior management with regard to such areas as "disposal site monitoring, data collection and management, insurance coverage and the handling of contingent liabilities on financial statements," gives support to the argument that senior management does not really understand all of the risks involved and that hazardous waste control programs and policies need to be reviewed.[45]

VI. POLLUTION LIABILITY INSURANCE

Coverage

General liability policies were written on an "accident" basis prior to 1966. This meant that coverage was intended only for events that were sudden and accidental in nature. When the Insurance Rating Board revised the general liability policy in 1966, it included coverage on an "occurrence" basis.

> By definition, occurrence includes both sudden and prolonged exposure to conditions that ultimately result in bodily injury or property damage that is neither expected nor intended from the standpoint of the insured. Many [insurers] were satisfied that the wording was sufficiently clear to rule out cases involving intentionally caused injury or damage. But there were times when insureds successfully argued that, while their *acts* may have been intentional, they did not expect or intend the resultant *damages.* As the national concern over environmental pollution heightened, ultimately bringing about a number of new laws, insurers soon realized that the occurrence provision could very possibly subject them to claims for virtually every pollution or contamination incident. At the very least, insurers would sustain heavy expenditures in providing defense coverage. It therefore was decided that a change in policy provisions was needed.[46]

In 1970 two pollution exclusion endorsements were also introduced by the Insurance Services Office (ISO), formerly known as the Insurance Rating Bureau (IRB). One endorsement involved an absolute exclusion relative to oil pollution. The use of this endorsement was triggered by certain rating classifications appearing on a general liability policy. The other exclusion addressed all other pollution except oil pollution. This exclusion served to exclude "bodily injury or property damage arising out of any contamination or pollution into or upon land, the atmosphere, or any body of water—except when the discharge, dispersal, release, or escape is sudden and accidental."[47]

The pollution exclusion was made an integral provision of the 1973 revision of the comprehensive general liability policy. The exclusion is stated as follows:

(f) to **bodily injury** or **property damage** arising out of the discharge, dispersal, release or escape of smoke, vapors, soot, fumes, acids, alkalis, toxic chemicals, liquids or gases, waste materials or other irritants, contaminants or pollutants into or upon land, the atmosphere or any water course or body of water; but this exclusion does not apply if such discharge, dispersal, release or escape is sudden and accidental.[48]

The intent is to exclude gradual pollution. In order for coverage to exist, the *intent* is that the discharge, dispersal, release, or escape of the pollutants, contaminants, or irritants must be both sudden *and* accidental. The exclusion has not been completely successful in its intent. More will be said about this in the section "Future."

Of course, the introduction of such an exclusion opened the way for firms to offer gradual pollution coverage to fill the gap. This coverage is usually only offered on a claims-made basis. Wohlreich & Anderson, Ltd. led the way in the mid 1970s and was followed by Shand, Morahan; Stewart Smith Mid America, Inc.; Swett & Crawford; and AIG in the early 1980s. The Insurance Services Office (ISO) introduced its pollution liability policy in the latter half of 1981, the effective date of the EPA financial responsibility regulations.[49]

The Marketplace

Until August 1981, whatever limited market for pollution liability insurance that existed involved primarily excess and surplus lines insurers. The insurance industry worked with the federal government to develop financial responsibility standards that would be reasonable, thereby enabling a domestic primary market for pollution liability insurance to develop. It was with this objective in mind that the insurance industry requested ISO to develop an industry pollution liability policy. The market, however, has been slow to develop.

Several of the major domestic primary writers, such as The

Hartford Insurance Group, The Aetna Casualty and Surety Company, and The Travelers originally opted to become a market for pollution liability insurance. Some of these companies, such as The Hartford and The Travelers, developed their own policy forms instead of using the ISO forms. The motivation for becoming involved in this marketplace in many instances turned on the insurers' need to protect their commercial and industrial accounts for which a pollution liability insurance policy would become part of an overall insurance program.

Surplus lines insurers were also a market for pollution coverage. They were an especially important market for standalone pollution requests (that is, where companion insurance business is not included in the offering).

The Pollution Liability Insurance Association (PLIA) was formed in 1982 as a pool to write pollution liability insurance for member companies. Approximately nineteen companies are members of PLIA and share premiums and losses on a predetermined basis. The London market was a key factor in the EIL insurance marketplace in one way or another. A number of these markets depended on the London market for their capacity. In addition, London developed its own form and wrote coverage itself. See Exhibit 9-4 for a sample of one pollution liability policy.

Beginning in 1984, the market for pollution liability insurance began to constrict. The overall crunch in liability insurance and in the reinsurance markets also affected the pollution liability insurance. A number of markets (of the few that were offering coverage) stopped writing EIL insurance, often citing lack of reinsurance as a reason. Other markets became more restrictive in terms of coverage, limits of liability offered, and premiums charged. This trend continued to the point where the market for EIL coverage as of this writing consists of PLIA and one domestic primary insurer. An additional market is beginning to develop, although it is too early to tell what impact it might have.

As mentioned, SARA specifically authorized risk retention groups for the purpose of insuring the pollution liability exposure. A few such groups are being organized as of this writing. Alexander & Alexander is organizing a risk retention group called EPIC that is intended for middle-sized environmental impairment liability risks that are either sudden or gradual in nature. The policy will be written on a claims-made basis, with no prior acts coverage. EPIC will exclude Superfund sites from the program. Johnson & Higgins is also organizing a risk retention group for the EIL exposure. Additionally, Planning Corporation of Reston, Virginia is attempting to organize a risk retention group for service station risks.[50]

One difficulty experienced by insurers in this marketplace has been

Exhibit 9-4
Pollution Liability Coverage Form (Designated Sites)

Various provisions in this policy restrict coverage. Read the entire policy carefully to determine rights, duties and what is and is not covered.

Throughout this policy the words "you" and "your" refer to the Named Insured shown in the Declarations. The words "we," "us" and "our" refer to the Company providing this insurance.

The word "insured" means any person or organization qualifying as such under SECTION II -- WHO IS AN INSURED.

Other words and phrases that appear in quotation marks have special meaning. Refer to SECTION VI -- DEFINITIONS.

SECTION I - POLLUTION LIABILITY COVERAGE

1. **Insuring Agreement - Bodily Injury and Property Damage Liability**

    a. We will pay those sums that the insured becomes legally obligated to pay as compensatory damages because of "bodily injury" or "property damage" to which this insurance applies. We will have the right and duty to defend any "suit" seeking those damages. But:

        (1) The amount we will pay for damages is limited as described in SECTION III - LIMITS OF INSURANCE;

        (2) We may investigate and settle any claim or "suit" at our discretion; and

        (3) Our right and duty to defend end when we have used up the applicable limit of insurance in the payment of judgments, settlements or "clean-up costs."

    b. This insurance applies only to "bodily injury" and "property damage" caused by a "pollution incident" that commences on or after the Retroactive Date shown in the Declarations. The "pollution incident "must be from an "insured site" or "waste facility" in the "coverage territory."

        The insured's responsibility to pay damages because of the "bodily injury" or "property damage" must be determined in a "suit" on the merits in the "coverage territory" or in a settlement we agree to.

    c. This insurance applies to "bodily injury" and "property damage" only if a claim for damages because of the "bodily injury" or "property damage" is first made in writing against any insured during the policy period.

    (1) A claim by a person or organization seeking damages will be deemed to have been made when written notice of such claim is received by any insured or by us, whichever comes first.

    (2) All claims for damages because of "bodily injury" to the same person, including damages claimed by any person or organization for care, loss of services, or death resulting at any time from the "bodily injury," will be deemed to have been made at the time the first of those claims is made against any insured.

    (3) All claims for damages because of "property damage" causing loss to the same person or organization as a result of a "pollution incident" will be deemed to have been made at the time the first of those claims is made against any insured.

2. **Insuring Agreement** - Reimbursement of Mandated Off-Site "Clean-up Costs."

    a. We will pay for "clean-up costs" that the insured becomes legally obligated to pay because of "environmental damage" to which this insurance applies. The amount we will pay for such "clean-up costs" is limited as described in Section III - LIMITS OF INSURANCE.

    b. This insurance applies only to "environmental damage" caused by a "pollution incident" that commences on or after the Retroactive Date shown in the Declarations. The "pollution incident" must be from an "insured site" or "waste facility" in the "coverage territory."

        The insured's obligation to pay "clean-up costs" because of the "environmental damage" must be asserted under statutory authority of the government of the United States of America, Canada or any political subdivision of the United States or Canada. Notice asserting such obligation must be first received by you during the policy period.

        We have the right but not the duty to investigate, settle, contest or appeal, at our expense, any obligation asserted against an insured to pay "clean-up costs."

3. No other obligation or liability to pay sums or perform acts or services is covered unless explicitly provided for under SUPPLEMENTARY PAYMENTS.

continued on next page

4. Exclusions.

This insurance does not apply to:

a. "Bodily injury," "property damage" or "environmental damage" caused or contributed to by any "pollution incident" that commenced prior to the Retroactive Date shown in the Declarations.

b. "Bodily injury," "property damage" or "environmental damage" expected or intended from the standpoint of the insured.

c. "Bodily injury," "property damage" or "environmental damage" for which the insured is obligated to pay damages by reason of the assumption of liability in a contract or agreement. This exclusion does not apply to liability for damages that the insured would have in the absence of the contract or agreement.

d. Any obligation of the insured under a workers compensation, disability benefits or unemployment compensation law or any similar law.

e. "Bodily injury" to:

(1) An employee of the insured arising out of and in the course of employment by the insured; or

(2) The spouse, child, parent, brother or sister of that employee as a consequence of (1) above.

This exclusion applies:

(1) Whether the insured may be liable as an employer or in any other capacity; and

(2) To any obligation to share damages with or repay someone else who must pay damages because of the injury.

f. "Property damage" or "environmental damage" to:

(1) A "waste facility;"

(2) Property you own, rent, or occupy;

(3) Premises you sell, give away or abandon, if the "property damage" or "environmental damage" arises out of any part of those premises;

(4) Property loaned to you; or

(5) Personal property in your care, custody or control.

g. "Clean-up costs" or any other expense incurred by you or others to test for, monitor, clean-up, remove, contain, treat, detoxify or neutralize pollutants on or at:

(1) A "waste facility;" or

(2) Premises you own, rent or occupy;

or to any recovery claimed for such cost or expense.

h. "Bodily injury," "property damage" or "environmental damage" included within the "products-completed operations hazard" and arising out of an emission, discharge, release or escape which originates away from any "insured site."

i. "Bodily injury," "property damage" or "environmental damage" arising out of the ownership or operation of any offshore facility as defined in the Outer Continental Shelf Lands Act Amendment of 1978 or the Clean Water Act of 1977 as amended 1978 or any deepwater port as defined in the Deepwater Port Act of 1974 as amended or as may be amended.

j. "Bodily injury," "property damage" or "environmental damage" arising out of a "pollution incident" from an "insured site" or any part of an "insured site" that was used by you for the storage, disposal, processing or treatment of waste materials and was:

(1) Sealed off, closed, abandoned or alienated prior to the Retroactive Date shown in the Declarations of this Coverage Part; or

(2) Sealed off or closed subject to statute, ordinance or governmental regulation or directive requiring maintenance or monitoring during or after sealing off or closure.

k. "Bodily injury," "property damage" or "environmental damage" arising out of the ownership, maintenance, use or entrustment to others of any aircraft, "auto," rolling stock or watercraft owned and operated by or rented or loaned to any insured. Use includes operation and "loading or unloading."

This exclusion does not apply to:

(1) Parking an "auto" on, or on the ways next to, premises you own or rent, provided the "auto" is not owned by or rented or loaned to you or the insured; or

(2) "Bodily injury" or "property damage" arising out of the operation of any of the equipment listed in paragraph f. (2) or f. (3) of the definition of "mobile equipment" (Section VI.8).

l. "Bodily injury," "property damage" or "environmental damage" arising out of the emission, discharge, release or escape of drilling fluid, oil, gas or other fluids from any oil, gas, mineral, water or geothermal well.

continued on next page

m. "Bodily injury," "property damage" or "environmental damage" arising out of a "pollution incident" which results from or is directly or indirectly attributable to failure to comply with any applicable statute, regulation, ordinance, directive or order relating to the protection of the environment and promulgated by any governmental body, provided that failure to comply is a willful or deliberate act or omission of:

(1) The insured; or

(2) You or any of your members, partners or executive officers.

n. "Bodily injury," "property damage" or "environmental damage" arising out of acid rain.

SUPPLEMENTARY PAYMENTS

We will pay, with respect to any claim or "suit" we defend:

1. All expenses we incur.

2. All reasonable expenses incurred by the insured at our request to assist us in the investigation or defense of the claim or "suit," including actual loss of earnings up to $100 a day because of time off from work.

3. All costs taxed against the insured in the "suit."

4. Pre-judgment interest awarded against the insured on that part of the judgment we pay. If we make an offer to pay the applicable limit of insurance, we will not pay any pre-judgment interest based on that period of time after the offer.

5. All interest on the full amount of any judgment that accrues after entry of the judgment and before we have paid, offered to pay, or deposited in court the part of the judgment that is within the applicable limit of insurance.

6. Expenses incurred by the insured for first aid to others at the time of any accident, for "bodily injury" to which this insurance applies.

These payments will not reduce the limits of insurance.

SECTION II - WHO IS AN INSURED

1. If you are designated in the Declarations as:

a. An individual, you and your spouse are insureds, but only with respect to the conduct of a business of which you are the sole owner.

b. A partnership or joint venture, you are an insured. Your members and your partners and their spouses are also insureds, but only with respect to the conduct of your business.

c. An organization other than a partnership or joint venture, you are an insured. Your executive officers and directors are insureds, but only with respect to their duties as your officers or directors. Your stockholders are also insureds, but only with respect to their liability as stockholders.

2. Each of the following is also an insured:

a. Your employees, other than your executive officers, but only for acts within the scope of their employment by you. However, none of these employees is an insured for:

(1) "Bodily injury" to you or to a co-employee while in the course of his or her employment.

(2) "Property damage" or "environmental damage" to property owned or occupied by or rented or loaned to that employee, any of your other employees or any of your partners or members (if you are a partnership or joint venture).

b. Any person or organization having proper temporary custody of your property if you die, but only:

(1) With respect to liability arising out of the maintenance or use of that property; and

(2) Until your legal representative has been appointed.

c. Your legal representative if you die, but only with respect to duties as such. That representative will have all your rights and duties under this Coverage Part.

3. Any organization you newly acquire or form, other than a partnership or joint venture, and over which you maintain ownership or majority interest, will be deemed to be a Named Insured if there is no other similar insurance available to that organization. However:

a. Coverage under this provision is afforded only until the 90th day after you acquire or form the organization or the end of the policy period, whichever is earlier; and

b. Coverage does not apply to "bodily injury," "property damage" or "environmental damage" that occurred before you acquired or formed the organization.

No person or organization is an insured with respect to the conduct of any current or past partnership or joint venture that is not shown as a Named Insured in the Declarations.

SECTION III - LIMITS OF INSURANCE

1. The Limits of Insurance shown in the Declarations and the rules below fix the most we will pay regardless of the number of:

a. Insureds;

b. Claims made or "suits" brought;

c. Persons or organizations making claims or bringing "suits;" or

continued on next page

d. Governmental actions taken with respect to "clean-up costs."

2. The Aggregate Limit is the most we will pay for the sum of:

   a. All damages because of all "bodily injury" and "property damage;" and

   b. All "clean-up costs" incurred because of all "environmental damage."

3. Subject to the Aggregate Limit above, the most we will pay in any one "pollution incident" for the sum of:

   a. All damages because of all "bodily injury" and "property damage;" and

   b. All "clean-up costs" incurred because of all "environmental damage;"

   will be the lesser of:

   (1) The Each "Pollution Incident" Limit, reduced by the deductible amount, if any, shown in the Declarations; or

   (2) The sum of those damages and "clean-up costs" minus any such deductible amount.

We may, or will if required by law, pay part or all of any deductible amount, if applicable, to effect settlement of any claim or "suit." Upon notice of our payment of a deductible amount you shall promptly reimburse us for the part of the deductible amount we paid.

The limits of this Coverage Part apply separately to each consecutive annual period and to any remaining period of less than 12 months, starting with the beginning of the policy period shown in the Declarations, unless the policy period is extended after issuance for an additional period of less than 12 months. In that case, the additional period will be deemed part of the last preceding period for purposes of determining the Limits of Insurance.

SECTION IV - POLLUTION LIABILITY CONDITIONS

1. Bankruptcy.

Bankruptcy or insolvency of the insured or of the insured's estate will not relieve us of our obligations under this Coverage Part.

2. Duties In The Event Of A Pollution Incident, Claim Or Suit.

a. You must see to it that we are notified promptly of a "pollution incident" which may result in a claim or any action or proceeding to impose an obligation on the insured for "clean-up costs." Notice should include:

   (1) How, when and where the "pollution incident" took place; and

   (2) The names and addresses of any injured persons and witnesses.

Notice of a "pollution incident" is not notice of a claim.

b. If a claim is made or "suit" is brought against any insured or if an action is initiated, you must see to it that we receive prompt written notice of the claim or "suit" or notice of action.

c. You and any other involved insured must:

   (1) Immediately send us copies of any demands, notices, summonses or legal papers received in connection with the claim or "suit;"

   (2) Authorize us to obtain records and other information;

   (3) Cooperate with us in the investigation, settlement or defense of the claim or "suit;" and

   (4) Assist us, upon our request, in the enforcement of any right against any person or organization which may be liable to the insured because of injury or damage to which this insurance may also apply.

d. No insureds will, except at their own cost, voluntarily make a payment, assume any obligation, or incur any expense, other than for first aid, without our consent.

3. Legal Action Against Us.

No person or organization has a right under this Coverage Part:

a. To join us as a party or otherwise bring us into a "suit" asking for damages from an insured; or

b. To sue us on this Coverage Part unless all of its terms have been fully complied with.

A person or organization may sue us to recover on an agreed settlement or on a final judgment against an insured obtained after an actual trial; but we will not be liable for damages that are not payable under the terms of this Coverage Part or that are in excess of the applicable limit of insurance. An agreed settlement means a settlement and release of liability signed by us, the insured and the claimant or the claimant's legal representative.

4. Other Insurance.

If other valid and collectible insurance is available to the insured for a loss we cover under this Coverage Part our obligations are limited as follows:

continued on next page

a. Primary Insurance

This insurance is primary except when b. below applies. When this insurance is primary our obligations are not affected unless any of the other insurance is also primary. Then, we will share with all that other insurance by the method described in c. below:

b. Excess Insurance

This insurance is excess over any of the other insurance, whether primary, excess, contingent or on any other basis:

(1) That is effective prior to the beginning of the policy period shown in the Declarations of this insurance and applies to "bodily injury" or "property damage" on other than a claims-made basis, if:

    (a) No Retroactive Date is shown in the Declarations of this insurance; or

    (b) The other insurance has a policy period which continues after the Retroactive Date shown in the Declarations of this insurance.

(2) If the loss arises out of the maintenance or use of aircraft, "autos" or watercraft to the extent not subject to Exclusion k.

When this insurance is excess, we will have no duty under Section I. to defend any claim or "suit" that any other insurer has a duty to defend. If no other insurer defends, we will undertake to do so, but we will be entitled to the insured's rights against all those other insurers.

When this insurance is excess over other insurance, we will pay only our share of the amount of the loss, if any, that exceeds the sum of:

    (a) The total amount that all such other insurance would pay for the loss in the absence of this insurance; and

    (b) The total of all deductible and self-insured amounts under all that other insurance.

    We will share the remaining loss, if any, with any other insurance that is not described in this Excess Insurance provision and was not bought specifically to apply in excess of the Limits of Insurance shown in the Declarations of this Coverage Part.

c. Method of Sharing

If all of the other insurance permits contribution by equal shares, we will follow this method also. Under this approach each insurer contributes equal amounts until it has paid its applicable limit of insurance or none of the loss remains, whichever comes first.

If any of the other insurance does not permit contribution by equal shares, we will contribute by limits. Under this method, each insurer's share is based on the ratio of its applicable limit of insurance to the total applicable limits of insurance of all insurers.

5. Premium Audit.

a. We will compute all premiums for this Coverage Part in accordance with our rules and rates.

b. Premium shown in this Coverage Part as advance premium is a deposit premium only. At the close of each audit period we will compute the earned premium for that period. Audit premiums are due and payable on notice to the first Named Insured. If the sum of the advance and audit premiums paid for the policy term is greater than the earned premium, we will return the excess to the first Named Insured.

c. The first Named Insured must keep records of the information we need for premium computation, and send us copies at such times as we may request.

6. Representations.

By accepting this policy, you agree:

a. The statements in the Declarations are accurate and complete;

b. Those statements are based upon representations you made to us; and

c. We have issued this policy in reliance upon your representations.

7. Separation Of Insureds.

Except with respect to the Limits of Insurance, and any rights or duties specifically assigned to the first Named Insured, this insurance applies:

a. As if each Named Insured were the only Named Insured; and

b. Separately to each insured against whom claim is made or "suit" is brought.

8. Transfer Of Rights Of Recovery Against Others To Us.

If the insured has rights to recover all or part of any payment we have made under this Coverage Part, those rights are transferred to us. The insured must do nothing after loss to impair them. At our request, the insured will bring "suit" or transfer those rights to us and help us enforce them.

9. Coverage Form Issued To Comply With Law Or Regulation.

If this policy is issued to comply with any law or regulation which requires notice of cancellation to any governmental body, cancellation may not be effected until the required notice has been provided by you or us.

continued on next page

SECTION V - EXTENDED REPORTING PERIOD OPTION

1. This Section applies only if:

    a. We cancel or non-renew this Coverage Part for any reason except non-payment of the premium; or

    b. We renew or replace this Coverage Part with other Pollution Liability insurance that:

    (1) Provides claims-made coverage for Bodily Injury and Property Damage Liability; and

    (2) Has a Retroactive Date later than the one shown in this Coverage Part's Declarations.

2. If we provide the Extended Reporting Period Endorsement, the following is added as part (4) of paragraph 1.c. SECTION I - POLLUTION LIABILITY COVERAGE:

    A claim first made within one year after the end of the policy period will be deemed to have been made on the last day of the policy period, provided that the claim is for damages because of "bodily injury" or "property damage" that occurred before the end of the policy period.

    The Extended Reporting Period Endorsement will not reinstate or increase the Limits of Insurance or extend the policy period.

3. We will issue this Endorsement if the first Named Insured shown in the Declarations:

    a. Makes a written request for it which we receive within 30 days after the end of the policy period; and

    b. Promptly pays the additional premium when due.

    The Extended Reporting Period Endorsement will not take effect unless the additional premium is paid when due. If that premium is paid when due, the Endorsement may not be cancelled.

    The Extended Reporting Period Endorsement will also amend paragraph 4.b. of SECTION IV - POLLUTION LIABILITY CONDITIONS (Other Insurance) so the insurance provided will be excess over any other valid and collectible insurance available to the insured, whether primary, excess, contingent or on any other basis, whose policy period begins or continues after the Endorsement takes effect.

4. We will determine the actual premium for the Extended Reporting Period Endorsement in accordance with our rules and rates. In doing so, we may take into account the following:

    a. The exposures insured;

    b. Previous types and amounts of insurance;

    c. Limits of Insurance available under this Coverage Part for future payment of damages; and

    d. Other related factors.

    The premium for the Extended Reporting Period Endorsement will not exceed 50% of the annual premium for this Coverage Part and will be fully earned when the Endorsement takes effect.

5. If we fail to offer to renew this Coverage Part at the same rates or with the same form, that will not constitute cancellation or non-renewal by us.

SECTION VI - DEFINITIONS

1. "Auto" means a land motor vehicle, trailer or semitrailer designed for travel on public roads, including any attached machinery or equipment. But "auto" does not include "mobile equipment."

2. "Bodily injury" means bodily injury, sickness or disease sustained by a person, including death resulting from any of these at any time.

3. "Clean-up costs" means expenses for the removal or neutralization of contaminants, irritants or pollutants.

4. "Coverage territory" means the United States of America (including its territories and possessions), Puerto Rico and Canada.

5. "Environmental damage" means the injurious presence in or upon land, the atmosphere, or any watercourse or body of water of solid, liquid, gaseous or thermal contaminants, irritants or pollutants.

6. "Insured site" means the specific location specified in the Declarations.

7. "Loading or unloading" means the handling of property:

    a. After it is moved from the place where it is accepted for movement into or onto an aircraft, rolling stock, watercraft or "auto;"

    b. While it is in or on an aircraft, rolling stock, watercraft or "auto;" or

    c. While it is being moved from an aircraft, rolling stock, watercraft or "auto" to the place where it is finally delivered;

    but "loading or unloading" does not include the movement of property by means of a mechanical device, other than a hand truck, that is not attached to the aircraft, rolling stock, watercraft or "auto."

8. "Mobile equipment" means any of the following types of land vehicles, including any attached machinery or equipment:

    a. Bulldozers, farm machinery, forklifts and other vehicles designed for use principally off public roads;

    b. Vehicles maintained for use solely on or next to premises you own or rent;

c. Vehicles that travel on crawler treads:

d. Vehicles, whether self-propelled or not, maintained primarily to provide mobility to permanently mounted:

(1) Power cranes, shovels, loaders, diggers or drills; or

(2) Road construction or resurfacing equipment such as graders, scrapers or rollers;

e. Vehicles not described in a.,b.,c. or d. above that are not self-propelled and are maintained primarily to provide mobility to permanently attached equipment of the following types:

(1) Air compressors, pumps and generators, including spraying, welding, building cleaning, geophysical exploration, lighting and well servicing equipment; or

(2) Cherry pickers and similar devices used to raise or lower workers.

f. Vehicles not described in a.,b.,c. or d. above maintained primarily for purposes other than the transportation of persons or cargo.

However, self-propelled vehicles within the following types of permanently attached equipment are not "mobile equipment" but will be considered "autos:"

(1) Equipment designed primarily for:

(a) Snow removal;

(b) Road maintenance, but not construction or resurfacing;

(c) Street cleaning;

(2) Cherry pickers and similar devices mounted on automobile or truck chassis and used to raise or lower workers; and

(3) Air compressors, pumps and generators, including spraying, welding, building cleaning, geophysical exploration, lighting and well servicing equipment.

9. "Pollution incident" means emission, discharge, release or escape of pollutants into or upon land, the atmosphere, or any watercourse or body of water, provided that such emission, discharge. release, or escape results in "environmental damage." The entirety of any such emission, discharge, release, or escape shall be deemed to be one "pollution incident."

Pollutants means any solid, liquid, gaseous or thermal irritant or contaminant, including smoke, vapor, soot, fumes, acids, alkalis, chemicals and waste. Waste includes materials to be recycled, reconditioned or reclaimed.

10.a. "Products-completed operations hazard" includes all "bodily injury," "property damage" and "environmental damage" occurring away from premises you own or rent and arising out of "your product" or "your work" except:

(1) Products that are still in your physical possession; or

(2) Work that has not yet been completed or abandoned.

b. "Your work" will be deemed completed at the earliest of the following times:

(1) When all of the work called for in your contract has been completed.

(2) When all of the work to be done at the site has been completed if your contract calls for work at more than one site.

(3) When that part of the work done at a job site has been put to its intended use by any person or organization other than another contractor or subcontractor working on the same project.

Work that may need service, maintenance, correction, repair or replacement, but which is otherwise complete, will be treated as completed.

c. This hazard does not include "bodily injury," "property damage" or "environmental damage" arising out of:

(1) The transportation of property, unless the injury or damage arises out of a condition in or on a vehicle created by the "loading or unloading" of it;

(2) The existence of tools, uninstalled equipment or abandoned or unused materials.

11. "Property damage" means:

a. Physical injury to, destruction of, or contamination of tangible property, including all resulting loss of use of that property; or

b. Loss of use of tangible property that is not physically injured, destroyed or contaminated but has been evacuated, withdrawn from use or rendered inaccessible because of a "pollution incident."

12. "Suit" means a civil proceeding in which damages because of "bodily injury" or "property damage" to which this insurance applies are alleged. "Suit" includes an arbitration proceeding alleging such damages to which you must submit or submit with our consent.

13. "Waste facility" means any site to which waste from the operations of an "insured site" is legally consigned for delivery or delivered for storage, disposal, processing or treatment, provided that such site:

a. Is licensed by state or federal authority to perform such storage, disposal, processing or treatment; and

b. Is not and never was owned by, rented or loaned to you.

14. "Your product" means:

a. Any goods or products, other than real property, manufactured, sold, handled, distributed or disposed of by:

(1) You;

(2) Others trading under your name; or

(3) A person or organization whose business or assets you have acquired; and

b. Containers (other than vehicles), materials, parts or equipment furnished in connection with such goods or products.

"Your product" includes warranties or representations made at any time with respect to the fitness, quality, durability or performance of any of the items included in a. and b. above.

"Your product" does not include vending machines or other property rented to or located for the use of others but not sold.

15. "Your work" means:

a. Work or operations performed by you or on your behalf; and

b. Materials, parts or equipment furnished in connection with such work or operations.

"Your work" includes warranties or representations made at any time with respect to the fitness, quality, durability or performance of any of the items included in a. or b. above.

the lack of revenue, which is critical to sustaining and adding capacity. This situation can probably be attributed to a variety of reasons:

- The cost of coverage tends to be higher for pollution than for other coverages.
- The on-again/off-again implementation of many of the financial responsibility standards has confused people.
- Some risks may not be aware that they come under the law because of the complexity of federal and state regulations.
- Some risks fail to understand that even if they do not fall under pollution financial responsibility guidelines, they may still have a common-law exposure and therefore a need for the coverage.
- Because of the complexity of environmental laws, financial responsibility requirements, pollution exposures, coverages (there are many different forms in the marketplace), and different insurance company approaches and underwriting philosophy, producers and company personnel are not as comfortable with the subject as perhaps they are with other less complex insurance lines.
- Due to some of the court interpretations of the general liability policy's sudden and accidental pollution exclusion, some risks may feel they already have some elements of gradual pollution protection under their general liability policy.

Marketing Pollution Liability Insurance

From a producer's standpoint, the selling of pollution liability insurance makes sense because the coverage can be used as a door opener for new business as well as for various target marketing opportunities. It fits in nicely with the risk management approach to account handling, and because the coverage tends to be a higher priced insurance product, larger commissions are generated. And finally, but not least of all, is the need of producers to be concerned with enhancing their professionalism by selling the coverage and protecting themselves from errors and omissions (E&O) liability suits.

Producers who want to market this coverage and learn more about the subject should contact insurance companies they represent to determine answers to the following questions:

1. Does the insurer write pollution insurance?
2. Does the insurer provide any training materials or background material that may be of help to the producer or a client?
3. What underwriting information does the insurer require?
4. What does the insurer's underwriting program consist of:
   - types of risks desired,

- limits of liability available,
- coverage program requirements,
- commission payable, and
- deductible options?

5. What is the insurer's loss control capabilities in this area?
6. How are risk assessment/site evaluation fees handled?

Next, producers should review the insurer's policy form(s), paying particular attention to the following:

1. Retroactive coverage.
2. Extended reporting period (tail or discovery period) coverage.
3. Punitive damages.
4. *Pay on behalf of* versus *indemnification.*
5. Defense (included *within* or *in addition to* limits of liability).
6. Exclusions, for example, acid rain (and how is it defined), violation of environmental protection laws/regulations, offshore facilities/deep water ports, or Superfund sites.
7. Cleanup cost coverage.
8. Limits of liability available.
9. Sudden/accidental versus nonsudden/gradual coverage—are they both provided by one policy or must they be provided by separate policies and/or insurers? This could possibly create a coverage dispute.
10. Deductible *inclusive* or *exclusive* of policy limits).
11. Off-premises disposal site coverage.

Producers may find it useful to clip newspaper and periodical articles to build a file to convince clients of the need for coverage.

Producers should try to make the pollution exposure and its treatment part of their risk management approach to selling accounts. Options include the following:

1. Altering the manufacturing process (less toxic materials)
2. Substituting substances or processes
3. Contracting with others to handle hazardous phases of a process
4. Transferring part or all of the risk contractually
5. Recycling materials or altering storage and disposal practices
6. Changing the structure of the facility

Producers should also consider a few other important steps when dealing with clients and insurers:

1. A signed letter should be obtained from clients declining coverage if a proposal has been provided and declined.

2. Clients should not be advised as to whether they come under federal or state environmental laws or financial responsibility requirements. Otherwise, the producer may incur unnecessary errors and omissions liability.
3. Almost any client may be a "suspect" (a member of a market). The producer may want to target market environmental impairment liability insurance to risks that appear to be good "prospects" for coverage.
   - The risk should be discussed in advance with the underwriter to determine if the risk appears acceptable from an underwriting standpoint.
   - At the time the risk is being evaluated from a loss control standpoint for other lines of coverage, it could be evaluated from a pollution standpoint.
   - If the producer does not target market, he may end up with a risk for which pollution insurance cannot be placed.

Coverage Issues

Pollution liability policies differ significantly from one company to another. From a competitive standpoint and in terms of selecting the best coverage vehicle for a client, as well as from an errors and ommissions (E&O) standpoint, producers and risk managers need to be alert to these differences. Pollution liability policies covering gradual pollution are written on a claims-made basis.

One issue that should become less of a concern is that of having the sudden/accidental coverage provided by the comprehensive general liability policy and the gradual pollution coverage provided by a separate policy, possibly with a different insurer. The new commercial general liability policy introduced by ISO in 1986 contains what amounts to a total pollution exclusion, thus preventing it from being an alternative.

Other coverage issues involving claims-made pollution liability policies include the following:

- How much retroactive (*prior acts*) coverage is available and at what price? Most claims-made forms contain a retroactive date, meaning that the coverage will go back to, but not beyond, a certain date. This is a narrowing of coverage; other forms contain no retroactive date for coverage for pollution incidents first discovered and reported during the term of the policy.[51]
- If "tail" (*extended reporting period* or *discovery*) coverage is available, for what period, under what qualifications, and at what price? In some instances, the coverage is available only if

the insurer terminates the policy (at least one state insurance department has objected to this), whereas in other instances, the coverage is available regardless of which party terminates the policy. Usually the option can be elected by an insured only for a stipulated period following the termination of the policy— this "time period" varies among companies.

- Does the policy respond to "punitive damages?"
- Is defense coverage unlimited (in addition to policy limits) or is it limited in some manner? This is an important consideration due to the high cost of defending pollution liability suits.
- Is the policy written on a *pay-on-behalf-of* basis or on an *indemnification* basis? Aside from the obvious differences between coverage written on these two bases, one author noted that the obligation to defend is not always as clear under a policy written on an indemnification basis as compared to a policy that is written on a pay-on-behalf-of basis. Whether or not defense coverage is included within the limits of liability, is an important consideration and, therefore, the language regarding defense coverage should be closely examined.[52]
- What exclusions does the policy contain? Exclusions should be carefully examined since policies vary considerably in this area. Some forms exclude "acid rain" activities that violate environmental laws, and pollution involving deep water ports or offshore facilities. Other insurers control these exposures through underwriting and making their policies scheduled location policies. Some policies may contain a "Superfund" site exclusion that would preclude coverage for a risk if it becomes involved with a Superfund site.
- Does the policy afford limited reimbursement of on-site cleanup expenses? Some policies afford no such coverage.
- What are the limits of liability? Different companies, because of varying financial strength, general underwriting philosophy, and treaty reinsurance agreements, will make available differing limits of liability. The limits may also be stated in different terms.
- What deductibles are used? Most pollution coverage is written with a per claim or per occurrence deductible. The deductible amount can differ significantly and usually is a function of individual risk considerations and underwriting philosophy. The deductible may or may not impair the limits of liability.
- On what basis is coverage for off-premises disposal sites provided (that is, third party sites to which a risk would deliver or consign toxic waste for handling)? Such coverage may be provided on a blanket basis, a scheduled basis, or not at all.

Exhibit 9-5 shows how eleven primary pollution policies differed on ten issues at one point in time. Some insurers that afford sudden and gradual coverage under their pollution policy will attach an absolute pollution exclusion to the general liability policy if they also write this coverage for the same risk and if the general liability policy provides sudden pollution coverage. In effect, such an exclusion would eliminate all sudden and accidental coverage protection for a risk even for those sites not scheduled and covered specifically on the pollution liability policy. One approach that can be used is to attach an endorsement to the general liability policy that only excludes sudden and accidental coverage with respect to those specific locations insured under the pollution liability policy (see Exhibit 9-6).

Underwriting the Pollution Exposure

Information Needed Underwriters generally require a completed pollution application, although some insurers in the past have been willing to provide quotations based upon a company's annual report and a Securities and Exchange Commission's 10K report, subject to a loss control inspection or risk assessment report if the business is written. However, in light of some of the pollution losses that have developed, this practice is quickly disappearing.

Underwriters also need financial information concerning prospects for pollution insurance. A healthy financial posture is important in order to be certain funds will be available to (1) properly maintain the premises/facility, (2) support loss control recommendations, (3) pay premiums, and (4) fund deductibles.

A risk assessment will be needed and may be performed by the insurer's loss control department, or the risk will be requested to arrange directly with an outside firm to perform a risk assessment. A risk assessment is basically a "statement of health" or a snapshot of a firm's potential to cause sudden and gradual environmental impairment. Such an assessment will identify the following:

- Potential ways that pollutants can escape from the site
- The characteristics of the hazardous materials
- Populations affected
- Current practices from a handling, storage, transportation, and disposal standpoint and how these practices can be changed to minimize risk
- Environmental physical integrity of the locations involved

Pollution underwriters work very closely with their company's environmental science loss control personnel when evaluating a pollution submission. This is necessary because of the technical aspects of

Exhibit 9-5
How Eleven Primary Pollution Policies Differ on Ten Issues*

Coverage	ERAS	AIG	Shand, Morahan	Swett & Crawford	The Home	PLIA	Hartford	Travelers	Dryden	J.H. Blades[1]	Stewart Smith
Primary limits (Occurrence/aggregate)	$20 million/$40 million	$20 million/$20 million	$30 million/$60 million	$15 million/$15 million	$10 million/$20 million	$6 million/$6 million	$10 million/$10 million	$10 million/$10 million	$5 million/$10 million	$10 million/$20 million	$15 million/$30 million
Excess limits (Occurrence/aggregate)	None	None[2]	None[2]	$10 million/$10 million	$10 million/$20 million	None	None	None	$5 million/$10 million	None	$25 million/$50 million
Minimum deductible	$10,000	$5,000	$5,000	$5,000	$1,000	None	Varies	Varies	$5,000	Varies	NA
Allows self-insured retention?	Yes[3]	Yes[4]	No[2]	No[2]	Yes[4]	No	Yes[5]	No	Yes[6]	Yes[3]	Yes[7]
Cleanup on insured's property? (First-party)	No	No	No[2]	No	Yes	No	No	No[2]	No	No	Yes[8]
First-party cleanup to prevent third-party liability	Yes	No	No[2]	No[2]	Yes	Yes	Yes	No	No	Yes	Yes[8]
Defense costs included in policy limits?	Yes	Yes[2]	Yes[2]	No[9]	No[9]	No[9]	No[10]	Yes	Yes	Yes	Yes[2]
Retroactive date specified?	No	No	Yes	No	Yes	Yes	Yes	No	No	Yes	No
Covers on-site cleanup of Superfund sites?	No	No	No	No	Yes[11]	No	Yes[11]	Yes[11]	No	No	No
Covers third-party liability arising from Superfund sites?	No	No	Yes	Yes	Yes	Yes	Yes	Yes	No	Yes	No

[1]New policy; anticipated conditions listed. [2]Conditions may be changed subject to negotiation. [3]Minimum negotiated. [4]$5,000 minimum. [5]No minimum.
[6]$25,000 minimum. [7]$10,000 minimum. [8]Up to 10% of policy limit. [9]Unlimited. [10]Coverage ends when claims exhaust limits. [11]In limited circumstances.
NA: Not applicable; self-insured retention required.

* Reprinted with permission from *Business Insurance*, 28 November 1983, p. 3.

Exhibit 9-6
Endorsement Limiting Pollution Coverage*

LIMITATION OF COVERAGE FOR POLLUTION

THE HARTFORD

Named Insured and Address

Policy Number

This endorsement forms a part of the policy as numbered above, issued by THE HARTFORD INSURANCE GROUP company designated therein, and takes effect as of the effective date of said policy unless another effective date is stated herein.

Effective Date

Effective hour is the same as stated in the Declarations of the policy.

Endt. No.

This endorsement modifies such insurance as is afforded by the provisions of the policy relating to the following:

COMPREHENSIVE GENERAL LIABILITY INSURANCE
COMPREHENSIVE-PLUS SPECIAL GENERAL LIABILITY INSURANCE
SMP LIABILITY INSURANCE

It is agreed that the exclusion relating to the discharge, dispersal, release or escape of smoke, vapors, soot, fumes, acids, alkalis, toxic chemicals, liquids or gases, waste materials or other irritants, contaminants or pollutants is deleted and replaced by the following exclusion:

This insurance does not apply to **bodily injury, property damage** or loss, costs or expenses of any nature for which the **insured** may be held liable by reason of the acts or omissions of any person or organization including but not limited to the **insured,** if the **bodily injury** or **property damage** arises out of the discharge, dispersal, release or escape of pollutants into or upon land, the atmosphere or any water course or body of water. "Pollutants" include smoke, vapors, soot, fumes, acids, alkalis, toxic chemicals, liquids or gases, waste materials and all other irritants or contaminants. This exclusion does not apply if the release or escape is an **accident** which occurs at a location not covered as an insured site in a pollution liability insurance policy issued by any company which is a member of The Hartford Insurance Group.

As used herein, **"accident"** means a sudden event which happens at a definite time and place and results in immediate **bodily injury** or **property damage.**

Nothing herein contained shall be held to vary, waive, alter, or extend any of the terms, conditions, agreements or declarations of the policy, other than as herein stated.

This endorsement shall not be binding unless countersigned by a duly authorized agent of the company; provided that if this endorsement takes effect as of the effective date of the policy and, at issue of said policy, forms a part thereof, countersignature on the declarations page of said policy by a duly authorized agent of the company shall constitute valid countersignature of this endorsement.

Countersigned by..

Authorized Agent

Form L-4410-0 Printed in U.S.A. (NS)

*Reprinted with permission from The Hartford Insurance Group.

the exposure as well as the complexities that are involved. In many instances, one key benchmark or standard that is used to measure whether a risk meets underwriting and loss control standards involves the degree to which the risk meets RCRA guidelines or standards. While RCRA is not the only standard against which a risk will be measured, it is an important one.

In many instances the information requirements are dictated by the type of operation and exposure involved. Additional underwriting information frequently sought by a pollution underwriter includes the following:

1. Did the risk file with the EPA? RCRA requires that risks that fall under its regulations file notice with the EPA in a prescribed fashion acknowledging this fact.
2. What is the risk's chemical flow analysis or hazardous waste cycle? This would include information concerning the following areas:

    • raw material storage,
    • production process(es),
    • hazardous chemical generation,
    • hazardous chemical storage,
    • hazardous chemical transportation, and
    • hazardous chemical treatment and disposal.

    Note that the concern is not just with hazardous wastes but rather "hazardous chemicals"—some as mundane as printer's ink.
3. What are the details of off-premises disposal sites used by the risk to treat and dispose of chemicals and waste?
4. Has the risk been cited by any authority for being in violation of any environmental laws?
5. What is the risk's historical pollution exposure? While the risk may be conforming to currently acceptable standards, past practices may have created environmental liability problems yet to surface.
6. Is the risk involved with any existing environmental litigation or has it been in the past? What are the details?
7. Is the risk's record keeping adequate? Accurate record keeping is important to constructing a good defense.
8. How well does the risk monitor its environmental liability program on an on-going basis? Are the proper individuals in the company involved (including senior management) and is corrective action promptly taken?

Factors to Be Considered Some of the critical factors that underwriters take into consideration in evaluating a prospect for pollution liability insurance include the following:

- *Type of waste*—for example, is the hazardous chemical or waste toxic, corrosive, or reactive, and to what degree?
- *Amount and toxicity of waste generated*—the amount could be small but highly toxic.
- *Kinds of dikes or containment systems*—these are important in the event of a spill.
- *Environmental routes*—based on the location and topography, what are the pathways, such as air, surface water, and groundwater, by which hazardous chemicals or waste could move off the premises of the facility and into the environment?
- *Target populations*—what are the potentially exposed human, animal, and plant populations or ecological systems that could be harmed by any such materials moving off premises? An example of this might involve a dry cleaning firm polluting the drinking water of a nearby school.
- *Facility or plant operation and practices*—what is the design, construction operating plan, and general state of upkeep of the facility or location?
- *Characteristics and toxicity of the hazardous chemicals and waste materials*—what are the genetic hazards of the materials that could migrate off premises and thus affect off-site target populations? The exposure could result from inadequate facility operations, design, maintenance, or because of the characteristics of the environmental routes.
- *Coverage, limits, and deductible requested*—this would include retroactive (prior acts) and tail (discovery period) coverage desired.
- *Management qualifications and attitude*—these constitute the cornerstone of any acceptable risk.
- *Probability of loss*—what is the likelihood of a loss occurring and how often could it happen?
- *Severity of loss*—if a loss does occur, how large is the loss likely to be (including defense costs)?
- *Complaints/past claims*—have there been any and what are the circumstances? Were the losses preventable and has corrective action been taken?

The problem areas that underwriters frequently encounter involve the following:

- *Historical exposures*—past practices may have contributed to an actual or potential pollution situation that is imposible to quantify or is the basis for existing environmental problems.
- *Off-premises disposal site(s)*—many such sites have environmental problems, and underwriters will opt to exclude such sites from coverage.
- *Poor controls*—risks may wish to substitute insurance for poor handling practices, forgoing needed corrective action.
- *Underground fuel tanks*—many of these tanks are old and may either be leaking or be close to it. While a "pressure test" may substantiate tank integrity *today*, the tank may start leaking *next week*. It is extremely difficult to adequately predict the life of a tank. Underground fuel tanks present special problems for underwriters.
- *Past losses*—these may indicate future problems. This generally is a red flag for the underwriter. Further losses may be likely.
- *Target risks' visibility*—in today's climate, a large chemical firm may be more likely to invite pollution litigatin than more innocuous risks with a lower public profile.
- *Existing litigation*—underwriters feel that existing litigation may signal additional litigation and will scrutinize such situations very carefully.

The final step in the underwriting decision-making process is to arrive at a price for the pollution coverage. While some companies have elaborate rating programs to establish pricing benchmarks, in the final analysis, the resultant price is very much a product of informed judgment. No two risks are identical, and in many instances a wide range of premiums between insurers will be quoted for a given risk.

VII. FUTURE

Pollution exposures are going to continue to develop, and the demand for pollution coverage will continue to grow. It is likely that municipalities, chemical firms, farms, various industrial operations, and underground fuel tanks will increasingly be found to be sources of significant pollution contamination. The existing market is fragile at best and is in a process of transition. It is too premature to predict whether it is likely to become a mature market.

EIL Insurance and the Pollution Exclusion

There are certain to be some coverage changes brought about that will affect pollution coverage. Likely changes affecting pollution liability policies include the following:

- Blanket coverage for third party off-premises disposal sites is likely to become a thing of the past; coverage, if provided, will probably be on a specific-designated location basis only.
- Retentions for insureds will increase.
- Lower limits of liability will be available.
- A Superfund exclusion (excluding "Superfund" sites and attendant cleanup costs) may be required in certain cases.
- Defense coverage may be included within the limit of liability.

When the Insurance Services Office introduced its commercial general liability policy intended to be effective in 1985, it originally contained a revised pollution exclusion, the purpose of which was still to distinguish between sudden/accidental and gradual pollution and to exclude the latter. Many within the insurance industry preferred a total pollution exclusion. As mentioned, courts were tending to find gradual pollution coverage under the general liability policy and these people in the industry had doubts as to whether anything short of a total pollution exclusion would be effective. In addition, by having a total pollution exclusion, risks that desire pollution coverage must specifically ask for such coverage, and this forces a conscious decision and evaluation on the part of the underwriter before granting the coverage.

The authors of one article on the subject concluded the following:

> From the cases discussed, it is fair to conclude that the pollution exclusion is not much of an exclusion. Under the pollution exclusion, as interpreted by the courts, policyholders will be covered for legal liability arising out of pollution, unless it is determined that the policyholder deliberately intended to pollute and deliberately intended to cause injury. In the absence of fairly extreme circumstances, pollution probably will be considered sudden and accidental, and thus, the pollution exclusion will be inapplicable. Even if the pollution is gradual, the pollution exclusion will not obviate coverage because of the courts' narrow reading of the pollution exclusion.[53]

Another author concludes:

> The clearest case where the pollution excusion will be held to exclude coverage is that which involves an industrial enterprise discharging substances commonly considered environmental pollutants, knowing that the emissions are a potential hazard. Absent this scenario, various factors must be considered. What was the cause of the discharge or release of the substance in question? Once released, were the effects or extent of the discharge anticipated? Did anyone make the insured aware of the existing or potential problem? If so, were any remedial steps taken? What was the nature of the substance emitted or discharged? Was the contamination or pollution

itself the injury or damage at issue or did the contamination or pollution merely set the stage for other injuries?

The frequency with which these questions must be answered will undoubtedly increase in the coming years. The public's awareness of the problem of pollution is increasing. As more suits are brought to recover for injuries arising from environment-contamination, insurers will be more likely to consider whether the claims being alleged fall within the pollution exclusion. The stakes are high, as entire communities can be forced to evacuate and clean-up costs can be enormous. We can expect to see many more cases litigating the meaning and scope of the pollution exclusion in years to come.[54]

A court case involving the older pollution exclusion and its interpretation is illustrative of this point. Buckeye Union Insurance Company wrote a comprehensive general liability policy for Liberty Solvents & Chemical Company. The policy contained the usual exclusion for nonsudden pollution. An 11 July 1984 decision by the Ohio State Appellate Court ruled that Buckeye must defend Liberty in a lawsuit seeking cleanup of a hazardous waste site. This decision was a reversal of a lower court's decision that had upheld the pollution exclusion.

In overturning the lower court's decision, the higher court stated, "Policy provisions which exclude coverage are to be strictly construed against the insurer where the language is ambiguous." The ambiguousness referred to by the court in its decision was the lack of a definition for "sudden and accidental" in the policy. The court referred to the *Jackson Township* case mentioned earlier and *Lansco, Inc.* v. *the Department of Environmental Protection*, where an oil spill that was neither expected nor intended from the standpoint of Lansco was considered sudden and accidental with regard to the pollution exclusion, even if it was deliberately caused by a third party.[55]

Another writer expresses the opinion that "while the pollution exclusion is probably not as restrictive of coverage as many insurers would probably like, it is not almost useless, as many articles seem to imply. He goes on to say:

A significant portion of the blame for the apparent dilution of the pollution exclusion clause by the courts must lie with the insurance companies themselves. In less than half the cases discussed above, do the facts of the incident support a reasonable interpretation of the pollution incident not being sudden and accidental. Coverage in a case like *Lansco*, where a tank was vandalized, should not be denied on the basis of the pollution exclusion. By forcing the courts to decide coverage issues, the insurance companies are putting their fate in the hands of the same institution that is looking for any and all possible solvent contributors to finance the cleaning up of environmental hazards.

It is clear that despite some readings to the contrary by some courts and commentators, the pollution exclusion in the CGL policy was meant to and does deny coverage for claims arising out of pollution events that are not of a brief temporal duration and unexpected and unintended in nature. In addition, the financial responsibility regulations promulgated under the Resource Conservation and Recovery Act and many state laws for the owners or operators of hazardous waste facilities make a sudden/nonsudden distinction, and base it on the time course of the event. This distinction does have enough imprecision so that there will still be litigation over when sudden ends and nonsudden begins, or what is expected and what is not.

Given this more unambiguous (and more reasonable) reading of the exclusion, the insurance companies should not allow the courts to muddy up their insurance contracts, which will continue to occur if coverage is unreasonably withheld. The insureds, on the other hand, should realize that, despite reports to the contrary, the courts are generally not broadly giving away coverage under the CGL for any pollution event. Given the current availability of a product to cover nonsudden pollution, the EIL [environmental impairment liability] policy, the courts may be less sympathetic to claims that coverage is warranted under the CGL for pollution events that are obviously nonsudden. Both sides should be more hesitant about running into court.[56]

Robert S. Faron of the law firm of Lane & Mittendorf in Washington, D.C., on the other hand, notes in a memorandum dated 6 January 1984 that "absent a drastic revision of the CGL or more successful defenses based on emphasizing a distinction between gradual and sudden pollution-causing events, the need for a separate pollution liability market will be questioned."

He goes on to say:

Nevertheless, there are many distinguishing features of current pollution liability policies which could be emphasized in marketing. Therefore, the extent to which this market may grow will depend more on the value of the coverage in the EIL in terms of limits, structure of coverages, and availability, rather than on the need to fill a gap in the CGL coverage.

If the sudden/accidental and gradual distinction had remained in the pollution exclusion, insureds and producers would have faced the question of whether to separately purchase gradual pollution coverage. Most insureds (or their producers) could not afford to gamble that they would be successful in finding pollution liability coverage under their general liability policy for the following reasons:

- The exclusionary language may be upheld.
- The insured at a minimum would have to sue its insurer and it may not be successful.

- The magnitude of the exposure may be so large (remember the risk management maxim "don't risk a lot for a little") as to render the risk of loss prohibitive—the insured in such an instance cannot affort to lose.

In response to many of these concerns, ISO changed the pollution exclusion on the proposed policy to one that amounts to almost a total pollution exclusion with no distinction between gradual and sudden. The exceptions revolve around the off-site emissions exposure and the products/completed operations exposure. Exclusion "f" now states that the insurance does not apply to the following:

(1) "Bodily injury" or "property damage" arising out of the actual, alleged or threatened discharge, dispersal, release or escape of pollutants:
   (a) At or from premises you own, rent or occupy;
   (b) At or from any site or location used by or for you or others for the handling, storage, disposal, processing or treatment of waste;
   (c) Which are at any time transported, handled, stored, treated, disposed of, or processed as waste by or for you or any person or organization for whom you may be legally responsible; or
   (d) At or from any site or location on which you or any contractor or sub-contractor working directly or indirectly on your behalf are performing operations:
      (i) if the pollutants are brought on or to the site or location in connection with such operations; or
      (ii) if the operations are to test for, monitor, clean up, remove, contain, treat, detoxify or neutralize the pollutants.

(2) Any loss, cost, or expense arising out of any governmental direction or request that you test for, monitor, clean up, remove, contain, treat, detoxify or neutralize pollutants. Pollutants means any solid, liquid, gaseous or thermal irritant or contaminant, including smoke, vapor, soot, fumes, acids, alkalis, chemicals and waste. Waste includes materials to be recycled, reconditioned or reclaimed.[57]

Insureds are able to "buy back" pollution coverage either through an endorsement to the general liability policy or through one of two pollution liability coverage parts (the primary difference being coverage for cleanup costs). This is possible if one assumes that the insured finds an insurer willing to provide the coverage.

Shortly after the policy was introduced, the pollution exclusion was amended to clarify that the policy would respond to bodily injury or property damage as a result of smoke from a hostile fire. That amendment states:

The following is added to exclusion f. of COVERAGE A (Section I):

Subparagraphs (a) and (d)(i) of paragraph (1) of this exclusion do not apply to "bodily injury" or "property damage" caused by heat, smoke or fumes from a hostile fire. As used in this exclusion, a hostile fire means one which becomes uncontrollable or breaks out from where it was intended to be.[58]

In the future, the concerns of federal, state, and local governments with environmental issues will continue to grow. It is a certainty that states will continue to enact more legislation pertaining to the environment. A key issue that remains for the insurance industry is whether the new laws will provide a role for private insurance and permit the effective operation of the insurance mechanism.

The Pollution Exposure

One source states that there is no such thing as a completely secure landfill. Use of a landfill is probably one of the least desirable means of disposing of hazardous wastes from an insurance standpoint. The source describes landfills as "long term storage." It goes on to say, "It is widely acknowledged that current technology is not capable of constructing a landfill that will never leak. In almost every case, landfill failure is a matter of time."[59] As time goes on, more emphasis will be placed on better disposal methods. Advanced manufacturing techniques will reduce the amount of hazardous waste generated through recycling and other methodology. The use of incineration as a disposal technique will increase. Over time, America's economic base will become more service-oriented and industry will decrease, but this transition is unlikely to have a significant positive impact on the pollution problem for some time to come. While government officials at all levels recognize the need for more disposal facilities, the public concurs but qualifies it with, "Just don't put it in *my* backyard."

Adequate enforcement of environmental laws continues to be a prime concern for insurers writing pollution insurance. One of the factors that originally encouraged the insurance industry to provide a market for environmental impairment liability insurance was that the EPA indicated that it would strictly enforce its regulations. Unfortunately, this enforcement has not been forthcoming for a number of reasons. It was never the intent of the insurance industry to perform the role of "surrogate regulator." The lack of realistic enforcement by the EPA may diminish the industry's incentive to provide an environmental impairment liability market; only time will tell the effectiveness of the pronouncements by the EPA that it is going to take a tougher stance on enforcement.

Many of the pollution exposures existing today do not meet the test for insurability. An insurer does not knowingly insure a building on fire; likewise, an insurer is not likely to insure a pollution site that has already caused injury or damage or is on the verge of doing so. Many such sites exist today. For these sites, pollution coverage is unlikely to be available. The lack of readily available funding mechanisms may create problems for society, and there may be pressure placed on the insurance industry to participate in involuntary insurance arrangements. The industry will most likely vigorously resist this, and this issue will become a source of friction for the industry.

One writer has proposed a concept called *channeling*, which could address environmental injury compensation:

> Under the "channeling" concept strict, exclusive liability is imposed, either directly by national law or by special mandatory financial protection requirements, on one and only one firm at a time. There is an absolute ceiling on the liability of the "enterprise" (that is, of all firms whose liability is "channeled" to the target defendant). The target defendant must maintain financial protection, generally at high limits. It becomes the responsibility of the national government to provide supplemental compensation when claim payments reach the ceiling.[60]

One writer summed up the feelings of many when he said that if the insurance industry, the courts, and the persons doing the polluting do not come up with some workable solution, Congress will try to do so legislatively. According to that writer, Congress may place some type of victims' compensation in the next version of Superfund due to pressure from various groups, including environmentalists.[61] (The "next" version to which this writer refers is SARA. While his prediction did not come true, there were indeed attempts to include such provisions. Such attempts may be more successful in the future if there is still a large group of uncompensated victims.)

There are concerns that a victims' compensation program could simply become another entitlement program, and therefore, "manufacturers and the insurance industry are scrambling to come up with a workable solution to the pollution liability problem before a hasty, ill-conceived and unworkable plan is mandated by Congress or the courts."[62]

VIII. SUMMARY AND PERSONAL OBSERVATIONS

The opinions expressed in this summary are those of the author and are not necessarily those of The Hartford Insurance Group.

The growing impact of pollution liability is being increasingly felt by the public, government, and the insurance industry. It seems that the pollution exposure is omnipresent with few individuals and areas totally insulated from some form or type of pollution. Lawsuits involving environmental impairment liability claims will continue to escalate. These lawsuits will be predicated on a growing body of tort law and principles.

At the same time, it is likely that statutory law regulating the environment will continue to be enacted by federal, state, and local government on an increasing basis. Some of this legislation will not be favorable to the insurance industry, and is likely to inhibit the effective role and development of the insurance mechanism for funding pollution liability losses.

New problems are developing. According to some EPA officials, some of the wastes that have been hauled away under Superfund to new sites are beginning to leak at the new site. It appears that the millions already spent may have just shifted the problem to new locations that will require cleanup under Superfund.[63]

Acid rain is another problem likely to gain prominence in the near future. A report by the Acid Rain Peer Review Panel, a group of experts appointed by the Reagan administration to look into the problem of acid rain, was reportedly suppressed by the Reagan administration according to two New England congressmen. One proposed solution to the acid rain problem is the Waxman-Sikorski bill, which would impose a limit on the amount of sulfur dioxide emissions allowed. The bill was defeated in subcommittee. The electric industry in opposing the bill called the limitations too expensive and perhaps unnecessary since the cause and effect of acid rain is unknown. The acid rain controversy is likely to be debated for some time to come.[64]

Business firms will be forced through necessity to address their pollution liability exposures utilizing more effective risk management techniques. The need for thorough risk assessments will be accentuated. It is likely that firms offering such services will proliferate. From a risk management standpoint, better risk control methodology will be emphasized and employed, and risk financing will involve increasing retentions.

The transfer of the pollution risk via insurance then becomes the next issue. Will insurance be available? One writer stated that while agents were still able to find pollution coverage, it was like finding "spare parts for an Edsel." He said this was understandable given the "incalculable" potential for damage and the inability to predict the size of the bill. He did believe it was agreed among many that "pollution is the biggest risk" the insurance industry has faced.[65]

Another writer stated that in the Midwest, legislatures facing pollution problems were turning more and more to the insurance industry for the funds to solve these problems. Most of the problems being addressed are from the past, and the writer believes that while the insurance mechanism could probably handle problems arising from future events, there is probably not enough money within the insurance industry (and perhaps other sectors of the private economy) to handle the problems arising from past pollution events. The writer does not believe that insurers and their policyholders can be an "alternate funding source" for the pollution problem. Finding a solution to please all parties will not be easy, but "the process is underway."[66]

One crucial question for the industry will be whether reinsurance will be available (and at what price) for pollution liability insurance. There is fear, according to one underwriter, that one underwriter will "burn the reinsurers" and that the event will have "repercussions throughout the entire market."[67] Reinsurance is crucial to the writing of EIL insurance; without reinsurance, it is unlikely that many markets will offer the cover.

Although it did not become law as it was proposed, H.R. 5640— Superfund Expansion and Protection Act of 1984, is interesting to examine as a reflection of the sentiment of some legislators. Introduced by Congressmen Florio, Howard, and thirty-four others on 10 May 1984, it contained provisions with respect to victims' compensation. It would have extended Superfund for five years and increased the fund by about $9 billion for the five-year period. Title I of this bill established mandatory schedules by which the EPA must plan and implement cleanup of Superfund sites. Title III of the bill provided additional impetus in this regard as it authorized citizen suits whereby individuals were permitted to compel action required by the bill where there had been inaction on the part of the responsible agency despite sufficient notification that a problem existed. The bill would have imposed joint and several liability on responsible parties for the recovery of the costs of cleanup of the site. (Currently, several courts have repudiated the mandatory joint and several standard, deciding that the imposition of the entire cleanup burden on only one of a number of contributors to the problem is not equitable. These courts prefer an apportionment of liability. The codification under H.R. 5640 would have prohibited court discretion in selecting the standard of liability.)

Title II of the bill, however, posed the most controversy. Essentially, it created a federal cause of action for individuals claiming injury from exposure to hazardous releases at a waste disposal or treatment facility. The remedy would have supplemented state tort and statutory remedies, amounting to "absolute" liability. Liability would attach to anyone who ever generated, stored, transported, or treated any hazardous substance disposed of at the facility regardless of whether the substance released was contributed by the defendant and regardless of the quantity involved. An illustration of this might, for example, involve a laboratory that might have disposed of a pint of a substance; under Title II, the laboratory could be liable for any and all damages caused by a release of *any* hazardous substance from that facility, including cleanup cost liability.

The only defenses available to "responsible" parties were limited to acts of God, war, or unrelated third parties. As to liability, the plaintiff's behavior was irrelevant, as was conclusive proof that the substance that the defendant disposed of could not have caused the injury or the damage. In the final analysis, the end result was "absolute" liability and liability without causation—basically allowing plaintiffs to sue any party still available or select a "deep pocket."

Business Insurance had an excellent editorial with regard to this portion of the bill. It disagreed with Congress' apparent attempt to adopt the "deep pocket" theory for pollution liability. The editorial stated that it appeared that Congress had decided it was easier to go after the large corporations in pollution cases than to "fuss" with smaller ones who might not be able to pay for the damages they caused. It also warned that such a move might make the exposure uninsurable and would definitely create uncertainty when a firm was trying to determine its potential pollution liability. A firm possibly could be assessed for damages caused by other firms about which it has no knowledge and over which it has no control. The editorial proposed that companies pay their "fair share" of damages caused by toxic wastes based upon each company's actual contribution to the damage. If a responsible firm were bankrupt or unable to pay, some form of "rational victims' compensation fund" should be established.[68]

Harsh provisions like this would make it highly unlikely that the insurance community would want to provide EIL insurance in such an environment. Unfortunately, it is also probable that more legislative efforts following this tack will be made in the future.

There is little question that the insurance industry cannot cover all of the costs associated with toxic waste cleanup. One attorney put the costs at roughly "36 with nine zeros after it."[69] Adding to the problem is the fact that no legislature or court has said definitely when bodily injury or property damage occurs with regard to pollution. The courts have, in the case of asbestosis, issued several differing opinions as to how insurance coverage should apply:

- *Exposure theory*—The injury occurs essentially at the time of exposure and thus the insurer providing coverage at the time of exposure is liable (*Insurance Co. of North America* v. *Forty-Eight Insulations, Inc.*).
- *Manifestation theory*—The injury occurs when the disease or injury "manifests" itself (essentially when the disease becomes reasonably capable of medical diagnosis, for example, when symptoms appear) and the insurer at that time should provide

coverage (*Eagle-Picher Industries, Inc.* v. *Liberty Mutual Insurance Co.*).

- *Triple-trigger theory*—All insurers providing coverage from the time of exposure through the time of manifestation should provide coverage (*Keene* v. *Insurance Co. of North America*).
- *Date medical injuries occurred theory*—Insurers providing coverage when the victim's medical injuries, sickness, or disease actually occur (which medical science reportedly can pinpoint) are the insurers responsible (*American Home Products Corporation* v. *Liberty Mutual Insurance Company*).[70]
- *Continuous*—All insurers providing coverage from the time of exposure until the date of the claim or death, whichever occurs first (ruling by a California superior court judge in May 1987 in a consolidation of lawsuits filed separately by asbestos producers).[71]

One of the continuing, troublesome aspects of pollution liability situations involves the apportionment of liability in an equitable manner that addresses the actual contribution of the wrongdoer relative to the amount of harm done. Is it equitable to assign the brunt of the burden involving damages and cleanup costs to a single defendant on a strict, joint, and several basis when the contribution of that defendant to the problem has been miniscule or unrelated to the toxic waste actually causing the harm? Another potentially troublesome area is the issue of punitive damages. The fear is that such damages will be exacted where the behavior of the defendant does not justify them.

What then are the alternatives that can be called upon to address the potential bodily injury and property damage liability losses that are certain to develop, particularly those situations involving sites where the wrongdoer(s) cannot be identified, is out of business, or lacks the financial capability to respond (sometimes called *orphan sites*)? In these latter situations especially, there is little consensus on what constitutes the best approach.

There are many who insist and feel confident that the existing tort liability system is the best system to respond. Certainly, while imperfect, it has endured better than any other system up to now.

If the pollution problem exceeds the capacity of the tort system to respond, other mechanisms could be employed. It should be kept in mind, however, that the price tag for many of the alternatives will be exorbitant—perhaps far in excess of what society is willing to shoulder. Some possible alternatives include the following:

- A first party group health program whose bill could be financed by the government (state and federal). The government could purchase a group health policy for the benefit of the general public.

- The workers compensation system expanded to allow workers a federal cause of action.
- The channeling concept already described. One advocate of the approach suggests that when compared with conventional tort system, it provides "a more predictable system with substantially lower frictional costs."[72]
- A state program providing funds within prescribed parameters that would respond to cleanup costs and damages over which the federal government could step in or participate. Possibly excess EIL coverage could be provided over this pool of funds/retention.
- An arbitration panel or tribunal approach.
- The chemical industry alone or in conjunction with the state and/or federal government could agree to provide exposed employees with the following services (separate from their workers' compensation coverage):
  1. Physical exams to detect illness
  2. Medical benefits insurance
  3. Disability wage loss insurance

This insurance would be excess of any other insurance available to the employee, and in exchange for these benefits, the employee would waive his or her tort right against the employer. This approach would probably assuage the fears of the majority of the workers who may perceive injury when no real injury has occurred.

Variations of these alternatives are possible, and some of these alternatives could be combined. These constitute only some of the possible alternatives available. However, in most instances, they are expensive, and it is questionable as to what real benefit society would receive. This author is of the opinion that until something better, more efficient, and with clearly definable advantages (including a reasonable price tag) comes along to supplant the existing tort system, then the existing tort system is the best answer. The Draconian provisions of some of the proposals that have been presented as solutions effectively preclude any real involvement on the part of the private insurance sector in terms of providing an EIL market. It should be noted that the standard of liability to which the insurance industry is best able to respond is "several" liability.

Reinsurance, improved risk control, legislation, EPA enforcement, and loss development will be critical factors in determining the availability and affordability of pollution liability insurance. The insurance industry cannot be responsible for all of society's past pollution sins, but it can, if it is allowed to, provide a reasonable insurance market for this cover. Government, business, society, and the insurance industry must be willing to work together to see that this happens. The author is sanguine that a great deal can be achieved by the insurance industry if it is willing to take an interactive as well as a proactive approach to the various pollution issues discussed in this monograph.

Monograph Notes

1. Rachel L. Carson, *Silent Spring* (New York: Fawcett, 1962), p. 24.
2. Henry E. Beal, "The Coming Trend in Lawsuits," *Business Insurance*, 28 November 1983, p. 41.
3. Lynne M. Miller and Douglas E. Gladstone, "Keeping Up Your Guard: Expanding Pollution Laws Demand Risk Managers' Vigilance," *Business Insurance*, 28 November 1983, p. 40.
4. Miller and Gladstone, p. 40.
5. Rick Janisch, "Protection From Pollution Risk: A Team Effort," *Professional Agent*, June 1984, p. 29.
6. Janisch, p. 29.
7. Carson, p. 157.
8. Janisch, p. 26. Also see, Robert A. Finlayson, "Joint and Several Liability Dumped from Superfund Bill," *Business Insurance*, 20 August 1984, p. 81.
9. "EPA Adds 133 Sites to Hazardous Waste List," *New York Times*, 2 September 1983, p. 16-A. Also, data base report on "Environmental Pollution," III Data Base, January 1987.
10. "Hazardous Waste Tally Keeps on Growing," *New York Times*, 4 September 1983, p. 16-E.
11. III Data Base.
12. "Landfill Disposal," American Insurance Services Group, Inc., Engineering and Safety Service Division, *Pollution Control Bulletin PC-24*, November 1983, pp. 3, 4.
13. Beal, p. 41.
14. Janisch, p. 29. Also see Ellis Simon, "Ruling Forces Utica to Defend Love Canal Suits," *Business Insurance*, 5 May 1980, p. 1.
15. Ellis Simon, "Love Canal: Hooker Battles Insurers for Pollution Coverage," *Business Insurance*, 14 January 1980, p. 1.
16. Ellis Simon, "Township May Fight Pollution Suit Alone," *Business Insurance*, 25 February 1980, p. 1.
17. Robert A. Finlayson, "Court Ruling in Buckeye Case Narrows Pollution Exclusion," *Business Insurance*, 30 July 1984, p. 24.
18. Elisabeth M. Wechler, "Livestock Poisoning Kicks Off $1 Billion Battle," *Business Insurance*, 19 May 1975, pp. 1 and 8.
19. Carson, p. 163.
20. See Michael Brown, "Toxic Waste: Organized Crime Moves In," *Readers' Digest*, July 1984.
21. Matthew Lenz, Jr., *Environmental Pollution: Liability and Insurance* (New York: Insurance Information Institute, February 1982), p. 12.
22. Interestingly, although Love Canal is probably one of the most widely recognized examples of toxic waste pollution, a study conducted at Love Canal produced the following: "Although improper disposal of toxic chemical wastes poses a clear risk for human health, the risk is not easily

measured.... [S]tudies at Love Canal ... have thus far defined no firm evidence of increased disease incidence or mortality." (Sean F. Mooney, *Toxic Wastes: The Insurance Issues* [New York: Insurance Information Institute, January 1984].) Another study ("A Study of Cytogenetic Patterns in Persons Living Near the Love Canal") conducted by the Centers for Disease Control also concluded in its summary that frequencies of chromosomal aberrations or of sister chromatid exchange of those living near Love Canal did not differ from control levels significantly.

23. Harry H. Wellington, "Asbestos: Private Management of a Public Problem," *Insurance Times*, 1 January 1985, p. 15.

24. This section was adapted from a paper on this subject written by Antoinette L. Ruzzier, Assistant Counsel, The Hartford Insurance Group.

25. John M. Kobayashi states:

There is not presently a substantial body of appellate case law specifically related to the theories of "common law" liability for toxic substances or hazardous wastes *per se;* the area of law is developing rapidly and various pending and decided cases are noted. There is also rapid development in some of the litigation doctrines that are particularly important to cases arising from toxic substances and hazardous wastes.

A variety of established common law doctrines related to toxic substances and common law theories of action have been applied and there are others that are presumptively applicable to various activities associated with toxic substances and hazardous waste, manufacture, processing and disposal that will, in this lawyer's opinion, become the basis for extraordinarily complex litigation and trials and enormous potential liabilities within the relatively near future.

(John M. Kobayashi, Esq., "A Witches' Brew Now Bubbling: Summary Lecture Outline Notes Re: Selected Private Party Theories or 'Common Law Civil Liability' and Various Potentially Applicable Criminal Provisions With Selected Related Litigation Questions for Environmental, Toxic Substance and Hazardous Wastes Problems," Risk Insurance Managers [sic] Society National Convention, Washington, DC, April 1982, p. 3).

26. Kobayashi, pp. 1-3.

27. *Environmental Law—Defense and Insurance Problems*, Volume 1977, No. 3, (Milwaukee: The Defense Research Institute, 1977), p. 7.

28. *Martin v. Reynolds Metals Co.*, 342, p.2d 790, 797 (1959).

29. *Environmental Law—Defense and Insurance Problems*, p. 12.

30. *Knabe v. National Supply Division of Armco Steel Corporation*, 592 f.2d 841 (c.a. 5, 1979).

31. William L. Prosser, *Law of Torts*, 4th ed. (St. Paul, MN: West Publishing Co., 1971), p. 512.

32. *Restatement of Torts*, section 519 (1938).

33. Restatement (Second) of Torts, section 519 (1977).

34. Beal, pp. 41, 42.

35. Simon, "Love Canal: Hooker Battles Insurers for Pollution Coverage," p. 1.

36. *Don't Find Out About Pollution Liability By Accident* (Hartford: The Hartford Insurance Group, 1982), p. 4.
37. Doris Fenske, "Don't Think About It Late At Night," *Best's Review Property/Casualty Insurance Edition,* August 1983, p. 26.
38. Mooney.
39. Mooney.
40. Mooney.
41. Mooney.
42. Gahin, M.F.S.S., "A Theory of Pure Risk Management in the Business Firm," a thesis submitted in partial fulfillment of the requirement for the degree of Doctor of Philosophy (Commerce) at The University of Wisconsin, 1966, p. 8.
43. *Don't Find Out About Pollution Liability By Accident,* p. 11.
44. Douglas McLeod, "More Firms Seeking Risk Assessments," *Business Insurance,* 28 November 1983, p. 30.
45. Eckardt C. Beck, "Hazardous Waste Disposal—Most firms urgently need to review loss control programs," *Business Insurance,* 20 July 1983, p. 17.
46. Donald S. Malecki, James H. Donaldson, and Ronald C. Horn, *Commercial Property Risk Management and Insurance,* 1st ed., Vol. II (Malvern, PA: American Institute for Property and Liability Underwriters, 1978), p. 259.
47. Malecki, Donaldson, and Horn, p. 259.
48. Comprehensive General Liability Coverage Form, GL 00 02 01 73, Copyright, Insurance Services Office, Inc., 1973.
49. Lenz, p. 13.
50. Janet Aschkenasy, "EPIC To Start Writing EIL By Oct. 1 From Ill. Base," National Underwriter Property & Casualty/Employee Benefits Edition, 25 May 1987, pp. 1 and 89.
51. William A. Mahoney, "A Risk Manager's Guide to Pollution Liability Policies," *Risk Management,* July 1982, p. 18.
52. Mahoney, p. 12.
53. Eugene R. Anderson and Abraham C. Moskowitz, "How Much Does the CGL Pollution Exclusion Really Exclude?" *Risk Management,* April 1984, p. 36.
54. Joanne L. Goulka, "The Pollution Exclusion," *For The Defense,* September 1983, p. 27.
55. Finlayson, "Court Ruling in Buckeye Case Narrows Pollution Exclusion," pp. 2, 24.
56. Douglas E. Gladstone, Ph.D., "The Pollution Exclusion," an unpublished paper which will appear at a later date in *Business Insurance* (Washington, DC: Risk Science International), pp. 11 and 12.
57. Commercial General Liability Coverage Form CG 00 01 11 85, Copyright, Insurance Services Office, Inc., 1982, 1984.
58. Amendment of Pollution Exclusion endorsement CG 00 41 05 86, Copyright, Insurance Services Office, Inc., 1986.
59. "Landfill Disposal," American Insurance Services Group, Inc., Engineering and Safety Service Division, *Pollution Control Bulletin PC-24,* November 1983, p. 3.
60. Richard A. Schmalz, "Some Thoughts on Compensation Systems and

'Channeling,' " American Insurance Association, National Conference on Environmental Injury Compensation, The Insurance Point of View—Companies, 20 March 1984. This paper draws heavily from the author's article, "Superfund and Tort Law Reforms—Are They Insurable?" 38 *The Business Lawyer*, 175, November 1982.

61. Janisch, p. 32.
62. Janisch, p. 32.
63. "Toxic Waste Clean Up May Need Doing Again," *Hartford Courant*, Knight-Ridder Newspapers, 19 July 1984, p. A12.
64. "Acid Rain Cover-Up Charged," *Hartford Courant*, Knight-Ridder Newspapers, 18 August 1984, p. 1.
65. Janisch, pp. 27-28.
66. Jaelene Fayhee, "Industry Faces Pollution Cover Woes," *National Underwriter*, Property & Casualty Insurance Edition, 6 July 1984, pp. 3, 12.
67. Robert A. Finlayson, "Reinsurance crunch tightening market for pollution cover," *Business Insurance*, 9 July 1984, pp. 1, 33.
68. " 'Deep Pocket' Theory is Unfair," *Business Insurance*, 9 July 1984, p. 8.
69. "Toxic Waste Costs Could Outstrip Insurers' Funds," *Business Insurance*, 28 May 1984, p. 76.
70. "Toxic Waste Costs Could Outstrip Insurers' Funds," p. 76.
71. Stephen Tarnoff, "Asbestos firms win broadest coverage," *Business Insurance*, 1 June 1987, pp. 1 and 93.
72. Fenske, p. 76.

Selected Readings

Alliance of American Insurers. "Hazardous Waste Exposure Assessment and Control—A Loss Control Guideline," 1981.

All-Industry Research Advisory Council. *Pollution Liability: The Evolution of a Difficult Insurance Market*, 1985.

———. *Risk Assessment for Pollution Liability*, 1985.

American Insurance Services Group, Inc., Engineering and Safety Service Division. "Landfill Disposal." *Pollution Control Bulletin PC-24*, November 1983.

Bader, Allan H. and Priesing, Charles P. "Attacking the EIL Problem Head On," *Risk Management*, January 1984, pp. 18-28.

Bardenwerper, Fred L. and Hirsch, Donald J. eds. "Environmental Law—Defense and Insurance Problems." The Defense Research Institute, Inc., Volume 1977, Number 3.

Dietz, Stephen, et al. "Final Report—National Survey of Hazardous Waste Generators and Treatment Storage and Disposal Facilities Regulated under RCRA in 1981." Submitted by: Westate, Inc., Rockville, Maryland, 20 April 1984.

The Hartford Insurance Group. *Don't Find Out About Pollution Liability By Accident*, 1982.

Huston, J. Spenser. "Documentation and Recycling of Hazardous Wastes." Presentation Prepared for Interforum Group, Inc., Toxic Waste Disposal Conference, January 1981

Lenz, Jr., Matthew. *Environmental Pollution: Liability and Insurance.* New York: Insurance Information Institute, Monograph No. 2, February 1982.

MacBeth, Angus and Rogers, James A. (Co-chairmen). "Expanding Liability in Environmental Law—New Financial Exposures for Hazards and Toxics Under Statutory and Common Law," *Law and Business, Inc.*, 4.

Miller, Lynne M. and Murphy, Michael J. "Environmental Impairment Liability Insurance." Chapter 31, *The Business Insurance Handbook*, Castle, Gray; Cushman, Robert F.; and Kensicki, Peter R., eds. Homewood, IL: Dow Jones-Irwin, 1981.

Mooney, Sean. *Toxic Wastes: The Insurance Issues.* New York: Insurance Information Institute, January 1984.

Pfennigstorf, Weiner. "Insurance of Environmental Risks: Recent Developments." *Research Contributions of the American Bar Foundation*, 1982, No. 1.

MONOGRAPH 10

Property-Liability Post-Assessment Guaranty Funds*

by Michael P. Duncan, J.D., CPCU

I. INTRODUCTION

This monograph deals with the development, operation, and experience of post-assessment property-liability guaranty funds. Insurance guaranty funds are one of a number of insolvency mechanisms developed over the last fifty-five years to protect customers from loss in certain financial dealings. Among the best known insolvency mecha-

*The author acknowledges the significant help of Anne Bazil and Robin Dodge, his colleagues; Richard Marcus, Executive Secretary of the National Committee on Insurance Guaranty Funds; and Shirley Work, the author's secretary, in getting this monograph into final form. Portions of this monograph have appeared in an article by the author, "An Appraisal of Property-Casualty Post-Assessment Guaranty Funds," *Journal of Insurance Regulation*, Vol. 2, No. 3, March 1984, pp. 289–303. Portions were also presented in June 1986 to the American Bar Association, Tort and Insurance Practices Section, National Institute on Insurer Insolvency, and appeared in the publication *Law and Practice of Insurance Company Solvency*, which was a compilation of the papers presented at that Institute under the title, "The NAIC Model Property and Casualty Post-Assessment Guaranty Funds," reprinted with permission of the American Bar Association Section of Tort and Insurance Practice Section, ABA National Institute on Insurer Insolvency.

nisms outside the insurance industry is the Federal Deposit Insurance Corporation (FDIC), which protects the deposits of bank customers if a bank becomes insolvent. Similar mechanisms exist for savings and loan deposits, brokerage accounts, pension funds, and life insurance, as well as for and property and liability insurance. There are significant differences in how each mechanism works and how much protection each provides. The common element in all of them is that insolvency of the financial institution triggers the protection.

II. DEALING WITH INSOLVENT INSURERS

The normal forum for marshalling assets and paying debts of an insolvent entity, or for reorganizing it, is a federal court. This is not so for insolvent insurers, which are not covered by federal bankruptcy laws.[1] While the Supreme Court's ruling in *Paul v. Virginia* in 1868[2], holding that insurance was not commerce, precluded regulation of the business of insurance as interstate commerce, Congress could have asserted control over insolvent insurers under its power under the Constitution to establish uniform laws on the subject of bankruptcy. In any event, there was no clear statement of legislative purpose for the insurance exclusion over the years.

Since the 1944 decision in *U.S. v. South-Eastern Underwriters Association*,[3] which held that insurance was commerce, thus reversing *Paul v. Virginia,* arguments have been made for subjecting insurers to federal bankruptcy provisions. When a commission created by Congress to review the Bankruptcy Act considered the matter of the insurance exclusion, it recommended, and Congress agreed, to leave the subject of insurer bankruptcies to the states.[4] This was consistent with Congress' response to the *South-Eastern Underwriters* case, which was the adoption of the McCarran-Ferguson Act that generally left the regulation of the business of insurance to the states.

This commission on bankruptcy had sought the views of Professor Spencer Kimball on the issue of the exclusion on insurers from the Act. He suggested "that while there were some arguments for federal liquidation of insurance companies, on balance it was preferable to continue to liquidate insurers at the state level because liquidation law is an integral part of insurance regulation, now carried on primarily at the state level, and further because it is preferable to do at the state level whatever can be done there tolerably well."[5]

When an insurer is financially troubled, the insurance regulator can take action under state law to "supervise" and work with company management to correct specific problems, or to take over management of a financially troubled insurer by instituting a conservation, rehabilitation, or liquidation under court proceedings. In a liquidation proceeding, which frequently follows an unsuccessful attempt to rehabilitate the company, five steps are involved: (1) marshalling assets, (2) identifying and evaluating claims, (3) distributing assets, (4) disposing of company records, and (5) closing the liquidation.[6]

An insolvent company is generally one without enough assets to pay claims. Before guaranty funds, this meant that when a company was liquidated, insureds and claimants were unpaid or underpaid after a long wait.

III. CONCEPT AND ORIGIN OF INSURANCE GUARANTY FUNDS

An insurance guaranty fund is a mechanism for pooling money of solvent insurers for the purpose of paying certain claims against an insolvent insurance company. The rationale behind this device stems from the nature of the insurance business. When a person buys insurance, he or she exchanges immediate payment for the insurance company's promise to pay for a loss or liability of serious economic impact on the insured. If the insured pays a premium to a company that later becomes insolvent and has insufficient funds to fulfill its promise, the insured suffers a tremendous hardship. In this case it is generally believed that the insured is an innocent victim of either bad management by the insurance company, outright fraud by people controlling the company, or regulatory failures relating to maintaining solvent insurers.

An argument against the need for guaranty funds is that it is up to the individual to be a smart shopper and to be sure that the company from which insurance is bought is financially solid. In some cases, when the customer purchases a policy from the company that has the lowest rates, the inadequacy of those rates to create a pool of money sufficient to pay claims is the cause of the insolvency of the company. In this situation it could be argued that the insured gets what was paid for and that others should not pay more to make up for a willingness to bargain for low premiums. Whether or not one supports the need for guaranty funds, it is a political reality that, due to a perception of wholesale insolvencies in the 1950s and 1960s, public policymakers at the federal and state levels saw a need for action that ultimately led to the creation of guaranty funds in every state.

Insurance guaranty funds first came into existence in the United States in the 1930s. They were limited to a single mandated insurance line, such as workers compensation (New York and Wisconsin) or taxi cab liability (New York), and pre-funded through assessments of solvent insurers paid to a state fund for use in case insolvencies occurred.[7] In the 1940s and 1950s Maryland, New Jersey, and New York created pre-funded auto insurance guaranty funds. In 1969 the National Association of Insurance Commissioners (NAIC) adopted a model act relating to state guaranty funds for property and liability insurance, which provided for funding after the insolvency.[8]

Federal Proposals and NAIC Reaction

No one disputes that the NAIC Post-Assessment Property and Liability Insurance Guaranty Association Model Act (hereinafter cited as Model Act) is predominantly the result of congressional activity in the 1960s first initiated by Senator Thomas Dodd (D. CT), who served on the Antitrust and Monopoly Subcommittee of the Senate Judiciary Committee. Senator Dodd was responding to a compilation of data by the Committee that showed that from 1960 to 1965, fifty-eight auto insurers became insolvent. A subsequent expanded study indicated that from 1958 to 1968, 109 property and liability insurers were liquidated due to insolvency. Of those, 108 were automobile insurers and all but 2 serviced the substandard market.[9] Senator Dodd introduced a bill that would have created a federal motor vehicle insurance guaranty corporation to pay auto claims that were unpaid because of insurer insolvencies. Funds would have been provided by adding a .125 percent charge to all automobile insurance premiums.[10]

The insurance industry and its regulators through the NAIC responded to the Dodd bill first by minimizing the nature of the problem, referring to data showing that unpaid claims due to insolvency represented about .10 of 1 percent of automobile loss payments.[11] The NAIC, however, did offer a solution to the problem. In 1967 it recommended mandatory uninsured motorists coverage, already being marketed by some insurers, with coverage triggered by the insolvency of the tortfeasor's insurer. To complement this solution, it was recommended that states review their local needs and entertain the possibility of other solutions to the insolvency problem including the possible adoption of state guaranty funds.[12]

The activity of the NAIC and the promise of activity by the states apparently did not satisfy all of the congressional concerns. In 1968 Senator Magnuson, chairman of the Committee on Commerce, introduced Senate Bill 2236, which would have created the Federal Insurance Guaranty Agency. Modeled somewhat after the Federal Deposit Insurance Corporation, which was created in 1933 to deal with bank failures, the agency would have had power to assess insurance companies for payments of claims against insolvent property and liability insurers and surety companies. Although there was no indication that the problem of insurer insolvencies then had any significance beyond automobile coverage, the Magnuson proposal went beyond automobile insurance and applied to all property and liability coverages. The bill also provided for some federal regulation regarding financial examinations and reporting. The examination and reporting features would have been a massive federal intrusion into the regulation of the business of insurance by the states.

As a result of the introduction of Senate Bill 2236, the NAIC created a committee to draft model guaranty fund legislation. In testimony before the Senate Commerce Committee, the chairman of the NAIC Executive Committee testified against the Magnuson bill and summed up his testimony by saying:

> Although the magnitude of the insolvency problem has been over-stated, nevertheless the problem is a very real one which deserves and is receiving the attention of both the NAIC and the individual states. There is an emerging consensus for guaranty fund legislation at the state level. Three types are under consideration—a prefunded plan, a post-assessment plan, or an interstate nonfederal fund.

> We are convinced that given time, the NAIC and the states will continue to meet the challenge and close the gap which even now has been narrowed to include a very small percentage of our populace. We ask therefore that you give us time and that you not act precipitously and thereby destroy the historic pattern of state insurance regulation.[13]

The growing concern of state regulators was further indicated by the adoption of post-assessment guaranty fund acts in California, Michigan, and Wisconsin while the NAIC was drafting its model. In December 1969, within a month after the testimony before the Senate Commerce Committee, the NAIC adopted the Model Act.[14] Senator Magnuson, apparently not yet appeased, secured passage of his bill out of the Senate Commerce Committee in December 1970 without a provision for federal financial examination of insurers. It was never brought to a vote on the floor of the Senate.[15]

The events that occurred between 1966 and December 1969 that led to the adoption of the Model Act would make an interesting study for students of political science. It has recently been pointed out that the guaranty fund system that now accounts for redistribution of hundreds of millions of dollars was created with "no significant public policy debate."[16] As to the change in scope of coverage from auto insurance to all property and liability insurance, the same person said that the "quantum leap to provide protection for all policyholders and claimants of property and casualty insurers, with a few minor exceptions, appears to have received no attention whatsoever in the Congress."[17] The system is in the main the obvious result of the threat of federal regulation, initially as to the consequences of automobile insurer insolvencies and, later, as to solvency regulation generally for the industry.

The perceived need for a solution to the hardship created by insurance company insolvencies was rapidly met. Twenty-two states had post-assessment guaranty funds by the end of 1970, thirty-five a year later. Eventually Puerto Rico, the Virgin Islands, the District of Columbia, and (with Maryland and New Jersey replacing their pre-assessment funds with Model Act-type statutes) every state except New York had one. (For convenience, in comments that relate to these various jurisdictions, the word "state" will be used). All funds closely resemble the Model Act. New York maintains a preinsolvency assessment fund that has existed since 1947.[18] In 1969 New York expanded its fund from coverage of auto insurance to all property and liability insurance. This monograph deals primarily with those guaranty funds that are like the NAIC Model Act.

IV. NAIC MODEL ACT

The Model Act provides for the creation of an involuntary, not-for-profit association consisting of all licensed companies writing the lines of insurance covered by the guaranty fund.[19] The association acts through a board of directors consisting of insurance company representatives and, in some states, the commissioner of insurance.[20] The association primarily pays insurance claims and refunds the unearned premium of insolvent insurers within the limitations described in the following text. The obligation to pay claims is triggered by the fact that a court of competent jurisdiction declares the insurer to be insolvent and orders it liquidated.[21] The source of the funds to execute this obligation is assessments paid by the member insurers based on each one's proportionate net direct premium writings in the state.[22] This is the essence of the guaranty fund mechanism put forth in the Model Act, but there are some limitations, exceptions, and conditions. The ones that primarily affect the insured or claimant are examined first, and those relating more to insurers and the fund itself are examined second.

The guaranty fund is directed to pay only "covered" claims.[23] A covered claim is defined in the Model Act as an unpaid claim arising out of and being within the coverage and subject to the applicable limits of the insured's policy.[24] Furthermore, the claimants or the insured must reside in the state at the time of the insured event unless the claim is for property permanently located in the state.[25] For corporations, residence is defined as principal place of business. Punitive damages and premium refunds under retrospective rating plans are excluded from covered claims. Amounts due other insurers either through subrogation, reinsurance, or another mechanism are also excluded.[26]

The Model Act applies only to licensed insurers and does not protect insureds of surplus lines insurers or provide for payment of claims arising from insolvencies of such insurers.[27] Unpaid expenses incurred by the insurer before liquidation, such as attorney's and adjuster's fees, are not covered.[28] Payment of an insured's liability by another does not entitle that person to guaranty fund coverage.[29] There are caps of $300,000 on coverage-related claims and $10,000 (with a $100 deductible) on unearned premium claims. There is no cap on workers compensation claims.[30] An insured with a net worth of $50 million or more will have liability claims paid by the guaranty fund but must reimburse the fund.[31]

When an insurer is declared insolvent, the liquidation order normally cancels the insurer's policies effective thirty days after the entry of the order of liquidation. The Model Act requires the guaranty fund to extend coverage up to thirty days after the entry of the liquidation order. This provides time for an insured to secure other insurance.[32]

The Model Act requires a claimant to seek recovery of a claim from a solvent insurer if any insurance policy other than that of the insolvent insurer covers the loss. An example of this would be uninsured motorists coverage, which is triggered by insolvency of the tortfeasor's insurer. After exhausting rights under the other policy or policies, the insured may recover the balance of the claim from the guaranty fund to the extent the sum of all payment is within the cap on covered claims.[33] It is possible to recover from more than one guaranty fund, but the Act provides that the caps of the various guaranty funds may not be stacked on top of each other. Therefore, recovery is permitted from more than one fund only if the funds in question have different caps and all prior recoveries are deducted.[34]

Additional provisions in the Model Act, primarily importance to insurers, should be noted. The Model Act gives the commissioner enforcement powers including suspension of a member insurer's license for failure to pay an assessment.[35] The Model Act gives alternatives regarding "assessment accounts." If a state has enough written premium to fund them, three accounts are recommended: auto, workers compensation, and all other lines. Otherwise, one account is recommended to cover all claims.[36] Assessments against any member insurer in any year may not exceed 2 percent of that member's net direct written premiums for the preceding calendar year in the lines subject to assessment.[37] Finally, member insurers are given the right to recoup their assessments through rates and premiums charged for insurance policies.[38] This is an exception to the general insurance ratemaking rule that rates may not include an amount to recoup past payments or losses.

State Variations

While Model Act-type laws were adopted in forty-nine states, the District of Columbia, Puerto Rico, and the Virgin Islands, state variations have developed. Some will be noted.

The Model Act determines which lines of insurance are covered by stating that "all kinds of direct insurance" are covered. The noncovered lines are then excepted.[39] States have generally used the Model Act approach but have varied the lines of insurance not covered. The Model Act originally excluded coverage for life, title, surety, disability, credit, mortgage guaranty, and ocean marine. This provided very broad coverage consistent with the approach Senator Magnuson proposed to the Congress. The Model Act was amended in December 1985 to further restrict its scope. As of this writing, few states have had an opportunity to consider those changes (which are itemized in the section, NAIC Activity Since 1969). Six states have enacted some of the changes.[40] Until more states do so, there will be significant deviations from the Model Act in scope of coverage.

Caps on covered claims range from $50,000 to $1 million (see Exhibit 10-1). Michigan has a formula to determine the cap, which is .05 of 1 percent of the aggregate premiums written by member insurers in the state in the preceding calendar year. Michigan further excludes from coverage under the guaranty fund act "any claim of any person who has a net worth greater than .10 of 1 percent of the aggregate premiums written by member insurers" in the state in the preceding calendar year. Georgia excludes claims from those insureds with a net worth over $3 million dollars. Indiana restricts and Missouri precludes recovery for noneconomic loss.

The variations in deductibles per claim vary from none to $200. The most common is $100, the amount suggested in the Model Act for all claims until 1980, when the NAIC made the deductible applicable only to unearned premium claims. Additional variations include applying neither caps nor deductibles to workers compensation claims. Some states have a separate fund covering workers compensation claims against insolvent insurers. At least one state, Massachusetts, provides no protection for workers compensation claimants.

Most states have created separate assessment accounts in their guaranty funds (see Exhibit 10-1). Twenty-two states assess companies separately for covered claims in three separate accounts as suggested in the Model Act: automobile lines, workers compensation, and all other

Exhibit 10-1
Post-Assessment Insolvency Funds Enacted (1969 Through 1986)

State	Maximum Covered Claim	Deductible Per Claim	Recoupment Provision	Maximum Annual Assmt.	Number of Accounts+
Code of AL §27-42-1	$150,000*	$100*	Premium Tax	1%	3
AK Stat. §21-80-010	$300,000*	$100*	Rates	2%	3
AZ Rev. Stat. Ann. §20-661	$100,000*	$100	Premium Tax	1%	2
AR Rev. Stat. 66-5501	$300,000	None	Premium Tax	2%	1
CA Ins. Code §1063	$500,000*	$100*	Rates	1%	3
CO Rev. Stat. Ann. §10-4-501	$50,000*	$100*	Rates	1%	3
CT Gen. Stat. Rev. §38-273	$300,000* 50% unearned premium ($1000 max)	$100*	Rates	2%	3
DE Code Ann. Title 18 §4201	$300,000	$100*	Premium Tax	2%	1
DC Ann. Code §35-1901	$300,000*	$100*	Rates	2%	3

FL Stat. §631-50	$300,000*	$100*	Rates (income tax credit for domestics only)	1%	4
GA Code Ann. §56-3401a	$100,000*	None	Rates	2%	3
HI Rev. Stat. §431D-1	$300,000*	$100*	Rates	2%	1
ID Code §41-3601	$300,000*	$100*	Rates	1%	3
IL Rev. Stat. Ch. 73 §1065.82	$150,000*	$100*	None	1%	2
IN Code Stat. Ann. §27-6-8-1	$500 Unearned premium $50,000 all other $100,000 max. per occurrence	$100	Tax Offset	1%	3
IA Code §515-B.1	$300,000*	$100*	Rates	2%	1
KS Stat. Ann. §40-2901	$300,000*	$100*	Premium Tax	2%	1
KY Rev. Stat. Ann. §304.36-010	$100,000	None	Yes	1%	1
LA Rev. Stat. §22:1375	$150,000* $1500 unearned premium	$100* None for unearned premium	Premium Tax	1%	1

continued on next page

ME Rev. Stat. Ann. title 24-A	$300,000*	None	Rates	1%	3
MD Code Ann. Art.48A §504	$300,000*	$100	Rates	2%	5
MA Ann. Laws Ch.175D §1	$300,000	None	Rates	2%	1
MI Comp. Laws Ann. §500.7901	Formula	$10	Rates	1%	5
MN Stat. §60C.01	$300,000	$100	Rates	2%	5
MS Code Ann. §83-23-101	$300,000*	$100*	Rates	1%	1
MO Rev. Stat. §375.785	$300,000*	$200	Premium Tax	1%	4
MT Ins. Code 33-10-101	$300,000*	$100*	Rates	2%	1
NE Rev. Stat. §44-2401	$300,000*	None	Premium Tax	1%	3
NV Rev. Stat. §687A.010	$300,000	None	Premium Tax	2%	1
NH Rev. Stat. Ann. §404-B:1	$300,000*	$50	Rates	2%	3
NJ Stat. Ann. §17:30A-1	$300,000	None	Policy Surcharge	2%	1

continued on next page

NM Stat. Ann. §59-A43-1	$100,000*	None	Rates	2%	3
NC Gen. Stat. §58-155.41	$300,000	None	Rates	2%	2
ND Cent. Code Ann. §26-36-01	$300,000	$100	Rates	2%	1
OH Rev. Code Ann. 3955.01	$300,000	None	Rates	1½%	2
OK Stat. Title 36 §2001	$150,000*	None	Rates	2%	3
OR Rev. Stat. §734.510	$300,000*	None	Premium Tax	2%	1
PA Stat. Ann. Title 40§1701 101	$300,000	$100	Rates	2%	2
PR Laws Ann. Title 26 §3801	$150,000	$50	Rates	2%	3
RI Gen. Laws Ann. §27-34-1	$1,000,000	1/12 of unearned premium*	Rates	2%	3
SC Code §38-19-10	$300,000*	$100*	Rates	1%	3
SD Comp. Laws Ann. §58-29A-1	$300,000*	$100*	Rates	1%	3

continued on next page

TN Code §56-12-101	$100,000*	$100*	Premium Tax	1%	2
TX Ins. Ann. Art. 21.28-C §1	$100,000* $1,000 unearned premium	None, except 75% of un-earned premium	Premium	2%	3
UT Code Ann. §31A-28-201	$300,000*	$100*	Premium Tax	2%	3
VT Stat. Ann. Title 8 §3611	$300,000*	$25	Rates	2%	3
VA Code §38.2-1600	$300,000*	$50 unearned premium	Rates	2%	3
WA Rev. Code Ann. §33-26-1	$300,000*	$100*	Premium Tax	2%	3
WV Code Ann. §33-26-1	$300,000	$100	Rates	2%	2
WI Stat. Ann. §646.01	$300,000	$200	Rates or Premium Tax Rate	2%	4
WY Stat. Ann. §26-31-101	$100,000*	$100*	Rates	1%	1

+ Excludes administrative accounts
* Except in cases of a workers compensation claim

lines. States with more accounts still have the three basic ones. Arizona, Ohio, Pennsylvania, and West Virginia have two accounts with no workers compensation coverage by the Model Act-type guaranty fund. Illinois and North Carolina, which provide workers compensation coverage in their Model Act-type statutes, have accounts for auto and for all other lines, thereby being the only states using accounts to combine workers compensation with other lines of insurance. Tennessee has two accounts, one of which is workers compensation. Michigan has taken a unique approach by breaking the all-other-lines account into two, one primarily for personal lines coverages and the other for commercial. Sixteen states do not use separate accounts.

States vary in their treatment of unearned premium as a covered claim. Eight states have no coverage at all. Some allow only a portion to be recovered.

The provision in the Model Act requiring the guaranty fund to provide coverage under a policy for an additional thirty days after an order of liquidation has been modified by two states. New Jersey provides for the runoff of coverage for the full term of an automobile policy and ninety days on other policies. Virginia has extended the period to ninety days on all policies.

While most states provide for recoupment of assessments through rates, others use a surcharge on policyholders or a premium tax offset. The tax offset allows recoupment through deductions from premium taxes over a number of years. Specifically, New Jersey, Hawaii, and California follow the surcharge approach. Fifteen states have premium tax offsets.

Finally, there are differences as to the specific situations that trigger the guaranty funds' obligations to pay covered claims. They will be discussed in a subsequent section.

V. HOW POST-ASSESSMENT GUARANTY FUNDS WORK

The Model Act is self-executing in only two respects: it creates the guaranty fund and provides for members. All insurers licensed to transact the insurance specified are, by virtue of their continued licenses, members of the guaranty fund. The board that governs the guaranty fund is selected by the members and is subject to approval of the commissioner of insurance. After being selected, the board has only one mandatory activity. It must prepare a plan of operation for the commissioner's approval. Since the plan of operation must establish regular places and times for meetings of the board of directors, it is implied that the board will meet at least once a year. Unless an insolvency triggers the payment of covered claims, the fund can remain dormant for years. Once all covered claims from an insolvency are disposed of through payment, the guaranty fund can return to its dormant state. No administrator or other employees need be permanently hired.

Many guaranty funds have been active from their inception. Some states find it appropriate to hire full-time or part-time personnel to handle the business of the fund. In some instances the person handling the affairs is shared with other insurance pooling organizations, such as a residual market mechanism. Other funds have a full-time manager, and in some cases regional guaranty funds are combined under one manager. Ohio and West Virginia funds operate separately, but use one manager. The six New England guaranty funds, Virginia, and the District of Columbia have come together under the Guaranty Fund Management Services, a separate, not-for-profit association. Colorado, Idaho, Kansas, Montana, and Wyoming operate through the Western Guaranty Fund Services.[41] A fund can handle covered claims by hiring claims people temporarily or by hiring the services of an insurer to avoid the cost of a permanent staff.

Another operational matter for the guaranty fund is the assessment of member companies. Here again, there have been a variety of approaches and various degrees of sophistication in calculating and communicating each member company's assessment. In each case, however, the net direct written premium in the state that is subject to assessment is provided by the official reports of the state insurance department.

Because guaranty funds receive money from member companies that is then held for a period of time in order to pay claims in the future, a part of the guaranty fund's responsibility is investing the money received. However, as tax-exempt organizations, they should not unnecessarily accumulate money. Therefore, it is common to assess the member companies for the expected claims of an insolvency, but to call for payment in installments over a period of time as the funds are actually spent.

An important operational aspect of the guaranty funds is the relationship between the fund and the insurance department's liquidation bureau. In some respects both organizations perform the same function by evaluating and paying claims against the insolvent company. Anyone with a claim that exceeds the guaranty fund cap or is subject to a guaranty fund deductible has a valid claim against the liquidation estate. The liquidator takes control of the insolvent company's assets and, ultimately, the guaranty fund is entitled to reimbursement from the liquidation estate for the covered claims paid and expenses incurred.

Exhibit 10-2
Insolvency Assessments and Refunds
(From November 1969 Through 31 December 1985)

State	Amounts Assessed by Guaranty Association	Amounts Refunded by Guaranty Association to Member Companies	Net Assessments
Alabama	$ 11,802,996	$ -0-	$ 11,802,996
Alaska	2,359,182	1,146,766	1,212,416
Arizona	3,553,000	-0-	3,553,000
Arkansas	9,594,773	-0-	9,594,773
California	185,857,918	41,778,844	144,079,074
Colorado	5,398,787	1,207,401	4,191,386
Connecticut	5,383,604	3,431,157	1,952,447
Delaware	4,193,800	-0-	4,193,800
Dist. of Columbia	1,672,020	80,555	1,591,465
Florida	158,760,284	6,875,825	151,884,459
Georgia	18,584,704	4,834,264	13,750,440
Hawaii	20,604,520	500,000	20,104,520
Idaho	3,907,707	46,280	3,861,427
Illinois	36,953,086	6,963,265	29,989,821
Indiana	3,739,862	1,245,000	2,494,862
Iowa	6,193,705	525,441	5,668,264
Kansas	2,836,627	72,179	2,764,448
Kentucky	9,222,656	662,440	8,560,216
Louisiana	11,330,857	3,500,000	7,830,857
Maine	2,153,913	109,724	2,044,189
Maryland	16,401,586	1,090,300	15,311,286
Massachusetts	30,064,357	10,186,963	19,877,394
Michigan	30,010,758	8,491,652	21,519,106
Minnesota	36,771,000	6,029,776	30,741,224
Mississippi	4,392,310	586,621	3,805,689
Missouri	7,222,570	849,281	6,373,289
Montana	3,088,560	257,556	2,831,004
Nebraska	7,465,720	4,745,370	2,720,350
Nevada	7,157,669	1,908,358	5,249,311
New Hampshire	3,272,153	315,545	2,956,608
New Jersey	17,097,431	12,478,931	4,618,500
New Mexico	1,594,507	-0-	1,594,507
New York	*	*	*
North Carolina	5,156,871	709,073	4,447,798
North Dakota	302,303	-0-	302,303
Ohio	22,859,650	5,878,141	16,981,509
Oklahoma	13,602,284	-0-	13,602,284
Oregon	12,332,492	-0-	12,332,492
Pennsylvania	39,174,851	7,301,239	31,873,612
Puerto Rico	37,679,525	15,703,173	21,976,352
Rhode Island	2,761,023	1,090,581	1,670,442
South Carolina	3,636,756	782,436	2,854,320
South Dakota	166,908	-0-	166,908
Tennessee	850,396	280,352	570,044
Texas	30,441,799	-0-	30,441,799

Utah	120,182	-0-	120,182
Vermont	2,931,019	-0-	2,931,019
Virginia	7,398,483	-0-	7,398,483
Washington	5,667,435	292,352	5,375,083
West Virginia	4,884,329	782,106	4,102,223
Wisconsin	11,424,524	2,999,053	8,425,471
Wyoming	1,909,824	41,126	1,868,698
TOTAL	$871,943,276	$155,779,126	$716,164,150

Adapted from information compiled by the National Committee on Insurance Guaranty Funds

* New York has a pre-assessment fund.

VI. HOW FUNDS HAVE PERFORMED

One measure of how the post-assessment guaranty funds have performed is how and if they have met the goals stated in Section 2 of the Model Act.

The purpose of this act is to provide a mechanism for the payment of covered claims under certain insurance policies to avoid excessive delay in payment and to avoid financial loss to claimants or policy-holders because of the insolvency of an insurer, to assist in the detection and prevention of insurer insolvencies, and to provide an association to assess the cost of such protection among insurers.

Paying Claims Against Insolvent Companies

The most significant purpose of the guaranty funds is paying covered claims. According to a report by the National Committee on Insurance Guaranty Funds (NCIGF), shown in Exhibits 10-2 and 10-3, post-assessment property-liability insurance guaranty funds from 1969 through 1985 collected a net amount of $716 million from member companies. That figure can serve as an estimate of the amount of claims paid or in the process of settlement during that period.

The smallest amount collected during that period was $120,000 by Utah. Florida collected the largest amount, $152 million. Between 1969 and 1985, payments by guaranty funds were made on behalf of 125 insolvent insurance companies. As of 1 January 1987, the largest assessment for a single insolvency was $120 million for the Ideal Mutual Insurance Company.

Clearly, by raising these amounts to pay claims, guaranty funds have met the goal of avoiding loss to claimants or policyholders because of insolvencies within the limitations set out by the drafters.

As noted in the Model Act's purpose section, it is important that payment is made without "excessive delay." Once triggered to action, guaranty funds have not been criticized for slowness in making

Exhibit 10-3
Total Assessments by Insurer Insolvency*
(From November 1969 Through 31 December 1985)

Year	Insolvent Insurer	Total Assessed	Domicile
1969	Key Insurance Exchange	$ 1,350,649	California
1970	Fidelity General Insurance Company	199,580	Illinois
	Liberty Universal Insurance	247,388	Texas
	Ohio Valley Insurance Company	1,362,602	Ohio
	Sutton Mutual Insurance Company	583,363	New Hampshire
1971	Citizens Casualty of New York	2,435,056	New York
	First American Insurance Company	2,569,023	Florida
	Homeowners Insurance Company	601,102	Illinois
	LaSalle National Insurance Company	10,043,847	Illinois
	Los Angeles Insurance Company	1,692,463	California
	Maine Insurance Company	1,880,626	Maine
	Trans Plains Insurance	49,592	Texas
	United Bonding Company	616,151	Indiana
1972	Maryland National Insurance Company	466,921	Georgia
	Metro Casualty Group	500,000	Missouri
1973	Commercial Underwriters	2,998,766	Michigan
	First Fire & Casualty Company of San Antonio, Texas	—	Texas
1974	Gateway Insurance Company	38,679,583	Pennsylvania
	Granite Mutual Insurance Company	1,880,802	Pennsylvania
	Professional Insurance Company	1,594,436	New York
	Rockland Mutual Insurance Company	14,041,436	Massachusetts
	United American Insurers	2,462,946	Iowa

continued on next page

Year	Company	State	Amount
1975	Associated Merchants Mutual Insurance Company	Massachusetts	999,822
	Capitol Mutual Fire Insurance Company	Pennsylvania	409,735
	Epic Insurance Company	Arizona	—
	Financial Fire & Casualty Insurance Company	Florida	2,414,820
	Glaco Automobile Insurance Company	Montana	346,576
	Guardian Mutual Insurance Company	Pennsylvania	114,685
	Interstate Insurance Company of West Collingswood	New Jersey	1,835,071
	Manufacturers & Wholesalers Indemnity Exchange	Colorado	2,710,599
	Medallion/Missouri General Insurance Co.	Missouri	6,041,485
	Mobile County Mutual/Mobile Insurance Company	Texas	8,063,409
	National Mutual Insurance Company	Michigan	200,000
	Pennsylvania Taximen's Mutual Ins. Co.	Pennsylvania	199,620
	Resource Insurance Company of New York	New York	4,320,854
	Satellite Insurance Company	Pennsylvania	257,497
	Security Fire & Casualty Ins. Company	South Carolina	19,921
	State Security Insurance Company	Pennsylvania	548,948
	Summit Insurance Company of New York	New York	12,380,159
	Transnational Insurance Company	California	3,262,647
	Westgate-California	California	2,536,802
	Wisconsin Surety Company	Wisconsin	1,650,252
1976	Bankers Fire & Casualty Insurance Co.	Florida	2,036,284
	Manchester Insurance & Indemnity Co.	Ohio	11,214,030
	Southern American Fire Insurance Co.	Florida	297,812
	Woodland Mutual	Michigan	746,382
1977	All-Star Insurance Corporation	Wisconsin	12,560,767
	Builders Insurance Company	Puerto Rico	1,883,178
	Empire Mutual Insurance Company/Allcity Insurance Company	New York	4,824,324

continued on next page

Year	Company	Amount	State
	Maryland Indemnity Insurance Company	1,005,149	Maryland
	New York National Insurance Company	—	New York
	Old Security Life Insurance Company	71,549	Missouri
	Penn State Mutual Insurance Company	183,847	Pennsylvania
1978	Bakers Mutual Insurance Company	—	New York
	Commonwealth Insurance Company	24,358,242	Puerto Rico
	Consolidated Mutual Insurance Company	9,491,029	New York
	Consolidated Underwriters	185,079	Missouri
	Eldorado Insurance Company	19,213,619	California
	Signal Insurance Company/Imperial Insurance Company	53,478,429	California
1979	Long Island Insurance Company	582,444	New York
	Reserve Insurance Company/American Reserve Insurance Company	85,197,399	Illinois/ Rhode Island
1980	Atlantic and Gulf States	749,764	South Carolina
	Concord Mutual Insurance Company	9,987,912	Pennsylvania
	Cosmopolitan Insurance Company	12,218,367	New York
	State Farmers Insurance Company	2,873,674	Nebraska
1981	Church Layman Insurance Company	585,489	West Virginia
	Eastern Insurance Company	817,308	Florida
	Fauquier Mutual Insurance Company	339,902	Virginia
	Market Insurance Company	1,250,000	Illinois
	Proprietors Insurance Company	29,195,701	Ohio
	Security Casualty Company	11,941,734	Illinois
1982	Amherst Insurance Company	1,499,419	Pennsylvania
	Cotton Belt Insurance Company	364,584	Tennessee
	Equitable Insurance Exchange, Inc.	15,000	Texas
	Great Indemnity Insurance Company	3,170,041	Puerto Rico

continued on next page

Year	Company	Amount	State
	Kenilworth Insurance Company	4,599,254	Illinois
	Lloyds of America (Texas only)	1,084,484	Texas (only)
	Main Insurance Company	2,431,266	Illinois
	Safeguard Mutual Insurance Company	7,978,698	Pennsylvania
	Stuyvesant Mutual Plate Glass Insurance Company	1,999,957	Pennsylvania
1983	Interco Underwriters Exchange	4,216,027	California
	Lincoln Insurance Company	4,202,265	Puerto Rico
	Superior Lloyds	—	Texas (only)
	Western Carriers Insurance Exchange	9,862,520	California
1984	Ambassador Insurance Company	10,795,161	Vermont
	Aspen Indemnity[1]	2,870,396	Colorado
	Colonial Assurance Company	2,348,123	Pennsylvania
	Dome	—	Virgin Island
	Excalibur	29,029,008	Minnesota
	Financial Security Insurance Company	15,705,027	Hawaii
	Gibralter Mutual Insurance Company	224,595	Pennsylvania
	Golden West Insurance Exchange	1,999,812	California
	Guaranty Assurance Company	2,613,101	Puerto Rico
	Gulf American	4,253,591	Florida
	Horizon Insurance Company[1]	3,634,906	New York
	Ideal Mutual Insurance Company[1]	119,913,293	New York
	Independent Indemnity Company	91,904	California
	Lawyers Professional Liability Insurance Company	16,545,490	Florida
	Nassau	13,230,271	New York (only)
	North-West Insurance Company	1,998,497	Oregon
	Northeastern Fire Insurance Company of Pennsylvania	—	Pennsylvania
	Oklahoma Insurance Logistics Company	—	Oklahoma
	Surety Insurance Co. of California	—	California

continued on next page

	Company	Amount	State
1985	Universal Casualty Insurance Company	41,149,005	Florida
	American Consumer Ins. Co.	—	New York
	American Fidelity Fire Ins. Co.	—	New York
	American Protective Excess Ins. Co.	—	Delaware (only)
	Columbus Ins. Co.	3,568,464	Ohio
	Commercial Standard	2,802,889	Texas
	Commonwealth Marine	400,000	Delaware
	Consumers Ins. Group (Kent Ins. Co.)	3,297,451	Florida
	Early American[1]	11,318,640	Alabama
	Eastern Indemnity[1]	6,397,017	Maryland
	Glacier General Assurance Co.	23,792,579	Montana
	Guard Casualty & Surety Co.	—	Indiana
	Iowa National Mutual Ins. Co.	13,031,043	Iowa
	Pacific American[1]	4,193,355	Delaware
	S&H Ins. Co.	9,999,174	California
	Southwestern Ins. Co.	—	Oklahoma
	Southwestern National Ins. Co.	16,056,395	Oklahoma
	Standard Fire	931,817	Alabama
	Temple Mutual Ins. Co.	—	Pennsylvania
	Transit Casualty Co.	6,941,512	Missouri
	Union Indemnity[1]	4,350,995	New York
	United Employers Ins. Co.	—	Texas (only)

[1]These figures do *not* include amounts assessed by the Louisiana and Missouri guaranty funds to pay for claims arising out of the noted insolvencies. Data showing *total* yearly assessments by these funds has been reported to the NCIGF and is reflected elsewhere in this report. Information from these funds indicating assessment allocation *by insolvency*, however, is not available.

* Adapted from information compiled by the National Committee on Insurance Guaranty Funds

payments.[42] In fact, the greatest problem for insureds of insolvent companies prior to guaranty funds was that the liquidator was short on assets. The second greatest problem was that delivery of any payment was long in coming even if the assets were there. The delay was necessary in many cases to avoid creditor preferences as the liquidator would have to wait until all claims were presented and evaluated. Since the guaranty funds are not limited by the amount of the insolvent insurer's assets and can gather enough funds from member companies to pay all covered claims, there is no need to wait. Indeed, the funds take over claim files and begin paying as soon as possible. They provide claim service as it would be provided by a solvent insurance company.

Guaranty funds provide this service at limited expense. Those that are triggered process claims either through staff or by using servicing insurers. There is no national organization.

Prevention and Detection of Insolvencies

One area in which the purpose of the Model Act has not been achieved is in prevention and detection of insurer insolvencies. When the NAIC Committee was drafting the Model Act, it had the advantage of recently enacted post-assessment guaranty fund laws in California and Michigan that authorized the guaranty fund to submit reports and recommendations to the regulator on the financial condition of an insurer.[43] In pursuit of the goal of insolvency prevention and detection, Section 13 of the Model Act created a duty on the part of the board of directors upon majority vote "to notify the commissioner of any information indicating if any member insurer may be insolvent or in a financial condition hazardous to the policyholders or the public." It contained permissive provisions for requesting the commissioner to examine a member insurer and to make recommendations to the commissioner "upon any matter germane to the solvency, liquidation, rehabilitation or conservation of any member insurer."

There was always a measure of uneasiness regarding Section 13, partly based on antitrust concerns relating to board members who could be acting together against the interests of a competitor. Despite a legal opinion secured by the NCIGF in 1975 obviating some of that concern,[44] Section 13 proved to be of questionable value in prevention and detection of insolvencies over the years. Legal concerns persisted, and one guaranty fund counsel believed that there were significant risks that legal action would be taken against board members performing Section 13 duties, and that board members' duties to the guaranty fund and to their companies could seriously conflict.[45]

In 1982 the National Committee on Insurance Guaranty Funds reviewed the issues surrounding Section 13. Section 13 had produced little if any activity in which a regulator received new information about a troubled company from a guaranty fund. To the extent that Section 13 was based on the premise that the industry had better information about the financial condition of particular companies than regulators, a new situation prevailed. Better solvency monitoring techniques had been developed by regulators since the adoption of the Model Act in 1969. Given legal and other concerns, the NCIGF recommended that Section 13 be modified. This was accomplished by the NAIC in 1984. The new provision places no responsibility on the board for prevention and detection in general and allows the board, in its discretion, to respond to a regulator's request to discuss the financial condition of a specific insurer. Clearly, the original concept of the guaranty fund mechanism having a significant role in prevention and detection of insolvencies has been abandoned.

VII. CHALLENGES OF A MULTI-STATE SYSTEM

The same state system that allows for variation and experimentation and provides for cost efficiency in claims handling creates some burdens. The challenges of a multistate liquidation and guaranty fund system have been minimized through cooperation fostered by the NCIGF. Two stated goals of the NCIGF are:

> ... to provide a national forum for discussions and interchange of information on all problems arising out of the implementation of state guaranty fund laws; and to provide information and assistance with respect to the operation and administration of insurance guaranty funds and related activities.[46]

Operating through a board of insurer representatives and an executive secretary provided by the three major property-liability trade associations (Alliance of American Insurers, American Insurance Association, and National Association of Independent Insurers) on an alternating basis, the NCIGF fulfills these goals in a number of ways. It publishes newsletters, special bulletins, guaranty fund-related court decisions, and reports on the costs of insolvencies. It holds general workshops and seminars on administrative techniques and coordinates guaranty fund activities.

Residence of a Corporation

Significant challenges to the multi-state system arose with the insolvency of the Reserve Insurance Company in 1979. Reserve was the first large national commercial insurer to become insolvent. It wrote business in every state. All state post-assessment guaranty funds were triggered by Reserve, many for the first time. As noted, the original concern giving rise to the Model Act was the impact of insolvencies of automobile insurers. With Reserve it became apparent that the drafters of the Model Act had not contemplated many problems that arise in administering commercial insurance claims.

The elementary question concerning which guaranty funds were responsible for which claims became a matter of serious contention. The Model Act for most situations provides that a claimant should seek recovery from the guaranty fund of the state of residence of the insured,[47] but the residence of a corporation is not always certain. A corporation is said to be "domiciled" in the state of its creation, but can have a "residence" in one or more other states. Reserve had some corporate insureds operating on a national basis, so claims occurred in various places. Some guaranty funds took the position that the domiciliary state of a corporate insured was the place of residence. The NCIGF attacked the residency problem from a short-term and long-term standpoint.

Solving the Reserve Problem The short-term concern about corporate residence, of course, was to resolve the confusion then existing among the states over Reserve Insurance Company claims and the question of which state had responsibility for a particular claim. The NCIGF appointed a subcommittee to review the issue. It recommended in February 1980 that each guaranty fund adhere to the principle that a corporation's residence be considered to be "the principal place of business most closely associated with the risk."[48]

The Guiding Principles After the immediate problems of Reserve's claims were fairly well resolved, work on dispute resolution continued, resulting in 1985 in the *Guiding Principles for Settling Disputes Between and Among Property and Casualty Insurance Guaranty Associations as to Responsibility for Claims.*[49] The Guiding Principles would be used whenever two or more guaranty funds having some relationship to the claim could not agree among themselves as to which had the primary responsibility. The dispute would be settled by binding arbitration. Six criteria would be considered in determining the result:

1. state where executive offices or corporate headquarters are located,
2. location of the operation where the insured event occurred,
3. state of incorporation,
4. state where the applicable insurance policy was issued or delivered,

5. state where the applicable premium taxes were paid or should have been paid pursuant to annual statement allocation rules, and

6. state that is considered the insured entity's primary domicile for state income tax purposes.

Thirty state guaranty funds have adopted the Guiding Principles and have agreed to binding arbitration to settle disputes.

One author has found the following deficiencies in the Guiding Principles. First, no weight is assigned to the various criteria. Second, there is a lack of focus in the criteria in that some address the relationship between the insured and the state and others address the relationship between the insured and the insurer. Third, the multiplicity of unweighted criteria adds complexity to the situation, perhaps getting in the way of agreement and promoting arbitration.[50]

These deficiencies are being addressed by the NCIGF and the signatories to the Guiding Principles. The new standard, which would control disputes if a majority of the funds subscribing to the Guiding Principles agree, will be the place of the insured's principal office and where the highest level decisions are made for the corporate entity.[51]

Without a high degree of cooperation among guaranty funds, litigation resulting in severe delays in paying claims against Reserve and subsequent insolvent companies could have occurred. An illustration of the kinds of problems that could have resulted is provided by the following incident. In January 1979, a New Jersey court equated residence with domicile and decided that the New Jersey guaranty fund was not responsible for a claim asserted against a corporate insured domiciled in Delaware even though it had extensive business and its executive office was in New Jersey. The New Jersey appellate court reversed the lower court. Looking "to the aim and context of the statute in which the residency requirement is contained" and to the "extent and character" of the business transacted, the court decided that based on the facts, the Delaware domiciled corporation in question was a resident of New Jersey.[52]

As a result of confusion about corporate residency, Delaware, domicile to many national corporations, changed its guaranty fund law to define residency of a corporation as the "principal place of business most closely related to the claim."[53]

The Legislative Solution   To resolve the long-term implications of corporate residence, the Legal Subcommittee of the NCIGF pursued changing the language in the statute regarding residence as it relates to corporations. The subcommittee's recommendation that the Model Act be amended to specify that the residence of a corporation is its "principal place of business" was agreed to by the NCIGF.[54] The recommendation was endorsed by the Industry Advisory Committee to the NAIC Guaranty Fund Task Force in 1985, and the NAIC adopted that change in the Model Act.[55]

Triggering Guaranty Fund Obligations

New York Rehabilitations Questions have arisen about what events trigger the obligation to pay covered claims. In the Model Act, guaranty fund coverage was originally triggered upon the declaration of a company's insolvency by a court of competent jurisdiction. Some states required that this court not only declare the company insolvent but also order it liquidated and that the order be final and unappealable before the payment of covered claims begins. When the New York Superintendent of Insurance secured a court order declaring the Empire Mutual Insurance Company insolvent, but not ordering liquidation, most of the guaranty funds in states in which Empire did business were triggered. The overwhelming reaction of the guaranty funds was negative because the New York receiver used Empire's assets to pay claims in New York while relying on the guaranty fund system to pay claims of the insurer in other states. The NCIGF voiced its dissatisfaction with this approach: "[a] rehabilitation order which in effect forces the guaranty funds to spend their member's money on a speculative rescue attempt that admittedly has New York policyholders and claimants as the principal beneficiary is contrary to the whole purpose of guaranty funds and should be prevented from happening again."[56] As a result of this event, other states adopted the triggering requirement of a final order of liquidation, and the Model Act was changed.[57]

Guaranty funds not triggered by the court order finding Empire Mutual insolvent developed a precedent-setting technique to provide payment of Empire Mutual claims in their states. They negotiated an agreement with the New York liquidator for repayment of amounts advanced to pay claims that would have been payable if the funds had been triggered. Empire Mutual was eventually released from rehabilitation on condition that triggered guaranty funds also be reimbursed for claims they paid.

Appealed Liquidation Orders Complications regarding triggering developed in Illinois when an order to liquidate Security Casualty Company was appealed. The NCIGF and affected guaranty funds had been working on an agreement under which funds that were not triggered until a final (after appeals are exhausted) order of liquidation was entered would pay covered claims of Security Casualty in their respective states, subject to the Illinois liquidator's agreement to honor those payments as claims against the estate if the liquidation order were upheld. If the order were not upheld, the Illinois receiver would reimburse the funds since the company would still be in rehabilitation. While those negotiations were underway, the Illinois legislature attempted to resolve the issue by passing an act calling for an "appeal pendency plan" supervised by the court to provide for continued payment of claims.[58] Because the appeal pendency plan created potential inequities among guaranty funds, it became necessary for the triggered guaranty funds to work out agreements as well, thus complicating the resolution of the issue.

Stagnated Rehabilitation Some regulators have been frustrated about the inability to trigger guaranty funds when a company is in rehabilitation in its state of domicile and no claims are being paid. Claimants against the Main Insurance Company (an Illinois company that was in court-ordered rehabilitation from 1977 to 1982 and not paying claims) were left with no remedy for a number of years. Since the company was not declared insolvent or ordered liquidated in that period, no guaranty funds were triggered. As a result, claimants were left unpaid. If, however, the company had been either rehabilitated (so that it could properly operate and pay claims) or declared insolvent and ordered liquidated within a reasonable time after the original 1977 court order (so the guaranty funds could discharge the company's duties), the problem would not have occurred.

Florida's commissioner, in order to trigger that state's guaranty fund to cover Main Insurance Company claims, obtained an order of liquidation from a Florida court.[59] The guaranty fund appealed the order of liquidation, and the appellate court reversed the trial court because both Illinois and Florida had adopted the Uniform Insurers Liquidation Act,[60] which requires reciprocal recognition of the state of domicile's right to control rehabilitation or liquidation. The goal of the Florida commissioner was to get at assets of Main Insurance Company that were in Florida. But under the Uniform Insurers Liquidation Act, an ancillary (nondomiciliary state) liquidation of an insurance company's assets could not occur unless the domestic state had instituted liquidation proceedings. Thus, claimants in Florida who filed against Main Insurance Company could receive payment neither from the rehabilitator in Illinois (under court order not to pay claims) nor from the guaranty fund in Florida because the Florida fund could not be triggered without a court finding of insolvency and an order to liquidate the insurer. Situations like this, where payment of claims is delayed due to triggering requirements, illustrate some of the burdens created by the multistate system.

While the problem of appealed liquidation orders may require further legislative solutions, the guaranty funds working through the

NCIGF have shown a spirit of cooperation in seeking solutions. The result was that Security Casualty claimants suffered little inconvenience. Cooperation also allowed the system to work in the case of Empire Mutual. The Main Insurance Company problem was not solvable through agreements. A possible solution to the problem of continuing rehabilitation where no claims are being paid is to amend the Insurers Supervision, Rehabilitation, and Liquidation Model Act to require liquidation if a company fails to pay adjudicated claims within a certain period. Giving a right to claimants or to another state's regulator to seek such an order in the state in which the company is domiciled would avoid delays caused by a reluctant domiciliary regulator or put pressure on a reluctant judge.

VIII. NAIC ACTIVITY SINCE 1969

Early Activity

Over the years changes to the Guaranty Fund Model Act have been proposed in an attempt to adapt it to varying circumstances. In the mid-1970s GEICO Insurance Company was in a difficult financial situation that could have created the largest ever property-liability insolvency. The industry was concerned that the guaranty fund assessments required to meet GEICO claims would be an unacceptable burden. Although GEICO was "rescued" and the guaranty funds were not triggered, the experience led to two significant additions to the Model Act, early access and priority.

Recognizing that an insolvent company normally has insufficient assets rather than no assets, the NAIC enhanced the capacity of guaranty funds to meet their obligations by providing for early access.[61] This provision requires the liquidator to distribute funds from the insolvent insurer's assets to the guaranty funds in a timely manner, thus reducing the amount of funds that need to be assessed member companies. This short-circuits the process by which guaranty funds would assess member companies and later seek reimbursement when the insolvent estate is settled. At the same time, the NAIC changed the Insurers Supervision, Rehabilitation, and Liquidation Model Act to give the guaranty funds a right to file claims on assets of the insolvent insurer equal to that of insureds. This increases the likelihood of guaranty funds receiving some reimbursement for paying covered claims.[62]

A number of notable provisions were not adopted by the NAIC. As the early access and priority proposals were made, the NCIGF proposed a premium tax offset under which guaranty fund assessments from companies would be offset against premium taxes, and thus the funding for guaranty funds would be shifted wholly or partially to the state. The NAIC never adopted the proposal, but a number of states did.

There was an early recommendation that guaranty funds "receive the benefit of any reinsurance contracts or treaties entered into by the insolvent insurer which covered any of the liabilities incurred by the insolvent insurer with respect to covered claims."[63] Although this concept was reaffirmed in 1972, it was not pushed because many felt that it was "too soon to make definitive recommended change" in the guaranty fund laws.[64] The issue of reinsurance proceeds was raised again in 1978 and, lacking industry agreement, the NCIGF again recommended no action.[65]

In the mid 1970s, the NAIC considered institutionalizing the possibility of rescuing troubled insurers with funds provided by charges to policyholders. Each insurer would add an amount of money to every insured's premium bill and retain that money in a guaranty fund reserve. The NAIC would coordinate activities on a national basis, analyze troubled insurers, and make recommendations as to whether or not a rescue was appropriate. The commissioner in the state of domicile would then call on the guaranty fund to draw the money out of the various insurer guaranty fund reserve accounts (prefunded by the surcharges) and use that for the rescue. The guaranty fund of each of the various states would contribute in proportion to the troubled insurance company's premium volume in the state.[66] No support for such a rescue mechanism was found within the industry. The industry's position was summed up in a statement by the American Mutual Insurance Alliance (now known as the Alliance of American Insurers) to the NAIC:

> It is our opinion that in normal economic times, the companies which should be rescued, have been rescued for good business and economic reasons. The profit motive in our economy encourages others in the business community to rescue based on hard business and economic judgments. If it makes good business sense—a company will be rescued. This also holds true in unusual economic times. To date, no one has been able to demonstrate to us that anyone of the twenty-three companies now being handled by the Guaranty Funds might have been a potential rescue candidate.

> Some companies which went insolvent were basically unable to compete in a free enterprise economy. Who is to say if a rescue fund were established we would not be throwing good money after bad? What would make the rescue board any more omniscient than present regulators? Who will say that politics would not enter into the picture? But even more basic, a regulator who is not doing his job

might be encouraged to divert his attention from examination for solvency to superficial but politically popular pursuits.[67]

The GEICO rescue was "private," like that referred to in the statement by the Alliance. It involved an offer of stock of which 82 percent was subscribed to by current shareholders and the remainder by companies that reinsured GEICO's book of business.

Deductibles

The next significant action by the NAIC regarding the Model Act occurred in 1980. Most insurance regulators have an employee in charge of the liquidation bureau that handles insolvent companies. The liquidators of various states proposed to eliminate the $100 deductible on covered claims that was provided for in the Model Act. Their goal was to eliminate what they perceived as an inefficiency since a claimant who did not get $100 from the guaranty fund would still have a claim against the liquidation estate for that amount. The NCIGF vigorously opposed the elimination of deductibles on the basis that it would unnecessarily and significantly increase the cost to guaranty funds. An example of that increase was shown through a study of insolvencies in Florida. It was estimated that the Florida guaranty fund would have had to pay an additional $7.6 million from 1969 to 1980 for unearned premium claims and administrative expenses, a 165 percent increase over what the cost actually was.[68] Each side appears to have won part of the battle since the NAIC eliminated the deductible for insurance claims but not for unearned premium claims.[69]

Scope of Coverage

The NAIC created a guaranty fund task force in 1984 chaired by Illinois Director of Insurance John E. Washburn and reporting to the Financial Regulation Committee.[70] The impetus for this action was the insolvency of the Balwin-United subsidiary life insurance companies and the inability of the life guaranty fund system, if triggered, to handle the resulting claims. The task force thoroughly revised the life and health model guaranty act and also looked at the property and liability guaranty funds.

The Industry Advisory Committee to the task force directed the task force's attention to the potential for enhancing property and liability guaranty fund capacity by reducing fund obligations. A thorough public policy analysis was proposed to examine the lines and types of insurance covered; the types of claims or claimants covered; the caps, deductibles, and time limitations on coverage; the problems of companies organized under special provisions and not subject to full solvency regulation; and the matter of assessment accounts.[71]

Recent experience with commercial insurer insolvencies led to reconsideration of the scope of the Model Act as properly reflecting the underlying public policy behind guaranty funds. Consideration was also given to the extraordinary nature of a mechanism by which money is transferred from one group to another by means of the private sector. As a result, certain changes regarding coverage were made in the Model Act,[72] some of which have been previously described. The complete list is as follows:

New exclusions from coverage included:

- Annuity and health insurance (they are covered by the life and health guaranty fund)
- Financial guaranty or other forms of insurance offering protection against investment risks
- Fidelity insurance
- Any bonding obligations
- Insurance of warranties or service contracts
- Transactions indicated as insurance but which transfer nothing more than investment or credit risks (for example, fronting or retroactive insurance)
- Any claims by an affiliate of the insolvent insurer
- Punitive or exemplary damages
- Premium returns due under a retrospective rating plan
- Any claims covered by a government insurance or guaranty program (aimed primarily at the federal flood and crop-hail insurance program)

The following new limitations were adopted:

- A cap on recovery of unearned premiums of $10,000 (formerly $300,000)
- In the following liability coverage situations, the guaranty fund will be obligated to pay claims up to $300,000 (as was formerly the case) but will now have the right to recover such payment from the insured under the liability policy:
  - Where the insured is an affiliate of the insolvent insurer
  - Where the insured has a net worth of $50 million or more

Four public policy concepts are embodied in these changes: (1) a desire to avoid covering investment risks, (2) withholding coverage from wealthy insureds, (3) excluding noninsurance transactions that have the appearance of insurance, and (4) excluding for public policy or administrative reasons certain kinds of recoveries not worthy of support through an extraordinary mechanism like a guaranty fund.[73]

Financial guaranty insurance, some bonding obligations, and retroactive insurance are examples of coverage for investment-related risks. Financial guaranty insurance became an important topic among regulators at the time the Industry Advisory Committee and the task force were engaged in revising the Model Act. There had been a tremendous growth of financial guaranty insurance that provided coverage for certain economic transactions (for example, a guarantee that the insurer of a bond would pay when the bond became due, or that the value of a particular asset would be a certain amount at the end of a lease). A separate task force of the NAIC was considering regulatory aspects of this type of insurance. They attempted to determine the extent of insurer obligations for this kind of coverage and to define it for regulatory purposes. The NAIC ultimately adopted a model bill for regulating financial guaranty insurance.[74]

An example of retroactive insurance sought to be excluded is that relating to the Las Vegas MGM Grand Hotel fire in 1980. In this case, subsequent to the loss, an insurance company provided coverage for losses that had already occurred.[75] This was essentially a speculation (at a time when interest rates were high) that the insurer could invest the premium dollars in a manner sufficient to gain more than would later be paid out in claims.

The Industry Advisory Committee proposed other kinds of exclusions under the concept of financial guaranty. For example, no coverage was to be provided by guaranty funds for professional liability insurance for accountants and financial advisors or for directors and officers coverage. The idea was that these types of insurance are primarily guarantees that benefit stockholders and other investors and speculators in the marketplace. Medical malpractice could not be excluded since it protects innocent third parties who have suffered bodily injury. The task force rejected these proposed exclusions.

The second concept, excluding coverage for the wealthy insured, was not adopted as recommended by the Industry Advisory Committee. Rather than exclude coverage completely, the task force sought to protect innocent third parties from having to seek collection from the wealthy tortfeasor rather than the guaranty fund. As a result, the guaranty fund is still obligated to pay claims but is allowed to make a claim against the wealthy insured for reimbursement. The threshold of $50 million of net worth to determine who is "wealthy" still leaves coverage for eleven of the Fortune 500 companies. The task force also rejected a proposal that first-party claims of certain wealthy insureds not be covered by the fund. The threshold suggested for that coverage was $10 million of net worth.

The concept of excluding certain types of claimants from coverage by the guaranty fund is not new. The original Model Act excluded claims by insurers and reinsurers so that the funds would not be collecting money for the benefit of insurance companies. This type of exclusion was upheld in a court challenge based on unequal treatment.[76] The court stated as follows:

> The legislature is not bound, in order to adopt a constitutionally valid statute, to extend it to all cases which might possibly be reached, but is free to recognize degrees of harm and to confine its regulation to those classes of cases in which the need is deemed to be the most evident.

The third concept is to exclude noninsurance transactions. These are represented by fronting arrangements under which, due to regulatory constraints, an insurer uses a locally licensed company to write business and then reinsures it 100 percent. There is no real intention on the part of the fronting company to undertake the insurance risk. Retroactive insurance, which was already discussed, also fits into this category.

Additionally, there are a number of items found not to be worthy of support through the extraordinary device of guaranty fund coverage. The exclusion of punitive damages was supported on the basis that such awards are theoretically not meant to make a person whole for his or her injuries and are foreign to the insurance concept. Some states, in fact, forbid insurers on the basis of a public policy decision from covering punitive damages. The Industry Advisory Committee also recommended excluding coverage for noneconomic loss. In the recent debate over the tort system, attention has been focused on the erosion of concepts of fault and on the lottery aspect of awards of damages based on highly speculative, nonmeasurable injury. It was felt that the guaranty fund system should not to be used to support a tort system gone awry and add to the dislocation by further transfer of such payments. The task force did not agree.

Because some losses are of little consequence to the insured, they are not worthy of coverage. The unearned premium deductible is an example. The task force added insurance of service contracts and warranties to the exclusions for the same reason. These are relatively small, high volume claims and are not of serious economic consequence to the insured. Therefore, the guaranty fund should not be used to pay them. Additionally, there is normally a seller or servicing agent still responsible for making good on such contracts.

Finally, the insolvency of Ideal Mutual Insurance Company brought to light a problem regarding coverage for certain premium refunds. This insurer wrote a large amount of retrospectively rated commercial insurance business. Guaranty funds challenged claims under such rating plans on the basis that they were not unearned premium claims. Even if they were, guaranty funds would have neither the expertise to handle them nor the relevant records. In the 1985 changes the NAIC voted to exclude premium refunds under retrospective rating plans as not suitable for coverage.

Claims-Made Policies

After the substantial changes in the December 1985 amendments were made, the Task Force asked the Industry Advisory Committee to consider an additional item. The NAIC and some states had been considering the ISO-proposed claims-made version of the commercial general liability policy. The concept of a claims-made policy is simply that only claims made against the insured during the policy period will be covered by the insurer (ISO's original version of the proposed policy also allowed the claims to be made during the sixty-day period after the policy expired). Under an occurrence policy, events giving rise to the claims must occur during the policy period, but such events may be reported and the claim made against the insured any time during or after the policy period without limitation and still be covered.

The task force was concerned that an insured with a claims-made policy would have less coverage under the guaranty fund than an insured with an occurrence policy. In its negotiations with regulators and other industry people, ISO addressed this concern to some extent by providing for an additional five-year reporting period for claims arising from occurrences reported to the insurer within sixty days after the end of the policy period. Finally, a provision was added that allows the insured to purchase a "supplemental extended reporting period"— an unlimited tail. When combined, these two tails basically turn the claims-made policy into an occurrence policy.

Even with these changes, a gap in coverage could develop. It is possible that the insured would be unable to purchase the supplemental tail coverage due to the insolvency of the insurer. At the same time, market conditions might preclude the insured from buying a new policy covering those claims that would have been covered under the supplemental tail of the expiring policy of the insolvent insurer. In such a case any claims that would have been picked up under the supplemental tail of the insolvent insurer's policy would be uncovered. The task force proposed that claims-made insureds be considered as if they had occurrence policies.

The Industry Advisory Committee opposed using the guaranty fund for this purpose. It would be the first time the guaranty fund would be obligated to pay any claims under a coverage not in the policy issued by the insolvent company. The Industry Advisory Committee, however, accommodated the regulator's request for assistance and presented a draft under which the Insurers Supervision, Rehabilitation, and Liquidation Model Act would be revised to authorize the liquidator at his discretion to sell tail coverage. The Model Post-Assessment Property and Liability Guaranty Association Act would then be amended to indicate that the guaranty fund would cover claims arising under such coverage. The Industry Advisory Committee, in presenting its draft, recommended not to adopt it for a number of reasons. It was suggested that to do so would be to use guaranty funds to solve market problems, which would be a bad precedent. It was further suggested that the approach would do a disservice to insureds in that it could lull them into a false sense of security and result in their failure to seek new coverage in the voluntary market. The sense of security would be false since the value of coverage provided by the liquidator would be limited by the covered claims limitations, claim filing deadlines, and other restrictions in guaranty fund laws which differ in each state. Those limitations would make it difficult for an insured to determine the extent of any coverage to be received when electing to purchase coverage from the liquidator. Finally, it was suggested that the task force may have underestimated the administrative difficulties of pricing and communicating the coverage to insureds. It would be important to make such a communication early, and yet, reliance would have to be placed on records of an insolvent insurer, which are commonly inadequate and often missing. The ISO representative on the task force also indicated that it would be very difficult to price such coverage.[77]

When the issue came up at the June 1986 meeting of the NAIC, it was deferred for further consideration. Action was taken on the matter at the December 1986 meeting, at which time the task force voted to include the tail coverage in the two Model Acts as an optional solution and provision for each state to consider.[78]

Funding

As the NAIC task force considered Model Act changes regarding the scope of coverage, it decided to review issues of financial capacity from the funding side, too. A policy committee on guaranty funds comprised of chief executive officers of insurers (NAIC Policy Committee on Guarantee Funds) was impanelled to help in the effort after the Hartford Insurance Company proposed prefunding through a surcharge on policies.[79]

The reasons for the Hartford proposal were conveyed to the NAIC in the fall of 1984. Reference was made to stories in the trade press about the condition of the industry, the ISO study indicating serious deficiencies in loss reserves, and the Conning & Company report titled

"1984: Disasters and Opportunities in the Property and Casualty Business," which stated, "We believe that industry fundamentals have now deteriorated to a point where many less disciplined companies are on the brink of financial disaster."[80] The Hartford presentation went on to question the reliability of the state property and liability insurer insolvency system. There was no dispute that the system had performed well. The question was whether it could handle the impending doom suggested by the evidence at that time. The presentation concluded, "It would be foolish not to recognize that there can be serious capacity problems under property and liability insurance post-assessment insolvency fund laws."[81] The Hartford subsequently outlined a proposal for prefunding guaranty funds that became the primary subject of the NAIC Policy Committee on Guaranty Funds. The proposal was later supported by the American Insurance Association (AIA), which provided legislative language for consideration by the policy committee.

The Hartford Proposal   The prefunding approach that Hartford suggested would transfer surcharges on premiums from the insurers to a centralized state fund said to be an "irrevocable trust fund." The trust fund would be managed by a board of political appointees. Money would be transferred to the guaranty fund as necessary to pay claims. The surcharge, levied at the rate of the state's annual assessment cap, would be cut off when the fund reached an amount equal to three times the assessment cap. The surcharge would be reinstituted when the amount in the fund dropped to a certain level. If the fund generated investment income in excess of the target amount, the excess would spill over into the general revenue fund of the state. The guaranty fund would have power to assess insurers if the surcharge funds failed to meet needs. Any assessment would be recouped from subsequent surcharges.

The relationship between the proposed solution and the statement of the situation in the presentation to the NAIC is not readily apparent to this author. A proposal of this magnitude would require debate at the NAIC, amendment of the current Model Act, and then enactment by each state. Even with unified insurance industry backing, successful implementation of the program would be an uncertain, lengthy process. The time factor alone makes the proposal unresponsive to the economic conditions that gave rise to the creation of the policy committee.

The policy committee created a technical subcommittee to analyze the Hartford proposal and to raise other issues. The technical subcommittee consisted of representatives from the same insurers as the members of the policy committee. Representatives also came from the three major property and liability trade associations. In its analysis of the Hartford proposal, the technical subcommittee made the following list to summarize arguments for and against prefunding.[82]

A. The Case for Prefunding Guaranty Funds through Policyholder Surcharges

1. Major insolvencies can be expected to continue. According to regulators, the number of insolvencies could exceed 80 from June 1985 to June 1986, and could include some big companies. In addition, 186 property-liability insurers have been flagged by the NAIC Examiner Team for immediate regulator attention, based on indicators that the short-term survival of these companies is threatened. Insolvencies are also far more costly than in the past: the potential liabilities involved in two recent insolvencies (Ideal Mutual, $155 million; Union Indemnity, $135 million) are equivalent to more than 70 percent of the costs to insurers of all insolvencies from 1969 through 1982.

2. The cumulative effect of numerous insolvencies would produce guaranty association obligations faster than funds can be raised under current assessment caps and separate account limitations. Funds raised under early access laws, which permit liquidators to make the insolvent insurer's assets available to guaranty associations, would not be timely to help meet these accelerating obligations.

3. The potential maximum, annual "national" cost to insurers of numerous insolvencies is $1.7 billion. This cost would be a charge on earnings or surplus. In some states, insurers would be able to recoup some of this cost through mechanisms such as premium tax offsets, mandatory policyholder surcharges, or rate increases.

4. There is evidence of serious guaranty association funding inadequacy when an individual state's capacity is examined in terms of the state's assessment cap and the use of separate accounts. (See the ISO Study on State Guaranty Funds, subsequently discussed in this monograph.) For example, Florida has four separate accounts—automobile, workers compensation, auto physical damage, and all other kinds of insurance. The cap on each is 1 percent of assessable premiums per year. The automobile account produces around $18 million per year. Approximately $48 million is produced each year for all accounts.

a. The Florida automobile account is already "maxed out" for the next several years in order to pay for existing insolvencies. It will be assessing the maximum possible (1 percent) in each of these years, and it is not yet known whether funds continually will be available to pay covered claims on a timely basis. Imagine the likely effect on capacity when subsequent insolvencies occur.

b. Insurers will also be assessed the maximum (1 percent) for the workers compensation and auto physical damage accounts this year (1985).

5. Beyond an inability to pay covered claims, inadequate capacity can also result in regulatory delay in seeking adjudications of insolvency. Delay further increases the cost of an insolvency as more assets are dissipated and opportunities for fraud develop.

6. Guaranty association assessments to pay for new insolvencies will be a significant drain on insurer earnings or surplus. This creates additional hardship in an environment in which all property-liability insurers experienced $3.8 billion in operating losses (1984), and 50 of the 100 largest insurers operated in the red (1984).

7. Prefunding through mandatory policyholder surcharges funds the cost of insolvencies, and facilitates the gradual buildup of financial capacity to many times the present capacity under post-insolvency assessments, by generating additional capital rather than by cannibalizing earnings or surplus of solvent insurers.

8. Prefunding ensures that all policyholders and insurers participate in paying for the costs of insolvencies. The mandatory policyholder surcharge provides up front disclosure of the fact and the amount of payment by policyholders to fund the cost of insolvencies.

9. Policyholder surcharges would be dedicated up front to an irrevocable policyholder trust fund, a mechanism intended to insulate monies in the trust fund from subsequent legislative diversion. Capping the size of the trust fund and having excess investment income spill over into a state's general revenue will discourage legislative interest in diverting "excess" funds to other purposes. The AIA's draft bill includes unique provisions (that were not in prior insurance laws creating prefunding mechanisms) designed to obviate subsequent interference with the trust funds.

10. Prefunding is a far more constructive response to capacity limitations than increasing burdens on insurer earnings or surplus by increasing assessment caps, or merging separate accounts into a single account. It should also be an

attractive alternative to premium tax offsets when they are endangered.

B. The Case Against Prefunding Guaranty Funds

1. Prefunding guaranty funds may create large amounts of state-controlled funds, which are susceptible to raiding for other purposes. Raiding encompasses any taking of funds for purposes other than those considered in the original statute creating the prefunding mechanism. Examples of legislative raiding include (a) direct appropriation from the prefunded mechanism, (b) expanding the obligations of the guaranty fund, or (c) amending the investment authority of the guaranty fund. Methods of raiding are limited only by legislative imagination.

2. Prefunding guaranty funds increases the likelihood that insurers and their policyholders will be required to fund involuntary rescues to troubled companies, thus increasing the total cost to the guaranty fund system. This can be contrasted to those instances where a voluntary rescue is economically feasible, and the industry and regulators can work together on an arm's length basis to avoid the consequences of an insolvency.

3. Prefunding guaranty funds may jeopardize the tax-exempt status of guaranty associations. Efforts to insulate the funds from taxation by making the guaranty fund a quasi-state agency may increase the likelihood of successful state raids on prefunded pools.

4. Prefunding guaranty funds increases the cost of insurance for policyholders. The AIA draft addresses this problem by exempting from payment of the surcharge large insureds for whom self-insurance is an option. An additional problem is that the increased cost of the prefunded proposal is not related to any systemic changes geared to either improving regulation for solvency or improving claim handling services of guaranty funds in the event of insolvencies.

5. Prefunding guaranty funds can relieve some of the capacity pressures on regulators and the industry to find other solutions for problems related to solvency regulation and improved operation of the guaranty fund system.

6. Prefunding guaranty funds by means of mandatory identifiable policyholder surcharges may create quasi-contractual promises of insolvency protection making it difficult to implement or enforce subsequent limitations in the scope of guaranty fund coverage.

7. The AIA draft includes use of a board of public trustees. A board of public trustees appointed by a variety of public officials may be more susceptible than an industry board of directors to political pressures regarding payment of claims, investment decisions, and implementation of illegal raids on guaranty funds. Such a board of public trustees may be less inclined to put the economic and legal interests of policyholders above the short-term political interests of their sponsors.

8. The primary advantage of prefunding is that it expands the capacity of the insurance guaranty association to meet its statutory obligations. Depending on the extent to which the capacity in the current post-assessment guaranty fund system needs to be supplemented, there are alternative methods to increase capacity that do not have some of the disadvantages associated with prefunding, that is, improved early access distribution of assets, post-assessment policyholder surcharges, restrictions and limitations in the scope and definition of covered claims under guaranty fund laws, and increased caps on guaranty fund assessments. Capacity problems related to the possibility of multiple insolvencies following a major natural catastrophe may be better handled by prefunding the catastrophe exposure, for example, a federal disaster insurance Fund corporation.

9. The current system has worked well and has a significant overall capacity between one and two billion dollars. Although there may be regional and state dislocations since it is not administered on a national basis, they are not inevitable. Additionally, the current system provides borrowing power and early access has been improving. Where early access is not working well, it can be improved.

10. Should the system be designed for the worst possible case? Is the current prediction of "doomsday" any more valid than those in the past? Cannot regulatory action and the current reported trend in more adequate pricing help alleviate the current problems?

A number of members of the policy committee found the concept of prefunding guaranty funds to be attractive. After considerable discussion, however, the concept was rejected. The primary concern of the committee was the potential for raiding such funds. The three kinds of legislative raiding that are mentioned in Section B.1. of the analysis are described below.

Direct Appropriation First, there is raiding by directly appropriating prefunded monies. States with budget problems always go after pools of "idle" funds. While funds raised through taxes are subject to legislative will and may be applied to whatever purpose a legislature chooses, it is more difficult for a legislature to raid the monies of a fund financed by private resources. There have been several attempted raids of state workers compensation insurance funds, which have resulted in lawsuits.[83] The general bases for finding these raids unconstitutional were that the legislative actions impaired the funds' contractual obligations and/or constituted a taking without due process of law. The courts concentrated on the fact that, although the funds may have been publicly administered, they were created by contributing organizations for mutual benefit. The contributing parties had a property interest in the monies, and consequently, the monies could not be diverted for general or other purposes of the administering state. In a Wisconsin case the court said, "All money in the funds is attributable to contributions from insurers. No state money is involved."[84] This case is distinguishable from the Hartford proposal, which calls for surcharges on policyholders directly and provides that any earnings on the money raised over a certain amount goes to the state.

While most raids have been unsuccessful, when the Arkansas legislature appropriated money from the workers compensation trust fund to pay for the Workmens Compensation Commission office rental, the appropriation was unsuccessfully challenged. The Arkansas Supreme Court found such use of the fund permissible.[85]

In terms of state guaranty funds, the New York Pre-Assessment Property and Liability Security Fund has been raided by the New York legislature. A 1982 statute used certain accounting methods and a so-called "dry appropriation" to give the appearance that the monies of the security fund, as well as two workers compensation funds, had not been disturbed.

Employer policyholders and their insurers challenged the legislation, but the appellate division of the New York Supreme Court held that the monies were state funds, the fund itself a state agency since its eight commissioners were approved by the governor with the advice and consent of the senate, and the appropriation of $204 million a valid state action.[86] The New York Court of Appeals affirmed.[87] It should be noted that the Hartford proposal calls for the funds generated by the premium surcharge to be controlled by public officials and appointees of public officials, thus inviting this type of legislative raid.

Expanding Obligations The second raiding technique is to expand obligations against the funds. This can be done in a number of ways. First, the scope of the guaranty fund can be expanded by amending out some of the exceptions. For example, if a large pool of money is idle and a financial guaranty insurer becomes insolvent, the out-of-luck insureds would surely seek access to the idle funds. Another approach would be to expand the "covered claim" definition. This would be attractive for certain medical malpractice joint underwriting associations that are overextended and underfunded. The lobbies of the medical associations would surely push this approach. Also, when a natural disaster occurs and money is needed to help the victims, there would be temptation to make their losses "covered claims." A third approach would be to amend the mechanism that triggers the spill-over of investment income into the state's general revenue fund to provide for earlier state access to this money. New York is an example of this technique. In 1979 the legislature provided that $15 million annually of the income from assets of the property/casualty security fund would be used to subsidize the New York FAIR Plan.[88]

Amending Investment Authority Finally, while the draft of the proposal would limit investment of funds collected through surcharges to United States government obligations, state obligations, and interest-bearing certificates of deposits of banks, it could be amended to provide for investment in certain unmarketable obligations of local governments. This type of "raiding" happened in New York with the bonds issued to bail out New York City when it became insolvent. Money in the security fund was used to buy those bonds, making those funds nonliquid at the time. Further amendments could provide for investment in obligations issued to create housing opportunities in certain areas, to guarantee student and small business loans, and to support any socially desirable venture that could arise in the mind of a legislator.

Other Funding Proposals While the Hartford prefunding proposal was the primary focus of the committee's attention, other proposals were reviewed. The State Farm approach, which that company has consistently advocated for fifteen years with few changes, calls for each insurer to establish with a custodian an account of marketable securities (called a policyholder security account) that is equivalent to the higher of either its policyholder obligations or 70 percent of its written premiums. The custodian would report to the insurance regulator concerning transactions on a monthly basis and on March 15 each year would report the value of the account. Failure to maintain the account at the appropriate level would trigger the regulator to have the company comply with the law and a need for prior approval of other transactions in the account. Noncompliance would require issuance of an order to cease doing business.

State Farm has analyzed past insolvencies that indicate that the policyholder security account, had it been required, and would have forced the regulator to deal much earlier with the problems of the insurer, which would have likely resulted in greater available assets to pay claims if the insurer became insolvent. The analysis of the Reserve Insurance Company, which was put into rehabilitation and liquidation in 1979, shows that a policyholder security account law would have required regulatory action in 1974.

Some concerns about the State Farm proposal arise from a fear that freedom to deal with company investments may be affected. Also, in order to convince some opponents, the proponents agreed to cap the custodial account at $100 million, thereby favoring large companies. Finally, some are concerned that logic compels movement toward valuation of bonds at market rather than amortized value if the proposal is adopted. The industry has opposed this.

Nationwide Insurance Company has recently modified a proposal it first recommended in 1977 that calls for reinsuring the insolvency risk. The modified proposal would create a single, state-chartered, not-for-profit mutual reinsurance company. Every insurer would be required to add a charge per policy for the purchase of solvency reinsurance from the newly created company. The reinsurer would accumulate funds that would be available to a state guaranty fund unable to fulfill its obligations, with a 1 percent assessment against member insurers. Unlike the Hartford approach, which presumes that each state has need of a large capacity that is immediately available, the Nationwide approach creates a more modest pool of funds that is, however, "movable" in that it can be applied where needed, as needed.

Although this approach is simpler than the original one, it still creates a whole *new* mechanism, which in itself becomes a hurdle. Concern has been expressed about creating a central insolvency mechanism even as a backup to the state system. Furthermore, the creation of a reinsurance company that would receive premiums creates the potential that the federal government could tax dollars raised for insolvency.

The proposal offering the least radical change is that of Crum & Forster, which suggests that all states institute a policyholder surcharge of up to 2 percent of premium to be levied subsequent to an insolvency and the amount of which would be directly related to estimated needs based on claims against the insolvent company. The surcharge proceeds would be turned over to the guaranty fund. Since the proposal implies that the assessment power remains with the guaranty funds, this approach would increase capacity. Any assessments levied against insurers would be recoupable from subsequent surcharges, thereby shifting the recoupment mechanism from subsequent ratemaking to automatic surcharges.

While each of these issues was discussed by the policy committee and the technical subcommittee, there was not agreement on an approach to enhance the funding of guaranty funds. The fact that the present system has worked well, coupled with the difficulty of determining any future need, made it difficult to determine how and even if the system should be changed. On the other hand, the policy committee acknowledged that guaranty funds have a potential liquidity problem. That potential was illustrated by three studies.

Attempts to Quantify the Funding Issue

The ISO, the Alliance of American Insurers, and the Illinois Insurance Department did separate analyses that attempted to test the guaranty fund system against the occurrence of certain large insolvencies. Each analysis presented a different conclusion as to the scope of the problem. Each made assumptions that affected the results.

ISO Study This study sought to estimate the impact of assessments if a large insurer were to become insolvent and had to be liquidated. After looking at the thirty largest property-liability insurers and both post-assessment and pre-assessment guaranty funds, the study concluded that no single insolvency would invoke the full national capacity of the guaranty fund system. Yet, because of the distribution of business among the states and the various state caps, on average only 51.2 percent of the covered liabilities of guaranty funds could be handled by assessments during the first year.[89]

The ISO study was ambitious, but it left many unanswered questions. The study was based on a model that necessarily included many assumptions and statistical techniques to arrive at conclusions. For example, it assumed that the payout pattern of claims for the insolvent insurer would be the same as the industry pattern, and that the reserves of the insolvent insurer were adequate. The study also admitted that it ignored many relevant factors. Some were early access to the insolvent insurer's money and the ability of guaranty funds to borrow money, and the existence of large uncommitted assets in pre-assessment funds and in the New Jersey post-assessment fund. Premium balances held by agents would be an asset of the insolvent insurer, but they were also ignored. The ISO study was an attempt to show the worst-case scenario for an insolvency of any one of the largest insurers. Many on the policy committee were impressed with the ISO study but felt that a more refined approach might be necessary.

Alliance Study   The Alliance of American Insurers attempted to "estimate whether, and to what extent, the guaranty funds may have a capacity problem in handling a major insolvency," by using a different computer model than the ISO study and assuming one large company became insolvent. The Alliance also noted the need to make many assumptions that might not be valid. For example, it was noted that "payout patterns with respect to an insolvent company may differ from that of a solvent company, thereby changing the cash flow needs of the guaranty funds."[90] The study also noted that there was "no way of determining the test company's liabilities, by state, by line."[91] The study also did not take into account early access, did not consider unearned premium losses subject to guaranty fund coverage, or the benefit that guaranty funds would receive from covered claim deductibles and caps on amounts recoverable. "As a result of using nationwide data, the liabilities in all states, for like accounts, have the same relationship to premium. In actuality, the liabilities by state may be higher or lower than those estimated by the model and thus affect whether or not the guaranty fund will have sufficient funds by account to cover those liabilities."[92]

Using these assumptions, the Alliance concluded that "thirty-eight accounts in thirty-one states could not respond in the first year after making the maximum assessment, and thirty-one accounts in twenty-nine states could not respond after a maximum assessment in the second year."[93]

The Alliance study focused on accounts rather than the total state assessment. It showed different kinds of conclusions and potentially more serious problems for guaranty fund liquidity than the ISO study did because the ISO study incorrectly assumed that guaranty funds were not responsible for claims that were ceded through reinsurance by the insolvent company to a reinsurer. In focusing on accounts, the Alliance study produced, in addition to its state-by-state analysis based on the insolvency of one large insurer, a financial capacity threshold indicating what market share an insolvent insurer would need to have in order to put the guaranty fund capacity and liquidity in jeopardy based on three possible caps on assessment. The conclusions shown in Exhibit 10-4 are based on the assumptions used in the Alliance study.

Illinois Study   After the Alliance study was considered by the policy committee and questions were raised again about the many assumptions in such a study, the Illinois Department of Insurance began a new study building on the ISO and Alliance approaches. It attempted to address "three principal shortcomings" in them: loss reserve inadequacy, availability of assets of the insolvent company, and payout patterns. The Illinois study used data from the Reserve

Exhibit 10-4
Maximum Market Share of Insolvent Insurer that Guaranty Funds Can Handle*

Line of Business Account	Assessment Rate		
	1%	1.5%	2%
All Lines	3.1%	4.6%	6.0%
Workers Compensation	2.0%	3.0%	4.0%
Auto	2.7%	4.0%	5.3%
All Except Auto & Workers Compensation	3.6%	5.3%	7.0%
All Except Workers Compenstion	3.2%	4.7%	6.2%
All Except Auto	3.1%	4.6%	6.0%

* Adapted with permission from Alliance of American Insurers.

Insurance Company insolvency to provide model information on these three categories. The reserves of the insolvent insurer turned out to be significantly understated. Losses paid were 131 percent of the company's reserves as reported at the time of insolvency. The actual Reserve Insurance Company payout pattern was used and applied to the company used by the Alliance in its study. The Illinois project concluded that the data "paint a much grimmer picture of the capacity of the current guaranty fund system to handle an insolvency of significant size especially considering that the insolvent company's available assets are taken into account."[94] The Illinois study, which was designated as "a preliminary report," concluded that additional questions warrant further study:

> How much capacity should the guaranty fund system have? Should it be structured to handle a failure of a very large company?

> How adverse a scenario of insolvencies can the present structure handle? Given the current industry conditions, can the present structure handle a most likely scenario of insolvencies?

> What impact will a sequence of yearly maximum assessments have on the industry and individual companies from a surplus and operational standpoint?

> Are the methods and assumptions employed in this study, i.e., the Reserve Insurance Company insolvency data, reasonable and appropriate? Is the data reflective of likely net costs to guaranty funds for most insolvencies, and are the payout patterns appropriate?[95]

The Illinois study come closer to a good model for determining the financial capacity of guaranty funds. However, it too, as its authors recognized, raises more questions. One is whether there is a "typical insolvency." The Reserve Insurance Company, for example, was accused of irregular dealings in subsequent litigation surrounding reinsurance schemes that were said to be fraudulent.[96] Can that situation be ascribed to every insolvency that occurs? Currently, much of the concern about the industry's condition arises not from practices of questionable legality, but from market conditions and underpricing. It is fair to assume that if those conditions bring a company to a state of insolvency, the accuracy of its books and records will also be subject to question because of improper dealings?

Policy Committee Report

Taking note of potential liquidity problems, the policy committee identified funding options that could be helpful to guaranty funds.[97] They looked at short-term and long-term options. In the short-term it was noted that some states had been successful in preventing problems due to assessment caps by borrowing among guaranty fund accounts. An excess of funds in the auto account can be used to pay claims in a workers compensation account, and the "loan" can be repaid by use of future assessments in the account that benefited from the loan. This arrangement does not require new legislation. The Florida guaranty fund, which has operated with a 1 percent assessment cap and a burden of a large number of costly insolvencies, has used excellent cash management to enable it to pay claims in a timely fashion. The Florida auto liability account has been at maximum assessment since the mid-1970s. Since 1981, the workers compensation account has been at the maximum, and in 1985 the all-other account required the full assessment. These recent developments and projections of an overall shortfall in mid 1987 have led the commissioner of insurance to recommend an increase of the assessment cap to 2 percent.[98]

Guaranty funds have the power to borrow from commercial sources. The policy committee urged the NCIGF to look into types of security instruments that might be used by the guaranty funds under their borrowing authority.

The policy committee report noted that forty-two states have early access laws allowing guaranty funds access to an insolvent insurers' assets. "Better and more expeditious use of early access statutes" was recommended.[99]

As to long-term options, the policy committee endorsed the recommendations of the Industry Advisory Committee that were made in September 1985 for changes in the Model Act, including those that were not adopted by the NAIC in December 1985.

The committee noted two other options about which there was no agreement, and no recommendation was made. The first was increasing assessment caps. The Model Act calls for a 2 percent assessment cap, yet only twenty-one states have enacted that provision. (See Exhibit 10-1) It was noted that an increase to 2 percent in those states that now have a 1 percent cap could double the capacity of the post-assessment guaranty fund system. Finally, in recognition of the evidence in some of the studies that some states would have problems in certain accounts if there were a large insolvency, the committee noted that elimination of separate accounts would increase the flexibility and capacity of guaranty funds that now use those separate accounts. One reason there was no agreement on this issue is a public policy concern that personal lines insureds should not be unnecessarily charged for commercial insurance losses such as product liability and medical malpractice. Under the current system in states with only one assessment account, personal lines auto and homeowners premiums support commercial claims. In states with separate assessment accounts, homeowners help pay for commercial lines insolvencies since they are in the same account as commercial lines (that is, the "all other" account).

Concern over the financial capacity of insurance guaranty funds will likely be renewed as a result of the liquidation of Mission Insurance Company. While the full impact of this insolvency on guaranty funds is not certain, the California Insurance Commissioner estimates it initially to be approximately $650 million.[100] This would be the largest insolvency yet.

IX. PROSPECTS FOR THE FUTURE

Looking back at the development of property and liability guaranty funds, it is clear that the present national system did not result from a significant public policy debate. It came from the fear that there was a federal threat to state regulation. There was a rush to address any congressional concern, real or imagined. States adopted the NAIC Model Act so rapidly that, overwhelmingly, most property and liability insurance in the country was subject to protection by guaranty funds within a short period of time.

As measured by legislative and regulatory feedback about the system, one would have to conclude that it was very effective for more than a decade. While many ideas were brought up at the NAIC, no significant support to change the system emerged, and no serious complaint about an inadequacy was apparent among the insuring public and their elected representatives. Adjustments were made in the system in response to events. The early success of the system can be explained by the fact that it was addressing the perceived need for which it was created, automobile insurer insolvencies. It was not until the insolvency of Reserve Insurance Company, a commercial writer, that it became evident that the drafters did not contemplate that the system would have to respond to multistate commercial insurance problems.

While the Reserve insolvency posed some challenges, they were largely met through cooperation among guaranty funds and regulators under the auspices of the NCIGF. But the Reserve insolvency was only a sign of events to come. During the 1980s, the type of insurer insolvency accounting for most of the dollars assessed was no longer a single state or regional automobile insurer but a multistate and, sometimes, national commercial insurer. The faults of the system became magnified. The issue of a corporation's residence was but one of a number of matters that called for cooperation among guaranty funds and liquidators to make the system work.

Issues in a Multi-State Liquidation System

In June 1986, the American Bar Association (ABA) Tort and Insurance Practice Section sponsored the National Institute on Insurer Insolvency in which papers on insurer insolvency and guaranty funds were presented. Many of the writers focused on the flaws of the multistate system. Concern was expressed over the lack of uniformity in laws relating to rehabilitation and liquidation of insurers and in the guaranty funds themselves. Over the years the NAIC has recommended three separate statutes for dealing with insurer insolvencies. In the 1930s, the Uniform Act proposed by the commissioners on uniform state laws providing for interstate cooperation was recommended. In the 1960s, Wisconsin adopted a statute in relation to insurer rehabilitation and liquidation that was drafted by Spencer Kimball.[101] The NAIC recommended the Wisconsin Act as a model in 1968. In 1978, the NAIC promulgated its own model fashioned to a great extent after the Wisconsin statute. In one way or another, thirty-two states have adopted a law incorporating the basic provisions of the Uniform Act. Ten other states have statutes based primarily on the 1977 Insurers Supervision, Rehabilitation and Liquidation Model Act (Model Liquidation Act) of the NAIC. The rest of the states do not have acts that could be said to be similar enough to either the Uniform Act or the Model Liquidation Act so as to be "reciprocal states." The purpose of reciprocity, recognized in these acts, is to provide one process for liquidating an insurer.

Among the issues raised about the liquidation process was that disputes can arise over a receiver's rights to assets of the insolvent insurer when the insurer is domiciled in a state that has adopted neither the Uniform Act nor the Model Liquidation Act, and assets of the insurer are located in a state that has adopted one of those acts. Since the Model Liquidation Act and Uniform Act provide for multistate liquidation, they also provide for the domiciliary liquidator to have the primary authority in marshalling assets of the insolvent insurer wherever the assets are situated. In a case where the insurer is domiciled in a nonreciprocal state, that receiver will not acquire unfettered rights to assets of the insurer that are in a state that has a Model Liquidation Act or Uniform Act. The result can be bifurcated liquidation of the insurer. Cooperation is not precluded, but it is not required.[102]

Even if receivers in the different states cooperate, creditors may be able to complicate the proceedings.

> If the state where the assets are held has not adopted the Uniform Act (or an equivalent provision), creditors may be free to institute proceedings to seize the assets there. Moreover, if the domiciliary state is not a reciprocal state, the courts have allowed creditors to satisfy their claims against the insolvent insurer by obtaining an interest in assets located in other states even if such other states have adopted the Uniform Act.[103]

Problems can also arise when insurers that are affiliates are domiciled in different states. This occurred with the Reserve insolvency—the Reserve Insurance Company was domiciled in Illinois, and its subsidiary, American Reserve Insurance Company, was domiciled in Rhode Island. Each state had separate liquidation proceedings for its respective company. The books and records of both companies were located in Illinois and were not well segregated. The Illinois and Rhode Island liquidators each set up operations in the defunct companies' Chicago office and independently made demands of employees and worked on files. When that problem arose in relation to life insurance company subsidiaries of Baldwin-United Corporation, the issue was resolved by redomiciling certain affiliates into the state of one of the other affiliates.[104]

In multistate liquidation situations, problems have also arisen out of the ability of a liquidator to control litigation against the insolvent company. While most states honor an order from the domiciliary state's court staying all litigation against the insolvent company, one state has not.[105] Some federal courts have also refused to honor stay orders from state liquidation courts.[106]

Another issue that arises even among reciprocal states is a dispute about the right to special deposits some states require of insurers. This is an anomaly since the NAIC called for abolition of special deposits when it created the Model Liquidation Act.[107]

Guaranty Fund Issues

Papers delivered at the ABA also called attention to variations among guaranty fund provisions that many feel should be made more uniform. Differences in coverage by guaranty funds among the states were addressed. It was noted that many states have a different definition of a "covered claim" as well as different caps on the amount of coverage provided. This can cause those with guaranty fund claims to seek recovery from the most generous state.[108] A potential gap in coverage was also noted. "An individual automobile insured who has moved from state A, where the insolvent insurer is domiciled, to state B, where the insolvent insurer is not licensed, and has an accident in state B, may not be covered" because the fund applies only to licensed insurers.[109]

The issue of absent or delayed claims payments due to triggering differences among the states was also brought up. This was already discussed in this monograph.

The advent of significant commercial insolvencies has also led to complaints about the failure of guaranty funds to provide coverage for certain kinds of insurance. Surplus lines insurers are not members of the guaranty fund, and claims under their policies are not covered. The rationale for not covering surplus lines, according to one of the drafters of the Model Act, was "that licensed companies, which submitted to the state regulation for solvency and their policyholders who bear the ultimate cost of insolvency ... should not be required to pay for the losses resulting from the insolvency of insurers which do not submit to such regulation."[110] However, in New Jersey when an insolvent surplus lines insurer's claims were not covered, the legislature reacted by creating a surplus lines guaranty fund. The existence of a surplus lines guaranty fund in only one state has caused claimants to try to tie their claims to New Jersey since it is the "only game in town."[111]

Liquidator and Guaranty Fund Relations

Perhaps most disturbing fact about the presentations at the ABA Institute were the many comments about the failure of cooperation among the participants in the system.

> Some of the areas where problems have arisen in the past in obtaining cooperation between the guaranty funds and the liquidator are (1) delays in providing guaranty funds with claim files or estimates of potential liabilities on which an assessment can be based;

(2) liquidators refusing to allow guaranty funds to process payment of claims without using the domiciliary liquidators prescribed proof of claim form for both unearned premium claims and loss claims; (3) liquidators failing to seek court approval for early distribution of assets to guaranty funds which would eliminate unnecessary assessments and facilitate payment of policyholder claims; (4) problems in determining exactly what claims' activities should be reported directly to the reinsurer or the liquidator to preserve rights of recovery under reinsurance agreements; (5) problems concerning pursuit and recovery of subrogation and salvage; (6) failing to accord the administrative expenses of guaranty funds the same priority as administrative expenses of the liquidator; and (7) imposing unnecessary burdensome requirements on the guaranty fund as a claimant against the estate, such as requiring individual proofs of claim for each payment rather than an aggregate claim, or refusing to honor guaranty fund claim payments made after the final date for filing of claims even though claims were presented to the guaranty fund prior to the cutoff date.[112]

Early Access A separate paper was presented at the ABA Institute on early access. A significant part of it was devoted to the problems in this very important provision. The speaker attributed part of the problem to the "generalized language of the early access statutes," but also noted a potential "institutional reluctance to accelerate the winding down of insurer insolvency proceedings" on the part of the liquidators.[113] Liquidators often are reluctant to propose and implement early access. The speaker concluded, "Although the early access procedure is simple in concept, its implementation has proven troublesome and in operation it has not provided as much financial support as had originally been envisioned."[114] With the recent growth in the amount of money required to pay covered claim obligations of guaranty funds, early access is more important than ever before.

New York Finally, there is growing concern about the ability of the multistate system to work when a major and populous state is not part of the system. One speaker at the ABA Institute addressed this issue in his speech on "the New York problem."[115] He indicated that New York, which never changed from its pre-assessment security fund to a post-assessment Model Act-type fund, "remains outside the mainstream of the insurance guaranty association system and often works at cross purposes to it."[116] He pointed out that New York did not sign the NCIGF Guiding Principles regarding disputes over the obligation for covered claims. While other guaranty funds will respond to claims of their residents or claims concerning property with a permanent location in the state, New York has taken the position under its definition of an "allowed claim," that the incident that gives rise to liability under the insurance policy must occur within New York before a claim can be made against the New York security fund. For example, if an insolvent insurer had provided products liability coverage to a manufacturer whose product gave rise to a claim, New York would provide coverage from the security fund only if the product had been manufactured in New York and was located in New York at the time of the incident causing the injury. It was pointed out that as states begin to enact the newly adopted definition of corporate residence in the Model Act, "there will be the risk that those [guaranty funds] will have no responsibility to pay the claims and New York will [also] disclaim responsibility."[117]

The continuing concern about New York's role was brought up in November 1986 by the NCIGF. In a communication to guaranty funds, concern was expressed that the guaranty funds were having difficulty meeting their obligations as to covered claims for six insolvent New York companies.[118] The problems were itemized as follows: the peculiar New York requirement for a proof of claim for each claim to be submitted on New York's form was slowing down claim payments and increasing expenses for the guaranty funds; the failure of the New York liquidator to cooperate in providing early access increased guaranty fund assessments; using a finding of insolvency to trigger other state guaranty funds to fund New York rehabilitations; and the lack of cooperation on sharing information about coverage limitations in insolvencies of commercial insurers where multistate claims would arise under a policy, and coverage limitations in that policy and claims made within those limitations would have to be shared for guaranty funds to know when their obligations ceased because of exhaustion of coverage under the policy. Additionally, the situs of claims problems and the claim reporting problems mentioned previously were reiterated.

The Future

What are the prospects for the future of post-assessment insurance guaranty funds? The financial capacity of these guaranty funds has been examined. The studies show that there is room for concern given the potential for numerous insolvencies of good-sized companies. Yet, excluding New York, these post-assessment guaranty funds have an annual capacity to raise over $2 billion to pay covered claims.[119] That is no small amount. Small and medium-sized company insolvencies can be handled. Of concern, of course, is the so-called "jumbo" insolvency or insolvencies. In estimating the capacity of guaranty funds to handle them, the capacity would have to be reduced by the amount that would be contributed by the insolvent insurer or insurers for the first year. There are other limits of this capacity that should be noted.

Some large insurers pay out more than $2 billion in claims in a year. It would be theoretically possible, therefore, to exhaust one year's capacity with one insolvency. Additionally, if insolvent insurers had a large share of business in certain states, the capacity of those states' guaranty funds would be severely diminished. In that regard, the large "national" capacity of the guaranty funds can be misleading in terms of the ability to respond to large insurer insolvencies or to combinations of insurer insolvencies.

On the other hand, the capacity of the guaranty funds can be enhanced by borrowing among accounts, from outside sources, and by gaining early access to the assets of the insolvent company. The usefulness of the system has not suffered from bad design but from lack of cooperation.

No one can predict exactly what capacity is needed. It is clear that if the capacity were doubled or tripled, one could hypothesize a set of circumstances that would indicate the inadequacy of that capacity. As pointed out in the committee comments to the Wisconsin guaranty fund law, "No funding that is reasonable in amount could ever be adequate for a catastrophic rash of insolvencies touched off by a major and unprecedented depression or other serious change of direction of our society. All that any security device can do is to take care of the risk to policyholders that is inherent in the insurance mechanism itself, that is, the risk that bad management or peculation in a given firm will result in bankruptcy and loss to policyholders."[120]

The current system's capacity can be enhanced by a number of devices mentioned in the policy committee report to the NAIC Guaranty Fund Task Force. One device would raise the assessment cap in states that have a 1 percent cap, many of which are large states with large premium bases. Another way to immediately increase capacity would be provided by the Crum & Forster approach to institute a post-insolvency surcharge on policyholders that would be the immediate source for funding covered claims. That surcharge would provide funds immediately and be backed up by a continued authority to assess companies for additional amounts as a secondary source, doubling capacity.

On review it appears that the basic design of the post-assessment guaranty fund system appears to be sound. Many of the problems discussed relate more to the liquidation mechanism and its operation than to the guaranty fund system. The system finally was publicly debated in 1985, which led to changes in the Model Act regarding the scope of coverage of guaranty funds. The financial capacity of guaranty funds will be increased as the states adopt those changes by addressing the obligation side instead of the funding side of the guaranty fund mechanism. More can be done along that line.

It is the author's view that the future of the post-assessment guaranty fund system is not in doubt because of a lack of financial capacity, but as a result of parochialism and lack of cooperation among participants in the system. In 1979, the liquidator from New York discussed the need for cooperation between liquidators and guaranty funds. They met and agreed on the "desirability of a procedure to develop a quick response to 'brush fire' problems that have a tendency to arise between guaranty associations and regulatory receivers and liquidators."[121] While the need for cooperation was recognized, it seems that efforts to work together have deteriorated since 1979. The resulting problems for guaranty funds were recognized by the NCIGF in its report to the NAIC in December 1981:

> Finally, we would return to the idea that the guaranty fund system involves the joint efforts of liquidators and the several guaranty funds. The success of the multi-state system, particularly if it is compared with the concept of a single, federally administered system, depends in a great part upon the extent of the comity and cooperation among the states or, more specifically, the full faith and credit which each liquidator gives to the others. The domiciliary liquidator, whether his state has a large stake in an insolvency or not, has the duty to handle the estate in a prompt and efficient manner. By the same token, all potential ancillary liquidators should show reasonable restraint, even in the face of what may seem to be unnecessary delay on the part of the domiciliary liquidator, in order to avoid Balkanizing the system, with the resulting deterioration in overall results.[122]

Similar concerns were expressed by the NCIGF at the NAIC meeting in June 1983.[123] At that meeting, the NAIC Task Force organized by liquidators proposed that before liquidating an insurance company, there would be a meeting with all interested parties, including ancillary liquidators and state guaranty funds. Indeed, this task force has developed a checklist of what to discuss at such meetings and an operations manual for liquidators in an effort to systematize relationships and eliminate problems. These efforts were recognized by the NCIGF in 1983 at the December NAIC meeting.[124] It is clear, however, from comments made at the American Bar Association Institute and by the NCIGF in November 1986 concerning New York, that the hoped-for cooperation has not materialized enough to solve problems generated by commercial insolvencies.

Some changes appear to be essential to the future of the system. It would be helpful if New York would become a part of the system and adopt the Post-Assessment Model Act. Additionally, some method of coordination needs to be developed so that, in the case of commercial coverages, guaranty funds around the country can be made aware of what payments have been made on policies by the company prior to insolvency, by the liquidator or by other guaranty funds in order that payments not be made greater than called for under the underlying policy.

A number of differences among states are acceptable. Part of having a state-based system is accepting differences. For example, if a state in its public policy determination decides that payments by guaranty funds ought not to exceed a certain amount, that should be acceptable. Likewise, exclusions from coverage should be within the province of a state's public policy. Uniformity should be sought but should not be considered a precondition to the functioning of the system.

On the other hand, whatever the amount to be paid, greater uniformity in defining a covered claim would be very useful. New York and California have provisions that could cause a claim intended to be covered by the system to fall through the cracks. These states should be brought in line with the approach of the Model Act.

Finally, regulators and the insurance industry should push for all states to adopt the Insurers Supervision, Rehabilitation and Liquidation Model Act.

Without these minimal changes and cooperation and good will among the liquidators and guaranty funds, the future of the multistate post-insolvency guaranty fund system is in doubt.

This matter has once again generated congressional interest. As part of hearings on the "insurance crisis," Representative Florio has had one day of testimony on solvency regulation, including guaranty funds. While no legislation has been introduced on the issue, interest in it may increase. This time the states have the basic mechanism in place, but they need to fine-tune it and show that those in charge of it can make it work under current circumstances as it did in the 1970s.

Monograph Notes

1. For a history of the Federal Bankruptcy Act and the Insurance Exclusion, see Spencer Kimball, "History and Development of the Law of State Insurer Insolvency Proceedings—An Overview," *Law and Practice of Insurance Company Insolvency* (Chicago: American Bar Association, 1986), pp. 9, 12-17, and M. Sovern, "Section 4 of the Bankruptcy Act: The Excluded Corporations," 42 *Minn. L. Rev.*, pp. 171, 172-182.
2. Paul v. Virginia, 75 U.S. (8 Wall.) 168 (1868).
3. U.S. v. South-Eastern Underwriters Assoc., 322 U.S. 533 (1944).
4. 11 U.S.C. (1983), enacted by Act of 6 November 1978, 92 Stat. 2557.
5. Kimball, "History and Development," p. 54.
6. Jack Traylor, "The Liquidation Process," *Law and Practice of Insurance Company Insolvency* (Chicago: American Bar Association, 1986), pp. 63, 66.
7. Alfred Bennett, "Liquidations of Insurance Companies," Vol. II, No. 3, September 1960, *Insurance and Government*, eds. Charles C. Center and Richard M. Heins, University of Wisconsin School of Commerce, Bureau of Business Research and Service, 1960, pp. 1, 14-17.
8. Report of the (D6) Subcommittee to Prepare Model Legislation for Guaranty Funds, *1970 Proceedings of the National Association of Insurance Commissioners* (hereinafter referred to as Proceedings of the NAIC), Vol. I, pp. 251, 298.
9. Douglas Olson, *Insolvencies Among Automobile Insurers* (Washington, D.C.: Department of Transportation, 1970), p. 3.
10. See S. 3919, 89th Cong., 2d sess., 1966, and S. 688, 90th Cong., 1st sess., 1967).
11. "Report of the Federal Motor Vehicle Insurance Guaranty Act (J) Committee," *1967 Proceedings of the NAIC*, Vol. II, pp. 587, 589.
12. "Report of the Federal Motor Vehicle Insurance Guaranty Act (J) Committee," pp. 600-601.
13. U.S., Congress, Senate, Committee on Commerce, Lorne R. Worthington speaking during hearings on S. 2236, 91st Cong., 2d sess., 1970, reprinted in Report of the Special (A8) Committee on Automobile Insurance Problems, *1970 Proceedings of the NAIC*, Vol. I, pp. 137, 146-147.
14. "Report of the (D6) Subcommittee to Prepare Model Legislation for Guaranty Funds," *1970 Proceedings of the NAIC*, Vol. I, pp. 251, 258.
15. See Report of the Committee on Commerce on S. 2236, S. Rep. No. 91-1421, 91st Cong., 2d sess., 1970.
16. Jean C. Hiestand, "The Need for Revision of State Insolvency and Guaranty Fund Laws," *Law and Practice of Insurance Company Insolvency* (Chicago: American Bar Association, 1986), pp. 563, 571.
17. Hiestand, p. 572.
18. N.Y. Ins. Law § 7601 *et. seq.* (McKinney 1985). Originally limited to

automobile insurance, the New York fund was expanded to cover other property and casualty lines in 1969 when the Model Act was adopted by the NAIC.

19. Model Act, § 6. Official N.A.I.C. Model Insurance Laws, Regulations and Guidelines, Published by the NAIRS Corporation, Minneapolis, MN (1977).
20. Model Act, § 7.
21. Model Act, §§ 5(7) and 8(1)(a).
22. Model Act, § 8(1)(c).
23. Model Act, § 8(1)(a).
24. Model Act, § 5(6).
25. Model Act, § 12(3).
26. Model Act, § 5(6)(b). Constitutionality of the exclusion as to amounts due insurers upheld. See Central Nat'l Ins. Co. of Omaha v. Cal. Ins. Guar. Assn., 117 Cal. App. 3d 729, 173 Cal. Rptr. 35 (1981).
27. Model Act, § 5(8). See for example Adams v. Ill. Ins. Guar. Fund, 85 Ill. App. 3d 867, 407 N.E.2d 638 (1980); Osborne v. Edison, 211 N.W.2d 696 (Iowa 1973), Allen v. Mich. Property and Casualty Guar. Assn. 129 Mich. App. 271, 321 N.W.2d 500 (1983); Railroad Roofing & Bldg. Supply Co. v. N.J. Property-Casualty Ins. Guar. Assn., 85 N.J. 384, 427 A.2d 66 (1980). New Jersey created a separate guaranty fund for surplus lines insurers in 1984. See N.J. Stat. Ann § 17:22 - 6.70 *et seq.* (West Supp. 1985).
28. See, for example, White v. Alaska Ins. Guar. Assn., 592 P.2d 367 (1979); Commissioner of Ins. v. Mass. Insurers Insolvency Fund, 373 Mass. 798, 370 N.E.2d 1353 (1977); Metry v. Mich. Property and Casualty Guar. Assn., 403 Mich. 117, 267 N.W.2d 695 (1978); Ohio Ins. Guar. Assn. v. Simpson, 1 Ohio App. 3d 112, 439 N.E.2d 1257 (1981); Greenfield v. Pa. Ins. Guar. Assn., 256 Pa. Super. 136, 389 A.2d 638 (1979).
29. See, for example, Fla. Ins. Guar. Assn. v. Dolan, 355 So.2d 141 (1978); Beatrice Foods v. Ill. Ins. Guar. Fund, 460 N.E. 2d 908 (1984).
30. Model Act, § 8(1)(a).
31. Model Act, § 11(2)(a).
32. Model Act, § 8(1)(a), drafters' comments.
33. Model Act, § 12(1). See, for example, Murray v. Mont. Ins. Guar. Assn. et al., 573 P.2d 196 (1977); Lucas v. Ill. Ins. Guar. Fund, 367 N.E. 2d 469 (1978); State Farm Ins. Co. v. N.J. Property-Lia. Ins. Guar. Assn., 402 A.2d 952 (1979); Henninger v. Riley, 464 A.2d 469 (Pa. Super. 1983); Prutzman v. Wash. Ins. Guar. Assn., 579 P.2d 359 (1979).
34. Model Act, § 12.
35. Model Act, § 10.
36. Compare Model Act, § 8(1)(c) with Model Act, alternate § 8(1)(c).
37. Model Act, § 8(1)(c).
38. Model Act, § 16.
39. Model Act, § 3.
40. Ark. H.B. 1573 approved 7 Apr 87; Iowa H.B. 2354 approved 6 May 1986; Oklahoma H.B. 1983 approved 13 June 1986; Virginia S.B. approved 17 April 1986; Wisconsin A.B. 595 approved 10 April 1986; Utah H.B. 100 approved 16 March 87.

41. Section 9(4) of the Model Act provides that the plan of operation of the association may provide for certain powers and duties to be "delegated to a corporation, association or organization which performs or will perform functions similar to those of this association. . . ."

42. This is not to say that some policyholders and claimants of troubled companies that have had financial difficulty have not had any problems. The problems, however, have not been a result of the design of the guaranty fund as much as they have been a result of a lack of cooperation or of problems generally in the liquidation process that predates creation of the guaranty funds. Both of these issues are subsequently discussed.

43. Memorandum of NAIC Executive Secretary Richard Marcus to members of the Model Legislation for Guaranty Funds (D6) Subcommittee, reprinted in *1970 Proceedings of the NAIC*, Vol. I, p. 262.

44. "Report of Insurance Guaranty Funds (B3) Subcommittee—Part F-1" reprinted in *1975 Proceedings of the NAIC*, Vol. II, pp. 259, 267.

45. Comments by John G. Smith, partner of Lord, Bissell & Brook, Chicago, Illinois, NCIGF Seminar for Guaranty Fund Counsel, Atlanta, Georgia, February 1979 (discussing Section 13 Detection and Prevention Authority).

46. NCIGF Rules 3A and B.

47. Model Act, § 12(3).

48. Minutes of the NCIGF Meeting, National Association of Independent Insurers, Des Plaines, Illinois, 14 February 1980.

49. Hereinafter referred to as "Guiding Principles." Letter from NCIGF Executive Secretary Richard Marcus to State Guaranty Fund chairmen and managers (6 September 1985).

50. Thomas Ridgley, "Interstate Conflicts and Cooperation," *Law and Practice of Insurance Company Insolvency* (Chicago: American Bar Association, 1986), pp. 529, 542-543.

51. Discussion between author and Richard Marcus, NCIGF executive secretary, Northbrook, Illinois 19 December 1986.

52. Eastern Seaboard Pile Driving Corp. v. N.J. Property-Lia. Guar. Assn., 421 A.2d 517 (1980).

53. 18 Del. Code Ann., § 4212(c) (Supp. 1982). The Delaware approach was the primary standard for handling Reserve claims.

54. Minutes of the NCIGF Meeting, Marquette Inn, Minneapolis, Minnesota, 14-15, August 1980.

55. *1986 Proceedings of the NAIC*, Vol. I, pp. 23, 148, 294.

56. Statement regarding proposed liquidation act by George T. Keyes, chairman of the NCIGF, Regular Meeting of the NAIC, Miami Beach, Florida on 6 December 1977, reprinted in *1978 Proceedings of the NAIC*, Vol. I, pp. 288-289.

57. Twenty-five states now have such a provision. Section 5(7) of the Model Act was amended to require an order of liquidation which "has not been stayed or been the subject of a writ of supersedeas or other comparable order." *1979 Proceedings of the NAIC*, Vol. I, p. 217.

58. Ill. Ann. Stat. ch 73, § 802.1 (Smith-Hurd Supp. 1983-84). The liquidation

order was upheld. See Schacht v. Security Casualty Co., 455 N.E.2d 574 (1982).

59. Fla. Ins. Guar. Assn. v. Fla. Ins. Dept., 400 So.2d 813 (1981).
60. *Uniform Laws Annotated*, Master Edition, Vol. 13, 429, 434.
61. "Report of the Insurance Guaranty Funds (B3) Subcommittee," reprinted in *1978 Proceedings of the NAIC*, Vol. I, p. 238.
62. "Report of the Insurance Guaranty Funds (B3) Subcommittee."
63. "Suggested Amendments to the NAIC Model State Post-Assessment Guaranty Association Bill," *1972 Proceedings of the NAIC*, Vol. I, pp. 479, 481.
64. "Report of Industry Advisory Committee to NAIC Property and Liability Guaranty Fund (B3) Subcommittee," *1972 Proceedings of the NAIC*, Vol. II, p. 378.
65. Statement by Armor M. Hank, chairman of the NCIGF, at the regular meeting of the NAIC, Las Vegas, Nevada, 5 December 1978, reprinted in *1979 Proceedings of the NAIC*, Vol. I, pp. 235-237.
66. Memorandum of Robert E. Dineen to Insurance Guaranty Funds (B3) Subcommittee, reprinted in *1977 Proceedings of the NAIC*, Vol. II, p. 380. See also "Report of Insurance Guaranty Fund (B3) Subcommittee," Appendix § 2 *1975 Proceedings of the NAIC*, Vol. II, p. 256.
67. Statement by Kenneth Nails, assistant general counsel for the American Mutual Insurance Alliance, at a meeting of the Insurance Guaranty Funds (B3) Subcommittee in Dallas, Texas, 17 April 1975, reprinted in *1975 Proceedings of the NAIC*, pp. 267, 268.
68. Statement by Jean C. Heistand, chairman of the NCIGF, at a meeting of the Guaranty Fund Liquidation and Rehabilitation (A4) Subcommittee, Detroit, Michigan, 9 June 1981, reprinted in *1981 Proceedings of the NAIC*, Vol. II, p. 375.
69. "Report of Insurance Guaranty Fund Liquidation and Rehabilitation (A4) Subcommittee, *1981 Proceedings of the NAIC*, Vol. I, p. 225.
70. The task force members were John E. Washburn, Chair (Illinois); James P. Corcoran, Vice Chair (New York); Bruce A. Bunner (California); Bill Gunter (Florida); Bruce W. Foudree (Iowa); Fletcher Bell (Kansas); Michael J. Dugan (Nebraska); John C. Neff (Tennessee); Doyce R. Lee (Texas); Thomas P. Fox (Wisconsin). The Industry Advisory Committee consisted of: Michael P. Duncan, Chair (Allstate Insurance Co.); Carole Banfield (Insurance Services Office); Tom Bond, Atty.; David Bowers (Zurich Insurance Co.); David Brummond (NAII); William Courtney (CNA); Robert M. Hall (American Reinsurance Co.); Jon Harkavy (Risk & Insurance Management Society); Richard P. Hefferan (Alliance of American Insurers); John G. Lewis (GEICO); James Mack (State Farm Insurance Co.); William Pugh, Atty.; Phillip Schwartz (American Insurance Association); John Smith, Atty.
71. Letter from Michael P. Duncan to NAIC Guaranty Fund Task Force Chairman John E. Washburn, 9 May 1984, reprinted in *1985 Proceedings of the NAIC*, Vol. II, pp. 505-506.
72. "Report of Guaranty Fund (EX4) Task Force," reprinted in *1986 Proceedings of the NAIC*, Vol. I, p. 293.

73. Discussion of these considerations can be found in the Duncan letter, *supra;* in "Report of the Property and Liability Advisory Committee to the NAIC Guaranty Fund Task Force," *1985 Proceedings of the NAIC*, Vol. II, pp. 473-474; and in "Report of the Property and Liability Advisory Committee to the NAIC Guaranty Fund Task Force," *1986 Proceedings of the NAIC*, 295-296, 420-422.

74. "Report of Financial Condition (EX4) Subcommittee," reprinted in *1986 Proceedings of the NAIC*, Vol. II, pp. 203, 206.

75. Stephen Tarnoff, "Hall, Insurer Ask Court to Void MGM Coverage," *Business Insurance*, 13 June 1983, p. 1.

76. Central National Ins. Co. of Omaha v. Cal. Ins. Guar. Assn., 117 Cal. App. 3d 729, 173 Cal. Rptr. 35 (1981).

77. Letter from Michael P. Duncan to NAIC Guaranty Fund Task Force Chairman John E. Washburn, 25 March 1980, reprinted in *1986 Proceedings of the NAIC*, Vol. I, p. 409.

78. "Report of the Guaranty Fund Task Force," *1987 Proceedings of the NAIC*, Vol. I, p. 419.

79. The NAIC Policy Committee consisted of Richard J. Haayen, Allstate Insurance Company; John H. Bretherick, Jr., The Continental Insurance Company; Ian R. Heap, Crum & Forster Insurance Company; John H. Jones, Employers Insurance of Wausau; John R. Graham, Farm Bureau Mutual Insurance Company, Inc.; DeRoy C. Thomas, Chairman, The Hartford Insurance Group; Ian M. Rolland, Lincoln National Life Insurance Company; Alden A. Ives, Patron Mutual Insurance Company of Connecticut; Edward B. Rust, Jr., State Farm Mutual Automobile Insurance Company; and Jack B. Riffle, Utica Mutual Insurance Company.

80. Panel presentation by Stephen I. Martin, vice president, The Hartford Insurance Group, 1984 Fall Meeting of the NAIC, Omaha, Nebraska, 11 September 1984.

81. Martin presentation, p. 5.

82. Summarizeed and edited from *Report of Technical Subcommittee to NAIC Policy Committee on Guaranty Funds and Solvency* (Chicago: National Association of Insurance Commissioners, 25 July 1985).

83. See, for example, Kentucky Reinsurance Assn. v. Thompson, 710 S.W.2d 854 (1986); Moran v. Derryberry, 534 P. 2d 1282 (Okla. 1975); Gronning v. Smart, 561 P. 2d 690 (Utah 1977); Employers Insurance of Wausau v. Mitchell, 113 Wis. 2d 732.

84. Employers Insurance of Wausau v. Mitchell, 113 Wis. 2d 732.

85. McArthur v. Smallwood, 281 S.W. 2d 428 (Ark. 1955).

86. Methodist Hospital of Brooklyn v. State Insurance Fund, 102 A.D.2d 367, 479 N.Y.S.2d 11 (1984).

87. Methodist Hospital of Brooklyn v. State Insurance Fund, 64 N.Y.2d 634, 486 N.Y.S.2d 905 (1985).

88. N.Y. Ins. Law 7603(d)(1)(A) (McKinney 1985).

89. Insurance Services Office, Inc., *ISO Study on State Guaranty Funds* (New York: Insurance Services Office, Inc., 1985), p. 3.

90. Letter from Kenneth H. Nails, senior vice president, Alliance of American Insurers, to Stephen I. Martin, vice president, The Hartford Insurance

Group, and Laura Sullivan, secretary and counsel, State Farm Mutual Insurance Company, 31 July 1985.

91. Nails letter, p. 2.
92. Memorandum from Roger K. Kenney, Alliance of American Insurers, to Kenneth H. Nails, 25 July 1985.
93. Nails letter, p. 3.
94. "Illinois Department of Insurance Property & Liability Guaranty Fund Capacity Study Preliminary Report," reprinted in *1986 Proceedings of the NAIC,* Vol. I, pp. 323-324.
95. "Illinois Department of Insurance Property & Liability Guaranty Fund Capacity Study Preliminary Report," p. 6.
96. Schacht v. Brown, 711 F.2d 1343 (1983).
97. See, generally, "Report of the Policy Committee on Guaranty Funds and Solvency," reprinted in *1986 Proceedings of the NAIC,* Vol. II, p. 411.
98. Telephone conversation of Michael P. Duncan with Phillip Meuniere, III, Florida Insurance Guaranty Association Claims Manager, 5 January 1987.
99. "Report of the Policy Committee on Guaranty Funds and Solvency," p. 415.
100. Letter from Commissioner Roxanne Gillespie to Congressman James Florio, 1 April 1987, p. 2.
101. Wis. Stat. Ann. 645.01 *et seq.* (West 1985). The present law is substantially the same as it was when first adopted.
102. Charles Havens III, "Insurer Insolvencies: Inter-State Cooperation," *Law and Practice of Insurance Company Insolvency* (Chicago: American Bar Association, 1986), pp. 119, 132.
103. John Gavin, "Competing Forums for the Resolution of Claims Against an Insolvent Insurer," *Law and Practice of Insurance Company Insolvency* (Chicago: American Bar Association, 1986), pp. 151, 179.
104. Havens, "Insurer Insolvencies," p. 127.
105. Fuhrman v. United American Insurers, 274 N.W.2d 842 (Minn. 1978).
106. Gavin, "Competing Forums," p. 169.
107. Traylor, "The Liquidation Process," p. 78.
108. Ridgley, "Interstate Conflicts," pp. 534, 552.
109. Hiestand, "The Need for Revision of State Insolvency," p. 594.
110. William Pugh, Jr., '*Surplus Lines and Insolvency Funds* (Des Plaines, IL: National Association of Independent Insurers, 1981), p. 16.
111. Richard Spencer, Jr., "Surplus Lines Insurers and Guaranty Funds—The New Jersey Experience," *Law and Practice of Insurance Company Insolvency* (Chicago: American Bar Association, 1986), pp. 503, 518(b).
112. Hiestand, "The Need for Revision of State Insolvency," p. 590.
113. Joseph Tanski, "Early Access and Guaranty Association Proofs of Claim," *Law and Practice of Insurance Company Insolvency* (Chicago: American Bar Association, 1986), pp. 481, 484.
114. Tanski, "Early Access," p. 484.
115. Ridgley, "Interstate Conflicts," pp. 549-550.
116. Ridgley, "Interstate Conflicts," p. 546.
117. Ridgley, "Interstate Conflicts," pp. 549-550.

118. Letter from Richard Marcus, NCIGF executive secretary, to State Guaranty Funds chairmen and managers, 14 November 1986.
119. Post-assessment capacity for the states with Model Act-type statutes was calculated by state and assessment account base on 1981 data and totaled $1.2 billion. Michael P. Duncan, "An Appraisal of Property-Casualty Post-Assessment Guaranty Funds," *Journal of Insurance Regulation*, Vol. 2, No. 3, March 1984, pp. 289-303, Appendix (1984). Based on Best's data, increases of net premium written since 1981 indicate a current capacity of over $2 billion.
120. Wis. Stat. Ann. ch. 646, Committee Comment—1969 (West 1980).
121. "Report of Insurance Guaranty Fund Liquidation and Rehabilitation (A4) Subcommittee," 1979 *Proceedings of the NAIC*, Vol. II, pp. 219, 220.
122. Statement by Jean C. Hiestand, chairman of the NCIGF, to the Financial Condition (EX4) Subcommittee, New Orleans, Louisiana, 17 December 1981, reprinted in *1982 Proceedings of the NAIC*, Vol. I, pp. 248, 249.
123. Statement by Robert Eisenstadt, chairman of the NCIGF, to the Financial Condition (EX4) Subcommittee, St. Louis, Missouri, 16 June 1983, reprinted in *1983 Proceedings of the NAIC*, Vol. II, p. 350.
124. Statement by Robert Eisenstadt, chairman of the NCIGF, to the Financial Condition (EX4) Subcommittee, St. Louis, Missouri, 16 June 1983, reprinted in *1984 Proceedings of the NAIC*, Vol. I, p. 197.

MONOGRAPH 11

Captive Insurance Companies: Concepts, Developments, and Risk Management Applications*

by M. Moshe Porat, Ph.D., CPCU

I. INTRODUCTION

The captive company is not a new technique for handling the loss exposures of business firms. We can trace the origin of captives to the early twenties and even earlier both in the U.S. and other nations. A number of early mutual insurance companies began as captives. For example, the first of the "factory mutual" companies was established as a captive by a group of manufacturers who owned well-constructed, highly protected properties. In the late twenties the Church Insurance Company was formed by the Protestant Episcopal Church, and in 1919 in Denmark the F. L. Smidth Company formed Forenede Assurandorer A/S, presently one of the largest non-U.S.-owned captives.

While the captive concept is an old one, it has not always been widely used in corporate risk management. In fact, few captive companies have been operating for longer than two or three decades. Only during the last twenty years or so has there been a tremendous

---

*An early version of this monograph was originally written by Drs. Edward M. Glenn, CPCU, CLU, and Robert W. Cooper and appeared in the first edition of *Issues in Insurance*. It was revised twice, for the second edition by Mr. D. Hugh Rosenbaum and for the third edition by Dr. M. Moshe Porat.

increase in the use of captives to solve various risk management problems. The literature indicates that interest in the captive technique and the resulting formation of captive companies, really began during the late 1960s and increased up through the late 1970s. For example, in Bermuda, which has been the predominant domicile of most captives for the past three decades, only six captives were formed in 1967. But those six captives constituted about a third of all captives formed there in all previous years combined. The real growth of captives started in the early seventies when more than fifty new captives a year were formed. The growth continued to the late seventies at a rate of more than 100 captives per year in each of the years from 1977 to 1980. The peak occurred in 1978 with 158 new captives. Since then, the rate of growth has declined to a minimum of fifty-nine new captives a year, as in 1984. In 1985, the formation of new captives in Bermuda reached seventy-two, and in 1986, 125 new captives were formed (the highest since 1978).[1]

Although no precise worldwide aggregate statistics are available, the current number of captive companies is estimated at about 2,100 generating an estimated amount of net premiums in the range of 8 to 10 billion dollars in 1986. At the beginning of 1977 about 490 captives were registered in Bermuda. By the end of 1980 that number had grown to about 980. As of early 1987, the number of registered captives in Bermuda is greater than 1,200. Of these, only 750 to 850 captives are active, that is, writing business or maintaining investable assets. Of these, an estimated 150 to 200 are owned by insurance interests for the purpose of writing business for the general public. This estimate varies depending on one's definition of a "real" captive or even an "active" one.[2] In addition, about 350 captives are located in the Cayman Islands, some 125 in Guernsey, 50 in Barbados, and 25 in the Bahamas. Also, about 220 captives are domiciled in the U.S., where some states have passed special captive insurance legislation. One is Vermont with 67 captives, Colorado with almost 30, and Tennessee with about 10 captives. Delaware, Hawaii, and the U.S. Virgin Islands have most recently registered captives under special legislation. These new additions totaled about ten combined.[3] The number of firms offering managerial and other essential services to captives has also grown. In 1978 the number of management companies offering such services to captives was about 50, and by early 1980 that number was in excess of 100. The present estimate (1987) is about 160 companies.[4]

In 1972 the Internal Revenue Service (IRS) issued a supplement aimed at disallowing tax deductions for premiums paid to captives domiciled outside the United States. The IRS maintained an unfavorable attitude toward domestic and offshore captive companies. Most cases that went to court challenging the IRS were ruled in the IRS's favor. This trend was finally manifested in tax law in the Tax Reform Acts of 1984 and 1986, where any perceived or actual tax advantages of captive insurers have been practically all but eliminated.[5] Many experts felt that IRS attacks on the somewhat advantageous tax position of foreign captives and the changes in tax laws might bring an end to the captive movement. While it is still too early to evaluate the full impact of the 1986 Tax Reform Act on captives, it is becoming clear that diminishing tax advantages have had little negative impact on the formation of captives. If anything, it has been an impetus for innovation in terms of new ownership structures, writing formats, product, and services for captives.

Most of the large, multinational companies have formed captive insurers in the past two decades. More than two-thirds of the Fortune 500 companies have done so as have a great many on the Fortune 1000 list. Among the firms that have formed captives in the past decade are Rockwell International Corporation, E.I. DuPont de Nemours and Company, Levi Strauss and Company, Brunswick Corporation, Royal Industries, Gould Inc., Wang Laboratories, Smith Kline, Corning Glass, I.U. International, and United Parcel Service. Some firms, including Monsanto and Archer Daniels Midland Company, have established two captives each in order to separately handle U.S. loss exposures and foreign loss exposures. Some companies formed multiple captives domestically and offshore to separate not only domestic and foreign exposures but also to separate property and liability from life, health, and other employee benefit exposures. In addition, a number of captives were formed during the late 1970s by hospitals and other medical associations to write malpractice coverages. In the late 1970s and early 1980s the need for product liability and professional liability (especially medical malpractice coverage) protection provided strong motivation for the establishment of captives.

The Deficit Reduction Act of 1984 and the tightening of the insurance market in 1985 and 1986 have resulted in a renewed surge in the formation of group captives. These are captives owned by associations, groups of individuals or companies, or joint ventures among individuals and/or companies that were formed for insurance purposes and the associated tax benefits. Some examples of group captives are Energy Insurance Mutual Ltd. (EIM) formed by a group of eighty-five electric power stations; Attorney Liability Assurance Society Ltd. (ALAS) formed by a group of large law firms; Genesis Ltd., formed by nine northeastern universities; Gulf South Insurance Ltd., which is a joint venture between auto dealers, insurance agents, and insurance companies; and the recently formed CPA Risk Retention Group formed by the American Institute of Certified Public Accountants.

The crisis in directors and officers liability and in excess liability coverages in general has introduced, in addition to more group captives, a new breed of large, private insurers. These are formed directly by insured companies or through their individual captives for the purpose of solving insurance capacity problems in particular industries or in particular lines of coverages. About 90 such organizations are either formed or in the process of being formed. They are, in principle, pools of private investors formed by industries and actually function as group captives to handle large excess liability layers.

Some of the more well known of these are American Casualty Excess Company Ltd. (ACE), Excess Liability Company (X.L.), Bankers Insurance Company Ltd. (BICL), Tortuga Casualty Company, and Railroad Association Insurance Ltd. (RAIL). Although these large groups have attracted much publicity, the concept of pooling is not new. First Island Reinsurance Association (FIRA) was one of the earliest pooling organizations of member captives organized by the brokerage firm of Johnson and Higgins in 1978. Another is Corporate Insurance and Reinsurance Company, Ltd. (CIRCL), which served as a reciprocal pool for primary and excess captive business. A group of large oil companies formed Oil Insurance Ltd. (OIL) in response to a much earlier liability crisis. (OIL is discussed in detail later in this monograph.) Associated Electric Gas Insurance Services Ltd. (AEGIS) is a group captive formed by electric utilities. The latter two recently formed excess facilities—Oil Casualty Insurance Ltd. (OCIL) by the oil association and groups of insurance companies, and Directors and Officers Liability Insurance Company Ltd. (DOLI) formed by electric utilities for directors and officers excess liability coverage.

The Tax Reform Act of 1986, which eliminated most tax advantages for captives including group captives, and the Liability Risk Retention Act of 1986 are expected to encourage the formation of domestic group captives in response to a possible decline in formation of offshore captives. But this prediction has been wrong in the past. If anything, the signs of softening in the insurance market by the end of 1987 can have a slow down effect on the formation of new captives and/or the growth of existing ones.

While presenting the principal concepts and recent developments associated with captive insurers, this monograph will explore the use of captives in risk management programs. It will also examine various aspects of captive company operation. The financial and nonfinancial reasons for forming a captive are discussed in addition to the disadvantages of the captive technique. Finally, the considerations involved in assessing the feasibility of establishing a captive company are presented.

II. CONCEPT OF THE CAPTIVE COMPANY

A review of insurance literature reveals that the term "captive" has been used to describe many different kinds of wholly owned subsidiaries. If a captive company is to be thought of as a risk management tool, however, only a few types of subsidiaries deserve the title "captive." Thus, the concept of captivity as it applies to the study of risk management programs must be defined.

Definition

The captive has been defined in a number of ways. In some instances it has been referred to as simply "formalized self-insurance." More typically, the captive company has been defined as "a wholly owned insurance subsidiary with a primary function of insuring the... exposures of the parent organization.[6]

While this definition has some shortcomings, it nevertheless makes the important point that not all insurance subsidiaries can properly be classified as captives. Subsidiaries that insure exclusively or almost exclusively the exposures of the general public rather than those of their corporate parents are not captive companies in the sense the term is used in this definition. Examples of insurance subsidiaries that are not captives include Allstate, owned by Sears, Roebuck and Company; Great American Insurance Company owned by American Financial Corporation; and the Hartford Insurance Group owned by ITT.

The preceding definition does, however, have at least two important shortcomings. First, it suggests incorrectly that a captive must be a "wholly owned" subsidiary. While most captives are wholly owned subsidiaries of individual business firms, captive companies can also be jointly owned by several organizations or individuals (and thus partially owned by each). In fact, in recent years the jointly owned captive has become increasingly popular, particularly for the treatment of medical malpractice, products liability, professional liability, directors and officers liability, and excess liability exposures.

Second, the definition is too broad because it incorrectly includes finance company-owned insurers that insure exposures "owned under conditional sales contracts issued by financial institutions." Goshay points out that such insurers are not captive companies for several reasons.[7] First, the notion of captivity applies only to the owner relationship between the finance company and the insurance subsidiary. There is no captive relationship between the insured and the insurance company. Secondly, finance company-owned insurers frequently compete with other nonfinance-controlled insurers for the business of the general public. Finally, the insureds of an insurer owned by a finance company "presumably have the option of insuring elsewhere should they so desire."[8]

In an effort to overcome these shortcomings, Goshay suggests that the captive company "might be generally defined either as an insured-controlled carrier or as a carrier owned by interests owning or controlling the...(exposures) insured therein."[9] The problem with this definition is that it is too general. That is, it fails to differentiate clearly between a captive company and a commercial insurer organized as a mutual company. Goshay recognized this problem and attempted to remedy the situation by supplementing his definition with a list of purported distinguishing characteristics.[10]

As indicated by the previous discussion, it is difficult, if not impossible, to formulate a concise definition of a captive company that is both accurate and distinctive. The captive concept can, however, be illustrated quite clearly by referring to Exhibit 11-1.[11] Circle A represents an individual, corporation, group of corporations, or other association that owns or controls the company denoted by circle B. Circle C represents the general public. Areas 1, 2, 3, and 4 indicate the various relationships that can occur among A, B, and C. If A is composed of more than one member, the members are likely to have common business interests.

Area 1 represents those exposures owned or controlled solely by circle A interests that are handled in a risk management sense by the company owned or controlled by A. The general public has no direct ownership or controlling interest in the exposures denoted by area 1. Area 2 represents the interaction between circle A interests and the general public. This interaction is not necessarily an insurance relationship. Rather, it involves the normal business relationships that exist between the circle A interests and the general public. Area 3 signifies the insuring of exposures that involve the interests of the general public as well as those of the persons or firms represented in circle A. An example would be the insuring of property under a conditional sales contract. Finally, area 4 represents exposures of the general public that are insured or reinsured in the insurance company owned or controlled by the circle A interests. The latter group, however, has no direct ownership or controlling interest in the exposures denoted by area 4. For clarity's sake one can regard the space within circle B but outside of areas 1, 3, or 4 as being empty. That is, B is deemed to engage only in those activities that are related to the risk management or insuring or reinsuring of loss exposures represented by the areas 1, 3, or 4. Circle B has no other business interests or activity.

In terms of Exhibit 11-1 for purposes of this monograph, a captive will be viewed as being an enterprise whose area 1 is larger than the

Exhibit 11-1
The Captive Concept*

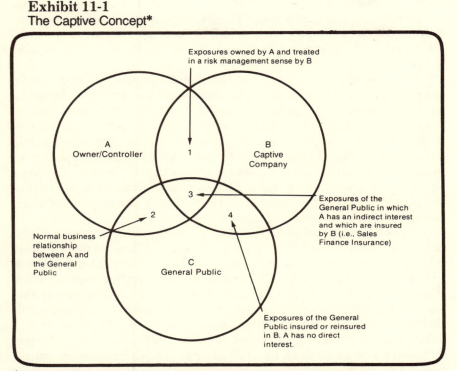

* Adapted, with permission, from Robert C. Goshay, "Captive Insurance Companies," *Risk Management*, H. Wayne Snider, Ed. (Homewood, IL: Richard D. Irwin for S. S. Huebner Foundation for Insurance Education, 1964), p. 83.

sum of areas 3 and 4. Thus, the captive is a company with the following basic characteristics:

1. It is owned or controlled by another corporation, an individual, or group of corporations or individuals (circle *A*)
2. It primarily treats exposures that are owned or controlled by the interests that own or control the captive itself (area 1)

In other words, a captive is a formal insurance subsidiary established in order to finance exposures *primarily* of its owners/controllers. Many insurance subsidiaries are not captives, because they do not possess the second characteristic listed above. For example, Ford Motor Company owns the American Road Insurance Company that provides automobile physical damage coverages on vehicles sold by Ford and financed by the Ford Motor Credit Company. The American Road Insurance Company, however, is not a captive insurer. It insures exposures located only in area 3 of Exhibit 11-1. Likewise, insurance subsidiaries that primarily insure or reinsure exposures located in area 4 are not captives. Clearly, subsidiaries such as Allstate and The Hartford are not captive insurers. Any insurance coverage each provides to its corporate parent is purely incidental to its primary function of selling insurance to the general public.

Some confusion does exist in the literature, however, concerning the proper classification of insurance subsidiaries commonly referred to as "profit-center" or "profit-making" captives or "senior insurance subsidiaries." These enterprises were originally formed to handle exclusively, or at least primarily, the exposures of their owners, but subsequently they shifted their primary underwriting emphasis to insuring or reinsuring the exposures of the general public. Although these subsidiaries were originally captive companies, they can hardly be classified as such because they primarily insure or reinsure exposures located in area 4 of Exhibit 11-1.

However, a lack of published data on companies that have evolved in this way (and on captives in general) makes it difficult to determine at what point a company "stops" being a captive. Clearly, Sears' Allstate or G.M.'s Motors Insurance Corporation are not captives anymore even if they started as such. Some of the better known insurance subsidiaries that started as captives and expanded their activities to become full-fledged insurance subsidiaries suffered considerable losses in recent years and went out of business, notably Gulf Oil's Insco, Phillips Petroleum's Walton, Murphy Oil's Mentor, and Ideal Mutual, which became an independent public company prior to its failure. Some others may have curtailed their nonrelated business writings or retrenched their activities, and it is rather difficult to determine their status with regard to our definition of a captive. In the next section this definition is expanded to include how a captive actually works—in its environment and individually.

The Captive Movement and the Structure of Captives

Many use the term "captive movement" without actually explaining what it means. Captives have been criticized as hardly more than files of offshore attorneys. To explain the captive movement and the captive company, the structure of both must be described.[12] Structure in this case means people and their positions, and the patterns of their interactions.

Exhibit 11-2 depicts the captive movement, and the captive company, and their structural relationship. The environment in which captives function includes "forces" that affect and are affected by captives, that is, the organizations that support, maintain, and control captives. Support organizations include parents or owners of captives, affiliates of parents, suppliers, customers of parents and captives, and employees of all these. Maintenance organizations are ones that supply the captives with services. They include management companies; brokerage firms; insurance and reinsurance companies; claims handling and adjusting firms; statistical and actuarial service providers; banking, accounting, and data processing organizations; and tax, legal, and money management services. The control organizations are authorities that exercise direct or indirect control over captives and the way they conduct their business. These include the IRS, the Financial Accounting Standards Board, state and domicile insurance departments, various federal regulatory agencies that monitor labor, safety and health care such as ERISA, OSHA, HCFA, and so on.

Not all of the above entities exercise the same degree of influence on captives, nor are they influenced to the same degree by them. To clarify this area, a criterion used by behavioral scientists to determine the intensity of interaction between structural components is the frequency of transactions.[13] The higher the frequency the greater the mutual influence. Based on empirical evidence, parent companies and management companies have had the most transactions with captives; the insurance industry as a whole and the IRS are important but less frequent interactors. For this reason, the captives, the parents, and the management companies are the most organic parts of the captive movement.

The most important part of the structure of a captive is its people—those who have the most influence on decisions and who regularly take part in company operations. Also important is the fact that a captive is not a closed system. It is a system open to its environment. It is much more flexible and organic than both most insurance organizations or parent organizations of captives because individuals in the captive structure often belong to other organizations as well. Probably the three key people that comprise the captive structure are the operator, most often the parent company's risk and insurance manager; the operator's superior at the parent company, most often the parent company's financial officer; and the management company's representative to the captive, an account executive or top officer of the management company.[14] In group-owned captives (defined in detail later) the operator may actually be a team of individuals. A captive's board of directors will often be composed of superior officers of the member owners or association, and the managers can be either contracted for or the captive's own personnel. Clearly, the larger the captive and the more complex the types of business it writes, the closer its structure will be to the traditional structure of insurance companies. However, this is currently only true for a minority of the captives. The types of captives are described in the next section.

Exhibit 11-2
The Captive Movement and the Captive Organization—Structural Framework*

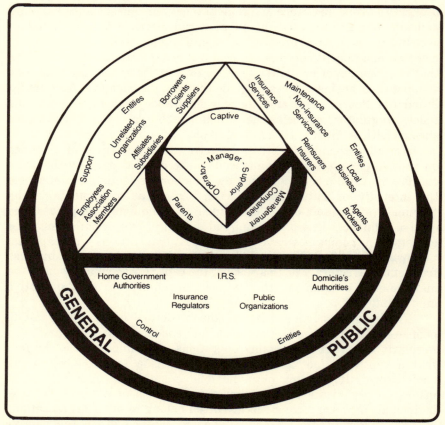

* Reprinted with permission from M. Moshe Porat, "The Bermuda Captive—A Comprehensive Evaluation and Analysis," *Risk Management*, March 1982, p. 47.

Pure Captives The two basic types of captive companies are pure captives and broad captives. Circle *B* in Exhibit 11-1 would be a pure captive if it treated only exposures located in area 1; in this case, areas 3 and 4 (and the remainder of B) would be empty. Thus, a captive is classified as pure if it handles only those exposures that are owned or controlled solely by the interests that own or control the captive itself. Most captives are established as pure captives. Many change to include in their underwriting portfolios varying portions of business unrelated to interest that own or control it. In most cases less than 25 percent of the total volume is unrelated business.

In a count of all Bermuda captives in 1980, some 52 to 61 percent of all captives were identified as pure captives.[15] In a 1985 update on Bermuda's statistics on captives, pure captives constituted about 55 percent of all captives. It appears that the negative experience some captives had with unrelated business during the soft insurance market from 1980 to 1984 diminished, at least temporarily, the interest in underwriting unrelated business.

Pure captives consist of two basic types. In this monograph they will be called single-owner pure captives and group pure captives. The majority of captives are still single-owner pure captives even though since the early 1980s the relative share of group pure captives and group captives in general has been rising. In 1980 count more than 83 percent of all captives were singly owned.[16] In the 1987 Captive Insurance Company Directory, which includes statistics on the entire captive movement in 1986, showed that group captives constituted about 26 percent of the approximately 2,000 captives (excluding credit life companies). Furthermore, based on Bermuda's registration statistics for two months in 1987, more than half of the newly registered captives were group captives. Among the pure captives, group captives accounted for as much as 30 percent.[17]

Single-Owner Pure Captives. As its name implies, the single-owner pure captive is owned by a single corporation or individual and handles only exposures that are owned or controlled by that corporation or individual. Because of their predominance in the pure captive category, single-owner pure captives often have been referred to simply as pure captives in the literature.

While some single-owner pure captives have been located in the United States, most have been domiciled offshore, principally in Bermuda. Organized ostensibly as either insurers or reinsurers, single-owner pure captives traditionally have focused primarily on providing property, marine, and workers compensation coverages for their owners. For example, the Petroleum Casualty Company formed in Texas in 1925 writes workers compensation and ocean marine coverages on exposures owned or controlled by its parent, the Exxon Corporation. In the early 1950s Exxon also organized Ancon, a single-owner pure captive in Bermuda. As of the end of 1985, Ancon's assets stood at about $600 million. A year earlier this figure was shy of one billion dollars. These figures make Ancon one of the largest captives in the world. It should be pointed out that in the period between its formation and the 1985 figure, Ancon started, and then stopped, writing unrelated business.[18] Although Texaco's captive, Heddington Insurance Ltd., derives most of its business from parent sources, it had earned premiums of $235 million and total assets of $870 million in 1985.

In the late seventies single-owner pure captives became increasingly involved in writing various types of liability coverages in response to problems encountered by their owners in the commercial liability markets. For example, Arroyo Insurance Company was formed in 1976 to provide Royal Industries, Inc. with coverage of $250,000 per occurrence for general liability (including products liability), auto liability, auto physical damage, and workers compensation claims. The captive was formed primarily because Royal Industries found it very difficult to get products liability insurance at reasonable rates in the commercial markets.[19] Similarly, in response to rapidly escalating malpractice premium rates, the Sisters of the Holy Cross established the Havican Insurance Company in 1976 to provide malpractice coverage for the nine hospitals operated by the order.[20] The captive serviced the hospitals for losses up to $1 million per occurrence with an annual aggregate limit of $5 million.

Group Pure Captives. Often referred to also as an association or industry captive, the group pure captive is a pure captive that provides risk management services to a group of corporations or individuals or both, often with similar business interests. In the past, group pure captives were domiciled largely in the United States. Those formed recently, however, tend to be domiciled offshore, particularly in Bermuda and the Cayman Islands.

Several approaches have been used in establishing group pure captives. In some cases trade or professional associations have established group pure captives to meet the needs of their members. For example, in 1970 Verlan, Ltd. was established in Bermuda by the National Paint, Varnish and Lacquer Association to provide property coverages for its members. The reason given by the Association for the formation of Verlan was "the bad experiences of its member companies with the conventional insurance market, particularly with regard to substantial premium rate increases and unwarranted cancellations of policy coverage."[21] As another example, in 1980 the California Dental Association formed a captive (The Dentists Insurance Company) domiciled in California to write professional liability insurance for participating members of the California Dental Association.[22] This type of group pure captive is generally owned by the trade or professional association, rather than by the individual members of the association. As an alternative, some groups of corporations or individuals have formed group pure captives that are independent of any organized trade or professional association. An example is ALAS, a Bermuda-based mutual insurer created to provide professional liability insurance for participating law firms.[23] In early 1980 ALAS was serving about forty law firms. This type of group pure captive is jointly controlled by the group members themselves. In the 1980 Bermuda captive population, 125 captives were identified as group captives. Some 60 percent of them were of the association or industry type while the rest, 40 percent, were formed by a group of individuals (56 percent) or groups of corporations (44 percent).[24] Group pure captives have been especially prominent in the treatment of energy-related exposures and medical malpractice exposures.

Energy-Related Captives. In the 1970s the group pure captive became an increasingly popular tool in efforts to solve the insurance problems of firms in various energy-related industries. In 1970 a substantial number of firms in the electric utilities industry established the United Services Insurance Company in Bermuda because adequate insurance coverages, particularly with regard to turbines and boilers, were not available in the conventional insurance markets. In 1972 eleven utility companies formed Nuclear Mutual Ltd. to provide more flexible and, so the incorporators hoped, lower cost property insurance coverages for their nuclear power plants than available in the regular market. This captive has seventeen participants as of this writing. Even more recently, Gas Ltd. (whose name was changed to AEGIS) was established in Bermuda by a group of six gas companies in order to provide themselves with a more stable source of liability coverages. In the past the gas companies found that their markets for obtaining liability insurance tended to disappear whenever the insurance industry experienced a "capacity crunch."

An interesting example of the use of a group pure captive in attacking the insurance problems of the firms in an energy-related industry is provided by Oil Insurance Ltd. After finding that the traditional insurance markets of the world were unable or unwilling to provide petroleum companies with catastrophe coverages on what petroleum industry officials regarded as reasonable commercial terms, a study group appointed by the American Petroleum Institute recommended in 1970 that consideration be given to creating a captive company to meet the needs of the petroleum industry. Shortly thereafter, a mutual insurance company named Oil Insurance Ltd. (OIL) was established in Bermuda by a group of American petroleum companies.[25] The eligibility rules for participation in OIL were designed to enable the captive to serve the widest possible segment of the international petroleum industry. Membership in OIL is open to both privately owned and government-controlled petroleum companies throughout the world. The current members include not only American oil firms such as Standard Oil of California, Atlantic Richfield, Marathon Oil, Cities Service, and Standard Oil of Ohio, but also foreign companies such as Petrofina (Belgium), Burmah Oil (United Kingdom), and Compagnie Francaise des Petroles (France). Thus, OIL has become a multinational company. It is a group pure captive in the sense that it serves only the members of the petroleum community that sponsor it. The fact that these members are competitors and are only loosely associated for the purpose of using OIL does not preclude OIL from being, by the definition suggested above, a pure group captive.

OIL provided its members with very comprehensive worldwide coverage that was instituted in 1980. At that time, limits of insurance were based on 10 percent of a member's gross assets, subject to the maximum of $150 million per occurrence.[26] The coverage applied to property losses on an "all-risks" basis as well as to pollution liability claims, well control losses, debris removal expenses, and "sue and labor" types of expenses. Deductibles of $1 million, $5 million, and $10 million were available. In addition to providing coverages directly to its member companies, OIL is also authorized to issue reinsurance policies to the insurance subsidiaries of its members.

The premium rating scheme employed by OIL was simple. No rating of individual exposures or even any attempt to determine insurable values was undertaken. Instead, each year a premium rate per $100 of gross assets was established for each of the three deductibles. To determine the premium rates, OIL essentially computed the average annual amount of its losses during the five most recent years, doubled the figure, and divided the result (subject to a minimum) by the gross assets of its member companies. The basic annual premium for a member company was calculated by simply multiplying the rate for the appropriate deductible by the amount of the member's gross assets. The basic premium was experience rated to determine the annual premium actually paid by the member company.

On 1 January 1976 Gulf Oil Company withdrew from OIL. Since Gulf was OIL's largest member, concern was voiced about the captive's future, particularly with regard to its ability to continue to attract new members.[27] It appears, however, that Gulf's withdrawal had little, if any, effect on the captive.[28] In fact, OIL has attracted new members. At the beginning of 1980 OIL had about forty members with aggregate gross assets of about $150 billion.[29]

Malpractice Captives. In response to rapidly rising premium rates and vanishing sources of medical malpractice insurance, in the late 1970s and early 1980s a number of groups of hospitals and physicians established captives to provide themselves with professional liability coverages. One source indicated that so many group medical malpractice captives had been formed by the end of 1980 that perhaps 40 percent of the total medical malpractice premiums in the United States was written by professional sponsored companies.[30]

In some cases the group captives were established because the participants were unable to obtain medical malpractice insurance in the commercial market. For example, the Health Care Insurance Exchange was formed by the New Jersey Hospital Association in 1976 after the market for malpractice insurance virtually disappeared in the state.[31] A number of group medical malpractice captives have also been formed because their owners felt that rapidly rising commercial premium rates based on countrywide averages did not accurately reflect their superior loss experience. The Controlled Risk Insurance Company Ltd. (CRICO), for example, was established on Grand Cayman Island to provide malpractice coverages to eleven Harvard-affiliated hospitals and their 2,800 closely associated doctors because the rapidly escalating annual premiums being paid by these institutions dwarfed the adverse judgments and settlements against them in recent years.[32] The Harvard affiliates felt that they could expect better than average claims experience because of the quality of the personnel on their staffs, their emphasis on quality control, and the fact that frequency of malpractice claims against doctors in teaching hospitals is considerably lower than that of doctors in general. Initially, premium rates were set at 73 percent of those charged by the Massachusetts Joint Underwriting Association. This association had provided malpractice coverage to the Harvard affiliates prior to the formation of the captive. By 1981 the hospitals served by CRICO were reported to have achieved about a 40 percent reduction in their rates compared to what participating hospitals had been paying prior to the formation of CRICO. Comparable rates in the regular market also declined during this period.

Joint Venture Captives.   In the past two to three years a new type of group captive known as the joint venture captive became rather popular. The joint venture captive is often a collaboration between a group of individuals or corporations and a "promoter" who might be an insurance agent, broker, an investor, or other financial or insurance interest who promotes the joint venture captive as a way to retain control over the members as well as a way to receive financial and operational benefits. For example, First Virginia Re Ltd. was originally formed to serve physicians and hospitals and was later approached by lawyers to write their professional liability. Other examples are Jefferson International Insurance Company Ltd., which is a joint venture of freight forwarders and insurance interests, and Kitty Hawk Insurance Company Ltd., which is a joint venture of California aerial companies and some commercial insurers. Many of the joint ventures have been formed in the Cayman Islands which offers certain advantages since that is where a captive can be formed in conjunction with a holding company and enjoy some technical advantages.[33] As of 1986, some 5 to 8 percent (about thirty-five to forty) of all group captives were joint venture captives.

Broad Captives As mentioned, most captive companies are formed as pure captives; many eventually broaden their underwriting activities beyond the exposures of their owners. In 1980 as many as 48 percent of Bermuda captives were writing some amount of unrelated business.[34] In a recent update on Bermuda captives' statistics about 45 percent of the captives were reporting writing some amounts of unrelated business.[35] The operations of captives have been expanded to include insuring and reinsuring the exposures of the general public for a number of reasons. Quite often the owners of the captive are interested primarily in the profits that may be generated by the insurance or reinsurance business. In addition, however, captive operations have been expanded in order to obtain a better spread of loss exposures and thus more stable underwriting results and more credible statistics. Expansion also permits the captive's fixed operating costs to be spread over a broader premium base. Some firms have expanded the underwriting activities of their captives because they felt that reinsurance would be more readily available to a publicly operating insurance company than to a pure captive, particularly during times of limited capacity in the reinsurance markets. Finally, in response to IRS attacks on the tax status of offshore captives, the insurance and reinsurance portfolios of a number of captives have been broadened to include some exposures of the general public in an effort to convince the IRS that the captive is a legitimate insurance company and not just a sham corporation formed solely to avoid or at least defer taxes.

A captive company is classified as a broad captive if it insures or reinsures exposures of the general public as well as those of its owning or controlling interests. The company depicted in Exhibit 11-1 would be a broad captive if, in addition to handling exposures located in area 1, it also insured or reinsured some exposures located in areas 3 and/or 4. Diversity Insurance Company, Ltd., owned by U.S. Industries, Inc., provides an example of a broad captive. Formed in 1971 for the primary purpose of serving the exposures of its parent, Diversity generated about 25 percent of its 1976 premium volume by reinsuring foreign insurance companies through treaties originating in the London market. For 1981 the figure was about 30 percent. Later it was reported, however, that Diversity's owner had decided to wind down Diversity's unrelated business. Just how much "outside" business a captive must generate to cease being "pure" and to become "broad" is an unsettled matter. If these labels are to be strictly construed, *any* outside premium volume would be sufficient to convert a pure captive into a broad captive. Most interested persons are willing to accept such an interpretation.

Incidentally, reinsurance commissions can be highly important to a captive company. Such commissions may amount to 20 percent of the business ceded by the captive to a reinsurer. These commissions can be a source of low-risk income to a captive properly launched into the reciprocal reinsurance business. Additional income may be forthcoming from reinsurance profit-sharing (that is, contingent) commissions.

While some companies remain in the broad captive category for a considerable number of years, or even permanently, many broad captives are transients. Quite often, former pure captives pass briefly through the broad captive stage on their way to becoming full-fledged commercial insurance companies. The line of demarcation between a broad captive and a full-fledged commercial insurance company is less distinct than between a pure and a broad captive.

Group captives (both pure and broad) formed by associations comprise about half of all such captives. The other half includes those group captives formed by individuals, corporations, or both, and joint ventures between individuals, corporations, and promoters. Some of these group captives which were originally pure captives have expanded to become broad captives. Additional organizations that can be considered group captives include what this author refers to as "second generation" formats—businesses that function in a captive-like manner. They are group broad captives because they are formed or owned by other organizations with related interests; they also write some amount of unrelated business. These organizations are often referred to as rent-a-captives, exchanges, and policyholder-owned insurers.

Rent-a-Captives. The concept of "renting" a captive has existed for almost ten years. This is a situation where an existing captive or, more likely, another insurance-related entity offers to another enterprise access to the various advantages of operating a captive without the trouble of setting it up. This can be useful to an enterprise when forming a new captive is not economically feasible or desirable, or when it wants to experiment with a captive-like program prior to actually owning one. The facility making the offer provides the services needed to administer and fund the program for a fee. Typically, each renter's account is kept separately and there is hardly any sharing of risk—each renter is responsible for its own losses. The keys to the renting arrangement are the services provided by the facility, the reinsurance arrangement, and the security provided by the renter to guarantee that it will meet its obligations under the agreement. Some renting facilities provide their renters with an opportunity to share in other renters' risk experience and to use the facility's funds to finance the program for a fee. Fees for the various services including fronting arrangements and reinsurance have ranged from 25 to 40 percent of the gross premium. In recent years the difficulties in securing aggregate excess reinsurance and insurers willing to "front" for a captive slowed down the use of these rent-a-captive arrangements. (Fronting is described in more detail later in this monograph.) However, in view of recent softening of the market and the change in tax laws, the author expects an increase in the use of some rent-a-captive facilities. Mutual Indemnity Ltd. (formerly Aneco Mutual Ltd.) is one of the major participants in this market. It is owned by a publicly traded U.S. company managed in Bermuda, and operates a marketing arm in the U.S. The organization has been operating since 1980, has grown considerably, and has very loyal renters. In their 1986 report to shareholders Mutual Indemnity claimed to have 140 participant accounts, written premiums of some $84 million, and assets in excess of $131 million.[36] Other participants in the rent-a-captive market include Trenwick Guaranty Insurance Company Ltd.; Arkwright Boston's HPR Mutual Limited; A.I.G.'s Interhemispheric Company; Alexander and Alexander's Hemisphere Marine and General; Johnson and Higgins' Universe; and Bermuda Fire and Marine Company.

Exchanges and Pools. Exchanges include facilities that, in principle, are entities owned by a group of captives or insureds to provide a medium for unilateral or multilateral exchange of risks among participants with or without the help of intermediaries. The term exchange has become more commonly used since the formation of the Risk Exchange Association in Bermuda in 1984. The Risk Exchange operates as a facility for the reinsurance of risk of its members and their parent or affiliated companies. By 1987, the Risk Exchange included twenty-seven member captives from the U.S., Canada, and several European countries. Although they could almost be considered a pool, exchanges differ from other pools such as CIRCL, Hopewell, or First Island in that they do not have a risk-bearing function. They function as pools in that they facilitate the risk-sharing mechanism and have access to the purchase and sale of reinsurance. The Risk Exchange was created by and for the use of its own members unlike excess pool captives such as Hopewell or First Island, which were created with the help of intermediaries or insurers.

In all of the above cases, however, the pooling and reinsurance were limited to the less problematic layers of risk in terms of limits, or the property and few liability lines of business where capacity has been relatively stable. When the capacity shortages reached record levels in 1984-1985, excess liability in general, and, specifically, directors and officers liability and other professional liability lines faced a capacity crunch of unprecedented proportions. Clearly insureds on their own, including those with captives and pool participants, could not resolve the problem. Solutions called for a cooperative effort between insurance intermediaries, financial and investment institutions, insurers and reinsurers, and the insureds themselves. This was the background for development of new organizations referred to as excess pools or policyholder-owned insurers. Some of the well known ones are ACE, XL, DOLI, ERIC, and CODA.

The formation of pools to solve coverage availability and affordability problems is not new. Mutual fire companies were formed by textile manufacturers and evolved into the well-known factory mutual system. Mutuals also were formed in response to statutory workers compensation insurance, and more recently, captive insurers have been formed by hospitals, doctors, and manufacturers in response to the malpractice and product liability crises during the 1970s.

The recently formed pools, however, are different from the traditional pools in several respects. While the traditional pools were by and large a regional solution to problems facing specific, largely homogeneous industries, the current pools are more of a national or global response to problems facing a diverse range of industries. While the traditional pools (1) were relatively small, (2) had low capital requirements combined with significant assessment options, and (3) were formed mostly as mutuals or reciprocals, the current pools have high initial capitalization requirements with little or no post assessment options, and were formed as stock companies. The original pools dealt primarily with the primary layers of insurance and relied heavily on treaty reinsurance. A special characteristic of current pools is the focus on the excess layers of insurance (that is, those with low frequency, high severity, and low predictability) with substantial "net line" retention. Because of low initial capitalization, little net line underwriting, and similarity of interest among participants, the traditional pooling arrangement was arranged by participants with little or no outside help. Because of the diversity of interests and the high stakes in terms of capitalization, exposures, and contract provisions, current pools require a leader-promoter with excellent negotiation and communication skills and great technical expertise in order to generate the financial and legal support needed to keep the organization afloat while the group goes through the formation stages. Thus, it is not a coincidence that the primary building block for many current pools are some of the largest brokers, insurers, banking investment institutions, and risk management consultants in the world. Marsh & McLennan, Johnson and Higgins, Frank B. Hall, Alexander and Alexander, the Reiss Group, Tillinghast, Conning and Company, Continental, Aetna, Chase Manhattan, Morgan Stanley, and Smith Barney are some of the names associated with current pooling activities. Lawrence L. Drake, managing director of Marsh & McLennan, in a recent presentation proposed a set of ground rules to test any proposal for an excess pool facility.[37]

1. The facility should fill a long-term need for substantial insurance capacity.
2. The prospective pool should be conservatively capitalized—to allow substantial net line underwriting.
3. The pool should be specialized in purpose, single or few lines only.
4. The pool should incorporate a diverse range of industries.
5. The pool should be formed as a stock company because of its inherent long-term organizational advantages.
6. The prospective pool should operate in a way that complements rather than competes with the commercial insurance market.
7. The sponsoring broker should bear the cost of formation and be rewarded appropriately if the project is successful.
8. The pool should utilize a distribution system that encourages utilization, and the brokerage system performs this function best.

The writings of the various pooling facilities can generally be grouped under those that write (1) primary or excess liability only, (2) excess liability and D & O coverage, (3) primary D&O coverage only, and (4) environmental impairment liability coverage.[38]

The first group would include some of the older pools that have been in existence for a decade or more, such as AEGIS and First Island. More recent examples of pools in this category include Primex, Tortuga, and Corporate America's Risk Exchange (CARE). Primex is a pool sponsored by Johnson and Higgins to write excess general liability coverage for small to mid-sized chemical companies. It is domiciled in Barbados and is open through a broker to companies in that category. At present, some twenty-seven policyholders subscribe. Tortuga is a pool domiciled in the Cayman Islands and is sponsored by the Reiss Group for captives managed by Reiss. CARE is a pooling facility under study to write excess liability for chemical companies. The impetus for this group came from a risk manager of one chemical company.

Among the pooling facilities in the second category that write excess liability and directors and officers coverage, the best known is probably the American Casualty Excess Insurance Company (ACE). ACE currently has about $730 million in capital and surplus generated by its approximately 240 shareholders (out of a total 280 policyholders). ACE is no longer selling stock but requires a reserve premium equal to the annual premium ($220 million in 1986). ACE was sponsored by

Marsh & McLennan and Morgan Guaranty. Access to ACE, which operates out of Bermuda (its domicile of registration is the Caymans), is through brokers. XL, which stands for excess liability, is similar to ACE in its structure and coverage, except for the limits offered. Marsh & McLennan also sponsored XL, which currently has about 200 policyholders. Additional pools in this category are in formation and include Energy Insurance Mutual (EIM) for utilities, European Excess Ins. Ltd. (EUREX) for European companies, and SCUL for colleges and universities.

Several pools were formed as a response to the extreme shortage of directors and officers liability insurance coverage, even at the primary layer limits. These pools write D&O coverage without other liability lines or specialize in related areas. For example, Bankers Insurance Company Ltd. (BICL) is based in Bermuda and writes D&O as well as bankers blanket bonds for bank members. CODA, ERIC, and DOLI are also in this category.

A few pools were formed to write solely environmental impairment liability coverage. Most of these are still in the formation stage or have just started to operate. Some of the names in this group include Waste Insurance Liability Ltd. (WILL) formed in Vermont by the National Solid Wastes Management Association; North American Casualty Cooperative (NACC); Intel Plan formed by the Intel Corporation; and Hypercept formed by Aralie for manufacturing companies.[39]

Most of the activity associated with these pooling facilities started in 1986. Toward the end of the year with the passing of the Tax Reform Law of 1986, some pools got "cold feet" because of the unfavorable tax treatment of offshore group captives. In the author's view, this will be a temporary slowdown until the tax status will clear and become, as it should be, only a marginal issue. Signs of a softening insurance market may slow down new pool development as they have slowed down formation of captives in the past. But the formation and growth of pools is a fundamental answer to the problem of low frequency-high severity unpredictable risks. The insurance industry will have no choice other than to recognize and ultimately cooperate with excess pools that have the support of insureds, brokers, and financial institutions.

Which Type of Risk Management Technique?

The techniques for handling loss exposures can be classified as avoidance, control, retention, noninsurance transfers, and insurance. The captive device does not fit neatly into these categories. In some cases captives truly provide their owners with insurance protection, while in others, they merely retain the loss exposures of their parents.

In still other instances captives are essentially hybrids displaying the characteristics of both insurance and retention.[40]

Captives frequently cede to reinsurers a major portion of the coverage they write. For example, a single-owner pure captive writing property coverage may cede all but $50,000 or $100,000 of the coverage to reinsurers. To the extent that the coverage written by a captive is reinsured, insurance truly exists because the loss exposures of the captive's owners are transferred to independent insurance companies. The reinsurers, however, rather than the captive are providing the insurance in this case. The captive merely serves as an insurance conduit with respect to the portion of coverage that it cedes to reinsurers.

To the extent that coverage is not reinsured, the single-owner pure captive is a funded retention device. In reality, the financial burden of unreinsured losses paid by the captive falls on its owner because the captive is merely a subsidiary funded by its owner. No transfer of exposure out of the corporate family occurs.

In contrast to the single-owner pure captive, the group pure captive can often be viewed as an authentic insurance device, particularly when there is a large number of participants involved. For example, OIL is jointly owned by numerous, unrelated petroleum companies. Since the losses incurred under policies issued by OIL are shared by all of the owners, a substantial transfer of loss exposure from the owner-policyholder to the captive occurs. Also, the breadth of the exclusions permits some useful predictions of future losses. Thus, the coverage provided by OIL to its owners is insurance.

When a group pure captive has only a few participants, however, the amount of loss sharing is limited and the amount of retention may be substantial. In that case the group pure captive would be a hybrid; it exhibits the characteristics of both insurance and retention. Similarly, in the absence of a large number of owners, the broad captive would also be a hybrid. The losses of the owners would be shared at least to some extent by those members of the general public that purchased coverage from the captive.

Group broad captives, by and large, have many owners and write enough outside business so the owners' risks are fully shared and distributed among others. Thus, for each member-owner, the transaction is indeed a complete transfer of risk, that is, the coverage provided by the captive is insurance. Perhaps the recently formed pools such as ACE, and XL are classic examples of group broad captives who retain fully the risk underwritten, but because of numerous stockholders and other policyholders, the risks are sufficiently shared and distributed so that each member-owner is involved in a complete insurance transaction.

III. THE NATURE OF CAPTIVE OPERATIONS

Captive companies operate in a variety of ways. In this section the author examines some key aspects of their operations, including forms of organization, places chosen as domiciles, types of coverages underwritten, and approaches to management.

Form of Organization

While some captives have been organized as mutuals and reciprocals, most have been formed as stock companies. In the 1980 Bermuda captive population, only 4 percent of all captives were mutuals while the overwhelming majority of 96 percent were organized as stock companies.[41] In recent years all captives but a few exceptional cases, are formed as stock companies. Several reasons have been offered to explain the overwhelming popularity of the stock form of organization. Reiss, for example, contends that "the primary reason for forming a stock insurance company is the fact that...the stock insurance company ensures complete ownership [and control] by the parent company that may not be true in either the mutual or reciprocal company."[42] Similarly, Lalley suggests that most captives are formed as stock companies because "there is absolutely no ambiguity in the control of a stock insurance company, while such ambiguity can exist in the case of a mutual insurance company and a reciprocal or interinsurance exchange."[43]

The ease of liquidation of a stock corporation is also mentioned as an advantage of this form. Reiss states:

> If in the life of a Captive Insurance Company the parent company decides to liquidate the Captive..., the liquidation procedures of a stock company are clearly drawn out by law and follow a well traveled path. In a mutual company, state liquidation laws are very unclear to say the least. How a mutual company liquidates is so unclear that I personally know of three mutuals that have been dormant for a period of 10 years and permission to liquidate has not yet been granted.[44]

Goshay points out that some observers suggest that "the stock insurer, with its attendant equity and surplus position, enjoys a superior position in reinsurance relations."[45] He questions, however, the validity of the purported advantage of the stock corporation, arguing that reinsurers are concerned with an insurer's management, personnel, and underwriting standards rather than with its corporate form.

While most captives are stock companies, some have been organized as mutuals and reciprocals. For example, Kraftco Corporation's captive, Ideal Mutual Insurance Company, was incorporated as a mutual in 1944 because, at that time, mutual insurance companies enjoyed a federal tax advantage that was not available to stock companies.[46] In essence, mutual property-liability insurers were not taxed on underwriting income prior to 1963.

In 1950 the Belk Stores organization established its property insurance captive as a reciprocal. The Belk organization consisted of a chain of about 400 separately owned and operated department stores in 18 states. In view of this diversity of ownership interests, Belk found the reciprocal characteristics of several, rather than joint liability and surplus allocation through separate accounts to be quite appealing. In addition, a reciprocal would not require the stores to freeze capital in equity and surplus as in the case of a stock company. Finally, the reciprocal offered the Belk organization several tax advantages that could not be obtained by forming its captive as a stock or mutual insurance company.[47]

During the period 1950 through 1969, few, if any, new captives were formed as mutual companies. Subsequently, however, a number of group pure captives, including several of the ones already discussed, were organized as mutuals. For example, several of the captives that have been formed since 1970 by firms in various energy-related industries are mutuals. These include AEGIS and Nuclear Mutual, Ltd. Similarly, several of the recently established medical malpractice captives have been organized as mutual companies. With regard to captives serving a group, mutuals have a particular advantage in providing ease of entry and exit and in allowing easy alteration of the relative participation by the members of the group. Despite this upsurge in the use of the mutual form of organization in recent years, most new captives are still being formed as stock companies for the reasons already mentioned.

Domicile

A captive company may be domiciled either in the state or country of its parent organization or elsewhere, notably offshore. In this monograph the term domestic captive is used to refer to a captive domiciled in the United States, and the term foreign captive is used to refer to a captive domiciled in another country. In the literature foreign captives are often called offshore captives. The author acknowledges that this terminology differs from that used in the licensing, regulation, and taxation of insurance companies by the various states, where three categories of insurers are recognized: (1) domestic (headquartered within that state), (2) foreign (domiciled or headquartered in one of the other forty-nine states), and (3) alien (domiciled outside the U.S.). Federal laws and regulations, however, use only the terms domestic (domiciled in the U.S.) and foreign (headquartered outside the U.S.) where captive companies are concerned. The domestic-foreign terminology is also used exclusively in the growing body of literature on the subject of captives. The author will use the domestic-foreign terminology throughout this monograph, even though it may, eventually, prove to be less precise.

Traditional Problems of Domestic Domicile While a number of successful captives are domiciled in the United States, most are domiciled in foreign countries. At the time of this writing (early 1987) it is estimated that 90 percent of all captives are domiciled in foreign countries.[48] Choice of a foreign as opposed to a domestic domicile is usually motivated by a desire to avoid various problems traditionally encountered in connection with establishing and operating a domestic captive. The following are some of the factors tending to discourage the formation of domestic captives:

1. Obtaining a charter in most states is usually more difficult, time-consuming, and expensive than obtaining it in any one of several foreign countries.
2. Most states have substantial initial capital and surplus requirements that exceed the relatively low levels of capitalization desired by the owners of most captives.
3. State regulations pertaining to insurance company investments are often quite stringent and detailed and might unduly limit a captive's investment activities.
4. Detailed financial disclosure by domestic captives is required in the form of annual statements and periodic examinations.
5. Rates and forms used by a domestic captive may have to be filed and approved in accordance with state regulations, thereby limiting price and product flexibility.
6. The volume of premiums that a domestic captive can write is limited by state regulation to some multiple of the amount of its capital and surplus.
7. In many states, a domestic captive is required to participate in FAIR Plans and/or other residual market plans if it writes insurance in the lines associated with the plans.
8. A domestic captive is generally required to participate financially in state insurer insolvency funds.

Foreign Domicile While a number of foreign countries have served as domiciles for captive companies, the most popular location by

Exhibit 11-3
Locations of Captives—End of 1986

Domicile	Number Estimated
Bermuda	1,200
Cayman Islands	350
Barbados	50
Bahamas	25
Guernsey	125
Vermont	70
Colorado	30
Tennessee	10
Other U.S.	120
Other non-U.S.	130
Total	2,110

far has been Bermuda, followed by the Cayman Islands. Recent estimates are shown in Exhibit 11-3.[49]

Bermuda. Since 1969, Bermuda has clearly been the most popular domicile for captive companies. A captive is formed as an "exempted company" in Bermuda, which means exempted from the General Companies Act requiring local companies to be at least 60 percent Bermudian owned. It also enjoys tax-exempt status under the provisions of the Exempted Undertakings Tax Protection Act of 1966, the effect of which is to exempt income and capital gains from all taxation until 2006. The only official charges are annual government fees, which have been raised over the years to the level of $3,800 as of 1987.

As an exempted company, the captive may write all lines of insurance, including life and health coverages, and may enter into other lines of business not directly related to insurance, except that, since 1979, it cannot act in the capacity of insurance broker. A captive is prohibited from doing business with any person or firm in Bermuda except to further its business carried on outside of Bermuda. This means it is not allowed to sell insurance to Bermudians, but may hire a local law firm and engage in reinsurance business with other exempted companies.

Bermuda captives are subject to the Insurance Act of 1978, which actually became effective at the end of 1980. The act and the regulations that followed it are meant to fit within a framework of self-regulation, rather than to be repressive regulation reminiscent of American state insurance law and practice. The act imposes mild operating and financial constraints on all captives and requires that a statutory statement of compliance by the company auditors be filed annually with the government. The statements, however, do not have to include much detail. The emphasis is on solvency margins and protection of the Bermuda image rather than on how captives should run their business. Premium-to-surplus ratios must be no more than five to one, up to a premium of $6 million per year, and the solvency margins must be no less than $120,000 for a property-liability captive, $250,000 for a life or health insurance captive, and $370,000 for a combination of the two. (A "solvency margin" is the excess of assets over liabilities, although definitions of this term vary widely.) In addition to these general solvency measures, the act requires that assets equal at least to 75 percent of the captive's insurance *liabilities* be "admissable," that is, be in the form of cash, time deposits, quoted securities, or first mortgage notes or bonds.[50]

The procedure for incorporating a captive insurance company in Bermuda used to be simple, quick, and inexpensive. With the enactment of the new legislation, the continuing rush of business to the island, particularly between the late seventies and early eighties, and the popularity of locating other exempt companies in Bermuda, the administrative burdens in creating new captives have been growing.[51] As of this writing, the process requires involvement of a local law firm and a local insurance management representative (sometimes provided by the law firm). A complete dossier on the proposed company must be prepared and submitted to the Insurers Registration Subcommittee. The soundness of the business, the owners, and financial projections are closely scrutinized by this committee, especially as to formation of captives that are to be heavily involved in professional or product liability coverages.

A captive must maintain a registered office in Bermuda and have on its board of directors at least two residents of Bermuda. Only the share register of the company is open to inspection by the public; none of the statutory statements is public information. Board meetings need not be held in Bermuda. Common practice, however, calls for appointment of the Bermuda lawyer or head of the management company to an officer position such as secretary to be able to carry out necessary filings and other paperwork that may be of interest to the island.

Once incorporation has taken place, the Bermuda captive can conduct its operation relatively free of further governmental regulation. The captive can invest its funds in any way it desires, except the constraint mentioned above about admissable assets. Investing in local Bermuda companies is generally prohibited, but loans to its parent or other affiliated companies are not. No rate, policy, or coverage filing or approval is required. As mentioned, an annual statutory financial return is required. In it the captive has to report gross premium written for the year, reinsurance ceded, net premium written, and statutory capital and surplus. In addition three ratios are reported, premiums to capital and surplus, five-year operating ratio, and the change in the statutory surplus ratio. The act requires an annual audit. The auditors are required to certify that the operations and accounts have been in conformance with the law and the regulations. No other requirements exist for public financial disclosure.

Bermuda's main attractions as a domicile for captive insurance companies are the following:

1. freedom from regulation, in the American sense;
2. freedom from local taxation;
3. relative ease of incorporation, management, and operations;
4. an adequate "infrastructure" of insurance company support activities including legal, accounting, management, underwriting, reinsuring, and clerical as well as adequate office space; and
5. excellent commercial transportation and banking support services.

In response to a question presented to operators of 204 Bermuda captives in 1980, the "economic and political stability" of Bermuda was the most frequent attraction followed closely by "minimum regulation" and the "advanced financial communication and management facilities." "Freedom from local taxation" was the fourth-ranked reason for forming a captive in Bermuda out of eight main reasons mentioned.[52]

Other Foreign Domiciles. While Bermuda is clearly the most popular domicile for foreign captives, others are being used as well. The major ones include, in order of importance to U.S. owners, the Cayman Islands, Barbados, the Bahamas, Turks and Caicos Islands and Guernsey. Some others are: Panama, Switzerland, the Netherlands Antilles, the British and U.S. Virgin Islands, and islands in the Pacific such as Nauru, the New Hebrides, and Hong Kong.

Similar to Bermuda, the Cayman Islands adopted an insurance law (The Insurance Law of 1979) and some regulations to apply to the growing number of captives domiciled there. Captives in the Caymans also enjoy tax-free status. (The guaranteed period of continued tax-free status is thirty years, even longer than that in Bermuda.) Minimal regulation is exercised, although it is significantly different from the regulation in Bermuda. One difference is that in the Cayman Islands much stricter secrecy is imposed on captive operations. No information of any kind concerning the captive may be divulged by the government or by anyone else (The Confidential Relationships [Preservation] Law of 1978). Also worth mentioning is the fact that the Cayman insurance infrastructure is much thinner than that in Bermuda, although banking facilities are considered superior because of the presence of some 450 foreign banks in the Cayman Islands. These islands are first a bank subsidiary domicile and second an insurance subsidiary domicile. The statutory financial statements for a captive company do not have to be filed with the authorities, although an auditor's statement that they exist in the required form must be filed.[53]

The Bahamas. Until 1969 Nassau in the Bahama Islands was a favorite place for establishing a captive. Its popularity stemmed not only from the income tax-free status enjoyed by captive corporations but also from the complete lack of insurance regulation in the islands. No minimum capital and surplus requirements existed; no investment regulations were imposed; and no financial disclosure was required. In fact, the government did not even engage in any clerical screening before granting a charter.

As a result of the government's failure to weed out undesirable elements, a series of spectacular insurance scandals erupted in the Bahamas in 1968. Although they did not involve legitimate captives, the scandals gave the Bahamas the reputation of being a haven for "suitcase" insurance companies. As a consequence, the legislature passed the Bahamas' Insurance Act in 1969 to provide the government with regulatory powers over all insurance companies. The act required all insurance companies to register with the government and annually publish their financial statements in an official newspaper. In addition, the act required insurers to maintain minimum capital and surplus. Life insurers had to maintain capitalization of at least $300,000, while other insurers had to maintain minimum capitalization of $140,000 or 20 percent of their annual nonlife premium volume, whichever was greater.

Disturbed by the new insurance regulations and the rumors, particularly the financial disclosure requirement, most of the existing captives eventually left the Bahamas. In 1978 the Insurance Act was amended to remove the taxation of captives. Even so, there was no rush to return to the Bahamas. Labor problems, the difficulty of obtaining residence and work permits, and the history of the legislative changes are still considered obstacles to growth of "the industry" in the Bahamas.[54]

In 1983 the Bahamian government passed the 1983 External Insurance Act. The act was designed particularly for single parent captives. The new act also regulates captive management companies. Thus, nonresident insurers in the Bahamas are licensed under either the 1969 Insurance Act or the External Insurance Act of 1983. The new law reduces minimum capitalization to $100,000 for property-liability captives and to $200,000 for a life insurer although regulators seek at least $250,000 in initial capital before approving a nonresident insurer under either law. An annual registration fee of $2,500 is required. Although the government currently is actively welcoming captives, the number of nonresident insurers still totals about twenty-five writing some $120 million dollars in premiums. Of the twenty-five insurers, only about half are not owned by insurance interests, that is, are true or real captives.[55]

Barbados. This site is particularly interesting because in just two years Barbados has built a strong foundation for a captive domicile. There are close to sixty nonresident insurers, most of which are true captives, as well as some twenty management companies, accounting firms, and other captive-supporting systems. It is clear that the growth of Barbados is not only due to the recent tight insurance market, which generated worldwide growth in captive formation, but primarily to the tax treaty between Barbados and the U.S., as well as treaties with Canada and some European countries. The treaty with the United States exempts U.S. companies from paying the 4 percent federal excise tax on direct premiums and the 1 percent excise tax on reinsurance premiums paid to foreign insurers and reinsurers. In an era of disappearing tax advantages and increasing premiums, such exemptions are excellent incentives. The treaty agreement with the U.S. runs through 1990, which gives Barbados a few years to build a solid reputation as a quality domicile for captives.

The Barbados Exempt Insurance Act of 1983 calls for a minimum capital requirement of $125,000, which may be met with a letter of credit if approved by the Minister of Finance. The registration and incorporation fees amount to about $3,100; there is an annual fee of $2,500. Some of the details regarding solvency and premium-to-capital requirements resemble those in Bermuda. The Act also allows licensees to become operational at any time, thus allowing organizations to form captives which remain dormant until needed—reducing costs.

Barbados has received a substantial boost in its status as a captive domicile by attracting large group captives and pools such as XL, PRIMEX, and EIM.[56]

But Barbados is not yet a Bermuda or a Cayman, and the double taxation treaty it has with the U.S. is subject to some criticism in view of the fact that Bermuda has sought a similar arrangement with the U.S., and Congress has not yet approved it. Some observers believe that the treaty with Bermuda is unlikely to be approved in light of the U.S. government's attempt to eliminate corporate tax shelters and that even the treaty with Barbados will be in jeopardy when it has to be renewed in 1989. The other forces that may hamper the growth of Barbados' captive movement as well as other offshore domiciles is the Risk Retention Act passed in 1986. It makes forming retention groups in the U.S. more attractive than doing so offshore. The Tax Reform Act of 1986, which eliminated the tax advantages of offshore group captives, may also inhibit Barbados' captive movement.

In general, the softening of the worldwide insurance market, leveling of prices, and availability of capacity may hamper the formation of all types of self-insurance mechanisms including captives. Nevertheless, it is unlikely that the foreign captive movement will be abandoned or that the formation of captives will be significantly reduced in the next few years.

Domestic Domicile Colorado was the first state to favor the creation of captives. It was followed by Tennessee, Virginia, Vermont, Delaware, and Hawaii. It has been reported that Oregon and New Mexico are studying the formation of special legislation for captives. New Jersey, however, is expected to pass a bill in 1987 that will ease the creation of captives.[57] Common features of the legislation pertaining to captives in these states are (1) exempting captives from participation in residual market plans and from guaranty fund and other insurance assessments; (2) requiring lower initial capitalization than for ordinary insurers; and (3) levying insurance premium taxes at only 1 percent or less. Captives domiciled in these states, however, cannot be certain that they will have income tax advantages. Just like their offshore counterparts, the IRS may disallow the deductibility of the premiums paid by the parent organization to the captive. The belief was once widely held that a domestic captive, subject to regulation by a state insurance commissioner, would be treated differently by the IRS than would an offshore tax-avoidance captive. Experience has proved otherwise. However, a domestic domicile can still be highly practical, especially for medical malpractice captives seeking reimbursement from third-party payers whose regulations specifically or by inference prohibit foreign insurance subsidiaries.

Colorado. The Colorado experience, which the other states have used as a model, began in 1972 with the passage of the Colorado Captive Insurance Company Act. This act permits corporations and associations to form pure captives. The single-owner parent of a pure captive must demonstrate to the satisfaction of the insurance commissioner that the coverages it will provide for its owner are not reasonably available elsewhere, and that annual premiums paid by the parent will total at least $500,000 (although all of them do not have to involve the captive). The minimum capital and surplus requirement are $400,000 and $350,000, respectively, the same as for commercial property-liability companies domiciled in Colorado. Part of these amounts may be satisfied by means of a letter of credit. In practice, the commissioner usually requires capitalization of up to $1 million total. The law prohibits the captive from writing personal coverage and from writing life, accident, and health insurance, whether or not it is personal. Unrelated business may be written only as reinsurance, and such unrelated business is carefully supervised by the commissioner.

The operations of captives domiciled in Colorado have been regulated more closely than those in offshore domiciles and even in other competing domestic domiciles, notably, Vermont. Since 1972, only twenty-eight captives have been formed in Colorado, while Vermont, which passed legislation in 1981, was the domicile of some sixty-seven captives by the end of 1986. The new insurance commissioner of Colorado and members of the Risk and Insurance Management Society (RIMS) in particular have called for liberalizing the state's captive insurance law to make it more competitive with other domestic domiciles. The legislation currently being considered would repeal all restrictions on captive investments, would repeal the requirement by the applicant to show that insurance is unavailable or available at excessive prices, and would lower the minimum requirements to $300,000 and $200,000 in capital and surplus, respectively. This would put Colorado's requirements in line with those of Vermont. In addition, the new legislation would remove the requirement that an association must exist for a year before it can form a captive. It would also require a quicker response to applicants and allow a letter of credit to be used as the minimum surplus requirement. The new legislation will probably facilitate the formation of risk retention groups in the state.

Economics and competition play an important role in captive legislation. The number of states that followed Colorado and continue to consider laws to encourage captive formation is still growing.[58]

Tennessee. In 1978 Tennessee passed the Tennessee Captive Insurance Company Act. In many respects it is similar to the statute in Colorado on which it was modeled. One difference is that association-type captives were openly favored by Tennessee. Among the early ones to be formed in Tennessee were medical malpractice captives for associations of hospitals. A total of only five captives had selected Tennessee to be their domicile up to mid-1981 despite an amendment to the law favoring the formation of mutuals under the Tennessee captive legislation. In 1982 the state also dropped the requirement to prove lack of adequate U.S. markets before allowing the formation of a captive, in addition to simplifying reporting and filing requirements. As of the end of 1986 some ten captives were operating in Tennessee.[59]

Vermont. Vermont's captive legislation was passed in 1981 and went one step beyond Colorado and Tennessee in creating a new form of captive, the "industrial insured captive." This form was essentially a joint venture insurance company owned by several noninsurance parents. It was designed to respond to the perceived need for a domicile for such ventures that would arise with the passage of the 1981 Federal Risk Retention Act (for product liability coverage). Vermont's capital requirements are lower than for the other states. They are $250,000 for a pure captive, $500,000 for an industrial insured captive, and $750,000 for an association captive. Moreover, no requirement exists that the insurance placed in the captive be otherwise unavailable or reasonably priced, as in the case for Colorado and Tennessee captives. Vermont's captive legislation was supported and aided by efforts of RIMS, whose leaders perceived heavy ultimate use of the Vermont approach. Proponents of the Vermont effort predicted that captives domiciled offshore would switch to an onshore domicile, and Vermont's legislation would be the most favorable.

Vermont's success had to do with good timing. A cooperative and positive approach by the insurance commissioner and industry people produced legislation that was more liberal and reasonable than other domestic alternatives. Indeed, by the end of 1986 there were some 67 captives registered in Vermont. The insurance commissioner of Vermont expects as many as 200 captives by the end of 1987 (although his estimate may be somewhat liberal). That Vermont is serious about its function as a domicile for captives is supported by the fact that some very large captives that have been formed there, including Mobil's Bluefield International Co., American Hospitals Association's Health Providers Insurance Co., and ALCOA's Three Rivers Insurance Co. In addition, most large captive managers have established offices in Vermont, which demonstrates commitment and expectation of growth on their part.

But even given the effects of these states, the offshore captives still retain the advantage of flexibility, secrecy, and minor tax advantages. In spite of regulation enacted in Bermuda and the Cayman Islands, captives there are free to write insurance and reinsurance (including life and health coverages) for anyone. They may invest their assets with more freedom. Bermuda has become recognized as an insurance center, with major insurers and reinsurers opening offices. Colorado, Tennessee, and Vermont are still considered by some persons as outposts of big-city insurance centers in the United States. Naturally, the attitudes are subject to gradual or even abrupt change.

In February 1984 the U.S. Virgin Islands territory passed an exempt insurance act granting favorable tax status to captives. While many regulatory elements of this act resemble similar principles in other offshore and onshore captive regulation, what makes the U.S. Virgin Islands captive legislation interesting is its potential implication for writing employee benefits exposures by captives. The U.S. Virgin Islands can be a domicile that is offshore for tax code purposes but may qualify as a domestic domicile for funding employee benefits, which, so far, have been practically banned in non-U.S. domiciles.[60] As of this writing, however, both the implication of this legislation on formation of captives in the U.S. Virgin Islands and the implementation of the above idea remain to be seen. In fact, by the end of 1986 only four captives were located in the U.S. Virgin Islands. The local government suggests that lack of information prevents companies from coming. Critics relate it to some complications in interpretation of the insurance law.[61]

Removing Barriers to Domestic Domiciles—The Risk Retention Act The Risk Retention Acts of 1981 and 1986, although responding to specific circumstances involving unavailability and affordability of coverage, may have been the first federal attempts to encourage domestic captive insurers. The original Product Liability Risk Retention Act of 1981 was a response to the critical lack of product liability coverage in the late 1970s. When the bill was actually passed, the crisis was almost over. This fact combined with the limited nature of the act (product liability only) and the many remaining regulatory burdens limited its use to a great extent.

The Risk Retention Amendment of 1986, creating the Liability Risk Retention Act of 1986, was passed in October of that year. The scope, publicity, and particularly the timing were much better than its predecessor. Both acts have similar objectives—to enhance insurance options for companies, trade associations, municipalities, and other organizations by developing mechanisms to provide insurance and self-insurance arrangements on a group basis.[62]

The 1986 Risk Retention Act facilitates the formation of group captives known as risk retention groups and of mass purchasing organizations known as purchasing groups. The act removes a number of barriers that confronted insureds, insurers, and promoters in certain states. These include countersigning laws, "fictitious group" laws for group purchases, restrictions regarding nonadmitted insurers doing business in other states, registration requirements for federal securities laws, and state "blue sky laws (laws prohibiting a person selling securities from promising the 'blue sky')." There is no longer regulation that prohibits or hinders the sale and purchase of liability insurance on a group basis.[63]

A risk retention group can offer almost all forms of liability insurance except personal lines, workers compensation, private passenger auto insurance, and employee benefits.[64] Membership and ownership in a risk retention group is limited to persons engaged in similar or related businesses or activities. The group does not have to exist for any other purpose. The risk retention group must be formed as a corporation or association and be chartered and licensed as a liability company in at least one state. A risk retention group can act as a reinsurer for liability insurance to other risk retention groups and to groups or members whose liability risks are similar or related to those of the risk retention group. The risk retention group must provide a full business plan with actuarial support to the state where the license is sought. A copy of this document must also be submitted in other states where the group intends to do business.

As mentioned, the act also facilitates the formation of purchasing groups. This is any group whose members have similar or related loss exposures and obtain coverage from one or more admitted or nonadmitted insurers. Such a group does not have to be licensed or set up according to a particular legal form of business. The purchasing group is exempt from state laws requiring rate and policy form approval; it can offer coverage at rates better than standard rates for the same class of risks.[65]

It is clear that the Risk Retention Act can substantially boost the formation of domestic group captives; perhaps it will encourage the return of offshore captives to the U.S. Not only does it reduce the regulatory burdens, but it also may eliminate the substantial fronting fees that may range to as much as a third of the premium. Also, as mentioned, the Tax Reform Act of 1986 (to be subsequently discussed) makes offshore captives less attractive. For instance, the risk retention group will be subject to the same income tax liabilities as any other liability insurer, equalizing its tax status to offshore captives, but with the other presumed advantages of being domestically located.

As a means to encourage the domestic captive movement, the Risk Retention Act is a move in the right direction. Its main advantage is essentially removing some barriers and regulations, thus attracting captives who did not like the offshore sites, but who had no real choice in terms of location. Still, there are many constraints even compared to the relatively regulated offshore captive site of Bermuda. For instance, the Risk Retention Act left considerable regulatory requirements by the state of domicile and by nonchartering states. These include issues of unfair claims settlements, payment of premium taxes, participation in mandatory liability pools, and submitting to an insurance department examination. There are also several gray areas such as the issue of what is unacceptable reinsurance; how many members and who can qualify as a member of a risk retention group; and the exact way state regulators are to be involved in the business of nondomiciled risk retention groups.

The author believes that the success of domestic domiciles for captives will depend on the insurance market, the strength of promotion by the organizers and supporters of captives, and the degree of cooperation by state insurance departments. At present, the act is clearly good for organizers, promoters, brokers, and agents who will profit from studying the market and forming such groups. The lukewarm reaction to the act by most state insurance departments introduces some uncertainty into the success of captives.[66] Key factors in the success of domestic captives are that more than a few high visibility groups will form risk retention groups, that some of the offshore captives will return, or that they will form an additional domestic branch. Some of these events are happening, and the interest in domestic captives is high as of early 1987. But, as in the past, a soft insurance market can slow this trend. And of this writing, (mid-1987) there are some early signs of market softening in the liability business.

Methods of Providing Coverage

In providing coverage for the loss exposures of its owners, a captive may deal directly with its owners, may deal indirectly through some fronting intermediary, or both. Terminology becomes awkward in any discussion of this topic. A convenient approach is to divide the subject into insurance and reinsurance. Yet, we already have noticed that in the view of many observers a pure captive is neither an insurer nor a reinsurer. A captive becomes an insurer or a reinsurer only to the extent that it accepts exposures other than those of its owner or owners. Drawing a distinction between a pure captive and a broad captive in each appropriate passage of the ensuing discussion would become tedious. With this in mind, readers are asked to accept in this section of the monograph the following usage of insurer, insurance, reinsurer, reinsurance, and related terms. The use of these terms in this discussion as it applies to pure captives is simply a matter of expediency.

Insurer Captive companies provide direct coverage on a primary or an excess basis. In many cases captives issue primary property contracts covering the loss exposures of their owners. These property contracts are written either with no deductible or with a small deductible of $5,000 or less. The captive may typically retain only $50,000 to $250,000 of the coverage and reinsure the balance in the conventional reinsurance market.

Primary policies are also issued by some captives to provide liability coverages for their owners. For example, Arroyo Insurance Company has issued a primary product liability policy to its parent, Royal Industries, Inc. The policy covers the first $250,000 of loss per occurrence and contains an annual aggregate loss limit of $1.25 million. Similarly, a number of group malpractice captives are providing their participants with primary professional liability coverages. The malpractice policies issued by these captives may have per claim and annual aggregate limits of $100,000 and $300,000, respectively.

Captive companies frequently provide property or liability coverages on a direct excess basis. Some captives issue policies that provide their owners with coverages for property losses in excess of a retention of $50,000 or more. For example, one major manufacturing firm that handles its property losses up to $100,000 through unfunded retention purchases property coverage with a $100,000 deductible from its captive. In this case the direct excess policy issued by the captive provides coverage for property losses in excess of the parent company's substantial retention. The captive retains the first $150,000 of the excess coverage and cedes the balance to reinsurers. Some companies provide liability coverage on a direct excess basis. For example, AEGIS originally provided its members with liability coverage for the first $1 million of losses in excess of minimum retention of $100,000 per occurrence. Similarly, Hospital Underwriting Group originally provided its owners with malpractice coverage for losses above a minimum retention level of $500,000 up to $7.5 million per occurrence.[67]

Reinsurer In providing coverage on the loss exposures of their owners, captives frequently operate as reinsurers.

U.S. Loss Exposures. The most common exposures ceded as reinsurance to captives formed in recent years have been liability exposures of United States origin such as product liability, professional liability, workers compensation, and auto liability, in that order. Generally, a quota-share reinsurance treaty is arranged between the primary insurer and the captive company under which the captive accepts a percentage (sometimes as high as 100) of the primary insurer's exposures, premiums, reserves, claims, and expenses in exchange for a fixed fee or a commission. These "fronting arrangements" are usually entered into by domestic companies (that is, companies domiciled in the United States). Frequently, irrevocable bank letters of credit in favor of the fronting insurers are obtained by the captive or the parent equal to ceded loss reserves, but sometimes up to the limit of the primary policy. For example, as of 1976, Royal Industries, Inc., was purchasing workers compensation and auto liability insurance from National Union Fire Insurance Company. That primary insurer, in turn, was ceding 100 percent of the coverages to Royal's captive, Arroyo Insurance Company.[68] Similarly, Brunswick Corporation's captive, Centennial Assurance, Ltd., in 1976 was accepting reinsurance of Brunswick's workers compensation and auto liability coverages, the primary insurance having been written by Northwestern National Insurance Company.[69]

The fronting company approach to providing coverage is required for workers compensation and auto liability insurance in most states because of local restrictions on nonadmitted insurers writing these lines. (Most captives are by their very nature foreign, or nonadmitted, and undercapitalized from a local insurance regulation point of view.) Unregulated lines, such as product liability and professional liability, do not require fronting companies, but the fronts are sometimes used anyway to provide certificates of insurance and claims handling. Whenever legal problems related to a captive selling insurance arise, they often can be solved by use of a fronting company. Brokers and agents involved in a captive arrangement are prohibited from selling insurance coverage directly from the offshore (or even domestic) captive, but they can safely sell fronting programs with the coverages issued by admitted insurers.

Fronting arrangements usually cost the parent from 5 percent to 35 percent of original gross premium depending on the degree of service, the brokerage commission, and the desirability of the business to the fronting company. Flat fees for fronting are rare but may be preferable to the buyers of the coverages, especially in a time of rising premiums without a corresponding improvement in fronting services.

Occasionally, captives are operated as direct insurers or reinsurers for other kinds of domestic exposures, notably property, crime, marine, and employee benefits exposures in that order of importance. The last category, employee benefits, has been used infrequently due to the requirements of ERISA.

Foreign Loss Exposures. One of the original drives to create captives was to insure or reinsure exposures of property located outside the United States but belonging to the parents of captives. The impetus also came from the fact that insurance rates in the other countries could be high, no allowance might be made by the foreign insurers for loss prevention or deductibles, and premium taxes could be exorbitant. Incidentally, foreign liability type coverages were only of minor interest in these early captives. Since the late 1970s, however, the previously unfavorable conditions have changed in many foreign countries: property rates have become competitive in many countries by many captive owners, and worldwide deductible credits are available through international property programs without the necessity of using the captive vehicle. Foreign property insurance may still be a candidate for multinational single-owner captive parents, but the driving force to create a new captive primarily will be the desire to consolidate, coordinate, and control the overall risk management program. Savings can possibly be a factor when price differences are still significant.

The ceding by foreign insurers of reinsurance to the captive is commonly resorted to because of local regulations forbidding export of direct premiums to nonadmitted insurers. Rather than incur the cost and inconvenience of having their captives licensed to operate in foreign countries, U.S. business firms generally comply with the foreign insurance regulations by having their captives enter into fronting company arrangements with locally admitted insurance companies.[70] Under this type of arrangement a U.S. firm with loss exposures in a given foreign country purchases direct coverage from an insurance company licensed to operate in that country. The locally admitted (fronting) company then reinsures a substantial portion of the coverage with the U.S. firm's captive. The captive, in turn, retains a portion of the reinsured coverage (generally an amount between $50,000 and $250,000) and cedes the balance to other companies.

To illustrate a typical fronting company arrangement, suppose a U.S. corporation has a $10 million plant in a foreign country that prohibits nonadmitted insurance. The corporation might obtain full coverage from a local insurer with the understanding that the insurer will cede 95 percent of the coverage to the corporation's captive on a quota share basis. Under the quota share reinsurance arrangement, the local insurer would retain $500,000 of the coverage and cede $9.5 million to the captive. The captive, in turn, might retain $500,000 of the coverage and retrocede $9 million to commercial reinsurers on an excess of loss basis.

While some captives use local insurers in foreign countries as fronting companies, many use the services of large U.S. domiciled insurance companies such as Commercial Union, CIGNA, and Continental Insurance Company, or U.S. groups such as AFIA (formerly the American Foreign Insurance Association and currently part of the CIGNA organization) and American International Underwriters that have admitted facilities in various foreign countries. For example, in order to achieve its "objective of having a more fully admitted insurance program in its overseas location," Levi Strauss & Company used AFIA as a fronting company for its Bermuda captive, Zenith International Insurance, Ltd.[71]

The captive compensates the fronting company for its services through the payment of a fronting fee. This fee is expressed as a percentage of premium and varies according to the services provided by the fronting company. A typical fronting fee might be 12.5 percent of premium composed of 5 percent for profit and administrative expenses and the rest for commissions to local brokers, for fire brigade charges, and for miscellaneous other uses. This payment of the fronting fee could be in addition to the provision of the letter of credit, as mentioned, or to a cash advance in lieu of the letter of credit.

Large multinational companies that operate in many foreign countries have been using in recent years sophisticated programs that are arranged by some of the large international brokers (for example, Marsh & McLennan, Johnson & Higgins, Alexander & Alexander, and so on) often using international insurers such as AFIA, American International Underwriters, or Continental. It is common for the international brokers and the international insurers to have either a branch office or a correspondent that operates in these foreign countries, is familiar with local conditions, and is also admitted locally. The local broker or agent, with the cooperation of the local insurer, writes the underlying policy for the foreign subsidiary at the specifications of the global program but in compliance with local customs and regulations. The local insurer or branch of the international insurer issues the policy, retains a small percentage (usually up to 10 percent), and after compliance with other possible reinsurance regulations, reinsures the rest to the captive. The captive will pick up only a portion of the 90 percent (or less), perhaps up to $100,000 of each loss. It is the international broker who from that point provides intermediate reinsurance facilities in the form of both aggregate stop loss for the captive as well as a worldwide reinsurance treaty for the 90 percent (or less) of the exposure. Exhibit 11-4 shows the distribution of risk in such a program. The treaty involves the corresponding international insurers as well as other insurers and reinsurers worldwide. Such a complex program provides the multinational with a worldwide coordinated program that is up to U.S. or equivalent standards, that is relatively easy to control and administer, and that achieves utmost savings both at the level of the foreign subsidiary and at the level of the parent/captive. It is known that such programs have achieved savings at the range of 20 to 50 percent for the multinationals as compared to the precaptive, nonconsolidated programs. Exhibit 11-5 illustrates the premium distribution of an international captive program.

Combination Insurer and Reinsurer Many captives are operated as both insurers and reinsurers. For example, a captive owned by a multinational corporation might be operated as an insurer for purposes of handling property exposures located in the United States and those foreign countries that permit nonadmitted insurance. As a reinsurer, it would handle exposures located in countries that prohibit nonadmitted insurance. Alternatively, a given parent may use two captives: one for foreign exposures and another for United States and perhaps Canadian exposures.

Still other variations are possible. For example, since some

Exhibit 11-4
International Captive Insurance Program Risk Distribution*

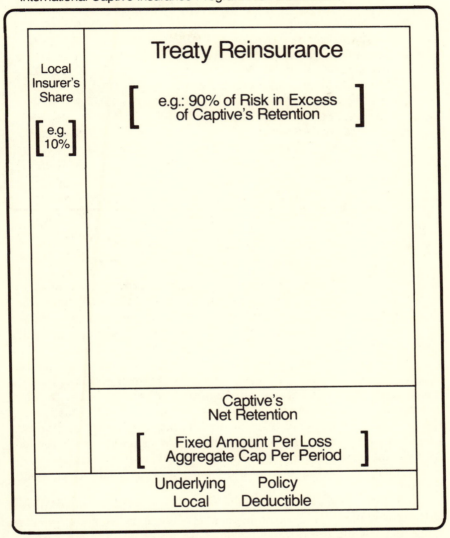

* Adapted with permission from M. Moshe Porat, "The Impact of Captive Insurers on Insurance Markets in Developing Countries," Report to the United Nations Conference on Trade and Development, Geneva, Switzerland, April 1984.

countries only prohibit nonadmitted insurance for coverages available from locally licensed companies, a captive may reinsure a fronting company for locally available coverages and issue direct insurance in

Exhibit 11-5
International Captive Program Premium Distribution*

Gross Local Premium	$100,000
Less: Local Retention (10.0%)	-10,000
Gross Premium Assumed by Captive	$ 90,000
Less: Brokerage Fees (12.5%)	-11,250
Fronting Fees (7.0%)	-6,300
Captive's Net Premium Written	$ 72,450
Less: First Loss Retention Allowance (35%)	-25,358
Gross Reinsurance Premium	$ 47,092
Less: Ceding Commission (10%)	-4,709
Net Reinsurance Premium	$ 42,383
Less: Contingent Profit Commission (15%)	-6,357
Net/Net Reinsurance Cost	$ 36,026

* Adapted with permission from M. Moshe Porat, "The Impact of Captive Insurers on Insurance Markets in Developing Countries," Report to the United Nations Conference on Trade and Development, Geneva, Switzerland, April 1984.

the form of a difference in conditions policy to provide coverages not available in the local market. Another variation is a captive that provides both property and workers compensation coverages on parent loss exposures in the United States. This type of captive frequently issues direct contracts to cover property losses and also accepts reinsurance from primary insurers that have issued workers compensation insurance on the parent's exposures. Similarly, some liability insurance captives operate as both insurers and reinsurers. A fronting arrangement is used for liability lines like auto coverage that involve the filing of certificates of insurance with state regulatory authorities. Direct insurance is issued for other lines. For example, as mentioned, Arroyo Insurance Company provides Royal Industries, Inc., with product liability coverage on a direct basis and auto liability coverage through reinsurance.

In a 1980 survey of all Bermuda captives, pure captives used direct writing (41 percent) or reinsurance (48 percent) in about similar proportions while the combination of both insurance and reinsurance was practiced by only 11 percent of the population. However, among broad captives, sole direct writing was limited to only 6 percent of the captives, but reinsurance and the combination approaches were quite prevalent, 45 percent and 49 percent, respectively. When surveyed for a more detailed method in providing coverage, it became apparent that the fronting method was the most popular among all captives—used by 30 percent of the population. The method commonly described as "flow

Exhibit 11-6
International Captive Insurance/Reinsurance Program Flow*

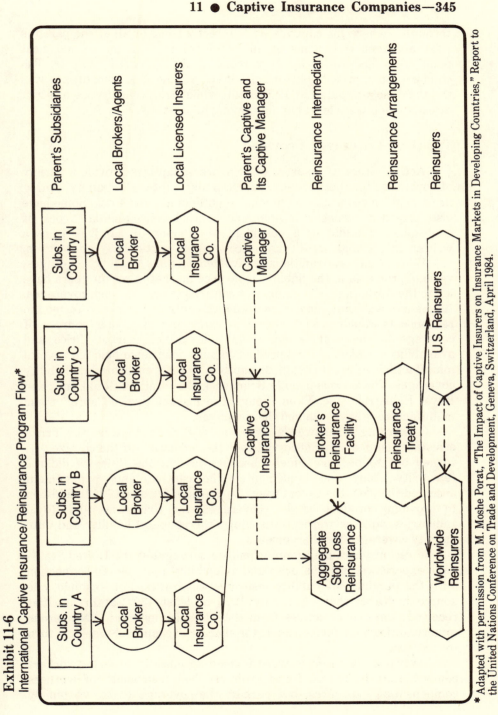

* Adapted with permission from M. Moshe Porat, "The Impact of Captive Insurers on Insurance Markets in Developing Countries," Report to the United Nations Conference on Trade and Development, Geneva, Switzerland, April 1984.

through," where the captives write directly some or all of the parent's risks and then cede some or all to reinsurers, was the second most popular method—used by 21 percent of the surveyed captives. The combination approach of fronting, direct writing, and reinsurance was the third most popular, at 19 percent, while strict reinsurance or strict direct writing were least popular among all captives.[72]

Types of Coverages Provided

Acting either as insurers or reinsurers, captives provide a variety of coverages for their owners. Traditionally, captives began by writing fire and allied coverages on buildings, equipment, and stock. Some have also provided business income and related consequential types of insurance. In addition, a considerable number of captives have a written inland and ocean marine coverages, particularly on cargoes.

While captives traditionally avoided writing liability coverages, various problems in the liability insurance market in recent years have led to the formation, of a number of captives to provide such coverages. As mentioned, many medical malpractice captives have been formed in response to rapidly rising premium rates and vanishing sources of coverage in the professional liability insurance market. Price and availability problems in the product liability insurance field led several manufacturing firms to establish captives to write their product liability coverages. These firms include Brunswick Corporation; Gould, Inc.; and Royal Industries, Inc. Even though the market turned "soft," these manufacturers have retained their captives.

Concerning Brunswick's decision to form a captive, the firm's assistant risk manager observed that the formation of the captive ". . . turned out to be very timely, because just at the time we did the feasibility study and implemented the captive, and management accepted the idea, the excess casualty markets fell apart."[73] In addition to providing product liability coverages, the Brunswick and Royal Industries captives were also issuing other general liability and auto liability coverages for their owners.

In recent years many municipalities throughout the United States have experienced serious price and availability problems in connection with the purchase of liability insurance coverages. For example, one source indicates that on 1 July 1976 at least 150 California cities received nonrenewal notices from their liability insurers.[74] Numerous municipalities have formed pools for sharing exposures. Some may turn to captives.

Several early captives were formed specifically to write workers compensation in Texas. Texas prohibits "self-insurance" of workers compensation exposures, but permits the coverage to be written by private insurers. Thus, the formation of a single-owner pure captive provides a convenient means of complying with the law in that state. In addition, however, many captives that write property or liability coverages for their owners also write workers compensation coverage. Goshay indicates that "while the workmen's compensation risk does involve long-term obligations, the existence of a highly structured reinsurance market, predictability of costs, a tradition of self-insurance, and the high degree of control over the...[exposure] which the parent is capable of exerting make the...[exposure] attractive for captive insurers."[75]

Employee Benefit Plans   Several firms have used their captives to provide coverages in connection with employee benefit plans. Among these are U.S. Industries, Inc., TRW, Inc., and North American Phillips. Since the Employee Retirement Income Security Act (ERISA) was passed in 1974, however, there has been concern about the legality of handling employee benefits through a captive company.[76]

ERISA regulates any employee benefit plan that is established or maintained by an employer engaged in commerce, an employer engaged in any industry or activity affecting commerce, or an employee organization representing employees engaged in commerce. ERISA also covers employee benefit plans that qualify for tax favored status. ERISA generally prohibits certain broad classes of transactions between a plan and a "party in interest" or a "disqualified person." These two terms include any fiduciary, trustee, or officer of the plan; anyone providing services to the plan; an employer (firm) whose employees are covered by the plan; any firm owning 50 percent or more of such an employer; relatives of such persons described; any employees, directors, officers, or 10 percent or greater shareholders of persons or organizations described; and any organization that is 50 percent or more controlled by the persons just described.

ERISA generally prohibits transactions between a plan and a party in interest that constitute directly or indirectly sale, exchange, or leasing of property; extension of credit; furnishing goods, services, or facilities; any transfer or use of plan assets; or the acquisition or holding by the plan of "excess employer securities." ERISA also prohibits "self dealing" by plan fiduciaries; that is, a fiduciary is neither permitted to deal with plan assets for self interest nor on behalf of persons whose interests are adverse to the plan or its participants.

These limitations clearly apply to transactions between a parent and its captive insurer in employee benefit plans.[77] ERISA granted the Secretary of Labor and the Secretary of Treasury the authority to provide general or specific exemptions from the prohibited transaction rules. Since ERISA's enactment in 1974, the Department of Labor has issued various class and individual rulings that, in combination, do not reflect any clear policy but rather a struggle in the attempt to develop a policy for employee benefit plans written by captive insurers functioning as direct insurers or reinsurers. These attempts are, in part, reflected in the following summary of several key rulings.

There are several ways in which captives may handle employee benefits without participating in a prohibited transaction. These include a limited exclusion, a statutory exemption, a class exemption, on an individual exemption. Certain types of employee-paid plans, particularly group insurance programs offered by an insurer directly to employees, will not be considered ERISA plans. Thus, participation in this type of plan is not considered a prohibited transaction if certain conditions take place. For instance, no contribution may be made by the employer, participation is completely voluntary, the program cannot be endorsed by the employer, and the employer receives no special consideration other than reasonable compensation for administrative services. A specific case was a Department of Labor Advisory Opinion 83-3A in January 1983 known as Integon Ruling. Ashland Oil's captive, Integon Life Insurance, issued the type of plan just described and received a ruling that it was not a plan subject to the requirements of ERISA. However, the Department of Labor ruled differently for a similar case where the plan was issued by an unrelated insurer and then, in turn, reinsured with the captive (Department of Labor Advisory Opinion 83-28A, 9 June 1983).

There is, however, a limited statutory exemption in ERISA to the prohibited transaction rules. ERISA's rule 408(b)(5)(B) permits a plan to buy life or health insurance or annuity contracts from a captive insurer that is qualified to do business in at least one state—defined by ERISA to include also the District of Columbia, Puerto Rico, the U.S. Virgin Islands, American Samoa, Guam, Wake Island, and the Canal Zone—provided that the insurer is either the employer or a party of interest wholly owned by the employer, that the plan pays no more than adequate consideration, and that the total premiums and annuity considerations paid by the affiliated employers, which are parties in interest, do not exceed 5 percent of the total premium for all lines written in that year from sources other than those employers.

Obviously, very few captive insurers could meet the 5 percent limit. Lobbying by the insurance industry resulted in the Department of Labor class exemption known as Prohibited Transaction Exemption (PTE 79-41) of August 1979. This expands the statutory exemption of ERISA regarding direct sale by an insurance company that is a party of interest. The PTE applies only to insurance companies licensed in at least one state (and the other territories as in the statutory exemptions) that have a 50 percent or more stock or partnership affiliation with the employer. The PTE allows the captive to sell life, annuity, and health contracts to affiliated employers if certain conditions are met. For instance, the insurance company must obtain a certificate of compliance from the domicile state eighteen months prior to the transaction, or the insurance company must have undergone financial examination in that state within the five-year period prior to the transaction date; the plan must pay adequate consideration for the contract; no commissions are to be paid on such contracts; and, most importantly, the total life, health, and annuity premiums received from the affiliated employers cannot be more than 50 percent of all premiums received by the captive for all lines in that year. PTE 79-41 covers life, health insurance, and annuity contracts. The term "health insurance" also includes forms of accident, disability, hospital, and dental expense policies.

The last requirement clearly relaxed the 5 percent limits and was designed to ensure that the captive deals also with the general public and is not solely dependent on its affiliates for its financial and customer base. It also ensures that the transactions are done on an arm's length basis. Based on private rulings, it appears that the 50 percent requirement is satisfied if the premiums from all unrelated risks together with the premiums from related property and liability risks equal or exceed the premium from related benefit risks. Apparently, employee-paid premiums are not unrelated for purposes of meeting the 50 percent requirement (PTE 85-90 of May 1985).

Reinsurance of employee benefits through a captive has been a controversial issue. A recent interpretation by the Department of Labor (November 1986 Bulletin 2509.75-2, 51 Fed. Reg. 41280) suggests that if a plan purchased an insurance contract with a third party insurer through the insurer's general account, and if a subsequent transaction is made involving the general asset account and a party of interest (such as a captive), then, generally, this is not necessarily a prohibited transaction. However, if a plan agrees to purchase an insurance contract from a third-party insurer "pursuant to an agreement, arrangement, or understanding, written or oral, under which it is expected that the unrelated company will subsequently reinsure all or part of the risk related to such insurance with an insurance company which is a party in interest of the plan, the purchase of the insurance contract would be a prohibited transaction." This has been the interpretation according to paragraph F of the commentary to PTE 79-41. Thus, such a reinsurance transaction could be a direct or indirect transfer of plan assets or use of plan assets by a party in interest, and it may also be an act of the fiduciary's dealing with the assets in his or her own interest.[78] Reinsurance transactions with captives therefore are not dealt with specifically within the PTE 79-41, but are interpreted through individual exemptions and rulings.

Rulings regarding the 50 percent requirement, the eighteen-month residing requirement, financial examination and other requirements have been handled on an individual basis. For the 50 percent requirement some rulings allowed in the total lines calculation premiums of all employee benefits and other property-liability lines. It seems, therefore, that the Department of Labor allows a generous interpretation of the 50 percent requirement in terms of excluding related business that is not life and health benefits. It appears, therefore, that it would be acceptable for new captives that were formed to write employee benefits to write equal portions of related and unrelated risks of similar or dissimilar business in order to meet this requirement. In some cases larger percentages of reinsurance were exempted. For example, the J. C. Penney case where 100 percent of the risk was reinsured through a captive, PTE 84-86 of June 1984.

The use of captives in employee benefits insurance and reinsurance has not been prevalent. This is partly because of the limiting ERISA regulations and their interpretation, but more so because firms have made only limited attempts to use some of the exemptions available. To a great extent, this is a result of the fact that benefit managers and risk managers neither coordinate their activities, nor do they usually function in the same departments.[79]

The existence of domestic captive laws in several states and the U.S. Virgin Islands, in addition to the growth of group captives and pools, and some of the few recent Department of Labor interpretations should generate more action in using captives to handle the insurance of employee benefits. The Risk Retention Act, which will further facilitate the development of domestic group captives, will likely advance the use of captives in employee benefits since, in most cases, employers will own less than 50 percent of the captive. Therefore such transactions should usually not be considered prohibited.

In 1980, of 592 Bermuda captives actively writing business, more than 95 percent were writing only general coverages, a term used for property-liability lines. A small minority of less than 2 percent wrote solely long-term coverages (life, health, and accident lines), and only 1 percent of the captives wrote both general and long-term coverages. Five years later, still an overwhelming majority of the 697 active captives wrote general business lines. Only about 7.5 percent of all active captives wrote life, health, and accident coverages, which highlights how relatively few captives are used in employee benefits.

Based on the specific coverages written by captives both in 1980 and subsequently in 1985, it is apparent that the traditional lines of business were the dominating lines among captives as well. Liability lines were written by some 50 percent of all captives and had been the most popular lines of business. Property lines were more prevalent in

1980, but they were still the second most popular coverages provided by captives in 1985. Workers compensation, marine, and auto coverages were specific lines that followed liability and property in terms of popularity among captives both in 1980 and 1985. In 1985, however, specific lines such as product liability and professional liability became more frequently written by captives. In both years only about 12 percent of all active captives were writing what is known as specialty lines. These were coverages such as errors and omissions, directors and officers liability, performance bonds, strike insurance, libel and slander, political risks, war risks, maternity risks, currency risks, players' contracts, and crop insurance. Thus, although some captives do engage in some coverages that are not of the ordinary, the most popular lines of business are still, as always, the traditional liability, property, marine, workers compensation, and auto coverages.[80]

Reinsurance of Captives

The discussion thus far has included the issue of acceptance by captives of reinsurance ceded to them by insurers of the exposures of the parents of the captives. Of equal or greater importance is the purchase of reinsurance *by* the captives of cover exposures directly "insured" by the captives. Adequate reinsurance is vital to the successful operation of a captive company. Ingrey indicates that "the primary purpose of the reinsurer is to provide the capacity by which the captive can insure the parent on a gross basis."[81] Proper reinsurance arrangements enable a captive with limited capitalization to issue policies providing millions of dollars of coverage on the loss exposures of its owner(s).

In addition to its primary function of providing increased under-writing capacity, reinsurance enables a captive to stabilize its loss experience and thus, its underwriting results, over time. Moreover, quota share reinsurance can be used to provide unearned premium reserve relief and ceding commission income for newly formed domestic captives. Reinsurers also provide a captive's management with a useful source of information and advice on a wide variety of insurance and reinsurance matters.

Reinsurers give careful consideration to a number of factors in determining whether or not to provide coverage for a captive. Among the factors generally considered are the following:

1. the reasons for establishing the captive,
2. the intent of the parent company or association to operate the captive on a long-term basis,

3. the extent of the captive's financing and the availability of additional capital,
4. the nature of the coverages contained in the policies and forms used by the captive,
5. the adequacy of the premium rates charged by the captive, and
6. the adequacy with which loss prevention, safety engineering, claims adjustment, and accounting functions are performed.

Types of Reinsurance Programs   Although the specific details of captive reinsurance programs vary considerably, most programs are based on an excess of loss reinsurance arrangement. Unless it is quite small, the captive is likely to retain at least the first $100,000 to $250,000 of each loss and then purchase excess of loss reinsurance on either a per exposure or per occurrence basis. In addition, a captive will frequently purchase annual aggregate stop loss reinsurance to protect against an accumulation of losses within the first loss retention. Another common modification is for the captive to retain a small percentage of any loss in excess of its first loss retention. Barile provides the following example:

> A rather large captive insurance company, established some years ago, has a reinsurance program which provides reinsurance protection for 99% of any loss in excess of $50,000 to the captive company. The captive must retain, in addition to the first loss of $50,000, a 1% participation in all losses in excess of $50,000. Since the captive company receives a 34% credit for the $50,000 retention, the reinsurer receives a premium amounting to 99% of 66% of the captive's premium, less a 25% ceding commission and a 15% profit commission.[82]

Excess of loss reinsurance is available on both a treaty and a facultative basis. Normally, domestic facultative arrangements are between $500,000 and $2.5 million per reinsurer although in some cases, it can be clearly higher than that.

Sources of Reinsurance   Reinsurance has not always been readily available to captives. Barile explains:

> In the early part of 1955, before the emphasis toward captive insurance companies was really to begin, the reinsurance industry began to be approached to reinsure captive companies. The initial reaction within the industry was highly controversial and some reinsurance companies advocated the philosophy that they would not entertain such a proposition as it promoted the self-insurance concept. They feared, in the long run, this could conceivably take business away from the conventional insurance companies, many of whom were clients of the reinsurance companies.[83]

Most reinsurers now support captives. John Lepine, chairman of Reinsurance Corporation, Ltd. and chairman of the prestigious Reinsurance Offices Association, indicated in 1975 that "London reinsurers are very interested in reinsuring captives, and are in favor of captives, as long as they are set up as good business operations."[84] This interest has continued and even intensified in the early 1980s. Frequently, Lloyd's syndicates and other London companies serve as the lead underwriters in reinsurance programs for captives. Professional reinsurers and large U.S. insurance companies that write reinsurance also provide important markets for captives.

In many cases captives have obtained reinsurance coverage from pools established by independent captive management companies and international brokers that provide management services to captive insurers. The pools were formed by the captive managers to provide their clients with ready access to reinsurance. While the details of such reinsurance pool arrangements are generally kept confidential, a 1977 letter from Mr. Arthur Deters provides some information on the nature of the pool established by the American Risk Management Group (ARM). Some of the information reported in Mr. Deters' letter may now be dated. In early 1977 the pool consisted of about 140 domestic and foreign reinsurers including twenty-six ARM-managed captives. The 1977 ARM reinsurance pool had an "unlimited" total capacity, which, as shown in Exhibit 11-7, was divided into four layers. The first and fourth layers of coverage were provided by the participants in the basic treaty that is outlined in Exhibit 11-8. That figure illustrates the flow of reinsurance from the various participants in the basic treaty to the ARM-managed captives. As indicated in Exhibit 11-8, Hopewell International Ltd., ARM's subsidiary, served as a focal point for the "Bermuda Pool" reinsurers. In addition, Hopewell participated as a reinsurer in the basic treaty to the extent of 1 percent. For competitive reasons, reinsurance pools similar in principle have been formed by several international brokers including Johnson & Higgins, Alexander & Alexander, and the Pinehurst Group.

The Bermuda-based captive movement has produced ceded reinsurance premiums in the range of $2 billion annually for the past five years with about $2.3 billion in 1985. About 60 percent of the business has remained with Bermuda-based professional reinsurers. Some twenty active reinsurers operated in Bermuda in early 1987; GTE Reinsurance Co., Ltd. was the largest reinsurer of captives and noncaptives writing some $194 million in 1986.

As of mid 1987, about fifteen other previous reinsurers of captives have stopped writing new business and are in the process of running off their portfolios, while two companies are in liquidation process. However, other captives, particularly such facilities as Hopewell, First Island, the Risk Exchange, and CIRCL, have been writing reinsurance

Exhibit 11-7
1977 American Risk Management Reinsurance Pool Capacity*

Capacity	Participants
$15,000,000 Primary	Basic Treaty (See Exhibit 11-8)
$20,000,000 Excess of $15,000,000	Sixty-Seven Reinsurance Companies
$25,000,000 Excess of $35,000,000	Seventy-Eight Reinsurance Companies
Unlimited Excess of $60,000,000	Basic Treaty

* Reprinted with permission from a letter from Arthur H. Deters, CPCU, Executive Vice President and Director, American Risk Management Group, Englewood Cliffs, New Jersey, 6 January 1977.

for their captives. In addition, several rent-a-captive entities and pools have been writing reinsurance for captive companies.[85]

Management of Captives

A captive company can be self-managed or administered under contract by an outside management firm. Some single-owner captives are administered through or at least are "influenced" by the parent corporation's insurance department. The corporate risk manager may be appointed as an officer of the captive. In this capacity the risk manager may be looked upon by the parents as being responsible to provide input for the major decisions of the company. The various traditional insurance company functions are performed for the captive by the employees of the parent corporation's insurance department. A notable exception is loss prevention and safety engineering services that are often obtained on a fee basis from consulting firms. This internal management approach is particularly common among single-owner captives domiciled in the United States. Several major corporations, however, manage their foreign captives themselves. These include, among others, Exxon Corporation, Ford Motor Company, Gulf Oil, Johnson and Johnson, Merck and Company, Continental Oil, and DuPont. Some thirty-eight self-managed captives were operating in 1985 in Bermuda alone.

Self-management is also employed by some group captives, particularly those formed by large trade associations to solve industry-wide insurance problems. For example, Mutual Insurance Company, Ltd., and Potomac Insurance Company, Ltd., both owned by the American Newspaper Publishers Association; United Insurance Compa-

Exhibit 11-8
Reinsurance Flow Chart for the American Risk Management Basic Treaty, 1977*

Captives Domiciled in the U.S.,
the Cayman Islands, Bermuda
or the Isle of Jersey†

↑

Reinsurance Covering
Up to 99%
of the Captive's Exposure

Hopewell International Ltd.
Hamilton, Bermuda

"Bermuda Pools"

| 26 ARM Managed Captives including Hopewell International Ltd.—21% | Lloyds Syndicates— 7% | 12 British Companies other than Lloyds—12% | Captive Company Retrocessions to 86 Reinsurers—60% |

† The percentages indicate the percentage participation of the various basic treaty participants.

* Reprinted with permission from a letter from Arthur H. Deters, CPCU, Executive Vice President and Director, American Risk Management Group, Englewood Cliffs, New Jersey, January 6, 1977. As noted in the text, some of this information may now be obsolete.

ny, Ltd., owned by Printing Industries of America; and IARW Insurance Company, Ltd., owned by the International Association of Refrigerated Warehouses were operated under their own management.

The popularity of external management stems principally from the fact that the business operations of most captives can be conducted more economically by using the services of a management company. In addition, however, some captive management companies have argued, apparently with some success, that the use of a management company enables a corporation to demonstrate more easily to the Internal Revenue Service that it is dealing at arm's length with its captive. Use of the management company is said to help the parent establish the legitimacy of the parent's operations outside the United States.

Captive management services are provided by a considerable number of international insurance brokers and independent captive management companies. As of the end of 1986, about 160 management firms were located in Bermuda and other domiciles worldwide.[86]

In 1985 only about 6 percent of the active captives in Bermuda were self-managed, while the majority of 94 percent were managed by some 160 registered professional management companies representing about 47 separate management groups. The management business was dominated by companies originating in the U.S. (70 percent), followed by United Kingdom companies (21 percent) and Bermudian organizations (4 percent). Three management firms owned by two large U.S. brokers and a risk management organization controlled more than 20 percent of the market in terms of both the number of captives managed and net premium volume. To a great extent they have led the market in size as well as in insurance and reinsurance arrangements and the variety of services provided to captives. In the highly competitive field of captive company management, International Risk Management, Ltd., a subsidiary of American Risk Management, Inc., Johnson & Higgins, Marsh & McLennan, Alexander & Alexander, Fred S. James & Company, and Frank B. Hall & Company are among the leaders.[87]

Management companies in general maintain close and often complex relations with captives. They are deeply involved in captives' decision-making processes and often are represented on captives' boards of directors. Such mutual dependency sometimes results in areas of friction and dissatisfaction. Nevertheless, the overall satisfaction level of owners of captives from their management companies is quite good. Despite the competitive atmosphere there has been relatively little turnover or switching of captives among management companies.[88]

Most management companies have grown from providing only the basic services of registration, administration, issuing policies, cover notes, or maintaining books and records to providing underwriting services for related and unrelated business. They arrange fronting and reinsurance for captives and often supply loss control and claims handling services. Some management companies have expanded to provide actuarial and information system analysis. Others have expanded into legal services, investment advisory, tax planning, and, recently, strategic planning, social arrangements, and if needed, winding up of captive services.

Captive managers are compensated for their services through the payment of fees. Few management firms charge fixed fees for their services. Instead, fees generally vary according to the amount of work performed by the manager and the expenses involved in performing this work. Some captive management firms charge a flat monthly or annual fee plus out-of-pocket expenses.

The "Insurance Factor" in the Captive Movement

It has been apparent for some time that the insurance industry is involved in the offshore captive movement. However, the magnitude and diversity of this involvement have hardly been analyzed, nor has the rationale for this involvement been evaluated. Although it would appear that such involvement would be against the insurance industry's interest, initial negative attitudes toward captives by the insurance industry have changed over the past two decades. Furthermore, the insurance industry, primarily brokers, might have been the catalyst in the growth of the captive movement.[89] In fact, insurers, reinsurers, brokers, and agents are clearly involved with captives. They are the direct owners of offshore subsidiaries that write reinsurance for captives, provide fronting facilities, coinsurance, and/or other insurance-related services. Insurers and primarily agents are also involved in the joint ownership of captives with noninsurance owners. The noninsurance owners usually own the majority interest, but the insurance-related owners provide the sponsorship and/or management. Insurers and primarily brokers also provide management services to captives.

Terminology can become a problem when trying to examine the extent of this involvement. Most observers do not consider a "captive" owned by insurance-related interests to be a true captive and do not include these in a listing of captive companies. A rough estimate of the number of such insurance related firms out of the 2,100 "captives" worldwide is 10 to 15 percent. In Bermuda, this estimate may be as high as 15 to 20 percent because of the relative direct involvement of many insurers there. Involvement of insurers in Bermuda and other domiciles is more usually indirect, executed through holding and trust companies, management companies, and related financial services companies.

Therefore, it is often quite difficult to ascertain if the actual owner of the "captive" is insurance-related.

In 1985 there were 1,180 insurance organizations in Bermuda, of which 313, or in excess of 26 percent, were organizations owned directly by insurance-related interests. The breakdown of ownership of these 313 organizations was: insurers (53 percent), agents and brokers (30 percent), financial services companies (9 percent), and management companies (8 percent). Not included in this figure are those organizations that were owned jointly by insurances and noninsurance-related organizations where the nonrelated company had more than 75 percent of the stock.

This percentage of organizations with insurance-related ownership does not fully reflect the real situation because many of the 1,180 organizations were inactive. Of the 1,180 organizations, there were only 697 that had any written net premium and only 798 that maintained investable assets. Of the 697, there were 119, or about 17 percent, that had insurance-related ownership. Of the 798, there were 153, or about 19 percent, that had insurance related ownership.[90]

Although organizations with insurance related interests accounted for only about 17 percent of the organizations that had any net written premium, these same organizations accounted for close to 40 percent of the $6.7 billion of net premiums written in 1985 in Bermuda. In terms of those organizations with investable assets, the 19 percent with insurance-related ownership controlled some 30 percent of the total $24.2 billion in assets in 1985.

Insurance-related organizations were also deeply involved in the management of captive insurers. Of the 47 management groups that controlled approximately 160 separate management firms, 25 percent were owned by insurers/reinsurers and 60 percent were owned by brokers/agents.

Comparing these organizations that have insurance-related ownership with typical captives, it is apparent that the former were significantly larger and wrote a broader scope of business. The average captive in 1985 wrote some $7 million in net premium compared to $22.5 million for the noncaptive (that is, the insurance related organization). The mean asset value for a captive was $26.3 million compared to $46.9 million of assets value for an insurance related organization. In addition, they also tended to have larger net premiums to net worth ratios than typical captives, 1.55 for an average captive compared to an average of 2.43 for a noncaptive. This larger ratio is typical of most insurance companies.

It is evident that the captive movement owes much of its growth to the influence of the insurance industry and especially brokers. The insurance industry continues to be involved with the captive movement through direct ownership of insurance organizations at captive domiciles, through joint ventures with captives and their parents, and most of all through the management and provision of a variety of insurance-related services to captives.

IV. REASONS FOR ESTABLISHING A CAPTIVE: FINANCIAL BENEFITS

Captives are established for a variety of reasons. They can provide a number of financial benefits for their owners. In addition, they can be used to solve many different corporate problems. Some captives have been formed because they provide their owners with a particular financial benefit or a solution to a specific corporate problem. In other cases, formation of a captive was in response to implicit social-psychological motives of the personalities involved (usually the risk manager). In most cases, however, a captive is established because its owner(s) expect(s) that a number of financial and nonfinancial benefits will result from its use in the risk management process.

Financial benefits usually provide the principal inducement to form a captive. These benefits can be quite substantial. For example, the observation has been made that "a captive can trim its parent's foreign insurance bills by as much as 30%"[91] One risk manager of a large U.S. drug company was quoted as saying that his firm saved about 25 percent of the premiums previously paid by using a captive.[92] Similarly, at the time of its formation in 1974, Levi Strauss and Company officials expected a premium saving of 10 to 20 percent from the use of the newly formed Bermuda captive, Zenith International Insurance, Ltd.[93] The savings are usually not as pronounced in years of a soft domestic market.

The financial benefits associated with a captive result from lower costs of financing losses, improved cash flow, and various possible tax benefits. The first two sources of financial benefits are examined in this section. The various tax benefits that may be derived from the use of a captive are discussed in the next section. The nonfinancial reasons are subsequently presented.

Lower Costs of Financing Losses

Use of a captive can reduce the cost of financing losses in several ways.

Lower Expenses As mentioned, to the extent that the coverage provided by a single-owner pure captive is not reinsured, the captive is a retention device. As such, it offers essentially the same opportunities to save on insurance-related expenses as do other forms of retention.

The most common argument is that a captive permits its parent to save the acquisition expense loaded into premiums by insurers to cover the commissions that must be paid to agents and brokers. While this contention is substantially correct, the use of a captive does not always permit the parent to save the entire amount of the acquisition expense loading. For example, in addition to placing coverage with a direct insurer, the agent or broker may also render other services such as conducting risk surveys and providing advice with regard to loss prevention. To the extent that these services have to be taken over by the captive or an outside management company, the entire amount of the agent's or broker's commission is not "saved" by the parent. In addition, local regulations in some foreign countries require that a captive's fronting company deal with the insured (that is, the parent company or one of its subsidiaries) through an intermediary. While this requirement involves the payment of a broker's commission, the fronting company can usually arrange for a reduction in the commission rate, thereby providing some acquisition expense savings.

The use of a captive may also enable the parent to save some of the administrative expenses that are loaded into direct insurance premiums. These savings may result for a number of reasons. First, by using a captive, a business firm can avoid paying for insurance company expenses that do not benefit it directly such as an insurer's advertising outlays. Second, a captive may provide savings in cases where insurance-related services are being duplicated by a business firm and its commercial insurer. Barile provides the following example:

> Typically, the large corporate insured possesses an adequate safety and engineering department which often performs inspection services for the benefit of the corporation's insurance department. It is conceivable that these services are actually duplicating those performed by the insurance company, who charges for such engineering services in the cost of its product.[94]

By using a captive, a corporation with a competent engineering staff can perform its own inspections and avoid paying a commercial insurer for services that may be unnecessary and duplicative.

Finally, a captive may provide administrative expense savings for its parent if it can either perform certain services more economically than a commercial insurance company or obtain services on a fee basis for less than a commercial insurer would charge. For example, Barile indicates that a captive may reduce administrative expenses by eliminating unnecessary overhead generated in adjusting losses:

As far as cutting down on loss adjustment expenses, we must realize that insurance companies maintain large claim staffs, including attorneys, which contribute to the substantial operating costs of the companies. These overhead costs must also be injected into the price of the product. It is conceivable that the captive insurance company can adequately handle routine losses and the more complex cases can be contracted out, on a fee basis, to reputable loss adjustment firms.[95]

Similarly, Brunswick Corporation's assistant risk manager indicated that, while insurers generally charge about 11 percent of losses for loss adjustment services, Brunswick's newly formed captive was paying the General Adjustment Bureau only 9 percent of losses for these services.[96]

Group captives also appear to be providing their participants with expense savings. For example, AEGIS was reported in 1978 to be using about 8 percent of its premium income to cover expenses as compared with acquisition and administration expense rates of 30 to 40 percent said to be common in the commercial markets.[97] Similarly, in 1975 Oil Insurance, Ltd., was said to be devoting less than 4 percent of premiums to fixed operating expense.[98] Many captives maintain expenses at 10 to 15 percent of their premiums. But it should be noted that additional costs such as brokerage fees and excise taxes are not always included as expenses.[99]

Lower Loss Costs In many cases captives have been formed because their owners believed that their expected losses were less than those assumed by insurers in calculating their premium rates. They felt that, by establishing a captive to write their coverages, they could save the difference between the two expected loss estimates.

Traditionally, this rationale has been applied primarily to property coverages in which even large corporate insureds are charged premium rates based on average, rather than individual, loss experience. The failure of commercial liability insurers to reflect the better-than-average claims experience of some hospitals in their professional liability insurance rating schemes in the past has led several hospital groups to form captives to write malpractice coverages at rates they feel are more in line with their own claims experience.

Better Credits for Retention In some foreign countries credits for deductibles are not available under local tariffs. In many others deductible credits are difficult to obtain and, when allowed, are usually unrealistically low. As might be expected, these conditions are particularly prevalent in countries that either prohibit nonadmitted insurance or make it difficult to arrange. A study by John B. Laadt in 1975 provides the following examples of problems encountered by U.S.

corporations in attempting to obtain deductibles and deductible credits in various parts of the world:

Venezuela, Colombia, and Brazil:

> No deductible credits are available under local tariffs. There is however, the possibility of special filings for which approval is hard to get.

Belgium, The Netherlands, Germany, France, Italy, and Spain:

> Deductible credits generally do not exist under local tariffs. Where they are allowed they are decided on a case-by-case basis by the tariff committee or subcommittee, and the credits are almost always ludicrously low. Perhaps a typical credit of $500,000 deductible on a large sum insured (more than $5,000,000) would be 7 to 10 percent.

Japan:

> There is no deductible credit available under the Japanese Fire Insurance Tariff.[100]

Laadt indicates that by establishing a captive to handle its foreign loss exposures, a corporation "can bypass restrictive tariff regulations in many countries and implement deductibles with intelligent credits where they would otherwise be unavailable."[101] The way in which a captive is used to establish a deductible and produce a meaningful deductible credit in such countries is best explained through the use of an example.

Reference is made to the example cited where a U.S. corporation owns a $10 million plant located in a foreign country that prohibits nonadmitted insurance. Suppose that local tariff rules do not provide for deductibles. The corporation's captive as noted earlier, could enter into a fronting arrangement with a locally admitted insurance company. The U.S. corporation is presumed to purchase $10 million of direct insurance coverage from the locally admitted company with the understanding that the fronting company would cede 95 percent of the coverage to the corporation's captive on a quota share basis. Under the quota share reinsurance arrangement, the locally admitted insurer would retain $500,000 of the coverage and cede $9.5 million to the captive. As a variation from the example cited earlier, suppose that the captive would, in turn, keep a first loss retention of $250,000 and retrocede the remaining $9.25 million to commercial reinsurers on an excess of loss basis. In this case a deductible has been implemented by the captive's assuming 95 percent of each loss that occurs up to a retention of $250,000. The credit for this deductible is reflected in the difference between the captive's net income from reinsurance assumed and its net expense for reinsurance ceded.

This phenomenon is illustrated in Exhibit 11-9. As shown, the

Exhibit 11-9
Source of Deductible Credit*

Captive's Transactions with Fronting Company:	
Reinsurance Assumed Premium Income	
(95% of $100,000 direct insurance premium)	$95,000
Less Fronting Fee (32.5% of $95,000)†	30,875
Net Income (Before Losses) from Reinsurance Assumed	$64,125
Captive's Transactions with Reinsurers:	
Reinsurance Ceded Expense	$44,000
Reinsurance Ceded Commission Income (25% of $44,000)	11,000
Net Expense for Reinsurance Ceded	$33,000
Captive's Net Reinsurance Income (Before Losses):	
Source of Deductible Credit ($64,125 − $33,000)	$31,125

† The relatively high fronting fee reflects the fact that the fronting company was required by local regulation to pay a broker's commission.

* Adapted from John B. Laadt, "Captive Insurance Companies as a Method of Insuring Foreign Risks" (Master's thesis, DePaul University, Chicago, Illinois, 1975), p. 37.

captive received net income of $64,125 for reinsurance assumed from the fronting company and incurred a net expense of $33,000 for reinsurance retroceded. The difference of $31,125 contains the deductible credit (that is, the compensation for the captive's retention). One should notice, however, that in addition to the deductible credit, this difference may also reflect credits given by the reinsurers for other factors such as good experience or superior protection. In this analysis no attention is given to the losses that might be payable by the captive under its exposure as a reinsurer.

Lower Cost of Reinsurance As a logical alternative to establishing a captive, a business firm might consider purchasing direct excess insurance with a deductible equal to the captive's retention. Some observers suggest, however, that the captive approach is preferable because reinsurance is often less costly than direct excess insurance. The supporters of this argument attribute the lower cost of reinsurance to the stability of the relationship between a captive and its reinsurer. They indicate that less continuity exists in the direct excess markets where corporate insureds often move from one insurer to another in search of the best terms currently available. Under these conditions, a direct insurer has difficulty in recouping losses from a given insured following a year of bad experience. As a result, direct excess insurance premiums must include a charge to cover the losses of insureds who terminate their coverage with a given company after a year of bad experience. Such a charge, however, need not be reflected in the basic cost of reinsurance, so advocates of the reinsurance approach argue, because reinsurance arrangements tend to be more stable and thereby provide reinsurers with a better opportunity to recover losses from individual insureds.

The net cost of reinsurance is a function of ceding commissions and profit-sharing (or contingent) commissions, all of which are open to negotiation. Use of these commissions is common practice in professional reinsurance, although some captives are transacting reinsurance net of all commissions. Ceding commissions, actually withheld by the captive at the time of payment of the reinsurance, range from about 5 percent to about 25 percent and represent risk-free income to the captive. This income, in turn, can have an important effect on some of the key ratios by which a captive is judged. Suppose, for instance, that a captive had been receiving direct annual premiums from the parent of $1,000,000 and that the parent had been buying excess insurance in the conventional market for $500,000 per year. If the parent pays $1,500,000 to the captive, which then purchases reinsurance for $500,000 and receives a $100,000 ceding commission, the corporate family has saved $100,000 (the amount of the reinsurance commission earned by the captive) and the captive has $100,000 of non-U.S. source income. The premium-to-capital ratio of the captive this year is no different from what it would have been had the parent purchased the $500,000 of excess insurance in the conventional market, but next year it has $100,000 additional surplus on which to write additional business. Captives have fewer expenses, and theoretically, do not deserve the same ceding commissions paid to conventional insurers that buy reinsurance. As long as the reinsurance mechanism includes the ceding commissions in normal computation, however, this advantage will remain.

Many insurance experts disagree with the notion that a captive is preferable to a program of retention and direct excess insurance because of the lower cost of reinsurance. For example, Edward P. Lalley has stated:

> It is difficult to rationalize what there is about a reinsurance arrangement that permits me to take the 600 National Dairy properties into the reinsurance market (through Ideal Mutual as the insurer), reinsure the risks above $100,000, and pay less reinsurance premium than I would pay if I took the self-same risk into virtually the same market on an insured program with $100,000 deductible....
> Under either arrangement the conventional insurance market pays

the same losses; consequently, if there is an advantage to the reinsured arrangement, it is an artificial advantage and will not continue for long.[102]

While cases undoubtedly arise in which reinsurance can be obtained at a lower price than direct excess insurance, the price differential will usually be relatively small and may exist only temporarily. Thus, financial benefits stemming from the lower cost of reinsurance should probably not be the only, or even the principal, reason for choosing a captive insurance program over a program of retention and direct excess insurance.

Better Terms for a Consolidated Program A captive may produce lower loss financing costs for a business firm by enabling the firm to consolidate the coverages of its subsidiaries into a single large program. The rates that a large corporation can negotiate for a single consolidated insurance program may be lower than those that could be obtained by its subsidiaries for their individual programs. For example, John B. Laadt indicates that multinational corporations often obtain volume discounts for their insurance coverages by consolidating the insurance programs of their foreign subsidiaries through the use of captives.[103] In such cases, the volume discounts are allowed in the form of reduced fees charged by the captive's fronting company and reduced premiums charged by the captive's reinsurers. The volume discounts in addition to the ceding commission, contingent profit commission, and credit for the deductible can result in considerable savings estimated in the range of 20 to 50 percent over the precaptive, nonconsolidated program.[104]

Bargaining Wedge Once a captive has been established, savings in loss financing costs can often be realized by using the captive as a bargaining wedge in negotiating with other insurance companies. For example, a firm that uses its captive to write only some of its coverages may threaten to shift other coverages from the commercial market to its captive unless commercial insurers are willing to offer the conventional coverages at more reasonable rates. In one case reported by a foreign subsidiary of a U.S. company in South Africa, merely approaching the local insurer about a captive program achieved a discount of 40 percent in the existing coverage. Thus, a decision was made not to change the coverage at all, at least for the time being.[105]

In several instances the formation of a group captive by some of the firms in an industry has led commercial insurers to make coverage available on more reasonable terms to other firms in the same industry. For example, in 1972 a group of utilities wanting lower premiums for property insurance on their nuclear power plants dropped their policies with the Nuclear Energy Liability-Property Insurance Association

(NEL-PIA) (the name of which was subsequently changed to American Nuclear Insurers), one of the insurance pools serving the nuclear energy industry, and set up a captive, Nuclear Mutual, Ltd. Concerned that other insureds might drop their policies and join the captive, NEL-PIA instituted a credit rating plan later the same year. In 1976 NEL-PIA's insureds enjoyed a 29.5 percent reduction in their property insurance rates as a result of the credit rating plan established in response to competitive pressures from the industry captive.[106] Similarly, the existence of Oil Insurance, Ltd., and AEGIS perhaps has enabled nonmember petroleum and gas companies to obtain insurance coverages from commercial insurers at lower rates than might have otherwise been available.

Increased Investment Yield

Another argument advanced for use of a captive is that the captive may be able to earn a higher yield on the loss reserves than would its parent in holding the funds or in allowing a conventional insurer to hold them. One possible source of the incremental yield is said to be the flexibility of the captive in investing the money in international instruments that usually provide higher rates than the equivalent securities that the parent or its domestic insurer would be likely to hold. With the captive holding assets for months or years pending the settlement of workers compensation and liability claims against the parent, the compounding of the incremental investment income could become important. Observers who are skeptical of this argument insist that seldom is a captive able to earn a higher yield on the assets in question that the yield that the parent could earn by using the assets in the parent's regular productive process. The implication is that if the parent cannot do better than the captive with regard to the money, the parent is in the wrong business. In an analysis conducted on a sample of ninety Bermuda captives with regard to their investment income performance for the financial year ending in 1980, their rates of return, when measured according to standard measurements of rate of return, were not in excess of normal returns achieved elsewhere by regular insurers in similar periods.[107] Furthermore, it appeared that captives tended to make rather conservative, short-term investments (often in U.S. currency) having high liquidity and security as compared to the general investment practices of the property-liability industry.[108]

Improved Cash Flow

In addition to the tax deferral benefits discussed in the next section, the use of a captive may improve a business firm's cash flow in several ways. As is the case whenever retention is used as the method for handling loss exposures, a single-owner captive enables a firm to retain for its own use the funds that would normally be paid out as insurance premiums until such time as those funds are actually needed to pay losses and expenses. Goshay indicates that this financial benefit is often explained in terms of "control of loss reserves, contingency reserves, underwriting profits and so forth."[109] Regardless of how the situation is viewed, opportunity income is realized with respect to the portion of the coverage that is retained by the captive.

The use of a captive may also provide a firm with a cash flow advantage as compared with a program of retention and direct excess insurance because it may enable the firm to deal with reinsurers. The advantage stems from differences in the timing of premium payments. Premiums for direct excess insurance usually must be paid annually in advance. However, a captive pays premiums to its reinsurers at the end of a predetermined period. Commonly, reinsurance premiums are paid either monthly or quarterly in arrears. Thus, a captive may enable a firm to retain the use of its funds for a longer period of time than would be possible with the purchase of direct excess insurance.

A firm that uses an unfunded retention program to handle its loss exposures may experience serious cash flow problems if its losses fluctuate widely from year to year. The firm might have to borrow money, sell property on unfavorable terms, or forgo planned investments in order to generate the cash to pay losses as they occur. As a funded retention program, use of a captive enables a firm to spread the impact of its retained losses over time and thus avoid the cash flow problems that might be encountered with a program of unfunded retention, assuming the level of funding is adequate.

Finally, by insuring or reinsuring the loss exposures of the general public, a broad captive may generate underwriting and investment profits that improve its parent company's cash flow.

V. TAX CONSIDERATIONS

Taxation of captive insurers is a complex topic with several interrelated dimensions. There are issues pertaining to income taxation and those relating to excise taxes. Income tax aspects can be further classified into issues that relate to tax deductibility of premiums paid by the insured, direct taxation of the captive, and indirect taxation of captive's shareholders. In tax deductibility of premiums, the key issue is whether there has been an act of insurance between the captive and its parent. Direct income taxation of captives varies according to whether the captive is domestic or foreign. With regard to foreign captives, the key issue is whether the captive, by its conduct of business, is considered as one engaged in "U.S. trade or business." Also the element of taxation in the foreign domicile is important. Last but not least is the indirect income taxation to the shareholders or insureds of the captive. The key issue here is the status of the captive as a "controlled foreign corporation."

This section briefly covers tax treatment of payments by parents to their captive for "insurance" coverages. Tax factors at one time were probably a primary reason for forming a captive. Deductibility of premiums by the parent plus the possibility of underwriting and investment profits by the captive that could be also tax deferred seemed a double advantage. In the United States, however, the IRS has never been content to let deductibility of premiums by the parent pass without challenge. The IRS frequently audits captives—several years at a time for each—and disallows the deductions. Battle lines between captive owners and the IRS have been drawn. At the time of this writing (mid-1987) it appears that combined efforts of the IRS and the U.S. Congress have virtually removed any tax advantages captive insurers have enjoyed. Significant additions to case law since the early 1970s, some IRS class and individual rulings, and the Tax Reform Acts of 1984 and 1986 have finally made the tax situation regarding captive insurers more clear. However, taking tax deductions on premiums paid by parent to group pure captives and broad captives is still in a state of flux. What follows is a review of the developments and basic considerations in the area of captives and taxation.

Tax Deductibility of Premiums

When a business firm uses a funded retention program other than a captive to handle its loss exposures, contributions to the retention fund cannot be deducted in calculating the firm's federal taxable income. Instead, only losses and expenses actually *paid* are tax deductible.[110]

By contrast, premiums paid to a captive by its parent may be deductible by the parent as a business expense.[111] Thus by formalizing its retention program through the use of captive, a firm may be able in special cases to take a current tax deduction for its contribution to the retention fund. The tax treatment of the captive, however, must also be considered in order to determine the extent of the tax benefits, if any, that actually accrue to a captive's parent company.

The present status of the tax deductibility premiums to captives' owners depends, broadly speaking, on the question of whether there has been an act of insurance, both "risk-shifting and risk-distribution," from the parent to the captive. In general the IRS will deny tax deductibility to single-owned pure captives but will be inclined to allow such deductibility to group-owned pure captives and possibly to broad captives. What is open to debate and speculation are the definitions or specifications of group or broad captives under which the IRS will allow tax deductibility of the premium. Specifically it refers to the minimum number of owners, their shares in ownership, and in the risks insured. Also the debate continues as to the minimum proportion (if any) and the type of risks that will constitute unrelated business in the captive's portfolio that will turn the captive into a separate insurance entity for the tax deductibility of the parent's premiums.[112]

Taxation of Domestic Captives

A captive domiciled in the United States is taxed in the same manner as any U.S. insurance company. Therefore, the premium that is deductible as an ordinary and necessary business expense in the parent company's tax return is treated as income in computing the captive's federal income tax liability.[113] Nevertheless, the use of a captive can still provide a business firm with a tax benefit that is not available with other funded retention programs. While firms using other types of funded retention programs must generally wait until losses actually occur or are paid in order to take their tax deductions, a captive is permitted to deduct additions to reserves for unpaid losses in computing its federal income taxes. Thus, if a considerable lag ensues between the time a loss occurs and the time the claim is paid by the captive to the parent, the captive's ability to take a tax deduction for the unpaid loss will leave it—until the time the claim is paid—with additional funds available for investment.

When a domestic captive is used to write property insurance, the resulting tax benefit will generally be quite limited because, in most cases, relatively little time elapses from the time a property loss occurs until the time the claim is paid. More substantial tax advantages will result, however, when a domestic captive is used to write workers compensation and liability coverages, due to the longer lag between the time such losses occur and the time such losses are paid. For example, Lalley states:

> ... There is a considerable tax advantage arising to a casualty insurer in the initiation of an $80,000 workman's compensation reserve on a 40-year-old claimant who will, actuarially speaking, be paid $62 a week for 30 years. Under a self-insurance program (unless the amount is unequivocably payable, which is seldom the case since claimants may suffer premature death or achieve complete recovery) the $62 a week is deductible only when it has been paid.[114]

However, this argument, which is based on the "time value of money," holds less weight as a result of the revisions of the 1986 Tax Reform Act. Among other changes, the act requires all insurance companies, including captives, to discount loss reserves and reduce unearned premium reserves for calculating taxable income.

Taxation of Foreign Captives

Prior to the enactment of the Revenue Act of 1962, a foreign captive (that is, one domiciled outside the U.S.), that handled a U.S. firm's domestic and foreign loss exposures could accumulate both its underwriting and investment earnings without incurring any U.S. income tax liability. The Revenue Act of 1962 restricted the tax advantages of foreign captives considerably by adding Subpart F of Subchapter N to the Internal Revenue Code. Subpart F makes certain sources of undistributed income of a "controlled foreign corporation" (CFC) taxable to its U.S. owner(s) each year. Conceptually, Subpart F creates an "imputed dividend" and defines how it will be measured. Of course, dividends actually paid by a foreign captive to its U.S. owner(s) have always been and continue to be taxable income to the U.S. shareholder(s).

In addition to the federal income tax indirectly imposed by Subpart F, foreign captives are also affected by the federal excise and withholding taxes. A federal excise tax must be paid whenever a premium for insurance applicable to loss exposures located in the United States is paid abroad. The organization paying the premium is responsible for remitting the federal excise tax. The excise tax is 4 percent of premiums for direct property and liability insurance, 1 percent of premiums for "life, health, and accident" insurance, and 1 percent on all reinsurance premiums.[115] U.S. withholding taxes were applied (at the rate of 30 percent) to all dividends and interest payments made abroad including payments made in Bermuda, the Cayman Islands, or the Bahamas. No withholding was applied to interest on bank deposits on certificates of deposit in the United States. However, the Tax Reform Act of 1984 repealed the 30 percent U.S. withholding tax on interest paid by U.S. borrowers to nonresident aliens and foreign corporations, subject to certain adjustments.[116]

A foreign corporation is considered "controlled" and thus subject to the provisions of Subpart F of the Internal Revenue Code when more than 50 percent of the voting power of its stock is owned by U.S. shareholders (counting only those shareholders whose ownership interest is 10 percent or more).[117] There is a special rule applying if 75 percent or more of the gross premiums are derived from insuring U.S. risks. In this case the 50 percent figure was reduced to 25 percent. Since many foreign captives fall within the scope of this definition, they are usually treated as CFCs for federal tax purposes.

Subpart F specifies the types of income of a CFC and the conditions under which that income will produce taxable income for the captive's U.S. owner(s). When a CFC does have taxable Subpart F income, that income is taxable to the captive's U.S. owner(s) in the year it is earned, as if it were a dividend, whether or not it is actually received. Furthermore, the normal dividend exclusion for corporations (85 percent) does not apply to Subpart F dividends, real or imputed. The principal types of income governed by the provisions of Subpart F (Section 952) of the Internal Revenue Code are the underwriting income derived from insuring or reinsuring "U.S. risks" (as determined under Section 953) and certain investment income (as determined under Section 954).

Prior to the revisions of the 1984 Tax Reform Act, Subpart F of Subchapter N of the Internal Revenue Code, which defines the types of undistributed income that will be taxable to the captive's U.S. owner(s) each year ran briefly as follows. First, the Subpart F income tax applied only to "controlled foreign corporations." Second, only that portion of the controlled foreign captive's underwriting earnings attributable to U.S. risks was recognized in determining Subpart F income, and then only if the captive's premium income derived from U.S. risks exceeded 5 percent of its total premium income. Third, only a portion of the investment income of the CFC was considered as Subpart F income. While an oversimplification, it generally could be stated that a CFC's investment income and the value of its investments in U.S. property were excluded from Subpart F income to the extent that the invested assets were equivalent to the unearned premium reserves and other reserves that were ordinary and necessary for the captive's business.

However, when the Tax Reform Act was enacted in 1984, it required companies to include as Subpart F income underwriting and investment income attributable to insurance or reinsurance of U.S. risks as well as underwriting and investment income on foreign related risks.[118] Thus, the revision was a major defeat to single-owned captives who were controlled foreign corporations and, as such, all underwriting and investment income attributable to insurance or reinsurance of foreign risks was not considered Subpart F income. Federal income taxation on this income was generally deferred until a distribution was made to the U.S. shareholder. Nevertheless, underwriting income from insurance or reinsurance of nonrelated, non-U.S. risks and investment income attributable to reasonable reserves of such risks escaped taxation under Subpart F.[119]

Because of the nature of group captive ownership and by dispersing the ownership of the captive among shareholders owning less than 10 percent of the stock, managing the level of written premiums related to U.S. risks in relation to total written premium and avoiding the more than 50 percent (or 25 percent) voting stock ownership test, most group captives have avoided being considered CFCs and therefore were not impacted by the 1984 revisions regarding shareholder's current income taxation derived from insurance or reinsurance of related, non-U.S. risks. As could have been anticipated, this situation boosted the formation of group captives of all sorts (associations, exchanges, pools, rent-a-captives, joint ventures, and agent-owned) in order to benefit from practically the last tax advantage of offshore captives.

As soon as the 1984 act was passed, proposals began to appear to close this last loophole which existed for group captives. As a result, the Tax Reform Act of 1986 introduced major changes affecting captives, particularly group captives. The key changes expanded Subpart F to include all kinds of captive income earned by all types of owners. The new law expands the definition of a CFC for the purpose of determining insurance income to include any corporation in which U.S. shareholders own 25 percent or more of the voting power or value of the stock of the company. The net effect is that any U.S. shareholder owning an interest in an offshore captive, directly or through subsidiaries, regardless of how small that interest is, generally will be taxed on its proportionate part of the captive's income if 25 percent or more of the captive is owned by U.S. shareholders.[120] (This is in contrast to the earlier provision of Subpart F that applied only to shareholders with an interest of 10 percent or more.) The definition of the CFC as it relates to unrelated parties or noninsurance income has hardly been changed. It is to "related person insurance income" that the new 25 percent rule applies. Related person insurance income (RPII) is any income earned from insuring or reinsuring a risk where the primary insured or a party related to primary insured is a shareholder of the foreign insurer. Thus RPII is all underwriting and investment income derived from insuring property and liability risks of the captive's shareholders and related parties.[121] The new law does not apply if less than 20 percent of the captive's stock in vote and value is owned by the insureds or related persons; or if less than 20 percent of its business comes from insuring primary insureds who own, directly indirectly, shares of the captive; or if the foreign captive exercises its option to be taxed as a foreign corporation engaged in a trade or business in the U.S. In the last case, the company will be subject to U.S. income tax, but the shareholder will not be subject to the Subpart F income tax provision. In effect, the new provisions make owners of any share in an offshore captive include in their income their pro-rata share of the offshore captive's RPII in the year it was earned.

The Tax Reform Act of 1986 affects most owners, regardless of the size of the share, in offshore captives. Group captives have felt the impact most, but single-owned captives are also affected. All income of a single-owned captive is Subpart F income, so deferrals for income generated from unrelated, non-U.S. risks are eliminated.

Elimination of Other Tax Advantages

In addition to the elimination of income tax benefits discussed in the preceding section, a few other incidental tax advantages of foreign captives have been eliminated.

Recapture of Foreign Tax Credits   In general, income taxes (or other taxes in lieu of income taxes) paid to a foreign government may be credited against U.S. income taxes. This credit, however, was limited to the lesser of the amount of the foreign income taxes actually paid or the amount of U.S. income taxes that would be payable on that same amount of (foreign) income. Because several foreign countries had higher income tax rates than those in the United States, foreign tax payments for this purpose were deemed to be in excess of the amount of foreign taxes that can be credited toward U.S. income taxes. The foreign income and the associated foreign income tax was determined on an overall basis rather than on a country-by-country basis.[122] Thus, a captive located in a country that did not have an income tax, such as Bermuda, could produce foreign income without incurring any additional foreign income tax. This additional source of foreign income had the beneficial effect of permitting the U.S. parent corporation to use more or even all of its foreign tax credits.

By characterizing foreign-generated income as Subpart F income, the Tax Reform Act of 1984, in effect, reclassified and reduced the amount of income against which a corporation's foreign tax credit could be applied.

Offsetting Subpart F Income from Other Sources   Before the 1986 tax law was passed, even if a CFC had Subpart F income, the amount reportable by its U.S. shareholders could have been reduced by application of its own accumulated deficit in earnings and profits or by a deficit of another CFC that was a member of a "chain" of corporations. The Tax Reform Act of 1986 does not allow deficits from insurance operations to be used to offset Subpart F income from other sources.

Avoidance of Forced Distribution to Stockholders   Before the tax revisions made in 1984 and 1986, the rules and procedures for determining Subpart F income permitted some revenue to be sheltered from taxation (necessary insurance reserves and other sources of income are good examples). The net result of this situation was that the foreign captive could retain and invest these funds, and the funds so accumulated could be paid as dividends to the U.S. shareholders at the most advantageous time. This flexibility and control over the timing of dividends to be paid could have had a beneficial effect on the level and stability of the U.S. parent corporation's earnings and its payment of taxes. The Tax Reform Acts of 1984 and 1986 eliminated the potential advantage.

Reduction of Taxes of Foreign Subsidiaries Acting through its investment operations, a foreign captive could help to reduce the tax burden of affiliated foreign companies. Whenever foreign subsidiaries of the captive's U.S. owners were located in countries with high income tax rates, the captive could use its investment flexibility to reduce foreign tax payments in either of two ways. First, the captive could lend working capital to the other foreign company. The loan provided the captive with interest income and the other company with a tax deductible interest expense. Second, the captive could purchase equipment or build facilities needed by the affiliated foreign company for its operations and lease the equipment or plant facility to the affiliate. Either method provided the affiliate with a tax deductible expense, thus lowering its income tax payments to a foreign government, while producing income for the captive. This income to the captive was not subject to a foreign income tax and could have been sheltered from U.S. income tax by virtue of being excluded from Subpart F income. After 1986, any sheltering of that kind was eliminated. However, the captive can still offer operational and financial help to the parent in dealing with its foreign subsidiaries.

Increase in Taxable Income The Tax Reform Act of 1986 introduced several new provisions that affected all insurers, including captives, by way of increasing their taxable income. Loss reserves must be discounted at a predetermined average federal discount rate. Long-tail lines such as products liability and workers compensation are given an eleven-year discounting period and short-tail lines (fire, for example) have a four-year discount period. The company has the option to continue to use its historical payout patterns.[123]

All property and casualty insurers have to include 20 percent of their increase in unearned premium reserve in their reported income.[124] This will increase the taxable income since only 80 percent of an annual increase in the unearned premium reserve will be deductible. The deduction for losses incurred by property-casualty companies is reduced by 15 percent of the sum of the company's tax exempt interest received or accrued—a fact that will add to the taxable income reported by general insurers and captives alike.[125]

The Tax Reform Act of 1986 left little ambiguity about captives' tax advantages. They have all but completely disappeared. In a sense, the revisions have had a positive effect. Captives will be formed and maintained with a clear knowledge that they have to be a more efficient and effective mechanism of risk management financing and control than other techniques; otherwise, their existence will not be justified over the long run. Clearly, most captives will now have to pay income tax. It is hopeful that promoters of captives will stop promoting the so-called tax benefits, and critics as well as policymakers will take a second look at the nontax advantages of captive insurers.

Some tax issues were left open. The ability to elect to be taxed as a foreign corporation engaged in a trade and business in the U.S. and its full economic implications is not clear yet. The tax revisions do not apply to public companies. Therefore, the degree to which large group captives and pools will become public and/or move onshore is unclear. The new act can also be looked at as excluding the life and health lines of business. This may cause some adjustments and/or encourage more use of captives in life and health insurance. The new tax law maintains the old status quo for captives whose RPII is less than 20 percent. This hardly affects real captives, but it might encourage some promoters to push joint ventures or other quasi-captive organizations that conform to the 20 percent exceptions.

The full impact of the Tax Reform Act of 1986 on the captive movement remains to be seen. It may have negative effects, although these may not be as significant as some might have suggested. It is clear that the captive movement will be affected by the Risk Retention Act of 1986, the softening of the insurance market, as well as the tax revisions, which may turn out to be the least significant of the three factors.

IRS Attacks on Foreign Captives

The Internal Revenue Service has never seemed pleased about the perceived or actual tax advantages that were available to foreign captives. Over the years, the IRS has alleged that many such companies were a sham, having been formed for the purpose of avoiding federal taxes. The IRS can use several means to challenge captives—by direct taxation of foreign captives, by direct taxation of U.S. shareholders in foreign captives, and by denying the owners of captives tax deductions on premiums paid to offshore captives. The IRS can tax directly foreign insurers only if they conduct a trade or business in the U.S. In that case, the foreign corporation's income would be subject to current U.S. tax law. However, the IRS would have to prove that "trade or business" was conducted. With careful planning, most captives avoided this type of finding by conducting business activities offshore. Thus, the

IRS, by and large, has not challenged offshore captives along this line. Some observers do believe that this will change in the near future.

A better strategy was to directly tax U.S. shareholders of foreign captives. The simplest way to do this was to change the definitions of a controlled foreign corporation and income from a U.S. source. This was accomplished once in 1984 and more successfully in the Tax Reform Act of 1986.

A more complicated strategy but probably one that had good potential for collecting additional tax revenues was to challenge owners of captives on the tax deductibility of premiums paid to their offshore captives. This challenge has been expedited through formal class positions, individual rulings, and fierce fights in the courts. The following discussion summarizes the key steps in that process beginning with IRS's first positions vis-à-vis offshore captives; the position was unofficial in 1972 and became official in 1977.

Revenue Ruling 77-316 The official IRS position on foreign captives is presented in Revenue Ruling 77-316. It was issued on 29 August 1977.[126] This ruling essentially denies a U.S. parent company a deduction for any premiums it or its U.S. subsidiaries may pay, directly or indirectly, to a wholly owned foreign captive. The ruling is limited in scope to this single issue, the deductibility of premiums; it does not address any other tax aspects of captives. Prior to this ruling, the only written statement to reflect the attitude of the IRS toward such captives was contained in the IRS Manual Supplement 42G-256, Amendment 1 entitled, "Captive Offshore Insurance or Reinsurance Companies," issued on 10 January 1972. The same basic premise underlies both the 1972 manual supplement and the 1977 revenue ruling. That rationale is that premiums paid to a foreign captive constitute nothing more than a formalized corporate retention plan and, as such, they fail to meet the requirement for a true shifting to a third party of financial liability for any actual losses. Therefore, such payments cannot be deducted in the calculation of an organization's federal income tax liability. Because the basic IRS position has remained unchanged since the 1972 internal memorandum, it is useful to describe briefly that document before examining in more detail Revenue Ruling 77-316.

The 1972 IRS manual supplement listed the following audit rules and instructed IRS agents to use any one or more of them when auditing the tax returns of a corporation having transactions with a foreign captive.[127]

1. Disallow deductions for premiums paid to the captive under Internal Revenue Code Section 162 on the ground that they are merely retention expenses that are not deductible.

2. Disallow deductions for premiums paid to the captive under Section 269 on the ground that the principal purpose of acquiring the captive company is to obtain a deduction not otherwise available.
3. Treat premium payments from foreign subsidiaries to the captive as constructive upstream dividends to the parent under Section 316.[128]
4. Impute commissions to the domestic parent company for directing business to the captive under Section 482.
5. Disallow, under Section 482, deductions for premiums based on the claim that they were not negotiated at arm's length.
6. Disallow deductions for premiums paid to a captive by foreign affiliates for the purpose of determining effective foreign tax rates, minimum distributions, foreign tax credits and Subpart F income, under Sections 901, 902, and 963.
7. Treat the captive as a "sham" corporation and attribute its income to the parent under Section 61.
8. Treat the captive as engaged in business in the United States, under Section 882, and therefore, subject its income to regular U.S. corporate tax rates.
9. Treat the acquisition of the captive's stock as subject to Interest Equalization Tax.[129]

The IRS internal audit rules concerning foreign captives include some obvious inconsistencies. For example, the first two rules, which would disallow the deductions for premiums paid to a foreign captive by a U.S. organization, and the third rule, which would treat the premium payments made by foreign subsidiaries as imputed dividends to the U.S. parent corporation, are based on the contention that the captive is not a true insurance company operation. Conversely, the fourth and fifth audit rules, which are concerned with the amount of the premium paid and whether or not it was established at arm's length, implicitly assume that the captive is a true insurance company operation.

Equally important as the inconsistencies, however, are the unanswered questions raised by the IRS audit rules. For example, if premiums paid to a foreign captive are not allowable expense items, how should they be treated by the captive—as contributions to capital, gifts, or other receipts? Also, how should the payment of losses be treated both by the captive and its U.S. owner/policyholder—as a dividend or in some other manner? If premiums are disallowed as expense deductions, should the U.S. organization be allowed to deduct the property and liability losses it incurs? Finally, should the audit rules be applied to domestic as well as foreign captives? For example, it would appear to be highly inconsistent for the IRS to apply the first audit rule to premiums paid to a foreign captive and not to apply the same rule to premiums paid to a domestic captive.

Revenue Ruling 77-316 finally provides a clear, public statement of the IRS position on foreign captives and the tax treatment that should be accorded the premiums paid to such companies.[130] The ruling thus eliminates the inconsistencies that previously existed between different IRS audit rules. It also answers some of the questions raised by the previous audit rules. What the ruling does not do, however, is resolve the basic issue once and for all; it merely states the IRS position on the matter. Revenue Ruling 77-316 may be directly challenged in court; in fact, Carnation Co., in its appeal of the case discussed in the text that follows, attempted to litigate the central theme of Revenue Ruling 77-316 but failed. The court chose to rule strictly on the facts of the case.[131]

Revenue Ruling 77-316 basically states that a U.S. parent company and its U.S. subsidiaries cannot deduct, as ordinary and necessary business expense, premiums paid to an offshore insurance company that is wholly owned by the parent. The ruling sets forth three hypothetical "fact" situations and explains the IRS position and the tax treatment for each of these three cases. The three situations are:

1. The U.S. parent and its subsidiaries insure their loss exposures directly with the foreign captive. The captive does not enter into any reinsurance arrangements with respect to this coverage. In this case, the IRS position is that none of the premium is deductible.

2. The U.S. parent and its subsidiaries insure their loss exposures with an unrelated U.S. insurance company under a "fronting" arrangement that calls for 95 percent of the coverage to be reinsured with the parent's foreign captive. In this case, the proportion of the premium that remains with the unrelated fronting company (5 percent) is deductible.

3. The U.S. parent and its subsidiaries insure their loss exposures directly with the parent's foreign captive, and the captive reinsures some part (say 90 percent, for example) of this coverage with an unrelated insurance company. In this case, the reinsurance premium is deductible by the U.S. parent and its subsidiaries.

The IRS ruling treats the premiums paid to a foreign captive by its U.S. owner as contributions to the captive's capital. Premiums paid by a subsidiary are treated first as a constructive dividend to the parent, and then as a contribution to the captive's capital. Because premiums paid to and retained by the foreign captive are not allowable deductions, the losses covered by the captive are deductible by the U.S. parent and its subsidiaries.

The theory underlying Revenue Ruling 77-316 is that any arrangement with a wholly owned foreign subsidiary cannot be insurance because there is no transfer outside the economic family of the U.S. parent of any ensuing financial loss. Based on this theory, the ruling (which specifically addresses only U.S. companies that "insure" with a wholly owned foreign captive) should also apply to premiums paid to a wholly owned domestic captive, and to premiums paid to a foreign captive by the U.S. parent's other, wholly owned foreign subsidiaries. These matters, however, are simply not addressed by Revenue Ruling 77-316.

Over the years Revenue Ruling 77-316 has received important support from various sources. For example, in its statement on "Accounting for Contingencies," the Financial Accounting Standards Board (FASB) clearly considers insurance purchased from a single-owner pure captive (foreign or domestic) to be a deposit made to the corporate retention plan, rather than a true insurance expense.[132] More attention is given to this FASB rule later in this monograph.

Those opposed to the position stated in Revenue Ruling 77-316 generally believe that premiums paid to a captive should be deductible as business expenses as long as the transactions are conducted on an arm's length basis and the captive is a bona fide insurance operation adequately capitalized and operated as an insurer under laws of the jurisdiction in which it is incorporated. Many legal and tax experts who hold this viewpoint believe that the only valid way to challenge the deductibility of premiums paid to a captive is by applying Section 482 of the Internal Revenue Code.[133] This section of the Code permits the IRS to reallocate the income and expense items resulting from transactions between related companies to reflect more accurately the true income and expense of each company.

Carnation Case   Few captive owners have won arguments with IRS auditors over disallowed deductions. A very conspicuous case on the deductibility of premiums paid to a captive is *Carnation Company v. Commissioner of Internal Revenue.*[134] Carnation contested an IRS action to disallow $1.755 million in premiums that it paid to its foreign captive, Three Flowers, in 1972. In this case, the IRS claimed that the $1.755 million was money placed in a retention fund and, therefore, the amount could not be deducted. The IRS simultaneously reduced Carnation's Subpart F income to $50,616 and reduced by $1,647,216 the numerator of the fraction used in determining the limitation on foreign tax credits. Carnation lost the case in the tax court and also lost its appeal in the Ninth Circuit of the U.S. Court of Appeals.[135] The U.S. Supreme Court refused to consider the case.[136]

Many practitioners feel that the central issues in the use of offshore captives were not squarely addressed in the Carnation case. They feel that the definitive litigation needed to settle the issues has yet to be pursued. For this reason various supporters of captives are continuing their efforts to persuade the IRS to change its position. The opposing views were succinctly summarized in the briefs filed in the Carnation case (but were not directly addressed by either the tax court or the appellate court). Several quotations are useful to contrast the opposing views.

The Commissioner argued:

> The second principle applicable to the determination of whether payment constitutes deductible insurance premiums is that payments set aside pursuant to a self-insurance plan are not deductible business expenses. Not only is there no risk-shifting or risk-distributing on a self-insurance plan, but payments set aside pursuant to such a plan are not business "expenses" where the taxpayer retains a proprietary interest in the fund, or where the payments are merely a reserve for contingent or future liabilities. Payments made pursuant to contractual arrangements, which result in the neutralization of the risk customarily inherent in an insurance contract, are not deductible expenses for federal tax purposes....

> When the insurer is the wholly-owned subsidiary of the insured there is no risk-shifting; when the subsidiary insures only its parent corporation, there is no risk-shifting. The result is that those who bear the ultimate economic burden of loss are the same persons who suffer the loss. There is no "insurance" as that term is used for federal tax purposes.[137]

Carnation challenged the basic IRS position with the following arguments:

> [The economic family doctrine] violates tax law principles because it ignores the separate corporate identity of Three Flowers.... The economic family concept conflicts with the authorities which allow loss deductions in transactions between related corporations.... [It] further conflicts with the recognition ... that insurance may exist between related corporations ... it also cannot be applied intelligently in the context of the Code....

> Existing tax law principles, and not the economic family concept, provide the answer to the Commissioner's question ... as to whether it is merely enough to incorporate a self-insurance reserve with minimal capital in order to obtain a current deduction. If an insurance subsidiary is a sham, lacking a legitimate business purpose, the Commissioner may ignore its separate existence.... If the principal purpose for the acquisition of an insurance subsidiary is the evasion or avoidance of federal income tax by securing a deduction ... the Commissioner may disallow the deduction.... If insurance premiums

are not based on arms-length rates, the Commissioner may reallocate income and deductions.... The Commissioner has not attempted to apply any of these principles in the instant case and has effectively conceded their non-applicability....

This appeal is the first time that a court has had the opportunity to pass on the principle asserted in Rev. Rul. 77-316. Judge Goffe did not even discuss it in his opinion.... this is the first of a myriad of cases in which the so-called "captive" insurance company issue will be litigated. The Commissioner is attempting here to obtain a broad authorization to upset all insurance transactions between related corporations.... [He] is engaged in nothing more than a transparent attempt to circumvent the requirement imposed by existing authorities that he analyze individual insurance transactions between separate corporations under existing tax principles. At the same time he refuses to defend the underlying principle of Rev. Rul. 77-316.... The defective principle of Rev. Rul. 77-316 is the same, however, whether the corporations in question are related by 100 percent ownership or by some lesser percentage, and whether or not the insurance corporation insures the risks of unrelated as well as related entities.[138]

Another celebrated case that reached a court ruling on the issue of premium tax deductibility is the case of *Stearns-Roger Corporation, Inc. v. United States,* decided in late 1983 by the U.S. District Court in Denver, Colorado.[139] The case involved Stearns-Roger, a worldwide manufacturer of mining, petroleum, and power generation plants, which filed suit against the IRS seeking refund for taxes it had already paid when audited by the IRS. The IRS had disallowed the tax deduction for premiums paid to its insurance subsidiary, Glendale Insurance Co., a Colorado-domiciled captive. The denial of the tax deductibility was based on the principles of Rev. Rul. 77-316, upholding the concept that Glendale, a wholly-owned subsidiary, and its parent company were members of the same "economic family;" therefore, there was no "shifting and distribution of risk" that is necessary for the existence of true insurance between the two entities. Many observers believe that the Stearns-Roger case has been a considerable blow to the issue of tax deductibility of premiums paid by a parent to wholly owned captives. The Stearns-Roger case was much clearer than the multifaceted case of Carnation, because the judge found the captive to be a legitimate insurance subsidiary, and because the decision for the first time applied also to a domestic captive. Many previously believed that domestic captives would be treated more favorably by the courts than offshore captives.[140]

In late 1984 the taxpayer lost yet another round in court regarding the deduction of premiums. The case was *Beech Aircraft Corp. v. the United States.* Beech claimed as a deduction the premium paid to its captive, Travel-Air in Bermuda. Beech attempted to build a case of "risk shifting and risk distribution" by demonstrating arms-length relations and the existence of an insurance transaction. The court ruled against Beech by emphasizing the key concept established in the Carnation and Stearns-Roger cases: "the gain or loss enjoyed or suffered by the captive is reflected directly on the net worth of the parent ... the net worth of Beech was reduced by approximately the same extent as though Beech had paid the loss itself." Furthermore, the court judged that the captive, which had only $150,000 in capital and purported to cover several million in exposure, could not cover the loss. Only Beech could have responded to a loss of this nature if one had occurred.[141]

This trend changed with the case of *Crawford Fitting Company v. the United States*, decided in January 1985. Crawford won this unique case in which the structure of ownership and presence of unrelated policyholders made the difference. The case involved the sole owner of Crawford, who also owned four other companies directly and indirectly through close relatives. These four companies owned 80 percent of the Colorado-domiciled captive, Constance. The other 20 percent was owned by Crawford employees (15 percent) and Crawford lawyers (5 percent). Since Crawford was neither sole nor majority owner of the captive, and since the captive had other unrelated business, the court held that risk was shifted and distributed outside the economic family. The court held that risk was distributed within the captive and that the insureds were "not so economically related that their separate financial transactions must be aggregated and treated as the transactions of a single taxpayer."[142]

The deductibility of premiums was once again challenged in *Clougherty Packing Co. v. Commissioner*. In this case premiums were paid by the parent to an unrelated fronting insurer who, in turn, ceded 92 percent of it to Clougherty's captive, Lombardy, domiciled in Colorado and wholly owned by Clougherty's Arizona subsidiary. Though resembling the Carnation case, the capitalization in this case was more than adequate, and there was no agreement or understanding between the parent and the fronting company about indemnifying the fronting company or adding any capital to secure the transaction. Although the taxpayer lost the case; it was a split decision. The majority of judges relied on the opinion in the Carnation case and concluded that there was no shifting of the risk outside the taxpayer family. The dissenting opinion, seven of the eighteen judges, stated that the fronting company was still primarily responsible for paying claims even if the captive failed; thus, there was risk shifting.[143]

Mobil Oil v. the United States, decided in the U.S. Court of Claims in August 1985, was a long awaited case. Both the IRS and Mobil positioned themselves with numerous experts and arguments drawing on economic theory of insurance and the conceptual integrity of the tax code. The case involved Mobil's captive, Blufield, which was owned by another Mobil subsidiary. Blufield, located in Bermuda, wrote insurance and reinsurance business for Mobil, many of its related companies, and other parties related to Mobil through business dealings. Mobil maintained that the premiums paid to the captive should be deductible based on the doctrine of separate corporate entities, and that the transactions were not different from other legally accepted transactions between affiliated corporations. The court denied deductibility of the premium stating that any losses suffered by the insurance affiliate would be reflected on Mobil's financial statement. This case turns more on the issue of reclassifying a transaction and less on the separate nature of corporate entities. The court stated that "in the present situation there was no risk transference and thus no insurance when a wholly owned affiliate reinsured the risk of the parent." The bright spot for Mobil in the decision, however, was the court's refusal to accept the IRS contention that the premiums paid by Mobil's sister companies constituted constructive dividends to the common parent.[144]

In the case *Humana Inc. v. Commissioner*, the court upheld the IRS position that Humana could not deduct the premiums paid to its captive in Colorado, Health Care Indemnity. Although the captive wrote coverage for other professionals and employees, the court was not persuaded that this distinguished the case from others such as the Carnation and Clougherty cases.

As of this writing, it is quite clear that case law has supported the IRS point of view on disallowing a deduction for premiums paid to wholly owned captives. It is also clear that the key issues in deciding cases were evidence of an insurance transaction, that is, risk shifting and distribution, which, according to the court, does not take place in a wholly owned subsidiary even if the transaction involves some degree of unrelated parties or a fronting company. Based on some private rulings and case law, it is evident that each case will be determined in its own right, considering both policyholders and shareholders to determine the presence of requisite risk shifting and distribution. This is determined not only by the capital structure of the company but also by the premium and resulting surplus and investment income paid to policyholders. Thus, it is possible, based on IRS expressed opinions, that risks can be shifted and distributed in cases of multiple ownership among unrelated parties and/or when a wholly owned insurer has enough unrelated policyholders.[145]

Unrelated Business   In recent years the concept of "unrelated business" has significantly changed the captive industry. Before addressing the concept directly, we should bring attention to a type of captive that is likely to avoid the premium deductibility issue altogether. If a captive is organized as a foreign *group* captive, little room exists for argument about its being a bona fide insurance company operation. A favorable U.S. Treasury ruling was issued to Atlantic Richfield Company (ARCO) on this very point. In May 1972 ARCO requested that the premiums it paid to Oil Insurance Ltd. (OIL) of Hamilton, Bermuda be ruled deductible as ordinary and necessary expenses under Section 162 of the Internal Revenue Code. The Treasury ruling of 30 March 1973 stated in part:

> ... after consideration of all the information submitted in this request, we conclude that there is sufficient risk shifting and risk distribution to constitute insurance and that the consideration paid by ARCO for this insurance can be characterized as premiums and will be deductible as ordinary and necessary business expenses under Section 162 of the Code, provided they are reasonable in relationship to the insurance coverage obtained.[146]

This Treasury ruling applies to the premium payments made to a group captive (OIL) owned by, and operating to insure the loss exposures of, approximately 25 oil companies. This favorable ruling established that OIL was a legitimate insurance operation largely because it embodied loss sharing through an insurance mechanism and a transfer of the financial consequences associated with the loss exposure of its policyholders to a third party. This favorable response by the IRS did not mean that OIL has not been subject to other IRS criticism. For example, ARCO's payments to OIL were attacked by the IRS as being excessive for each of the first three years they were made. Many critics point out that the 1986 tax revisions regarding CFC are designed after "OIL type" group captives.

Short of using the foreign group captive approach, many have believed a foreign captive might demonstrate its independent status as an insurance company by expanding its insurance operations to provide insurance coverages to unrelated companies (by acting as a direct insurer, by becoming a reinsurer, or by doing both) and thereby demonstrate that it is, in fact, a bona fide insurance company because it handles "unrelated business."

Unrelated business has been advocated principally by some interpreters of Revenue Ruling 77-316 as a defense against disallowance deductibility of the parent's own premium payments to a captive. Such defense remains theoretical and quite doubtful because the IRS might choose to disallow the portion of the captive's income that is parent-related, no matter how small the portion might be. Aside from tax considerations, the service of unrelated insureds is said to be justified by the possible increase in spread of exposures therefore affecting the overall "risk" of the captive,[147] and the prospects for underwriting profit. The principal sources of unrelated business are the following:

1. commercial reinsurance from contacts in London, the U.S., and elsewhere;
2. direct writing of unrelated risks;
3. pooling plans organized by brokers and service providers; and
4. bilateral or multilateral pooling of business with other captives. (These exchanges are similar to but not identical to the activities of group captives.)

Both sources three and four involve pooling of captives' exposures. They differ mainly in one respect. In source three the pooling is arranged and serviced by a broker or some other intermediary. In source four the pooling is either spontaneous or administered by the participating captives. Bilateral pooling involves two captives; multilateral involves three or more.

An example of a pooling administered by a broker is the First Island Reinsurance Association organized and operated in Bermuda by Johnson & Higgins. Association members were pooling workers compensation (and certain other) premiums and exposures. They were doing so by ceding *to* the First Island pool premiums and exposures up to $25,000 per occurrence and by receiving premiums *from* First Island as consideration for its promise to pay its share of losses suffered by others in the pool. If, for example, a captive cedes $1 million to the pool, and if this amount represents 10 percent of the pool's business, the captive participates in the pool's quota share reinsurance for 10 percent, which in this example produces roughly $1 million of premiums for "unrelated business." Total premiums flowing through such pooling arrangements in 1980 were estimated at about $250 million.

Bilateral or multilateral pooling can be thought of as being "captive controlled." That is, the captives somehow deal directly with each other to do their own pooling rather than using brokers or other "outside" intermediaries. This situation has caused some observers to believe that outsiders may perform less of a function in captive operations in the future than in the past. Other observers, however, see the broker role as critical to any systematic and large-scale pooling.

In any case the pooling (whether or not it is broker-administered) is perceived as "good business" for the simple reason that the underlying parent-related business is "good business." As B. M. Brown stated:

Do not overlook the fact that captives probably represent the best risks and the best business. Inter-captive transfers of risk and reinsurance of captives will therefore also be the best business and may be the only safe haven in a time of crazy rates and markets.[148]

A good example of this kind of pooling is CIRCL, some of whose members frequently pool their primary and excess liability premiums and coverages above the primary layers of insurance or self-insurance. CIRCL's list of participants was composed of large and medium-sized U.S. parents and originally included the following:

Alco Standard Corporation
Allegheny Ludlum Industries, Inc.
Archer Daniels Midland Company
Charter Oil Company
General Tire & Rubber Company
The Hanna Mining Company
Ideal Mutual Insurance Company
International Harvester Corporation
Minnesota Mining & Manufacturing Company (3M)
National Steel Corporation
Owens-Illinois, Inc.
A. O. Smith Corporation
Sybron Corporation
Wheelabrator-Frye, Inc.

The reinsuring that takes place within CIRCL results in the premiums constituting unrelated income to the captive. Even so, the primary purpose for organizing CIRCL was said by its founders to be the provision of a market for excess liability insurance for the parent companies.

An example of a multilateral exchange facility is the Risk Exchange Association formed in Bermuda in 1983, but which started to operate in 1984. The exchange was originally comprised of seventeen captive members. The exchange was formed to give captives access to profitable third-party business that they otherwise could not obtain in the marketplace.

Unrelated business has become of such interest that many misleading ideas are heard in the marketplace. The most misleading of all concerns the "safe percentage," that is, the minimum percentage of a captive's total earned premiums that should be attributable to unrelated business in order to satisfy the IRS. Folklore suggested that the figure was 25 percent. Some observers say that it has recently crept up to 50 percent. Whether cited by a tax counselor, a purveyor of reinsurance treaties, or someone else, all such figures are theoretical, even though the "50 percent" was implicitly mentioned in the private IRS memorandum, PLR 8111 087. The IRS however has given no official or formal indications as to what percentage of outside business it deems as generally sufficient to support deductibility of premiums paid by a parent to its captive.[149]

If the unrelated business concept should ultimately change the mix of captive business, the change could defeat the purpose of a parent's use of its captive in the first place. To the extent a captive writes insurance or reinsurance on unrelated business, the captive takes on the coloration of a conventional insurer or reinsurer and assumes the extra underwriting risk that goes with it. Indeed, more than a few broad captives, too eager to position themselves favorably in terms of taxes launched a less than prudent underwriting of unrelated business, which ultimately resulted in great losses and even bankruptcies.[150]

VI. THE USE OF CAPTIVES TO SOLVE CORPORATE PROBLEMS

The discussion in the two preceding sections of this monograph focused on the tax benefits and other financial advantages of a captive. Equally important, however, are the ways in which a captive may be utilized to minimize or resolve other types of corporate risk management problems. Frequently, one or more of these corporate problem-solving capabilities serves as the primary reason for establishing a captive. In this section consideration is given to the ways in which captives can be used to help solve several common, but nonetheless significant, corporate risk management problems.

Coverages

Captives have often been formed to obtain insurance coverages (or broader forms of coverage) not available in the traditional insurance marketplace, or not available at prices the insured considers reasonable. Some examples of the types of perils, losses, and loss exposures that at one time or another have fallen into this category include, but are not limited to, the following: coinsurance deficiency as a result of improper valuation, inadequate insurance, or currency realignment; confiscation and expropriation; earthquake and flood; libel and slander; pollution damage; product liability, guarantee, or recall; professional liability; strikes; turbine and boiler explosion; and wild well control (oil wells). In some instances the loss exposures involved are considered to be uninsurable by either commercial insurers or state regulatory officials, while in other cases, the commercial market may be temporarily restricted with respect to the loss exposures or the industry in question. (Readers should bear in mind that the fact has already been established that treatment of an exposure by a captive is not necessarily insurance. Pure, single-owner captives use noninsurance techniques. Thus, an uninsurable exposure can be "treated" by captives.) Limited and fluctuating availability of an relatively high price levels for certain coverages have tended to be a cyclical phenomenon generally recognized as characteristic of the property-liability field. In the early 1980s the formation of new captives has been largely attributed to this type of market condition.

Almost all of the growing number of captives formed in recent years by state hospital and physician associations were created to provide their members with professional liability coverage that commercial insurers were either unable or unwilling to offer at prices and on terms that hospitals and physicians considered reasonable. The Products Liability Risk Retention Act, enacted in 1981 and amended in 1986, facilitated somewhat the formation of group captives organized in Vermont and other states to provide the product liability protection envisioned by the proponents of the bill.[151] Several engineering groups have formed captive companies to cover loss exposures considered to be uninsurable or prohibitively expensive in the traditional insurance marketplace. Several other captives (some of which have already been mentioned in this monograph) have been formed primarily for these reasons. Among them are the following:

1. Oil Insurance, Ltd., of Bermuda, formed by members of the American Petroleum Institute and now jointly owned by a number of American, Belgian, Canadian, Dutch, English, French, and Italian corporations with active petroleum operations.[152]
2. Nuclear Mutual, Ltd., of Bermuda, formed by some of the members of the Edison Electric Institute (an association of utility companies).
3. Mutual Insurance, Ltd., of Bermuda, formed by members of the American Newspaper Publishers Association to write strike as well as libel and slander for its members.
4. Arch Insurance Company, formed by the Associated General Contractors to write strike coverage.
5. Verlan Insurance Company, formed by the Paint, Lacquer and Varnish Association to write difficult-to-place coverages for its members.
6. WESCAP Insurance Company, formed by the National Welding Supply Association to write property-liability coverages for its members who were previously unable to buy the coverages in commercial markets.[153]

About 520 group captives were estimated to be in operation in early 1987, up from some 150 in 1984, many of them domiciled in the U.S.[154] About 40 percent of the medical malpractice premiums from U.S. sources were reported to have been paid to such captives in

1980.[155] The American Society of Association Executives has even published a booklet, *How to Form and Operate an Association Captive Insurance Company.*[156]

In terms of providing coverage, captives do not possess any inherent advantages over commercial insurers. Whatever advantage exists in this regard stems from the absence of regulation and market constraints. The ability of a captive, especially a foreign captive, to tailor the insurance coverages for its owners is attributable mainly to its freedom from regulation. The ability of the captive to purchase an appropriate reinsurance package, which the insured can hardly do on its own, is the result of an imperfection of the market. Domestic insurance companies licensed to operate on an "admitted" basis within a given state are subject to the strict insurance regulations of that state. Typically, these regulations apply both to rates and policy coverages. Generally, any deviations from policy wording such as extensions of coverage to new hazards or loss exposures must be filed with and approved by the insurance commissioners in the appropriate states in order to be used. A foreign captive is not subject to this type of regulation.

Even though it was mentioned in the discussion of financial advantages of captives, one of the lower-cost-of-loss-financing arguments is worth repeating here because of its relevance to coverage motivations for captive formation. A number of captives have been formed because their owners felt that the rating structure of commercial insurers failed to reflect adequately their superior loss experience or because it denied to them what they considered to be "fair" credits for the larger deductible amounts they were willing to assume. One example of this point is the Controlled Risk Insurance Company (CRICO) that was established by the eleven Harvard-affiliated hospitals principally to recapture "excess" premiums.

Despite the popular thinking that captives have been formed to obtain coverage not available in the marketplace or available only at unreasonable prices, the captive movement as a whole underwrites mostly the same common coverages that most property-liability insurers do—namely, fire and allied lines, general liability, marine, workers compensation, products and professional liability, and auto coverages. Only a minority of all captives write solely specialty, rare, or hard to place coverages.[157]

Capacity

The lack of sufficient underwriting capacity has frequently been cited as another reason for establishing a captive. Capacity can be defined in either of two ways. First, from an aggregate viewpoint, capacity is the overall ability of the insurance industry to insure or reinsure loss exposures or, in other words, to write premium volume. In a financial accounting sense, the industry's aggregate capacity is thus limited by its capitalization, reserve requirements, and the level of premiums written. Of course, capacity also is limited by the psychological outlook of the industry. Over time, the aggregate capacity of the industry will vary in response to changes in portfolio values, underwriting profitability, and the catastrophe potential of loss exposures. The experience with the first two factors has been both favorable and unfavorable over time, while the trend of the last factor has been continually increasing with the growing concentrations of insurable values, larger and more costly ships and aircrafts, increasingly large third-party liability judgments, inflation, and so forth.

Capacity can also be defined in terms of the ability of the industry to underwrite and reinsure the loss exposures of an individual organization. This individual underwriting capacity is limited by all of the factors mentioned and, at times, further limited by the need of the industry to allocate its capacity among policyholders. The allocation problem, when it exists, is in turn influenced heavily by the relative attractiveness of different lines of business, client industries, and even subgroups within those industries. For example, the level of premiums and the resulting profitability of the different lines of insurance, the industries, and the individual firms have a bearing on how scarce capacity is allocated.

Thus, when a business or an industry association considers a captive for capacity reasons, it may be looking at capacity from an individual underwriting viewpoint, even though this view is not entirely divorced from the aggregate capacity of the industry. The concern of the firm or association in such an instance is to obtain adequate amounts of insurance on a consistent basis.[158] Gas Ltd. (now AEGIS) of Bermuda, for example, was formed in 1975 to secure adequate insurance coverage for its six gas company members.[159]

An interesting question is the extent to which captives add to the capacity of the insurance industry. The point is irrefutable that captives in the aggregate have enormous capital. By the end of 1986, total capital and surplus of captives worldwide was estimated at about $9 to $10 billion. Not all of this, however, adds to *insurance* capacity because, as emphasized, not all captives engage totally in insurance activities. That is, some captives merely operate formalized retention programs as part or all of their activities. The activities of all captives, however, bear on insurance capacity in the sense that the exposures treated by the captives are withdrawn from the conventional insurance market. To that extent, insurance industry capital is released to be available to support the insuring of other exposures.

The discussion needs to be carried at least one step further. A significant feature of captives may be the access they afford their owners to the reinsurance market. Without a captive a firm may have to buy coverage from an insurer. With a captive the firm may be able to buy essentially the same coverage from a reinsurer. While the pure premiums may be about the same in each case over the long run, the expense elements may not be. If the firm buys reinsurance through use of its captive, it may (again, through its captive) earn a commission on the reinsurance bought. The commission has the effect of reducing the cost of the coverage. In the direct market the commission goes to an intermediary. In short, captives may alter (reduce) the transactional costs of the protection purchased by their parents.

Control

A captive provides a vehicle for consolidating and unifying its owner's worldwide risk management program. By writing either direct coverages or by accepting coverages written by "fronting" insurers, and then, in turn, by retroceding some of its volume, a captive can serve its owner's overall corporate risk management policy while simultaneously accommodating the special needs of any corporate subsidiaries and the differing foreign insurance law. One of the most important advantages in using a captive may be the psychological one that results from a greater top management awareness of and concern for the risk management function. Establishment and operation of a captive insurer may bolster the status of the risk manager(s) and the risk management function. A positive attitude toward the corporate risk management program and a belief that the captive may be a potential profit center, as opposed to an unavoidable and largely uncontrollable expense, can be a highly important matter to the risk manager.

Several aspects of the captive's operation lend themselves to improved risk management. First, the existence and use of the captive may bring about a more nearly optimal allocation of the risk management and loss costs to each subsidiary while allowing the corporation as a whole to achieve a more nearly optimal retention level as befits the total corporate need. This "total corporate approach" may also serve to motivate managers of the corporate subsidiaries to be more aware of and concerned with the cost and performance of their risk management programs. Finally, many corporations have labeled their captives as "profit centers." The propriety of such an appellation, however, is open to serious question. It is probably an inaccurate description in the case of single-owner pure captives because there can be no increased profit in the consolidated corporate financial statements, except for that which can be attributable to a reduction in the costs of the risk management program (that is, pure captives may generate savings but not true profits). The profit-center label could be an accurate label in those relatively few situations in which a captive writes insurance or reinsurance for the general public and does so consistently at a profit. One can see, then, that this label fits only a broad captive that is also profitable.

Overcoming Currency Control Problems

Some countries, especially those with a high rate of inflation and a weakening currency, have currency exchange control programs. Many of these programs, however, treat differently the payment of insurance or reinsurance premiums in their control laws. Consequently, the risk management process becomes an important part of international corporate financial management in that the captive can be used advantageously in making foreign currency available for exchange into dollars. For example, the foreign captive can be used as a currency hedge. The corporate parent can move funds from an otherwise currency-blocked country by paying premiums to the captive after all local compulsory insurance and reinsurance requirements have been satisfied. (This option is based on the assumption that the parent or a noncaptive subsidiary as well as the captive operate in the currency-blocked country.) The parent can even pay premiums for perhaps three years in advance. While the parent or its foreign subsidiary could not have moved the funds out of the currency-blocked country, the captive may be able to do so. As another example, reinsurance premiums can often be paid by a fronting company to a domestic captive. The fronting company in the foreign country would also be less subject to the currency controls. The common arrangement involves an offshore captive domiciled in a tax-free country receiving reinsurance premiums of the noninsurance foreign subsidiary via a fronting company admitted at the foreign country, and which writes the underlying coverages retaining only a small part of the risk. This arrangement partly circumvents the currency control laws and simultaneously satisfies the local insurance requirements.

Still another example might involve loss adjustment. When an insured loss occurs in the foreign country, the needed repair parts and equipment may not be available or may become available only after a long delay. In such cases the foreign subsidiary must either wait or apply for foreign exchange in order to obtain U.S. dollars with which to buy the needed parts and equipment. In either event a long delay may ensue. If affiliated with a captive, the foreign subsidiary can avoid these delays by having the captive purchase and supply the needed repair parts and equipment.

Stabilization of Financial Statements

The U.S. tax laws do not permit amounts contributed to a contingency reserve for future losses under a corporate retention plan or "self-insurance" to be deducted for tax purposes. Of course, the losses that do occur can be deducted, but only in the year in which they occur. Premiums for insurance to cover such losses, however, are deductible for corporate income tax purposes in the year they are paid. Accordingly, captives have been used as a means of evening out the impact of retained losses on the financial statements and earnings per share of the corporation (a chronological stabilization program) and to fund extraordinary loss exposures such as strikes (when accounting rules permit).

The use of a captive to accomplish chronological earnings stabilization can be illustrated by an example. A corporation's losses might run to $20 million over a ten-year period, while the annual losses could fluctuate widely, ranging from $100,000 to $9 million. The payment of an annual $2 million premium to the captive permits the firm to eliminate the adverse impact of wide fluctuations in earnings due to random losses averaging out its loss experience with a more stable and tax deductible annual premium expense. Thus, assuming the IRS allows the parent to deduct the payment to the captive, the captive can lend stability to the parent corporation's earnings by controlling the timing of premium and claim payments compared to the results of a retention program. Purchase of insurance from a regular insurer could also provide financial stability.

Financial Accounting Standards Board Standard Number 5 The point has been made that the Financial Accounting Standards Board issued a rule that pertains to captives. Specifically, in March 1975 the Financial Accounting Standards Board issued its Standard Number 5, "Accounting for Contingencies."[160] As observed, this statement has to do with accounting for retained "self-insured" losses, foreign expropriation losses, and catastrophe losses. Financial accounting standards issued by the FASB become an established part of the body of generally accepted accounting principles. Thus, a member of the American Institute of Certified Public Accountants cannot state that a firm's financial reports to stockholders have been prepared and presented in accordance with generally accepted accounting principles if this standard or any other has not been substantially adhered to, unless a compelling reason can be cited for any exception.[161]

Standard Number 5 basically supports the position that uninsured losses should be charged against revenues in the period in which they occur. This position is consistent with the tax laws, but at odds with the risk manager's objective of achieving stability in the cost of such losses. The primary rationale underlying Standard Number 5 is the uncertainty about the magnitude and timing of such losses.

Financial Accounting Standard Number 5 states that:

> [A]n estimated loss from a loss contingency shall be accrued by a charge to income if both of the following conditions are met:
> a) Information available prior to issuance of the financial statements indicates that it is probable that an asset had been impaired or a liability had been incurred at the date of the financial statements.
> b) The amount of loss can be reasonably estimated.[162]

The appendix to the statement of Standard Number 5 contains several examples and situations that explain its application. Example 27 describes what is to be considered an "uninsured loss." This paragraph states that "uninsured risks may arise in a number of ways, including (a) noninsurance of certain risks or coinsurance or deductible clauses in an insurance contract or (b) *insurance through a subsidiary* or investee *to the extent not reinsured* with an independent insurer." (Emphasis added.)

Paragraph 28 states that no amounts can be charged against income for estimated incurred but not reported losses because a firm does not actually know that an asset has been impaired (or a liability incurred) in such cases; nor does it know the amount of such losses. Furthermore, unlike an insurance company, the enterprise has no contractual liability to others for such losses.

Paragraphs 44 and 45 state that "payments to insurance companies may not involve a transfer of risk" in all cases and "if, regardless of form, the substance of the contract is that all or part of the premium paid by the insured or the ceding company is a deposit, it shall be accounted for as such" rather than as a premium payment.

In summary, Financial Accounting Standards Board Standard Number 5 defines the terms "contingency" and "uninsured losses" (including payments to captive insurers to the extent that they are not reinsured). It then states that all "uninsured losses" shall be charged to income during the period when the loss or liability become known and the amount of the loss can be determined with reasonable accuracy. Contributions or deposits made to a "contingency" reserve shall not be deductible items, but a segmented part of retained earnings. Furthermore, payments to any insurance company may be either totally or partially a deductible expense depending upon the substance of the contractual agreement.

Impact of FASB Standard Number 5 While the implications of FASB Standard Number 5 on the use of captives were still not completely evaluated, the point was settled that the standard was aimed at discouraging reliance on pure captives. Despite this discouragement, however, the formation of new captives and growth of old ones has continued.

Readers should take pains to recognize that broad captives are not threatened by FASB Number 5. They may be regarded as independent insurers and are therefore immune from any negative aspects of Standard Number 5 altogether. Group captives to an extent are recognized as independent insurance companies. These captives can continue to establish recognized and tax-deductible reserves for incurred but not reported losses. The question of unearned premium reserves is not raised by Standard Number 5, but creation of these reserves would not seem to pose any problem, especially with captives that characteristically use monthly premium payment plans.

Summary

The various financial and operational advantages of captives just outlined have been recognized for many years. However, in recent years, particularly during the soft insurance market of the early 1980s, it became apparent that captive insurance companies were neither necessary for a good risk management program nor the best technique to finance risks. Self-insurance and other creative financing methods offered by competitive insurance companies could be equally advantageous. Yet, both single-owned and group captives have continued to be formed. The author surveyed risk managers and promoters in an attempt to understand the rationale for the continued interest in captives despite disappearing tax advantages and the rise of competing techniques. It become apparent from the responses that the advantages currently brought by captives to a risk management program primarily relate to the control advantage. Closely related to this advantage is the attention or focus given to the risk management function as a result of the captive and its control over a number of functions.

These are two interrelated aspects. As discussed, control refers to the ability of the risk manager to monitor all aspects of the risk management program through stabilization, standardization, and centralization. The centralization of all key aspects of the risk management program into one place brings attention to or focus on the importance of the risk manager and the risk management function. These key aspects involve all corners of the organization and include claims payments and administration; cash flow and investment planning; tax, legal, and budgetary planning; information systems; and cost of risk and profit allocations. Some of these key aspects may have been previously handled by a different function or department within the organization. With the increased control over more aspects of the organization's operations comes greater responsibility on the part of the risk manager. In turn, the increased focus on the risk management function because of this greater control brings about an expectation of accountability for the results of that function. The chances for recognition (either through failure or success) of the risk manager and the risk management function are thus increased.[163]

Thus, in the era of reduced economic advantages of captives, which may be temporary, still there are other noneconomic advantages. Some of these are grouped under the next discussion of social-psychological advantages.

VII. SOCIAL-PSYCHOLOGICAL ADVANTAGES

The preceding three sections dealt with the two major reasons for forming captives—financial (savings in costs and expenses, potential profits, and tax benefits) and operational (coverages, capacity, control, and other services). Several other reasons or motives are often mentioned, though hardly in an explicit form. In private interviews with captive operators and management company executives such motives as empire building, personal ambition, prestige among peers, enhanced status within the parent organization, ego, inertia, momentum, and so on were often mentioned "off the record." These social-psychological reasons can be grouped into two representative categories. The motive, status, reflects all personal reasons originating *within* the organization; and the motive, prestige, reflects all reasons originating *outside* the organization.

In two independent surveys operators of captives and executives of management companies were asked to indicate reasons for forming their captives. Operators were also asked to compare the reasons that, in their opinions, had triggered the formation of their captive at the time of its establishment with the reasons they believe are relevant at the present time.[164] Exhibit 11-10 summarizes the responses.

It is apparent that financial benefits have been the major reasons for forming captives in the past and still may be important. The operational solutions to corporate problems that captives are said to provide are equally important and are probably becoming more so in view of the disappearance of tax advantages as a reason for forming a captive. In fact, tax advantages as a reason for forming a captive were (even prior to the tax law changes) 20 percent less frequently mentioned as a present motive than as compared to the time of formation. The change in the social-psychological motives is notable. The increase from the prior to the post formation responses has been

Exhibit 11-10
Reasons for Forming Captives: Survey Responses*

Reasons	Survey of Captive Operators				Survey of Management Companies	
	At the time of captive's formation		At the present		At the time of captive's formation	
	No. of responses	PCT	No. of responses	PCT	No. of responses	PCT
I. Financial Benefits (savings, profits, tax)	224	48%	235	45.0%	30	40%
II. Operational Solutions (coverage, capacity, control, services)	219	47	239	45.5%	42	56
III. Social-psychological motives (status, prestige)	23	5	49	9.5	3	4
Total	466	100%	523	100%	75	100%

* Adapted with permission from M. Moshe Porat, "The Bermuda Captive's Organizational Structure and Goals" *Risk Management* (April 1982), p. 37.

almost 100 percent and the particular motive, status, has been more frequently reported as a reason by a rate of more than 200 percent.

These social-psychological motives have been given almost no explicit consideration even though they may have dominated the decision process. Apparently, many operators still tend to attribute the formation of captives to financial and recently more to operational motives. However, some have reached the realization and had the frankness to point explicitly toward personal, often subconscious motives.

In the past seven years the insurance market has gone from being very soft to tight. There are now signs (mid-1987) of renewed softening. Many have wondered why new captives continue to be formed and existing ones continue to operate. The answers vary. Some point to the future expectation of financial benefits when the market will turn, to underwriting profits, or to savings in writing new lines such as employee benefits. Still others explain the continued growth of the captive movement primarily in operational terms such as the captive's flexibility in providing coverage or the importance of the coordination and allocation of the overall cost of risk among all corporate units, namely focus and control. Also mentioned are the potential noninsurance or financial services in which the captives may be involved. What is clear, however, is that captives continue to be formed and to operate despite the changing market and the disappearing tax advantages partly because of momentum, inertia, empire building, personal ambition, and the like.[165] Thus, these social-psychological motives are beginning to be explicitly stated. It is quite likely that they have always existed but have been overshadowed by the more apparent "rational" motives.

VIII. DISADVANTAGES OF CAPTIVES

The preceding sections of this monograph have dealt with the nature and benefits of captive company operations. Captive companies also involve certain disadvantages, some of which can be serious. The purpose of this section is to discuss the major disadvantages associated with captives. These disadvantages may be broadly classified as either financial or operational.

Financial Disadvantages

The formation of a captive represents a sizable financial undertaking on the part of the parent corporation. Funds are needed for any preliminary studies of the idea and for meeting the initial start-up costs. These costs include the direct costs of incorporating the captive and satisfying necessary and reasonable capital and surplus requirements, including some provision for meeting the initial operating expenses. The parent corporation should also anticipate the incurring of certain indirect costs associated with forming a captive, such as the salaries of risk management department personnel and other members of the feasibility study group. Start-up costs for an average captive formed in Bermuda in 1987 would be in the area of $160,000 to $190,000 including minimum capitalization of $120,000. Annual operating cost would be in the range of $35,000 to $60,000. Finally, the parent should ask itself if this project is an attractive use of its corporate resources. If the answer to this question is negative, the captive idea should be rejected in favor of other risk management alternatives, unless other overriding reasons argue for allocating captive to this purpose. Stated somewhat differently, the fundamental question should be: Will this investment create a risk management tool that can reasonably be expected to generate worthwhile savings over and above its own operating expenses as well as nonfinancial benefits that exceed other risk management options?

An equally important question for the parent corporation has to do with the captive's ability to withstand an abnormally bad period of loss experience. The answer to this question will depend upon several variables, including the captive's ability to arrange for a stable reinsurance program. It would be difficult to overstate the importance of this critical factor as discussed earlier in this monograph. For this reason and those mentioned above, the financial projections that should be made to assist management in reaching an informed decision on whether or not to form a captive should be made for at least a ten-year period. Furthermore, different sets of financial projections should be made to reflect the different patterns of loss experience that might result.

Another disadvantage that results from using a pure captive follows from Standard Number 5 issued by the Financial Accounting Standards Board. As discussed, individual pure captives are not considered to be insurance operations under FASB Number 5. Broad captives and group pure captives apparently could qualify. It follows, then, that the premiums paid to captives cannot be treated as expenses but are regarded as contributions to a retention "self-insurance" fund in the parent company's financial reports to its stockholders. This treatment causes the parent company's financial statements to give the appearance of less stable earnings because the parent is able to deduct as loss costs or expenses only those amounts actually paid or incurred, rather than the more uniform stream of premium payments.

Another financially related disadvantage of captives concerns the uncertainty about their treatment and the treatment of premiums paid to them under the federal tax laws. As discussed, the IRS is waging its attack against captives by use of the 1972 internal memorandum and the 1977 Revenue Ruling 77-316. Similarly, the FASB, by issuing Standard Number 5, has taken a hostile position toward pure captives. The IRS challenge to the legitimacy of pure captives is being tested in court. Practically all court decisions regarding the deductibility of premiums in single captives favor the IRS. The Tax Reform Act of 1986 hardly left any tax deferred advantage for either single or group captives. At the time of this writing, any company considering the formation of a pure captive would have to consider the positions of the FASB and IRS toward captives to be discouraging.

Operational Disadvantages

The operation of a captive company involves many new, complex, and technical activities for the parent organization. The parent must decide whether to have the captive enter into a management contract with one of the several firms offering such services or to let the captive be self-managed. If the captive is to manage its own activities and affairs, it will still be obliged to purchase certain services (perhaps actuarial, loss prevention, and claims handling) or hire expert consultants for assistance and advice. The formation of a captive is really a new venture for the parent, and its staffing problems will very likely consume a considerable proportion of the parent's executive and risk management time, at least initially.

Captive companies are frequently used to write some insurance coverages for the parent but rarely to meet all of the parent's insurance needs. Essentially then, the captive leads to some "unbundling" of the parent's insurance programs and coverages. This process may hurt the relationships that have been established over the years with commercial insurers, agents, and brokers. It may also lead to higher administrative costs (in a relative sense) for the coverages, if any, that will continue to be placed in commercial markets. On the other hand, if the captive is formed to treat the more difficult-to-place coverages and loss exposures, it could be a pleasantly received development. Even in this event, however, the captive is likely to be used, sooner or later, to also handle some of the conventional coverages and thus to become a source of irritation to the commercial insurers serving the corporate family of which the captive is a member.

Captives must deal with the regulatory structure, and this requirement must be viewed as a distinct disadvantage. For example, if a captive wants to treat the parent's foreign loss exposures, the captive must comply with a variety of generally restrictive insurance and currency exchange laws. At the very least, these laws reduce the captive's flexibility to deal with different types of coverage situations. A captive is also exposed to various other laws and regulations within the U.S. that restrict or define the nature and scope of its activities.

Other operational disadvantages of captives have become apparent as the captive movement has matured. Among these disadvantages are the simple day-to-day costs and troubles associated with captive ownership. Some single-owner parents of captives are grumbling about the administrative burdens. Doubtless, apprehension about these costs and administrative problems have prevented several associations or groups from establishing captives. Another disadvantage is that expansion of a captive into unrelated business can cause the captive to develop a "mind set" that is detrimental to the captive owner's risk management program. The captive cannot serve two masters (for example, its own parent and its set of unrelated insureds). Some captive managements have grown schizophrenic in trying to do so. Several captives in the early 1980s experienced considerable underwriting losses due to inexperience in underwriting coupled with an unreasonable desire for fast expansion, lack of control on expenses, and in many cases, miscalculation with regard to interest rates. A serious disadvantage is the danger of investment losses on the part of the captive. The substantial investment losses suffered by numerous captives in 1979-1980 are still fresh (and grim) reminders of the vagaries of investments, especially in the face of rising interest rates. Another disadvantage is that forming a captive may be an easier process than getting rid of one that is no longer needed. Eliminating a captive can be an expensive and lengthy process.[166]

IX. THE FEASIBILITY OF ESTABLISHING A CAPTIVE

Consideration of Various Risk Management Approaches

Regardless of the initial motivation, use of a captive should be considered as only one of several alternative risk management approaches. Moreover, since pure captives are really a sophisticated, formal means of funding the parent corporation's loss retention capability, they should not be viewed as alternatives to commercial insurance in an absolute sense, but rather as a method, possibly but not necessarily the most cost-beneficial method, of implementing a loss retention plan. Neither should captives be viewed as potential profit centers as some proponents would suggest unless the parent organization fully intends to form a *broad* captive that ultimately will do most of its business with the general public. It is appropriate, however, to regard a captive as a cost center capable of saving corporate dollars on the owner's risk management program and also capable of providing a useful means of allocating loss costs among subsidiary operations in an equitable manner. Thus, while captives may be well suited for some circumstances, they are not universally the best approach for all corporate situations. Furthermore, the advantages that a captive may offer in a given situation generally stem from artificial market, institutional, or regulatory constraints applicable to other risk management techniques, rather than from any inherent superiority of the captive concept.

Essentially, then, the captive technique is a highly sophisticated form of retention, but one that involves additional costs that can be outweighed by the savings produced by use of the technique. In order to consider establishing a captive, an organization should be fairly large with a good spread of loss exposures and, thus, financially capable of retaining sizable losses. In general, it should have at best all the conditions that make retention ideal. An annual premium volume of $1 to $2 million is often cited as the minimum required for starting a captive; otherwise, the initial start-up costs and continuing administrative costs would be disproportionately large.[167] Captives also become a more attractive option as the firm develops extensive foreign operations and a favorable underwriting and loss history. Even then, however, the fundamental question is not whether it is possible for a given organization to establish a captive. Rather, the question is whether the captive technique is the best method of treating the organization's loss exposures and otherwise serving the financial objectives of the firm.

The decision on whether or not to form a captive is an individual one that depends upon the circumstances of each particular case. Accordingly, no organization should proceed to form a captive without first thoroughly analyzing the organization's specific needs and objectives and the full range of risk management alternatives available to it. These alternatives should include such approaches as (1) a commercial insurance program, (2) an administrative-services-only contractual arrangement with an insurer or brokerage firm (for actuarial, claims, adjusting, loss prevention, and possibly other risk management services), (3) a funded retention plan, (4) a 501(c)9 trust (or an employee association for funding and administering employee benefit programs), (5) various retrospectively rated plans, and (6) some combination of these alternatives. The basic objective of the organization's feasibility study and analysis should be to determine the optimal way of treating its property-liability loss exposures and possibly its employee benefit plan. Thus, the person or team making the feasibility study should fully consider the costs, benefits, and any other advantages and disadvantages of the alternative risk management approaches in evaluating and selecting the course of action that will best fulfill the sponsoring organization's risk management needs.

Feasibility Study

Once an organization has become interested in exploring the feasibility of establishing a captive, the initial step is usually for the firm's risk manager to conduct a preliminary investigation (a review of the available literature and a comparison of what other companies have done with captives, their objectives or reasons, and their experience). After this preliminary effort has been completed, a feasibility study proposal is usually prepared for consideration by the organization's top management. The items to be studied should include but not be limited to the following:

1. Probable form of organization (stock, mutual, or reciprocal).

2. Possible sites for locating a captive.
3. Types of coverage most likely to be placed with the captive.
4. Types of services required to operate the captive (legal, management) and the alternate methods for securing the services.
5. Potential for savings and the probable capital investment required.
6. Expense estimate for the feasibility study, a description of how the study will be staffed and conducted, and a timetable for completion of the study.
7. Benefits to be gained from the study, even if those conducting it should recommend against establishing a captive (that is, the benefits of a thorough review and analysis of the existing risk management program with the possibility of resulting improvements, and a complete review of the organization's risk management philosophy and retention policies).

Once the necessary approval has been granted and the project team organized, the feasibility study can be undertaken.[168] It should involve two distinct parts: (1) a risk management analysis and (2) an operational analysis. The basic purpose of the risk management analysis is to determine the organization's loss retention capability and the types of coverages most suited to treatment through a captive. This purpose requires that those doing the study gather and analyze the available information concerning the organization's loss history, its current loss exposures, and the method of treating these exposures. This process begins with the identification of the firm's loss exposures (including those uninsured as well as those presently insured) and extends to the accumulation of relevant data to permit a thorough analysis. The summary report of this information provides the basis for discussions with reinsurers, captive management companies, and other specialists representing other risk management alternatives. This comprehensive approach to the feasibility study also enables the organization's management to view its risk management program as a whole rather than in segments.

The purpose of the operational analysis is to assemble the information necessary to make operational cost-benefit comparisons for the several risk management alternatives available to the firm. This requires that those doing the study secure price and fee quotations from reinsurers, captive management companies, and other service organizations about all activities relevant to the various risk management approach. This information permits the study team to compare the costs and benefits of the alternative approaches. If the formation of a captive is the favored approach, the study team should also consider how the captive should be organized, capitalized, managed, and so on.

The final report and recommendations of the feasibility study team should include a brief narrative summary, including the recommendation to management followed by an indexed report of the analysis. The analysis should include a brief discussion of the alternative risk management techniques and the costs and benefits associated with each alternative. The report should also contain opinions on the legal and tax implications of the captive operation for the captive and the parent corporation. Finally, a management decision on the study must be obtained to enable the organization to proceed to implement its chosen course of action.

One should remember that not all captive feasibility studies include a favorable recommendation for developing a captive insurer. While little information is available about such studies, two airline industry captives and a captive for a group of chemical companies were planned but never activated. While a number of factors were no doubt responsible for the airline captives never becoming operational, the two principal reasons apparently were the sizable capital requirements at a time when the industry had spent heavily on jumbo jets and a marked improvement in the conventional aviation insurance markets that resulted in sharply reduced premium.[169] Commercial insurance alternatives and elimination of tax deferral advantages were main reasons in aborting the plan for the chemical companies.

Key Factors for Success

When exploring the feasibility of forming a captive it is important to consider the key factors that contribute to a successful captive. Since group captives have been the major focus of attention in recent years and more than half of the newly formed captives in 1986 were group captives, the following factors were originally intended to apply to group captives. Nevertheless many of these factors also apply to single-owned captives. The list is based on Felix Kloman's writings and various observations reported in Captive Insurance Company Reports.[170]

The general elements for success are long-term commitment, conservative funding and underwriting, efficient operations, high standards of loss prevention and reduction, and political support from the parent organization. More specifically, the list includes the following factors.

Long-Term Commitment by the Parent Long-term orientation is essential to any retention plan. It is even more critical for group captives. With group captives, it is essential that members have penalties or other forms of disincentive for early withdrawal from the captive.

Prudent Funding Most successful captives are formed with sufficient capitalization, surplus, and annual premiums. In eras of limited reinsurance these aspects have proven essential. For members of group captives, it is much easier to commit initially, rather than later, to sufficient funding.

Careful Underwriting Too many captives suffered large losses during the early 1980s because of lack of prudent underwriting. For a group captive it is important to adopt entry and retention underwriting standards as well as risk assessment procedures. Equity is critical for the continued coherence of the group.

Efficient Operations Captives have historically maintained better control on expenses than regular insurers. It is important that they maintain that control because it can make a difference in the ability to survive. Group captives have to operate efficiently while maintaining a reasonable quality of service to its members.

Risk Sharing For group captives it is essential that there be a mechanism established at the outset for sharing all losses. An equitable formula has to be established. The group has to avoid pressures to maintain separate accounts that will ultimately lead to a breakup.

Risk Control As in any successful retention plan, there should be a high awareness of loss control. Loss prevention and reduction techniques are in the interest of the single-owned and group captive.

Homogeneity of Interest It appears that too much diversity among the group members may lead to conflicting interests and confusion. Successful group captives are apparently more often those with homogeneous membership.

Sense of Urgency Long lasting, successful captives have been those who turned to the captive solution as a serious attempt to resolve major problems of capacity inconsistency. Those who formed captives for minor cost savings or tax advantages have not lasted.

Profit Allocation For group captives it is critical to state in advance the formula for profit distribution as much as loss sharing. The distribution should be equitable and formed in recognition of the differences in loss experience, premium size, capital, surplus, and tenure in the group.

Political Support The captive cannot survive successfully without political support from influential members in the parent organization. This is more critical in group captives. The captive should be backed by these influential members in order to overcome initial and subsequent difficulties. The captive must be perceived as a "winner," and this image can be created and furthered with support from influential members of the parent organizations.

Creative Promoter Successful captives have always had an individual who assumed the responsibility and leadership to bring the organization from concept to reality. It is often the risk manager, the finance officer at the parent, a broker, or an agent. In group captives it might have been one or more of the members in the group. It could also be a consultant or a hired executive-organizer. What is clear is the need for a figure with the energy, commitment, and communication skills to lead, coordinate and to actively persuade the doubters. This individual is the cheerleader and the coordinator among all members, participants, and professionals involved such as legal staff, financing, and insurance personnel. Clearly Marsh & McLennan and other major brokers provided those skills that brought into being such entities as ACE, XL, and others.

The factors-principles mentioned above have been observed by many as keys to successful captives. Adopting them can save time, effort, and cost if taken into consideration as early as possible, even at the feasibility study stage.

X. THE OUTLOOK FOR CAPTIVES

Likely Future Developments

As stated at the beginning of this monograph, the current number of captives is estimated at around 2,100. Only a few of them have been operating for longer than twenty-five years. Therefore, the rapid growth in the number of captive insurers formed in recent years strongly suggests that the fundamental reasons underlying the creation of captives have more to do with meeting risk management and other needs than with seeking favorable tax treatment. This observation seems all the more accurate when one recalls that several incursions have been made in recent years on the favored tax status of domestic and especially foreign captives. Attention was called to the restrictive influence of Subpart F of the Revenue Act of 1962, to the 1972 IRS memorandum, "Captive Offshore Insurance or Reinsurance Companies," to Revenue Ruling 77-316 issued in August 1977 and to the fatal blow to tax deferral advantages for captives as a result of the Tax Reform Acts of 1984 and 1986. The fact that captives have continued to increase in number despite the unfavorable tax implications of these developments attests to the importance of nontax considerations in the establishment of captives. Captives are a natural outgrowth of the demand for self-insurance, which is expected to grow by as much as one-third to one-half of the property-liability market in the next five years. The demand for captives vis-à-vis other forms of self-insurance vary over time. The formation rates of new captives are on the rise when financial reasons justify them as during the upturns of the insurance cycle. When the cycles are turning downward, that is, when capacity is in abundance and price competition is strong, captives are financially relatively unattractive. Although formation rates decline, they definitely do not cease. Even at such times, captives have continued to be formed for operational or social-psychological reasons.

Exhibit 11-11 shows the relationship between the formation rates of new captives in Bermuda and the U.S. property-liability industry's operating income ratios as a percentage of earned premium for the past twenty-six years. There is a clear correlation between the formation rates and the relative profitability of the industry which is reflected by the cyclical nature of the property-liability industry.[171] This supports the proposition that the formation of new captives is influenced by the economic turns of the U.S. property-liability industry.[172]

In the next five years the key to captive development will be the insurance marketplace. Despite the recent growth of group captives, joint ventures, and various pools, early signs of a soft market coupled with the dampening effect of the 1986 tax reforms may somewhat reduce the interest in captives, particularly those offshore, even though we still may expect new captives at the rate of at least 50 to 70 annually in Bermuda and 100 to 120 annually worldwide.[173] This rate may be substantially higher if the Risk Retention Act of 1986 has the expected effect on the formation of domestic group captives. Signs in early 1987 suggest a great deal of interest in captives, but to what degree this interest becomes a reality remains to be seen. Over the longer run, the author believes that captives will be a permanent part of the risk management process and insurance industry. They will continue to grow with the growing demand for self-insurance. It is reasonable to expect further increases in group and joint venture captives, and in pools, exchanges, and rent-a-captive facilities. Still, the single-owned captives will remain because they will continue to provide the desired control and centralization of all aspects of the owner's risk management program. More captives will be formed in Europe and the Far East, but the more mature, U.S.-originated offshore captives will continue to make the innovative steps that have been restructuring the industry.

In the distant future,[174] the author believes that the captive movement will cooperate with insurers, reinsurers, and financial institutions in the risk-bearing business. Their efforts will focus on supplying mostly aggregate coverages for catastrophic risks to individ-

Exhibit 11-11
Captive Formation Rates and the U.S. Property and Liability Insurance Industry Cycles*

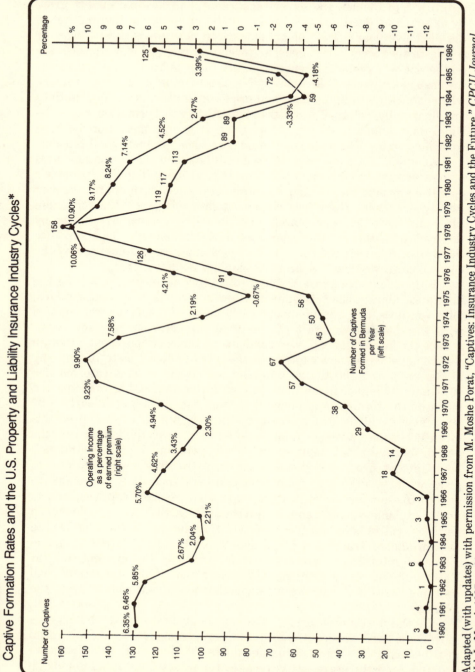

* Adapted (with updates) with permission from M. Moshe Porat, "Captives: Insurance Industry Cycles and the Future," *CPCU Journal,* Vol. I, March 1987, p. 39.

uals and organizations. However, captives will also compete with insurers, brokers, financial institutions, and others in the supply and distribution of insurance and risk management products and services other than in a risk-bearing capacity. Captives will establish their market share by providing expert services, by using their relative competitive advantage, and by supplying products to their own "captive clientele," that is, to parent company's employees and their families, customers, suppliers, and associated members.

Captives and the Public Interest

Having presented a view of what to expect with regard to the captive movement, the author raises a related but far more complex issue underlying this topic: do captive companies serve the public interest? Since the author believes that this question is one about which knowledgeable persons may hold different, valid views, a definitive answer will not be provided. Nevertheless, the issue will be raised and the opposing points of view briefly outlined.

Proponents of the captive concept could point out several aspects that are beneficial to the public interest. First, it could be argued that any measure that improves the economic efficiency of an organization or reduces the ancillary costs of its support services is of some benefit to society. If captives can accomplish such objectives for their owners, they can also achieve worthwhile results for society (through lower prices, increased output, and so on). Captives may also be considered socially beneficial whenever they provide coverage not otherwise available. Captives can provide a means of funding potential losses, the adverse consequences of which would undoubtedly be worse for society (or some of its members) than would be the case in the absence of such coverages. Similarly, if captives can help the earnings of a firm become more stable over time, captives thereby serve the public interest because stable corporate earnings help to create a more stable economy. Finally, it can be argued that captives provide additional financial capacity for the insurance industry. Most people would probably agree that to the extent this statement is true, society indirectly benefits.

In a survey of 204 Bermuda captives, operators were asked to express their opinion regarding the contribution, if any, of their captives to the public interest. Public interest was identified along three dimensions: (1) availability of insurance coverage, (2) reliability of the insurance product, and (3) its affordability. A contribution to the public interest is made by a captive when it increases the availability of some coverages that otherwise would not be available; if it operates more efficiently, or is well capitalized and well managed and thus reliable; or

Exhibit 11-12
Captives Contribution to Public Interest Survey Responses*

Criterion	Yes	Somewhat/ Not Sure	No
Increase Insurance Availability	45.8%	26.7%	27.5%
Promote Insurance Reliability	76.1	5.3	18.6
Promote Insurance Affordability	61.8	17.6	20.6

*Reprinted with permission from M. Moshe Porat, "Serving the Public Interest," *Business Insurance* (2 April 1984), p. 65.

if it adds to competition that results in lower prices and, in turn, affordability. The results of the survey are summarized in Exhibit 11-12.

It appears that most of the respondents believe that captives, to some degree, serve the public interest in each area. Somewhat surprising is that only 45.8 percent of the operators supported the claim that captives increase insurance availability. This may indicate that obtaining difficult-to-find coverage was not a major factor in forming a captive. This is even more apparent in a soft market.

It is natural that operators or managers cannot be completely unbiased in answering this question. But the contribution of some types of captives (the group and associations) to public interest was also stated by the 1977 Federal Interagency Task Force on products liability. It raised four possible purported contributions of captives:

1. they will operate more efficiently than standard insurance companies
2. they will encourage the parent to utilize better loss prevention plans,
3. they will give the parent more control over litigation and settlement, and
4. they will allow the parent company to deal directly in the reinsurance market.

The task force also noted that captives "provide a potential for relieving availability and affordability problems for some product liability insureds," and that "it may be constructive to establish such requirements at the federal level and permit captives to obtain charter at that level."[175]

Opponents of the captive concept could conclude that captives fail to serve the public interest and only benefit the interests of their owners. Perhaps the major reservation expressed about captive companies concerns the inadequacy of their financial strength in view of the catastrophic loss possibilities they face. Those who believe that captives lack adequate financial strength could also find examples of captives lacking a diversity of loss exposures in their portfolio of coverages. Some would consider their reinsurance arrangements to be inadequate, too. On a related point, one could argue that the surplus of captives is vulnerable to expropriation by way of the "declaration" of special dividends whenever the owners encounter a period of embarrassing financial circumstances. Others would assert, as has the IRS, that captives are really nothing more than an artificial means of avoiding taxes. Some would also suggest that captives are a means of bypassing some form of bothersome regulatory controls. Still others might say that captives do not augment the capacity of the insurance industry, but that they only serve the interests of their owners. Finally, others who oppose the captive concept would simply say that captives do not achieve their stated goals and, therefore, they constitute a wasteful side activity for industry to pursue.

Convincing arguments can be offered both for and against the captive concept, but the history of captive companies is too brief to support any conclusive evaluation of the captive movement. If captives do legitimately serve the public interest, their use should be encouraged. On the other hand, if captives merely serve the self-interests of owners at the society's expense, their use should be discouraged.

The tax laws currently favor the use of commercial insurance over funded retention programs or captives by permitting deductions for premiums paid to commercial insurance companies but not for contributions to funded retention programs. Captives do not fall neatly into either category and, as noted, the matter of income tax deductions for premiums paid to them is still not completely settled. If captives are deemed ultimately to serve the public interest, they will undoubtedly flourish. For that matter, they may even be encouraged through government fiscal policy. If captives do not serve the public interest, their future will be threatened and possibly discouraged by public policy.

Monograph Notes

1. These data were gathered by M. Moshe Porat from the files of the government of Bermuda. For further details, see M. Moshe Porat, "Offshore Captive Insurers' Structure: Macro and Micro Perspectives," in *Risk Retention: Alternative Funding Methods*, CPCU Monograph, Winter 1983 and M. Moshe Porat, "Captives, Insurance Industry Cycles, and the Future," *CPCU Journal*, Vol. 40, No. 1 (March 1987), pp. 39-45.
2. See *1987 Captive Insurance Company Directory* (Darien, CT: Tillinghast/TPF&C, 1987). Some estimates of the number of captives in existence include in their tallies wholly owned insurance subsidiaries whose primary underwriting emphasis is on insuring or reinsuring exposures of the general public. In this monograph the emphasis is on captives that handle all or significant portions of the exposures of the interests that own or control the respective captives themselves. The author's estimate is at the upper end of that range, $10 billion. Some include in their tallies about 700 credit life insurers. This would raise the 1986 estimate of the number of "captives" to about 2,700.
3. *Captive Insurance Company Reports* (Darien, CT: Tillinghast/TPF&C, January 1987).
4. *1987 Captive Insurance Company Director*, pp. 157-202.
5. The latest IRS pronouncement on the subject of captives is contained in Revenue Ruling 77-316. Basically, that ruling states that certain captive companies are not insurance companies; rather, they are a means of implementing a funded retention program. Revenue Ruling 77-316 is discussed in detail in this monograph as are the principles of the recent tax laws.
6. Frederick M. Reiss, "Corporations and the Captive Insurer," *Proceedings of the 12th Annual Insurance Conference*, The Ohio State University (1961), p. 15.
7. Robert C. Goshay, "Captive Insurance Companies," in *Risk Management*, H. Wayne Snider, ed. (Homewood, IL: Richard D. Irwin, Inc., 1964), p. 82.
8. Goshay, "Captive Insurance Companies," p. 82.
9. Goshay, "Captive Insurance Companies," p. 82.
10. The validity of the distinguishing characteristics provided by Goshay is questionable. For example, Goshay states that "the owners or controllers of a captive insurance company are banded together for a purpose other than insurance, which is quite opposite from the situation in a mutual insurance company." This observation, however, does not hold in the case of the many jointly owned captives that have been formed to solve insurance problems faced by the owners. The observation does hold, however, for an "association or group captive."
11. This approach for illustrating the captive insurance concept is borrowed,

with minor modifications, from Goshay, "Captive Insurance Companies," pp. 83-84.

12. For a detailed discussion of these concepts see M. Moshe Porat, "Offshore Captive Insurers' Structure," pp. 55-114.
13. Porat, "Offshore Captive Insurers' Structure," pp. 56-59.
14. Porat, "Offshore Captive Insurers' Structure," pp. 89-91.
15. M. Moshe Porat, "The Bermuda Captive—A Comprehensive Evaluation and Analysis," *Risk Management* (March 1982), pp. 45-54; and "The Bermuda Captive's Organizational Structure and Goals," *Risk Management* (April 1982), pp. 32-40. The interval stems from insufficient information regarding some captives owners' identity and the proportions of unrelated business in their portfolios.
16. Porat, "The Bermuda Captives—A Comprehensive Evaluation and Analysis." A 1984 estimate of the proportion of group captives was about nineteen percent of all known and listed captives. See also *1987 Captive Insurance Company Directory.*
17. Based on 1985 statistics collected by Dr. Porat from data provided by the Government of Bermuda.
18. *Captive Insurance Company Reports* (October 1984). Some suspected this move as a prelude to Exxon pulling out or closing the captive altogether.
19. "Royal Industries Slates Captive to Underwrite Products Liability Risk," *Business Insurance* (9 February 1976), p. 2.
20. Susan Alt, "Catholic Hospitals Form a Captive for Malpractice Cover," *Business Insurance* (26 July 1976), p. 1.
21. Andrew J. Barile, *Managing Captive Insurance Companies* (Hartsdale, NY: 1972), p. 42.
22. "Dentists Form Captive for Malpractice Risks," *Business Insurance* (11 August 1980), p. 3.
23. "Lawyers' Mutual Draws Members Despite Objection," *Business Insurance* (7 January 1980), p. 24.
24. Porat, "Offshore Captive Insurers' Structure," p. 72.
25. For a detailed discussion of the early operation of OIL, see Roy D. Jackson, Jr., "OIL: An Insurance Mechanism to Meet the Energy/Capital Crisis," *Risk Management*, Vol. 21 (October 1974), pp. 22ff. For more recent information, see *Captive Insurance Company Reports* (June 1980), pp. 4-5.
26. *Captive Insurance Company Reports* (June 1980), pp. 4-5.
27. Margaret LeRoux, "Gulf Pulls Out of OIL," *Business Insurance* (20 October 1975), pp. 1, 12.
28. Margaret LeRoux, "OIL Ltd. Continues as a Viable Alternative," *Business Insurance* (18 October 1976), p. 2.
29. *Captive Insurance Company Reports* (June 1980), p. 4.
30. "Statistical Studies, *"Best's Insurance Management Reports* (7 September 1981).
31. "First Hospital Owned Captive Formed in U.S.," *Business Insurance* (23 February 1976), p. 16.
32. "Harvard Hospitals' Malpractice Captive Projects Lower Premiums for

Insureds," *National Underwriter* (Property & Casualty Insurance Edition) (16 April 1976) pp. 11-12.

33. *Captive Insurance Company Reports* (May 1985).

34. Porat, "The Bermuda Captives—A Comprehensive Evaluation and Analysis," p. 52.

35. Bermuda government statistics (1985).

36. *Mutual Indemnity Ltd., Annual Report 1986.*

37. Lawrence L. Drake, Managing Director, Marsh & McLennan, from his presentation at the 11th International Captive Insurers Conference, Bermuda, March 1987.

38. For details see Janet Aschkenasy, "Capacity Crisis Spurs Explosion of Insurance Alternatives for Buyers," *National Underwriter* (Property & Casualty Insurance Edition) (29 August 1986), p. 3.

39. For more details see John Burville, "Creative Group Funding Excess Limits Higher Excess Retention in Captives" *Proceedings of the 11th International Conference on Captive Insurance Companies*, Bermuda, March 1987. (Darien, CT: Tillinghast/TPF&C).

40. Thus, one should continue to bear in mind that a "captive" and a "captive insurance company" are not necessarily the same thing. Unless the subsidiary enterprise engages in at least some insuring activities (as opposed to retention or noninsurance transfer of exposures), one should not refer to it as a captive *insurance* company. The difficulty, however, of distinguishing between insurance and noninsurance leads to a rather loose use of the term "captive insurance company." The author of this monograph does not purport to have used the terms, "captive" and "captive insurance company" correctly in every instance.

41. Porat, "Offshore Captive Insurer's Structure," p. 71.

42. Reiss, "Corporations and the Captive Insurer," pp. 19-20.

43. Edward P. Lalley, *Captive Insurance Companies* (New York: American Management Association, 1967), p. 10.

44. Reiss, "Corporations and the Captive Insurer," p. 20.

45. Goshay, "Captive Insurance Companies," p. 89.

46. Letter from W. F. Hanson, Vice President, Ideal Mutual Insurance Company, New York, 5 October 1976. Legislation effective in January 1963 eliminated the tax advantage. Since then, mutuals have been taxed on underwriting profits in the same manner as stock companies. Ideal Mutual, which was one of the leading fronting companies for captives during the 1970s and early 1980s, was liquidated in 1985 due to financial difficulties.

47. For more discussion of Belk's reasons for choosing the reciprocal form of organizations for its captive, see A. Grant Whitney, *The Captive Reciprocal* (New York: American Management Association, 1959), especially pp. 102-107.

48. Largely based on *Captive Insurance Company Reports* (January 1987) with author's adjustments. It is worth noting that the author does not include credit insurance companies (about 700) in this estimate because they are different from typical captives. Their development and changes

are independent of what is referred to in this monograph as the captive movement concept.

49. The estimates are based partly on an annual directory published by Tillinghast/TPF&C and other sources. Accurate statistics on captives are hard to find. Hardly any official source publishes such statistics, and there is no one accepted definition of a captive. Some of the statistics published or publicized include companies operated or owned by insurers or brokers, which function as regular insurers or reinsurers. It is debatable as to whether or not to include credit companies, how to consider dormant or inactive captives, and how to account for entities owned by other captives. As far as Bermuda is concerned the 1,200 estimate includes as many as 400 inactive or dormant entities and an additional 150 entities which are owned by insurance-related interests. Secrecy associated with captives adds considerably to the difficulty of establishing accurate estimates.

50. The text of the Bermuda Insurance Act of 1978 and of the current regulations can be obtained by writing to the Registrar of Companies, Bermuda Government Office Building, Parliament Street, Hamilton 5, Bermuda.

51. "Too Many Captives in Bermuda? Two Viewpoints," *Captive Insurance Company Reports* (April 1979), pp. 2-3.

52. For more details on motives in general, see Porat, "The Bermuda Captive—A Comprehensive Evaluation and Analysis," pp. 46-54.

53. Steve Sherwood, "Cayman Officials Say Quality Improving as Growth Slows," *Business Insurance* (2 April 1984), p. 45. The full text of the law, regulations, and statutory forms, including a review of Cayman business topics, can be obtained from Coopers and Lybrand, Chartered Accountants, P. O. Box 219, Grand Cayman, BWI. One packet is entitled "Captive Insurance Companies in the Cayman Islands."

54. "Special Issue on the Bahamas," *Captive Insurance Company Reports* (August-September 1980), pp. 44-47. See also Kathryn J. McIntyre, "Bahamas, Business and Government Stalk Captive Insurers," *Business Insurance* (6 April 1981), p. 44.

55. Steve Taravella, "Bahamas Prepares for Day in the Sun," *Business Insurance* (30 March 1987), p. 85.

56. Robert A. Finlayson, "Tax Treaty Helps Barbados Flourish," *Business Insurance* (30 March 1987), p. 82.

57. Judy Greenwald, "New Jersey Expected to Approve Captive Bill," *Business Insurance* (30 March 1987), p. 105.

58. Robert A. Finlayson, "Colorado Plans to Amend Statute," *Business Insurance* (30 March 1987), p. 98.

59. Dave Lenckus, "Tennessee Expects More Captive Growth," *Business Insurance* (30 March 1987), p. 100.

60. Len Strazewski, "New Law in U.S. Virgin Islands Gives Parents Another Choice," *Business Insurance* (2 April 1984), p. 74.

61. Michael Bradford, "Few Captives Seek Virgin Islands Home," *Business Insurance* (30 March 1987), p. 87.

62. James T. McIntyre, Jr., "Opportunity Knocks: The Risk Retention Act of 1986," *Risk Management* (March 1987), pp. 42-44.

63. *Captive Insurance Company Reports* (October-November 1986), pp. 1-3.
64. Jon Harkavy, "The Risk Retention Act of 1986: The Options Increase," *Risk Management* (March 1987), pp. 22-34.
65. Michael J. Mullen, "An Overview of the Risk Retention Act," *Risk Management* (January 1987), pp. 36-40.
66. Jerry Geisel, "Groups Mobilize to Use New Risk Retention Act," *Business Insurance* (20 October 1986), "Risk Retention Groups Could Fail: Regulator," *Business Insurance* (13 April 1987), p. 31.
67. Susan Alt, "Hospital Chains Use Own Insurer for Excess Covers," *Business Insurance* (23 August 1976), p. 1.
68. Telephone conversation with Richard Smith, Director of Insurance and Risk Management, Royal Industries, Inc., 13 October 1976.
69. Susan Alt, "Brunswick Enjoys 'Unbundled' Plan," *Business Insurance* (14 June 1976), p. 18.
70. Norman A. Baglini, "Problems and Practices in International Risk Management," *Best's Review* (Property/Casualty Insurance Edition), Vol. 77 (September 1976), pp. 94ff. Any one or more of several barriers could either prevent or dissuade U.S. business firms from having their captives licensed to do business in various foreign countries. Among these are "legislation prohibiting foreign insurance companies or prohibiting majority ownership by foreigners; regulations requiring investment of reserves in the country of premium origin or stipulating the statutory investment of such reserves; controls over remittances; lack of foreign exchange; and high deposit requirements." See pp. 94, 96.
71. "Levi's Foreign Risks Put into Offshore Sub," *Business Insurance* (14 July 1974), p. 26.
72. M. Moshe Porat, "Offshore Captive Insurers Underwriting Operations," *Best's Review*, (Property/Casualty Insurance Edition, May 1982), pp. 20-24.
73. Susan Alt, "Brunswick Enjoys 'Unbundled' Plan," p. 1.
74. "150 California Cities Told of Non-Renewals this Summer," *Business Insurance* (20 September 1976), p. 4.
75. Goshay, "Captive Insurance Companies," pp. 96-97.
76. See, for example, "Pension Law Restricts Corporate Use of Captives for Group Benefits," *Business Insurance* (2 September 1974), p. 1.
77. For a detailed analysis of the issues involving the use of captives in employee benefit programs, see Yale D. Tauber, Cynthia M. Combe, and Jude Anne Carluccio, *Utilization of Captives to Write Employee Benefit Business* (New York: LeBoeuf, Lamb, Leiby and MacRae). Mr. Tauber presented parts of this paper at the 11th Captive Insurance Conference in Bermuda, March 1987.
78. Tauber, p. 22.
79. Douglas McLeod, "Law Restricts Benefits Written by Captives," *Business Insurance* (30 March 1987), p. 65.
80. Porat, "Offshore Captive Insurers: Underwriting Operations," pp. 96-98, and recent updates.
81. Paul B. Ingrey, "Reinsurance of Captive Insurers," *Risk Management*, Vol. 19 (January 1972), p. 19.

82. Barile, *Managing Captive Insurance*, pp. 40-41.
83. Barile, *Managing Captive Insurance*, p. 38.
84. "Captives Warned to Avoid Conflict Areas," *Business Insurance* (10 March 1975), p. 54.
85. Kathryn J. McIntyre, "Bermuda Reinsurers Focus on Captive Business," *Business Insurance* (30 March 1987), p. 30.
86. *1987 Captive Insurance Company Directory*, p. 2.
87. Porat, "Offshore Captive Insurers' Structure," pp. 81-86. Also in *Business Insurance* (30 March 1987), p. 14.
88. M. Moshe Porat, "Operation and Management of Captives: Problem Areas," *Captive Insurance Company Review*, Vol. II, No. 9 (July 1983), pp. 10-16.
89. M. Moshe Porat, "The Insurance Factor in the Captive Movement," *The National Underwriter* (Property & Casualty Insurance Edition) (9 March 1984), p. 6.
90. For a detailed analysis of the insurance (or non-captive) sector in Bermuda see M. Moshe Porat and Anthony F. Gasich, "The Real Captive Movement in Bermuda," *Captive Insurance Company Reports*, September and October, 1987.
91. "Captive Insurers Cut Costs Abroad," *Business Week* (8 November 1976), p. 109.
92. "Captive Insurers Cut Costs Abroad," *Business Week* (8 November 1976), p. 109.
93. "Levi's Foreign Risks Put into Offshore Sub," p. 26.
94. Barile, *Managing Captive Insurance*, p. 9.
95. Barile, *Managing Captive Insurance*, pp. 9-10.
96. Alt, "Brunswick Enjoys 'Unbundled' Plan," p. 18.
97. *Captive Insurance Company Reports* (August 1978), p. 4.
98. *Captive Insurance Company Reports* (June 1980), p. 5.
99. *Captive Insurance Company Reports* (November 1985), p. 4.
100. John B. Laadt, "Captive Insurance Companies as a Method of Insuring Foreign Risks" (Master's Thesis, De Paul University, Chicago, IL, 1975), pp. 67-68.
101. Laadt, "Captive Insurance Companies as a Method of Insuring Foreign Risks," pp. 67-68.
102. Lalley, *Captive Insurance Companies*, p. 6.
103. Laadt, "Captive Insurance Companies as a Method of Insuring Foreign Risks," pp. 66, 144.
104. M. Moshe Porat, "The Impact of Captives on Insurance Markets in Developing Countries." Report to the United Nations Conference on Trade and Development, Geneva, Switzerland, April 1984.
105. Porat, "The Impact of Captives on Insurance Markets in Developing Countries," pp. 10-16.
106. Marie Krakowiecki, "Nuclear Insurance Pool Responds to Competitive Pressures from Captive," *Business Insurance* (19 April 1978), p. 61.
107. M. Moshe Porat, "The Investment Strategy, Instruments, and Rates of Return in Offshore Captive Insurers," *CPCU Journal*, Vol. 36 (March 1983), pp. 21-30.

108. Based on a summary of results from a 1986 survey of 80 captives on their investment practices conducted by M. Moshe Porat, Temple University.

109. Goshay, "Captive Insurance Companies," p. 118.

110. In the case of Kaiser Steel Co., the 9th Circuit Court in California in 1983 ruled in favor of a self-insurer's deductibility. The taxpayer was allowed to deduct currently self-insured loss reserves before they were actually paid. This was allowed under the accrual method of accounting, which allowed an expense to be deductible currently if "all the events" had occurred that determined the fact of liability and the amount had been determinable with reasonable accuracy. Following the 1984 Tax Reform Act, a new criterion for deductibility was established and referred to as the "economic performance" test, which simply means that losses and expenses are deductible only when actually paid.

111. The Internal Revenue Service has stated (in Revenue Ruling 77-316, discussed in this monograph) that it does not consider certain types of captives to be "true" insurance companies, and therefore premiums paid to such companies would not be considered a deductible expense. As brought out later, the courts have generally supported this revenue ruling.

112. Discussions of the issues involved can be found in many sources. For a good overview see "Captive Insurance Update," Peat, Marwick, Mitchell & Company, 1982.

113. In those cases where the parent company and the captive file a consolidated tax return, the parent company's premium expense and the captive's premium income offset each other, and thus the tax benefit resulting from the deductibility of the premium paid by the parent is eliminated.

114. Edward P. Lalley, *Self-Assumption, Self-Insurance and the Captive Insurance Company Concept* (New York: Risk and Insurance Management Society, 1975), p. 12.

115. Marianne Burge, "Foreign Risks and the Captive Insurance Company," *The Price Waterhouse Review* (Autumn 1970), p. 42.

116. For a more detailed discussion of the federal excise tax and the withholding tax, see Burge, "Foreign Risks," or Gerald I. Lenrow and Ralph Milo, "The Offshore Captive Insurance Company—What Are the U.S. Tax Consequences?" *Best's Review* (Property and Casualty Insurance Edition), Vol. 78 (March 1978), pp. 56ff. For an update on the status after the 1984 tax reforms, see P. Bruce Wright, "Choosing the Domicile that Suits Your Captive," *Risk Management* (July 1985), p. 31.

117. When a foreign insurance company derives more than 75 percent of its premium income from insuring or reinsuring "U.S. risks," it will be considered a CFC if U.S. shareholders (with 10 percent or more voting power) own more than 25 percent of the total voting power (IRC, Section 957[b]).

118. Internal Revenue Code Sections 953 and 954.

119. Internal Revenue Code Section 954 (c)(3).

120. For more details see William L. Burke and John J. Sarchio, "Life for Offshore Captives Under the New Tax Law," *Risk Management* (February 1987), p. 20.

121. Jim Leak, Addison Shuster, and Simon Israel, "New Tax Rules," *Business Insurance* (29 December 1986), p. 17.
122. The option of calculating the foreign tax credit on either basis was eliminated by the Tax Reform Act of 1976.
123. Internal Revenue Code Sections 807(c), 832, and 846.
124. Internal Revenue Code Section 832(b).
125. Internal Revenue Code Section 832(b).
126. A Revenue Ruling is an official interpretation of the tax law. While a Revenue Ruling can be contested and overturned in the courts, its impact nevertheless is more significant than any internal instructions the IRS may prescribe for its agents. Revenue Ruling 77-316 is also discussed in Section V of the monograph titled "Soft Spots in Insurance Theory," found in the second edition of this text.
127. Each of these audit rules is discussed in an article by Jerome S. Horvitz, entitled "Captive Insurance Companies: Their Economic and Tax Consequences," *CPCU Annals*, Vol. 27 (September 1974), pp. 197-202.
128. The amount so treated would be the captive's net premium income from its insurance and reinsurance operations (that is, reinsurance premium expense would be exempt).
129. The Interest Equalization Tax law expired in January 1974. Basically, this tax was one applied to the investments made by a U.S. entity in the securities of a foreign company (at the rate of 11¼ percent of the funds so invested). The tax was not to apply when the U.S. investor owned more than 10 percent of the foreign company, unless the foreign company was formed as a means of avoiding the interest equalization tax. While this tax never applied to premium payments, the IRS could have alleged that the foreign captive was formed to avoid this tax, especially if the capitalization of the foreign captive could be considered excessive.
130. For further information on Revenue Ruling 77-316, see (1) Kathryn N. Roberts, "IRS Axes Deductions for Premiums Paid to Captives; Court Test Awaited," *Business Insurance* (19 September 1977), pp. 1ff; (2) "A Special Report: Captive Insurance Companies," *The John Liner Letter*, Vol. 14, No. 10 (September 1977); (3) Gerald I. Lenrow and Ralph Milo, "Have Offshore Captives Been Captured—The Service Issues a Ruling," *Best's Review* (Property and Casualty Edition), Vol. 78 (November 1977), pp. 78ff; (4) Warren, McVeigh, and Griffin, "IRS Analysis of Dividends Is Sleeper in Captive Ruling," *Business Insurance* (6 March 1978), p. 34; (5) Sidney R. Pine, Abraham N. Stanger, and P. Bruce Wright, "IRS Revenue Ruling 77-316: Avoiding Its Consequences," *Risk Management*, Vol. 25 (April 1978), pp. 11ff.
131. The Ford Motor Company had a dispute with the IRS about deductibility of premiums paid to Ford's foreign captive, Transcon Insurance Company, Ltd., by Ford's foreign subsidiaries. The IRS assessed Ford about $6.6 million in additional taxes. The IRS said that the premiums paid by the subsidiaries to Transcon were really dividends constructively received by Ford. The IRS argued further that Ford then constructively paid the dividends to Transcon as additional contributions to Transcon's capital. The case was settled out of court. One of the conditions was reported to

have been that the terms of settlement were not to be discussed. This settlement, therefore, cannot serve as much of a precedent.

132. Financial Accounting Standards Board, Statement of Financial Accounting Standard No. 5, "Accounting for Contingencies" (March 1975), paragraph 27, pp. 13-14.

133. Sidney R. Pine, "The Case for Captive Insurers," *Harvard Business Review*, Vol. 50 (November-December 1972), pp. 142-148 at 147.

134. 71 U.S.T.C. 400 (1978).

135. Carnation Company v. Commissioner of Internal Revenue, 640 F.2d. 1010 (9th Cir., 1981). Reh. denied 13 May 1981.

136. The Carnation case is also discussed in Section V of the monograph titled "Soft Spots in Insurance Theory," found in the second edition of this text.

137. Extracted from briefs filed in litigation cited in Note 99. See also *Captive Insurance Company Reports* (October-November 1980), pp. 1-4.

138. *Captive Insurance Company Reports* (October-November 1980), pp. 1-4.

139. Civil Action 81-C-2046, Judge Jim R. Carrigan, Stearns-Roger v. U.S. For a discussion see Sidney R. Pine and P. Bruce Wright, "Legal Considerations: IRS Rules Colorado Captive's Premiums Not Deductible; Group Owned Insurer Seen as Taxable; Casualty Loss Rulings," *Risk Management* (January 1984), p. 14. Subsequent to the ruling (January 1984), the case was certified by the judge for appeal. This left the way open to Stearns-Roger to file a petition for leave to appeal.

140. Rhonda L. Rundle, "Stearns-Roger Loses Captive Insurer Tax Case," *Business Insurance* (21 November 1983), pp. 1, 30.

141. Beech Aircraft Corporation v. U.S. 84-2, U.S.T.C. Para. 9803.

142. Crawford Fitting Company v. U.S. 8J-1 U.S.T.C. Para. 9189.

143. Clougherty Packing Corporation v. Commissioner No. 1954-82.84 T.C.

144. Sidney R. Pine and P. Bruce Wright, "Court of Claims Rules on Deductibility of Premiums Paid to Wholly-Owned Insurance Subsidiaries," *Risk Management* (October 1985), pp. 14-18.

145. See IRS Rev. Rul. 78-358 and private rulings 8111087, 8250021, 8215066.

146. Letter to ARCO dated 30 March 1973 from Mr. A. Fichel, Chief Corporate Tax Branch, U.S. Treasury, quoted in John B. Laadt, "Captive Insurance Companies," p. 132. Two additional revenue rulings, 78-338 and 80-20, support the tax deductibility of premiums paid to group owned captives.

147. The theoretical effects on and practical implications on the overall risk portfolio of the captive by underwriting third-party business have been discussed in Alfred E. Hofflander and Blaine F. Nye, "Self-Insurance, Captives and Income Taxation," *The Journal of Risk and Insurance* (December 1984), pp. 702-709, and Barry D. Smith, "Analyzing the Tax Deductibility of Premiums Paid to Captive Insurers," *Journal of Risk and Insurance* (March 1986), pp. 85-103.

148. *Risk Management Reports*, Vol. VIII (1981), p. 11.

149. Indeed, in a 1981 Technical Advice Memorandum No. 8215066, the IRS casts doubt on the 51 percent benchmark that most interpreters of Revenue Ruling 77-316 believed to be the portion of unrelated business that would guarantee tax deductibility of premiums paid by parent to a single owned captive. The IRS in this memorandum refused to grant

support for such claims and said that it is up to the district IRS offices to determine the deductibility issue on a case by case basis no matter what the proportion of unrelated business. This attitude is further displayed in the Mobil case arguments.

150. Following the trend toward underwriting unrelated business, few captives and, more so, some mature captives began to be less prudent in underwriting third-party business. Almost inevitably, in periods of declining interest rates, that practice resulted in considerable losses and some tough decisions by the parent companies. A celebrated case was Walton Insurance Ltd., a wholly owned subsidiary of Phillips Petroleum Company, which practically went out of the business. Although such cases were a small minority of the captive population, which by and large is rather conservative in its underwriting practices, it led some observers and journalists to quick, pessimistic, and rather wrong conclusions about the captive movement generally. See, for example, John Dizard, "Danger Signals for Bermuda's Happy Captives," *Fortune* (23 January 1984). For an empirical analysis of captives' underwriting, see M. Moshe Porat, "Bermuda Captive Insurers: An Analysis of Underwriting Exposure Ratios," *CPCU Journal*, Vol. 35, No. 2 (June 1982), p. 95.

151. For a comprehensive discussion of the act, see Eric A. Wiening, "The Risk Retention Act—A Solution to What Problem?" *CPCU Journal*, Vol. 35, No. 3 (September 1983), pp. 174-192.

152. For a discussion of OIL's operations, see Roy D. Jackson, Jr., "OIL, Ltd. Has 85% of North Sea Spill," *Business Insurance* (16 May 1977), pp. 1, 36. For a list of OIL participants as of early 1980 and a description of OIL operations see *Captive Insurance Company Reports* (June 1980), pp. 4-5.

153. For a discussion of WESCAP's structure and operations, see Susan Alt, "First Association Captive in Colorado," *Business Insurance* (30 May 1977), pp. 2, 84.

154. *Captive Insurance Company Reports* (January 1987), p. 2.

155. Rosenbaum, *Risk Management Reports*, Vol. VIII, No. 1 (1980), p. 14.

156. The association's office is located at 1575 I Street, N.W., Washington, D.C. 20005.

157. Porat, "Offshore Captive Insurers' Structure," p. 78.

158. Capacity as a topic is treated in depth in the monograph titled "Insurance Capacity: Issues and Perspectives," found in the second edition of this text.

159. The problem may be illustrated by the experience of one of the gas company members that had $10 million insurance coverage from a large insurer in 1967 but was offered only $300,000 coverage in 1970; see "Insurance Largest Business Cost for Gas Companies; Captive Helps Some," *Business Insurance* (5 May 1975), p. 38.

160. The FASB was formed on 30 June 1972 as an independent organization within the private sector to develop standards of financial accounting and external reporting for industrial and commercial entities. It is the successor organization to the Accounting Principles Board of the American Institute of Certified Public Accountants.

161. Readers should be aware that the principles and practices for financial

accounting and external reporting are not always identical to accounting procedures required for compliance with the federal income tax laws. FASB Standard No. 5 speaks to the former, while the latter is governed by federal tax laws.

162. A contingency is defined as "an existing condition, situation, or set of circumstances, involving uncertainty as to possible gain or loss to an enterprise.... Resolution of the uncertainty may confirm the ... loss or impairment of an asset or the incurrence of a liability."

163. For more discussion of these issues see Mike Washom's editorial, "Nonfinancial Factor Count," *Captive Insurance Company Reports* (January 1987), pp. 3-4.

164. Porat, "Bermuda Captives Organizational Structure and Goals," *Risk Management* (April 1982), p. 37.

165. *Captive Insurance Company Reports* (November 1983), p. 7. See also Rosenbaum, "Captives Are Growing Despite Soft Market and New Funding Plans," *Business Insurance* (2 April 1984), p. 63.

166. See Rosenbaum, *Risk Management Reports*, Vol. VIII (1981), pp. 18-19 on the subject of "Captives as Cop-Outs."

167. For more discussion of premium volume required for a captive, see William A.D. Hare and Joseph C. Smetana, "Captive Insurance Companies." *An American Management Briefing* (New York: American Management Association, 1972), p. 9. As inflation proceeds, the suggested minimum should be raised accordingly.

168. The feasibility study team will usually be chaired by the organization's risk manager. Others generally involved are a corporate attorney, a company tax adviser, a company engineer with loss prevention experience, the current insurance company producer and/or other representatives, and an independent consultant familiar with captive insurers.

169. These two studies are discussed in Barile, *Managing Captive Insurance*, p. 44.

170. H. Felix Kloman, "The Future of Captives: 1986," *Risk Management Reports*, Vol. XIII, No. 1, January/February 1986. Also in *Captive Insurance Company Reports*, September 1986, p. 4.

171. M. Moshe Porat, "Captives, Insurance Industry Cycles and the Future," *CPCU Journal*, Vol. 40, No. 1, March 1987, pp. 39-45.

172. Porat, "Captives, Insurance Industry Cycles and the Future," p. 40. A test for statistical correlation (Spearman Rho statistic) measured the degree of correlation at about 50 percent and accepted the hypothesis of dependent relationship between operating income ratios and formation frequencies of new captives in Bermuda (1967 through 1986) with the probability of error less than 2 percent.

173. Porat, "Captives, Insurance Industry Cycles and the Future," p. 44.

174. Much of this discussion has been adapted from M. Moshe Porat, "The Captive Movement's Role in the Restructuring of the Insurance Industry," a forthcoming monograph of the Society of CPCU (Winter 1988).

175. M. Moshe Porat, "Serving the Public Interest." *Business Insurance* (2 April 1984), p. 65.

Selected Readings

Baglini, Norman A. *Global Risk Management: How U.S. International Corporations Manage Foreign Risks.* Risk Management Society Publishing, Inc., 1983.

Bawcutt, P.A. *Captive Insurance Companies.* Homewood, IL: Dow Jones-Irwin, 1982.

Burge, Marianne. "Foreign Risks and the Captive Insurance Company." *The Price Waterhouse Review,* Autumn 1970.

Business Insurance. Selected issues, notably annual Captives Markets Reports in April.

Captive Insurance Company Reports as published periodically by Risk Planning Group, Inc., Darien, CT.

Dauer, Robert, Editor and Publisher. *The John Liner Letter.* Selected Issues.

Doherty, Neil A. *Corporate Risk Management; A Financial Exposition.* McGraw-Hill, 1985, Chapter 16.

Goshay, Robert C. "Captive Insurance Companies." In *Risk Management,* Edited by H. Wayne Snider. Homewood, IL: Richard D. Irwin, Inc., 1964.

Greene, Mark R. and Serbein, Oscar N. *Risk Management: Text and Cases.* Reston, VA: Reston Publishing Company, Inc., 1978.

Horvitz, Jerome S. "Captive Insurance Companies: Their Economic and Tax Consequences." *CPCU Annals,* Vol. 27, September 1974, pp. 197-202.

The Impact of Captive Insurance Companies on the Insurance Markets of Developing Countries. United Nations Conference on Trade and Development. Geneva, Switzerland, December 1984.

Kloman, H. Felix and Rosenbaum, D. Hugh. "The Captive Insurance Phenomenon: A Cautionary Tale?" *The Geneva Papers on Risk and Insurance,* No. 23, April 1982, pp. 129-151.

Laadt, John B. "Captive Insurance Companies as a Method of Insuring Foreign Risks." Master's thesis, De Paul University, Chicago, IL, 1975.

Lalley, Edward P. *Captive Insurance Companies.* New York: American Management Association, 1967.

Leak, Jim; Shuster, Addison; and Israel, Simon. "New Tax Rules." *Business Insurance,* 29 December 1986, p. 17.

Lenrow, Gerald I. and Milo, Ralph. "Have Offshore Captives Been Captured?—The Service Issues a Ruling." *Best's Review* (Property and Casualty Insurance Edition), Vol. 78, November 1977, pp. 78-86.

———. "The Offshore Captive Insurance Company—What Are the U.S. Tax Consequences?" *Best's Review* (Property and Casualty Insurance Edition), Vol. 78, March 1978, pp. 56-64.

Pine, Sidney R. "Tax Factors of Foreign Captive Insurance Companies." *Risk Management,* Vol. 19, January 1972, pp. 22-24, 37-38.

———. "The Case for Captive Insurers." *Harvard Business Review,* Vol. 50, November-December 1972, pp. 142-148.

———. Stanger, Abraham M. and Wright, Bruce P. "IRS Revenue Ruling 77-316: Avoiding Its Consequences." *Risk Management*, Vol. 25, April 1978, pp. 11-23.

Porat, M. Moshe. "The Captive Movement's Role in the Restructuring of the Insurance Industry." A forthcoming monograph of the Society of CPCU, Winter 1988.

———. "Offshore Captive Insurer's Structure: Macro and Micro Perspectives." In *Risk Retention: Alternative Funding Methods*. Edited by N. A. Williams. Malvern, PA: The Society of Chartered Property and Casualty Underwriters, Winter 1983.

Risk Management Reports. Darien, CT: Tillinghast/TPF&C. Selected Issues.

Smith, Barry D. "Analyzing the Tax Deductibility of Premium Paid to Captive Insurers." *Journal of Risk and Insurance*, March 1986, pp. 85-103.

Wright, P. Bruce. "Choosing the Domicile that Suits Your Captive." *Risk Management*, July 1985, pp. 26-28, 30-32, and 34.

MONOGRAPH **12**

An Update on the Liability Crisis*

I. INTRODUCTION AND EXECUTIVE SUMMARY

In February of 1986, the Tort Policy Working Group issued a report entitled, "Report of the Tort Policy Working Group on the Causes, Extent and Policy Implications of the Current Crisis in Insurance Availability and Affordability."[1] As its title indicates, the report not only documented the existence of the crisis in insurance availability and affordability, but also analyzed its various causes and made a number of appropriate policy recommendations.

The following is an update of that report. It not only updates the Working Group's prior report in the sense of reviewing the past year's developments as to both the insurance crisis and tort law (and, most importantly, tort reform), but it also summarizes and analyzes recently published empirical data on our nation's tort system. In addition, it discusses new issues and questions relating to the liability crisis which have emerged in the course of the national debate during 1986 over the problems and the future of our civil justice system.

The material under the heading, An Update On the Availability and Affordability of Liability Insurance, summarizes the current state of insurance availability and affordability in the United States. It indicates that while availability problems have substantially ameliorated since a

*This monograph is adapted from a March 1987 paper prepared by the Tort Policy Working Group established by the Attorney General of the United States. The Working Group initially published a report titled, "Report of the Tort Policy Working Group on the Causes, Extent and Policy Implications of the Current Crisis in Insurance Availability and Affordability" in February 1986. This report is a follow-up to that initial report.

year ago, they continue to exist in certain lines or types of coverage, where they remain serious. Affordability problems also have ameliorated, but only in the sense that premiums appear to have stabilized at much higher levels. This increased availability and price stability has been accomplished by, and in no small part is a result of, the use of higher deductibles, lower coverage limits, and additional policy exclusions and limitations. Moreover, the past year has witnessed an increasing reliance on both self-insurance and captive insurer programs, though it remains to be seen whether such arrangements provide reliable long-term insurance coverage. Most importantly, this section shows that, despite some assertions to the contrary, the impact of the crisis in insurance availability and affordability continues to be felt—often acutely—throughout much of the American economy.

The material headed, The Insurance Industry's Economic Performance, updates the Working Group's prior analysis of the economic state of the property and liability insurance industry. It indicates that the industry's profitability in 1986 improved markedly from 1984 and 1985, although its 1986 rate of return was roughly equivalent to its ten-year average, and was slightly less than the ten-year rate of return for Fortune 500 industrial corporations. This section also shows that the two key lines that have been central to insurance availability and affordability problems—commercial general liability and medical malpractice—continue to generate disproportionately high underwriting losses. These two lines produced 13 percent of the industry's written premiums in 1986, but accounted for 33 percent of the industry's total underwriting loss. This section also briefly discusses the fact that while the industry's profitability has varied cyclically, the industry's economic downturn in the mid-1980s was far more serious than its downturn in the mid-1970s.

The material headed, The Contribution of Tort Law to the Crisis in Insurance Availability and Affordability, addresses a number of different issues relating to our tort system. The section on jury awards analyzes data recently published by the Rand Corporation's Institute for Civil Justice on jury award trends in Cook County, Illinois, and San Francisco from 1960 through 1984. The Institute's data, which are inflation-adjusted, show that during this period the average jury malpractice award increased by 2,167 percent (from $52,000 to $1,179,000) in Cook County and 830 percent (from $125,000 to $1,162,000) in San Francisco. The comparable increase in average jury product liability awards was 212 percent (from $265,000 to $828,000) in Cook County and 1,016 percent (from $99,000 to $1,105,000) in San Francisco.

Even more astounding is the increase in the "expected jury award"—the average jury award multiplied by plaintiff's likelihood of success. From 1960 to 1984, the expected jury malpractice award (also inflation-adjusted) increased by 4,254 percent (from $13,000 to $566,000) in Cook County and 1,172 percent (from $34,000 to $616,000) in San Francisco. The comparable increase in expected jury product liability awards was 445 percent (from $76,000 to $414,000) in Cook County and 927 percent (from $56,000 to $575,000) in San Francisco.

It is interesting to note that both the average jury award and expected jury award data show that most of the increase in jury verdicts from 1960 to 1984 occurred during the 1980 to 1984 period. For example, in many of the expected jury award categories, the increase in awards from 1980 to 1984 was double or triple the entire increase in jury awards from 1960 to 1980.

The Institute's data also show a very substantial increase in inflation-adjusted, million-dollar jury awards. Of particular interest is the fact that million-dollar awards accounted for 85 percent of the total damages awarded by Cook County juries in 1980 to 1984 (as compared to 4 percent in 1960 to 1964) and 58 percent of the total damages awarded by San Francisco juries during the same period (as compared to 14 percent in 1960 to 1964). Thus, a small percentage of all tort cases appears to account for a very large percentage of the total tort damages awarded by juries.

The material under the heading, Case Filings, addresses a number of arguments that have been raised regarding the Working Group's evidence of substantial growth in product liability and medical malpractice cases filed in federal court. This section discusses the recent study of the National Center for State Courts, which has been widely cited for the proposition that there is no "litigation explosion" in the United States. This section not only identifies a number of serious methodological deficiencies in the Center's study, but notes that because the Center's study aggregates all tort filings—including automobile accident cases—it cannot and does not provide any meaningful insights as to the growth in the type of complex tort litigation, such as product liability, medical malpractice and many municipal liability cases that have been at the center of the debate over tort reform.

This section also answers a number of assertions that have been made regarding the methodology and meaning of the federal district court caseload data compiled by the Administrative Office of the United States Courts.

The section headed, Punitive Damages, discusses the most recent data collected by the Institute for Civil Justice on punitive damage awards. It also notes the growing consensus within the legal community that punitive damages have become a source of substantial litigation abuse, and it discusses a number of reasons why punitive damages need to be reformed. Of particular importance is the fact that punitive damages not only exacerbate insurance availability and affordability problems, but that they often serve as a significant obstacle to settlement, even where the likelihood of a punitive damage award is relatively small.

The section titled, Transaction Costs, discusses data recently published by the Institute for Civil Justice on the overall transaction costs of the tort litigation system. The data show, for example, that out of a total tort litigation expenditure in 1985 of $29 to $36 billion, plaintiffs received at most $14 to $16 billion. If only nonautomobile tort cases are considered, the net compensation paid plaintiffs amounted to only 43 percent of the system's total expenditures.

The section headed, Doctrinal Changes in Tort Law, discusses the fact that many of the current problems of the tort system can be traced to the sweeping doctrinal changes in tort law embraced by the courts over the past two decades. These doctrinal changes almost universally seem to have shared one common objective—to increase plaintiff's likelihood of obtaining compensation. As noted in this chapter, this has led to a systematic undermining of the most fundamental principles of tort liability—most importantly, the roles of fault and causation. The section notes that this judicial attack on the traditional limitations and conditions placed on tort liability has not only had the effect of increasing the amount of tort liability, but has introduced considerable uncertainty and unpredictability into tort law. This uncertainty and unpredictability greatly exacerbates the already serious problems of the tort system, and substantially increases the cost of liability insurance. And, as importantly, the lack of predictability has undermined and perverted the deterrent role of tort law.

The section headed, Public and State Support for Tort Reform, summarizes the remarkable success of tort reform in 1986. It describes the wide-spread popular support for tort reform, as indicated by opinion polls, ballot initiatives, the breadth of many of the coalitions formed to advocate tort reform, and even the support for tort reform from much of the legal profession. The section also describes the National Governors Association's recent *unanimous* endorsement of product liability reform, as well as the support for tort reform of a number of State Commissions and Task Forces which were directed to analyze the insurance and liability crisis and make appropriate recommendations. In addition, this section summarizes the extraordinary record of tort reform initiatives in the State legislatures in 1986, a year in which over two-thirds of the States enacted tort reform legislation of one sort of another. Finally, the chapter briefly summarizes the state legislative activity last year relating to insurance regulation.

The next section, An Analysis of Various Tort Reform Provisions, analyzes six areas of tort reform which were the subject of considerable legislative activity in state legislatures in 1986. The analysis reviews the strengths and weaknesses of some of the different legislative reform formulations enacted by the states. Where appropriate, this section also sets out the legislative provisions drafted by the Working Group which were part of the Administration's civil justice reform package submitted both last year and this year to the Congress, and explains the reasons for the specific legislative language adopted by the Working Group.

The section headed, The Relationship of Tort Reform to Insurance Availability and Affordability, addresses an issue that has been central to the debate over tort reform—whether such reforms in fact have a significant effect on insurance availability and affordability. The chapter explains the reasons why tort reforms take some time to affect the insurance market. But it also notes that there is persuasive evidence that over the long-term tort reforms can have a very substantial impact on insurance. Specifically, the chapter compares the experience of California physicians, who have the benefit of a rigorous medical malpractice reform statute enacted in 1975, with that of New York and Florida physicians, who practice in States with far weaker medical malpractice reforms. The difference in the experience of California physicians to that of their New York and Florida colleagues is instructive, to say the least. The rate of increase of medical malpractice premiums paid by New York and Florida physicians from 1980 to 1986 was substantially higher than for California physicians; indeed, for high risk specialties such as obstetrics/gynecology and neurosurgery, the rate of increase was two to three times larger in New York and Florida than in California. And the premiums paid by obstetricians/gynecologists in 1985 was substantially less in California than in New York or Florida for similar coverage, both in absolute dollar terms as well as in the percentage of physician net income and physician gross revenue. Accordingly, it seems evident that strong tort reform measures, if given sufficient time, can have a very substantial impact on the insurance market.

The appendix to the report provides the results of an economic analysis by the Antitrust Division of the Department of Justice, prepared at the request of the Working Group, of the causes of the crisis in insurance availability and affordability. The analysis reviews the merits of the four most commonly alleged causes of the crisis— insurer collusion, imprudent insurer business practices and declines in investment income, State insurance regulation, and changes in tort liability. It finds that it is unlikely that any of the first three of these alleged causes in fact caused the crisis. The analysis concludes that only the last alleged cause—changes in tort liability—can be directly responsible for the recent availability and affordability problems in property and liability insurance. Based on its review of the property and liability industry's financial performance, the Antitrust Division's analysis concludes that two specific aspects of the tort system— changes in the average awards, and increased uncertainty—have contributed greatly to the crisis in insurance availability and affordability.

The Conclusion to the Report lists eight conclusions of the Working Group regarding the insurance and liability crisis and the appropriate response of the federal government to that crisis.

Richard K. Willard
Chairman
Tort Policy Working Group

Robert L. Willmore
Chairman
Task Force on Liability
Insurance Availability

II. AN UPDATE ON THE AVAILABILITY AND AFFORDABILITY OF LIABILITY INSURANCE

In its report last year, the Tort Policy Working Group documented the existence of a serious crisis in insurance availability and affordability. The report identified a number of industries, professionals, public entities, and other purchasers of liability insurance that were experiencing extraordinary premium increases (often in combination with lower limits and higher deductibles), or, in some instances, were unable to obtain any insurance coverage at all. The report concluded that there were two primary causes underlying this crisis: the economic difficulties of the insurance industry—essentially a short-term (but potentially recurring) problem; and, the deteriorating tort system—a long-term problem which appears to have worsened considerably in recent years. As noted in the conclusion to the report, "It is likely that these [economic problems of the insurance industry] will work themselves out in the short-term as the insurance industry restores its desired level of profitability, and as other insurance industry developments ... are implemented."[2] The Working Group Report also concluded, however, that while this might mean that some unavailability problems would be resolved, insurance premiums would remain high, and *affordability* problems accordingly would remain a serious and long-term concern.[3]

The past year has proved that the Working Group's predictions were correct. The insurance crisis has, in fact, ameliorated; that is, premiums appear to have stabilized at now much higher levels, and unavailability problems have limited themselves to specific lines or types of coverage. Much like the oil crisis of the early 1970s following the OPEC oil embargo, after experiencing an initial shock and immediate serious economic dislocations, the public appears to have resigned itself to an era of much higher prices.

It is important to note, however, that stability in prices and greater availability of insurance is not merely the result of the substantial premium increases of the past two years. For one thing, insurers appear to have abandoned certain risks they have found to be too unpredictable or open-ended to insure with any degree of certainty. In some instances they have abandoned these risks simply by refusing to write coverage; in other instances they have written some coverage but sharply reduced their exposure through low limits or the use of claims-made policies. All of these latter developments essentially achieve the same purpose—they force the purchaser of insurance to retain far more risk than it would prefer, thereby limiting the uncertainty faced by the insurer. While this may make insurance available where it otherwise might be unavailable, and bring down the cost of coverage to an affordable level, it means that many risks are either uninsured or underinsured.

Moreover, much of the new found stability in premiums, as well as some of the availability of insurance, is the result of recently instituted self-insurance programs. It remains to be seen whether these self-insurance programs will, over the long term, provide a stable source of insurance that the commercial market is unwilling to offer at affordable prices. If these self-insurance programs should fail, the results may be even more adverse for the United States economy than the most extreme aspects of the recent crisis in insurance availability and affordability. Unfortunately, the experience of the captive insurance companies (widely known as "bedpan mutuals") established by many physicians in the mid-1970s as a result of a crisis in medical malpractice insurance suggests that these efforts, through capable of providing short-term relief, are not always a viable long-term solution.

Finally, as noted, there continue to be serious availability problems in certain lines or types of coverage, particularly in those areas with "long-tail" exposure—that is, where the liability may not manifest itself for many years, perhaps not even for decades. For many of these purchasers of insurance, the crisis has not abated in the least, and may in fact be even more pressing today than a year ago.

The following is an update on the state of insurance availability and affordability.

Insurance Coverage Summaries

Year-end reports in the business press note increased capacity and greater availability of liability insurance than existed a year ago. Prices are still high, but the days of triple-digit percentage increases appear to be over. While serious problems remain in certain markets—environmental coverage, medical malpractice, and certain product liability risk classes—in general, availability is greater and prices have largely stabilized, albeit at a much higher level.

The National Association of Insurance Commissioners (NAIC) released two availability surveys in December, 1986. The survey of regulators concluded that improvement in availability has occurred overall as well as in several individual liability lines. Lines identified by 25 percent or more of the responding states as showing great or slight improvement were day care, nurse-midwives, restaurant liquor liability, truckers liability, and exterminators liability. However, additional problem areas were identified in the categories of recreational liability exposures, professional liability and product liability.

The following summaries of changes in particular types of liability coverage were derived from reports in the business press and insurer reports.

Environmental Impairment Liability Insurance (EIL) and Sudden and Accidental Pollution Coverage A recent NAIC survey of state insurance departments found that thirty-seven states reported availability problems with environmental liability. NAIC is currently conducting a study of the environmental liability market.

Most package policies (both commercial multiple peril and commercial general liability policies) now specifically exclude pollution risks of all types as part of their comprehensive coverage.

Directors and Officers Liability (D&O) While availability problems are easing somewhat, D&O liability remains tight according to the NAIC availability survey. Coverage is still not available for certain risks, and desired liability limits may not be available.

Year-end reports suggest that D&O coverage is improving; capacity is growing, and new facilities are developing. Reinsurance also is more available, but prices remain high. One D&O insurer has reentered the market covering small and emerging businesses after not writing any D&O for eighteen months.

The NAIC December 1986 report on the availability of D&O coverage concluded that the line is experiencing some improvements although coverage is still not available for certain risks, and deductibles and premiums have increased, with desired limits not always available. Underwriters have indicated to NAIC, however, that they have increased previous limits and are writing new business.

A recent poll of Fortune 1,000 companies conducted by Heidrick & Struggles (an executive search firm) found that D&O insurance premiums increased by an average of 506 percent in 1986. Twenty percent of the poll's respondents reported that their D&O insurance premium had increased by more than 999 percent over 1985.

Bank Fidelity Bond Coverage The American Bankers Association has created a captive to provide D&O coverage of up to $2 million and bankers blanket bonds of up to $3 million.

Motor Carrier Liability Coverage While there still are serious problems, there appear to be improvements in the availability of long-haul trucking coverage—primarily as a result of less difficulty in obtaining reinsurance.

Liquor Liability Coverage Coverage for liquor liability is still a severe problem in some areas of the United States. A recently completed NAIC survey of liquor liability coverage concluded that there is an availability problem, but it varies significantly among the states and by type of liquor establishment. Demand for liquor liability coverage has increased as more liquor vendors who previously were uninsured have sought to obtain coverage. As demand has increased, capacity, particularly in excess lines, has diminished.

Medical Malpractice Insurance Medical malpractice insurance remains exceptionally tight. The major commercial insurers are writing only renewals, and are not writing new policies. Substantial insurance is being written by physician captive mutuals. The formation of two medical malpractice risk retention groups should increase capacity.

Commercial General Liability (CGL) Commercial general liability policies are available for most but not all risks. Prices have stabilized at the higher levels, and no further major increases are predicted for the near future. The new CGL forms exclude pollution liability; while this may increase availability, it necessitates the purchase of pollution liability separately (where available) or self-insurance. Product liability coverage is still tight for long-tail products, as well as specific products such as pharmaceuticals and chemicals.

Excess Coverage Excess coverage for large risks continues to be difficult to find, but the availability situation has eased considerably. Brokers reportedly are able to assemble excess liability limits of $50 million to $100 million by using conventional markets, and even higher limits through the use of alternative markets. Capacity in excess coverage for liability risks has expanded with the entry of new insurers. Primary among these is X.L. Insurance Co., Ltd., an insurer formed by over sixty major corporations, and American Casualty Excess Insurance, Ltd., a syndicate of large insurers. These companies are reported to have begun offering policies covering claims in excess of $25 million.

Reinsurance Capacity is increasing both in the United States and London reinsurance markets. It is estimated that the United States market has twice the capacity for general liability and specialty casualty risks it had a year ago.

Capacity in the London market is up significantly, but a number of restrictive coverage clauses are in use. London reinsurers are providing reinsurance for the United States, but are restricting coverage through the use of sunset clauses, date of loss clauses, event definitions, exposure unit rating, and pollution exclusion clauses. London insurers have expressed a preference for covering homogeneous risks under a treaty, a preference that might make risk retention groups attractive risks.

Sectoral Summaries

Trade associations representing each of the sectors discussed in the Working Group's prior report were contacted for updated information. A few of the contacted associations had no new information. The following is a summary of the available updated information.

Municipalities Municipalities, with some exceptions, continue to face serious difficulties in obtaining insurance. There has been a substantial movement toward both self-insurance and pooling arrangements among municipalities. For example, in California, 21 municipal liability pools cover 350 of the state's 444 cities. NAIC's Subcommittee on Governmental Liability (chaired by the Alliance of American Insurers) conducted a survey of market conditions over the past eighteen months, and concluded that available capacity has *dropped* significantly. Several insurers and reinsurers have dropped out of the municipal liability market. The remaining insurers are raising prices and tightening underwriting terms, including moving to claims-made forms for some lines.

Transportation Railroads have experienced a complete unavailability of insurance for requirements in excess of $20 million in the past year. To solve this problem several railroads joined together to form the Railroad Association of Insurance Limited, a Bermuda captive, specializing in railroad insurance at the $50 to $100 million range only.

The industry is looking for a similar solution for their $25 to $50 million insurance requirements.

According to the General Accounting Office, about 1,300 motor carriers went out of business in 1985 due to lack of insurance. More than 12,000 trucking insurance policies reportedly were cancelled. Carriers have been forced to pay higher premiums for less coverage. The American Trucking Association is working to develop an insurance source for its members. In some states long-haul truck risks have been covered through assigned risk pools.

Publishing The United States book publishing industry is troubled by both sharply rising costs and unavailability of liability insurance. Policy increases in 1986 averaged 200 percent to 300 percent over 1985 premiums, and some publishers have had their deductibles raised from $25,000 to $100,000. Reportedly, some policies now pay only for liability judgments but not the cost of defending lawsuits. Publishers of "controversial" books are having difficulty getting liability insurance of any type.

Magazine and newspaper publishers continue to have cost and availability problems, particularly for libel insurance. Premiums for newspapers have risen 10 percent to 20 percent over the past year; those for magazines are up 30 percent to 200 percent. This is somewhat less than doubling and tripling of premiums experienced by both newspaper and magazine publishers in 1985. Deductibles continue to rise, but more modestly than in 1985, when they more than doubled for many companies.

Nurse-Midwives In July 1986, ten insurers formed a consortium to provide professional liability insurance for certified nurse-midwives who are members of the American College of Nurse-Midwives. Policies are written on a claims-made basis and offer three different limits of coverage. This action followed the release of a study funded by the insurance industry which identified risk characteristics and risk management techniques, and which also presented proposed liability rates. These actions are believed to have alleviated availability problems in this line.

Dairy and Food Industries A February 1986 survey of its members by the Drug and Food Industries Supply Association generated responses from 21 percent of its membership. Ninety-five percent of the respondents found liability insurance coverage to be available, and 93 percent of these had experienced premium increases for the same or less coverage. Thirty-four percent had increases of 10 percent to 50 percent; 22 percent had increases between 51 percent and 100 percent; 35 percent reported increases between 101 percent and 500 percent, and

3 percent had increases over 500 percent. Respondents reported difficulty in obtaining satisfactory coverage in:

Products	55%
General (Casualty)	32%
Officer and Director	15%
Umbrella or Excess	15%
Transportation	12%
Environmental	11%
Professional	6%

Architects and Engineers A survey of 1,600 firms conducted by the American Consulting Engineers Council found that engineers nationwide experienced average increases of 43 percent in the cost of their professional liability insurance in 1986 over 1985. Structural engineering and small firms were hit the hardest. Nineteen percent of the survey respondents reported "going bare" in 1986, compared with 13 percent in 1985.

Day Care Centers Problems continue with both availability and affordability for some day care centers, although the situation seems to have eased somewhat since 1985. Problems appear to be greatest for home day care providers caring for more than three children and for small commercial operations. As of May 1986, CAL-CARE, the California market assistance plan for day care centers, had received 320 completed applications—of those, 238 applicants received quotes, 43 were rejected for not meeting underwriting standards, and 39 were pending.

Toy Manufacturers The Toy Manufacturers of America reports that established members of the industry are having no problems obtaining liability insurance, but that some small companies just entering the market have been unable to obtain insurance. During 1986, of the ninety-nine companies that contacted the association about their premiums, 50 percent had increases of 25 percent or more, 30 percent had increases of 15 percent to 24 percent, and the remainder had no change in their premiums. Thirty-five to forty small companies are considering the development of a captive insurance plan for the industry.

Household Appliance Manufacturers The problem of insurance costs remains as serious as a year ago. Costs are reported to be still increasing. Companies are generally able to get primary coverage of $1 million, but they have difficulty getting coverage above that amount. The Association of Home Appliance Manufacturers is considering setting up a captive insurer if reinsurance can be obtained.

Medical Equipment Although product liability insurance remains an urgent problem for the medical equipment industry, the situation has improved slightly over 1985 and early 1986, when one in five members of the Health Industry Manufacturers Association had its insurance cancelled or not renewed. Insurance availability is expected to improve in 1987, so that the majority of companies will be able to obtain insurance, with rates expected to remain at current levels. But members more often are getting claims-made policies with legal defense costs included in the overall settlement limits. The Medical Device Mutual Assurance and Reinsurance Company, a captive, has seen its membership increase between September 1984 and September 1986 from 35 to 305 companies. As of December 1986, membership stood at 325 companies.

Chemical and Pharmaceutical Availability and adequacy of insurance continue to be problems for these companies. Sudden and accidental pollution coverage reportedly is almost nonexistent in the chemical industry. Premiums are increasing 200 percent to 500 percent, with some increases as high as 1,000 percent.

Biotechnology The two major trade associations, the Association of Biotechnology Companies (ABC) and the Industrial Biotechnology Association (IBA), report that availability and affordability of liability insurance remain problematic, particularly for small companies. ABC, which represents many small new firms, has set up a captive cooperative insurance company in Vermont to provide product liability and D&O liability coverage. IBA, which represents larger companies, decided against setting up a captive since its members have been able to get insurance. The associations report that no companies have curtailed operations because of insurance problems, but that some small companies are "going bare." The biotechnology sector's insurance difficulties are compounded by the presence of new small companies with high risk profiles, as well as research and development operations in high risk areas of pharmaceuticals, biologicals, chemicals, and environmental applications.

Oil and Gas Drilling A survey conducted in May 1986 by the International Association of Drilling Contractors found that the average premium more than tripled over the last two years, and that some premiums are almost twenty times higher than two years ago.

Construction Contractors A 1986 survey of 500 construction contractors found that "skyrocketing insurance premiums" is the most serious problem facing the construction industry. The average liability insurance premium for construction contractors increased by 50 percent in 1985, and nearly doubled for architect-engineering firms.

Availability has been especially difficult for new companies and companies involved in tunnelling, hazardous waste clean-up, and crane operations.

In April 1986 a $125 million water tunnel project for New York City was stopped for a month because a contractor's liability insurance policy had expired. The group of carriers that insures this type of work has discontinued insuring tunnel projects. There is an increasing tendency for small construction companies to continue working without liability insurance.

Tank Truck Carriers Tank truck carriers are required by the Department of Transportation to have either $1 million or $5 million coverage for public liability, property damage, and environmental restoration, depending on the type of hazardous material being transported. The National Tank Truck Carriers (NTTC) reported that the cost of renewed coverage after June, 1985, jumped 500 percent to 700 percent over the previous twelve-month period, with coverage over $5 million very difficult to obtain. An NTTC survey also found that many of those renewing after January 1, 1985 faced increased deductible amounts of over $21,000 per occurrence. Some carriers are not renewing policies. One New England company reported that its insurance premium is 21 percent of its gross annual revenue. Several companies have gone into bankruptcy, and two have gone out of business entirely.

Service Station Dealers According to the Service Station Dealers Association, its members are finding it difficult to find pollution liability insurance. Last year only 3.5 percent of these dealers had pollution insurance, and most of those that did had limitations which negated much of the coverage. Two firms have found it necessary to waive requirements that their dealers maintain specific coverage until coverage becomes more affordable.

General Manufacturing The Machinery and Allied Products Institute recently updated its survey of liability coverages of member companies. The survey was completed by companies which experienced policy renewals after April 1, 1986. The survey covered general liability, D&O liability, environmental impairment liability, products liability, and some other coverages.

Respondents experienced premium increases for all types of insurance, but the increases, except for products, were less than reported for 1985. Limits tended to be the same as previously for all coverages, with the exception of excess general liability—where a majority of the respondents found less market capacity. Increases in deductibles were most noticeable in D&O coverage, where 68 percent of the respondents experienced increases, and in products coverages, where 73 percent experienced increases.

An overwhelming majority reported an increase in exclusions. Fifty-eight percent indicated that their general liability coverage now excludes "sudden and accidental" pollution of the environment. Exclusions from D&O coverage included liability resulting from mergers and acquisitions, suits brought against a director by the corporation or other directors, suits against named directors, and suits for failure to maintain adequate insurance coverage.

Seventy percent reported that they have been compelled to shift to a "claims-made" form, and approximately 27 percent have had some coverage cancelled since April 1, 1986. More than half of the respondents indicated that they are either sponsors or shareholders of American Casualty Excess Insurance, Ltd., or X.L. Insurance Co., Ltd., or that they are considering these options. Other respondents are considering association captives.

Machine Tool Manufacturers   The 1986 product liability survey of the National Machine Tool Builders Association indicates that 23 percent of its members have no product liability coverage. For those who do have such coverage, premiums have risen by 55 percent over the last year, and have more than tripled since early 1985. The Association reports that 43 percent of its members with annual sales in excess of $2.5 million have no umbrella policy against catastrophic claims.

Steel Industry   The steel industry continues to have problems with the availability and affordability of liability insurance. Premiums remain high, and available coverage generally includes large deductibles.

General Aviation Manufacturers   General aviation continues to have serious insurance affordability problems. The General Aviation Manufacturers Association estimates that the average cost of product liability coverage in 1986 will approach $100,000 per airplane delivered compared to $70,000 per airplane in 1985, with fewer delivered airplanes in 1986.

Cessna's product liability insurance costs increased from $7.3 million in 1983 to $50 million in 1986. Piper's costs increased from $7 million in 1983 to $40 million in 1985. Beech experienced product liability insurance costs of $24 million in 1986.

Commercial Airlines   The Air Transport Association reports that there is sufficient capacity in the market for its members to buy what they need. Premiums in 1985 were 40 percent greater than in 1984.

Ice Skating Rinks Fifty percent of ice skating rinks report they cannot obtain liability coverage and may be forced to close.

Sports Leagues The Amateur Softball Association, composed of 182,000 teams with 3.5 million participants in 1985, had a premium increase of over 2,000 percent, from $7,000 in 1985 to $150,000 in 1986.

The Soccer Association for Youth Organization, which oversees 4,600 youth soccer teams, experienced an increase in its liability cost from $4,500 in 1984 to $22,000 in 1985 for the same coverage.

Sports Equipment A producer of baseball and softball equipment saw its premiums rise from $14,300 in 1984-85 for $500,000 worth of coverage to $70,000 for the same coverage in 1985-86. For 1986-87, it was quoted a premium of $159,000, the lowest from among only five companies that were willing to bid.

Premium increases of 200 percent to 500 percent have forced 20 percent of small diving equipment producers to "go bare" or self-insure.

The Impact of Insurance Availability/Affordability Problems

The above sectoral and industry descriptions, though informative, do not fully tell the story of the insurance availability and affordability problems that still beset many businesses, professionals, employees, and consumers. The following items, while admittedly anecdotal, perhaps give a better sense of the real and continuing costs associated with unavailable or unaffordable insurance.

- Several domestic sports equipment manufacturers have ceased doing business, discontinued some products, and failed to introduce other products, as a result of liability insurance problems. The Sporting Goods Manufacturers Association reports that the number of manufacturers of varsity football helmets has dropped from eighteen in 1976 to three in 1985. There are no longer any domestic producers of trampolines or ice hockey protective equipment. A lacrosse equipment manufacturer was unable to introduce a new helmet on the market because the plastic manufacturer was concerned about product liability. Spaulding Sports Worldwide indicates that it no longer manufactures and sells protective equipment because of increased insurance costs and increases in the number of associated product liability suits.
- A Massachusetts company has refused to place its metal folding crib on the market because of its inability to obtain

liability insurance. The product has been certified as meeting government safety standards, and a substantial number of orders for the product have been received.

- In a letter to a Congressional subcommittee, the Merchants Corporation of America stated that it had been prepared to begin production of a new infant car seat which it believed would be the highest quality unit available, but that it ultimately decided not to market the product because of the liability risks to which the company would be exposed.
- A Charlottesville, Virginia health products company refused to market a new product for use in dialysis until it eventually obtained insurance.
- A small Virginia business manufacturing driving aids for the handicapped removed its product from the market following a dramatic increase in its cost of insurance.
- Puritan-Bennett, a manufacturer of hospital equipment, stopped making anesthesia gas machines because of its inability to obtain insurance. Puritan-Bennett was the sole domestic manufacturer of such machines.
- The Dyneet Corporation has stopped producing its clutch for helicopters because the cost of insurance has become prohibitive. No damages claims for the product have been reported.
- General aviation manufacturers have stopped or suspended production of a number of product lines. For example, in early 1986, Piper Aircraft suspended production of general aviation aircraft models, and has now resumed production of only one of these models. Similarly, Beech Aircraft suspended production in 1985, with only one model in production at this time, while Cessna suspended production of all of its piston-powered aircraft in May of 1986 and has yet to resume production. Each of these manufacturers indicates that product liability costs have been an important factor in these decisions, in that the cost of insurance now often exceeds all other costs of manufacture. Employee layoffs accompanied these product removals.
- In January 1986, G. D. Searle and Company announced it would withdraw its Copper 7 IUD from the U.S. market, citing the unavailability of insurance and the threat of product liability lawsuits as the reason for its decision. Searle's withdrawal leaves only a single manufacturer of IUDs in the United States market.
- A recent editorial in the Journal of the American Medical Association states that because of liability concerns, 12 percent of obstetricians nationwide have stopped delivering babies and 38 percent of surgeons are avoiding high-risk cases, and that

the National Cancer Institute believes that liability fears have led physicians treating cancer to use far milder doses of chemotherapy.[4]

These are but a few examples of products or services that have been removed from the marketplace because of insurance availability/affordability problems. Ironically, many of these products or services would have promoted public health and safety.

The Adequacy of Insurance Coverage

The foregoing discussion has focused almost entirely on the availability and affordability of insurance. But as the Working Group's prior report noted, there is a third important facet to the insurance crisis—the adequacy of insurance coverage.

While insurance is more available than a year ago, it is important to note that much of this new availability has come with far higher deductibles, more exclusions, less coverage and additional policy limitations. Accordingly, the higher premiums discussed here reflect only a portion of the increased cost of insurance. To the extent that these premium increases are accompanied by higher deductibles, less coverage and new exclusions and limitations, the cost of insurance to its purchasers has increased beyond merely the growth in premiums. In other words, not only have insurance premiums increased, but the coverage that can be purchased with those premiums usually is less— often substantially less—than what it was a year or two ago.

While the growth in insurance premiums can be measured relatively easily, it is virtually impossible to express the reductions in insurance coverage in similar numerical terms. Thus, there is a tendency to focus on insurance premiums and to ignore changes in coverage. But the latter can be just as important—and can have an even larger effect on the ultimate cost of insurance—than raw premium data.

Accordingly, this discussion of insurance availability and affordability provides only a partial picture of the state of insurance in the United States in that it does not account for the reductions in insurance coverage which have helped both to increase the availability of insurance and to stabilize insurance premiums.

In sum, while the crisis in insurance availability and affordability has ameliorated as a result of the improved economic conditions of the insurance industry, the insurance problems of the past two years have by no means disappeared. Prices have largely stabilized, but remain very high, and for some lines continue to increase. The availability problems which one year ago affected almost every sector of the

American economy are now limited to specific lines or types of coverage. But for those lines or types of coverage the problem is still serious and often a matter of economic survival. Many of the newer developments, particularly the increasing use of self-insurance programs, have yet to prove their long-term reliability. And insurance coverage has been substantially reduced through higher deductibles, lower coverage limits, and additional policy exclusions and limitations. Thus, while the shock and many of the more extreme aspects of the insurance crisis have abated, the simple reality is that its effects are still felt throughout the American economy and likely will continue to be felt for some time to come.

III. THE INSURANCE INDUSTRY'S ECONOMIC PERFORMANCE

In its report last year, the Working Group discussed relevant data on the financial state of the property and casualty insurance industry. The following updates that discussion with available 1986 data.

The Industry's Operating Performance

In its February 1986 report, the Working Group noted that there were conflicting views of the economic performance of the property and casualty insurance industry in 1985. While overall premiums were up substantially, some of the problem lines were returning very high losses for their proportion of generated premiums. Consequently, the industry in 1985 had only a small operating profit after tax rebates.

In its year-end review of the 1986 performance of the industry, appropriately entitled "Up From the Ashes," A.M. Best Insurance Management Reports estimated the 1986 operating profit of the property and casualty industry to be $4.5 billion, with an expected $1.5 billion in tax rebates, for a total operating profit of $6 billion.

The property and liability industry had a statutory insurance underwriting loss in 1986 of $17 billion on net written premiums of $176.4 billion. The loss figure is the total of estimated claims losses (payouts), loss adjustment expenses, operating expenses, and policyholder dividends. The comparable underwriting loss for 1985 was $25.2 billion on $143.9 net written premiums. The corresponding 1984 figures were $117.7 billion in premiums with a $21.5 billion net underwriting loss. Exhibit 12-1 summarizes premium and cost data for the years 1981 to 1986.

The substantial growth in net written premiums from 1984 to 1986—a 50 percent increase—and the reduction in the loss and loss

Exhibit 12-1
Property/Casualty Operating Results*

Year	Net Premiums Written[1]	Loss and LAE[1]	Under- writing Expenses[1]	Statutory Under- writing Loss After Policyholder Dividends[1]
1981	$ 98.8	$ 75.8	$ 27.1	$ - 6.3
1982	103.1	82.2	29.0	-10.4
1983	107.8	87.7	30.8	-13.3
1984	117.7	103.7	33.0	-21.5
1985	143.9	126.8	37.4	-25.2
1986[2]	176.4	145.5	43.7	-17.0

[1] In billions of dollars.
[2] Estimated
* Source: Best's Insurance Management Reports

adjustment expense ratio—from 88.09 percent to 82.49 percent—have been major factors in restoring the industry's financial health. The industry also was able to generate substantial income through its investments, which gave it an overall net operating profit. Specifically, the industry's 1986 $21.6 billion investment gain offset the $17 billion underwriting loss for a net $4.5 billion profit. Further, tax recovery of $1.5 billion raised the total operating profit to $6 billion. Additionally, the industry realized capital gains of $5.5 billion, resulting in a final estimated after-tax profit of $11.5 billion.

The $11.5 billion in after-tax profits of the property and liability industry significantly improved the industry's rate of return on net worth. Its rate of return for 1984 was 1.8 percent, and increased to 3.8 percent in 1985.[5] The industry's rate of return on net worth for 1986 was 11.6 percent.[6] This rate of return is roughly equivalent to the industry's ten-year average for 1976 to 1985 (11.9 percent statutory accounting; 11 percent GAAP accounting), and is slightly less than the ten-year rate of return for Fortune 500 industrial corporations (13.2 percent).[7] Thus, while the industry significantly improved its rate of return, that rate was substantially less than its most recent high years (19 percent in 1977 and 18.1 percent in 1978[8]), and was still less than the rate of return of many companies competing with the industry for investment capital (see Exhibit 12-2).

One measure of the industry's performance is a ratio that measures all costs against premiums written and earned. This ratio—the combined ratio—dropped from the 1985 level of 114.8 percent to 107 percent in 1986. The ratio's recent peak was 116.1 percent in 1984. If premiums continue for another year at the current level, and natural

Exhibit 12-2

Annual Rate of Return as a Percent of Net Worth*

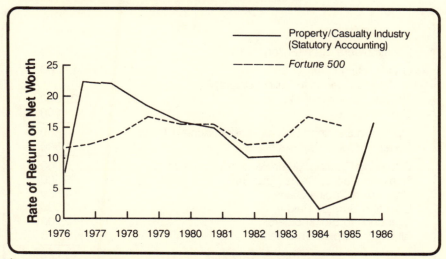

* Source: Insurance Information Institute (Based on Data Compiled by A.M. Best and *Fortune* Magazine)

catastrophic losses remain as low as they were in 1986, a further drop in the combined ratio can be expected.

The lower combined ratio for the industry can be partly attributed to the reduction in the ratios of the problem lines, though these lines continue to be a substantial drain on the industry's financial performance. Medical malpractice still has a combined ratio of 144.4 percent, but is down from 166.7 percent in 1985. Commercial multiple peril and other liability are the two lines that include products, municipal, D&O, general liability, and other problem coverages. The combined ratio for commercial multiple peril dropped from 122 percent in 1985 to a respectable 97.2 percent in 1986, with the combined ratio for other liability dropping from 147.2 percent in 1985 to a still high 120.3 percent in 1986. Further reductions in these ratios should add materially to the industry's stability.

Another important measure of the industry's performance is the change in policyholder surplus. That surplus generally is equated to net worth, and is a measure of the industry's ability to withstand future losses. Exhibit 12-3 provides the detailed calculation of policyholder surplus, which is estimated to have reached $91 billion at the end of 1986, a 21.5 percent increase over 1985.

Exhibit 12-3
1986 Estimated Changes in Consolidated Policyholders' Surplus*

	($ millions)
Policyholders' Surplus Jan. 1, 1986	74,878
Underwriting Loss	-17,000
(After Dividends to Policyholders)	
Net Investment Income	21,600
Other Income	- 100
Operating Earnings Before Federal Income Taxes	4,500
Federal Income Tax Recovery	1,500
Operating Earnings After Federal Income Taxes	6,000
Realized Capital Gains (After Tax)	5,500
Unrealized Capital Gains	4,500
Capital & Surplus Paid In	4,000
Dividends to Stockholders	- 2,700
All Other Surplus Changes	- 1,178
Total All Changes	16,122
Policyholders' Surplus Dec. 31, 1986	91,000

*Source: Best's Insurance Management Reports

Underwriting Results by Major Lines

In order to understand the relationship between the property and liability industry's financial performance and the problems in insurance availability and affordability, it is important to examine the underwriting results of the major commercial liability lines: Commercial multiple peril (CMP), commercial general liability (CGL) and medical malpractice. Particularly the latter two lines continue to be a substantial drain on the property and liability industry's financial performance. These two lines together produced only 13 percent of the industry's total written premiums, but accounted for 33 percent of its total underwriting loss (see Exhibit 12-4).

Commercial Multiple Peril CMP is a packaged line including general liability coverages such as product liability. The general liability lines are subject to long-tail losses which may be reported many years after the policy is written and often involve claims which are not resolved until long after having been reported. The line also includes property coverage that is typically reported and resolved in a short time

Exhibit 12-4
Written Premiums Compared to Underwriting Loss*

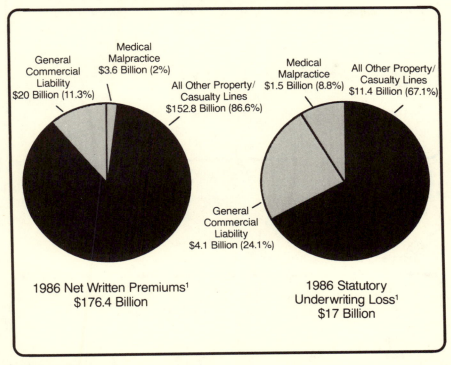

1986 Net Written Premiums[1]
$176.4 Billion

1986 Statutory
Underwriting Loss[1]
$17 Billion

[1] Estimated
* Source: Best's Insurance Management Reports

frame. CMP experience for the past six years is summarized in Exhibit 12-5.

Best's Management Reports predicted in 1985 that the short-tail portion of this coverage could provide a fast turnaround in the CMP line. The combination of a nearly 40 percent increase in net written premiums and the drop in natural disaster costs in 1986 apparently has led to the sharp improvement in the line.

Commercial General Liability This line includes most of the sectors that have experienced serious affordability and availability problems. It is also a long-tail line. The line's experience for the past six years is summarized in Exhibit 12-6.

Premiums in this line increased more than 20 percent in the past year after a similar increase from 1984 to 1985. But losses increased 43

Exhibit 12-5
Commercial Multiple Peril*

Year	Net Premiums Written[1]	Loss and LAE[1]	Under-writing Expenses[1]	Statutory Under-writing Loss After Policyholder Dividends[1]
1981	$ 6.8	$ 4.6	$ 2.5	$ -0.5
1982	6.9	5.3	2.7	-1.2
1983	7.2	5.9	2.9	-1.7
1984	8.2	7.9	3.2	-2.9
1985	12.0	9.0	4.0	-2.8
1986[2]	16.0	9.4	5.0	-0.1

[1] In billions of dollars
[2] Estimated
*Source: Best's Insurance Management Reports

Exhibit 12-6
Commercial General Liability*

Year	Net Premiums Written[1]	Loss and LAE[1]	Under-writing Expenses[1]	Statutory Under-writing Loss After Policyholder Dividends[1]
1981	$ 6.0	$ 5.1	$ 1.8	$ -1.0
1982	5.6	5.4	1.8	-1.7
1983	5.7	6.0	1.8	-2.1
1984	6.5	7.8	1.9	-3.2
1985	11.6	11.5	2.7	-4.9
1986[2]	20.0	16.4	4.2	-4.1

[1] In billions of dollars.
[2] Estimated
*Source: Best's Insurance Management Reports

percent during 1986, while underwriting expenses increased 52 percent. Accordingly, net underwriting losses in the line remain extremely high.

The statutory underwriting loss is based on *earned* premiums rather than *written* premiums. Earned premiums in 1985 and 1986 were substantially less than written premiums. Exhibit 12-7 summarizes the net earned premiums over the last six years for the property/casualty industry and the three analyzed lines.[9]

Exhibit 12-7
Net Premiums Earned*

Year	Property/ Casualty Industry[1]	CMP[1]	CGL[1]	Medical Malpractice[1]
1981	$ 97.0	$ 6.7	$ 6.1	$ 1.3
1982	101.0	6.8	5.7	1.4
1983	105.8	7.1	5.7	1.5
1984	114.3	7.8	6.2	1.7
1985	132.7	10.2	9.4	2.4
1986[2]	164.7	14.3	16.6	3.3

[1] In billions of dollars.
[2] Estimated
* Source: Best's Insurance Management Reports

Exhibit 12-8
Medical Malpractice*

Year	Net Premiums Written[1]	Loss and LAE[1]	Under- writing Expenses[1]	Statutory Under- writing Loss After Policyholder Dividends[1]
1981	$ 1.3	$ 1.6	$ 0.2	$ -0.5
1982	1.5	2.0	0.2	-0.7
1983	1.6	2.1	0.2	-0.8
1984	1.8	2.8	0.3	-1.1
1985	2.8	3.7	0.4	-1.7
1986[2]	3.6	4.3	0.4	-1.5

[1] In billions of dollars.
[2] Estimated
* Source: Best's Insurance Management Reports

Medical Malpractice Medical malpractice remains a major source of losses and continues to be a substantial problem for the medical profession and consumers. Only a few private insurers provide coverage, with state mutuals and self-insurance taking up much of the slack. Exhibit 12-8 summarizes the line's experience over the past six years.

Although the experience indicates a slight improvement in underwriting losses in 1986, the line continues to have the highest combined ratio of the problem lines.

Stock Market Performance

During the past four to six months some pessimistic reports from insurance stock analysts have contributed to a decline in many property and liability and multi-line insurance company stocks. Many analysts continue to recommend insurance stocks but caution that investors should be very "selective."

Most analysts, however, believe that the industry "learned a lesson" from the excesses of the early 1980s and that prices, which are stabilizing, will be maintained through 1987 and into 1988. They see interest rates remaining at current levels, and expect insurance profits to be healthy for the immediate future. They believe that the property and liability and multi-line companies will have low price-to-earnings ratios and, therefore, be attractive to investors.

While property and liability stocks generally outperformed the market from January 1, 1984, to January 1, 1986, for the first three quarters of 1986 property and liability stocks actually trailed the market's performance. A recent issue of *Business Insurance* reported that property and liability stocks seriously lagged behind the Standard and Poor's 500 and the Dow Jones Industrials during the second half of 1986.[10]

The Value Line, a comprehensive stock analysis firm, reports regularly on fourteen property and liability stocks. Its October 1986 report noted that these stocks have not performed well during the past six months. It believes that the insurance industry must build its reserves, and that to do so the industry will remain conservative in its underwriting. Accordingly, Value Line concludes that the market will remain tight for at least the near future. In commenting on the new tax law, Value Line predicts that the industry will be able to pass on the resulting increased costs but that the provisions may require the industry to focus on obtaining underwriting profits, and not to continue to rely—as it has in the recent past—on its investment income to achieve overall profitability.

Insolvencies

Accompanying the serious problems that have affected the property and liability insurance industry over the past few years has been a modest increase in the number of financially troubled companies or insolvencies. This conclusion is based primarily on a review of both

Exhibit 12-9
Property/Casualty Insolvencies*

Year	Insolvencies
1969	1
1970	4
1971	8
1972	2
1973	2
1974	5
1975	20
1976	6
1977	6
1978	6
1979	3
1980	4
1981	6
1982	9
1983	4
1984	20
1985	21
1986	16(Est.)

*Source: National Committee on Insurance Guaranty Funds.

Best's ratings and reports of the insurer committee tracking insolvencies and their claims on insurance guaranty funds.

For 1986, Best's evaluated the financial condition of 1,703 property and liability companies. As a result of this evaluation, 176 companies received higher ratings and 220 had their ratings lowered. In 1986, 124 companies were in the "Other Not Assigned" category, compared to 118 companies in 1985. This category covers companies below minimum standards, those with incomplete financial information, those not listed by company request, and those under state supervision.

As noted, there has been some increase in the number of insolvencies of property and liability insurers over the past few years, as well as a change in the type of companies facing insolvency. Exhibit 12-9 shows the number of property and liability insolvencies between 1969 and 1986. The listing does not include reinsurers, surplus carriers, or offshore captives.

During the 1960s and 1970s, most of the industry insolvencies involved companies writing high risk automobile insurance. This started to change in 1980-81 with a few insolvent commercial lines writers. In 1984 and 1985, there was an increase in insolvencies among commercial lines companies. Among the insolvencies in those years were both mixed and specialty commercial writers whose coverages included asbestos, long haul trucking, dram shop, and medical malpractice.

The Industry's Profitability Cycle

Much has been made of the property and liability industry's profitability cycle. Indeed, the Working Group's February 1986 report discussed the effect of that cycle on the availability and affordability of insurance. Some have suggested that the entire availability/affordability crisis can be attributed to that cycle, and that thus there is a certain inevitability to the reccurrence of such insurance problems.

It is important in understanding the contribution of the cycle to the recent availability and affordability crisis to appreciate how much more severe the insurance crisis of the mid-1980s was than the crisis of the mid-1970s. To give but two examples of the difference between the two periods: the industry's underwriting losses of $21.5 billion in 1984 and $25 billion in 1985 were vastly greater than its underwriting loss of $4.2 billion in 1975 (the previous record); and, the industry's operating losses of $4 billion in 1984 and $5.6 billion in 1985 also were far larger than its $300 million operating loss in 1975 (which is all the more astounding in light of the record investment income generated by the industry in 1984 and 1985).[11]

The insurance crisis of the mid-1980s thus was far deeper and much more severe than the crisis of the mid-1970s. Accordingly, it is misleading to suggest that such industry crises simply recur cyclically, and that no other explanation is needed for the recent problems in insurance availability and affordability. Something was substantially different between the two crises which led the latter to be very different from the former. One difference, as the next section discusses in detail, is that tort law in those ten years underwent a dramatic transformation, both in terms of doctrinal changes as well as in awarded damages. That transformation appears to have played a major role in making the industry's cyclical downturn in the mid-1980s a far more serious insurance crisis than the United States had every previously faced. This, unfortunately, has ominous implications for the likely effects of the industry's next cyclical downturn should the deterioration of tort law continue unchecked.

IV. THE CONTRIBUTION OF TORT LAW TO THE CRISIS IN INSURANCE AVAILABILITY AND AFFORDABILITY

In its February 1986 report the Working Group discussed the central role of tort law to the crisis in insurance availability and affordability. The report noted four problem areas in tort law which have contributed substantially to the insurance crisis. These four areas are:

- the movement toward no-fault liability,
- the undermining of causation,
- the explosive growth in damage awards, and
- excessive transaction costs.

The report also noted the growth in lawsuits in areas such as medical malpractice, product liability, and municipal liability. Finally, in discussing the problems of tort law and how they relate to the availability and affordability of insurance, the report focused on the instability and uncertainty which currently beset the tort system and which greatly exacerbate the already serious deterioration of that system.

Jury Awards

While the Working Group's report dealt with a number of troubling aspects of tort law, most of the critics of the report's discussion of tort liability have focused on its conclusions regarding the extraordinary growth in damage awards. Ironically, recently updated data issued by the Rand Corporation's Institute for Civil Justice—which represent by far the most reliable empirical data to date on civil jury awards—indicate the report, if anything, appears to have understated the magnitude of this particular problem.

Average Jury Awards The recently released analysis of the Institute for Civil Justice[12] summarizes civil jury verdict data over a twenty-five year period in two jurisdictions: Cook County, Illinois and San Francisco, California.[13] The Institute's data are adjusted for inflation, and expressed in terms of 1984 dollars. The data demonstrate an extraordinary growth in civil jury awards in recent years, particularly in two areas that have been of major concern with regard to insurance availability and affordability—malpractice[14] and product liability. For example, the data show that the average jury malpractice award in Cook County increased by 2,167 percent from the early 1960s

Exhibit 12-10
Average Malpractice Jury Award*

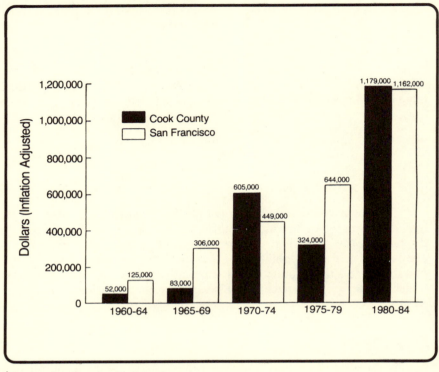

* Source: Institute for Civil Justice

to the early 1980s, and by 830 percent in San Francisco during the same period. In inflation-adjusted dollars, the average malpractice jury award in Cook County increased from $52,000 in 1960-64 to $1,179,000 in 1980-84, with a corresponding increase in San Francisco of from $125,000 to $1,162,000 (see Exhibit 12-10).[15]

Product liability jury awards underwent a similar extraordinary increase. Thus, in Cook County the average product liability jury award increased by 212 percent from the early 1960s to the early 1980s, while in San Francisco the increase during this period amounted to 1,016 percent. In inflation-adjusted dollars, the average product liability jury award in Cook County increased from $265,000 in 1960-64 to $828,000 in 1980-84, with a corresponding increase in San Francisco of from $99,000 in 1960-64 to $1,105,000 in 1980-84 (see Exhibit 12-11).[16]

Even when factoring in personal injury lawsuits that typically involve far lower monetary stakes—such as automobile accident and street hazard cases—the average jury award has increased substantial-

Exhibit 12-11
Average Product Liability Jury Award*

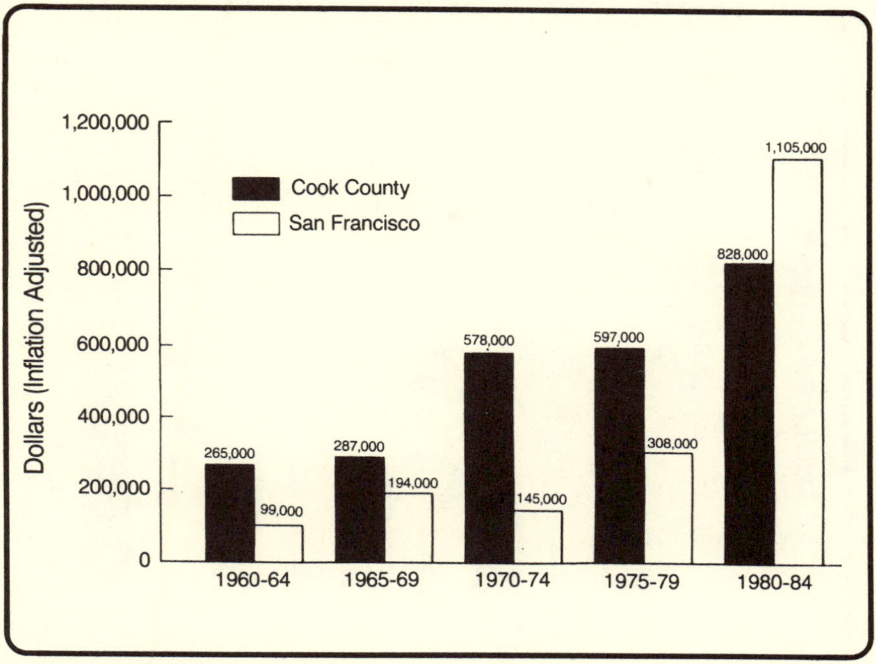

*Source: Institute for Civil Justice

ly over the past two decades. For example, the Institute found that the average personal injury jury award in Cook County increased by 217 percent from the early 1960s to the early 1980s (from $59,000 in 1960-64 to $187,000 in 1980-84), with a corresponding increase in San Francisco of 358 percent (from $66,000 in 1960-64 to $302,000 in 1980-84), as shown in Exhibit 12-12.[17]

Of particular interest is the fact that the rate of increase of average jury awards appears to have surged dramatically in the early 1980s. Thus, while the average product liability jury award in San Francisco increased by a total of $209,000 from 1960 to 1979, it increased by $797,000 from 1979 to 1984.[18] This trend was particularly evident in malpractice jury awards in both Cook County and San Francisco, where roughly half of the entire increase in average jury verdicts since 1960 occurred in the 1980-84 period.

The Institute's analysis also shows that along with increasing average jury awards, plaintiffs also have steadily increased the percentage of cases in which they prevail before juries.[19] Thus, in product liability cases in Cook County and in malpractice cases in both

Exhibit 12-12
Average Personal Injury Jury Award*

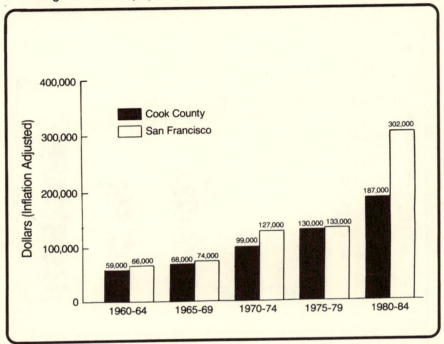

* Source: Institute for Civil Justice

Cook County and San Francisco, plaintiffs have roughly doubled the percentage of tried cases in which they prevail before juries (from approximately one-quarter of such cases in 1960-64 to one-half in 1980-84).[20]

Expected Jury Awards This offers another way of illustrating the change in jury verdicts over the past two decades—the "expected award"; that is, the average jury award multiplied by plaintiff's likelihood of success.[21] The expected award for malpractice jury verdicts increased from the early 1960s to the early 1980s by 4,254 percent in Cook County (from $13,000 to $566,000) and by 1,712 percent in San Francisco (from $34,000 to $616,000), as shown in Exhibit 12-13.[22] During the same period, the expected award for product liability jury verdicts increased by 445 percent in Cook County (from $76,000 to $414,000) and by 927 percent (from $56,000 to $575,000) in San Francisco (see Exhibit 12-14).[23] Similarly, from the early 1960s to the early 1980s, the expected award for personal injury jury verdicts

Exhibit 12-13
Expected Malpractice Jury Award*

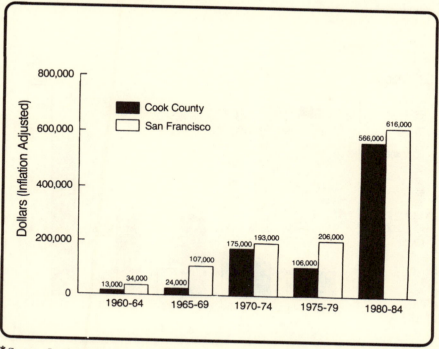

* Source: Institute for Civil Justice

increased by 307 percent in Cook County (from $28,000 to $114,000) and by 448 percent in San Francisco (from $33,000 to $181,000), see Exhibit 12-15.[24]

The expected award data illustrates even more clearly that the vast bulk of the increase in jury verdicts occurred during the early 1980s. In many of the above categories of cases the increase during the early 1980s in the expected jury award was *double or triple* the entire increase in the prior twenty years.

The degree to which average jury awards have increased dramatically in recent years is further illustrated by the data published by Jury Verdict Research, Inc. While the Jury Verdict Research data are not inflation-adjusted and do not meet the same rigorous methodological criteria used by the Institute for Civil Justice,[25] they also demonstrate an explosive trend in average verdicts. For example, the average medical malpractice jury award increased from $220,018 in 1975 to $2,056,525 in 1986, a 835 percent increase (see Exhibit 12-16).[26] The average product liability jury award increased from $393,580 in 1975 to

Exhibit 12-14
Expected Product Liability Jury Award*

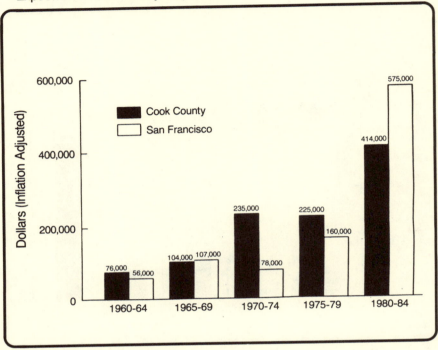

* Source: Institute for Civil Justice

$1,971,655 in 1986, a 401 percent increase (see Exhibit 12-17). Of particular interest is the fact that the average medical malpractice jury award grew by only $184,708 from 1975 to 1980 but by $1,651,799 from 1980 to 1986, while the average product liability jury award grew by only $169,858 from 1975 to 1980 but by $1,408, 217 from 1980 to 1986. Clearly, the 1980s have been a period of extraordinary and unsurpassed growth in jury awards which has troubling implications for the stability of the entire tort system.

Million-Dollar Jury Awards The empirical analysis of the Institute for Civil Justice also provides interesting data on the growth in million-dollar jury awards. In its earlier report, the Working Group noted the substantial growth of million-dollar verdicts, as reported by Jury Verdict Research, Inc. Because the Jury Verdict Research data are not inflation-adjusted, and because it is likely that its methodology *understates* the absolute number of such verdicts, the data were cited in the February 1986 report not as a statement of the absolute number

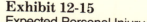

Exhibit 12-15
Expected Personal Injury Jury Award*

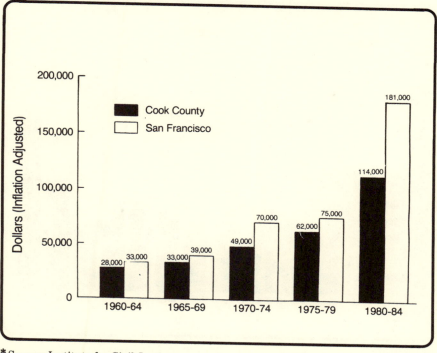

*Source: Institute for Civil Justice

of such verdicts, but primarily to demonstrate the rapid growth of "high-end" verdicts. As noted in the report, these verdicts appear to be largely responsible for the recent extraordinary increases in average jury awards. The Institute's data on million-dollar verdicts are more meaningful in that they are inflation-adjusted (expressed in 1984 dollars), and appear to include all million-dollar jury awards in the analyzed jurisdictions. Not unexpectedly, the data clearly confirm a very substantial increase in million-dollar jury awards.

In Cook County, the analysis shows that million-dollar awards increased from a total of two in 1960-64 to sixty-seven in 1980-84, while in San Francisco, such awards increased from a total of five in 1960-64 to twenty-one in 1980-84.[27] What is particularly important is the percentage of the *total* dollars awarded by juries that were awarded through verdicts of a million dollars or more. In Cook County, this percentage grew from only 4 percent in 1960-64 to 85 percent in 1980-84 (see Exhibit 12-18),[28] while in San Francisco the percentage grew from 14 percent in 1960-64 to 58 percent in 1980-84.

Exhibit 12-16
Average Medical Malpractice Jury Verdict*

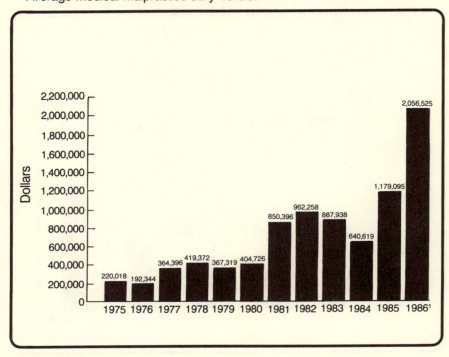

[1] 1986 information not complete
* Source: Jury Verdict Research, Inc.

The Institute's analysis also provides data on million-dollar *personal injury* awards as a percentage of all *personal injury* awards for the 1980-84 period (as noted, this category of cases also includes many lawsuits that typically involve lower monetary stakes). The data show that in Cook County 65 percent of the total dollars awarded by juries in all personal injury cases were awarded in verdicts of a million dollars or more, while in San Francisco the corresponding percentage was 47 percent.[29] What is particularly noteworthy is the small percentage of all tried personal injury cases which resulted in million-dollar awards. In Cook County, only 2.8 percent of all plaintiffs' personal injury jury verdicts resulted in an award of a million dollars or more, yet, as noted, those verdicts accounted for nearly two-thirds of the total of personal injury damages awarded by juries.[30] In San Francisco, only 3.8 percent of all personal injury verdicts for plaintiffs resulted in an award of a million dollars or more, yet those verdicts accounted for nearly half of the total damages awarded. The obvious conclusion to be drawn from

Exhibit 12-17
Average Product Liability Jury Verdict*

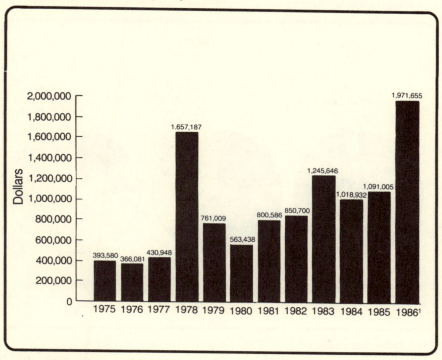

¹ 1986 information not complete
* Source: Jury Verdict Research, Inc.

this data is that a very small percentage of all tort cases account for a very large percentage of all awarded tort damages. Thus, it appears that much of the explosion in jury awards that has manifested itself so dramatically in recent years can be attributed in large part to a small percentage of all cases.

While the Institute's analysis does not distinguish economic from noneconomic damages awarded in these "high-end" verdicts, available data suggest that much of the increase in awarded damages is in the form of noneconomic damages—that is, damages awarded for pain and suffering, mental anguish, and other forms of nonpecuniary injury.[31] Since noneconomic damages are far more subjective and open-ended than economic damages,[32] it should be by no means surprising that a sudden surge in damage awards would be largely attributable to a change in the noneconomic rather than the economic components of such damage awards.

Exhibit 12-18
Percentage of Total Dollars[1] Awarded by Cook County Juries Attributable to
Million-Dollar Verdicts*

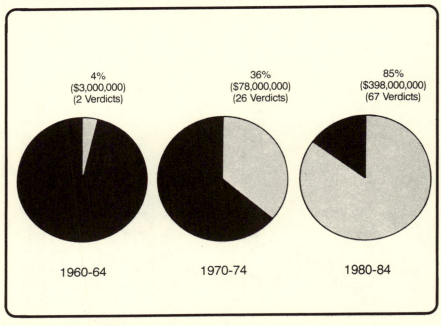

4%
($3,000,000)
(2 Verdicts)
1960-64

36%
($78,000,000)
(26 Verdicts)
1970-74

85%
($398,000,000)
(67 Verdicts)
1980-84

[1] Inflation Adjusted Dollars
* Source: Institute for Civil Justice

Median Jury Awards Many of the critics of the Working
Group's February 1986 report have focused on the report's use of
average (or *mean*) rather than *median* jury verdicts to illustrate the
extraordinary growth in jury awards and its effect on insurance
availability and affordability. Simply put, the *average* award is derived
by dividing the total dollars awarded in a particular category of
verdicts by the total number of such awards, while the *median* award
is the dollar level at which half of the awards are at or below and the
other half at or above. To illustrate, if there were three jury awards—
one for $50,000, one for $150,000, and one for $1,000,000—their
average would be $400,000, while their median would be $150,000.

Critics of the Working Group's report have argued that median
rather than average jury award data should be used to measure the
change in jury verdicts, and that median data do not demonstrate a
substantial change in verdicts over the past two decades.[33] They
contend that average jury awards, by including a small number of
"high-end" verdicts, provide a distorted picture.[34]

The use of median data essentially obscures—to the point of nonrecognition—the effect of "high-end" verdicts on the trend in jury awards. But, as noted, these "high-end" verdicts, while only a small percentage of all jury awards, represent a very large percentage of the total dollars awarded by juries.[35] Accordingly, median data substantially understate the growth of jury verdicts by eliminating or at least greatly obscuring the effect of the large awards which appear to be the major source of the problem. It is perhaps for that reason that critics of the Working Group's report have so enthusiastically embraced the use of *median* rather than *average* verdicts in analyzing the growth of jury awards.

The simple answer to these critics, however, is that median data cannot, by their very nature, provide any meaningful insight into the relationship between tort damages and insurance premiums. Thus, to the extent one is analyzing jury award trends to assess the effect of those trends on insurance availability and affordability, median data simply are incapable of providing useful information.

An insurer calculating its premiums or a self-insurer setting aside liability reserves is interested in obtaining as accurate a projection as possible of its total liability. If it were to use projected median awards and settlements, it would most likely vastly underestimate its total liability since such data do not reflect the small number of "high-end" settlements and awards that account for a large percentage of its likely total payout. On the other hand, an accurate projection of the average award or settlement would allow the insurer or self-insurer to determine its actual exposure if it could also accurately project the number of settlements and awards it would have to pay.

A simple example illustrates this point. Let us assume that an insurer projects that it will have to pay four claims on a particular policy—that three of those payments will be in the range of $100,000, but that at least one payment will be for a million dollars. If it were to use the median payment ($100,000) to calculate its premiums, the insurer would only collect sufficient premiums to cover a total payout of $400,000 (4 × $100,000). If its projections proved correct, it would lose $900,000 on the policy. On the other hand, if it based its premiums on the average payment ($325,000), the insurer would collect sufficient premiums to cover the projected payout of $1,300,000 (4 × $325,000). Assuming its projections proved correct, the insurer would break even.

Simply put, those who must pay the liability generated by the tort system cannot afford the luxury of using data which effectively ignore the cases that result in the largest payouts. Accordingly, it is virtually impossible to understand the effect (or even to appreciate the existence) of rapidly increasing settlements and awards on the availability and affordability of insurance if one relies on median data.

In sum, the recently published jury award data by the Institute for Civil Justice show an extraordinary growth in jury awards, much of which appears to have occurred in the 1980s.[36] The bulk of this growth seems to come from a small percentage of "high-end" verdicts that account for a very substantial percentage of all awards. Because such "high-end" verdicts tend to consist predominantly of noneconomic damages, such damages appear to be the most significant contributing factor to this surge in jury awards.

Case Filings

Some critics of the Working Group's February 1986 report have contested the report's conclusions regarding the increase in the number of product liability and medical malpractice lawsuits. The report noted that the number of product liability actions filed in federal court from 1974 to 1985 had increased by 758 percent, and that federal district court medical malpractice actions had increased almost three-fold in the past decade.[37] In addition, the Report cited separate data showing a 123 percent increase in malpractice claims against physician-owned companies from 1979 to 1983, and a doubling of malpractice lawsuits per 100 physicians from 1976 to 1981[38] (with a tripling per 100 obstetricians/gynecologists during the same period).[39] The report also cited data showing a substantial increase in recent years in tort claims filed against municipalities (New York City, for example, witnessed a 375 percent increase between 1979 and 1983).[40]

Nonetheless, these critics have denied that there has been any substantial increase in the number of filings, and they have relied almost entirely in this assertion on a study published last year by the National Center for State Courts.[41]

The National Center for State Courts Study The Center's study of tort lawsuits used state court data from thirteen states. Based on this data, the Center concluded that there had been only a 9 percent increase in tort filings between 1978 and 1984, and that this increase roughly mirrored population growth (8 percent) during the same period. The Center thereupon concluded that there was no "litigation explosion."

At the outset, it must be noted that the Center's study has serious methodological deficiencies, particularly when compared to federal district court caseload data. The Center's study, for example, was limited to only thirteen states, and only two of those states (Kansas and Ohio) provided complete and unqualified data. Eleven of the surveyed states either did not provide tort data for all available courts, or provided data that were otherwise incomplete.[42] In contrast, the federal data are obtained from all ninety-four judicial districts throughout the United States, and are compiled and maintained in a consistent manner which facilitates comparison over time and among regions or states.

An example illustrates the incomplete nature of the Center's data. The Center's data on filings in California include only superior court filings, not filings from the eighty-five municipal courts. By using only the superior court data, the Center "found" only a 12 percent increase in tort filings between 1978 and 1984, identical to the increase in population. But statistics from the 1976 and 1985 versions of the Annual Report of the Judicial Council of California, which include *both* superior court and municipal court filings, document an increase in civil tort filings between 1974 and 1984 of 55 percent, while the population only increased by 21 percent during this period.[43]

There are other problems with the data used by the National Center for State Courts. The Center used only three snapshots of caseload statistics to substantiate its conclusions. It provided no information on the intervening years (1979, 1980, 1982, and 1983), and, of course, there is no pre-1978 or post-1984 data. Unlike the federal data, which span twelve years, with statistics for each year, the Center's data are, at best, barely adequate to identify trends. Simply put, the Center's use of a very limited number of discrete data points makes it difficult to determine whether those points actually represent trends or, instead, unknowingly focus on aberrations in the data attributable to other factors.[44]

Even more importantly, however, the data used by the Center fail to account for the significant decrease in automobile accident lawsuits which has taken place in recent years. With the advent of no-fault automobile liability insurance, and a nationwide decrease in the number of automobile-related injuries,[45] there has been a corresponding large reduction in automobile accident tort lawsuits.[46] Since automobile accident cases reflect the vast bulk of all tort filings,[47] when these reductions are unaccounted for, they readily can mask substantial growth in other types of tort lawsuits, including product liability and medical malpractice actions. Because the Center's study provides no separate data as to areas of liability such as product liability, medical malpractice, and municipal liability, but instead aggregates these claims along with all other tort claims (including automobile accident cases), the Center's report provides no information on the trend of filings in these particular areas of liability.

Thus, because the Center's study aggregates *all* tort filings, it is impossible to derive any credible conclusions from its study as to the growth in tort claims alleging product liability, medical malpractice, other forms of professional liability or municipal liability—that is, the very areas of liability that have experienced serious insurance availability/affordability problems and which have been at the core of the debate over tort reform. Indeed, as noted, even a small reduction in filed automobile accident claims could more than mask a massive increase in lawsuits in these other areas of tort liability.

Federal District Court Caseload Data   Critics of the February 1986 report also have raised a number of other arguments regarding the federal district court data cited by the Working Group. They have suggested that the federal data are not meaningful because they represent only a small percentage of all filed tort claims, that the federal data are somehow different or atypical, and that the statistics compiled by the Administrative Office of the United States Courts are skewed by a recent surge in removals and the fact that some cases may be counted more than once.[48] All of these assertions simply miss the mark.

While most tort cases in fact are filed in state court, federal court tort filings provide a valuable source of reliable data on the trend in the public's propensity to sue. For example, whether originally filed in federal court, or later removed there, federal district courts handle a significant number of product liability cases each year. In the twelve-month period ending June 30, 1985, over 9,000 nonasbestos-related product liability suits were filed in federal court.[49] This, alone, represents almost a 500 percent increase over 1974. During the same period, total civil filings in federal court rose only 164 percent.[50] Obviously, whatever its share of total tort filings, district court product liability filings have risen at a rate which greatly exceeds the general rise in civil filings. To dismiss these figures, as some would suggest, simply because they represent a small percentage of *all* tort cases is specious.

As noted, critics also have claimed that the federal court statistics are inaccurate because they allegedly reflect a continued growth in removed cases and double or triple count transferred cases. These assertions are either completely wrong or insignificant. The percentage of civil filings in district court which are removals from State courts has remained virtually constant over the last ten years. Between 1976 and 1985 that percentage was never lower than 5.8 percent and never higher than 6.5 percent.[51] Moreover, the number of civil filings which are original filings also has been remarkably steady. Original filings (that is, not transfers, removals, remands, etc.), have constituted between 88.1 percent and 89.6 percent of all federal civil filings for each of the last ten years. This consistency clearly repudiates the assertion that the growth in federal filings is attributable to any increased inclination to remove cases to federal court.

Nor is the assertion of multiple counting significant. While it is true that a case which is both originally filed and transferred to another district in the same year is included twice in the *raw number* of civil filings reported by the Administrative Office, the absolute number of such cases is, at best, minimal.[52] More importantly, however, the percentage of civil filings which are transfers has been highly consistent over the years, and has never been high.[53] Equally consistent has been the combined percentage of civil filings which are either original filings or removals from state courts. These categories, which do not include *any* cases which are double counted, routinely have constituted 95 percent of all civil filings.

This consistency strongly corroborates the validity of the federal data when used to evaluate *trends*. There may be minor discrepancies between the raw numbers of "new" federal cases. But these discrepancies are statistically insignificant, and, in any event, have been present in each year's data. Accordingly, the Working Group's conclusions about the percentage growth in federal court litigation are absolutely valid.

In the absence of meaningful data on case filings in state court in areas such as product liability and medical malpractice, the federal district court data compiled by the Administrative Office of the United States Courts provide the most accurate data available on the growth in filed cases. While federal cases represent only a fraction of all tort cases in either of these categories, there is no reason to believe that they do not accurately reflect what is happening in the state courts. Despite its notoriety, the study of the National Center for State Courts simply does not provide the kind of meaningful data which justifies rejecting the obvious conclusions to be drawn from the very substantial increases in federal district court case filings.

Punitive Damages

In its prior report, the Working Group noted the extraordinary increase in recent years in the level of punitive damage awards. For example, the Working Group cited data published by the Institute for Civil Justice showing that the average punitive damage award has increased in Cook County from $63,000 in 1970-74 to $489,000 in 1980-84, while the average *personal injury* punitive damage award in Cook County increased from $40,000 to $1,152,174 during the same period.[54]

The Working Group did not, however, recommend that punitive damages be abolished. Rather, it recommended two reforms: that punitive damages be included within a cap on all noneconomic damages; and, that the standard used for awarding punitive damages be one of actual malice.[55] As discussed in Chapter 4, a number of states in 1986 enacted legislation addressing punitive damages. In addition, punitive damages have been a key issue in the debate over tort reform, and was a particularly important element of the recent Senate consideration of a federal product liability bill.

While there are some who believe that punitive damages do not present a significant problem, there appears to be a growing consensus within the legal community that punitive damages indeed are in need of reform. For example, the Task Force on Litigation Issues of the American College of Trial Lawyers recently made the following statement on punitive damages:

> The Task Force unanimously agrees that one of the greatest problems with the current tort system is the way in which punitive damages are handled. Awards often bear no relationship to deterrence and reflect a jury's dissatisfaction with a defendant and a desire to punish, often without regard to the true harm threatened by a defendant's conduct. There is a general feeling that punitive damage awards should be more difficult to obtain and that the amounts of such awards should be controlled much more than they are at the present time.... The most important reform should be to limit, either by a lid or some general formula (for example, three or four times actual damages), the amount of punitive damages that may be recovered.[56]

Most recently, the American Bar Association House of Delegates approved the recommendation of its Action Commission to Improve the Tort Liability System regarding punitive damages. Among other proposals, the ABA recommends tightening both the standard of conduct and standard of proof necessary to obtain punitive damages, as well as giving judges the authority in certain cases to allocate part of such damages to public purposes.[57]

Those who disagree with the proposition that punitive damages are a serious problem in need of reform generally base their argument on two assertions.[58] First, they contend that punitive damages have not really grown excessively if median rather than average award data are used. Second, they argue that because punitive damages are rarely awarded, and because the "typical" (that is, the median) punitive damage is not really that high), the problem has been overstated. Unfortunately, these critics do not appear to appreciate fully the nature of the problem.

At the outset, it should be noted that punitive damage awards, while generally infrequent, are not nearly as rare as often suggested. For example, the recent analysis by the Institute for Civil Justice indicates that the number of punitive damage awards in Cook County grew from three in 1960-64 to seventy-five in 1980-84, and in San Francisco grew from fourteen in 1960-64 to fifty-one in 1980-84.[59] In San Francisco, almost one out of every seven plaintiffs' verdicts (13.6 percent) in the 1980-84 period included a punitive damage award.[60]

While most punitive damage awards occur in business or intentional tort cases, in San Francisco nearly one out of every eight (12 percent) plaintiffs' product liability verdicts rendered in the 1980-84 period included a punitive damage award.[61]

It is not, however, the increasing incidence of punitive damage awards that has brought such damages to the forefront of the national debate over our tort system. Rather, it is the extraordinary growth in the size of such awards, as clearly reflected in the increase in the average punitive damage award. The available data indicate that in the last decade the size of punitive damages awards has undergone almost explosive growth, particularly in personal injury cases.[62]

The argument that punitive damages have not really grown excessively if median rather than average awards are considered fails to appreciate the very nature of the problem generated by punitive damages. To a large extent, it is the seemingly random, extraordinary high punitive damage award, that—while rare—has the truly pernicious effect on the tort system. It is this occasional immense award, even if eventually reduced on appeal, which is at the root of many of the concerns regarding punitive damages, particularly with regard to product liability.[63]

Such awards often far exceed any available insurance coverage, even in those states that permit insurance for punitive damages liability.[64] Immense punitive damages awards can threaten the economic viability of many small to mid-size businesses, and can represent a substantial burden to even large corporations (particularly if such damages are awarded in a number of similar cases). Thus there is often a very low threshold for any risk of incurring such an award, even if that risk is statistically very small. Such awards, however, are an irresistible temptation for many plaintiffs' attorneys, who recognize that the one-third to one-half contingency fee they would receive from the award would be quite substantial, even if subsequently reduced on appeal or in a post-trial settlement.

The inevitable and all too predictable result is that punitive damages are sought in many cases where there is very little likelihood of obtaining such an award. Plaintiffs' attorneys have very little to lose by pursuing a punitive damages claim—generally not much additional work is required—and there is much to gain if the claim should succeed. Moreover, because defendants may be particularly risk adverse to the possibility—no matter how small—of an immense adverse verdict, the claim may also be useful as a bargaining chip in settlement negotiations. Finally, since many jurisdictions permit a plaintiff asserting a punitive damage claim to introduce evidence of the defendant's net worth, the claim may be useful for no other purpose than to obtain a higher compensatory damage award from the jury by highlighting the defendant's "deep pocket."[65]

Thus, punitive damage claims have become a kind of legal lottery, where many plaintiffs' attorneys regularly file claims, recognizing that even if in any one lawsuit their probability of success is small, if enough such claims are filed eventually they may hit the jackpot.

Punitive damages, however, present a number of serious problems other than merely facilitating often abusive litigation. Among the most substantial of these problems is the effect of such damages on the insurability of risks. Because punitive damages awards are largely unpredictable, almost random events (especially in product liability cases), it is difficult for insurers to assess their likely exposure from underwriting such liability risks. This is particularly true for a single act or decision (such as a product design feature or the wording of a warning) which can result in punitive damage awards in a number of different lawsuits, each of which constitutes a separate "incident" for coverage purposes. Because insurers cannot assess their risk with any degree of certainty, and in light of the general deterioration of the tort system, their tendency often is to view such risks on an almost "worst case" basis. As a result, many risks are far more difficult or expensive to insure if the insurer is also faced with the possibility of an open-ended liability which may be virtually impossible to assess and which may expose the insurer to massive, unplanned for liability.

Punitive damages also can have highly perverse social effects. One of the most dramatic recent examples was the $8 million punitive damage award against the sole manufacturer of the polio vaccine on the theory that it had produced the wrong type of vaccine (the Sabin rather than the Salk vaccine), even though the manufacturer's decision complied with the well-established medical judgment of the United States government and virtually the entire medical community. The jury effectively sought to use a massive punitive damage award to coerce the manufacturer into producing the Salk vaccine, even though the Sabin vaccine has proved to be more effective in combating polio. Fortunately, the decision was reversed by the Kansas Supreme Court by a four-to-three vote. *Johnson* v. *American Cyanamid Co.*, 239 Kan. 279, 718 P.2d 1318 (1986). Had the decision been upheld, it could very well have jeopardized the viability of the entire polio vaccination program.

In addition, as previously noted by the Working Group, punitive damages can serve as a significant obstacle to the settlement process by giving the plaintiff unrealistic expectations of the value of his case even where the defendant has made a generous settlement offer.[66] And, for reasons already discussed, it often is not in the interest of plaintiff's attorney to advise his client of the unrealistic nature of his expectations, even if the likelihood of a punitive damage award is small. As one commentator has noted in the context of product liability, "[i]t is close to impossible to negotiate sensibly with a plaintiff who believes that he can shoot for the moon."[67]

Finally, it must always be remembered that punitive damages by their very nature do not serve to compensate plaintiffs. They are a pure windfall, whose only legitimate purpose is to deter truly outrageous and harmful conduct. To the extent that punitive damages are an ineffective or an abused vehicle for deterrence, as many believe to be the case, it is important to consider the social costs associated with such damages. Prime among those costs is the effect such damages have on the price of products, as manufacturers pass through higher insurance premiums or the cost of maintaining increased self-insurance reserves. These price increases effectively operate as a form of regressive sales tax, with a disproportionate effect on poor and lower middle class consumers. These consumers ultimately must pay the price for a system which, at times, seems to have degenerated into little more than a lucrative lottery for plaintiffs' attorneys.[68]

Transaction Costs

As noted, the Working Group in its February, 1986 report identified excessive transaction costs as a major problem of the tort system. Late last year, the Institute for Civil Justice published the most detailed analysis conducted to date on the transaction costs of the entire tort system.[69]

Using two different methods for assessing the costs associated with the tort system, the Institute estimates that the total expenditure nationwide for tort litigation in 1985 was between $29 billion and $36 billion. Of this amount, the Institute estimates that between $16 and $19 billion was spent for the various costs of the tort litigation system,[70] with only $14 to $16 billion paid in net compensation to plaintiffs.

For all tort cases, the Institute's best estimate is that the net compensation paid to plaintiffs amounted to only 46 percent of the total 1985 expenditure for tort litigation. If only non-automobile tort cases are considered, the net compensation paid to plaintiffs drops to 43 percent (see Exhibit 12-19). While the Institute's analysis does not provide data for categories of tort litigation other than automobile and nonautomobile cases, its earlier analysis of the asbestos litigations suggests that the net compensation percentage is even less for complex tort litigation such as product liability cases.[71]

As noted by the Working Group last year, "[i]t is difficult to justify such extraordinary transaction costs. But it is particularly difficult to

Exhibit 12-19
Costs and Compensation Paid for the Average Tort Lawsuit Terminated in 1985*

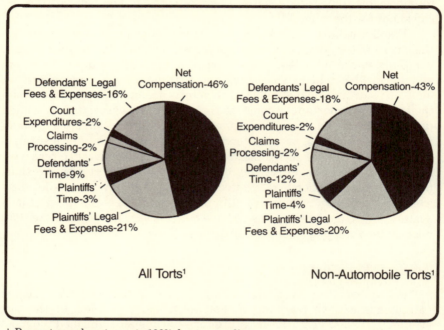

Defendants' Legal Fees & Expenses-16%
Net Compensation-46%
Court Expenditures-2%
Claims Processing-2%
Defendants' Time-9%
Plaintiffs' Time-3%
Plaintiffs' Legal Fees & Expenses-21%

All Torts[1]

Defendants' Legal Fees & Expenses-18%
Net Compensation-43%
Court Expenditures-2%
Claims Processing-2%
Defendants' Time-12%
Plaintiffs' Time-4%
Plaintiffs' Legal Fees & Expenses-20%

Non-Automobile Torts[1]

[1] Percentages do not sum to 100% due to rounding
* Source: Institute for Civil Justice

justify such costs when the costs often are borne largely by the seriously injured and by consumers who ultimately must pay for these costs through higher prices for goods and services.[72]

Doctrinal Changes in Tort Law

Heretofore, this section has focused primarily on changes in the tort system which can be measured in quantitative terms—the size of jury verdicts, the number of filed cases, the size and number of punitive damage awards, and the transaction costs of tort litigation. While such data add considerably to the public's understanding of many of the problems of the tort system, they also have an unfortunate tendency to distract attention from the underlying causes of the tort system's problems—the many doctrinal changes in tort law over the past two decades which, when taken together, have vastly expanded tort liability.

The past two decades have been an era in which traditional

limitations and conditions on tort liability have been swept aside in favor of far more expansive notions of liability. The empirical data discussed in this chapter provide an objective measure of *some* of the symptoms of this doctrinal revolution. The data, however, provide at best an imperfect picture in that they can only measure those aspects of the tort system that can be reduced to quantitative terms. But many of the most serious problems of tort law cannot be measured or demonstrated empirically, but can only be understood as qualitative deficiencies of our legal system.

The recent expansion of tort liability doctrines has been one of the most dramatic and far-reaching developments in modern American law. It has been almost entirely a product of judicial reconstruction of the common law. And it is only in recent years that this judicial movement has had its full impact upon American society and the United States economy.

The most active and visible area of expanding tort liability has been that of product liability. With the purported justification of risk redistribution and the internalization of injury costs, courts throughout the nation have relaxed concepts of fault and even causation to the point where many manufacturers have become virtual insurers for anyone injured while using their products.

But the expansion of tort liability is by no means limited to product liability. While considerable intellectual energy has gone into trying to justify more expansive liability for product-related injuries,[73] the same phenomenon—with far less of an attempt to develop an intellectually rigorous foundation—has manifested itself in other areas of tort liability such as governmental liability, medical malpractice, and other forms of professional liability.[74] One is left with an almost inescapable conclusion that the expansion of tort liability is less the consequence of the theoretical rationalizations developed in the context of product liability, than the result of a desire of many courts to use tort law to facilitate the transfer of assets from "deep pocket" defendants (including insurers) to injured or ill persons.[75] Whatever the reasons or justifications for this development, the last two decades have been a period of revolutionary change in tort law with one controlling theme— virtually every judicially created change has operated to expand rather than to limit tort liability.

In its prior report, the Working Group discussed these doctrinal changes in the context of the deteriorating role of fault and causation in determining tort liability.[76] While the report cited a number of cases as examples of this doctrinal evolution, it would require a virtual treatise to show the way in which tort liability has expanded in recent years in each of the states. But one case, in particular, illustrates well some of the worst excesses of our tort liability system—*O'Brien* v. *Muskin Corp.*, a 1983 decision of the New Jersey Supreme Court.[77]

O'Brien was a product liability case involving an above-ground swimming pool with an inner vinyl liner. The swimming pool was filled to a depth of approximately three and one-half feet. The manufacturer attached a warning in one-half inch high letters on the side of the pool with read "DO NOT DIVE." Nevertheless, the plaintiff (who was found to be a trespasser) dove in the pool (possibly off the side of an adjacent eight-foot high garage) and sustained a serious injury. The plaintiff alleged that his outstretched hands had slid on the vinyl bottom of the pool, thereby allowing him to strike his head. He sued the manufacturer of the pool on the theory that it was liable for his injuries because it had failed to warn him of the risks of diving into the pool, and because it had a vinyl liner for the pool.

The trial court allowed the failure to warn claim to go to the jury, but held that the defective design claim based on the use of a vinyl liner could not be presented to the jury on the ground that even the plaintiff's expert admitted that he knew of no alternative liner materials used for such above-ground pools other than vinyl.

The New Jersey Supreme Court reversed the trial court's decision on the defective design claim. The Court's holding was based on its conclusion that even where the plaintiff could not show a safer alternative design, he could prevail if he could convince a jury that the "risk posed by the pool outweighed its utility."[78] As justification for this result, the Court stated that the "cost [of liability of harm to others] might dissuade a manufacturer from placing the product on the market, even if the product has been made as safely as possible."[79] As noted by a dissenting member of the Court, this holding effectively transforms strict liability into absolute (or no-fault) liability if the jury determines that the "risk" associated with a product outweighs its "utility."[80]

One commentator has observed that *O'Brien* "reaches an astounding result," and that it "permits a jury to condemn at whim a common product that a manufacturer has honestly marketed and whose design it cannot improve."[81] As stated by that commentator:

> In short, courts may rely on *O'Brien* to declare defective in design a product used in millions of American homes even though the manufacturer provides adequate warning of the risks involved in its misuse and the plaintiff fails to present any evidence of an alternative design that would render the product safer.... Ultimately, *O'Brien* rejects the notion that the market, as an indicator of consumer values, provides an appropriate basis for concluding that widespread acceptance of a product indicates the social importance of a product or society's willingness to accept the risk the product presents, or both.[82]

O'Brien ably illustrates how "fault" in many instances has been reduced to an almost meaningless concept. It is difficult to conceive precisely what measures a manufacturer can take to avoid liability under *O'Brien,* other than not to manufacture a product which some jury might ultimately determine to pose risks outweighing its utility. In essence, the manufacturer becomes an insurer for everyone who injures himself—even when in total disregard of the manufacturer's instructions—while using its product.[83] The manufacturer's liability ultimately is not determined on the basis of its commitment to safety, but on the basis of a jury's abstract decision regarding the utility and risks of a product (which, in the case of *O'Brien,* reduced itself to the question of whether Americans should be permitted to own and use above-ground swimming pools). This decision is to be made in the context of a single case with the backdrop of an often sympathetic and severely injured plaintiff suing a "deep pocket" corporate defendant.

The purpose of the Court's holding in *O'Brien* seems relatively plain—to ensure that plaintiffs receive compensation. While some may welcome that result as well as the doctrinal changes that ensure such compensation, the price for these result-oriented legal decisions ultimately is borne by consumers. To the extent such liability results in higher prices, the cost will be borne disproportionately by lower income consumers, who will have to devote a larger percentage of their income to such tort driven insurance schemes. Moreover, the high transaction costs of the tort system ensure that for every three dollars consumers pay in higher prices to fund such compensation payments, consumers will recover only about one dollar in benefits.[84]

In a case such as *O'Brien,* however, it is distinctly possible that consumers may not even be permitted to purchase the product at a higher price, for what rational manufacturer will continue to produce a product whose "risks" are deemed to exceed its "utility," and which therefore will expose the manufacturer to virtually absolute liability in case after case.[85] Thus, result-oriented decisions such as *O'Brien* not only penalize consumers by making them pay higher prices for products, but in many instances totally deprive consumers of desired and useful products.

The above observations are, of course, equally applicable to other forms of economic activity, including the provision of professional services such as health care as well as municipal services such as police protection and the operation of playgrounds and public swimming pools. To the extent that courts devise new liability doctrines to ensure that plaintiffs will be compensated wherever possible, it is the consumer and the taxpayer who must bear the cost through higher prices and increased taxes, and through a reduction in the goods and services which otherwise would be available.

O'Brien illustrates an additional problem arising from the rapid expansion of tort liability doctrines in recent years—a problem which relates directly to insurance availability and affordability. Decisions such as *O'Brien* have introduced tremendous uncertainty into the tort system. Increasingly, insurers and potential defendants find it extremely difficult, if not virtually impossible, to predict liability. One commentator who has observed this phenomenon in recent changes in product liability doctrines condemns this "lack of comprehensibility of the law to those whose behavior the law seeks to control or modify."[86]

The lack of predictability, or comprehensibility, greatly exacerbates the already serious deficiencies of the tort system. It directly increases the cost of the tort liability system by generating uncertainty as to liability exposure, thereby increasing the cost of liability insurance or requiring larger self-insurance reserves.[87] But, as importantly, it undermines the deterrent value of tort law, for how can one modify one's behavior to avoid wrongful conduct when one cannot ascertain what type of behavior will be found to be wrongful. Of course, that is not to say that tort law no longer deters when its standards become increasingly uncertain and unpredictable. But it is to say that such uncertainty and unpredictability is as likely to deter socially beneficial activities and products as it is likely to deter undesirable and wrongful conduct.[88]

Thus, while expanding tort liability doctrines increase the burden of tort law on the American economy simply by generating additional liability which must be borne by the consumer and the taxpayer, it also has a second (and perhaps even more substantial) effect on generating uncertainty and unpredictability which, of itself, increases the costs of the tort system and undermines the deterrent role of tort law.

V. PUBLIC AND STATE SUPPORT FOR TORT REFORM

In its prior report the Working Group recommended a number of reforms of tort law. While some of these reforms appropriately can be implemented at the federal level,[89] the Working Group recognized that most of the reforms would have to be adopted by the States. In 1986, many states adopted tort reform proposals, many of which were similar to those recommended by the Working Group. In addition, the public repeatedly showed its strong support for tort reform initiatives in 1986. This chapter describes some of the more important and encouraging tort reform developments of the past year.

Public Support for Tort Reform

The public has shown strong support for reform of the civil justice system. A Lou Harris poll, conducted in May of last year, found that 69 percent of the people surveyed thought it was too easy for persons who claim to have been injured or wronged to sue for damages, while 63 percent thought that cash settlements in such cases were excessive.[90] The same survey found that the public placed the blame for the liability crisis squarely upon the shoulders of lawyers looking for big fees, clients who think such suits are the road to riches, and laws that make it too easy to sue.[91] Significantly, 65 percent of those surveyed indicated their support for a cap of $150,000 on awardable damages provided that the plaintiff's medical care is fully paid.[92]

In a separate study, conducted at about the same time, 85 percent of those surveyed favored a limit on attorneys' fees received from liability suits, while 63 percent (up from 57 percent in October 1985) favored limits on the amount of money an injured party can receive for pain and suffering in such suits. Similarly, 56 percent believed that pain and suffering awards were too high.[93]

More recent polls have produced the same results. A survey released in December of 1986, funded by the American Medical Association, is a good example. Of the survey's sample, 58 percent believed that jury awards were too large, and 70 percent agreed that jury awards should be limited.[94] Limits on attorneys' fees in successful suits were favored by 79 percent.

The public also demonstrated its support for tort reform at the ballot box. In June of last year, by a margin of 62 percent to 38 percent, California voters approved Proposition 51, an initiative which eliminates joint and several liability for all noneconomic damages in personal injury suits. This was a particularly important test of the public acceptance of tort reform because the debate had been so hotly contested. Indeed, the plaintiffs' bar initially characterized the Proposition as a referendum on the public support for tort reform.[95]

In August 1986, the White House Conference on Small Business, with 1,823 delegates representing ten times as many small businesses, voted tort reform as its number one priority for Congressional action. Outranking fifty-nine other recommendations, Resolution 180 included a package of eleven tort reform proposals, including the elimination of joint and several liability, a cap of $250,000 on noneconomic damages, a limitation on attorneys' contingency fees, and a return to the uniform, fault-based standard of liability. A separate resolution, recommending enactment of pending product liability reform legislation, also ranked in the Conference's top ten recommendations.

The American Tort Reform Association, a recently organized

coalition of trade associations, large and small businesses, professional groups, and individuals dedicated to obtaining tort reform legislation on the state and federal level, is further evidence of the broad base of support for civil justice reform. The Association's list of some 400 members covers the spectrum of American enterprise, and includes such diverse groups as the Boy Scouts of America, the American College of Obstetricians and Gynecologists, the National Ski Areas Association, the National Institute of Municipal Law Officers and the American Association of Community and Junior Colleges.[96]

In May of last year, 140 organizations representing a broad cross-section of American economic activity issued a report entitled "The Need for Legislative Reform of the Tort System: A Report on the Liability Crisis from Affected Organizations." Among other things, the report concludes that there is a very real tort liability crisis, and that legislative tort reforms are an important and effective response to that crisis.

In addition to these organizations, the AFL-CIO has endorsed specific tort reforms, particularly those that seek to increase predictability and reduce transaction costs.[97] The AFL-CIO's statement noted that "[u]ltimately, it is the American worker and the American consumer who suffer most ...," and that "[l]awyers, not victims, thus gain the most from the tort system." The statement was particularly critical of "the development of new theories of liability," and "dramatic increases in the size of the average award."

Notably, there has even been some limited support for tort reform from the practicing bar. The American College of Trial Lawyers issued a report in August which contained some modest recommendations for tort reform. For example, the College concluded that:

> [T]he joint and several liability rule should be modified, except in cases of concert of action, to reflect prevailing notions of comparative fault. There is good reason not to hold a defendant responsible for more than that defendant's proportional share of responsibility or fault.[98]

The College also concluded that some modification of the collateral source rule might be appropriate, and indicated that the concept of strict liability, which it concluded became popular because of assumptions about insurability and risk-sharing, needed to be reexamined in light of the current liability insurance crisis.[99]

In addition, the American Bar Association House of Delegates recently adopted the recommendations of its Action Commission to Improve the Tort Liability System, which proposed several modest tort reforms. Among these was a recommendation that joint and several liability be modified so that persons whose responsibility for an injury is "substantially disproportionate" to the liability for the entire injury may be found liable only for their equitable percentage share of the plaintiff's noneconomic damages.[100] (The ABA's recommendations regarding reform of punitive damages are discussed in the previous section.)

State Activity

In addition to the initiatives and referenda discussed above, tort reform and the liability insurance crisis were the subjects of much study and debate, as well as regulation and legislation, in the states during 1986. While legislative action probably was the most visible, there were other equally significant developments.

Commission Studies and Reports In August 1986, the National Governors' Association (NGA), *unanimously* adopted a resolution urging the Congress to adopt a national product liability code. The Governors noted that:

> The issue of product liability reform has increasingly pointed to federal action as a way in which to alleviate the problems faced by product manufacturers with regard to inconsistent State product liability laws. This lack of uniformity makes it impossible for insurers to predict accurately the potential liability of product manufacturers and insurers. Clearly, a national product liability code would greatly enhance the effectiveness of interstate commerce. Furthermore, the system causes inflated prices for our consumer goods, the discontinuation of necessary product lines, and adversely affects the international competitiveness of the U.S.[101]

In part, this resolution was based upon a report to the NGA presented by its Task Force on Liability Insurance.[102] The report, among other things, provided a synopsis of various tort reform measures, including most of those identified by the Working Group.[103]

The NGA noted that twenty governors had established task forces or commissions to review liability related issues. Many of these groups have since completed their work and have issued their reports and recommendations.[104] Perhaps the most thorough of these was New York's two-volume report of the Governor's Advisory Commission on Liability Insurance entitled "Insuring Our Future." Among other things, this report provides a compelling explanation and refutation of many of the criticisms that allege the crisis in insurance availability and affordability to be simply the result of the economic insurance cycle or that the crisis has been manufactured by the insurance industry.[105]

The Cuomo Commission report concluded that the crisis in liability insurance was the product of two unrelated but interacting causes. The industry's distinctive cycle was considered to be part of the problem.

But also a significant contributing factor was a long-term surge in civil liability costs, principally reflecting "the form and application of the law of torts."[106]

The Commission ultimately recommended a comprehensive scheme of tort reform and insurance regulation reform, both of which were viewed as critical to long-term stability in the liability insurance industry. The general tort reform measures which it recommended included modification of the rule of joint and several liability, amendment of the collateral source rule, caps on municipal liability, and sanctions for frivolous litigation.[107]

The Commission also addressed specific tort reform measures. For example, it concluded that in product liability cases more weight should be accorded the "state-of-the-art" at the time a product is manufactured in determining whether it is defective. In this regard, the Commission recommended establishing a rebuttable presumption that a product whose design complied with the "state-of-the-art" at the time of manufacture is *not* defective.[108]

Tort Reform Legislation   More visible than studies and reports was the activity of state legislatures and regulatory bodies. State legislative and regulatory activity concerning the liability insurance crisis in the last year was enormous. While a few states took little or no action,[109] most of the states examined the problems of the tort system, and tried to address them legislatively.

There was little uniformity among the states that adopted tort reform measures in 1986. While some states acted comprehensively, most adopted more discrete reforms. And even states which attacked the same aspects of the problem, such as the availability of punitive damages, did so with a number of different methods. A few of these state initiatives are described below. Also included is a list of those reforms recommended by the Working Group, and variations thereon, which were adopted in the last year by the states.

Connecticut.   Connecticut's tort reform bill has been described as the most sweeping in New England. Its major provisions include a sliding scale for attorneys' contingency fees (33.3 percent of the first $300,000, 25 percent of the next $300,000, 20 percent of the third $300,000, 15 percent of the fourth $300,000, and 10 percent of all amounts in excess of $1.2 million); a modification of joint and several liability (abolished, for both economic and noneconomic loss, unless another party's share is uncollectible, in which case the remaining parties pay only a share of the uncollectible amount equal to their percentage of fault); an extension to all personal injury actions of the collateral source reductions previously required only in medical malpractice cases; and, a provision which makes periodic payment of future damages in excess of $200,000 mandatory unless the parties agree otherwise. The same legislation also addressed dram shop liability, sanctions for frivolous litigation, and limits on the liability of directors and officers of nonprofit organizations.

Colorado. Colorado enacted more than a dozen measures in 1986 that addressed the liability insurance crisis. Most significantly, joint and several liability has been replaced with several liability in all wrongful death and personal injury actions. Noneconomic damages have been capped at $250,000, unless a court finds "clear and convincing" evidence that they exceed that amount, in which case the cap is raised to $500,000. Damage awards are now automatically reduced by collateral sources of compensation which are received because of the same injury, unless they result from a contractual source (insurance) funded by the plaintiff. Punitive damages cannot exceed the amount of compensatory damages awarded, except in very limited circumstances, and one-third of any punitive damage award goes to Colorado's general revenue fund. The statute of limitations in most product liability suits was lowered from three years to two years, which is now the statute for all tort actions, except intentional torts (one year). Also, municipal liability was limited, and dram shop liability was restricted to cases where the person to whom alcohol was served was either visibly intoxicated or a minor.

New York. Although not all of the Governor's Advisory Commission's recommendations were implemented, significant tort reforms were enacted in New York. Joint and several liability was modified, so that only defendants who are at least 51 percent liable may be held jointly liable for noneconomic damages. Periodic payment of future damages in excess of $250,000 is now mandated if a party requests it. Attorneys' fees and costs, up to $10,000, may be assessed for frivolous litigation. Director and officer liability has been limited to cases of "gross negligence." Evidence of collateral sources of compensation, except workers compensation benefits, may now be considered in determining the size of a damage award. In legislation aimed solely at medical malpractice cases, plaintiffs may now have their claims subjected to arbitration when defendants have conceded liability. The lost earnings component of a damage award may now be reduced by the taxes which would have been paid had the sum actually been normal earnings. And, new provisions have been enacted to monitor professional competence and to investigate professional misconduct.

Washington. Washington enacted significant tort reform measures in 1986. Joint and several liability was eliminated for all damages, except when defendants have acted in concert, the plaintiff is totally blame-free, or the case involves injury from toxic waste. Noneconomic damages are now limited by a formula which is tied to life expectancy and the average annual wage in Washington. Defendants are now protected from liability if the injured party was engaged in the commission of a felony which contributed to the accident, or if the plaintiff was intoxicated (by drugs or alcohol), and that intoxication contributed more than 50 percent to the accident. Periodic payment of all future damages in excess of $100,000 is now mandatory if either party requests it. Attorneys' contingency fee agreements may now be reviewed by the court to ensure they are reasonable. Also, liability of officers and directors of nonprofit organizations, school district employees, and hospital directors has been limited.

Other states also have been quite active in the area of tort reform. The following is a brief (though by no means exhaustive) summary.

Elimination of Joint and Several Liability. The Working Group recommended that the doctrine of joint and several liability be eliminated, except in cases where defendants have acted in concert. The issue of joint and several liability was addressed legislatively in the following states:

Alaska	Minnesota
California	Missouri
Colorado	New Hampshire
Connecticut	New York
Florida	Utah
Hawaii	Washington
Illinois	West Virginia
Michigan	Wyoming

As with every tort reform measure, the degree of response varied. In some states, a defendant's liability in a personal injury suit was strictly limited to his or her percentage of fault.[110] Other states abolished joint liability only with respect to noneconomic damages.[111] Still others eliminated joint liability only for certain types of defendants.[112] And, some states eliminated or modified joint liability only for certain types of personal injury cases.[113]

Limitations on Noneconomic Damages. The Working Group recommended that noneconomic damages (including punitive damages) be limited to a fixed amount. Several states adopted damage caps in 1986:[114]

Alaska ($500,000)	Maryland ($350,000)
Colorado ($250,000)	Minnesota ($400,000)
Florida ($450,000)	New Hampshire ($875,000)
Hawaii ($375,000)	Washington (variable)[115]

However, these caps do not include punitive damage awards and some apply only to certain types of noneconomic damages.[116] Other caps allow blanket exceptions to their application.[117]

Although not in conjunction with caps on noneconomic damages, punitive damages were addressed legislatively in the following states:

Alaska	Minnesota
Colorado	New Hampshire
Florida	Oklahoma
Illinois	South Dakota
Iowa	West Virginia
Maryland	

One state, New Hampshire, enacted an outright prohibition on punitive damages.[118] Several states tied the size of the award to the size of the compensatory damage award.[119] The most common reform was to elevate or more specifically define the standard of proof required for an award of punitive damages.[120] Also common was a requirement that some portion of a punitive damage award be paid to the state.[121]

Modification of the Collateral Source Rule. The Working Group recommended that the collateral source rule, prohibiting the consideration or the offset of collateral benefits, be modified or eliminated. The following states enacted legislation addressing the collateral source rule in 1986:

Alaska	Indiana
Colorado	Massachusetts
Connecticut	Michigan
Florida	Minnesota
Hawaii	New York
Illinois	

Some states, such as Alaska and Minnesota, now simply allow the trier of fact to consider evidence of collateral benefits when determining the amount of damages to award. Other states, such as New York and Indiana, allow or require the court to offset collateral benefits from the jury's award of damages. But not all collateral benefits are treated equally. Depending on the source, or the availability of subrogation, certain collateral benefits may not be offset from an award, or may not be considered by the jury.[122] Other states have adopted only modest changes to the traditional rule.[123]

Use of Periodic Payments for Future Damages. The Working Group recommended that structured payments be used when appropriate, so that a defendant may pay future economic damages as they accrue, instead of in a lump sum. The following states enacted provisions last year governing the use of periodic payment of damage awards:

Alaska	Michigan
Connecticut	New York
Florida	South Dakota
Hawaii	Washington
Iowa	

Most states required that estimated future damages exceed a certain minimum before the use of periodic payments is mandated, and then only at the request of a party. Some states have vested the court with complete discretion, or discretion only in cases where an award exceeds a certain minimum.[124]

Limitations Upon Attorneys' Contingency Fees. The Working Group recommended that attorneys' contingency fees be scheduled on a sliding scale, with declining percentages as the size of the award increases.[125] Attorney's fees were addressed in the following states in 1986:

Connecticut	Missouri
Hawaii	New Hampshire
Idaho	Washington
Maine	Wisconsin
Massachusetts	

Several states imposed a sliding scale for attorneys' contingency fees depending upon the size of the recovery.[126] Several others simply authorized or required the court to review fee agreements to ensure that they are reasonable and fair.[127]

Other Tort Reform Measures. A myriad of other tort reform measures were enacted by the states in 1986. Some of these were narrowly focused on special categories of cases. For example, dram shop liability was addressed in nineteen states. Most dram shop laws immunized social or licensed servers of alcoholic beverages from liability in alcohol-related personal injury suits, unless the person served was under the legal drinking age or was otherwise visibly intoxicated at the time of service. Several states created a legislative presumption that it is the consumption of alcohol, and not its service, which is the proximate cause of subsequent alcohol-related accidents. Similarly, at least twelve states provided partial or total immunity from liability to directors and officers of nonprofit organizations.

A number of tort reform measures of broader application were also enacted. For example, at least fifteen states established or strengthened the penalties available for filing frivolous lawsuits or asserting frivolous defenses. The most common penalty was to authorize or mandate the award of attorneys' fees to the party aggrieved by the frivolous litigation. A number of states reestablished or strengthened the availability of sovereign immunity for their political subdivisions.[128] In all, at least thirty-seven states took some legislative action related to reforming tort liability. Clearly, tort reform was an issue of broad national interest and appeal in 1986.

Insurance Regulation   Either separately or in conjunction with tort reform, many states also addressed the liability insurance crisis by taking action to further regulate the insurance industry. The most common activity was to regulate the circumstances or notice required for mid-term cancellation or nonrenewal of commercial liability insurance policies. Also common were statutes which authorized self-insurance, market assistance purchasing arrangements, or joint underwriting associations, and regulations requiring the insurance industry to report information concerning claims and settlements.

The following states authorized or expanded the development of self-insurance programs for certain categories of insureds:

Alabama	Missouri
Alaska	Montana
Arizona	New Mexico
Florida	New York
Georgia	Ohio
Hawaii	South Dakota
Iowa	Vermont
Kentucky	Washington
Maine	West Virginia
Maryland	Wisconsin
Minnesota	Wyoming

Most of these provisions dealt with self-insurance programs or the formation of risk-pools for public entities, municipalities, or other governmental subdivisions, and not for private groups or individuals.[129] However, the Liability Risk Retention Act of 1986 (Public Law 99-563)[130] assures that self-insurance and insurance purchasing groups are potential options for almost any entity.

Many states enacted legislation providing for greater direct regulation of the insurance industry. Thirty-seven states placed restrictions on the manner in which liability insurance policies can be cancelled or not renewed. For example, Delaware instituted a sixty-day-notice requirement for cancellation or nonrenewal of commercial, municipal, and professional policies. Other states enacted legislation requiring that specific "cause" be shown for mid-term cancellations.

Rate increases also are being subjected to greater scrutiny. New York now requires at least sixty days' notice before an increase in premiums of more than 10 percent. Also implemented were many directives aimed at obtaining information upon which to base future action. At least twenty-one states imposed some degree of new information reporting requirements upon the insurance industry. Most often, these requirements were directed at obtaining specific claims loss data.

VI. AN ANALYSIS OF VARIOUS TORT REFORM PROVISIONS

As is obvious from the last section, tort reform was an area of extraordinary legislative activity in 1986. It is difficult to think of another issue which has generated so much legislation in such a brief period of time in so many states. While some proponents of tort reform were disappointed by the tort reform statutes enacted in their particular states, the overall success of tort reform in 1986 was remarkable considering the complexity of the issues and the resources and aggressive opposition of the plaintiffs' bar.

There were, of course, substantial differences among the tort reform provisions enacted by the states. While many states addressed the same problems, the precise formulations of the "solutions" varied considerably. Some of these legislative provisions are better than others, in the sense that they are more effective, less ambiguous, and less susceptible to being undermined by trial attorneys and judges hostile to tort reform. But all these provisions to some extent reflect the compromises and vagaries inherent in the legislative process.

In drafting and then submitting to the Congress three tort reform bills,[131] the Working Group undertook the same effort undertaken by many tort reform proponents in 1986—to distill its general views about the deficiencies of the tort system into precise statutory reforms. In drafting this legislation, the Working Group attempted to meet several key criteria. First, the legislation should be relatively simple. Complexity breeds ambiguity and complicates the process of legislative deliberation. Second, the legislation should be as precise and clear as possible to maximize its likelihood of surviving judicial challenges seeking to limit its effect. This necessitates foreseeing the arguments that will be made by plaintiffs' attorneys, and drafting the legislation to allow as little interpretative ambiguity as possible. Finally, the legislation should seek to accomplish goals that can be achieved effectively through statutory standards. Thus, the legislation should focus on more mechanical types of reforms which can be expressed in clear statutory directives, rather than attempt to achieve broad doctrinal changes in tort law which are far more difficult to express in statutory language and which necessarily will involve considerable judicial interpretation. This means that many tort reforms that might be desirable in the abstract, cannot be implemented—at least effectively—through legislation.

As noted, there were substantial differences among the state tort reform statutes enacted in 1986. Although there is no single right solution which should be adopted in every state, some of the provisions enacted in 1986 were very effective, while others were so thoroughly compromised that they will have little if any impact on tort liability. The following is a discussion of six areas of tort reform which were the subject of considerable legislative deliberations in the states last year. The analysis discusses the strengths and weaknesses of some of the different legislative approaches in each of these areas. Where appropriate, it also sets out the legislative language drafted by the Working Group, and summarizes the reasons for the precise formulations adopted by the Working Group.

Joint and Several Liability

It is now widely recognized that the development of comparative fault has substantially undermined whatever justification may once have existed under the common law for joint and several liability. For that reason, abolition or modification of joint and several liability was a key component of many state tort reform statutes.

Despite the reverence in which the doctrine is still held by the plaintiffs' bar, few problems of the tort system have been as readily understood by the public as the patent unfairness of requiring a defendant who bears only minimal responsibility for an injury to pay all of plaintiff's damages. Particularly municipalities have been hard hit by the doctrine, and, accordingly, have been among its sharpest critics.

Joint and several liability also has led to abusive litigation practices in which "deep pockets" only marginally involved in the case are brought into the lawsuit because a 1 percent finding of liability will guarantee plaintiff a 100 percent recovery. Consequently, many plaintiffs' attorneys now use what is commonly known as "shotgun" pleadings, in which every possible person and entity—particularly those with assets or insurance—are named as defendants even if they have no readily apparent responsibility for the injury.

Finally, joint and several liability makes it extremely difficult for insurers to project liability, and undoubtedly increases the price of insurance. Joint and several liability, by exposing the insurer to liability for the wrongful acts of persons or entities it may not even be able to identify, much less take into account, substantially increases the unpredictability of tort liability.

A number of states which addressed joint and several liability abolished such liability, but only for noneconomic damages. While this undoubtedly was an attempt at compromise—and represents an improvement over no modification at all of joint and several liability—it nonetheless is a poorly conceived compromise. For one thing, there is no principled distinction between economic and noneconomic damages which justifies the application of joint and several liability as to the one component of damages but not as to the other. If it is unfair for a defendant to bear the cost of another person's responsibility for the plaintiff's noneconomic damages, it is equally unfair for that defendant to bear the cost of that person's responsibility for the plaintiff's economic damages.

As important is the fact that such a partial response to joint and several liability does not eliminate the problems such liability generates; it does not obviate the incentives for pursuing "deep pockets" only tangentially involved in an injury, nor does it cure the unpredictability stemming from such liability. Thus, such a partial abolition of joint and several is a compromise which leaves much of the unfairness in place and does not correct many of the abuses arising from the application of the doctrine.

The above observations are equally true for other types of compromises such as defendant-specific exceptions[132] or exemptions of certain classes or categories of cases. It is particularly unfortunate that some legislatures have recognized the unfairness of joint and several liability as to municipal defendants, but have failed to abolish the doctrine as to private parties. While, as noted, municipalities have been particularly hard hit by the doctrine, there is no reason to leave the doctrine in place for nongovernmental entities.

The following is the Working Group's draft provision abolishing joint and several liability.

Joint and Several Liability

(a) Except as provided in subsection (b) of this section, joint and several liability may not be applied to any action subject to this Act. A person found liable for damages in any such action may be found liable, if at all, only for those damages directly attributable to the person's pro-rata share of fault or responsibility for the injury, and may not be found liable for damages attributable to the pro-rata share of fault or responsibility of any other person (without regard to whether that person is a party to the action) for the injury, including any person bringing the action.

(b) This section shall not apply as between persons acting in concert where the concerted action proximately caused the injury for which one or more persons are found liable for damages. As used in this section, "concerted action" or "acting in concert" means the conscious acting together in a common scheme or plan of two or more persons resulting in a tortious act.

It should be noted that the provision specifically exempts concerted action from the abolition of joint and several liability. This means nothing more than that when two persons act together to achieve a common goal, one should not be able to avoid the responsibility for the other's actions when that common goal has been achieved. It is important, however, that the exemption for concerted action be drafted narrowly to avoid expansive interpretations that effectively impute concerted action.[133]

Noneconomic Damages

Perhaps the most controversial tort reform measure considered by the states in 1986 was whether and how to limit noneconomic damages such as pain and suffering, mental anguish, and so on. The debate over such a limitation often has been emotionally charged and divisive. Consequently, a number of state legislatures avoided the issue or limited their deliberations to punitive damages (discussed later in this chapter).

A limitation on noneconomic damages, however, if properly formulated, probably is the single most effective legislative reform of tort law. Not only does such a limitation significantly reduce the costs of the tort system,[134] but it also serves to expedite settlements by eliminating an unknown which undermines the ability of the parties to reach agreement on compensable damages. Such a limitation also mitigates the unfairness of the tort system for many plaintiffs and defendants arising from the fact that widely different damages are often awarded for nearly identical injuries.

The discussion in a previous section of the most recent jury award data makes it clear that damages in tort cases have, for whatever reason, undergone explosive growth in the 1980s. As noted in the chapter, much of this growth can be attributed to noneconomic damages, which in turn can be attributed to a small percentage of all tort cases. Accordingly, a reasonable cap on noneconomic damages will have only a limited impact on the vast majority of all tort cases. But its effect on those cases on which it does impact will have a very substantial influence on the viability and overall cost of the entire tort system. In other words, only a small percentage of all tort claims are responsible for much of the extraordinary recent growth in settlements and verdicts, and a reasonable limitation on noneconomic damages will affect precisely those claims.

Moreover, given that consumers and taxpayers must bear the cost of the recent explosive growth in damage awards, it seems more than appropriate for state legislatures to consider whether this growth in fact is in the public interest, or whether noneconomic damages should be stabilized at some fair and reasonable level. Ultimately, the question of whether noneconomic damages should be limited or allowed to continue their rapid growth involves the balancing of conflicting societal interests, including society's interest in maintaining a stable and affordable tort system. This is a balance which state legislatures seem to be far more capable of striking than courts engaged in case-by-case adjudications.

While there are other ways to limit noneconomic damages,[135] the simplest and most widely adopted method is an absolute cap on the amount of noneconomic damages that may be awarded with regard to a particular injury. In order for such a limitation to be effective, it should meet several criteria. First, it should include all noneconomic damages, and not be limited to a subset of noneconomic damages. Noneconomic damages are so subjective that it is relatively simple for a court or jury to avoid a partial limitation by shifting such damages between different categories of noneconomic injuries.[136] Second, the limitation should encompass all plaintiffs, all defendants, and all claims that may flow directly or indirectly from an injury. Unless this criteria is met, the limitation can be defeated by having different individuals (usually family members) sue separately, or by suing additional defendants, or by filing as many different separate claims as possible.

Finally, the limitation must be set at some reasonable level that is fair to the plaintiff yet not so high as to be counterproductive. This is particularly important since a limitation also serves to some extent as a floor, and thus may actually *increase* many noneconomic damage awards. This effect in fact may be beneficial in reducing the wide variance between tort awards for similar injuries. But if a limitation on noneconomic damages is too high, it may actually increase rather than decrease overall damage awards. In addition, a limitation that exceeds a reasonable level is in fact no limitation at all; it affects so few cases that it has almost no beneficial impact on the tort system.

The Working Group originally recommended a $100,000 limit on noneconomic damages. In light of the higher limitations enacted by most states that addressed the problem last year, the Working Group has increased its recommendation to $200,000. The precise level of such a limitation, however, is a quintessential legislative judgment which each state legislature must make on its own.

The following is the Working Group's draft of a statutory formulation for an effective limitation on noneconomic damages.

Limitation on Noneconomic Damages

(a) Non-economic damages may not be awarded in excess of $200,000 in any action subject to this Act.

(b) For purposes of this section, "any action" includes all actions (including multiple actions) for damages, and includes all plaintiffs and all defendants in such actions, which arise out of or were caused by the same personal injury or death.

(c) As used in this section, "noneconomic damages" means all damages other than damages for economic loss, and includes punitive or exemplary damages. "Economic loss" means past and future (A) expenses of health or other care, (B) expenses of rehabilitation, (C) loss of earnings, (D) loss of homemaker services, and (E) burial expenses.

The limitation includes a definition of economic loss because of the concern expressed by some that courts hostile to a limitation on noneconomic damages would create new forms of economic damages to substitute for limited noneconomic damages.

Punitive Damages

As is obvious from the language of the above draft limitation on noneconomic damages, the Working Group recommended in its prior report that punitive damages be included within the overall limitation on noneconomic damages. This remains the Working Group's preferred approach. While some have recommended a separate, perhaps higher, limitation for punitive damages, the Working Group is concerned that such an approach would lead courts and juries to award punitive damages as a way of circumventing a limitation on noneconomic damages. Certainly, it would lead plaintiffs' attorneys to add punitive damage claims almost routinely to every claim (which, unfortunately, increasingly is the case anyway).

There are, however, alternative approaches that have considerable merit. One obvious reform is simply to abolish punitive damages in all cases where the underlying claim for compensatory damages is based on negligence, malpractice, or strict product liability. Historically, punitive damages arose in the context of intentional torts. It is only relatively recently that they have found their way into nonintentional tort actions. Restricting their application to intentional torts would simply return them to their traditional role in the tort system.

Another alternative is to limit punitive damages to a portion or multiple of plaintiff's awarded economic damages.[137] Such an approach would have the benefit of ensuring that the larger punitive damage awards are made to seriously injured plaintiffs.

A third alternative is to have all or virtually all of the award paid to the state to be used for public purposes. Since punitive damages are a windfall for the plaintiff and his or her attorney, there is much to be said for ensuring that this windfall accrues to the public. However, this approach is unprecedented in our legal system (although several states enacted such provisions last year), and may generate difficult problems of application and administration, particularly for the vast majority of cases settled out of court.

A fourth approach is to restrict attorneys' contingency fees to no more than 5 percent of any punitive damage award. While it is unlikely that such a restriction would prevent plaintiffs from seeking punitive damages where they are merited, it would reduce the incentive many plaintiffs' attorneys now have to pursue such claims at the cost of a reasonable settlement in their client's best interest.

The Working Group is relatively skeptical about the value of changing the standard of conduct or burden of proof which plaintiff must demonstrate to obtain punitive damages. While commendable, such changes are highly subjective, and thus quite susceptible to abuse. The recent increase in punitive damages has taken place, for the most part, with no articulated change in the doctrinal standard pursuant to which they are awarded. Accordingly, the Working Group believes that the most effective legislative approach to reforming punitive damages is to place some objective restriction on such damages, as discussed above. However, if the only possible reform is to address the required standard of conduct or burden of proof, the Working Group strongly recommends that punitive damage awards be restricted to cases where the plaintiff can demonstrate by clear and convincing evidence that the defendant acted with actual malice.[138]

Periodic Payments

The use of periodic payments for future economic damages can produce savings for the defendant or his or her insurer without depriving the plaintiff of anything to which he or she otherwise is entitled. Periodic payment provisions address those cases where the judge or jury has found that at some point in the future the injury suffered as a result of a defendant's conduct will cause the plaintiff to incur certain expenses or to forgo certain income. The use of periodic payments simply allows these sums to be paid to the plaintiff as they accrue.

As a result, there should be little reason to oppose the availability of periodic payments when *either* party believes it to be a better course of action in a particular case. When cases are settled for large amounts, the parties frequently agree to structured terms which result in the payment of the settlement over a long period of time. There is no reasoned distinction for precluding the use of similar arrangements simply because the amount of damages has been determined by a jury instead of through a settlement.

There are several important criteria, however, to the effective use of periodic payments. First, their use should not be left to the court's discretion. Instead, they should be required, but only when at least one of the parties indicates that some form of periodic payments is desirable. It serves no purpose to require periodic payments in a case where neither party desires that they be used.

Second, whatever periodic payments schedule is fashioned, it must not be open-ended—that is, it must not be subject to subsequent modification, except upon agreement of the parties. To allow either party to seek changes to the agreement from the court will quickly consume in additional litigation and transaction costs any savings that result from the use of periodic payments. In other words, a periodic payments provision should under no circumstances undermine the finality of the court's damage award.

Third, the Working Group continues to believe that periodic payments should not be imposed when future economic damages do not exceed a certain minimum level. The Working Group recommends a minimum of $100,000, though some states have set an even higher level.

Finally, such a provision should protect plaintiffs from the possible insolvency of defendants by permitting the court under appropriate circumstances to require the defendant to purchase an annuity providing the periodic payments.

The Working Group drafted the following provision which meets its criteria for periodic payments.

Periodic Payments of Judgments

(a) In any action subject to this Act in which the damages awarded for future economic loss exceed $100,000, no person may be required to pay damages for future economic loss in a single, lump-sum payment, but shall be permitted to make such payments periodically based on when the damages are found likely to occur.

(b) The court may require such person to purchase an annuity making such periodic payments if the court finds a reasonable basis for concluding that the person may not make the periodic payments.

(c) The judgment of the court awarding such periodic payments may not be reopened at any time to contest, amend, or modify the schedule or amount of the payments in the absence of fraud.

(d) This section shall not be construed to preclude a settlement providing for a single, lump-sum payment.

Collateral Source Rule

The collateral source rule provides that a plaintiff's award may not be reduced by other sources of compensation the plaintiff receives as a result of the same injury. The Working Group sees no reason why plaintiffs should be permitted to receive double compensation, particularly where part of the compensation is paid by the government. It simply makes no sense to require consumers of goods and services to pay higher prices to compensate plaintiffs through tort settlements or judgments, and then to pay higher taxes to compensate plaintiffs a second time through government benefits for the same injury.[139]

There are two important qualifications to the Working Group's position on the collateral source rule. First, it does not believe that collateral sources purchased purely by the plaintiff or his or her family should be included in the offset. Only benefits paid for in whole or in part by the government or by some independent source (such as the plaintiff's employer) should be treated as collateral sources to be offset from the tort award.

Second, the Working Group is concerned that existing subrogation rights not be lost. Thus, a collateral source offset ideally should not apply where there is a subrogated claim for restitution of the collateral source. This makes sense since a source of income is not really "collateral" if the plaintiff is required to reimburse the collateral source from the tort award.

Some have suggested that such subrogation proceedings, particularly as they apply to workers compensation payments, involve such high transaction costs that it may be advantageous to prohibit subrogation in certain situations. Particularly in the context of product liability, there appears to be considerable support for the position that substantial resources would be saved by a prohibition on subrogation proceedings by employers against liable manufacturers as well as indemnification proceedings by liable manufacturers against employers. The reasoning is that such subrogation and indemnification lawsuits generate considerable attorneys' fees without providing much in the way of social benefit. Thus, it is argued that the prohibition of such suits would be a "wash" for employers and liable manufacturers while saving both sides substantial attorneys' fees.

The Working Group has considerable sympathy for this argument, and does not wish its position on subrogation to be understood as opposition to such an arrangement if mutually acceptable to both employers and manufacturers.

The following is the collateral source modification provision drafted by the Working Group.

Collateral Sources of Compensation

(a) Any award of damages to a person in an action subject to this Act shall be reduced by the court by the amount of any past or future payment or benefit covered by this section which the person has received or for which the person is eligible on account of the same personal injury or death for which such damages are awarded.

(b) As used in this section, "payment or benefit covered by this section" means—

(1) any payment or benefit by or paid for in whole or in part by any agency or instrumentality of the United States, a State or a local government, or

(2) any payment or benefit by a workers' compensation system or a health insurance program funded in whole or in part by an employer;

but does not include any such payment or benefit that is (or by law is required to be) the subject of a reasonably founded claim of subrogation, reinbursement or lien.

VI. Attorneys' Contingency Fees

There is growing recognition that attorneys' contingency fees are a source of abuse that needs to be addressed. Even the American Bar Association House of Delegates recently adopted a recommendation that such fees be scrutinized more carefully.[140] But there continues to be substantial disagreement about how these abuses should best be addressed.

The Working Group believes that a sliding scale is the best and most equitable approach to dealing with the problem of excessive contingency fees. On the one hand, it ensures that contingency fees will be high enough to induce attorneys to take smaller claims, while, on the other hand, precluding immense and unjustified windfalls to attorneys from very high verdicts and settlements. The Working Group believes that such a sliding scale will provide more than adequate compensation for attorneys, while significantly reducing the transaction costs that make tort litigation such an extraordinarily expensive dispute resolution system.

The Working Group does not believe that provisions that merely give greater discretion to courts to review contingency fees will be very effective. While some contingency fees undoubtedly would be reduced by some courts if given greater discretion to do so, such actions likely would be rare and would have virtually no impact on the overall cost of tort litigation.

The following is the provision drafted by the Working Group on attorneys' contingency fees.

Attorneys' Contingency Fee Arrangements

(a) An attorney who represents, on a contingency fee basis, a person bringing an action subject to this Act may not charge, demand, receive, or collect for services rendered in connection with such action in excess of 25 percent of the first $100,000 (or portion thereof) recovered, plus 20 percent of the next $100,000 (or portion thereof) recovered, plus 15 percent of the next $100,000 (or portion thereof) recovered, plus 10 percent of any amount in excess of $300,000 recovered by judgment or settlement in such action.

(b) As used in this section, "contingency fee" means any fee for professional legal services that is in whole or in part contingent upon the recovery of any amount of damages, whether through judgment or settlement.

(c) In the event that such judgment or settlement includes periodic or future payments of damages, the amount recovered for purposes of computing the limitation on the attorney's contingency fee shall be based on the cost of the annuity or trust established to make payments. In any case in which an annuity or trust is not established to make such payments, such amount shall be based on the present value of the payments.

VII. THE RELATIONSHIP OF TORT REFORM TO INSURANCE AVAILABILITY AND AFFORDABILITY

In its report of last year, the Working Group recommended eight reforms of tort law. The Working Group felt that these eight reforms "would bring a greater degree of rationality and predictability to tort law, and thereby significantly assist in resolving the availability and affordability crisis.[141] The Working Group recognized that its list of recommended reforms was by no means exhaustive, but concluded that their adoption would result in "a more predictable and affordable liability allocating mechanism."[142]

The eight reforms recommended by the Working Group were:

- Return to a fault-based standard for liability.
- Base causation findings on credible scientific and medical evidence and opinions.
- Eliminate joint and several liability in cases where defendants have not acted in concert.
- Limit noneconomic damages (such as pain and suffering, mental anguish, or punitive damages) to a fair and reasonable maximum dollar amount.
- Provide for periodic (instead of lump-sum) payments of damages for future medical care or lost income.
- Reduce awards in cases where a plaintiff can be compensated by certain collateral sources to prevent a windfall double recovery.
- Limit attorneys' contingency fees to reasonable amounts on a "sliding scale."
- Encourage use of alternative dispute resolution mechanisms to resolve cases out of court.

As related previously, a number of states enacted tort reform proposals in 1986, many of which addressed the same problems identified by the Working Group. Recently, however, there has been a growing sense of frustration in some quarters that these enacted reforms have not been followed by immediate substantial rollbacks in the price of insurance. In some instances, the insurance market has tightened even further despite the enactment of tort reform legislation. Not surprisingly, opponents of tort reform have seized upon these events to claim that tort reform has no effect on insurance availability or affordability. But even some strong supporters of tort reform have expressed their disappointment at the fact that insurance prices have not responded more rapidly to the enactment of tort reform legislation.

Unfortunately, the reality is that the deterioration of our civil justice system is a long-term problem, and that any legislative reforms simply will not cure that deterioration overnight. While the impatience and frustration of those who expect immediate results is understandable, it is also unrealistic. There are several important, inescapable reasons why tort reforms take time to affect insurance availability and affordability, and it is crucial to the national debate on tort reform to understand those reasons.

One important reason that enacted tort reforms frequently do not have an immediate impact on insurance is the time-consuming process of determining their constitutionality. It can take years, perhaps a decade or more, before the highest court of a state renders its opinion on the constitutionality of a particular tort reform provision. For the plaintiffs' bar, tort reform is a two-front war—the first front is the state legislature, but any loss there still can (and usually will) be challenged in the courts.[143]

The time-consuming nature of such constitutional litigation is amply demonstrated by California's experience. In 1975 California enacted a set of comprehensive medical malpractice reforms, entitled the Medical Injury Compensation Reform Act of 1975 (MICRA). These reforms were immediately challenged in the courts, and not until nearly a decade later did the California Supreme Court (by a four to three vote) and the United States Court of Appeals for the Ninth Circuit uphold the constitutionality of the statute. *Fein* v. *Permanente Medical Group*, 38 Cal.3d 137, 695 P.2d 665 (1985);[144] *Hoffman* v. *United States*, 767 F.2d 1431 (9th Cir. 1985).

Insurers, of course, are well aware of such constitutional challenges, and of the fact that many such challenges against the medical malpractice statutes enacted in the mid-1970s were relatively successful. They also are aware that if a particular tort reform provision is declared unconstitutional, their liability will be determined on the basis of pre-existing law, even if the insurance premium was calculated on the basis of the reformed law. Accordingly, many insurers are reluctant to write policies which take tort reforms completely into account until those reforms have been found to be constitutionally valid.

A second factor which often delays the impact of tort reform is the process of judicial construction and application. Frequently, even where the reform is thought to be constitutional, there is sufficient ambiguity in the statutory language to allow courts great leeway in construing and applying the statute. Unfortunately, judges opposed to tort reform often are quite creative in interpreting reform provisions so as to reduce or even virtually eliminate their effect. Other times, however, the problem can be traced to poor legislative draftsmanship and unclear or contradictory legislative history. Thus, many tort reform provisions are sufficiently confusing or ambiguous (or have minor ambiguities which are exploited by opponents of the provision) that their meaning often can be determined only after years of litigation.

Obviously, the process of judicial construction and application can delay the impact of tort reform legislation for years. Just as insurers are reluctant to write policies on the basis of statutes that may be declared unconstitutional, they also are reluctant to write policies on the basis of statutes whose meaning is ambiguous and whose effect may be eviscerated through hostile judicial interpretation.

A third reason tort reform provisions often take time to have their desired effect on insurance rates is that the impact of some reforms can be determined only through experience. The effect of certain reforms, such as a cap on liability or an offset of collateral sources of compensation, should be relatively easy to "cost out." The likely savings from other reforms, however, particularly those directed at changing standards of liability or proof, use of alternative dispute resolution, tightening of sanctions for frivolous or abusive litigation, and regulation of attorneys' fees, are far more difficult to assess. In essence, the insurer must make behavioral judgments about plaintiffs, juries, and attorneys that are inherently speculative. For example, to what extent does a more rigorous burden of proof (such as the use of "clear and convincing" rather than "preponderance of the evidence") affect the willingness of a plaintiff to bring a claim, or the willingness of his or her attorney to settle the claim, or, most importantly, the final determination of a jury? These are critical questions which are extraordinarily difficult to answer in the abstract.

Insurers often are reluctant to make such abstract behavioral judgments. Where possible they try to base their underwriting decisions on actual claims experience, and such claims experience can accumulate for several years before it provides meaningful insights. That is not to say that insurers cannot and do not attempt to assess the impact of tort reforms without the benefit of detailed claims experience. It is to say, however, that many insurers are unwilling to assume large (and sometimes optimistic) savings on the basis of behavioral assumptions for which there is no corroborating claims experience.

It is also important to note that tort liability is only one factor—

albeit the most important factor—that determines the price of insurance. There are other considerations that also change over time, such as the prevailing interest rates, the return available from investment securities, state regulatory practices (including reserve requirements), and taxes, which affect the price of insurance. If some or all of these considerations exert upward pressure on the price of insurance, tort reform provisions may do no more in the short-term than to reduce the rate of premium increases.

Finally, the effect of many tort reforms may be obscured by the continuing deterioration of other aspects of the tort system which have not been reformed. Thus, for example, a mandatory offset of collateral benefits may achieve substantial savings, but those savings may be overwhelmed by continuing increases in noneconomic damage awards. The collateral benefit reform may have reduced the price of insurance over what it otherwise would have been, but due to other aspects of tort law, the price of insurance nonetheless may have increased, perhaps even substantially.

None of the above should be interpreted to mean that tort reform does not affect the availability and affordability of insurance. To the contrary, as discussed below, there is persuasive evidence of such an effect. But the above considerations indicate that the impact of tort reform often can be very difficult to ascertain in the short-term, even if its long-term impact can be quite substantial.[145]

While there is some anecdotal evidence showing that the tort reforms enacted in 1986 already are having an impact on insurance availability and affordability,[146] it is far too early to have any solid statistical evidence demonstrating the existence and extent of the impact of these reforms on the insurance market. There is, however, a body of data which is quite useful in documenting the link between tort reform and insurance. This body of data can be derived from the medical malpractice reforms of the mid-1970s, which have been in place (at least in those states where their constitutionality has been upheld) long enough to provide some useful information.

Recently, the General Accounting Office (GAO) studied six state medical malpractice statutes and their affect on claims and the cost of medical malpractice insurance.[147] Of particular interest is the comparison between California, which enacted a very rigorous medical malpractice statute in 1975,[148] and Florida and New York, which enacted substantially weaker reforms in the mid-1970s.[149]

The three states are useful for purposes of comparison since all three are highly urbanized,[150] and have large populations and substantial insurance markets. It is worth noting that of the three, California has the tort system most generally advantageous to plaintiffs. Indeed, the California Supreme Court has for many years been one of the most

Exhibit 12-20
Percent Increase in Malpractice Insurance Rates for Selected Specialties Between January 1, 1980, and January 1, 1986

	California	Florida	New York
General Practice	173%	199%	335%
Internal Medicine	61%	199%	326%
General Surgery	88%	256%	175%
Anesthesiology	35%	217%	96%
Obstetrics/Gynecology	140%	395%	345%
Orthopedic Surgery	88%	198%	216%
Neurosurgery	113%	370%	273%

activist courts in the nation in developing new tort liability theories, and has issued many of the seminal opinions that have undermined the role of fault and causation in determining liability. MICRA, on the other hand, is one of the most rigorous medical malpractice statutes in the United States. (See note 148.)

The GAO study provides the data shown in Exhibit 12-20 as to the increase in malpractice insurance rates during the 1980s.[151]

While all three states witnessed an increase in the cost of medical malpractice insurance from 1980 to 1986, both New York and Florida far outstripped California. Particularly in the two high litigation risk specialties (obstetrics/gynecology and neurosurgery), the difference between California, on the one hand, and New York and Florida, on the other, is stark. For both of these specialties, the percentage rate of increase in insurance premiums was two to three times greater in Florida and New York than in California.

These findings are consistent with a 1985 report to the New York Medical Society.[152] Among other things, the report contains data on the 1985 premiums for a $1,000,000/$3,000,000 malpractice insurance policy,[153] as well as the size of the premiums as a percentage of physician net income and gross revenue (see Exhibit 12-21).

Both the GAO study and the report to the New York Medical Society show quite clearly that California physicians have fared substantially better than their Florida or New York colleagues as far as the cost of their malpractice insurance is concerned. Not only is the absolute cost of medical malpractice insurance significantly lower in California, but perhaps even more importantly from the standpoint of showing the link between tort reform and malpractice, the *rate* of premium increases has been far more moderate in California. The inescapable conclusion is that MICRA has had a very substantial

Exhibit 12-21
1985 Premiums

	Malpractice Insurance Premiums	Premiums as a Percentage of Net Income	Premiums as a Percentage of Gross Revenue
All Physicians			
California	$10,547	9.5%	5.0%
Florida	$16,018	11.9%	6.6%
New York	$17,109	18.0%	10.2%
Obstetrics/ Gynecology			
California	$36,685	27.7%	13.6%
Florida	$57,781	38.5%	20.9%
New York	$51,420	51.6%	23.5%

impact on the cost of medical malpractice insurance for California physicians.

Two useful conclusions can be drawn from the data applicable to more general tort reform efforts. First, strong tort reform measures that rigorously address the problems of tort law—such as California's MICRA—can have a very real and substantial effect on insurance costs. Second, weak tort reform measures—such as the medical malpractice statutes enacted in Florida and New York in the mid-1970s—probably will have only a very limited impact on insurance availability and affordability.

There are also some important additional observations on the link between tort reform and insurance availability and affordability. One observation is that patience is important; tort reform works, but only if given time. And, obviously, the sooner reforms are enacted, the sooner they will begin to have their effect on the insurance market. A second critical observation is that tort reform statutes will be far more effective, and achieve their purposes more quickly, when they are drafted clearly with all ambiguities resolved prior to enactment. Finally, and perhaps the most important consideration, the ultimate success of tort reform measures depends greatly on the sensitivity of the courts to the legitimate need for and very real benefits of such legislation. The natural inclination of many judges is to oppose tort reform. And judicial hostility to tort reform can defeat, or, at a minimum, substantially delay the implementation of even the most necessary and popular reforms of the civil justice system. In this regard, the recent success of MICRA before the California Supreme

Court, the United States Court of Appeals for the Ninth Circuit, and the United States Supreme Court, suggests that the courts may be much more receptive to such legislation than in the recent past.

VIII. CONCLUSION

While there are a number of conclusions and recommendations contained within this report, the following are the Working Group's primary conclusions regarding the insurance and liability crisis and the appropriate response of the federal government to that crisis.

First, the crisis in insurance availability and affordability, while substantially ameliorated, continues to impose significant costs on much of the American economy. The effects of the crisis likely will be felt throughout the economy—particularly in certain sectors—for some time to come.

Second, tort liability is a key underlying reason for the crisis in insurance availability and affordability. Its contribution to the crisis is two-fold: rapidly expanding liability, including dramatically higher damage awards, have substantially increased the cost of the tort liability system; and changing doctrinal standards have significantly heightened the uncertainty and unpredictability of the tort system, thereby exacerbating the already serious problems of the system.

Third, legislative tort reforms are a reasonable, legitimate, and effective response to many of the deficiencies of tort law. Such legislation, however, is by no means the only answer to the problems of the tort system; much of the responsibility for improvement remains with the courts.

Fourth, rigorous and meaningful tort reforms can have a real impact on insurance availability and affordability if given the opportunity and sufficient time to work.

Fifth, the Working Group continues to believe that there is no justification or need for federal insurance regulation or for the creation of federal insurance or indemnification programs.

Sixth, there is an appropriate role for federal tort reform legislation in those areas where there is a compelling federal interest. Such areas include product liability, the liability of federal government contractors, and the tort liability of the federal government and its employees.

Seventh, the Administration should continue to support and work actively with governors and state legislators to achieve reasonable and workable tort reforms at the state level.

Eighth, the Working Group continues to believe that the eight tort reforms recommended in its prior report represent the most sensible and effective potential reforms of the American civil justice system.

Monograph Notes

1. The Tort Policy Working Group consists of senior administration officials of eleven federal agencies, seven of whom serve as the chief legal officer of their agency.
2. "Report of the Tort Policy Working Group on the Causes, Extent and Policy Implications of the Current Crisis in Insurance Availability and Affordability," (Washington, DC: Tort Policy Working Group, February 1986), p. 80.
3. "Report of the Tort Policy Working Group . . . ," pp. 51-52, 60 and 80.
4. "Beyond Tort Reform," 257 *JAMA* 827 (1987).
5. Insurance Information Institute, *1986-87 Property/Casualty Fact Book*, p. 22. These figures are based on Generally Accepted Accounting Principles ("GAAP"). The comparable statutory accounting rates of return were 1.7 percent and 2.8 percent.
6. This is the statutory accounting rate of return. GAAP figures for 1986 are not yet available. From 1976 to 1985, the GAAP figures closely tracked the statutory accounting figures, and in seven of those ten years showed a lower rate of return.
7. *1986-87 Property/Casualty Fact Book*, at page 22.
8. The statutory accounting rates of return for 1977 and 1978 were 21.3 percent and 20.5 percent respectively. *Id.*
9. *Best's Insurance Management Reports.*
10. "Insurer Stocks Trail Wall Street Gains," *Business Insurance*, 23 February 1987, p. 2. The article indicates that some investors are skeptical that the industry's recent improvement in earnings will continue.
11. The Statistical Information Advisory Committee to the NAIC Legal Liability Insurance (D) Task Force, *The Report of the Statistical Information Advisory Committee* 2.47 (1986).
12. M. Peterson, *Civil Juries in the 1980s: Trends in Jury Trials and Verdicts in California and Cook County, Illinois* (Institute for Civil Justice, 1987).
13. The Institute for Civil Justice selected Cook County and San Francisco for its jury verdict studies "because they are major urban commercial centers in different regions and because (the Institute) could draw upon jury verdict publications in both to obtain information about long-term trends." *Id.*, at page 1. The jury verdict reporters for each jurisdiction are described by the Institute as "among the best publications of their sort in the country." *Id.*
14. The malpractice data include not only medical malpractice but all forms of malpractice liability. While the analysis does not provide separate data on medical malpractice, it is likely that the malpractice data consist predominantly of medical malpractice cases.

15. *Civil Juries in the 1980s*, at page 22.
16. *Id.*
17. *Id.*, at page 35.
18. *Id.*, at page 22.
19. Jury Verdict Research, Inc., corroborates that in product liability cases plaintiffs have increasingly fared better before juries. See Testimony of Philip J. Hermann (Chairman of the Board, Jury Verdict Research, Inc.) before the House Subcommittee on Economic Stabilization on August 6, 1986 ("recovery rate for product liability has substantially increased in the past eight years").
20. *Civil Juries in the 1980s*, at page 17. Product liability cases in San Francisco are an exception. Plaintiffs' rate of success there has remained roughly constant since 1960, at about one-half of all jury verdicts.
21. Critics of the February 1986 report have argued that the average jury awards cited in the report are "inflated" because they do not reflect cases in which defendants prevail before the jury. The argument misses the point, however, since the report sought to document the *trend* of rapidly increasing jury awards. As long as the same categories of data (that is, plaintiffs' verdicts) are compared over time, the report's conclusion as to the trend remains entirely valid. But since the report did not reflect that plaintiffs steadily have increased the percentage of jury verdicts in which they prevail, the report, if anything, *understated* the magnitude of the trend. In any event, "expected award" data fully take into account those cases in which defendants prevail before the jury.
22. *Civil Juries in the 1980s*, at page 26.
23. *Id.*
24. *Id.*, at page 35. As with the average jury verdicts, the expected awards are inflation adjusted and expressed in 1984 dollars.
25. While there may be some deficiencies with the methodology used by Jury Verdict Research, Inc., as noted in the February 1986 report, the methodology has remained consistent over the relevant period. See Working Group Report, at page 35 n. 33. Thus, it is entirely appropriate to use Jury Verdict Research data to show the trend in jury awards, since as long as its methodology remains consistent the trends derived from the data should be accurate. While critics of the February 1986 report have contended that Jury Verdict Research data are collected purely from newspaper articles, Jury Verdict Research in fact uses a variety of reporting services to obtain jury verdicts. As stated last year by the Chairman of the Board of Jury Verdict Research, Inc., before the House Subcommittee on Economic Stabilization: "We are confident that the data for the hundreds of cases that Jury Verdict Research receives and processes each week (about 2,000 a month) constitutes more than a representative sampling and enables our staff to compile valid statistical verdict information."
26. Jury Verdict Research, Inc., *Injury Valuation: Current Award Trends* (1987). The 1975 to 1979 data can be found in the 1986 issue of *Current Award Trends*, and are summarized in the Working Group's February 1986 report, at pages 35-39. The award data for 1986 are incomplete and subject to refinement.

27. *Civil Juries in the 1980s*, at page 33.
28. *Id.*
29. *Id.* at page 37.
30. *Id.* As a percentage of *all* personal injury trials, including those in which defendants prevailed, million-dollar awards occurred in only 1.7 percent of all such trials. The corresponding percentage for San Francisco was 2 percent.
31. Patricia Danzon, for example, in her analysis of medical malpractice damages, estimates that for jury awards involving more than $100,000 in noneconomic damages, on the average 80 percent of the entire award is for noneconomic damages. *See* February 1986 Working Group Report, at pages 67-68. She also estimates that noneconomic damage awards in excess of $100,000 account for between 28 percent to 50 percent of *all* paid out medical malpractice damages. *Id.*
32. While the valuation of components such as lost earnings and the cost of necessary medical care is a relatively straightforward process, compensation for pain and suffering, mental anguish and other forms of noneconomic damages is wholly subjective and often varies greatly between cases involving similar injuries. Moreover, once economic damages are adjusted for inflation, the objective criteria used to determine these components should preclude large fluctuations over time. Noneconomic damages, in contrast, are based on subjective criteria which can change dramatically over time.
33. This often repeated assertion appears to be highly questionable. The recently published Institute for Civil Justice analysis shows a very substantial increase in inflation-adjusted median jury verdicts from the early 1960s to the early 1980s. For example, median malpractice jury awards increased in Cook County from $35,000 in the early 1960s to $121,000 in the early 1980s, with a corresponding increase in San Francisco from $64,000 to $156,000. *Civil Juries in the 1980s*, at page 22. Median product liability awards in Cook County increased from $103,000 to $187,000 during this period, with a corresponding increase in San Francisco, from $27,000 to $200,000. *Id.* Jury Verdict Research data, which are not inflation-adjusted, show a very substantial increase during the 1980s in median jury awards for both medical malpractice (from $200,000 in 1980 to $515,000 in 1986) and product liability (from $225,000 in 1980 to $603,400 in 1986). For purposes of comparison, the Consumer Price Index during this period increased by 33 percent.
34. See, e.g., Public Citizen, *The Assault on Personal Injury Lawsuits: A Study of Reality Versus Myth; An Analysis of the Causes of the Current Crisis of Unavailability and Unaffordability of Liability Insurance* (1986) (prepared for the National Association of Attorneys General by a task force headed by former Attorney General of Massachusetts Francis X. Belloti); P. Hermann & Jury Verdict Research, Inc. *Report to the Subcommittee on Economic Stabilization of the Committee on Banking, Finance and Urban Affairs, U.S. House of Representatives* (1986).
35. For example, as noted, from 1980 to 1984, 2.8 percent of all Cook County personal injury jury awards accounted for two-thirds of all awarded

personal injury damages, while 3.8 percent of all San Francisco personal injury awards accounted for nearly half of all such awarded damages. Thus, the use of median jury awards effectively would eliminate from a trend analysis the impact of one-half to two-thirds of all the damages awarded by juries.

36. It is sometimes suggested that jury awards are irrelevant because only a small percentage of all claims result in a jury verdict, while most claims are settled before trial. But, as previously noted by the Working Group, "settlements by their very nature reflect the range of verdicts available to the plaintiffs. Thus, as jury verdicts skyrocket, so do settlements." Working Group Report, at page 49 n.56. The quoted passage goes on to observe that "[s]ettlements also reflect the plaintiff's likelihood of success." *Id.* As noted, the Institute's data show that plaintiffs have over the years increased their likelihood of success. Accordingly, the most accurate measure of the rate of increase of settlements probably is provided by expected award rather than by average award data.

37. See Charts J (page 46) and K (page 48) of the February, 1986 report.

38. A recently published American Medical Association report indicates that, on average, claims per 100 physicians increased from 3.2 in 1980 to 10.1 in 1985. *The Continuing Need For Legislative Reform of the Medical Liability System,* at page 7 (1987).

39. These statistics are not, of course, limited to federal court filings. It is worth noting, however, that these numbers are entirely consistent with the federal district court caseload data.

40. Working Group Report, at page 47.

41. National Center for State Courts, *State Court Caseload Statistics: Annual Report, 1984* (1986).

42. Idaho, Alaska and Hawaii provided data from all available courts, but the data itself were incomplete. For example, while both superior court and district court data were obtained for Alaska, "low volume" district court data were *not* included. The Center did not clarify what constitutes a "low volume" district court case, and how many such cases are filed in Alaska. *Id.,* at table 33, p. 184. For Florida, the data do not cover all appropriate courts, and what is provided is incomplete. Specifically, the data for Florida contain circuit court statistics, but no data from the 67 county courts which can also hear some tort cases. And even the Florida circuit court statistics do not include any "professional tort cases."

43. The superior court filings may show a smaller increase than the combined filings because of an increase in the jurisdictional limits of the municipal courts from $5,000 to $15,000 in 1978.

44. Thomas Marvell, in the 19 May 1986 issue of the *National Law Journal,* in an article entitled "There *is* a Litigation Explosion," highlighted the danger of trying to draw conclusions about trends from the limited data used by the National Center for State Courts. Marvell concluded that because of prevailing economic conditions, data from 1981 to 1984 could substantially understate long term litigation trends. He also concluded that "we can expect a very large increase [in civil filings] in 1986."

45. Automobile-related injuries dropped from 2,000,000 in 1980 to 1,600,000 in

1984. Automobile-related deaths dropped from 51,000 in 1980 to 43,900 in 1984. *Statistical Abstract of the United States*, 1986, page 592.

46. A Department of Transportation study indicates that implementation of some form of no-fault automobile insurance scheme, alone, resulted in reductions in automobile accident lawsuits of from 31 percent to 80 percent, depending upon the type of scheme and the jurisdiction. "Compensating Auto Accident Victims" (1985), pages 113-117.

47. It is generally thought that, at least in the absence of no-fault automobile liability insurance, automobile accidents account for one-half to two-thirds of all tort lawsuits.

48. *See* Public Citizen, *The Assault on Personal Injury Lawsuits: A Study of Reality Versus Myth* (1986).

49. Nonasbestos-related claims are cited since it has been asserted that the asbestos litigations make federal product liability data unrepresentative. *Id.* While many asbestos injury claims in fact are filed in State courts, it should be noted that the deletion of asbestos-related lawsuits does not appreciably alter the import of the federal data.

50. Total civil filings in federal district court rose from 103,530 in 1974 to 273,670 in the twelve-month period ending June 30, 1985.

51. *Annual Report of the Director of the Administrative Office of the United States Courts 1985*. Table 17, page 136.

52. The percentage of civil filings which were transfers in 1985 was less than 1.4%. *Id.* And, of these cases, only some were transferred in the same year as originally filed.

53. That percentage hovered around 2% in the late 1970s, but actually decreased to about 1.5% in the first half of the 1980's. *Id.*

54. Working Group Report, at pages 39-42. The awards are inflation adjusted and expressed in 1984 dollars. The Institute recently has published a more thorough analysis of punitive damage awards, which not only reviews available data for Cook County and San Francisco, but also includes data for all of California for the 1980-1984 period. M. Peterson. S. Sarma & M. Shanley, *Punitive Damages: Empirical Findings* (1987).

55. Working Group Report, at pages 68-69.

56. *Report of the Task Force on Litigation Issues*, American College of Trial Lawyers, at page 4 (1986).

57. The Action Commission originally recommended that *all* punitive damages be allocated to public purposes after paying "a reasonable portion of the punitive damage award to compensate the plaintiff and counsel for bringing the action and prosecuting the punitive damage claim." This recommendation was watered down in a compromise before being submitted to the House of Delegates.

58. See, e.g., Public Citizen, *The Assault on Personal Injury Lawsuits: A Study of Reality Versus Myth; An Analysis of the Causes of the Current Crisis of Unavailability and Unaffordability of Liability Insurance* (1986) (prepared for the National Association of Attorneys General by a task force headed by former Attorney General of Massachusetts Francis X. Belloti.)

59. *Punitive Damages: Empirical Findings, supra*, at page 9.
60. *Id.*
61. *Id.*, at page 14.
62. The Institute's updated data for Cook County indicate that the average personal injury punitive damage award grew from $28,000 in 1970-74 to $1,934,000 in 1980-84, a 6,900 percent increase. *Id.*, at page 21.
63. To give but a few examples of such recent awards: a Texas jury awarded $100 million in punitive damages to the survivors of a man who died of leukemia alleged to have been caused by his work-related exposure to benzene; a Cook County, Illinois, jury awarded $26 million in punitive damages to a man whose legs were amputated, allegedly because, after open heart surgery, he was prescribed a drug routinely administered to prevent blood-clotting; and, a Hennepin County, Minnesota, jury awarded $12.5 million in punitive damages to a man who was injured when a twenty-six year-old tire rim exploded while he was attempting to mount it on his truck.
64. Contrary to popular belief, most states now permit such insurance coverage. See Schumaier & McKinsey, "The Insurability of Punitive Damages," 72 *ABA Journal* 68 (1986).
65. This abuse of punitive damage claims has led the American Bar Association, as part of its recent tort reform proposals, to recommend that the plaintiff not be permitted to introduce evidence of the defendant's net worth until after the determination of liability and compensatory damages.
66. Working Group Report, at pages 66-67.
67. Twerski, "A Moderate and Restrained Federal Product Liability Bill: Targeting the Crisis Areas for Resolution," 18 *University of Michigan Journal of Law Reform* 675, 612 (1985). Twerski argues that punitive damages in fact "sabotage settlement negotiations by thrusting a huge 'unknown' into the negotiations." *Id.*
68. Some commentators even argue that punitive damage awards have become so excessive and unfair in certain cases that the awards may be subject to legitimate constitutional challenges. *See* Jeffries, "A Comment On the Constitutionality of Punitive Damages," 72 *Virginia L. Rev.* 139 (1986).
69. J. Kakalik & N. Pace, *Costs and Compensation Paid in Tort Litigation* (1986).
70. This amount includes $4 to $5 billion in the value of time spent on tort litigation by litigants and their employees.
71. The net compensation percentage received by asbestos plaintiffs is roughly 38 percent. This does not, however, include the cost of the litigants' time, which, if taken into account, would reduce plaintiffs' net compensation percentage even further. See Working Group Report, at pages 42-45.
72. *Id.*, at page 45.
73. A detailed history of the deterioration of fault-based liability for product-related injuries can be found in Priest, "The Invention of Enterprise Liability: A Critical History of the Foundations of Modern Tort Law," 14 *J. Legal Studies* 461 (1985).

74. It is interesting to note that Fleming James, whom Priest credits with having established much of the intellectual foundation for strict product liability, did not limit or even focus his arguments on product-related injuries. Rather, James believed that the fault system derived from archaic notions of behavior, and argued that the sole aim of tort law should be to compensate the injured and the ill. See *Id.*, at pages 465-83.

75. The "deep pocket" effect in fact has been empirically corroborated. A. Chin & M. Peterson, *Deep Pockets, Empty Pockets: Who Wins in Cook County Jury Trials* (1985). The study found that in cases involving severely injured plaintiffs, corporate defendants had to pay over four times the amount paid by individual defendants in similar cases. It also found that corporate defendants were more likely to be found liable than individual defendants.

76. Working Group Report, at pages 30-35, 61-65.

77. 94 N.J. 169, 463 A.2d 298 (1983). Although the New Jersey Supreme Court has been a leader in the movement toward no-fault liability, see, e.g., *Beshada* v. *Johns-Manville Products Corp.* 90 N.J. 191, 447 A.2d 539 (1982) (manufacturer liable for failure to warn of dangers technologically and scientifically unknowable at time of manufacture); *Johnson* v. *Salem Corp.*, 99 N.J. 78, 477 A.2d 1246 (1984) (despite jury finding that product was reasonably safe as manufactured, manufacturer liable for failure to meet *its* burden of proof that utility of product outweighs product's risks), other states have embraced similar liability doctrines. See, e.g., *Duncan* v. *Cessna Aircraft Corp.*, 665 S.W.2d 414 (Tex. 1984) (adopting pure comparative "causation" standard for strict liability cases despite concluding that legislative adoption of modified comparative negligence encompassed only negligence cases); *Hughes* v. *Magic Chef, Inc.*, 288 N.W.2d 542 (Iowa 1980) (limiting manufacturer's defenses for consumer product misuse); *Elmore* v. *Owens-Illinois Inc.*, 673 S.W.2d 434 (Mo. 1984) (*en banc*) (manufacturer can be held liable for defectively designed product, even though state-of-art at time of manufacture or sale was such that defect could not have been known); *Gustafson* v. *Benda*, 661 S.W.2d 11 (Mo. 1983) (*en banc*) (abolishing doctrines of contributory negligence and last clear chance and adopting comparative fault despite repeated legislative refusals to adopt comparative negligence).

78. *Id.*, 463 A.2d at 306.

79. *Id.* In a revealing passage, the Court indicated that one of the criteria which can be used to determine whether a product's risk outweighs its utility is "[t]he feasibility, on the part of the manufacturer, of spreading the loss by setting the price of the product or carrying liability insurance." *Id.*, 463 A.2d at 305.

80. *Id.*, 463 A.2d at 310-15. While the dissenting justice would have remanded the case for further review of whether there was a safer alternative design, the majority expressly rejected the principle that the plaintiff would have to show a safer alternative design in order to prevail on his defective design claim.

81. *Twerski*, at pages 588-89.

82. *Id.* Twerski notes further that because the plaintiff challenges an entire product line, the defendant "could face countless lawsuits without any

realistic defense... a frightening liability picture for even the most conscientious manufacturer." *Id.*

83. As noted by a dissenting member of the Court in *O'Brien,* "[i]t follows from the majority's rationale that a jury may be permitted to find that there is a 'defect' whenever there is an accident involving a product." 463 A.2d at 315.

84. See Working Group Report, at page 31 n.24. As noted in the report, this rate of return is all the more inadequate when compared to first-party health and disability insurance, where the consumer receives back $1 for every $1.25 paid in premiums. *Id.*

85. See note 82.

86. *Twerski* at page 580.

87. Professor George Priest of the Yale Law School argues in a soon-to-be-published article that this uncertainty is the primary cause of the crisis in insurance availability and affordability. He believes that the growing uncertainty of tort liability makes it increasingly difficult for insurers to form and maintain risk pools, and thereby undermines the entire under-writing process. If Priest is correct in his assessment of the problem, a continued expansion of tort liability doctrines may effectively destroy the ability of the property and liability industry to underwrite many risks. Priest, "The Current Insurance Crisis and Modern Tort Law," (December 9, 1986, working paper).

88. One of the costs of the tort system most difficult to measure is the opportunity cost arising from products and services that are withheld from the market as well as innovation and product improvements that are inhibited because of the possibility of tort liability. Since these costs are so difficult to identify and measure they tend to be ignored. But they may very well be orders of magnitude greater than the direct costs of the tort system. *See* Huber, "Safety and the Second Best: the Hazards of Public Risk Management in the Courts," 85 *Columbia L. Rev.* 277 (1985). In this regard, see also a recent series of articles published by the National Legal Center For the Public Interest under the title of "The Legal System Assault on the Economy."

89. The Administration last year submitted three bills to the Congress implementing its tort reform recommendations. *See* "The Product Liability Reform Act of 1986," H.R. 4766 (the Senate companion was introduced as an amendment in the nature of a substitute to S. 100); "The Government Contractor Liability Reform Act of 1986," H.R. 4765, S. 2441; and, "The Federal Tort Reform Act of 1986," H.R. 4770, S. 2440.

90. The Harris Survey, Tribune Media Services, Inc., No. 34 (June 9, 1986).

91. *Id.*

92. *Id.*

93. These polls were conducted by Cambridge Reports, Inc. for the Insurance Information Institute.

94. This compares to only 44 percent and 56 percent respectively, in a similar poll conducted in 1985.

95. Voters in two other states also considered questions related to tort reform

in the November elections. In Montana, with nearly 56 percent of the vote, a constitutional amendment was adopted authorizing the legislature to enact tort reform measures. In Arizona, on the other hand, a similar amendment failed by about 15,000 votes out of a total of 844,000 cast votes.

96. *Legislative Resource Book,* American Tort Reform Association (1986).

97. Statement by the AFL-CIO Executive Council, "Liability Insurance and Tort Law" (21 May 1986).

98. *Report of the Task Force on Litigation Issues,* American College of Trial Lawyers, at page 4 (1986).

99. *Id.,* at pages 3-6.

100. As an illustration of such "substantially disproportionate" responsibility, the Commission's report gives the example of two liable defendants where one is less than 25 percent responsible for the plaintiff's injury.

101. National Governors' Association, policy E.-9 *Liability Insurance,* rescinding policy B.-19 (August 1986).

102. The members of this task force include the governors of Illinois, Massachusetts, Michigan, Missouri, Nevada, New Hampshire, New Jersey, New York, Ohio, Rhode Island, and Virginia.

103. The Task Force discussed elimination or modification of joint and several liability, caps on noneconomic damages, reform of punitive damages, scheduling of attorneys' contingency fees, reform of the collateral source rule, use of periodic payments, and reestablishment of broader sovereign immunity.

104. For example, reports have been issued in Arizona, Colorado, Connecticut, Hawaii, Maryland, Massachusetts, Michigan, New York, Oregon, Tennessee, and Wyoming. As might be expected, these reports vary in their conclusions and recommendations. But, almost without exception, they have endorsed the enactment of at least some tort reform measures. For example, the final report of the Governor of Oregon's Task Force on Liability included a comprehensive discussion of tort reform as part of its consideration of measures necessary to ease the liability insurance problem in Oregon. Among the tort reform measures recommended were caps on noneconomic damages, the use of periodic payments for awards of future damages, elimination of the doctrine of joint and several liability, limits upon attorneys' contingency fees, and increased sanctions for bringing frivolous lawsuits in the hope of obtaining a "nuisance" value settlement. *Final Report of Recommendations to Ease the Liability Insurance Strain in Oregon* (1986).

105. The report also discusses the nature of the link between tort reform and insurance availability and affordability. "Insuring Our Future," Vol. II, at pages 10-15.

106. *Id.,* Vol. I, at page 8.

107. *Id.,* Vol. I, at pages 129-63.

108. *Id.,* Vol. II, at pages 119-21.

109. Rather than reflecting the absence of a liability insurance problem, some state legislatures simply had no scheduled session in 1986.

110. Such is the case in Colorado, Utah, and Wyoming.

111. This was the thrust of California's Proposition 51. Similar action was taken legislatively in Hawaii and New York.

112. Michigan completely abolished joint liability for municipal defendants. The partial abolition in Alaska, Hawaii, Illinois, New York, and West Virginia applies only to defendants who are found to be less than 25 percent (Illinois, Hawaii and West Virginia) or 50 percent (Alaska and New York) at fault.

113. For example, Washington's abolition of joint liability does not apply if the plaintiff is fault free, or in cases involving hazardous waste disposal and business torts. Michigan's abolition does not apply in product liability cases or any case in which plaintiff is fault free. Florida's abolition, which only applies in cases over $25,000, does not apply to intentional tort or pollution-related cases. Illinois exempts medical malpractice and environmental cases, West Virginia's modification applies only to medical malpractice cases, and New York lists a host of exemptions, including motor vehicle cases and product liability cases where the manufacturer cannot be joined as a party.

114. In addition to these states, the following states enacted limitations for medical malpractice cases: Kansas ($250,000), Massachusetts ($500,000), Michigan ($225,000), Wisconsin ($1,000,000) and West Virginia ($1,000,000).

115. The estimated range of the cap is between $117,000 and $493,000.

116. Hawaii's cap applies only to damages for pain and suffering, and not other types of noneconomic loss, such as loss of consortium or emotional distress. Conversely, Minnesota's cap applies *only* to noneconomic damages other than pain and suffering; there is *no* cap on damages for pain and suffering.

117. Colorado's cap increases to $500,000 in any case where "clear and convincing" evidence is presented that noneconomic damages exceed $250,000. Alaska's cap does not apply to cases of severe physical impairment or disfigurement.

118. Four other states, Louisiana, Massachusetts, Nebraska and Washington, do not allow punitive damages. Three additional states, Connecticut, Georgia, and Michigan, prohibit classic punitive damages, but have classified certain types of compensatory damages as "punitive" or "exemplary."

119. With some exceptions, a punitive damage award may not exceed the compensatory award in Oklahoma and Colorado, and may not exceed three times the compensatory award in Florida.

120. Such was the case in Iowa, South Dakota, Alaska, Illinois, Oklahoma, and Florida.

121. This was the case in Colorado (one-third of the award), Florida (three-fifths of the award) and Iowa (three-quarters of the award).

122. In New York, workers compensation benefits subject to subrogation may not be offset. In Florida, collateral benefits which are subject to subrogation are not offset, and the party seeking subrogation must share the attorneys' fees incurred by the plaintiff in obtaining third-party recovery.

123. In Illinois, only benefits greater than $25,000 that are not subject to subrogation can be offset, and then only if they will reduce the award by less than 50 percent. In Michigan, any collateral benefit offset will first be reduced by the sum of any premiums paid for this benefit by either plaintiff, his family, or his employer. The Massachusetts modification applies only in medical malpractice cases.

124. For example, Florida and New York set a $250,000 minimum.

125. The Working Group recommended that attorneys' contingency fees be limited to 25 percent of the first $100,000, 20 percent of the second $100,000, 15 percent of the third $100,000, and 10 percent of the remainder of any recovery.

126. Connecticut's scale starts at one-third of the first $300,000, and graduates to 10 percent of amounts over $1.2 million. Effective in 1988, Maine's scale starts at one-third of the first $100,000, one-quarter of the second $100,000, and one-fifth of any recovery over $200,000. The Massachusetts and Wisconsin limits apply only in medical malpractice cases.

127. New Hampshire courts must approve fee agreements when an award or settlement exceeds $200,000. Hawaii courts have been directed to limit both plaintiffs' and defendants' fees to a "reasonable" amount.

128. For example, legislation to limit or clarify the liability of states and their subdivisions or employees was enacted in Colorado, Connecticut, Georgia, Illinois, Iowa, Michigan, Mississippi, Missouri, South Carolina, South Dakota, Tennessee, West Virginia, and Wyoming.

129. For example, in Alaska, municipalities, school districts, and regional educational areas were authorized to self-insure jointly, or to purchase coverage on a group basis. Florida, however, expanded the availability of the self-insurance mechanism to a broad class of private interests, including many professionals.

130. The Liability Risk Retention Act allows the purchase of a group liability policy by a risk retention group or through a purchasing group. The original Act was largely limited, however, to product liability. See Working Group Report, at pages 58-59. The 1986 amendments expand the Act to include all liability coverage other than workers compensation. The amended Act continues to rely on the state insurance regulatory system to ensure the solvency of risk retention groups, but exempts the groups from state laws that would interfere with interstate operations.

131. See note 89. The product liability reform provisions also are included in the "Trade, Employment, and Productivity Act of 1987" (S. 539, H.R. 1155), submitted this year to the Congress by the Administration.

132. For example, some states have abolished joint and several liability only for defendants whose responsibility is less than some specified percentage threshold, or condition the abolition on the ability of all responsible parties to pay their pro-rata share

133. See, e.g., *Abel* v. *Eli Lilly & Co.*, 418 Mich. 311, 343 N.W. 2d 164, cert. denied, 105 S.Ct. 123 (1984) (suggesting that manufacturers of similar or generic products act in concert).

134. Patricia Danzon estimates that statutory limitations on awardable non-

economic damages in medical malpractice cases have reduced the size of average paid claims by 23 percent. P. Danzon, *New Evidence on the Frequency and Severity of Medical Malpractice Claims* 26 (Institute for Civil Justice, 1986).

135. Washington State, for example, enacted a limitation formula which pegs noneconomic damages to the average state wage and plaintiff's expected lifetime.

136. For example, it is relatively easy for noneconomic damages to be shifted from one characterization such as "pain and suffering" to other characterizations such as "loss of consortium" or "loss of enjoyment of life." Indeed, such partial limitations may only lead courts, at the urging of plaintiffs' attorneys, to create new forms of noneconomic damages.

137. The Working Group recommends that economic damages be used because the highly subjective nature of noneconomic could lead to an inflated noneconomic damage award to increase the punitive damage award.

138. Under an actual malice standard, the plaintiff must show that the defendant acted with an "evil motive," such as with an actual intention to inflict harm. See *Smith* v. *Wade*, 461 U.S. 30, 78 n.12 (1983) (Rehnquist, J., dissenting).

139. For this reason, the Working Group believes that an abolition of the Collateral source rule should be in the form of a mandatory offset rather than a provision which merely allows evidence of collateral sources to be submitted to the jury.

140. The tort reform recommendations recently adopted by the House of Delegates would, among other things, require that, upon a complaint by plaintiff, the fee arrangement and the bill be submitted to the court after judgment is entered, which would then have the power to disallow any "plainly excessive" fee in light of prevailing rates and practices.

141. Working Group Report, at page 60.

142. *Id.*

143. The September 5, 1986 issue of *Business Insurance* reported that the American Trial Lawyers Association has established a Constitutional Challenge Committee to coordinate efforts to overturn legislative tort reforms. The article indicates that, among other things, the Committee will provide legal research assistance as well as model briefs. *Id.*, at page 1. For a discussion of various theories and cases challenging tort reforms on State and federal constitutional grounds, see Smith, "Battling a Receding Tort Frontier: Constitutional Attacks on Medical Malpractice Laws," 38 *Okla. L. Rev.* 195 (1985).

144. The United States Supreme Court, in declining to review *Fein*, held that the decision did not raise a substantial federal question. *Fein* v. *Permanente Medical Group*, U.S. 106, S.Ct 214 (1985).

145. The Report of the Governor of New York's Advisory Commission on Liability Insurance provides a synopsis of the practical and methodological difficulties inherent in trying to quantitatively document a direct link between specific tort reform measures and insurance pricing. *Insuring Our Future*, Vol. II, at pages 58-70. Despite these limitations, the Commission was sufficiently persuaded of the link between tort reform

and liability insurance to recommend significant tort reforms as part of its overall solution to the liability insurance crisis. *Id.*, at pages 70-180.

146. For example, it has been reported that, as a result of the tort reforms enacted in Connecticut in 1986, the Hartford Insurance Group has reduced its liability insurance premiums for Connecticut municipalities by as much as 10 percent; Aetna Life and Casualty has agreed to freeze its liability rates for Connecticut policyholders; and, Fireman's Fund has started to underwrite certain risks for the first time. The elimination of joint and several liability in Wyoming has caused at least one company to lower its municipal liability insurance premiums in that State by 10 percent. And in New Hampshire, recent tort reforms are reported to have resulted in a 16 percent decrease in liability rates for both municipalities and day care centers.

In other states, such as Alaska, Colorado, and Washington, insurance companies are expressing a willingness to expand their underwriting in certain areas, and even to return to markets that previously had been abandoned as uninsurable. In each case, the reason for this increased availability has been attributed to the tort reforms enacted in those states.

147. GAO, *Medical Malpractice: Six State Case Studies Show Claims and Insurance Costs Still Rise Despite Reforms* (1986). The six analyzed States were Arkansas, California, North Carolina, Florida, Indiana, and New York. The GAO also issued a separate report covering each state. The title of the summary report is somewhat unfortunate, since it suggests that tort reform may not affect insurance costs. In fact, the data contained in the report lead to precisely the contrary conclusion. And as already discussed, there are a number of factors that determine the cost of insurance, including aspects of tort liability that were not reformed in some or all of the six selected states.

148. The California statute, MICRA, has been described by many in the medical community as a model malpractice reform statute. Its key provisions are a $250,000 cap on noneconomic damages, a sliding scale on attorneys' contingency fees which limits the attorney to 10 percent of any amount over $200,000, and a periodic payment requirement. The New York and Florida statutes enacted in the mid-1970s are significantly weaker in comparison.

149. Both Florida and New York enacted more rigorous tort reforms in 1985 and 1986. As noted, however, it is still too early to draw any conclusion from those statutes.

150. Patricia Danzon has found that urbanization is "the single most important factor contributing to interstate differences in malpractice claims." P. Danzon, *New Evidence on the Frequency and Severity of Medical Malpractice Claims*, 17 (Institute for Civil Justice, 1986).

151. The New York data did not include Nassau, Suffolk, Bronx, Kings, Queens, Richmond, Rockland, Sullivan, New York, Orange, Ulster, or Westchester Counties. Interestingly, some of these counties reportedly have had among the most substantial insurance problems in New York State.

152. Report to the Medical Society of the State of New York, *An Analysis of*

Medical Malpractice Insurance Expenses and Physician Income in New York and Selected States prepared by Healthscope Management Services Corporation in association with the Center for Health Policy Studies (1985).

153. The premium data in the report to the New York Medical Society show substantially higher premiums for New York physicians than the data collected by the GAO. The most likely explanation for the difference is that the GAO data do not include a number of New York counties that reportedly have experienced serious insurance problems. See note 151.

Appendix

THE CRISIS IN PROPERTY AND LIABILITY INSURANCE

Antitrust Division, United States Department of Justice

Extensive debate continues as to the causes of the crisis in property and liability insurance. The crisis is manifested by serious problems in affordability, availability, or both, in several lines. In most of those lines, these problems are of relatively recent origin. This report describes and evaluates the most commonly alleged causes of the crisis.

The Antitrust Division's preliminary economic assessment indicates that three of the four most commonly alleged causes of the crisis—collusion among insurers, imprudent business practices and declines in investment income, and state regulation—all are unlikely to have caused the crisis. In contrast, both theoretical economic analysis and empirical evidence support the conclusion that unanticipated changes in the manner in which tort liability has been established and damages assessed, along with the uncertainty engendered by these changes, are directly responsible for the current affordability and availability problems in property-casualty insurance.

Collusion

It has been asserted that a principal cause of the crisis has been concerted, anticompetitive actions by insurers to raise prices in certain lines of property-casualty insurance or even to refuse to write such insurance. Economic analysis of the relevant insurance markets, however, leads to the conclusion that such a scenario is implausible.

The Legal Environment for Collusion A major purpose of the antitrust laws is to deter concerted pricing and marketing decisions among competitors. Certain types of collusive conduct, particularly agreements to raise price and restrict output, are illegal per se and expose the participants to both severe criminal sanctions and civil actions for treble damages by injured parties. In the insurance area, however, the McCarran-Ferguson Act[1] provides a limited antitrust exemption for the business of insurance.

The McCarran-Ferguson Act of 1945 was a response to a Supreme Court decision that held that the business of insurance was within the regulatory power of Congress under the Commerce Clause and thus was subject to the antitrust laws.[2] The Act secured the primacy of the states in the regulation and taxation of the business of insurance: it delimited the influence of the federal government, relegating only a residual role to the federal antitrust laws. Under the Act, the Sherman, Clayton, and Federal Trade Commission Acts apply to the business of insurance only to the extent that such business is not regulated by state law,[3] or if the challenged conduct involves boycott, coercion, or intimidation.[4]

Because the McCarran-Ferguson exemption is premised on state regulation, however, its net immunizing effect is more limited than otherwise might be supposed. There appears to be a substantial overlap between the McCarran-Ferguson exemption and another antitrust exemption, the "state action doctrine," which holds that the federal antitrust laws do not prohibit anticompetitive conduct properly attributable to the states rather than to private parties.[5]

Recent state action cases have established a two-pronged test for determining whether private anticompetitive conduct that restrains competition is entitled to state action immunity. The restraint must be the product of a "clearly articulated and affirmatively expressed" state policy to displace competition, and the state must actively supervise any private anticompetitive conduct.[6]

In its 1985 *Southern Motor Carriers* decision,[7] the Supreme Court held that a state need not "compel" private anticompetitive conduct in order to satisfy this test. In that case, state regulation of collective ratemaking by intrastate motor carriers was considered sufficient. Thus, *Southern Motor Carriers* suggests that at least some forms of state insurance regulation could protect concerted decisions among insurers from antitrust liability, even if the McCarran-Ferguson exemption did not exist.

While *Southern Motor Carriers* may have narrowed the difference between McCarran-Ferguson immunity and state action immunity, significant distinctions remain. The McCarran-Ferguson Act applies only to conduct that constitutes the "business of insurance" within the meaning of the Act,[8] whereas the state action doctrine is potentially applicable to any conduct regulated by the states. Also, states may regulate some insurer conduct in a manner that is sufficient to trigger the McCarran-Ferguson exemption, but not sufficient to provide state action immunity. For example, it has been held that states do not have to regulate the specific practices challenged under the antitrust laws for the McCarran-Ferguson immunity to attach:

> Unless the practice amounts to a boycott, the states are free to regulate it or choose not to regulate. They do not have to expressly authorize a specific activity, or proscribe it, for the exemption to

apply.... It is enough that a detailed overall scheme of regulation exists.[9]

Without a detailed, state-by-state analysis of regulation in the crisis lines, however, it is difficult to assess the extent to which concerted insurer decisions would enjoy state action immunity from the antitrust laws. Antitrust immunity by itself, however, does not necessarily imply that insurance providers are currently colluding: Even in the absence of legal prohibitions, the structure of the market for property and liability insurance may render successful collusion difficult or even impossible.

Economic Indicators of the Likelihood of Collusion

Theory. Collusion can be difficult to detect: the conduct itself is usually covert, and the effects on prices can be difficult to discern, especially when competitive benchmarks for prices or output levels are not available. Economic theory, however, can help assess the likelihood of collusion from observable evidence on market structure.

In using evidence on market structure to evaluate the probability of collusion, correct market definition is crucial. Market definition involves identifying groups of products the sellers of which collectively would have market power in the sense that if they could coordinate their pricing decisions they would price significantly above competitive levels.[10] Not all of these firms may currently be selling the same product in the same geographic area. However, any firm that is selling—or could readily sell—the same product, or other products that are good substitutes for the product in question, may undermine collusion, at least to some extent.

There are four aspects of market structure that are highly relevant to the probability that collusion will be attempted or will be successful if attempted. First, the fewer firms there are in a market, the easier it is for them to agree to raise price or restrict output and the greater the probability of collusion. Second, holding constant the number of firms, the greater the dispersion of market shares, the more likely it is that agreement among only a subgroup of the full number of firms would be necessary for collusion to be successful. Thus, a market with ten firms where two firms each hold 45 percent of the market is more conducive to collusion than a market with ten equal-sized firms.

Third, the easier it is for colluding firms to detect and police any cheating on the collusive agreement by other cartel members, the greater the probability of collusion. In the insurance industry, for example, where the McCarran-Ferguson Act and state regulation often permit collective (i.e., bureau) ratemaking, colluding firms might find it easy to monitor each other's activities. This could facilitate successful collusion among insurers. On the other hand, in industries such as insurance, where the product is heterogeneous and multi-dimensional, individual firms can often increase quality in a continuous and subtle fashion, making cheating on a collusive agreement relatively difficult to detect and collusion less likely.

Finally, the entry of new firms into the market may limit or even completely deter collusion.[11] Collusion would be deterred either if entry were so rapid as to make a price increase impossible,[12] or if entry would eventually restore prices to their original or lower levels but leave the colluding firms with lower market shares so that long-term losses from collusion would outweigh any short-term gains. Furthermore, even if collusion would be profitable, rapid entry would shorten any collusive episode and reduce the probability of its recurrence.

Market Definition and Market Structure in the Property and Liability Insurance Industry. In assessing collusion as a possible cause of affordability-availability problems in the crisis lines, it is first necessary to delineate the relevant markets. Under principles outlined in the Department's Merger Guidelines, markets for purposes of competitive analysis are delineated by considering very narrow groups of products and expanding until a hypothetical monopolist of that group of products would have significant market power, i.e., the ability profitably to raise price. The analysis basically consists of assessing the extent to which a price increase for the product under consideration would cause a reduction in quantity that would be large enough to make the price increase unprofitable. In the case of insurance, a price increase could cause a quantity reduction either because of substitution to other types of insurance or because of substitution of self-insurance. The former type of substitution is not very likely: a doctor seeking malpractice insurance, for example, is unlikely to find fire insurance to be an acceptable substitute.

Self-insurance is likely to be the best substitute for any particular line of insurance. Self-insurance, however, is likely to be an unattractive alternative for the vast majority of individuals for most perils. The loss of one's home from fire or one's life savings from a malpractice suit, for example, likely would be too devastating an event for one to be willing to risk. For such individuals, the only alternative to accepting a collusive price increase may be to form a mutual, where the policy-holders share responsibility for the residual risk of the group by setting premiums ex post rather than ex ante.[13]

Self-insurance is much more attractive for large corporations and governments. For governments, the residual risk can be spread across the taxpayers in that governmental unit. The larger the unit, the lower the cost of self-insurance, since, as long as all the risks assumed are not perfectly correlated, the larger the unit the less the residual risk assumed by each individual taxpayer and the easier it is for the individual taxpayer to pool that risk with other imperfectly correlated risks. For corporations whose equity holders can diversify widely and inexpensively in stock and other capital markets, the attraction of self-insurance is even greater.[14]

Notwithstanding any potential ability of large corporations and governments to self-insure in response to even a small collusive price increase, it is clear that a hypothetical monopoly supplier of any particular line of insurance would price well above competitive levels because of the unattractiveness of self-insurance to individuals and smaller corporations or governments. A hypothetical insurance monopoly likely would be able to raise prices just for individuals if necessary, so large corporations and governments would not prevent the exercise of market power.[15]

The next step in the analysis of market structure is to identify the competitors in the relevant markets. All property and liability insurers in the United States should be considered as competitors in any relevant market if all easily could offer any particular line of insurance. To determine whether such is the case, the Division conducted telephone interviews with executives from a size-stratified sample of ten national and regional insurance companies, as well as with the insurance regulators of the ten most populous states plus West Virginia. The Division found strong indications that insurers normally can, quickly and easily, acquire the necessary licenses and expertise to either begin selling their existing lines of insurance in new states or to provide new lines in the states in which they are already licensed. This appears true even with respect to those lines considered in crisis. These facts suggest that, even though at any one time only a small number of firms may be observed writing a specific line in a particular state, all firms in the property-casualty industry in the United States should be included in the relevant market for any particular type of property and liability insurance.[16]

The third step in the analysis of market structure is the assignment of market shares. Market shares should be assigned to competitors according to their abilities to compete and, in particular, to undermine any anticompetitive activities of rivals. The ability of an insurance company to expand output is potentially limited, at least in the short run, by state solvency regulation, which is keyed to certain financial ratios. Thus, these financial ratios could be combined with data on net assets to provide a capacity-based measure of market share. Data on premiums is more readily available, however, and, to the extent that premium-to-surplus ratios are uniform across firms, provide a good proxy for relative ability to write insurance. Thus, premiums were used to measure market shares. To the extent that insurers can shift

Exhibit A-1
National Herfindahl-Hirschman Indices for Select Insurance Lines,
1980-1985*

	1980	1981	1982	1983	1984	1985
All Property/ Casualty	213	213	215	225	226	229
Medical Malpractice	513	523	500	567	663	622
Other Liability	224	219	220	220	236	278

*Source: *Best's Aggregates and Averages: Property-Casualty.* (1980-1986)

capacity across types of insurance, total premiums for all insurance would be the best measure. To be conservative, however, the premiums used were limited to the property and liability lines.

Could Collusion Be the Cause of the Crisis? Exhibit A-1 provides measures of market concentration for property and liability insurance. The first one shows the Herfindahl-Hirschman Index, or HHI,[17] for all property and liability insurance in the United States from 1979 to 1985. Exhibit A-1 also shows the HHIs for medical malpractice and other liability insurance, lines that are generally considered to be in crisis. Even if these lines were appropriate markets and competitors limited to current sellers of these lines, the low HHIs would imply that collusion would be an unlikely explanation for significant increases in prices.

The highest HHI for all property and liability was 229 in 1985. Even if medical malpractice and other liability were valid antitrust markets and competitors limited to just current sellers of those lines, their highest HHIs would be 663 and 278. These are low HHI values. The 1984 Department of Justice Merger Guidelines, for example, indicate that mergers raising the HHI to a level under 1,000 are not a cause of competitive concern. These low levels of market concentration imply that successful collusion among property and liability insurers is highly unlikely, even in the absence of any legal prohibitions.

Finally, even if collusion were likely in this unconcentrated market because of McCarran-Ferguson or state action immunity, there are several reasons why the current availability-affordability problems cannot be blamed on collusion. First, the antitrust immunities have applied to all lines of insurance since at least 1945, with de facto immunity since the 1869 decision of the Supreme Court in *Paul v. Virginia*,[18] while the crisis is of relatively recent origin and is occurring in only a few lines. Second, collusion cannot explain unavailability: Firms do not collusively raise prices above costs and then refuse to sell the product. Third, collusion as an explanation for the large price increases observed in recent years is directly contradicted empirically by both the fall observed over that period in the ratio of premiums to underwriting costs (discussed below) and by indications of significant underperformance by property and liability firms in recent years in the stock market. See Lacey (1986).

All things considered, it is highly unlikely that increased collusion could have been a significant contributor to the recent affordability or availability problems in property and liability insurance.

Imprudent Insurance Company Business Practices and Declining Investment Income

Some commentators cite short-sighted or otherwise imprudent business practices as possible causes of the crisis. In particular, they perceive the recent dramatic increases in premiums as a reaction by insurance companies to "inappropriate" (i.e., too low) pricing in previous periods. They further argue that declining investment income is a major cause of current affordability-availability problems.

It is maintained that during the late 1970s and early 1980s unusually high interest rates encouraged property and liability insurers to lower their premium rates substantially. Because high returns on investments could be expected to offset anticipated casualty losses, insurers charged "artificially" low prices to attract business. As long as interest rates remained high, insurance companies could cover casualty losses while maintaining relatively low premiums.

The lower initial premiums could be made up by the higher investment income that could be earned on those premiums between the time they were collected and when they would be required to pay policyholders for their covered losses. Insurers were able—and, in a competitive market, would be forced—to lower their rates. In this scenario, falling interest rates in 1985 and 1986 resulted in an unanticipated decline in investment income. Insurers facing large anticipated casualty losses found themselves with investment income insufficient to cover those losses, and were forced to turn to their only remaining source of funds—current policyholders—whose premiums escalated rapidly. In sum, it is theorized that the additional income from recent, very substantial premium increases has been sought by insurers to compensate for unexpected declines in investment income.

Theoretical analysis suggests that if property-casualty insurance markets are competitive—and the concentration data presented above support that assumption—it would not be possible for insurers to recover sunk losses due to past pricing mistakes by charging higher, supra-competitive premiums to current policyholders, especially if new insurers, not suffering from previous errors, could profitably undercut the inflated premiums of the old insurers.[19] Moreover, even if dramatic declines in investment returns could in theory have resulted in the observed availability and affordability problems, it is not clear that any such losses or declines have actually occurred. In particular, column 2 of Exhibit A-2 shows that net investment income as a percentage of premiums earned in the property and liability industry increased significantly after 1980, from 7.88 percent of earned premiums over the 1967-80 period to 14.62 percent of earned premiums over the 1981-85 period.[20] Thus, we must look to the property and liability industry's underwriting gain/loss experience, shown in column 1 of Exhibit A-2, rather than to the industry's past investment experience, in order to explain either any financial problems in the industry or their actions on pricing and availability.

Regardless of past experience, any decline in anticipated future investment returns would place upward pressure on overall premiums. But cyclical movements in anticipated investment income would not cause severe affordability-availability problems to appear suddenly in only certain lines. While some small part of the higher cost of property and liability insurance today may be due to anticipations of lower investment income, the primary causes of the "crisis" must be found elsewhere.[21]

State Insurance Regulation

We turn now to the third potential cause of the insurance crisis, changes in state regulation. Any full discussion of state regulation of the insurance industry would be far beyond the scope of this report, but we can at least briefly examine three types of state regulation—regulation of prices, regulation of quality (i.e., solvency), and regulations that attempt to redistribute wealth by widening risk pools—and their potential roles in the crisis in property and liability insurance.

Turning first to the potential role of price regulation, any regulatory change could result in both higher prices and unavailability if the regulators imposed regulations that raised costs or restricted output considerably and then allowed prices to rise by less than would have been required to clear the market. Alternatively, suppose that costs were rising—perhaps not necessarily because of increased regulation—and the regulators responded by imposing price ceilings to limit the price increase. The result would be both higher prices and an

Exhibit A-2
Time Series Variation in Property/Casualty Industry Operating Results*

Years	Underwriting Gain/Loss (Percent to Earned Premiums)		Net Investment Income (Percent to Earned Premiums)		Combined Net Income (Percent to Earned Premiums)	
	yearly avg.	std. dev.	yearly avg.	std. dev.	yearly avg.	std. dev.
1967 - 1980	- 1.70	3.35	7.88	1.78	6.18	3.59
1981 - 1985	-13.28	5.41	14.62	.65	1.33	4.93
Change	-11.58	2.06	6.74	-1.13	-4.85	.34
F statistic for equality of means or increase in variance	31.98†††	2.61†	66.10†††	7.70†††[1]	5.55††	1.89

††† Significant at .01 level
†† Significant at .05 level
† Significant at .10 level

[1]F statistic of decrease in variance

*Source: *Best's Aggregates & Averages: Property-Casualty*, 1986, p. 72

availability problem, i.e., even at the higher prices, insurers would not be willing to supply as much insurance as consumers would like to buy.

There has been considerable research on the effects of regulation on the price of property and liability insurance. Unfortunately, no consensus has emerged: some researchers have found that regulation has raised prices; others have found no effect. For example, Joskow (1973) found that prices for property and liability insurance were higher in New York, where prices were regulated, than in unregulated California. Similarly, Hill (1979), and Frech and Samprone (1980) found that prices or profits were higher under regulation in all the lines of property and liability insurance that they examined, but neither study examined any of the lines currently in crisis. Hill (1979) did not examine medical malpractice or general liability, and Frech and Samprone (1980) looked only at automobile liability insurance. Moreover, for automobile liability insurance, while Frech and Samprone (1980) found that output had been reduced in regulated states compared to unregulated ones, Ippolito (1980) did not find that prices were higher in regulated states. Finally, Munch and Smallwood (1980), looking at property and liability insurance, found that solvency regulation reduced the number of firms, but not necessarily output.

None of this research presents evidence that regulation has restricted output in those lines of property and liability insurance that are considered to be in crisis. The only available evidence of an output restriction was provided by Frech and Samprone (1980) for the noncrisis automobile liability line. The evidence is mixed on the effects of regulation on the price of property and liability insurance, although most of it suggests that regulation has raised prices. Joskow (1973) found that regulation seemed to increase prices for all types of property and liability insurance. Hill (1979), as well as Frech and Samprone (1980), has similar results when looking at just the noncrisis lines of property and liability insurance and automobile liability insurance, respectively. Ippolito (1980), on the other hand, did not find that regulation increased the price of automobile liability insurance.

While we cannot rule out the possibility that state regulation has increased costs and reduced output, attributing an availability problem in any particular state to state regulation would, as noted above, require that regulators in that state have also imposed price ceilings that prevented prices from rising to the same degree as costs. To the extent that regulation has directly affected prices, however, the effect historically has been more to facilitate pricing above competitive levels than to impose price ceilings below competitive levels. See Joskow (1973).

Moreover, as also noted above, it is often relatively easy for producers of complex and heterogeneous products to increase quality in a sufficiently subtle and gradual manner to avoid detection by other participants in a private collusive agreement to raise prices. Similarly, unless regulators can rigorously specify all aspects of a price-controlled product, their attempts to set maximum prices are likely to be frustrated by reductions in quality. Under such conditions, the effect of maximum price ceilings is more likely to be unavailability of quality than unavailability of quantity.

Some industry observers have argued that such binding price ceilings did exist, at least through 1985, in those states where availability problems were particularly severe. The Antitrust Division's ongoing interviews with state regulators and insurance company executives, however, have not found any supporting evidence to date for this claim in the lines and states of the crisis. Moreover, in some lines, such as environmental exposure, unavailability appears to be a national problem and thus cannot be explained by state-specific events. Thus, some if not all of the explanations for unavailability must be found elsewhere than in state regulation.

The next major type of state regulation that needs to be considered is regulation of quality. Although the competitive nature of the insurance industry precludes the need for any form of price regulation, solvency regulation may be defended as one way to protect the interests of policyholders and third-party liability claimants, as well as other insurance firms that contribute to guaranty funds. Every state has a guaranty fund for its property and liability insurers. If an insurer licensed to do business in a particular state goes bankrupt, the other licensed insurance companies in the state assume at least partial responsibility for the failed firm's policies through the guaranty fund. The inability to ex ante "experience rate" individual insurance companies' contributions to the guaranty fund creates an incentive for insurers to underwrite too many policies relative to their net assets.[22]

While solvency regulation can thus be defended in principle as a way to prevent insurers from free riding on each other, the efficiency or effectiveness of such regulation in practice is an empirical question. See Munch and Smallwood (1980). Moreover, as noted in the next section, state solvency regulations may have played a significant role in the crisis due to their interaction with the increased uncertainty induced by changes in tort liability.

Finally, we turn to a third type of state regulation, restrictions on the size of risk pools. In several states, regulators have frustrated efforts by insurance companies to keep risk pools as narrow as possible in order to minimize the self-selection problem that is endemic to all insurance. Mandating broader, more heterogeneous risk pools can transfer wealth from low-risk to high-risk individuals, but only at a real cost. Broader risk pools reduce the efficiency of the insurance contract by increasing the real cost of insurance to low-risk consumers and thus reducing their demand. As enough low-risk consumers reduce the amount of insurance they purchase or even drop out of the pool entirely, insurance, like solid-gold Cadillacs, can become economically unavailable.[23]

Without seeking to minimize the real costs of this type of regulation, however, it is difficult to identify regulatory broadening of risk pools as a major contributor to the current crisis. These regulations may well have contributed significantly to a long-term upward trend in insurance costs in a number of lines in particular states, but such increases do not appear to match the lines and states in crisis.

Finally, for all three types of state regulation, while significant research on their effects in the specific crisis lines is lacking, timing alone suggests the lack of a significant, or at least exclusive, connection. In the mid 1970s there was a crisis in medical malpractice insurance. See Freedman (1986). The 1980s brought another crisis in medical malpractice, as well as in several other lines of property and liability insurance. If regulation were to blame for these crises, one would expect to find that regulation increased during or slightly before each crisis and slackened at other times. This, however, does not appear to have been the case. The lack of any apparent correlation between changes in regulation and the development of resolution of availability-affordability problems in particular states indicates that state regulation is not directly to blame for the current crisis.

Change and Uncertainty in Tort Liability

Perhaps the most frequently offered explanation for the current crisis in property and liability insurance involves the legal system. Significant changes in the manner in which tort liability is established and damages are assessed are cited as causes of dramatic rate increases and reductions in insurance availability. Examples of these changes include the perceived movement from a fault-based standard to a no-fault standard, eased requirements for establishing joint and several liability, the award of very large damages for such noneconomic losses as pain and suffering, punitive or exemplary damages against insuring companies for bad-faith failure to acknowledge liability, and the shift from first-party to third-party tort insurance.[24]

In the rest of this section, we attempt to evaluate this explanation by examining the consistency of its implications with the available accounting data on changes over time in the costs and revenues of the property-casualty industry.[25] We begin with broad overall data categories and progress to specific lines and narrower categories of costs and revenues, looking first for changes in average levels and then for signs of increased uncertainty.

Changes in Average Levels The first implication of an explanation based on changes in the tort liability system is that we should observe a deterioration in the overall financial performance of the property and liability industry, with the greatest deterioration occurring in the crisis lines. As can be seen from column 3 of Exhibit A-2 for all property-casualty lines combined there has been a significant decline in combined net income (the sum of underwriting gains and net investment income) as a percentage of premiums earned, from 6.18 percent over the 1967-80 period to 1.33 percent over the 1981-85 period.[26]

This deterioration in overall financial performance can also be seen in the last column of Exhibit A-4 which compares the 1976-80 period with the 1981-85 period for all property and liability lines combined as well as for two crisis lines, Other liability and medical malpractice, and two noncrisis lines, private passenger auto liability and homeowners multiple peril. For all lines of property and liability, the overall operating ratio[27] suffered a statistically highly significant deterioration of 8.64 percentage points, from 94.18 to 102.82. This deterioration is particularly marked in the crisis lines. In the two noncrisis lines, auto liability and homeowners, overall operating ratios rose respectively by 9.42 points to 101.24 and by 6.88 points to 103.96. Both the increases and the final levels are considerably greater, however, in the two crisis lines, other liability and medical malpractice, where overall operating ratios rose respectively by 22.86 points to 113.52 and by 21.96 points to 113.58.

A second implication of an explanation based on changes in the tort liability system is that this deterioration in overall financial performance should be due to declines in underwriting gains (or increases in underwriting losses) rather than declines in net investment income. As discussed earlier, this implication is strongly supported by the data in Exhibit A-2 which shows a statistically highly significant increase in net investment income as a percent of earned premiums, from 7.88 percent over the 1967-80 period to 14.62 percent over the 1981-85 period, combined with a statistically highly significant increase in underwriting losses as a percentage of earned premiums, from 1.70 percent for 1967-80 to 13.28 percent for 1981-85.

Continuing this disaggregation process, Exhibit A-3 shows that, for all lines of property and liability insurance, this deterioration in the ratio of underwriting costs to premiums earned, by 11.64 percentage points, from 100.74 over the 1961-80 period to 112.38 for the 1981-85 period (as shown in the last column of Exhibit A-3) cannot be explained by increased administrative expenses, which actually fell somewhat as a percentage of premiums written. The source instead lies entirely with the increase in the ratio of underwriting losses and adjustment expenses to earned premiums by 12.56 percentage points, from 70.44 percent to 83.00 percent. This result is confirmed in Exhibit A-4. For all lines of property and liability, the underwriting losses incurred (the first column of Exhibit A-4) increased significantly by 8.60 points and by 1.56 points, respectively in both the non-crisis lines, homeowners and auto liability. In the crisis lines of other liability and medical malpractice, however, the increases in the underwriting loss ratio and the loss adjustment ratio have been much more dramatic: 21.74 percentage points and 9.70 percentage points for other liability, and 35.50 percentage points and 6.46 percentage points for medical malpractice.

The determination that the source of the deterioration in the overall financial ratios for the property and liability industry lies entirely in increases in underwriting losses and adjustment expenses, with particularly dramatic increases observed in the crisis lines, is consistent with the implications of a hypothesis that the crisis is due to changes in the tort liability system. By contrast, the data appear to directly contradict the implications of two other hypothesized potential causes of contributions to the crisis, collusion and declines in investment income. The collusion scenario would imply an increase in the ratio of premiums to underwriting costs rather than the statistically highly significant decrease actually observed, while the investment scenario would imply a decrease in the ratio of net investment income to premiums, rather than the statistically highly significant increase actually observed.

Increased Uncertainty If insurers were risk-neutral, the competitive premium for a policy would be the expected value of its cost. Bankruptcy costs and insurance regulations, however, require insurers to maintain minimum solvency levels in order to limit the probability of default. This requires insurers to load (raise) premiums by a factor over actuarially fair premiums in order to ensure a sufficiently low probability of failure. This load factor is higher, the greater the uncertainty with respect to the insurer's future net income. Thus, a costly change in the legal environment that also increased the variability in the financial results would induce a premium increase greater than the increase in the expected value of costs.[28]

An increase in variability of casualty losses and investment income thus could trigger a crisis because insurers would have to set higher premiums in order to maintain an acceptable fixed probability of financial solvency. If the increase in financial variability becomes sufficiently large, the premiums required to maintain solvency require-

Exhibit A-3
Time Series Variation in Property/Casualty Industry Loss and Expense Ratios*

Years	Loss and Adjustment Ratio to Premiums Earned		Administrative Expenses Ratio to Premiums Written		Premiums Dividend Ratio to Premiums Earned		Combined Ratio to Premiums Earned	
	yearly avg.	std. dev.	yearly avg.	std. dev.	yearly avg.	std. dev.	yearly avg.	std. dev.
1961 - 1980	70.44	3.78	28.54	2.26	1.76	.29	100.74	3.01
1981 - 1985	83.00	5.25	27.50	.96	1.86	.18	112.38	4.89
Change	12.56	1.47	-1.04	-1.30	.10	-.11	11.64	1.88
F statistic for equality of means or increase in variance	39.10[†††]	1.93	1.03	.18	.61	.39	47.79[†††]	2.64[†]

[†††] Significant at .01 level
[††] Significant at .05 level
[†] Significant at .10 level

* Source: *Best's Aggregates & Averages: Property–Casualty*, 1986, p. 75

Exhibit A-4
Time Series Variation in Underwriting Experience by Line*

Line	Years	Losses Incurred[1] avg	std. dev.	Loss Adjustment Exp.[1] avg	std. dev.	Commission & Brok Exp.[2] avg	std. dev.	Other Underwriting[2] avg	std. dev.	Dividends to Policy[1] avg	std. dev.	Net Investment Gain/Loss & Other Income[1] avg	std. dev.	Overall Operating Ratio[1] avg	std. dev.
Total All Lines	'76-'80	63.60	2.20	9.24	.21	12.94	.21	12.96	.55	1.42	.26	5.96	.92	94.18	2.45
	'81-'85	72.20	4.64	10.80	.65	12.52	.29	14.98	.70	1.86	.18	9.56	.84	102.82	4.06
Change		8.60	2.44	1.56	.44	-.42	.08	2.02	.15	.44	-.08	3.60	-.08	8.64	1.61
F		14.00†††	4.46†	26.00†††	9.88†††	6.78††	2.02	25.66†††	1.62	9.68††	.49	41.51†††	.84	16.57†††	2.75
Homeowners	'76-'80	58.48	5.37	7.00	.37	18.56	.36	12.86	.15	.64	.13	3.16	.29	94.36	5.21
	'81-'85	65.66	3.09	8.18	.66	17.42	.15	13.86	.34	.06	.01	4.46	.49	101.24	3.26
Change		7.18	-2.28	1.18	.29	-1.14	-.21	1.00	.19	-.58	-.12	1.30	.20	6.88	-1.95
F		6.72††	.33	12.17†††	3.09	41.92†††	.17	35.46†††	5.13†	.29	.56	25.92†††	2.92	6.25††	.39
Auto Liability	'76-'80	65.90	2.23	11.38	.34	10.42	.26	13.34	.28	.88	.37	6.32	.64	94.54	2.31
	'81-'85	76.12	4.05	12.08	.43	9.92	.18	14.24	.26	.84	.15	9.20	.74	103.96	3.23
Change		10.22	1.82	.70	.09	-.50	-.08	.90	-.02	-.04	-.22	2.88	.10	9.42	.92
F		24.42†††	3.30	8.06††	1.60	12.62†††	.48	27.74††	.87	.05	.17	42.89†††	1.35	22.42††	1.95
Other Liability	'76-'80	55.14	3.26	19.28	1.03	14.14	.29	12.86	.38	.54	.09	11.32	2.04	90.66	4.25
	'81-'85	76.88	12.52	28.98	3.87	12.38	.92	17.30	2.63	.64	.11	22.70	3.02	113.52	12.50
Change		21.74	9.26	9.70	2.84	-1.76	.63	4.44	1.25	.10	.02	11.38	.98	22.86	8.25
F		14.13†††	14.77††	29.27†††	14.06††	16.65†††	10.20††	11.20††	3.64	2.38	1.63	48.86†††	2.20	14.98†††	8.64††
Medical Malpractice	'76-'80	68.70	10.42	26.56	2.74	6.22	1.06	7.72	.97	1.08	.80	18.66	7.34	91.62	8.53
	'81-'85	104.20	9.36	33.02	3.70	4.98	.33	10.24	1.32	1.34	.39	40.18	3.27	113.58	10.73
Change		35.50	-1.06	6.46	.96	-1.24	-.73	2.52	.35	.26	-.41	21.52	-4.07	21.96	2.20
F		32.14†††	.81	9.82††	1.82	6.54††	.05	11.78†††	1.86	.43	.24	35.89†††	.20	12.84†††	1.58

††† Significant at .01 level
†† Significant at .05 level
† Significant at .10 level

[1] Percent of premiums earned
[2] Percent of premiums written

F statistics against null hypotheses of equal means increasing variance

*Source: *Best's Aggregates & Averages: Property-Casualty,* 1986, pp. 82-85.

ments might be so high that coverage would be unattractive to or even out of the reach of potential insureds. There would then appear to be an affordability crisis in the affected line. Should variability be so great as to exceed the ability or willingness of insurers to cope with it, coverage might be unavailable at any price. Questions would remain as to the underlying causes of large, perhaps greatly increased, variability, but an adverse effect on the affordability of insurance is predictable whatever those causes actually are.

To track down the source of any potential increase in uncertainty, we carry out the same disaggregation process as in the examination of changes in the average level of financial ratios. We measure the variability of each ratio by its standard deviation. Normalized comparisons of variability across ratios of different mean values can be made by computing each ratio's coefficient of variation, i.e., the standard deviation of the ratio divided by its mean.[29]

Exhibit A-2 shows that while the standard deviation (variability) of the underwriting gain/loss ratio has risen significantly during the 1980s relative to the 1967-80 period, the standard deviation of the net investment income ratio has actually declined significantly. This greater variability of the underwriting gain/loss ratio becomes clear when we note that the coefficient of variation for the underwriting gain/loss during 1981-85 was .41—ten times the coefficient of variation for net investment income, which measured only .04 over the same period. This suggests that any increase in overall uncertainty must have resulted from increased unpredictability of loss payouts and expenses rather than from any increase in the instability of investment income. Combined with the observation from Exhibits A-2 and A-4 that investment income increased significantly after 1980, this would appear to make it very difficult to blame imprudent investments for causing today's premium hikes and coverage withdrawals.

Exhibit A-3 shows that the variability of both the administrative expense ratio and the dividend ratio has actually decreased, though insignificantly. This result narrows the source of any increase in uncertainty even further, to the underwriting loss and adjustment ratio.

The pattern of increased uncertainty emerges most clearly in Exhibit A-4. While the increase in the variance of the overall operating ratio was not statistically significant for all lines of property and liability combined, variability in the loss incurred and loss adjustment ratios increased significantly. The two noncrisis lines showed no significant increases in variability in either their overall operating ratios or any of the component ratios. Furthermore, of the crisis lines, only other liability exhibited a substantial increase in overall variability as well as substantial increases in the variability of underwriting losses.

This suggests an anomaly. Why does the other crisis line, medical malpractice, fail to exhibit such increases in variability of its ratios? There is an explanation. Medical malpractice is a line of insurance that has popularly been thought to have been in a state of crisis since the mid-1970s. Thus, it is not anomalous that its variability has not increased greatly over the 1980s—it was highly variable to begin with. To see this, one need only look at the coefficient of variation exhibited by medical malpractice's overall operating ratio in 1976-80 and in 1981-85 as shown in Exhibit A-5. In both the earlier and later periods it was .09. Compare this with the coefficients of variation in the overall operating ratio for other liability. In the earlier period its coefficient of variation was only .05, but it soared to .11 in the later period.

In fact, if one examines the levels of all lines' coefficients of variation in the period 1981-85, one sees that these coefficients of variation are almost universally higher for each ratio in the crisis lines than for the corresponding ratio in the noncrisis lines.

Exhibit A-5 thus shows a sharp distinction between the crisis and noncrisis lines in terms of the variability of their financial ratios. As noted above, increasing variability reflects the increasing difficulty for insurers in accurately predicting their future liability, and therefore in their ability to underwrite the risks. To maintain an acceptable probability of solvency, insurers may choose either to raise premiums to "safe" levels, or to withdraw coverage from these lines.

One source of the greater financial uncertainty observed in the crisis lines may be the greater severity of delays before final settlement in the crisis lines. As shown in Exhibit A-6, for all lines of property and liability insurance, 18.30 percent of claims incurred in 1982, for example, were unpaid at the end of 1985. For other liability, however, 44.79 percent of expenses incurred in 1982 were unpaid at the end of 1985 while for medical malpractice 64.42 percent of expenses incurred in 1982 were unpaid at the end of 1985. Such delays suggest a more uncertain and thus more costly tort liability process.

The overall pattern in the data is thus one of high and increasing cost ratios for underwriting losses and adjustment expenses, especially in the crisis lines, and high and increased variability in these ratios for the crisis lines. These changes can cause dramatic increases in premium rates. Because of the increased load factors required by increased uncertainty, premium increase can be expected to be significantly greater than even the already large increase in costs in those lines. Increased cost ratios and uncertainty in crisis lines also can give rise to unavailability problems in those lines. Thus, given the findings from several studies that changes in the tort liability system have caused both higher expected awards and greater variability in such awards, the overall pattern of the data is consistent with explanations for the

Exhibit A-5
Coefficients of Variation in Underwriting Experience by Line*

	Losses Incurred		Loss Adj. Exp.		Comm. & Brok.		Other Underwriting		Dividends		Net Investments		Overall Operating	
	1976-80	1981-85	1976-80	1981-85	1976-80	1981-85	1976-80	1981-85	1976-80	1981-85	1976-80	1981-85	1976-80	1981-85
Total All Lines	.03	.06	.02	.06	.02	.02	.04	.05	.18	.10	.15	.09	.03	.04
Homeowners'	.09	.05	.05	.08	.02	.01	.01	.02	.20	.17	.09	.11	.06	.03
Auto Liability	.03	.05	.03	.04	.02	.02	.02	.02	.42	.18	.10	.08	.02	.03
Other Liability	.06	.16	.05	.13	.02	.07	.12	.15	.17	.17	.18	.13	.05	.11
Medical Malpractice	.15	.09	.10	.11	.17	.05	.13	.13	.74	.29	.39	.08	.09	.09

*Source: Computed from Exhibit A-3. The coefficient of variation is: (standard deviation)/(average).

Exhibit A-6
Fraction of Total Losses and Loss Expenses that Remain Currently Unpaid*

Year When Loss Was Incurred	Total All Lines	Various Multiple Peril	Auto Liability	Other Liability	Medical Malpractice
Prior to 1976	2.42	.55	.26	6.46	15.66
1976	5.05	.88	1.02	12.32	24.88
1977	5.45	1.20	1.34	13.34	27.62
1978	6.43	1.87	1.57	15.50	32.74
1979	7.75	2.26	2.21	19.78	39.21
1980	9.70	3.31	3.45	24.89	46.24
1981	13.40	5.74	6.19	33.80	54.52
1982	18.30	8.79	10.95	44.79	64.42
1983	26.42	13.54	19.77	59.92	76.57
1984	38.96	20.87	34.80	74.60	87.02
1985	65.69	44.26	65.68	90.80	96.98

*Source: *Best's Aggregates & Averages: Property–Casualty*, 1986, pp. 59-60.

property and liability crisis grounded in these changes in the tort liability system.

Appendix Notes

1. 15 U.S.C. §§ 1011-1015.
2. *United States v. South-Eastern Underwriters Ass'n* , 322 U.S. 533 (1944).
3. 15 U.S.C. § 1012(b).
4. 15 U.S.C. § 1013(b).
5. See *Parker v. Brown,* 317 U.S. 341 (1943).
6. *California Retail Liquor Dealers Ass'n v. Midcal Aluminum, Inc.,* 445 U.S. 97, 105 (1980).
7. *Southern Motor Carriers Rate Conference, Inc. v. United States,* 471 U.S. 48 (1985).
8. Not all insurer conduct necessarily constitutes the "business of insurance." See, e.g. *Group Life & Health Insurance Co. v. Royal Drug,* 440 U.S. 205 (1979).
9. *Klamath-Lake Pharm. v. Klamath Med. Serv. Bureau,* 701 F.2d 1276, 1287 n.10 (9th Cir.) *cert. denied,* 464 U.S. 822 (1983) (citations omitted). See also *Addrisi v. Equitable Life Assur. Soc.* 503 F.2d 725 (9th Cir. 1974), *cert. denied,* 420 U.S. 929 (1975); *Mackey v. Nationwide Ins. Companies,* 724 F.2d 419 (4th Cir. 1984); *Commander Leasing Co. v. Transamerica Title Ins. Co.* 477 F.2d 77 (10th Cir. 1973); *Feinstein v. Nettleship Co.,* 714 F.2d 928 (9th Cir. 1983), *cert. denied,* 466 U.S. 972 (1984).
10. See U.S. Department of Justice, Merger Guidelines (1984).
11. As noted above, it is appropriate to designate specific firms that readily could, but do not currently, sell the product in question as being "in the market" rather than "potential entrants." The difference between firms who do not currently sell a product being "in the market" and being "potential entrants" is mostly a question of time. According to the Department of Justice Merger Guidelines, if a firm could begin selling the product within one year, it is considered to be already in the market. If the firm would need more than one year, but less than two, it is considered a potential entrant.
12. Under some circumstances, entry may make price increases not only unprofitable but impossible. For a discussion of such "contestable" markets, see Baumol, Panzer, and Willig (1982). But see Schwartz (1986).
13. The Risk Retention Act Amendments of 1986, Pub.L. No. 99-563, were designed to allow related or similarly situated businesses and groups to purchase their liability insurance on a group basis or to provide security in lieu of insurance through interstate cooperatives called risk retention groups.
14. Indeed, one might ask why corporations would ever buy insurance. To the extent that the risks assumed by a corporation are ultimately assumed by shareholders who are capable of diversifying their portfolios directly, managers would appear to maximize share values by maximizing the expected value of earnings. Since the purchase of market insurance will

always require payment of a premium over the expected cost, self-insurance would appear to always dominate. Paying such a premium may be in the interest of shareholders, however, if insurance reduces managerial control problems by allowing more concentrated equity ownership, or if insurance provides an outside check on opportunistic behavior by managers toward shareholders or by shareholders toward bondholders. In addition, especially if bankruptcy is possible, some insurable risks may ultimately be borne by non-shareholders such as workers or managers, who cannot inexpensively diversify away such risks. If the price such input suppliers would charge to assume those risks is greater than the premium over the expected cost that must be paid to an insurance company, the purchase of market insurance can be consistent with maximizing share values. Finally, if costs would be involuntarily borne by third-parties, federal or state laws are likely to require firms or individuals to buy insurance.

15. If a sufficient number of large corporations and governments would self-insure in response to even a small collusive price increase, however, we would expect that an exercise of market power by insurers would not lead to a significant increase in all premiums, but rather to an increase in the premiums paid by individuals and small corporations and governments relative to those paid by large corporations and governments.

16. Companies that currently provide only life insurance but that could be expected to establish a property-casualty subsidiary in response to a collusive price increase could also be included in the property-casualty market.

17. The HHI is an index of market concentration calculated by summing the squares of the market shares of all of the firms in the market. It varies from near 0 (extremely unconcentrated) to 10,000 (total monopoly). The HHI is higher, the smaller the number of firms and the more unequal their market shares. The HHI thus provides a single summary measure for the first two of the four aspects of market structure discussed above.

18. 75 U.S. (8 Wall.) 168 (1869).

19. As noted in a later section, however, unanticipated changes in the manner in which tort liability has been established and damages assessed can lead to large ex post losses on policies, especially (see Exhibit A-6) in lines where there are long delays between the time premiums are set and received and the time claims are settled. Unless new capital can flow easily into the industry, such accumulated losses may deplete reserves and, in the presence of solvency regulation or other constraints on the ratio of premiums to reserves, contribute to a supply problem, at least in the short run.

20. As shown in Exhibit A-2, this increase of 6.74 percent is statistically highly significant. With an F-statistic of 66.10, the probability of such an increase being due to random movements is less than .01.

21. Even if anticipated net investment income were to fall to zero, however, the compensating proportional increase in premiums would not be greater than the previous ratio of anticipated net investment income to premiums. As shown in Exhibit A-4, the ratio of net investment to income has been highest in the crisis lines of medical malpractice and other liability, where,

as shown in Exhibit A-6, the time between when premiums are collected and when losses are paid out is the greatest. The premium increases observed in these lines, however, have been far greater than these net investment ratios.

22. The problem is analytically very similar to that created by the existence of federal deposit insurance that is available to all depository institutions. Financing such insurance with a flat-rate premium encourages depository institutions to assume more risk than if premiums were adjusted to reflect the risk of each bank's activities and investments. It can be argued that the appropriate response to potential moral hazard problems, whether in banking, insurance, or elsewhere, is to impose risk-based premiums. To the extent that risk-based premiums cannot be used, however, perhaps because of difficulties in accurately predicting the probability of bankruptcy, direct control measures such as minimum capital and surplus requirements or constraints on portfolio choice may be appropriate second-best solutions.

This type of market failure, however, cannot be used to justify regulations that maintain prices above competitive levels. There is a clear analogy here to the airline industry, where the recognition that price regulation was unnecessary and harmful to consumers led eventually to the dismantling of the CAB. In contrast, safety regulation by the FAA can still be justified since, because of limited liability, an airline with assets that were less than the maximum potential liability from a crash, including punitive damages, (literally a "fly-by-night airline) would have an economic incentive to provide less than the optimal amount of safety.

23. See Joskow (1973) and Priest (1986).

24. See U.S. Department of Justice (1986). For an extensive and insightful analysis of the effects of shifting from first-party insurance to third-party corporate-provided insurance administered through the tort system, see Priest (1986). For a comparative analysis of the Canadian liability insurance crisis, which in many ways parallels the U.S. experience, see Trebilcock (1987) who concludes that the Canadian crisis was caused by increased uncertainty in the judicial determination of liability and quantification of damages.

25. We should stress that empirical testing can only disprove hypotheses: If the implications of a particular hypothesis are inconsistent with the data, the hypothesis can be rejected, but since any given set of data may be consistent with the implications of a number of hypothesis, a particular hypothesis can never be empirically proven.

26. The F-statistic for a test of equality of means is 5.55, implying that the probability of this decline being due to random variations is less than .01.

27. The overall operating ratio is the ratio of total expenses (i.e., losses incurred plus loss adjustment expenses plus commissions and brokerage expenses plus other underwriting expenses plus dividends) minus net investment gain and other income, to premiums earned.

28. For a more rigorous mathematical modeling of the effects of uncertainty on load premiums, see Clarke, Simon, Smith, and Warren-Boulton (1986) and Winter (1986).

29. The relevant definition of uncertainty is uncertainty in the prediction of

ratios over the life of policies currently being issued. To the extent that these ratios are serially correlated, however, i.e., to the extent that they follow a predictable cycle or trend, the standard deviation will overestimate the absolute level of uncertainty. Under such conditions, a more accurate measure would be the standard error of a predictive equation for the ratios over time. Even if the assumption of serial independence is unwarranted, however, if the degree of serial correlation is held constant, changes in the standard deviation provide an unbiased measure of changes over time in the degree of uncertainty. More accurate measures of uncertainty may be developed in the near future. In addition to improving indexes for uncertainty that are based on accounting data, efforts are being made to develop ex ante measures of uncertainty using data from financial and capital markets.

Selected Readings

Baumol, William, John Panzar, and Robert Willig, *Contestable Markets and the Theory of Industry Structure* (1982).

Clarke, Richard N., Marilyn J. Simon, David D. Smith, and Frederick R. Warren-Boulton, "Sources of the 'Crisis' in Liability Insurance: An Economic Analysis," presented at the Allied Social Sciences Association Meetings, December 29, 1986.

Frech, H. E., and Joseph C. Samprone, Jr., "The Welfare Loss of Excess Nonprice Competition: The Case of Property-Liability Insurance Regulation," *The Journal of Law and Economics*, Vol. 23, October, 1980.

Freedman, Marian, "General Liability and Medical Malpractice Insurance Marketing—1985," *Best's Review*, October 1986, p. 138.

Hill, R. D., "Profit Regulation in Property-Liability Insurance," *The Bell Journal of Economics*, Vol. 10, Spring, 1979.

Ippolito, R. A., "The Effects of Price Regulation in the Automobile Insurance Industry," *The Journal of Law and Economics*, Vol. 22.

Joskow, P., "Cartels, Competition, and Regulation in the Property-Liability Insurance Industry," *The Bell Journal of Economics*, Vol. 4, Autumn, 1973.

Lacey, Nelson, J., "Recent Evidence on the Liability Crisis," mimeo, Department of General Business and Finance, The University of Massachusetts, December 1986.

Munch, Patricia, and Dennis Smallwood, "Solvency Regulation in the Property-Liability Insurance Industry: Empirical Evidence," *The Bell Journal of Economics*, Vol. 11, Spring, 1980.

Priest, George L., "The Current Insurance Crisis and Modern Tort Law," Working paper #44, Civil Liability Program, Center for Studies in Law, Economics, and Public Policy, Yale Law School, December 9, 1986.

Schwartz, Marius, "The Nature and Scope of Contestability Theory," EAG 86-8, May 20, 1986. *Oxford Economic Papers*, Vol. 38, Supplement, 1986.

Trebilcock, Michael J., "The Social Insurance-Deterrence Dilemma of Modern North American Tort Law: A Canadian Perspective on the Current Liability Insurance Crisis," University of Toronto Law School Working Paper, January 1987, and forthcoming, *San Diego Law Review*.

U.S. Department of Justice, "Report of the Tort Policy Working Group on the Causes, Extent and Policy Implications of the Current Crisis in Insurance Availability and Affordability" (February 1986).

Winter, Ralph A., "'Crises' in Competitive Insurance Markets," Working Papers in Economics E-86-74, Domestic Studies Program, Hoover Institution, Stanford University, 1986.

Index

E

F